Copyright, Congress and Technology: The Public Record

Volume I:
The Formative Years, 1958-1966

Volume II:
The Political Years, 1967-1973

Volume III:
The Future of Copyright, 1973-1977

Volume IV: CONTU:
The Future of Information Technology

Volume V: CONTU'S Final
Report and Recommendations

Edited with an introduction by
Nicholas Henry.

ORYX PRESS
1980

Operation Oryx, started more than 15 years ago at the Phoenix Zoo to save the rare white antelope—believed to have inspired the unicorn of mythology—has apparently succeeded. The operation was launched in 1962 when it became evident that the animals were facing extinction in their native habitat of the Arabian peninsula.

An original herd of nine, put together through *Operation Oryx* by five world organizations now numbers 47 in Phoenix with another 38 at the San Diego Wild Game Farm, and four others which have recently been sent to live in their natural habitat in Jordan.

Also, in what has come to be known as "The Second Law of Return," rare biblical animals are being collected from many countries to roam freely at the Hai Bar Biblical Wildlife Nature Reserve in the Negev, in Israel, the most recent addition being a breeding herd of eight Arabian Oryx. With the addition of these Oryx, their collection of rare biblical animals is complete.

Published by The Oryx Press
2214 N. Central Avenue at Encanto
Phoenix, AZ 85004

Published simultaneously in Canada

Printed and Bound in the United states of America

Distributed outside North America by
Mansell Information/Publishing Limited
3 Bloomsbury Place
London WC1A 2QA, England

Library of Congress Cataloging in Publication Data

Main entry under title:

The Future of copyright, 1973-1977.

   (Copyright, Congress, and technology : the public
record ; v. 3)
      Includes bibliographical references and index.
      1.   Copyright—United States—History—Sources.
2.   Fair use (Copyright)—United States—History—
Sources.   3.   Photocopying processes—Fair use (Copy-
right)—United States—History—Sources.   I.   Henry,
Nicholas, 1943-   II.   Series.
KF2994.A1C57   vol. 3   346'.73'0482   79-17301
ISBN 0-912700-31-9

To Adrienne

Contents

Science Foundation. NBS Special Publication 500-17, U.S. Department of Commerce, National Bureau of Standards. Issued October, 1977. Washington, D.C.: U.S. Government Printing Office, 1977.   **365**

An Act for the General Revision of the Copyright Law, Title 17 of the U.S. Code, and for other Purposes. S. 22. 94th Congress, Second Session, in the House of Representatives, February 23, 1976. Referred to the Committee on the Judiciary. Washington, D.C.: U.S. Government Printing Office, 1976.   **434**

Acknowledgements

I am indebted to a great many people in compiling these books, especially to Ms. Valari Elardo, my graduate assistant, who spent untold hours over a smoldering photocopying machine copying the necessary documents. Ms. Gwen Weaver has been both efficient and cheerful in putting out the necessary typing, and officials at the National Commission on New Technological Uses of Copyrighted Works have been cooperative and forthcoming in permitting me to reprint some of their important research in Volumes IV and V.

Ms. Phyllis Steckler, President of the Oryx Press, deserves recognition for her perceptiveness in seeing the need for this set, as well as her personal encouragement.

Of course, and as always, I am indebted to my understanding wife, Muriel, and my children, Miles and Adrienne, for their support in the completion of this project. This set is dedicated to them.

NH
Tempe, Arizona

Introduction to the Set

Copyright, Congress, and Technology: The Public Record is a compendium of selected public documents that were published during the remarkable effort to revise American copyright law which occurred during the twenty-one years between 1955 and 1976. Simply as an example of the policy-making process, the campaign waged to change U.S. copyright law is fascinating in and of itself; few pieces of legislation have taken as long to be enacted as a revised copyright law. This five-volume set, however, is designed not only to trace the development of the Copyright Act of 1976, but also is meant to set the record straight in the areas of how the new copyright law affects the use of new information technologies, notably photocopiers and computers, for the benefit of librarians, educators, authors, publishers, and public officials. The impact of copyright on these technologies is both profound and complex, and perhaps the most simple way of conveying the thinking of policy-makers and interest groups in their effort to resolve copyright and technology is to provide a format that allows them to speak for themselves.

These volumes also describe the actual policy-making process as it related to the attempt to revise the United States Copyright Act of 1909 in a manner that would accommodate the new information technologies, notably photocopying and computer-based information storage and retrieval systems. These are the primary "neo-publishing" technologies (in the sense that they permit the massive republishing of copyrighted works by the populace), and the "politics of neo-publishing" was the effort to reconcile these technologies with copyright law.

While there are other neo-publishing technologies, those that have engendered the greatest concern among copyright owners and copyright users are photocopiers and computers. Of these two, the photocopier is preeminent. There are approximately 600,000 photocopiers in this country alone, churning out an estimated 30 billion copies every year. Most of these copies are made in public and research libraries, and empirical studies of photocopying use patterns in libraries indicate that as much as 60 percent of all the photocopies made each year may be of copyrighted publications. Increasingly, publishers are convinced that their sales of periodical subscriptions and books are being undermined by popular and massive photocopying practices, and that this is particularly the case for publications in science and technolgy.

The other major neo-publishing technology is the computer. There are more than 100,000 computer-based information storage and retrieval systems in the United States. While we know that these systems are reformatting and disseminating vast quantities of the information on demand and at an incredibly rapid rate, we do not know what proportion of that information may be protected by copyright. Some material, certainly, that is processed by computers is protected by copyright, and it is highly unlikely that information system operators and programmers are soliciting the permission of the copyright owners to use their material to any significant degree, if at all.

Both copyright owners and copyright users perceive copyright law to be virtually the only public policy that is concerned with the relationships among the new neo-publishing technologies, intellectual creativity, intellectual property, and, to quote the Constitution (Article I, Section 8), the paramount social value of promoting "the Progress of Science and useful Arts . . .". Revising copyright law to accommodate the new information technologies thus is a public policy of some consequence.

Two conclusions may be drawn from the public record about copyright law revision. One is that the process represented, and no doubt will continue to do so, a politics of technological elites. Copyright is one of the least recognized but most important public policies of our time, affecting an industry of vast magnitude. In fact, the "knowledge industry" comprises the largest single segment of the American economy, and it has been estimated by economists that the knowledge industry accounts for a third of the Gross National Product. More than 40 percent of the nation's economic growth is attributable to advances in education, and the "copyright industries" alone are the equivalent size of mining, banking, and utilities. Copyright is not merely big business, it is the biggest.

In light of the implications of the new information technologies and copyright law, it is both discomfiting and surprising to learn how small the group is that has been debating how to reconcile technology and copyright during the past three decades. The elitism of this debate is brought out in these volumes. The same names appear and reappear with frequency, but the overwhelming reality remains that public policy for new information technologies has affected and will affect far more people than those who have been talking about it. We have here a case of very small elites "representing" very limited elements of society that nonetheless are forming public policy for the new information technologies.

Why is this elitism the case? A major reason appears to be that the sheer complexity of the subject inhibits participation. Yet, complexity is a growing fact of political life in techno-bureaucratic societies, such as ours. Political decision-making in twentieth century America deals with technology, and technology is complicated. Those who understand the complex technological issues of modern political life (or who say they do) become the policymakers. Nowhere is this better illustrated than in the instance of what some have called "the politics of neo-publishing." As the reader will quickly discern, very small elites have made a public policy that affects us all.

The second conclusion that one may draw from reading these public documents, is that the politics of neo-publishing is frankly Marxist. Revising copyright law was a political brawl involving the redistribution of political and economic power between haves and have-nots. While it was not a class war in the traditional sense, the politics of neo-publishing clearly is, to use Marxian language, a fight between the owners of a means of production and the users of their products. Indeed, the formal terminology of copyright law reflects the language of Marxism: copyright "owners" and copyright "users." The neo-publishing technologies have provided an opportunity to the "exploited masses" of copyright users. By dint of these technologies, proletarian copyright users may become bourgeois copyright owners. Publishers, the historic owners of the means of intellectual production, are witnessing the undermining of their ownership through the popular use of new information technologies. As Marshall McLuhan has noted "in an age of Xerox, every man is a publisher."

Copyright is the single public policy concerned with the economics of commercial publishing. It is predicated on the idea that a would-be publisher must put up a considerable amount of capital in order to begin publishing — that is, in order to control a means of production. It follows, therefore that publishers ought to be granted certain monopolistic rights or "exclusive license" to their products. This is what copyright does, or at least did, until the neo-publishing instruments made their debuts. These technologies are redistributing a means of production and, in so doing, are undermining copyright as a standing public policy. For these reasons, the documents included in this set can be understood most satisfactorily as a Marxian class conflict — owners against users.

While such conclusions may be interesting, and perhaps even important, the major reason why this set will be useful to most readers is that an enormous amount of confusion surrounds the impact of the new copyright law on librarians, authors, educators, and publishers. Thus, these volumes are organized in such a way that they will be of optimal use to these professionals in tracing how the thinking of their colleagues has evolved just as information technologies have developed.

Volume I of *Copyright, Congress, and Technology: The Public Record* focuses on those early public documents that emerged between 1958 and 1966. The discerning reader will note that the tone of the copyright proceedings in these years is substantially different from the tone found in public documents emerging in 1967 and beyond. I have referred to this phenomenon elsewhere as "noetic politics," or the peculiar style of politics that derives from knowledge, logic, and the scientific method.[1] We see in these documents a conscious effort by the participants in copyright politics to devise legislation that will work for the benefit of all society. The normal, grubbing interest-group politics that we associate with the legislative process is relatively absent, although there are many moments of passion and greed.

It was during this period that the Register of Copyrights commissioned thirty-four scholarly studies on copyright, and issued a major report in 1961 that was hailed as a seminal work in the area. Experts, lawyers, and policymakers of various stripes were consulted on a continuing basis during these years, and the Commission on New Technological Uses of Copyrighted Works (CONTU) was first proposed. All these instances and others represent an effort to form policy on the basis of knowledge rather than on the basis of the political power of particular interest groups.

As noted, however, this tone changes — and I think rather precipitously — in the years following. In the 1967 Congressional hearings, for example, we see spokespersons for various groups calling each other names during their testimony. The balance of power in the dispute appears to shift away from copyright owners (largely publishers and authors) and toward copyright users (largely librarians and educators), but not necessarily for reasons of wise public policy (although it may well turn out that way). Rather, the gains made by

---

1. See: Nicholas Henry, *Copyright/Information Technology/Public Policy. Part I: Copyright/Public Policies* and *Part II: Public Policies/Information Technology*. New York: Marcel Dekker, Inc., 1975 and 1976.

copyright users over the interests of copyright owners are made because the users have the votes and the owners do not. Thus, Volume II covers the years 1967 through 1973, and the tone throughout is overtly political, although there is some hard and creative analysis available in these years, which is included.

The third volume in the retrospect reprints documents emerging between 1973 and 1977, including pertinent selections from the several Congressional hearings on copyright law revision. An effort has been made to include those public documents that point the way toward the future of copyright. The entire Copyright Act of 1976 also is reproduced.

Volume IV, *CONTV: The Future of Information Technology*, reproduces the ground-breaking studies sponsored by the National Commission on New Technological Uses of Copyrighted Works, which dealt with computer soft-ware, photocopying and copyrights, public photocopying practices, library photocopying and the economics of periodical publications. The Commissions final report, the result of years of testimony by experts from across the nation, comprises Volume V.

Taken together, the five volumes are a collection that should be both convenient and authoritative in guiding copyright users and owners through the maze of copyright, technology, and public policy.

NH
Tempe, Arizona

Introduction to Volume III

The year 1973 begins Volume III of *Copyright, Congress and Technology: The Public Record*. It was a watermark year in the politics of neo-publishing. The participants clearly were starting to appreciate that enacting a revised copyright statute was approaching a point of now-or-never. Barbara Ringer, Register of Copyrights since late 1973, stated with considerable reason that "If there is continued inaction in the 94th Congress, I've got to get off the streetcar. It would be an abdication of the responsibility of the Copyright Office to blow death into a carcass . . . and I don't see any agency other than the Copyright Office that can provide the leadership to put through a legislative program." Yet, as Thomas Brennan, counsel to the Senate Subcommittee on Patents, Trademarks, and Copyrights, observed, it was also "absolutely critical" that a revised copyright law replace the 1909 act because "we can't continue to function with an archaic statute."

The uncertainty engendered by the *Williams & Wilkins* case was making its full impact felt on copyright politics as the statements made during the 1973 Senate hearings show. (Court documents germane to *Williams & Wilkins* conclude Volume II of this set, while the 1973 Senate hearings begin this volume.)

The positions of copyright owners and users were calcifying. A forum on licensing of copyrighted materials held in June, 1973, under the sponsorship of the Educational Media Producers Council and the Information Industry Association, indicated no progress at reconciliation between the 100-odd owners and users who attended. Harry N. Rosenfield, counsel for the Ad Hoc Committee on Copyright Law Revisions, snarled that the meeting was "obviously a set-up" for a drive for a licensing system "which would render incalculable damage to the nation's educational system." Ivan Bender, counsel for the Encyclopedia Britannica Educational Corporation, snapped back with the argument that "fair use is not free use," contending that licensing plans were designed to keep book publishing a healthy industry and to inhibit "unauthorized copying."

And so it went. In late 1974, the *New York Times* published an article beginning, "Authors and publishers are locked in a battle with the country's libraries over the photocopying of copyrighted materials, and both sides agree that the outcome will be felt for years to come." The article went on to quote the counsel for the Association of American Publishers (AAP) as saying, "The libraries seem to think they have a God-given right to reproduce material at will," while the lawyer for the American Library Association (ALA) was cited as stating that "there isn't the slightest bit of evidence of any damages to publishers from photocopying. We cannot figure out whether their motives are economic or philosophical."

Adding to this open hostility between copyright owners and users in the early 1970s was the obvious disinterest being shown by Congress in formulating a public policy for the new information technologies. The Register of Copyrights observed in 1974 that "Congress is terribly bored with the bill. It has been a failure of government in the past not to assume its responsibility in this area. . . ." She added that she was doubtful "that the revision package can hold together indefinitely," while an unnamed "industry expert" was quoted in *Publishers Weekly* as forecasting "a crisis in proprietary rights within six months unless the stalemate ends—a crisis growing out of the deteriorating legislative situation. . . ."

In part, at least, this "deteriorating legislative situation" was understandable. Copyright, information technologies, and economics are extremely complicated subjects. Invariably, articles about public policy for information technology written for even very well informed readers are described as "technical." A Senate staff aide remarked in 1974 that "One reason for the delay [the bill had been in the Senate for seven years] is that the bill is so complicated that every Senator is bound to hurt some constituent no matter how [s/]he votes."

Thus, it was to the relief of all parties that, in this atmosphere of legislative indifference (bordering on distaste) toward copyright revision and outright hostility between warring factions over the neo-publishing technologies, Senator John L. McClellan, chairperson of the Judiciary Committee's Subcommittee on Patents, Trademarks, and Copyrights, introduced S. 1361, the long-awaited Copyright Law Revision bill, on March 26, 1973. In introducing S.1361, McClellan reflected the mounting intensity of neo-publishing politics; he scored as "grossly inaccurate" a letter written to him by Jerome B. Wiesner, president of the Massachusetts Institute of Technology, which stated that the section on library photocopying "seems likely to result in the imposition of a fee or a delay whenever a student or scholar wants to copy part of a copyrighted work in order to facilitate [her/]his study or research." McClellan characterized the Wiesner letter as part of "an organized letter-writing campaign by presidents of universities and others in support of a substitute photocopying section."

Copyright owners, for their part, had been active too, although they had less widespread political resources on which to draw than did users. Nevertheless, an example is provided by Rand McNally & Company, whose president wrote, in "An Open Letter to All Rand McNally Authors," that "your support is needed now to prevent eroding amendments from being tacked on, such as a so-called General Education Exemption, which would allow large-scale photocopying without permission of, or payment to, the copyright proprieter. . . . If you agree with us, please take a few minutes *today* to write your Senator to seek [her/]his support in preventing amendments which would permit such uncompensated use of yours and other's intellectual product. Tell [her/]him in your own words that you accept the 'fair' free use now provided . . . without any such diluting amendments." As publisher Curtis G. Benjamin of McGraw-Hill noted, "a real rumble" on copyright was eminent, and that, with education's "big wallop . . . it's a real prospect that we could win the battle in committee but lose on the floor of the Senate."

S. 1361 represented the most conscientious effort up to that time to balance the needs of copyright owners and users in terms of the new information technologies. Section 107 on fair use was identical to that in the 1971 bill, as was Title II, establishing a National Commission on New Technological Uses of Copyrighted Works, and Section 504, which protected innocently motivated librarians and teachers who may have unwittingly violated a copyright.

Section 108 on library photocopying was enlarged from the 1971 bill. Sections 108(d) and (e) stated that a library has the right to make copies of an entire work, as well as "no more than one article . . . or a copy of a small part of any other copyright work," provided that the copy becomes the property of the user for purposes of private study, that the library "displays prominently . . . a warning of copyright . . ." and that the library determined, after a "reasonable investigation," that a copy of the work "cannot be obtained at a fair price." Also new, in that it was a significant expansion from Section 108(f) of the 1971 bill, was Section 108(g), which stated that "The rights of reproduction and distribution under this section extend to the isolated and unrelated reproduction or distribution of a single copy . . . of the same material on separate occasions, but do not extend to where the library . . . (1) is aware or has a substantial reason to believe that it is engaging in the related or concerted reproduction or distribution of multiple copies . . . or (2) engages in the systematic reproduction or distribution of single or multiple copies. . . ." Point (2) in particular was new.

Other sections of pertinence to the neo-publishing technologies and practices dealt with the concepts of "writing," "display," "performance," "adaptation," "reproduction," and "publication" (Sections 101, 102, 106, 107, and 110 being of special note in this regard, although Sections 107 through 117 are also relevant), computer usage (Sections 102 and 117), nonprofit public performances (Sections 106, 107, and 110), and performing rights (Sections 106 and 114).

Other important and new or continued sections concerned "common law copyright" (Section 301), the public domain policy (Section 105), and copyright duration (Section 302).

Important or not, however, legislative policymakers were bored with copyright; at least, the vast majority of them were. On May 29, 1973, Representative Bertram L. Podell of New York introduced to the House H.R. 8186, a Copyright Law Revision bill that was identical to McClellan's S. 1361. A spokesman for Podell stated that the Congressman did what he did "to remind his colleagues that copyright revision is still languishing in the Senate."

There were understandable reasons for the apparent legislative languor on copyright, such as the Agnew scandal, confirmation of a new Vice President, a steadily deteriorating economy, a skittery international situation (which included a massive and questionable military alert), the widening cesspool of Watergate, and a dawning realization by public officials that the American people were losing faith in them—their honesty, their integrity, and their ability. Nevertheless, those publics concerned with copyright had gotten little or no action on a revision bill for almost twenty years, and in the early 1970s various conferences were held that were attended by surprisingly broad-based segments of the public. Of note were two parliaments on "New Technological Uses of Copyrighted Works" and, as previously mentioned, a stormy "Forum on Licensing of Copyrighted Materials," attended by more than 100 people and sponsored by the Educational Media Producers Council and the Information Industry Association.

During this period, literally no one thought that any real action would be taken on copyright revision before 1974. The major trade journal for publishing, *Publishers Weekly,* queried rhetorically in 1973, "How much longer can Congress wait to act on copyright revision legislation? Currently, that legislation (S. 1361) is ever more deeply mired in the Senate Judiciary Subcommittee on Patents, Trademarks, and Copyrights, with virtually no hope of hearings before the Congressional recess in August." It was therefore surprising when the chairperson of that subcommittee, John McClellan, announced on July 10, 1973, that his group was going to hold hearings on S. 1361. *Publishers Weekly* ridiculed the "announcement [that] gave the many interested parties a bare 20 days to get ready for the big event," and McClellan had made "a spur-of-the-moment decision to hold the hearings"; the chairperson was "obviously eager now to rid himself of the copyright revision problem, which has been dragging on for years."

There were reasons beyond that of the simple impatience of an Arkansas Democrat that were more substantive. Representative Emanuel Cellar, the powerful chairperson of the House Judiciary Committee who had escorted the Copyright Law Revision bill through the House in 1967, had died, and as a partial result of his death, the structure of the House Judiciary Committee was being revamped in a way that could have an adverse effect on the revision process. Representative Robert W. Kastenmeier's Judiciary Subcommittee No. 3, which had conducted hearings on the House bill in 1965, was expanded and retitled the Subcommittee on Courts, Civil Liberties, and Administration of Justice. Its new duties included an investigation of the Justice Department in the wake of Watergate, and while Kastenmeier had always voiced a keen interest in copyright, S.1361 would play second fiddle to a number of Watergate-related agenda items. These developments were not lost on McClellan, who himself intended to relinquish the chair of his Senate Subcommittee on Patents, Trademarks, and Copyrights in order to concentrate on his responsibilities as chairperson of the Appropriations Committee. Additionally, a potential reorganization of the Senate Judiciary Committee was in the offing which quite possibly could result in the abolition of McClellan's copyright subcommittee.

Regardless of the reasons, the Subcommittee on Patents, Trademarks, and Copyrights held hearings on S.1361 on July 31 and August 1, 1973. None of the senators on the subcommittee evidenced any special interest in the proceedings, which was reminiscent of the subcommittee's copyright hearings of 1967, when the full contingent of senators had been present only once—when vocalist Julie London testified. In the 1973 hearings, only one senator, Quentin N. Burdick of North Dakota, besides the chairperson, attended the proceedings faithfully; the ranking minority member of the subcommittee, Hugh Scott of Pennsylvania, never put in an appearance, and Hiram L. Fong of Hawaii attended only briefly. It should be noted that the subcommittee had only five members.

The two-day hearings packed in the personal appearances of about 75 witnesses and another 50 statements that had been sent to the subcommittee were recorded. The principal points of discussion were library photocopying and general educational exemptions, although relatively limited testimony also was heard on the cable television royalty schedule, cable televised sports events, and the religious broadcasting exemption.

By 1973, educators and librarians had allied themselves into one massive association, which had been growing since its founding ten years earlier: the Ad Hoc Committee of Educational Institutions and Organizations on Copyright Law Revisions. At the time of the hearings, the ad hoc committee had 41 members plus 8 "interested observers," including the very biggest organizations in education and librarianship; together, these member organizations reached considerably more than 2 million, highly educated, articulate, and opinion-leading voters, not including students and library patrons.

Similarly, the two major associations of book publishers had merged into a single comprehensive organization since the last copyright hearings. The new Association of American Publishers (AAP) represented more than 260 book publishing houses, including university presses, educational publishers, and general book publishers. They accounted for, in the words of its spokesman, "the vast majority of all general, educational, and religious books and materials produced in the United States."

Beyond these two heavyweights, many of the member organizations (which often were heavyweights in their own right) such as Harcourt Brace Jovanovich, Macmillan, the American Library Association (ALA), the Association of Research Libraries (ARL), and the National Education Association (NEA), delivered their own statements to the senators. In addition, new and significant interest groups made their political debuts at the hearings, notably the Information Industry Association, with more than 60 member firms representing publishers, computer manufacturers, microfilm printers, photocopier manufacturers, software companies, and including such industrial giants as Xerox Corporation, Lockheed, Encyclopedia Britannica Education Corporation, McGraw-Hill, Macmillan, The New York Times, and Time, Inc.; the Educational Media Producers Council, with some 70 member organizations which produce roughly 80 percent of the nation's educational audiovisual materials; the Association of American University Presses, representing all 64 of the country's university presses, which account for almost half of the nation's annual output of nonfiction books addressed to a scholarly audience and which publish a total of 280 academic journals; and the American Chemical Society, with 110,000 members and a producer of 20 scientific periodicals. Finally, there were the representatives of groups, such as the Authors League of America, long-known in Congress.

The hearings began with witnesses interested in the section dealing with library photocopying. Copyright users in general, but librarians, in particular, were deeply concerned with developments in the courts, which had thrown them into considerable consternation that their traditional photocopying practices might be curtailed. Commissioner James F. Davis had made his pro-copyright owner recommendation for the U.S. Court of Claims on the *William & Wilkins* case and, at the time of the hearings, it looked likely that the Court would accept Davis's decision. As a result of this uncertainty, librarians as well as educators entered the hearings determined to make any legislative reference to library photocopying as pro-copyright user as possible. Two portions of Section 108 on library photocopying were of especial note in this regard: Subsection 108(g)(2), which prohibited "systematic reproduction or distribution of single or multiple copies," and Subsection 108(d), which did not specify categorically that a library could make a single copy of an entire journal article without fear of an infringement suit.

Librarians decided, as a matter of strategy, not to bring up the topic of "systematic reproduction" at the hearings, although they argued against the phrase in closed-door sessions with copyright owners. Stephen A. McCarthy, executive director of the Association of Research Libraries, snorted that "no one knows what it means," and argued that it potentially permitted the lodging of unfair infringement suits against libraries and would inhibit the growth of information networks.

At the hearings, librarians focussed their fire on Subsection 108(d), and McCarthy fired the opening shot followed by spokespersons for the American Library Association and the Medical Library Association. Both urged that Section 108(d) be redrafted so that "the library or archives shall be entitled, without further investigation, to supply a copy of no more than one article or other contribution to a copyrighted collection or periodical issue, or . . . of a similarly small part of any other copyrighted work," and that a library also be allowed "to supply a copy . . . of an entire work, or of more than a relatively small part of it," if the library has made a "reasonable investigation" that a copy of the work cannot be obtained readily from trade sources. This proposed amendment by librarians omitted references already in Section 108(d) to the copy becoming the property of the user and the library having no notice that the copy would be used for purposes other than scholarship. The remainder of the subsection was kept relatively intact.

Librarians argued that their amendment was designed "to insure by specific legislative language that a customary, long established library service of providing a photocopy for a reader who requests it may be continued without infringement of copyright." Adoption of the amendment would remove the threat of suit against libraries arising out of varying judicial interpretations of what is or is not fair use, "while simultaneously assuring librarians that they could continue to employ modern technology and methods in serving their readers."

The amendment, in short, was fundamentally a defensive maneuver aimed at the pending implications of the *Williams & Wilkins* case and the preservation of present library practices. Beyond that, however, librarians were worried over the requirement contained in Subsection 108(d) which stipulated that a user prove or demonstrate to a library that an unused copy is unavailable from a trade source. McCarthy queried, rhetorically, "How does the ordinary reader do this? How does the library evaluate the evidence?" and contended that the requirement would "impose a substantial added burden on libraries and on library users and will impede their access to information."

It was during McCarthy's opening testimony at the hearings that Senator Burdick brought up the question which would recur continuously in the ensuing discussions of library photocopying: "Suppose I go to the public library at Williston, North Dakota, and I want to get page 50 out of a book on zoology dealing with snakes, and I go to the library and I say, 'I want a copy of page 50 on snakes,' and the librarian says to me, 'I think that is available in the publishing house in New York or at the Library of Congress.' As you read that subsection . . . would you construe this section to mean that the library at Williston could not copy that page 50?" McCarthy replied, "Yes sir; that is right."

Burdick, however, also evidenced some concern over potential misuse should the librarians' amendment be adopted. Burdick stated to McCarthy that he wanted to get away from "what happens, what is practical," and into "what is possible. We have to think of that, too. Under your language, and under your contention, could an entire book be copied? Could it be?" McCarthy said no, that he was concerned with "the distinction between a complete book, sir, and a periodical article." Burdick expressed doubt over his response, reread the amendment to McCarthy, observed that "you get into a phasey area there of more than a relatively small part of it, et cetera, et cetera," and ultimately wrangled a different response out of Philip B. Brown, counsel to the ARL. Burdick, rephrasing the question, stated, "You would agree that it [the amendment] would apply if it was a total work or a substantial part of a total work," to which Brown replied, "Yes."

The representative from the American Library Association backed all that the ARL delegation had said, as did the spokesperson for the Medical Library Association. Only Frank E. McKenna, executive director of the Special Libraries Association (SLA)—with 8,000 members, the second largest library organization in the nation after the ALA—digressed from the librarians' "party line." The SLA sought "to reach an intermediate position of accommodation between the seemingly irreconcilable positions" of copyright users and owners. In this light, SLA neither was for nor against the other librarians' proposed amendment to Subsection 108(d). While the association was foursquare against having to seek permission from publishers to make a single copy of an in-print article, it conceded (as *Publishers Weekly* was quick to point out) that "there may be some validity in the claims of commercial publishers of periodicals that they may have some loss of income due to photocopying," and that "specialized libraries . . . can probably afford an added *cents-per-page* charge" for photocopying.

Copyright owners were eager to take issue with the librarians' proposals, and the lead-off witness for owners was Robert W. Cairns, executive director of the American Chemical Society. Cairns sounded a note so tough and unyielding that he probably did more good for librarians in the minds of the legislators than did the librarians themselves. As Cairns observed, however, his society had a lot to lose; ACS publications grossed about $30 million per year, and that, in the chemistry field generally, about 400,000 manuscripts were printed each year in approximately 10,000 different journals.

The ACS position was straightforward: "Photocopying should not be allowed under any circumstances unless an adequate means of control and payment is simultaneously developed to compensate publishers for their basic editorial and composition costs. Otherwise, fair use or library-photocopying loopholes, or any other exemptions from copyright control for either profit or nonprofit use, will ultimately destroy the viability of scientific and technical publications. . . ."

Senator Burdick again brought up the plight of the library patron copying a single page in Williston, North Dakota, and Cairns indicated he would accord her/him no leeway.

Senator Hiram Fong took up this train of thought, and, in terms of indicating the ideological position of the ACS, the exchange is interesting:

Fong: Now would you consider an exemption? Say, a little boy who takes the book home and copies, say, two or three pages of it, or he makes two or three Xerox copies. Would you exempt such a child from paying any fee?
Cairns: No, the exemptions that you exemplify by this particular case would represent the educational exemption. . . . We must be compensated the way anyone else is.
Fong: So you think that this little boy should pay for that?
Cairns: He must. . . .
Fong: So most of the people who copy your works do not make a profit. Is that correct?
Cairns: That is correct.
Fong: So you say that these people who copy your works should pay for them?
Cairns: They should pay the portion of the composition costs which their copying represents. . . .
Fong: Then you would not exempt any part of it at all?
Cairns: That would be about right. . . .

Other copyright owners were aware of the potentially detrimental import that this kind of candor could have on Congress. Later in the hearings, Charles Lieb, in connection with his appearance as a spokesperson for the Information Industry Association, returned to the subject of "the library in North Dakota." In the exchange, Lieb said to Senator Burdick that, while he could not speak for the American Chemical Society, he felt reasonably sure that the ACS would not object to the copying of a single page in a 10- to 30-page article in one of their journals, and that such an act would constitute fair use. Burdick replied, "This morning they said no, though." Lieb retorted, "No, they didn't. They were talking about the copying of whole articles." (This is not how the record reads.) The impression Cairns left was a lasting one. Burdick's parting shot was, "Well, someone here today—and I have been running back and forth to vote—but someone said, you can't make single copies."

The American Chemical Society's position on the responsibility of librarians in assuring adherence to copyright law also was conservative. In Cairns' view, the librarian ought to be responsible for collecting the fee from every user that amounted to "substantial payments"; e.g., "a clause which would rule out anything below $1 or $10." Cairns conceded that the situation "would be a little difficult to police. But that does not excuse not having a law to say that this is not legal."

Interestingly, Cairns was quite candid in his admission that the ACS desired only that the publisher get the money, and was not concerned whatsoever with compensating the author. This apparently came as a surprise to some of the senators, as the following exchange indicates. The subject under discussion is the page charge, a device by which the journal publisher is paid a per-page fee by the author (up to $75 per page) to publish his paper; usually, the federal agency sponsoring the research foots the bill.

> **Fong:**   So, actually, you have not paid for the article?
> **Cairns:**   We have not paid anything for the article. In fact, we usually get a page charge for publishing.
> **Fong:**   Yes, and he pays you for it, certainly—for the publication? . . . you say, since you publish it, the man who copies that article should pay you or pay him [i.e., the author]?
> **Cairns:**   The man who . . . recopies our publication should pay us . . . . The writer of the article invariably puts the copyright with the American Chemical Society.
> **Fong:**   I see.

Other periodical publishers also gave testimony on library photocopying, notably the Williams and Wilkins Company (which publishes some 30 academic journals) and the American Business Press (publisher of about 500 specialized periodical publications). Both are commercial periodical publishers, unlike the ACS, and their statements supported unequivocally Cairns' position.

Book publishers, most of them being represented by Ambassador Kenneth B. Keating and Bella L. Linden (for Harcourt Brace Jovanovich and Macmillan, two of the nation's five biggest publishing houses), and W. Bradford Wiley (for the Association of American Publishers), were less strident and more urbane in their remarks than the periodical publishers. The AAP was willing to compromise. While it suggested certain "technical" changes in the drafting of Section 108 (which appeared to be genuinely meant to clarify the intent of the section), the AAP was opposed to the librarians' proposed amendment, which it felt blurred the distinction between scholarly works and other kinds, ignored the degree of cost and effort put into the work, overlooked the type of library system doing the copying, omitted reference to systematic reproduction, and made inadequate reference to the library checking on the availability of a work through trade sources before copying it. In brief, the amendment "totally overlooked" the "basic differences and distinctions that exist between the kinds of material copied and their varying markets, the kinds of institutions which do the copying and the manner in which they distribute it." Provided that the drafting of technical changes in Section 108 could be implemented, the AAP supported S. 1361. The chairman of the Association of American University Presses' (AAUP) Committee on Copyright added that "We wish to associate ourselves, with certain reservations, with the Association of American Publishers in respect of Section 108."

Keating and Linden, speaking for Harcourt Brace Jovanovich and Macmillan, were less pleased with Section 108 than either the AAP or the AAUP, which hardly could be described as being wild about it. Keating took issue with a number of aspects of Section 108, notably the "inherent fallacy of the single-copy theory" that it embodied. He implied that it would be a serious mistake to have such a section at all, because "a compromise solution to the issue of photocopying at this point is likely to have the effect of freezing potentially detrimental measures into our laws for years to come and to remove any impetus for thorough consideration of this issue" by the proposed National Commission on New Technological Uses of Copyrighted Works. "I do not believe that library and allied interests will suffer materially from the omission of specific photocopying provisions in Section 108 at this time."

Linden, who always had shown herself extremely sensitive to the nuances of the congressional hearings in the past and displayed her acuity again in the 1973 proceedings, recalled Senator Burdick's remarks "with respect to the inquiries about the little boy who wants to photocopy one page." She went on to link the senator's inquiries with Keating's concern over "freezing" an untoward policy into law by, in effect, offering the policymakers a clever and graceful out in the form of a technological fix. She said that, as a result of her participation in the Committee on Scientific and Technical Information of the Federal Council on Science and Technology, she had learned that Xerox Corporation had invented a new machine with "a system of monitoring pages reproduced" by its photocopiers. "It is feasible today under the present technology to monitor uses, to pay for uses . . . the machine itself monitors effectively whether a book page or a loose piece of paper is photocopied. I am certain that the National Commission, which you in your mature wisdom and knowledge of the legislative process have recommended," can develop a new system of compensation "for photocopying uses that can be made practical. With all due respect, I urge that it be left to the Commission to report to you so that appropriate action can be taken at that time."

Burdick expressed an immediate interest in Linden's "great technological hope," and presumably her remarks had an effect on the other senators as well. Regrettably, her reliance on a social theory of *laissez innover* proved unfounded later. Ten days after Linden delivered her statement, the counsel of Xerox Corporation notified the counsel of the Senate subcommittee that "Xerox copiers do not have now—nor do we foresee the future technology having—the capability to discriminate automatically so as to classify copies made of works now in print in terms of source or of copyright status." Hence, if policymakers were going to resolve the issue of library photocopying they probably could not rely on a technological shortcut, no matter how tempting.

Finally, the Authors League made its inevitable appearance. It was noted, however, that at these hearings the League was the only group even making a claim that it had the *creators* of society's ideas at heart; publishers had spoken only for the *disseminators* of those ideas and, in some cases, such as that of the ACS, publishers had made it clear that the compensation of authors was of little concern to them. The League was more in sympathy with the remarks of Keating and Linden than with any other spokesperson for copyright owners; e.g., rejection of the librarians' proposed amendment to Section 108, reliance on the National Commission for a solution, elimination of ambiguities in Section 108, and opposition to the policy that libraries could make a copy of an entire article.

In summary, one point was obvious about the library copying issue: there was no agreement, not even among users and owners, much less between them. The Special Libraries Association represented a divergence from the mainstream of opinion in library circles, while Harcourt Brace Jovanovich, Macmillan, and the

xxiv   *Copyright, Congress and Technology*

Authors League differed with the majority's opinion in the publishing industry. As we have seen, these differences were not merely those of minor splinter groups. The SLA is the second largest library association in the country, the two publishing houses are among the five largest in America, and the Authors League is the only significant organization of writers in the nation. Yet, even the majorities of owners and users remained far apart, and the prospects of reconciliation appeared remote.

The other outstanding bone of contention in the hearings revolved around educators' demands for an educational exemption from copyright law. Essentially the same spokespersons who addressed library copying also gave testimony. An exception to this was the various representatives for copyright users; in place of librarians, the principal educational figures in the ad hoc committee expressed the users' case. Librarians, of course, had joined education's ad hoc committee some time ago, and so the committee's spokespersons were speaking for the libraries' interests, too. Copyright owners were represented by essentially the same people who had argued against the library copying provisos: the AAP, the Authors League, Macmillan, Harcourt Brace Jovanovich, plus the Educational Media Producers Council, and the Information Industry Association.

Harold E. Wigren, chairperson of the ad hoc committee, and seven other members of the committee, began the discussions on an educational exemption. Organized education was proposing a wholly new section to S. 1361 that, in effect, would be a resurrection of the "not-for-profit" principle, which education had abandoned in 1965 in its negotiations with copyright owners. The proposed and unnumbered section entitled "Limitations on Exclusive Rights: Reproduction for Teaching, Scholarship and Research" was a sweeping amendment. It stated that "nonprofit use of a copyright work for noncommercial teaching, scholarship and research is not an infringement of copyright." "Use," as defined for purposes of the amendment, included not only "reproduction, copying and recording," but storage, retrieval, processing, and transferring information in conjunction with any "automatic systems." Similarly, "portion" in this context meant "brief excerpts," "the whole of short literary, pictorial and graphic works," "entire works reproduced for storage" in automated information systems, and "recording and retransmission of broadcasts within five school days after the recorded broadcast." There were some modest restraints included in the amendment as concessions to owners, and these included clauses which excluded the copying of "consumable" works and reproduction for purposes of compilation—acts which already had been expressly forbidden in Senate *Report No. 93-983*.

Should legislators not see fit to incorporate a formal educational exemption into S. 1361, then the ad hoc committee had a backup alternative. The bill could be redrafted to provide "adherence to the concepts and meanings of 'fair use' which were written into House *Report No. 83* of 1967," but only "as amended in the following respects": the deletion of the famous phrase, "no matter how minor," which had so enraged educators; authorization of "limited multiple copying for short whole works," such as articles and stories; and the "application of the full impact of 'fair use' to instructional technology." There could also be a specific legislative rejection of Commissioner Davis's ruling in the *Williams & Wilkins* case "to the extent in which it differs from that House Report, as amended. . . ."

Wigren and most of the other spokespersons for the institutional members of the ad hoc committee made it plain that education would not support S. 1361 unless one or both of these alternatives were written into the bill. These representatives included the spokespersons of the National Education Association, the National

Council of Teachers of English, the Modern Language Association, the Joint Council on Education Telecommunications, and the National School Board Association. While some of these witnesses addressed themselves to issues not considered by the chairperson of their ad hoc committee, all of them were in accord with the proposal for an educational exemption.

An exception, if a partial one, was John Stedman, representing the Association of American Law Schools (AALS) but appearing also at the specific request of the American Association of University Professors (AAUP) and the American Council on Education (ACE). While making an appearance in conjunction with that of the ad hoc committee, neither the AALS nor the AAUP were members of the committee, although they maintained an interested observer status with it. The ACE, however, was a charter member, but Wigren long had characterized its stance as the "most conservative" of the committee's membership.

Stedman, in his capacity as the spokesperson at the hearing for the interests of higher education, came out neither for nor against the ad hoc committee's proposal for an educational exemption. The reasons behind this ambivalence are unclear, although it may reflect the ACE's disaffection with the decision of its committee members to unilaterally breach their 1966 agreements with copyright owners, a breach which the proposed exemption represented. In any event, Stedman spent his time on the concept of fair use in light of the *Williams & Wilkins* case, urging the "enactment of a statutory fair use provision accompanied by supportive language in the committee report comparable to that contained in House Report 2237 [which was the first legislative history to appear in the current copyright revision effort] expressing its concept of fair use as that term was understood prior to *Williams & Wilkins.*" Stedman termed this suggestion a "modest recommendation," which it was.

A similar exception to the ad hoc committee's proposed educational exemption was taken by the Association for Educational Communications and Technology (AECT), which is a member of the committee and an affiliate (though not a department) of the National Educational Association and, with some 8,000 members, is the major organization of educators concerned directly with the use of audiovisual materials. While the AECT did not send a spokesperson to testify, it issued a statement on the first day of the hearings which amounted to support for the position expressed by higher education interests and for the bill as written. The AECT, like the Special Libraries Association, was one of those few significant organizations of copyright users that maintained a sincere dialogue with copyright owners, while still retaining membership on the ad hoc committee.

While the AECT was characterized by the representative of the pro-copyright owner Educational Media Producers Council as being "in opposition to the so-called educational exemption," the similarly ambivalent stance of higher education in the ranks of the ad hoc committee was not commented upon the spokespersons for copyright owners at the hearings. Instead, owners focused their fire power on the alleged ignominies of the proposed educational exemption and hinted that these ignominies might extend to the character of educators themselves. As Irwin Karp, counsel for the Authors League, acidly observed, "It should be emphasized, at the outset, that what the educators are doing is asking this committee and the House Judiciary Committee to throw out a carefully worked out compromise on the problem of educational copying . . . Indeed, Mr. Rosenfield . . . speaking for the ad hoc committee, said that the *sine qua non* of our agreement on the compromise of educational copying, the *sine qua non* of our agreement, is the present language of

107, unchanged. The proposed educational exemption will change that agreement considerably and will change 107." Copyright owners, in brief, had not forgotten their 1966 accords with copyright users, and were ready to remind users and the subcommittee that users had broken those accords. Moreover, publishers stated that "it is important that you know that we have on many occasions offered to cooperate with the ad hoc committee to establish guidelines for the use of the classroom teacher. . . . Neither the NEA nor the ad hoc committee has been willing to cooperate with us in such an effort. . . ."

Authors, publishers, and educational media producers were unanimously opposed to the proposed educational amendment. They argued that, if enacted, it would go far beyond the normal guidelines of fair use and undercut many other sections of S.1361, that it was "unnecessary, redundant, swept-in, imprecise, overlapping, destructive, illogical, erosive, and preemptive," and that it represented "an attempt to revive a proposal which was considered a number of years ago by the House Committee on the Judiciary, was flatly rejected by the committee, and was then abandoned by the ad hoc committee in the hearings before this subcommittee." Owners urged that "the proposed educational exemption be rejected out of hand."

Publishers, but especially computer manufacturers, were particularly concerned with education's efforts to make a public policy for computer-based information systems. The spokesperson for the Association of American Publishers observed that education's proposal "would permit the free and unrestricted input of copyrighted works into computer systems. . . . What the ad hoc committee has in mind, obviously, is that input of works in copyright should be free (an encyclopedia or reference work, for example) and that bit-by-bit retrieval should be permitted, without payment, under the claim of fair use," and that also, "internal computer manipulation of the copyrighted material would also be free."

Paul G. Zurkowski, president of the Information Industry Association, elaborated on the point, stating that the amendment "would enable the educational institutions to put anything into a computerized data base," and that "if you take both the educational exemption and the library exemption together, you have an opportunity under the education exemption to put into the computer almost anything and then a right under the library exemption to make a single copy of it on demand. The combination of the two proposals would create quite a business operation for libraries and drain off a great deal of business from traditional publishers . . . as well as from information companies. . . ." The tendency of the new information technologies to homogenize and the trend's implications for public policy affecting private industry were not lost on Zurkowski, who was by far the most pointed and cogent of all copyright owners in his remarks on this topic of fundamental significance.

Zurkowski's observations on the combined effects of the proposed amendments concerning library copying and educational exemptions sponsored by copyright users came as close as any statement made by any witness at the hearings on the basic issue at stake: is copyright an adequate public policy for knowledge management in technological societies? No one answered the question beyond expressing the scope of his/her group's self-interest, but Zurkowski, at least, had come close to asking the question for the first time at a public hearing. He, like the other spokespersons for copyright owners, urged that the bill be left essentially intact and that these kinds of inordinately complex issues be left to the proposed National Commission on New Technological Uses of Copyrighted Works, as established in Title II of S.1361.

As the 1973 hearings on S. 1361 showed, the bill was complex. Fortunately, a concise and complete *Report No. 93-983* was issued by the Senate Committee on the Judiciary, which provided a clear exposition of the thinking behind the pertinent clauses in S. 1361. While it was contended in *Report No. 93-983* that "Other than for technical reasons, this bill is identical to S. 644 of the 92nd Congress," such a view was not entirely warranted.

Perhaps the most complicated aspects of S. 1361 dealt with policies for educational copying of copyrighted materials. Section 107 on fair use, Section 108 on library copying, and Section 504 protecting librarians and teachers from infringement suits, while contained for the most part in S. 644, still stood as substantial gains for copyright users. Beyond this, however, *Report No. 93-983* explicated the principal values underlying these and related sections in light of the most recent positions expressed by the contending interests. Of especial note was the rationale articulated in the *Report* concerning why the "use-profit" limitation was abandoned, and this was done largely in connection with the *Report's* explanation of the copyright owner's exclusive "bundle of rights" listed in Section 106 of S. 1361: reproduction, adaptation, publication, performance, and display. According to the *Report,* except for performance and display, these rights "extend to every kind of copyrighted work." But it is precisely these two rights wherein educators, researchers, and similar nonprofit groups find their latitude.

Nevertheless, the bill clearly abandoned, in the tradition of its more recent predecessors, the "for-profit" limitation. The *Report* explained that "The right of public performance . . . extends to literary, musical, dramatic, and choreographic works, pantomimes, and motion pictures and other audiovisual works and sound recording and, unlike the equivalent provisions now in effect, is not limited by any 'for-profit' requirements. The approach of the bill, as in many foreign laws, is first to state the public performance right in broad terms, and then to provide specific exemptions for educational and other nonprofit uses." The report went on to state that this approach was "more reasonable than the outright exemption of the 1909 statute" because "the line between commercial and nonprofit organization is increasingly difficult to draw," adding that many so-called nonprofit institutions are "highly subsidized and capable of paying royalties," and that "the widespread public exploitation of copyright works by . . . noncommercial organizations is likely to grow."

Most of these specific exemptions to the copyright owner's rights of performance and display were contained within the concepts of fair use and library copying as articulated in S. 1361, as well as in Section 110, which dealt specifically with exceptions regarding performance and display.

Section 107, on fair use, consumed more than five closely spaced pages of explanation and example in Senate *Report 93-983*. Some of it repeated what had been stated in the 1967 House *Report No. 83* (see Volume II), but not all. The four criteria of fair use were reiterated as guidelines, and the examples of legitimate fair use by a copyright user that had been forwarded in the Register's 1961 *Report* were cited approvingly in *Report No. 93-983* as giving "some idea of the sort of activities that the courts might regard as fair use under the circumstances." Quotation for purposes of review or illustration, use in a parody, summarizations in a news report, "reproduction by a library of a portion of a work to replace part of a damaged copy," and "reproduction by a teacher or student of a small part of a work to illustrate a lesson" were among those examples that were cited in the Register's *Report* that had appeared 13 years earlier.

Report No. 93-983 carefully explained that Section 107 was not intended to either freeze or change the fair use doctrine. "In particular, the reference to fair use 'by reproduction in copies or phonorecords or by any other means' should not be interpreted as sanctioning any reproduction beyond the normal and reasonable limits of fair use," and, in addition, the phrase was "not intended to give this kind of use any special or preferred status as compared with other kinds of uses." Furthermore, given rapid technological change, "the courts must be free to adapt the doctrine to particular situations on a case-by-case basis."

Since "there are few if any judicial guidelines" in the areas of copying by teachers and in public libraries, the Judiciary Committee deemed it advisable to consider these topics in relative detail as they pertained to fair use.

In this regard, several phrases found in House *Report No. 83* of 1967 cropped up in Senate *Report No. 93-983*, notably the ones stating that "fair use can extend to the reproduction of copyrighted material for purposes of classroom teaching," and that "the nonprofit character of the school" had an effect on the doctrine's applicability. Beyond such repetitions, however, the 1974 *Report* consistently tried to distinguish between the doctrine's applicability to the relatively spontaneous situation of a "teacher who, acting individually and at [her/]his own volition, makes one or more copies for temporary use by [herself/]himself or his[/her] pupils"—which was a legitimate application—as opposed to copying "done by the educational institution . . . or where copying was required or suggested by the school administration. . . ."

Another point concerned the vexing and long-standing problem of single and multiple copying. The Senate *Report* did not consider this facet in detail, but did note that the doctrine "should differentiate between the amount of a work that can be reproduced by a teacher for his[/her] own classroom use . . . and the amount that can be reproduced for distribution to pupils." Other factors to be considered vis-à-vis multiple copying were the numbers of students involved, whether the copies were circulated beyond the classroom's confines, and "whether the copies were recalled or destroyed after temporary use." This final caveat is especially interesting when we consider its practical application: pupils, for example, learning about ecology, forests, and the paper shortage through photocopied handouts are then instructed to burn their copies.

A final explanation concerning the nature of the use contained in the *Report* warned teachers not to gradually collect so many parts of a work that they accidentally collected an "anthology": such a practice "could turn into an infringement." On the other hand, certain "special uses," such as copying extracts of a work in a typing class, were legitimate under fair use.

Classroom teaching, the nonprofit element, spontaneous and individual as opposed to planned and institutional copying, single as opposed to multiple copying, the anthology aspect, and special uses all related to the first of the four guidelines of the fair use doctrine: the "purpose and nature of the use." A second guideline concerned the "nature of the copyrighted work"; that is, what kind of material—novels, poems, or textbooks, for example—was being copied. As the *Report* said, "The character and purpose of the work will have a lot to do with whether its reproduction for classroom purposes is fair use or infringement." In this light, it was important whether the work being used was, by its nature, "intended for performance or public exhibition," such as a drama.

Another criterion under this guideline was whether or not a work was "consumable." A student workbook, for example, could not be legally copied under fair use; a textbook "and other material prepared for the school markets would be less susceptible to reproduction for classroom use than material prepared for general public distribution." Hence, the doctrine could be "liberally applied" to such items as newspaper articles, but works designed specifically to be "consumed" by the educational process were relatively well protected by copyright.

Another factor concerned the material's availability. Out-of-print works and similar material normally would justify reproduction of the work by a user. Nevertheless, this seeming liberalism was considerably narrower than it might appear, as *Report No. 93-983* indicated. For example, organizations such as the Institute for Scientific Information, which were legally "licensed to provide photocopies," interjected a complicating variable if such a service could provide the needed copy. Moreover, the censorship aspects of copyright were enhanced by the *Report* in terms of the work's availability: "The applicability of the fair use doctrine to unpublished works is narrowly limited since, although the work is unavailable, this is the result of a deliberate choice on the part of the copyright owner. Under ordinary circumstances, the copyright owner's right of first publication would outweigh any needs of reproduction for classroom purposes." Thus, certain embarrassing documents, such as corporate statistics, conceivably could be shielded from public scrutiny by registering them in the Copyright Office.

A third fair use guideline, explained in *Report No. 93-983*, was the "amount of substantiality of the material used." If, for instance, "too much" of a work was copied, then there would be an infringement.

The substantiality guideline had been considered in the House's 1967 *Report* and said much the same. *Report No. 93-983* reiterated that educators could make a single copy of an entire work (such as a poem, story, or article) without fear of a law suit, provided that this practice did not extend to making a copy of an entire encyclopedia volume, periodical issue, novel, treatise, monograph, or similar publication. Educators could, however, make multiple copies of excerpts (such as an encyclopedia article) from such publications for classroom use under the fair use doctine, although this interpretation "should not be construed as permitting a teacher to make multiple copies of the same work on a repetitive basis or for continued use."

The Senate *Report* discussed the final guideline of fair use, that of the "effect of the use on the potential market for or value of the work," which generally has been perceived as the most critical of the four criteria. It was in connection with this guideline that the House Judiciary Committee had written the sentence which so angered educators in 1967: "Where the unauthorized copying displaces what realistically might have been a sale, no matter how minor the amount of money involved, the interests of the copyright owners needs protection." This phrase, as educators had been assured, was deleted from the Senate's *Report* of 1973.

In fact, much of the verbiage concerning the potential market guideline was eliminated from the 1974 Senate *Report*. It was emphasized, however, that this "factor must almost always be judged in conjunction with the other three criteria," although "a use that supplants any part of the normal market for a copyrighted work would ordinarily be considered an infringement." At root, however, fair use "is essentially supplementary by nature, and classroom copying that exceeds the legitimate teaching aims such as filling in missing information or bringing a subject up-to-date would go beyond the proper bounds of fair use. Isolated instances of minor infringements, when multipled many times, become in the aggregate a major inroad on copyright that must be prevented."

The Senate Judiciary Committee made no bones about the fact that it was concerned primarily with the fair use doctrine as it pertained to classroom teaching, but noted that its "concentrated attention" in this area "should not obscure its application in other areas," since "the same general standards of fair use are applicable to all kinds of uses of copyrighted material. . . ." In particular, these uses included educational broadcasting, transmitting instructional television programs into remote regions, uses by the blind, preserving early motion picture prints, and uses that might be involved in a person's or institution's defense of his/her/its reputation.

The second major section of S.1361 that dealt with "specific exemptions" to the copyright owner's "exclusive right" to control the performance and display of his/her work was Section 108 on "Reproduction by Libraries and Archives." Basically, Section 108 stipulated that a library and its employees may make one copy of a work, provided that such use is not designed for a "commercial advantage," that the library is open to all relevant publics, and that the reproduction or distribution of the work includes a copyright notice. The reasoning behind this section, as expressed in *Report No. 93-983*, was to authorize the copying of unpublished works for purposes of preservation or security; to replace a damaged or lost copy (provided that another copy cannot be obtained through normal trade channels); to copy and distribute copies of "not more than one article" of a copyrighted work for the convenience of patrons, whether on the library premises or through interlibrary loan, provided that the copy becomes the property of the user, that the library have no notice that the copy will be used for any purpose other than "private study," and that a "warning of copyright" be prominently posted; and finally, a library may copy an entire work, such as a novel, provided that it is out-of-print, that a user requests it for private study, and that a prior search by the library is made for a reasonably priced, unused copy which is available through commonly known trade sources, the publisher, the copyright owners, or an authorized reproducing service.

Beyond these qualifications, there were other clauses in the section that represented the outcomes of recent politicking by owners and users. Notable in this respect was Subsection 108(d). Librarians had objected, in shrill tones, to Subsection 108(d)(1) of the 1971 bill because of an offending phrase which stated that a library could make a copy of a work (it was unspecified whether the work could be an entire volume or only a small excerpt) provided that the "user has established to the satisfaction of the library or archives that an unused copy cannot be obtained at a normal price from commonly known trade sources in the United States, including authorized reproducing services." In the 1973 bill, this phrase was deleted and was replaced, in part, with Subsection 108(e), which states that an "entire work" could be copied by a library provided the "library or archives has first determined on the basis of a reasonable investigation that a copy . . . of the copyrighted work cannot be obtained at a fair price. . . ." While policymakers did not capitulate entirely to librarians, this nonetheless is a considerably less specific phrase, and in effect it applied virtually only to books. Hence, a quick perusal of *Books in Print* by a librarian would likely meet the letter of the proposed law. Indeed, *Report No. 93-983* specified that "commonly known trade sources" and "authorized reproducing services" be checked before making a copy, but these phrases no longer were in the Copyright Law Revision bill, and appear to refer only to entire works that are out-of-print. Moreover, the term "reasonable investigation" also is ambiguous. As the *Report* stated, the "scope and nature of a reasonable investigation to determine that an unused copy cannot be obtained will vary according to the circumstances of a particular situation."

Another outcome of interest group conflict between 1971 and 1973 is found in Subsection 108(f). The old version used in S. 644 had been slightly filled out and perhaps strengthened to protect librarians from copyright infringement suits stemming from library-related photocopying. Employees of the library were protected, but not, according to *Report No. 93-983*, "the person using such equipment or requesting such copy if the use exceeds fair use. . . . It is the intent of this legislation that a subsequent unlawful use by a user of a copy of a work lawfully made by a library, shall not make the library liable for such improper use."

Subsection 108(g) was, for the most part, new, and was basically pro-copyright owner in its thrust. The subsection prohibited any form of multiple copying by librarians, a limitation that also was contained in the 1967 bill, but then went on to ban "systematic reproduction" as well.

Senate *Report No. 93-983* explained what was meant by "systematic reproduction" in some detail: "Systematic reproduction or distribution occurs when a library makes copies of such materials available to other libraries or to groups of users under formal or informal arrangements whose purpose or effect is to have the reproducing library serve as their source of such material." While it was opined in the *Report* that "it is not possible to formulate specific definitions of 'systematic copying,'" some examples of the practice were offered as guidelines.

One such example would be the hypothetical case of a library which maintains a substantial collection of biology journals, and then informs other libraries that it will furnish them with copies of articles from these journals on request; as a result of this policy, the other libraries discontinue the building of their collections of biology journals, and discontinue or refrain from subscribing to biology journals. A similar instance would be the case of the research center that subscribes to only one or two copies of needed scientific journals and then photocopies articles from those journals for distribution to its staff, thus undermining the journals' multiple subscription potentiality. A final example would be agreement in which the branches of the same library system implement a practice of having only one branch subscribe to particular journals with the understanding that the remaining branches can obtain copies of articles from these journals on request. In sum, these examples added up to one very clear meaning of S.1361: that developing, library-based information systems and networks—which, by definition, exchange data over geographic space on demand—could not escape payment to copyright owners.

Report No. 93-983 concluded that, overall, Section 108 provided "an appropriate statutory balancing of the rights of creators, and the needs of users. However, neither a statute nor a legislative history can specify precisely which library photocopying practices constitute the making of 'single copies' as distinguished from 'systematic reproduction.'"

Interestingly, the committee appeared to display a concern for the ongoing development of information systems that were not necessarily library-based, stating that the "photocopying needs of such operations as multicounty regional systems, must be met." It was recommended in the *Report* that copyright owners get together with librarians in order "to formulate photocopying guidelines to assist library patrons and employees" and that "workable clearance and licensing procedures be developed." Moreover, it was urged that the proposed National Commission on New Technological Uses of Copyrighted Works "give priority to those aspects of the library-copyright interface which require further study and clarification."

The final principal section dealing with the role of the neo-publishing technologies in S.1361 was Section 110, which specifically concerned "exemptions of certain performances and displays." Of special import were Subsections 110(1), 110(2), and 110(4).

Subsection 110(1) broached the old saw of face-to-face teaching activities, and it was an attempt to set out the conditions under which instructional performances and displays, other than educational broadcasting, could be exempted from copyright. All varieties of copyrighted materials were covered by the clause, which exempted the performance or display of these works "by instructors or pupils in the course of face-to-face teaching activities of a nonprofit educational institution," where the teaching is occurring "in a classroom or similar place devoted to instruction."

The idea behind Subsection 110(1) was not only to protect educators and students from infringements suits, but to distinguish traditional modes of teaching from the new and evolving methods of electronic educational transmission.

It is noteworthy in this context that, as *Report No. 93-983* observed, the phrase "face-to-face" does not "require that the teacher and his[/her] student be able to see each other, although it does require this simultaneous presence in the same general place." Moreover, the teaching activities protected by the subsection included "systematic instruction of a very wide variety of subjects. . . ." Still, the Senate Judiciary Committee came out clearly on the side of boredom in school; the clause did not encompass teaching activities involving "performances or displays, whatever their cultural value or intellectual appeal, that are given for the recreation or entertainment of any part of their audience."

Provided these qualifications were met, there simply were "no limitations" to what copyrighted works could be used in teaching pupils. A teacher or student "could read aloud from copyrighted text material, act out a drama, play or sing a musical work, perform a motion picture or filmstrip, or display text or pictorial material to the class by means of a projector." Guest lecturers and similar "instructors" also were protected.

Subsection 110(2) was another clause of particular interest to educators. While it did not deal with the neo-publishing technologies as other portions of Section 110 did, the clause, which was continued in S.22 and ultimately enacted into law, probably will hold the greatest potential effect on the future development of instructional technologies and education. Subsection 110(2) concerned instructional broadcasting, and applied only to the "performance of a nondramatic literary or musical work or of a sound recording, or display of a work." This meant, in effect, that a copyright proprietor's permission would be required for the showing of movies, operas, musicals, and so forth, on educational television or radio, but nothing else. Nonetheless, legislative hair-splitting in the *Report* is evident on this point: "Thus, for example, a performer could read a nondramatic literary work aloud . . . (which would constitute a display) but the copyright owner's permission would be required for him to act it out in dramatic form (which would constitute a performance)."

To be considered exempt from copyright control under the instructional broadcasting clause, a transmission must meet three criteria: First a performance or display must be "a regular part of the systematic instructional activities of a governmental body or a nonprofit educational institution."

"Systematic instruction" could include material and methods "not related to specific course function," and cable television installation and similar "commercial facilities" could be used in these nonprofit transmissions and the exemption still would apply.

A second criterion amplified the first, and stipulated that the transmission be "directly related and of material assistance to the teaching content" of the broadcast.

The third and final condition was more complex. It required that an educational, nonprofit transmission be designed principally for reception in "classrooms or similar places normally devoted to instruction," or reception by people who are unable to be in an educational center because of "disabilities or other special circumstances" that prevent their attendance, or reception by government employees "as a part of their official duties." These stipulations were not quite so rigid as they may sound, however, because such transmissions needed to be oriented only "primarily" rather than "solely" to these recipients; in other words, the public could at least get in on the nonprofit, educational transmission.

The overall significance of Subsection 110(2) lay in its possible effect on the future homogenization of information technologies, such as the photocopier and the computer, with communications technologies, such as cable television and electronic data transmission systems. These technologies are gradually becoming integrated, and a majority of computer installations now have a communications capacity. Hence, while it seems almost inevitable that developing technology will impact heavily on the educational process and on the institutional form of education itself, how public policy will affect that impact remains unknown. Subsection 110(2) of the Copyright Act of 1976, as originally expressed in S. 1361, probably will prove to be the chief expression of public policy for this vital, if ill-understood, aspect of the new information technologies. It would appear at this juncture, regrettably, that a potential effect of the educational broadcasting clause may be to inhibit the educational uses of the evolving information/communications systems and networks.

The final major portion of Section 110 that affected educators and related professions was in Clause (4). As *Report No. 93-983* stated, this subsection "contained a general exception to the exclusive right of public performance that would cover some, though not all, of the same ground as the present 'for-profit' limitations, [and] applies to the same general activities and subject matter as those covered by the 'for-profit' limitation today; public performances of non-dramatic literary and musical works." There is a catch here, however, in that to be exempted, such performances must be "given directly in the presence of an audience whether by means of living performers, the playing of phonorecords, or the operation of a receiving apparatus, and would not include a 'transmission to the public'" This proviso was intended to be a tough one by the Senate Judiciary Committee; its *Report* flatly states that "public performances given or sponsored in connection with any commercial or profit-making enterprises are subject to the exclusive rights of the copyright owner even though the public is not charged for seeing or hearing the performance."

There was an exception, and a rather complicated one. The committee had tried to exempt those performances that were seen as legitimate educational functions from copyright control, and yet also recognize that on occasion the performers themselves sometimes must be paid no matter how eleemosynary the enterprise. On the one hand, Subsection 110(4) of S. 1361 stated that, to be free from copyright restricitons, the nonprofit performance had to be given "without payment of any fee or other compensation for the performance to any of its performers, promoters, or organizers," but, on the other hand, Senate *Report No. 93-983* stated that "the exemption would not be lost if the performers, or directors, or producers of the performance, instead of being paid directly 'for the performance' are paid a *salary* [emphasis is mine] for duties encompassing the performance.'' Thus, the policy-makers tried to exempt such activities as a performance by a school band and the participation by a school teacher in his/her capacity as band leader, but simultaneously keep a tight reign on the ''free use of copyrighted material under the guise of charity. . . .'' If the legislative distinction between ''fee'' and ''salary'' was nitpicking, at least it was nitpicking with a purpose.

Sections 107, 108, and 110 were and are of primary pertinence to the neo-publishing technologies and the interest groups concerned with them, but the sections had very little to say about the single information technology that perhaps was (and is) the most worrisome to copyright owners and tantalizing to copyright users: the computer. Only one section of S.1361 dealt with the computer, and it stood as a succinct statement of nonpolicy. Section 117 related that ''this title does not afford to the owner of a copyright in a work any greater or lesser rights with respect to the use of the work in conjunction with automatic systems capable of storing, processing, retrieving, or transferring information, or in conjunction with any similar device, machine, or process, than those afforded to works under the law whether Title 17 or the common law statutes of a state, in effect on December 31, 1974, as held applicable and construed by a court in an action brought under this title.''

Senate *Report No. 93-983* explained what was largely obvious in Section 117: that it was designed ''to preserve the status quo.'' Unfortunately, the Judiciary Committee did not explain what it deemed the status quo to be, other than to observe that ''the problems are not sufficiently developed for a definitive legislative solution,'' and shuffled the question off to the proposed National Commission on New Technological Uses of Copyrighted Works, which ''is intended, among other things, to make a thorough study of the emerging patterns in this field and . . . to recommend definite copyright provisions to deal with the situation.''

In any event, the *Report* noted that Section 117 ''is intended neither to cut off any rights that may now exist, nor to create new rights that might be denied under the Copyright Act of 1909 or under common law principles currently applicable,'' and that it ''deals only with the exclusive rights of a copyright owner with respect to computer uses . . . With respect to the copyrightability of computer programs, the ownership of copyright in them, the term of protection, and the formal requirements of the remainder of the bill, the new statute would apply.''

The time proviso in Section 117, that which concerned the appropriate and applicable statute in potential copyright infringement suits involving computer usage, seemed destined to become a craw in many federal judicial throats in the future. As the *Report* stated, ''An action for infringement of a copyrighted work by means of a computer would necessarily be a federal action brought under the new Title 17. The court, in deciding the scope of exclusive rights in the computer area, would first need to determine the applicable law, whether state common law or the Copyright Act of 1909. Having determined what law was applicable, its decision would depend upon its interpretation of what that law was on the point on the day before the effective date of the new statute.'' In other words, not only had the legislators deferred to the judges on the topic of public policy for computers, but also had left to them the choice of the law which they could use in formulating that policy.

While Section 117 was the sole section in S.1361 dealing specifically with computers, various portions of *Report No. 93-983* referred to the issue in connection with other sections of the bill. Some of these passages are important. For example, the *Report* recorded the existence of the controversy over the copyrighting of computer programs as a part of its discussion of Section 102(b). The argument, in essence, was whether a computer programmer could copyright his/her methodology, i.e., the processes which s/he uses to complete a program, or whether his/her copyright extended only to the actual program itself, i.e., the "writing" made by the programmer that expresses his/her ideas. The *Report* asserted that Section 102(b) made it "clear that the expression adopted by the programmer (i.e., his[/her] 'writing') is the copyrightable element in a computer program, and the actual processes or methods embodied in the program are not within the scope of copyright law. . . . The basic dichotomy between expression and idea remains unchanged."

Similarly, another passage in the *Report* made it plain (if in an offhanded way) that a "performance" and a "display"—the only two rights in the copyright owner's bundle of five rights that are less than totally exclusive—can include computer usage, and hence be in potential violation of copyright. "A performance may be accomplished 'either directly or by means of any device or process,' including all kinds of equipment for reproducing . . . visual images, any sort of transmitting apparatus, any type of electronic retrieval system, and any other techniques and systems not yet in use or even invented." The *Report*'s comment on what the term "display" encompassed rectifies the point: "In addition to the direct showings of a copy of a work, 'display' would include the projection of an image on a screen or other surface by any method, the transmission of an image by electronic or other means, and the showing of an image on a cathode ray tube, or similar viewing apparatus connected with any sort of information storage and retrieval system."

Also of note was the fact that the *Report* specifically excluded libraries from reproducing computer programs, even for the sake of archival preservation. While a library, under Section 108, could take photocopies of unpublished manuscripts for the purpose of preservation "by microfilm or electrostatic process," it "could not reproduce the work in 'machine-readable' language for storage in an information system."

While neither S. 1361 nor its accompanying Senate *Report* were the last official statements on copyright law revision, they were critical ones, and for that reason we have dwelt on them at length here. Within the next three years, another Copyright Law Revision bill (S. 22 and H.R. 2223) and three official *Report*s would be released by Congress. These and other documents are included in this volume, but they represent refinements on the 1973 policies. Hence, we shall not review them here in the same detail.

The 1973 Senate hearings on copyright law revision had displayed an antagonism between users and owners that probably could not be reconciled, and it was evident that this gap existed in some measure because of the uncertainty generated among copyright users by Commissioner Davis's recommendation in the *Williams & Wilkins* case. On November 27, 1973, the full Court of Claims announced its ruling in the case: by a 4:3 decision, the Court decided to overturn the recommendation of its commissioner, and ruled in favor of the defendant. Library and education interests were not only surprised, but cautiously jubilant, and their caution heightened when it was learned that the U.S. Supreme Court had agreed to hear the case on appeal. Nevertheless, the judiciary was perceived as swinging slowly to the side of copyright users, and this perception was reinforced a few months later when, on March 4, 1974, the U.S. Supreme Court announced its decision in the case of *Columbia Broadcasting System, Inc. v. TelePrompter Corporation*. The Court held 6:3 in favor of TelePrompter, a cable television company, stating that the Copyright Act of 1909 did not require cable operators to pay the networks a fee for boosting their signals to remote regions. While tenuous, it was nonetheless arguable that such pro-user logic could be extended to the machinations of photocopiers and computers.

With a possible trend emerging in court decisions concerning the two biggest issues of the copyright debate, Congress began moving on S.1361 at a pace which, given the Senate's history of lethargy on the topic, was comparable to that of a Xerox 4000. As the chief counsel of the subcommittee noted, "The incredible number of interests running around on this bill have made everyone punch-drunk and made them want to get rid of this bill."

On April, 8, 1974, the Subcommittee on Patents, Trademarks, and Copyrights referred the bill to the Judiciary Committee. As a result of the committee's debate of June 11, a few changes were made which granted certain benefits to cable television operators and recording artists at the expense of the broadcasting, sports, and movie industries; the clauses dealing with the neo-publishing issues emerged from the committee untouched, probably because of their complexity. An aide to a senator attending the session related that "the members did not have the expertise or time to deal with the issues."

During the following month, July 9 through July 24, the Senate Commerce Committee reviewed salient portions of S.1361 (which did not affect the sections dealing with the new information technologies), but held no hearings on them, and sent the bill to the Senate. Despite an onrush of events during the late summer of 1974 that were making political history, the Senate voted on S.1361 on Monday, September 9—the day following President Gerald R. Ford's pretrial pardon of former President Richard M. Nixon for possible Watergate-related crimes. In view of the intense and bitter controversy characterizing the politics of copyright law revision, the vote was abnormally near unanimity. By 70:1, with three senators voting present, the Senate passed S.1361. The full Senate did make some amendments to the bill, but the issues of photocopying, computer usage, educational exemptions, "for-profit" limitations, and fair use never were mentioned on the floor of the Senate.

The years 1974 and 1975 found copyright politics taking a different turn, moving more toward the movies, jukeboxes, and recordings, and away from photocopying and computers, though there were many machinations behind the scenes over the issue among copyright owners and users. Several key reports were issued by the House and Senate during this period, notably Senate *Reports No. 94-92* and *No. 94-473*, both issued in 1975, and *Reports No. 94-1476* and *No. 94-1733*, both issued in 1976. It is not our intention here to review in detail these *Reports*, other than in terms of how they differ from *Report No. 93-983* which had been issued in 1973 by the Senate and which accompanied S.1361.

On February 19, 1976, the Senate passed S.22 by a vote of 97 to 0, and in August of that same year, the House Subcommittee on Courts, Civil Liberties, and the Administration of Justice reported favorably on H.R. 2223, the House counterpart of the bill that had been passed by the Senate. Progress was being made, but even as late as 1975, most people would not have believed such progress was possible. Consider the House hearings of that year which indicated a substantial difference of opinion between copyright owners and users over the new information technologies. A representative of the National Education Association stated in words essentially identical to its 1973 testimony, that teachers' interests needed an overall educational exemption. In contrast, the representative of the Information Industry Association argued that such an exemption would be inconsistent with previous legislative thinking on the topic. Harry N. Rosenfield, counsel for organized education's Ad Hoc Committee on Copyright Law Revision, perhaps summarized the position of organized education—and for that matter library and archival interests—as succinctly as anyone when he stated that the ad hoc committee favored the limited educational exemption, the clarification of fair use, the committee's opposition to a copyright term of life of the author plus 50 years, a waiver of statutory damages for innocent infringements (which already had been incorporated into copyright law revision bills for some time), support of the librarians in their position on Section 108 (already discussed in this introduction), recognition of instructional television as a school activity, opposition to any kind of copyright clearinghouse notions, and finally, "that input into a computer not be infringement for the period of the study by the National Commission on New Technological Uses, . . . but that output be paid for the normal rules of the game."

Library photocopying proved to have a renewed controversial color during the 1975 hearings. Librarians were particularly outraged by a passage in the 1974 *Report No. 93-983,* which dealt with Section 108(g). Section 108(g) referred, of course, to "systematic reproduction or distribution of copies," and is reproduced in this volume.

The Association of Research Libraries was particularly concerned over this issue during its testimony to the House subcommittee, and stated that, "at issue is the making, whether at the request of a patron or at the request of another library, of single copies of copyrighted matter for the private use of a scholar or other reader." The Association of Research Libraries went on to contend that clause (g)(2) of Section 108 was a "restriction" written into the bill by the Senate Patents, Trademarks, and Copyrights Subcommittee "at the last minute" and was "only vaguely and confusingly explained in the committee report." Therefore, in the opinion of the Association of Research Libraries, it was "impossible to determine exactly what it means," but that it appeared "to be potentially applicable whenever a library makes a photocopy of an article or other portion of a published work in the context of a 'system'." The Association went on to note that there were "many such systems of libraries, from city or county branch library systems to the university with branch campuses to regional library consortia. Where it applies, Section 108(g)(2) would reach the making of a *single* copy for a *single* requester, of any part however small, of that copyrighted work. It is precisely the right to make such copies which Section 108 was intended to confirm." Relying on this logic, the Association of Research Libraries contended that a library was prohibited by the bill from making at a user's request a single copy of a journal article or an excerpt from another published work simply on the grounds that a library had obtained the copy from a branch library; this, in the Association's view, was against custom.

The Association of American Publishers argued back that not only was the "library world" wrong but divided on the issue, going on to summarize its position with the statement that, "We think it unnecessary to belabor the point that unauthorized systematic copying—the kind of copying that is done at a research center, or at a central resource point for use in a library network—is the functional equivalent of piratical reprint publication. . . . It is equally meretricious to complain that the 'systematic copying' that is to be paid for is too imprecisely defined, or that payment cannot be made because payment systems have not been established.''

While these statements are representative of the substance of the 1975 hearings as they pertain to neo-publishing technologies, some other testimony is worth a quick review here. For example, the representative of the American Chemical Society still was protecting the interests of copyright owners although he had, with uncharacteristic diplomacy, dropped his references to "the little boy in Williston, North Dakota,'' who might take home a library book and copy a couple of pages; America's chemists no longer were advocating that the little boy of the Dakota plains should be prosecuted to the hilt as they had urged in 1973.

The president of the Association of American Publishers made public for the first time the fact that a series of meetings between "copyright owners and users" had been held between 1972 and 1974, principally at the Cosmos Club of Washington (an exclusive club of scientists and academics) and at Dumbarton Oaks, during which agreements had been made among the Register of Copyrights, the Chairman of the National Commission on Libraries and Information Science (NCLIS), and the Association of American Publishers, on the copying of journal articles. Despite these meetings, the president of the Association of American Publishers noted that: "I regret to say, Mr. Chairman, that there has not been much progress to date, chiefly because the librarians have refused to accept either the Senate bill or the guidelines suggested by the NCLIS and Ms. Ringer [the Register] as in any way limiting frame of reference. . . . their consistent reply has been that they know of no copying done by libraries which extends beyond fair use.'' The president of the Association of American Publishers went on to note that "I suggest, Mr. Chairman, there are two possible explanations for this unforthcoming attitude. Either the library community as a whole is still attempting to secure total exemption from copyright, and expects to get its way with the Congress; or the attitude here expressed reflects a minority view within the library community and is not therefore representative of the whole. In this latter connection, I must say that we are struck by the difference in the attitudes we have found among local librarians and those expressed by the official spokesmen of library associations in Washington.''

Other representatives also made statements of interest during the final congressional hearings on copyright law revision, notably the representative of the American Association of Law Libraries; the chairperson of the Board of Williams & Wilkins Company; a number of spokespersons for the Ad Hoc Committee on Copyright Law Revision, which represented organized education and library interests; the peripetatic lawyer, Bella L. Linden, arguing the case for copyright owners; the chairperson of the Educational Media Producers Council, representing, in effect, copyright owners, although from a more moderate point of view; and the always intellectual Paul G. Zurkowski, president of the Information Industry Association. The testimony of each of these witnesses is included in this volume.

As we have noted earlier, a number of excellent reports were issued by Congress during 1975 and 1976, but perhaps the most significant of these was House *Report No. 94-1476*, published in 1976 by the Committee on the Judiciary. In this *Report*, the Judiciary Committee made public an agreement that had been reached on March 19, 1976, among the Ad Hoc Committee of Educational Institutions and Organizations on Copyright Law Revision, the Authors League of America, and the Association of American Publishers. This was a breakthrough. In their letter to the Judiciary Committee, these three umbrella organizations stated that, "We are now happy to tell you that the agreement has been approved by the principals." The agreement stated that a single copy could be made of: a chapter from a book; an article from a periodical or newspaper; a short story, essay, or poem, whether or not from a collected work; and a chart, graph, diagram, drawing, cartoon, or picture. Multiple copies that did not exceed in number more than one copy per pupil in the course could be made by or for the teacher for classroom use or discussion, provided that the copying met the fair-use tests of "brevity and spontaneity" and that each copy included a notice of copyright. There was, of course, more to the agreement than that, as in most agreements, and the details are included in this volume. The agreement between owners and users over the photocopying question was significant, and it resulted in an important parenthetical phrase in the revision bill that eventually was enacted into a new copyright law. That phrase was, "including multiple copies for classroom use." To put the phrase in context, Section 107, Limitations on Exclusive Rights: Fair Use, now read, "Notwithstanding provisions of section 106, the fair use of a copyrighted work, including such use by reproduction and copies or phonorecords, or by any other means specified by that section, for purposes such as criticism, comment, news reporting, teaching (including multiple copies for classroom use), scholarship, or research is not infringement of copyright." As noted, the parenthetical phrase was new—brand new—and represented a considerable conquest for copyright users. That parenthetical phrase now is the law of the land.

Also amended as the result of the 1975 hearings and agreements reached thereafter was the eternal Section 108(g) which dealt with multiple copies and systematic reproduction. As *Report No. 94-1476* noted, "this provision in S.22 provoked a storm of controversy, centering around the extent to which the restrictions on 'systematic' activities would prevent the continuation and development of interlibrary networks and other arrangement involving the exchange of photocopies." Therefore, after much consideration, the committee had amended S.22, Section 108(g)(2), to read: "provided that nothing in this clause prevents a library or archives from participating in interlibrary or archives receiving such copies or phonorecords for distribution does so in such aggregate quantities as to substitute for a subscription or purchase of such work." Beyond that amendment, the committee added a completely new subsection (i) to Section 108, requiring that the Register of Copyrights report to Congress at five-year intervals on the "extent to which this section has achieved the intended statutory balancing of the rights of creators, and the needs of users." The report stated that it was the intention of Congress that the National Commission on New Technological Uses of Copyrighted Works, which had been established only recently, provide "good offices" in developing guidelines so that these needs could be balanced. These agreements are refined in the *Conference Report* submitted by the House Committee of Conferences on September 29, 1976, and which is reproduced in this volume.

Nevertheless, House *Report No. 94-1476* remains a particularly useful documentary, quite aside from the fact that it records certain key alterations in copyright law. Compiled in the *Report* was a well laid-out comparison of the Copyright Act of 1976 with the Copyright Act of 1909 plus the Committee "amendments to the nature of substitutes to S.22." The comparison is among the more useful documents coming out of the entire revision process and it is reproduced in its entirety here.

The utility of *Report No. 94-1476* is rivaled by the *Draft of the Second Supplementary Report of the Register of Copyrights on the General Revision of the*

U.S. Copyright Law: 1975 Revision Bill, October-December 1975, written by the Register of Copyrights. Not all of the document is contained in this volume, but relevant portions of Chapters 1, 2, 3, 4, and 6 of the *Draft*'s 15 chapters, which specifically pertain to issues involved in photocopying and computer usage, are reproduced here. The succinctness and lucidity of the Register are well worth the attention of copyright owners, users, and, even lawyers.

Rounding out Volume III of *Copyright, Congress, and Technology* are a number of public documents written in the bowels of the bureaucracy that indicate as well as any of the congressional reports the future of copyright. The annual *Reports* of the Librarian of Congress from 1974 through 1976 are included at appropriate intervals in Volume III, and these are notable for their tone on the prospects of copyright law revision which ranges from despondent to subdued; the 1976 annual *Report,* while noticeably more optimistic than the reports for the preceding two years, nevertheless is cautious in its optimism.

Volume III also is unique in that excerpts from the *Congressional Record* of the Senate and House are included. These excerpts trace the debates on the floor concerning the passage of S.22 in 1976. By no means are all the floor debates recorded in this volume, merely those that are of particular interest to readers following the controversies surrounding the neo-publishing technologies. On September 22, 1976, the House of Representatives passed a Copyright Revision bill by a vote of 316 yeas, 7 nays, 3 who answered "present," and 104 who did not vote. On September 30th, the Senate passed S.22 with 75 yeas, and no nays. The roll call votes for both the House and Senate are recorded in the *Congressional Record,* excerpts of which are reprinted in this volume.

Also reproduced in this volume are two Library of Congress publications, *Circular R21* and *Circular R99,* which cover the topics of "Copyright and the Librarian" and "Highlights of the New Copyright Law." Both publications are of use to the reader interested in a quick and cogent summary of how the law affects users of the new technologies.

As copyright law revision neared the end of its peculiar political history, new government agencies became increasingly involved in the implications of copyright and the new information technologies. Notable in this regard were the National Commission on Libraries and Information Science and the National Bureau of Standards (NBS) of the U.S. Department of Commerce. In 1976, the National Commission on Library and Information Science published its official report to the President on *National Information Policy* which is reproduced in its entirety in this volume. Of particular interest are the recommendations of the Commission, which urge that the United States establish a coordinated national information policy that would include the formation of an Office of Information Policy within the Executive Office of the President, an Interagency Council on Information Policy, and an Advisory Committee to assist the Office of Information Policy. While the prospects of adopting the Commission's recommendations are not bright, the report issued by the Commission is of note in the way that it explicates the political, social, and economic impact of technology in an age of information. While *National Information Policy* does not address copyright extensively as such, it details in a particularly cogent fashion the role of information policy in a post-industrial era.

The report issued in 1977 by the National Bureau of Standards, *Copyright in Computer-Readable Works: Policy Impacts of Technological Change,* written by Roy G. Saltman, also addresses the relationships between copyright and technology, if in a more technical fashion than the report published by the National

Commission on Libraries and Information Science. The entire NBS report is not reprinted in this volume, but the more germane portions of it are. Of particular note in the portion of the report reproduced here are chapters 1, 2, 3, and 6, which summarize the NBS findings, review the historical foundations of copyright, discuss some significant court decisions, and consider the role of policymaking for copyright in a technological era.

Volume III concludes with the entire text of the Copyright Act of 1976 and provides an appropriate finish for the book, since all the documents compiled in Volume III of *Copyright, Congress, and Technology* amount to a vast storehouse of authoritative knowledge, speculation, law, and policy. The documents should be of use not only to the copyright expert, but to the casual user of materials that are protected by copyright law.

NH
Tempe, Arizona

Copyright Law Revision
pursuant to S. Res. 56 on S. 1361
July 31 and August 1, 1973

STATEMENT OF STEPHEN A. McCARTHY, EXECUTIVE DIRECTOR, ASSOCIATION OF RESEARCH LIBRARIES

Mr. Chairman, my name is Stephen McCarthy. I am Executive Director of the Association of Research Libraries, an organization of the principal university and research libraries of the country. We appreciate this opportunity to present the views of the Association on the Copyright Revision Bill, S. 1361, and we ask that this statement be made part of the official record.

Mr. Chairman, the Association of Research Libraries wishes to recommend to the Committee an amendment to section 108(d) of S. 1361, in the form in which it was submitted to the staff of the Committee during the past week. A copy is attached to this statement.

Mr. Chairman and members of the Committee, the purpose of the proposed amendment is to ensure by specific legislative language that a customary, long established library service of providing a photocopy for a reader who requests it may be continued without infringement of copyright. Adoption of the amendment would remove the threat of suit against libraries arising out of varying judicial interpretations of what is or is not "fair use." At the same time this amendment would assure libraries, which are public service agencies largely supported by public funds, that they can and should employ modern technology and methods in serving their readers. It should be emphasized further that this amendment does not seek to encourage or develop a new service. Instead it seeks to assure beyond doubt or question the legality of a traditional service which was not challenged for two generations under the 1909 Copyright Law until a suit was brought by the Williams and Wilkins Company against the National Library of Medicine several years ago.

The opinion of Commissioner Davis of the U. S. Court of Claims in the Williams and Wilkins case brings into question the fair use doctrine as applied to library photocopying. Despite the several criteria of fair use which have been developed by the courts and which are expressed in section 107 of S. 1361, Commissioner Davis apparently disregarded all criteria except one and focused his attention on the loss of potential income by the copyright proprietor. In view of this opinion it is apparent that fair use can no longer be considered adequate assurance for the continuation of customery library services. At best, fair use is a defense in case of a suit. The services of libraries to their readers are of sufficient importance to society and to the nation as a whole to make it desirable to remove any doubts about the legality of a long established and much used service.

Section 108(d) (1) of S. 1361 requires the user to prove or demonstrate to the library that an unused copy is not available from a trade source. How does the ordinary reader do this? How does the library know that he has done it? How does the library evaluate the evidence? Questions such as these and others will inevitably arise, if 108(d) (1) is permitted to remain unchanged in the copyright revision bill. Observance of its requirements will impose a substantial added burden on libraries and on library users and thus will impede access to information. At the very least, this requirement will cause delays and hang-ups in service, at a time when the pressure for prompt service is very great.

While it is true that section 108(d)(1) may not affect the library user who is physically present in the library because he can make a copy for himself on a self-operated copying machine, it will impose a serious handicap on a reader from a distant library who is seeking to obtain library materials through interlibrary loan. This reader will be dependent on the staff of the library from which the loan is requested. The requirements placed on the reader and the library by this section would be in many cases result in denial of the request because compliance with the request might constitute an infringement of copyright and be subject to a suit for damages. It is clear that 108(d)(1) would thus have the effect of penalizing the user who does not have direct, personal, physical access to a large comprehensive library. The number of library users who do not have such access is substantial.

Library support both locally and at the federal level is limited. Appropriate bodies, including the Congress, adopted measures designed to encourage the sharing of library resources. This is consistent with traditional library practices. The Revision Bill without the amendment we recommend would raise doubts about the continuation of this practice because photocopying has been one of the accepted ways of sharing scarce library resources.

The requirements of the Bill in its present form would also add substantially to the expenses of libraries because decisions regarding photocopy requests could only be made by highly qualified personnel.

It may be noted further that the copyright laws of most foreign countries contain a specific provision permitting library photocopying for purposes of personal study and research.

I would emphasize that the amendment we recommend refers to a single, i.e., one, photocopy; it applies to one article or item in a periodical, not to the whole issue; and it applies to a complete work, i.e., a book, only if the work is no longer available in book stores.

This amendment does *not* seek to legalize multiple copying. Libraries are *not* trying to become publishers; libraries do *not* wish to photocopy best sellers or complete issues of periodicals.

Revision of the copyright law has been underway for a period of years. In that time, copyright proprietors have repeatedly stated that library photocopying was causing serious financial damages to their enterprises. No evidence to support this contention has been presented. In the absence of evidence, it seems fair to conclude that the damage is not as serious as has been alleged.

For these reasons, the Association of Research Libraries recommends the adoption of the proposed amendment as a means of assuring library users of the continuation of an important service.

Thank you for your attention. Our legal counsel, Mr. Brown, will now discuss briefly some of the legal aspects of library photocopying and the proposed amendment.

AMENDMENT TO COPYRIGHT REVISION BILL, S. 1361

Substitute for section 108(d) the following:

(d) The rights of reproduction and distribution under this section apply to a copy of a work, other than a musical work, a pictorial graphic or sculptural work, or a motion picture or other audiovisual work, made at the request of a user of the collections of the library or archives, including a user who makes his request through another library or archives, but only under the following conditions:

(1) The library or archives shall be entitled, without further investigation, to supply a copy of no more than one article or other contribution to a copyrighted collection or periodical issue, or to supply a copy or phonorecord of a similarly small part of any other copyrighted work.

(2) The library or archives shall be entitled to supply a copy or phonorecord of an entire work, or of more than a relatively small part of it, if the library or archives has first determined, on the basis of a reasonable investigation that a copy or phonorecord of the copyrighted work cannot readily be obtained from trade sources.

(3) The library or archives shall attach to the copy a warning that the work appears to be copyrighted.

and renumber section 108(d)(2) to make it 108(d)(4).

STATEMENT OF PHILIP B. BROWN, ATTORNEY FOR THE ASSOCIATION OF RESEARCH LIBRARIES

Mr. Chairman, members of the Committee, my name is Philip B. Brown. I am a partner in the Washington law firm Cox, Langford & Brown, counsel to the Association of Research Libraries. I appreciate this opportunity to appear before you with the President and Executive Director of ARL and the Chairman of its Copyright Committee. My statement supplements that of Dr. McCarthy with emphasis on recent legal developments bearing on the status of library photocopying under existing law and under the pending bill.

The major legal development on this subject in recent years is, of course, the case *Williams & Wilkins* v. *The United States*, pending before the judges of the Court of Claims following a report of the Commissioner filed on February 16, 1972. The case has been briefed and argued to the Court and is awaiting decision. The Commissioner held that the photocopying of entire articles from medical journals by the National Institutes of Health and the National Library of Medicine at the request of doctors and medical researchers constituted infringement of copyright and he recommended that the Court conclude, as a matter of law, that plaintiff is entitled to recover reasonable and entire compensation for infringement of copyright, the amount to be determined in further proceedings.

Subject to the pending decision of the Court, the main effect of the Commissioner's report on library photocopying is twofold, first to rule that such photocopying as was involved in the case constitutes a violation of the copyright proprietor's rights under 17 U.S.C. § 1, and, secondly, to rule that such copying is not protected by the doctrine of "fair use." If the Commissioner's report should be adopted by the Court, the decision would constitute the first judicial interpretation of the 1909 Act as it applies to library photocopying and an interpretation contrary to both the libraries' understanding of the meaning of the 1909 Act and to the previously unchallenged long-standing photocopying practices of libraries.

These new developments underscore the importance of the libraries' request that Congress adopt a specific amendment to Section 108(d) of the pending Copyright Revision Bill authorizing a library to make a single photocopy of an entire journal article at the request of a user without such a practice constituting an infringement of copyright. Prior to *Williams & Wilkins* it could be argued that if libraries interpreted the 1909 Act to authorize such copying and could point for support to the fact that the publishers had not challenged that interpretation and had even participated in a Gentlemen's Agreement for a period of years which ratified the libraries' practice, there was no need to give the libraries explicit statutory protection on this point, since the revision bill did not take away from libraries any rights which they then enjoyed under the 1909 Act. Today, it is no longer possible to assert that position, and the libraries' need for explicit statutory protection for such photocopying is clear.

The amendment to Section 108(d) proposed by the American Library Association and endorsed by the Association of Research Libraries is essential to permit a library to make a copy of an entire journal article for a user. Such an amendment would be fully consistent with the literal wording of all copyright statutes prior to 1909 and fully consistent with the interpretation placed on the 1909 Act by users and publishers alike for a period of 60 years.

In addition to adopting the specific photocopying amendment, we respectfully submit that Congress should also clarify and endorse the application of the doctrine of fair use to library photocopying practices. This is important both because the doctrine had not previously been judicially applied to library photocopying and because the report of the Commissioner in *Williams & Wilkins*, if allowed to stand, would raise serious doubt whether the doctrine could ever apply to library photocopying of an entire article. The Commissioner determined that the copying involved in NIH and NLM constituted "wholesale" copying, apparently simply because of the large number of individual requesters for each of whom the library made a copy. The Commissioner also referred to the facts that, on rare occasions, the same requester received a second copy at a later date and that the library furnished a copy of the same article to a number of different requesters. If these facts constitute "wholesale" copying, sufficient to deny a library the defense of fair use, it would appear that the defense would not be available to any large library, such as any of the major research libraries of this country, simply because the total number of patrons of each of these libraries would be so numerous as to fall within the Commissioner's term "wholesale," and thus go beyond his interpretation of fair use.

In order to restore the application of fair use to library photocopying consistent with the intent of the bills considered by this Committee over recent years, it is essential that Congress reject the interpretation given to fair use by the Commissioner in the *Williams & Wilkins* case and that Congress further declare that the long-standing practice of libraries of making a single copy of copyrighted material, including an entire journal article, is within the meaning of fair use in this bill.

Accordingly, there are two changes in the bill which libraries are requesting of this Committee: The first is the specific amendment to Section 108(d) proposed by ALA and ARL. The second is clarification that fair use applies to the normal library practice of making a single photocopy of copyrighted material, including an entire journal article, for a user.

We respectfully submit that these protections are essential to permit libraries to continue to serve the needs of scholars and to make appropriate use of existing technological aids in doing so. We submit that there is no evidence of damage to publishers resulting from this practice and that, in fact, the practice promotes subscriptions to journals rather than replacing them. There is certainly no evidence that this practice is driving publishers out of business. Library photocopying deserves continuing protection from Congress. In view of the uncertain state of the law resulting from the Commissioner's report in *Williams & Wilkins*, the statutory protection should be clear and certain.

The need for clarity and certainty is underscored by the fact that, without the protection of the proposed amendment to Section 108(d), a librarian could well be liable for the extensive damages provided for in Section 504 of the bill. The sentence in Section 504(c)(2) which allows the librarian to prove that "he believed and had reasonable grounds for believing that the reproduction was a fair use under Section 107 . . ." is rendered virtually meaningless by the report of the Commissioner in *Williams & Wilkins*. Without the proposed amendment to the bill, the librarian would undoubtedly refuse to run the risk of rendering the service to the patron—to the great detriment of research and scholarship.

STATEMENT OF EDMON LOW, CHAIRMAN, COPYRIGHT SUBCOMMITTEE, AMERICAN LIBRARY ASSOCIATION

I am Edmon Low, director of the Library of New College, Sarastota, Florida, and chairman, Copyright Subcommittee of the American Library Association, a nonprofit, educational organization founded in 1876. Its membership includes some 30,000 librarians, trustees and other public-spirited citizens dedicated to the development of libraries as essential factors in the continued educational, economic, scientific and cultural advancement of the American people. The Association is concerned with the development of all types of libraries—public libraries; school and college and university libraries; medical and law libraries and other specialized libraries—and with the problems they encounter, such as financing, relations with their patrons, and the legal provisions under which they operate, including copyright.

We are concerned here today with the Copyright Revision Bill, S. 1361, and primarily with the provisions relating to photocopying in libraries. This is a subject of great concern to all librarians and to the patrons whom they serve—the general user of the public library, the student, the scholar, the research man, the lawyer, doctor, minister or other professional individual, or to the Congressmen himself, as he frequently turns to our great Congressional Library for aid in his important work.

This copying may be roughly divided into two groups, the first being that done either by a member of a library staff or by the user himself from material in the library for immediate use on the premises or nearby; the second, that done by one library for and at the request of another library, often some distance away, for use by one of its patrons there. The first is often designated "in-house" copying, while the second we usually refer to as "inter-library loan." The first is often only a convenience to the patron, as for instance a student writing a term paper, in that he does have the material in hand and could use it on the premises; the second is basically the more important in that the scholar or other user does not have the document in hand and therefore it is his only practical access to what may be highly important material for information or research.

It is now generally understood that a single collection of books or other recorded forms of thought as represented by a library can contain only a fraction of the total amount of material in existence. Even the Library of Congress, possibly the largest single collection of materials in the world, does not have many thousands of titles which exist in the United States, to say nothing of those elsewhere in the world, while on the other hand even a relatively small library will often have titles not found anywhere else in the country. The location and cataloging of these titles, and of articles in journals, and the making of same available readily through photocopying or loan—the dissemination of knowledge—is indispensable to education and research and often involves the reproduction by photocopying of a portion of a monograph or a journal article protected by copyright.

It should be noted that copyright is not an inherent right, such as trial by jury of one's peers. It is a statutory right—one created by law—and may be changed, enlarged, narrowed, or abolished altogether by the Congress here assembled. It is a law enacted not for the benefit of an individual or a corporation but for the public good and with the purpose, as the Constitution expresses it "to encourage progress in science and the useful arts." Consequently, in considering revision, the problem becomes one of providing protection to the author or publisher to provide reasonable return on the investment of time and money, and at the same time to provide for the widest possible access to and dissemination of information to the public.

At present I am Director of the New College Library at Sarasota, Florida. New College is a small, but very fine, private college and its problems in this connection are typical of the two thousand small and medium-sized colleges throughout the country. While our library is liberally supported and spends every cent it can afford on serial subscriptions, we cannot possibly have the large resources of a university like the one at Gainesville or at Tallahassee. Yet our faculty members, if they maintain a good quality of teaching and do the research which contributes to it, must have access by random photocopying at times to the larger collections in the State and elsewhere.

It is usually not known that the inter-library loan arrangement often encourages the entering of additional subscriptions by the library rather than reducing the number as is often charged. It is a truism that a librarian would rather have a title at hand rather than to have to borrow even under the most convenient circumstances. Consequently, when the time comes around each year to consider the serials list of subscriptions, the record of inter-library loans is scanned and titles are included from which articles have been requested with some frequency during the year. In our library the number is two; if we have had two or more requests for articles from the same title during the year, we enter a subscription. This not only indicates how the procedure can help the periodical publishers but also indicates that if only one article or none was copied from a title during a year, the journal could not have been damaged materially in the process. It is not only the small schools which would suffer if such photocopying were eliminated, however; the scholars at Illinois or Cornell would also be severely put to it to continue their research in the same way and it is these scholars which account for the major writing for the scholarly journals. The journals themselves, therefore, have a stake in seeing this procedure continued in a reasonable way.

Courts have long recognized that some reproduction of portions of a copyrighted work for purposes of criticism, teaching, scholarship or research is desirable and this judicial concept, known as "fair use," is incorporated in Section 107 of the revision bill. Libraries have operated all these years under this principle but it does lack the assurance of freedom of liability from harassing suits which the librarian needs in his work. This fair use concept necessarily is expressed in general language in the bill so a librarian will not be able to be sure, until a court decides a particular case, whether his action, undertaken with the best of intentions to aid the patron, is or is not an infringement. Fair use, then, is really not right to copy any given thing, but only a defense to be invoked if one is sued. This threat of suit, even if one is able to maintain his innocence in court, is very real because suits are costly in proportion to the amount for which one is sued. This revision bill provides not only for demand for actual damages but also one can be sued for statutory damages up to a limit of $50,000 for each imagined infringement.

This threat has now become much greater by the recommendation of Commissioner Davis in the Williams and Wilkins case now under appeal in the U.S. Court of Claims. In this he says "While it may be difficult (if not impossible) to determine the number of sales lost to photocopying, the fact remains that each photocopy user is a potential subscriber or at least is a potential source of royalty income for licensed copying." [1] Also, "Plaintiff need not prove actual damages to make out its case for infringement." [1] Since any copying may be viewed as potential income, and since no actual damages have to be proved, this recommendation seems to indicate that *any* photocopying is an infringement and that there is no longer any fair use except in some very limited instances mentioned later in the report.

In light of the above, we feel that librarians greatly need some further protection than that offered by fair use in Section 107. We need a definite statement in the law that making a single copy to aid in teaching and research, and particularly in inter-library loan, is permissible and not subject to possible suit for this activity in behalf of the public good. To my knowledge, it has not been shown anywhere that this activity is harmful to the copyright proprietor and, as detailed above, may be of definite help to him.

In light of the above, we wish to request that the attached amendment be substituted for Section 108(d) in S. 1361. We believe this will provide the protection needed by librarians in their efforts to serve their various publics while allowing equally good protection to the owners of copyright.

In conclusion, may I say that I think I speak for all librarians that we intend to faithfully observe the provisions of whatever law is finally passed, both in letter and in spirit, but an unduly restrictive law will make it impossible to serve the people of this country and aid in teaching and research to the maximum extent which is desirable for all.

It has been a pleasure to appear before you today and we appreciate your genuine interest in the problems which copyright presents to libraries.

AMENDMENT TO COPYRIGHT REVISION BILL, S. 1361

Substitute for section 108(d) the following:

(d) The rights of reproduction and distribution under this section apply to a copy of a work, other than a musical work, a pictorial, graphic or sculptural work, or a motion picture or other audio-visual work, made at the request of a user of the collections of the library or achives, including a user who makes his request through another library or archives, but only under the following conditions:

(1) The library or archives shall be entitled, without further investigation, to supply a copy of no more than one article or other contribution to a copyrighted collection or periodical issue, or to supply a copy or phonorecord of a similarly small part of any other copyrighted work.

(2) The library or archives shall be entitled to supply a copy or phonorecord of an entire work, or of more than a relatively small part of it, if the library or archives has first determined, on the basis of a reasonable investigation that a copy or phonorecord of the copyrighted work cannot readily be obtained from trade sources.

(3) The librarly or archives shall attach to the copy a warning that the work appears to be copyrighted.

and renumber section 108(d)(2) to make it 108(d)(4).

STATEMENT OF DR. McKENNA, EXECUTIVE DIRECTOR, SPECIAL LIBRARIES ASSOCIATION

I wish to present the position of the Special Libraries Association with respect to the provisions of S. 1361 as they relate to library photocopying and inter-library loan in lieu of photocopies. The policy position as adopted by the Association's Board of Directors in January 1973 is one which seeks to reach an intermediate position of accommodation between the seemingly irreconcilable positions of publishers and literary authors on the one side, and the positions of some parts of the library and educational communities on the other.

---

[1] U.S. Court of Claims. The *Williams & Wilkins Company* v. *the United States.* Report of the Commissioner to the Court, February 16, 1972, pp. 16–17.

Special Libraries Association, with 8,000 members, is the second largest library- and information-oriented organization in the United States. It is estimated that there are more than 10,000 special libraries in the U.S. The concept of special libraries or—in better words—the concept of specialized libraries is not well known among the general public or even in some segments of the library community itself. The interests and activities of specialized libraries are described briefly in this document and in the annexed brochure.[1] SLA is an association of individuals and organizations with educational, scientific and technical interests in library and information science and technology—especially as these are applied in the selection, recording, retrieval and effective utilization of man's knowledge for the general welfare and the advancement of mankind.

Special Libraries Association was organized in 1909 to develop library and information resources for special segments of our communities which were not adequately served by public libraries or by libraries in educational institutions. At first the emphasis was on special subject coverage in each special library as it related to the interests and business of its parent organization, for example: sources of statistical data for both corporations and the agencies of the national government and state governments; business data for banks and investment firms; chemical information for the then developing chemical industry; engineering information for the emerging complexes of engineering and construction companies, etc.

During the past 64 years—and with particular growing needs for rapid information delivery since World War II—specialized libraries and information centers have been established in all segments of our nation's affairs. They exist in for-profit enterprises and not-for-profit organizations, as well as in government agencies. Some are open to public use, and others have restricted access or are part of a for-profit organization. During this period of accelerated growth, the original emphasis on special subjects has been replaced more and more by the concept of specialized information services for a specialized clientele. An example of such a specialized information service for a specialized clientele is the Legislative Reference Service of the Library of Congress. Although the Library of Congress (as a whole) is often called a "national library," the entire Library of Congress itself is, perhaps, an outstanding example of a definition of service to a specialized clientele: The Congress of the United States of America.

The specialized clients are normally the employees of the parent organization. The specialized information services are based on the speedy availability of information, both for current projects and for management determination of decisions regarding future efforts of the parent organization. To these ends, the members of SLA include not only librarians, but also persons who are subject specialists—so that they can evaluate and screen out the irrelevant, the redundant and the too often useless portions of the voluminous published literature. The totality of the literature includes not only the publications of commercial publishers of copyrighted books and periodicals, but also the avalanche output of government agencies (often with security handling requirements) plus the parent organization's own internal corporate documents (with the obvious need to protect proprietary or competitive information).

As a parenthetical observation, it should be noted that the pioneering work in machine use for information storage and retrieval (now computerized) took place in specialized libraries and information centers in the 1940's and 1950's. Similarly, the need for miniaturization of the bulk of the literature in microforms occurred thru the influence of S.L.A.'s liaison with designers and manufacturers of microreading equipment.

Last, but not least, S.L.A. pioneered the concept of information networks— long before computers and other communication devices had been developed. S.L.A. has facilitated communications among its members through the Association's unique information network of Chapters and Divisions. Initiated more than 60 years ago, the network has been frequently updated in response to the needs of new informational requirements.

S.L.A. is organized in 25 Divisions which represent broad fields of specialization or information handling techniques. These fields range alphabetically from Advertising, Aerospace, and Biological Sciences thru Military Librarians, Museums, and Natural Resources, and on to Transportation, and Urban Affairs.

S.L.A. is also organized in 44 regional Chapters which range geographically from Hawaii across the continental United States (plus two Chapters in Canada) and on to a European Chapter (which encompasses geographically all the non-Socialist countries of Europe).

Special Libraries Association in its own right is a publisher of 3 periodicals and of an average of 6 books per year. Therefore the Association has its own interests as a publisher to conserve its sales income and royalty income. The Association's publications are needed by special groups, but they are in such areas of specialization that commercial publishers (or even vanity presses) would not touch them because of the small sales potential. Our subscription lists range from 11,000 as a high to 1,000 as a low. Our book sales average about 1,000 copies for each title with a range from 500 to our top category of "best sellers" at a level of about 3,000 copies sold per title.

Special Libraries Association and its individual members would prefer continuation of the long recognized concept that the preparation of a single copy constitutes "fair use." The Association recognizes that there may be some validity in the claims of commercial publishers of periodicals that they may have some loss of income due to photocopying of one article from a periodical issue that is still available in-print. If the publication is out-of-print (that is, if the publisher has not maintained his stock in-print), it is difficult to conceive how a photocopy of out-of-print material can cause any loss of income to the publisher.

Further, the slow delivery by publishers to fulfill an order for a single in-print issue is totally unacceptable to the needs of our specialized users who are responsible for fast management decision. There is little question that it is an administrative impossibility to secure publisher permissions to permit interlibrary response within any reasonable time. Moreover, the costs and delays in seeking such permissions would be prohibitive.

Four items must be emphasized:

(1) Totally unacceptable is the concept that has been proposed of an agency to determine whether an original is still available with a report period of, say, 21 days. The information needs and expectations of management are such that delivery in excess of 24 to 48 hours is incompatible with research and management decision processes.

(2) As a starting point, one potential solution is a provision for the payment of a per-page royalty on photocopies of copyrighted works. Such an arrangement has precedence already in the proposed Copyright Act in § 111 (relating to cable transmissions), § 114 (sound recordings), § 115 (phono records), and § 116 (coin operated phono record players). A Royalty Tribunal of the type proposed in Chapter 8 of the Copyright Revision Bill, (but with a different membership composition) could assure that the per-page royalty rate is reasonable.

(3) Any legislative proposal should assure that libraries are not required to separately identify and account for each photocopy which they prepare, or to determine the allocation of the royalties, or to distribute the royalties for which they may be liable among the copyright proprietors. If payment of a "cents-per-page" charge is enacted, the beneficiaries of such charges (that is, the publishers) must themselves establish the agency for the collection and for the determination of pro rated payments to each publisher (in an ASCAP-style operation). Specialized libraries (and their parent organizations) can probably afford an added "cents-per-page" charge. But they cannot afford the added costs of record keeping and bookkeeping to issue checks for small amounts to each one among the multitude of publishers.

(4) The legislation to be enacted must not prevent or penalize the preparation of a photocopy for or by specialized libraries—particularly those in for-profit organizations. There will be immeasurable damage to the ecoomy and the welfare of the nation if such intent is contained in the enacted version of S. 1361, or if such interpretation is possible after enactment of the law.

The rapid transmission of man's knowledge—either to not-for-profit or to for-profit organizations—must not be impeded by law.

Special Libraries Association is grateful to the Subcommittee for the opportunity to present our views. The Association will be pleased to submit additional comments in the future if such would be appropriate.

---

[1] Annex. *Special Library Sketchbook.* S.L.A., N.Y. 1972, 45 p. Editors note, the document referred to may be found in the files of the Committee.

STATEMENT OF ROBERT W. CAIRNS, EXECUTIVE DIRECTOR, AMER-
ICAN CHEMICAL SOCIETY; ACCOMPANIED BY RICHARD L. KEN-
YON, DIRECTOR, PUBLIC AFFAIRS AND COMMUNICATION DIVI-
SION; BEN H. WEIL, CHAIRMAN, ACS COMMITTEE ON COPY-
RIGHTS; STEPHEN T. QUIGLEY, DEPARTMENT OF CHEMISTRY
AND PUBLIC AFFAIRS; AND ARTHUR B. HANSON, GENERAL
COUNSEL

Dr. Cairns. Thank you, Mr. Chairman, for the privilege of testifying today.

I wish first to introduce my compatriots and colleagues here. Mr.
Ben H. Weil, who is chairman of the American Chemical Society
Committee on Copyrights. Sitting next to him is Arthur B. Hanson,
our ACS general counsel, with whom you and your staff, I believe, are
acquainted; Dr. Richard Kenyon, on my right, who is director of our
division of public affairs and communication. Sitting next to him
is Dr. Stephen T. Quigley, director of the department of public
affairs.

I brought these gentlemen along to answer questions, if they are
needed, and to display to you our serious concern with this legislation.

I wish to read one paragraph from the written testimony and ask for
its complete introduction into your record.

Senator McClellan. Your prepared statement—you want to read
from it, sir?

Dr. Cairns. I just wish to read one paragraph.

Senator McClellan. Very well.

Dr. Cairns. I am testifying here on behalf of the American Chemical
Society by authority of its board of directors. This is the largest scientific and educational society in America and I believe in the world—
110,000 members, approximately.

We have a very large publishing activity which aggregates close
to $30 million a year and hence we are very familiar with the economics
of journal publication and the dissemination of scientific and technical
information, which is a very vital link in the whole process of the development of science and technology in the world.

Now, I shall read from the central paragraph on page 11 of my statement. It is desirable that use be made of modern technology in developing optimum dissemination." We are certainly strongly in favor
of the most modern methods and are developing the most modern
methods of dissemination.

"This new technology includes the use of modern reprography, but
as technology inherently includes economics the means of financial support of the system must be a part of its design. Therefore, photocopying should not be allowed under any circumstances unless an adequate
means of control and payment is simultaneously developed to compensate publishers for their basic editorial and composition costs.
Otherwise, 'fair use' or library-photocopying loopholes, or any other
exemptions from the copyright control for either profit or nonprofit
use, will ultimately destroy the viability of scientific and technical

publications or other elements of information dissemination systems."

Now, I emphasize that I am speaking with regard to scientific and technical publications. In the chemical field, for example, there are a total of 400,000 manuscripts per year which are authored and printed ultimately, after due editing, in journals. There are approximately 10,000 journals which impinge on the chemical field. That means that, in the full field of science, there are perhaps five times as many journal articles and publishing societies. It is a very large group, and it is very vital in the dissemination field.

We have under our general guidance and responsibility the Chemical Abstracts service, which publishes 40,000 pages of abstracts and indices each year and issues this to all of the libraries, to all the scientists and engineers. This forms a vital link in dissemination.

We publish, in addition, separate journals that are issued approximately biweekly, which are 20 in number, and which aggregate about 40,000 pages a year, and which go to 330,000 subscribers.

Only 4 percent of the world's literature is published in this form by the ACS. However, we feel that this is of outstanding quality and represents the work of Nobel prize winners and other top scientists and engineers throughout the world. This is a vital link in the progress of science and technology.

Each worker writes reports and submits them to the journals. The editorial boards carefully screen and select them, edit them, and bring them into the line of quality of the journals they represent. The American Chemical Society assures the quality through peer analysis of the material submitted to the journals. All of science and technology rests on this communication link. It is essential to both research and education.

The first copy of each journal, counting all 20, costs the society $4 million a year. That is the first copy only. The overrun, or additional printing costs, amount to about $1 million a year. Somehow, we must recover both types of costs. Obviously, the collection, editing, formating, and composition of the journals has to be paid for by someone.

Today, it is paid for largely by subscribers. Even if libraries are to take over with their Xerox machines the entire publishing, it will be necessary for someone to compensate the publishers for the collection and editing and composition of the material which they copy. Otherwise, there will be nothing to copy.

The cost figures—if they are stated in terms of per page and per copy—are in pennies; somewhere in the realm of 1 cent to 10 cents a page is what it costs to create the editorial content. But, of course, if you have 10,000 pages and 10,000 copies, you come up to 100 million cents, or $1 million. So it is quite obvious that pennies per page can add up to very substantial amounts of money. And this is why I am talking to you now as I am.

The first copy cost must be collected if journals are to exist. Journals are essential because of the quality angle and the admission to the world's literature through peer review and analysis and editing. It is essential; otherwise, we would have an unsorted pile of millions of manuscripts a year, and who is going to do anything to them, in terms of intellectual analysis, if the publishing societies do not perform and cannot perform their tasks under the law and protect the results, which are the content of the copies of the journals which they submit?

Next month I am going to Russia. I am going to talk about copyrights. Last May, the Russians decided to join in the Geneva Copyright Convention, as you know. They came to the publishing societies of the United States and Canada and other places, to my knowledge, proposing that they enter into copyright licensing agreements for our publications. They have been admitting that they have copied for many years—multiple copies, not single copies—multiple copies are simply multiple copies of single copies.

They have been publishing and republishing our material in Chemical Abstracts, and now they come to us and ask for licensing considerations. And we are ready to answer them.

The strange thing is that in our own country, we have not been approached by anyone about copyrights, in spite of the tremendous amount of copying that is taking place. Now, it is rather strange if I go to Russia to negotiate something that we cannot even deal with here.

I think we can deal here. I think we can negotiate properly if the law protects our property correctly.

I think, then, in closing, all I would like to say is that we are in favor of this dissemination of information. We spend millions of dollars a year on it. The libraries are some of our best customers. But I think if they are going to copy and join in the supplementary publishing scheme that they should help to pay for the initial costs of collecting journals and the content that they represent.

Thank you for your time.

Senator McCLELLAN. Now, what journals do you have there that you are using as an illustration?

Dr. CAIRNS. The Journal of the American Chemical Society which is a broad coverage journal of all of the elements of subdisciplines of chemistry.

I have in addition, Chemistry, which deals with that particular branch.

Senator McCLELLAN. Let's just take one of them for an illustration; the first one.

Dr. CAIRNS. The Journal of the American Chemical Society is the major journal.

Senator McCLELLAN. How often is that published?

Dr. CAIRNS. Every 2 weeks.

Senator McCLELLAN. How many subscribers do you have?

Dr. CAIRNS. I will ask Dr. Kenyon.

Dr. KENYON. Between 16,000 and 17,000.

Senator McCLELLAN. I beg your pardon?

Dr. KENYON. Between 16,000 and 17,000.

Senator McCLELLAN. Between 16,00 and 17,000.

Are the subscriptions adequate to pay for the cost of publication and distribution?

Dr. CAIRNS. At present, there is a close balance on the economics of journal publication. We derive about half of our costs directly from subscribers.

I would guess in the case of the Journal of the American Chemical Society—because it is highly academic and has no advertising— that it would be about two-thirds.

Senator McClellan. What I am trying to get at—how is it financed now?

Have you been able to finance it?

Dr. Cairns. We finance by subscription, by page charges. In some of the technology publications, we have advertising. And we just balance the budget. It is very difficult.

Senator McClellan. Now, talking about balancing the budget, assuming an article that you publish in there it constitutes a page. It occupies one page in your journal. How do you arrive at, and what would you undertake to say would be a fair charge of a copyright fee for the copying of one page that a library might want to copy and give to a patron?

Dr. Cairns. A single page would be pennies per page, somewhere——

Senator McClellan. Would be what?

Dr. Cairns. Pennies per page.

Senator McClellan. A penny per page?

Dr. Cairns. Several cents a page.

Senator McClellan. Several cents a page.

How do you arrive at it? How would a librarian know how much to collect?

Dr. Cairns. I think we should have something approaching a uniform charge or a uniform set of charges for various journals. Each journal in science and technology carries a distinguishing mark, a coden, which is a six-letter term, which characterizes that journal. It would be easy enough to group these journals under their codens at a specific price of a certain number of cents per page. Somewhere between 1 cent and 10 cents, I assume, would probably generate enough money to take care of their share of the composition costs of the material being copied.

Senator McClellan. All right.

We have another book in the library, a book of poems, that has been copyrighted. Somebody wants to copy that poem.

How would you arrive at what would be a fair compensation or copyright fee for that?

It is five verses, but it is on one page of a small book.

Would you make any differentiation between that poem and a scientific article?

Dr. Cairns. I have to confine my testimony to scientific and technical communication.

Senator McClellan. All right. I will point out, though, to you the problems that we have. We are trying to legislate on every particular kind of journal and every particular kind of publication and information that may be copyrighted.

Dr. Cairns. I do not envy you that problem, but I do not think I want to try to answer for you.

Senator McClellan. We need some help, do you not see?

Dr. Cairns. We will help you on scientific and technological publications, because that is something that we know.

Senator McCLELLAN. Thank you very much.

All right, Senator Burdick.

Senator BURDICK. Just a minute. I want to get your position this morning as clearly as I can. I do it by example.

I am going back to Williston High School again. Suppose a senior is doing a paper on chemistry and he goes to the library in Williston, and he finds a copy of your journal, and he wants to take it home and type it. He wants one page.

Is it your contention this morning that, unless he pays for it, he should not have it?

Dr. CAIRNS. This would seem to me, perhaps, to come pretty close to a very limited fair use, but my contention is that if there is a change in ownership involved in the transfer of copied material that, thereby, there has to be some accounting. Since it is only a matter of a few cents, I think it would not stand in the way in the process of communication in this particular instance.

Senator BURDICK. Your answer, then, is yes. You would not let him have it until he paid for it.

Dr. CAIRNS. Yes.

Mr. WEIL. I would like to speak to this.

The mechanisms by which these pennies per page could be collected are severalfold. One of them that we have heard about in the Special Libraries Association was the idea of a royalties tribunal, which in turn would, through the various collection mechanisms and various distribution mechanisms, distribute the few cents per page in the aggregate to the owners of the copyright. The library chore of recording could perhaps be done mechanically. It could be done by sampling. There are many techniques. So that the students involved, while he might, indeed, have to pay a few cents, or he might not have to pay a few cents, depending on how that library chose to operate. The mechanisms for collection and payment would not need to be donors.

Senator BURDICK. Well, I gather from your testimony that you would not permit the young man to have this material without paying for it.

Now, to get to the next question. In the libraries across the country, in my sort of country, you could not possibly set up a mechanism for distributing the money. Suppose you get this one page out of this book and pay 5 cents for it. Why, the postage to give you that 5 cents by mail would be more than that. And to keep a running account and to be keeping books would be impossible for small libraries.

The question is, either he gets it or he does not get it. It is a practical matter.

Mr. WEIL. No. There are mechanisms. Right now, that student if he wishes to use a machine for himself drops into it a dime or a quarter. So that the collection mechanism could be part of that dime or quarter which he puts in. How that money is distributed right now—most of it goes to the vendor who supplies the machine.

But there are methods that I mentioned—sampling; the Coden that was mentioned that would identify the journal is a method, also which could be electronically counted by the machine at the time of copy. The student would not need to be bothered. Right now, he must drop a dime or a quarter into the machine.

Senator BURDICK. You mean to say that the library at Williston has electronics, has got money for stuff like that?

Dr. CAIRNS. May I ask Counsel to answer?

Mr. HANSON. Senator, believe it or not, it does. And if it does not, it should have. I would suggest to you that, obviously, in any approach to this, you have to use common sense and practicality.

Senator BURDICK. That is right.

Mr. HANSON. The American Chemical Society is not interested—and I do not believe any other publisher is—in picking up the single page that a student is going to use. But remember, your premise was that he was going to take this out and copy it himself at home.

Senator BURDICK. No, no.

Mr. HANSON. If he sat down in the library and wanted to take whatever notes he wanted to out of that page, that is obviously a fair use under the settled law of the land.

I would suggest that what we are speaking to here is the practice that has arisen in the last few years of heavy copying by certain major metropolitan libraries, for the most part, which have made inroads into the publisher's ability to meet his costs, to make his material available. And I think this is really the problem that the committee must address.

Senator BURDICK. I understand the problem.

But in my hypothetical question, I did not have the young man taking the periodical out. I had him take the photostatic part home.

Dr. CAIRNS. There are other ways to meet your question other than an educational exemption, which I believe you were speaking to. I do not believe that we can have or afford an educational exemption, because we, in producing journals, are an essential link in the educational process. Therefore, we must have some means of recovery.

It might be through licensing through the library to allow them to do this practice that you described, and it would be at their behest. And this, as a matter of fact, was at issue in the Williams and Wilkins case, of which we are a party in having submitted an amicus curiae brief. We are normally on the side of education and science, because this is our charter.

We are also interested in preserving the function of continued dissemination of scientific and chemical information, so we must come to a practical determination, just as you people must.

Senator McCLELLAN. Let your brief that you submitted be filed and be marked as an exhibit to your testimony. Or would you like to have it printed in the record?

Dr. CAIRNS. Yes, we have submitted the full testimony for the record, and we also would ask the privilege, if you are agreeable, to let other scientific societies submit statements for the written record in the period of time to August 10.

Senator McCLELLAN. That is agreeable. They may do so.

Senator Fong?

Senator Fong. Are the articles in your magazine originally written by your people?

Dr. Cairns. These are articles that are originally written by scientists and engineers throughout the world.

Senator Fong. For your magazine?

Dr. Cairns. No. They are written in the first instance to record the works of the scientists and engineers. They are submitted for acceptance or rejection, or editing by the editors of our prospective periodicals, and they may or may not be accepted.

Senator Fong. Do you pay them for this?

Dr. Cairns. We do not. As a matter of fact, in most of the scholarly journals of which I have spoken, there is a system of page charges, in which the author pays up to $50 a page to help absorb the cost of publication. And this is recognized as a policy by the U.S. Government,

as enunciated by the Federal Council on Science and Technology, I think, about 1963, that all these Federal grants can be used for the purpose of these charges—payment of page charges—on their scientific works into nonprofit journals.

Senator Fong. So actually, you have not paid for the article?

Dr. Cairns. We have not paid anything for the article. In fact, we usually get a page charge for publishing.

Senator Fong. Yes, and he pays you for it, certainly—for the publication?

Dr. Cairns. He pays page charges at a rate of $50 a page for the scholarly journals.

Senator Fong. You say, since you publish it, the man who copies that should pay you or pay him?

Dr. Cairns. The man who publishes—who recopies—our publication should pay us so that we can be compensated for the costs of creating the first copy, before the overrun cost of thousands of copies, which we also have.

Senator Fong. So, then, you would enter into an agreement with the writer of the article.

Dr. Cairns. The writer of the article invariably puts the copyright with the American Chemical Society.

Senator Fong. I see.

Now, would you consider an exemption? Say, a little boy who takes the book home and copies, say, two or three pages of it, or he makes two or three xerox copies. Would you exempt such a child from paying any fee?

Dr. Cairns. No, the exemptions that you exemplify by this particular case would represent the educational exemption, and the educational process is a part of what we contribute to in our dissemination of scientific and technical literature. We are a part of the educational process, and if we are to continue to exist, we must be compensated the way anyone else does.

Senator Fong. So you think that this little boy should pay for that?

Dr. Cairns. He must, if we are not to have a general educational exemption.

Senator Fong. Now, who is going to do the collecting?

Dr. Cairns. I would say that the person who is in the control point in this case would probably be the librarian.

Senator FONG. How would she know?

Dr. CAIRNS. Their Xerox machine is usually indoors.

Senator FONG. If he took the book home, how would she know?

Dr. CAIRNS. I do not think she would if he took the book home. It would be a little difficult to police. But that does not excuse not having a law to say that this is not legal.

Senator FONG. So, if he asks the librarian to Xerox the copy, then you want the librarian to collect the money?

Dr. CAIRNS. I see no other rational way to do this.

Senator FONG. Suppose in 1 month there is only one page that is copied, and you charge only cents for that copying. You expect the librarian to put all her time to collect that money for you and send it back to you?

Dr. CAIRNS. No. I would say that we would only be interested in substantial payments, and there might be a clause which would rule out anything below $1 or $10. We are talking here in terms of millions of dollars.

Senator FONG. This is what I am asking where is the exemption? Would you say that we charge those who make a profit out of it, and we do not charge those who do not make a profit of it? Where is the exemption?

Dr. CAIRNS. There is no profit here. This is only compensation for costs that are incurred in creating the journal.

Senator FONG. You say many of these are metropolitan libraries?

Dr. CAIRNS. They have photocopying devices, yes.

Senator FONG. And they have photocopying devices and they print thousands of copies and disseminate it. And these are the people you want to stop?

Dr. CAIRNS. No, I do not want to stop them. I wish it to continue.

Senator FONG. Stop them from copying without paying?

Dr. CAIRNS. I wish to receive enough compensation so that, in proportion to the total number of copies circulated, that these Xerox copies carry their share of the composition costs.

Senator FONG. These people—these Xerox copies of your publications—are they making a profit?

Dr. CAIRNS. I do not think the concept of profit is applicable here, because they are, in the first place, nonprofit organizations. But that does not save the American Chemical Society, which is a nonprofit organization, from going broke if all of our works are copied.

Senator FONG. We are trying to get at the facts. We do not know the facts. We are asking you as to whether they—are they making a profit, or are they not making a profit?

Dr. CAIRNS. No.

Senator FONG. So most of the people who copy your works do not make a profit. Is that correct?

Dr. CAIRNS. That is correct.

Senator FONG. So you say that these people who copy your works should pay for them?

Dr. CAIRNS. They should pay the portion of the composition costs which their copying represents, in terms of that number of copies to the total number of copies.

Senator Fong. Then you would not exempt any part of it at all?

Dr. Cairns. That would be about right, with the possible exception of the subscriber making copies for his own use for convenience.

Senator Fong. Thank you, sir.

Senator McClellan. Thank you very much.

Mr. Kenyon. May I enter a simple factual correction? You asked the subscription circulation of the Journal of the American Chemical Society. I stated it was between 16,000 and 17,000. That was true last year.

The circulation on journals is falling, and as of June 30, 1973, it was 14,726.

Senator McClellan. Very well.

I only wanted to use that as an illustration.

Dr. Kenyon. Well, I did not want an inaccuracy in the record.

[Exhibit A referred to by Ambassador Keating follows:]

EXHIBIT A

LIBRARY COPYING UNDER DOMESTIC COPYRIGHT LAW REVISION

I. THE LIBRARY COPYING PROVISION AS PASSED BY THE HOUSE OF REPRESENTATIVES

On April 11, 1967 the House of Representatives passed H.R. 2512 (90th Cong., 1st Sess.), an Act for General Revision of the Copyright Law. While Section 107 of this Act codified the general doctrine of "fair use" as it has been developed by the courts, Section 108 established a specific "limitation" on the rights of copyright owners in a carefully circumscribed area of library copying:

§ 108. Limitations on exclusive rights: Reproduction of works in archival collections.

Notwithstanding the provisions of Section 106 [delineating the exclusive rights of copyright owners], it is not an infringement of copyright for a nonprofit institution, having archival custody over collections of manuscripts, documents, or other unpublished works of value to scholarly research, to reproduce, without any purpose of direct or indirect commercial advantage, any such work in its collections in facsimile copies or phonorecords for purposes of preservation and security, or for deposit for research use in any other such institution.

Section 108 was thus limited to (i) facsimile reproduction of unpublished works by certain nonprofit institutions, for (ii) their own limited purposes.

In approving this version of Section 108, the House Committee on the Judiciary stated that it did "not favor special fair use provisions dealing with the problems of library photocopying" other than under the circumstances above-described. H.R. Rep. N. 83 (90th Cong., 1st Sess.) at 36 & 37. Similar sentiments were expressed by the Register of Copyrights. Thus, although the Copyright Office Preliminary Draft of the Revision Bill allowed libraries to make and supply single copies of periodical articles, or copies of entire published works considered to be unavailable from trade sources, upon request, the Register subsequently "became convinced that the provision would be a mistake"[1] in view of rapidly changing information technology.

The limited version of Section 108 set forth in H.R. 2512 is the only specific "library copying" provision to have received the formal approval of a Congressional Committee or either house of Congress.

II. THE LIBRARY COPYING PROVISION PRESENTLY BEFORE THE SENATE

The Copyright Revision Bill presently before the Senate Subcommittee on Patents, Trademarks and Copyrights [S. 644 (92nd Cong., 1st Sess.)], includes a much more extensive "library copying" provision in its version of Section 108. In brief, the "limitations" on the exclusive rights of copyright owners are extended to include (i) duplication of *published* works by certain public or semi-public institutions, at (ii) the request of *users* of the institution's collections.[2]

[1] Supplementary Report of the Register of Copyrights on the General Revision of the U.S. Copyright Law at 26 (May 1965).
[2] The current Senate version of section 108 also extends the limitation of H.R. 2512 to include duplication of published works for the purpose of replacing "damaged, deteriorating, lost, or stolen" copies of works under certain circumstances.

*This extension of the specific "library copying exemption" was expressly dis-
approved by Resolution 38 of the Section of Patent, Trademark and Copyright
Law of the American Bar Association in 1970:*

Resolved, that the Section of Patent, Trademark and Copyright Law disapproves in principle enactment of severe limits on the exclusive rights of
copyright proprietors with respect to reproduction and distribution of copyright
works by libraries and archives.

Specifically, the Section of Patent, Trademark and Copyright Law disapproves
Section 108 of the December 10, 1969 Committee Print of S. 543 (McClellan—
91st Congress, First Session).[3]

III. ANALYSIS OF SECTION 108 OF S. 644

A. *Synopsis.*—Section 108 of the Copyright Law Revision Bill now before
the Senate Subcommittee adopts the provision of the House Act allowing library
and archival copying of unpublished works for the purposes of preservation,
security or deposit in other institutions. However, the Senate Bill extends the
library copying exemption to allow unlicensed facsimile reproduction of published works for the purposes of replacing deteriorating, lost or stolen copies
if the institution has "after reasonable effort determined that an unused replacement cannot be obtained at a normal price" from certain sources.

The Senate Bill further extends the exemption to include unlicensed reproduction of published or unpublished books and periodicals[4] by libraries and archives
at the request of a user of the institution's collections. This "user request"
exemption is subject to the conditions that (a) the user must have "established
to the satisfaction" of the institution that an unused copy cannot be obtained
"at a normal price" from certain sources; (b) the reproduction must become
the property of the requesting user and the institution must have had "no notice
that copy would be used for any purpose other than private study, scholarship
or research," and (c) the institution issues certain "warning" notices.

B. *Considerations.*—At this point our purpose is not to re-draft or rehabilitate
the library copying provisions of S. 644. Our purpose is merely to isolate certain
aspects of the proposed Senate version of Section 108 in order to allow examination of their impact on the business operations of interested parties. In this
context, we believe the following considerations to be of principal significance:

(i) Section 108 condones *free* reproduction. It is *not* a "compulsory licensing"
provision; no compensation to copyright owners—whether by statute, regulation,
or otherwise—is contemplated. Similarly, the Section does not expressly require
accurate reproduction, original source credit, or use of copyright notice on the
reproductions.[5]

(ii) The provision allowing reproduction of published works for purposes of
replacement and the "user request" exemption require some determination that
unused copies are not obtainable. However, unavailability in fact is not required:
in the case of replacement the library need only conclude that such is the case
"after a reasonable effort," and in the case of copies made at a user's request the
library need only be "satisfied," by the user, that such is the case. In the latter
case, at least, there is no express requirement that the library's determination
be in good faith, *nor is there any requirement that the requesting user make any
actual effort to locate a copy, or give actual evidence thereof.*

Moreover, Section 108 provides no meaningful standards with respect to availability. In this respect we can only raise questions as to what circumstances may
be sufficient to render a copy available or unavailable: may inability to secure
a copy within "X" number of days render the copy unavailable; are there geographic limits on availability or the library's or user's efforts (is a work not
available at the neighborhood bookstore unobtainable; how many bookstores
should be checked; what types of sources other than bookstores are relevant
sources for certain works?); does a new version of a work satisfy the availability conditions with respect to prior editions; should a work be considered
available if it is included in a compilation or collection otherwise not needed by
the library or user?

Even where Section 108 does attempt to give some definition of availability, it
remains unclear or troublesome in operation. Thus, availability at announced
or catalog prices does not preclude unlicensed copying; the library may still determine that the price is not "normal."[6] To preclude copying, the work must be

[3] Section 108 of the Dec. 10, 1969. Committee Print of S. 543 is identical to the version
of section 108 currently set forth in S. 644.
[4] This provision of S. 644 extends to all walks other than musical, pictorial, graphic,
cinematographic, or audio visual works.
[5] We do not believe that any of these requirements will necessarily be deemed implicit
in the requirement of "facsimile" reproduction of section 108 (b) and (c). In any event,
the "user request" exemption of sec. 108(d) is not limited to "facsimile" reproductions.
[6] Sec. 108(c), (d) (1).

available from "commonly known" trade sources; specialized sources for works of more esoteric disciplines may not qualify. Indeed, it is not clear to whom the source is to be "commonly known"—the library, the requesting user, the

publisher, the "trade," or the courts? Certain sources are clearly insufficient, namely, those outside the United States. Thus, to preclude unlicensed copying, arrangements must be made for domestic availability of foreign publications, in any language, no matter how limited their normal market.

Similarly, the provision does not appear to have considered the particular problems raised by its application to back issues. Although a number of organizations have made great investments of time and cost in locating, accumulating, and storing back issues in specialized fields and servicing their clients, their efforts and investment are adversely affected if not completely ignored: (a) we doubt that many libraries will accurately estimate the "normality" of back-issue prices; and (b) one may question whether such suppliers will comprise "commonly-known" trade sources, particularly where inter-library requests may involve libraries which have had no knowledge or dealings with such specialized sources.

Availability on library loan or for in-library use also appears insufficient to preclude unlicensed copying at the request of a user. The references to "trade sources," "price," and "unused copy," and the fact that to make a copy the library must have a copy, or have access to one under inter-library affiliation, all seem to imply that a user may request and receive a copy of a work no matter how accessible such work may otherwise be for his use under loan, and regardless of the degree of inconvenience, if any, caused by such use being restricted to a certain location or for a certain time, or his having to wait for such access. In short, a user may even request and receive an unlicensed reproduction of all or part of a work which is available to him from his local library for home or business use for extended periods of time.

"Trade sources" are defined to include "authorized reproducing services"; [7] "reprint houses" are presumably included but are not expressly mentioned.

There are no excuses for unavailability. Thus a work may be withdrawn by a publisher for revision, while his potential market is sapped by duplication of prior editions.

(iii) Section 108 does not require initial recourse to the copyright proprietor. That the proprietor may be willing to consent to the desired reproduction, even on "reasonable" terms, is rendered irrelevant since his permission need not be first requested. (The previously-discussed "availability" conditions do require some initial degree of unsuccessful recourse to trade sources for copies. Author-proprietors would generally not be considered "trade sources"; under various circumstances, this may also be true of publisher-proprietors. In any event, we believe that the condition of unavailability which allows reproduction will be met where existing copies are considered unobtainable. Thus, a request for permission to create a *new* copy is not a condition precedent to free copying under the proposed law.)

Similarly, although Section 108 is apparently not intended to interfere with certain contractual arrangements between libraries and copyright owners, [8] there is no incentive to libraries to enter into such arrangements on even "reasonable" terms. Furthermore, the relevant subsection refers only to obligations assumed when the library "obtained [the] copy for its collections." Thus, agreements which may be entered into with respect to earlier-published works, such as "blanket" licenses covering a publisher's catalogue or subscribers, may be ignored by libraries if less favorable than the proposed law. Even with respect to new works, it may be questioned whether the language of the relevant sub-paragraph clearly indicates that more "difficult" contractual undertakings will prevail over contrary provisions of Section 108.

(iv) The "libraries" and "archives" entitled to invoke the exemptions of Section 108 are not restricted to nonprofit institutions. [9] So long as the particular act of reproduction in question is without purpose of "direct or indirect commercial advantage" [§ (a)(1)], even profit-making institutions may avail themselves of the provision. We do not believe that the quoted language was intended, or will be construed, to preclude the operation of photoduplication services by for-profit institutions in order to make their overall, profit-generating, services more attractive or competitive.

Nor are such "libraries" and "archives" limited to public institutions. The only restriction on the nature of the exempt institutions is the requirement that its collections be open to *at least* persons, other than affiliates of the institution,

---

[7] Sec. 108 (c), (d)(1).

[8] Sec. 644, sec. 108(e)(3): "Nothing in this section . . . in any way affects . . . any contractual obligations assumed by the library or archives when it obtained a copy or phonorecord of the work for its collection."

[9] In this respect, the Senate version of sec. 108 goes beyond the House act even with respect to archival reproduction of unpublished works.

"doing research on a specialized field." It would appear that many corporate collections will qualify, or can be made to do so with little effort or burden.

In a similar vein, there is no effective restriction on the "users" entitled to receive unauthorized reproductions under the "user-request" exemption. *Any* "user of the collections" of the institution qualifies, including users making their request "through another library or archives." As inter-library affiliation and "information networks" grow, the way is paved for single-copy purchase to satisfy public requirements.

Section 108(d)(1) does require that "the library or archives has had no notice that the [requested] copy would be used for any purpose other than private study, scholarship, or research." This does not impose any effective limitation on the nature of the user. Since there is no requirement that the library make any *inquiry* as to the purposes for which the copy is to be used, the condition is met by silence and is meaningless. Similarly, there is no limitation to any type of curricular or systematic instructional base for the private study. Again, the condition is rendered meaningless. Also, it is not clear that it is the "study, scholarship or research" of the requesting user which is to be served. We do not believe that the word "private" negates the possibility of even single-copy photocopying for group or successive uses.[10]

(v) Section 108 is not restricted to the reproduction of portions or excerpts of works; entire works may be reproduced without consent or compensation.

Nor is Section 108 entirely clear with respect to the manner of permitted reproduction (e.g., microform, recording, light and laser techniques, etc.). Thus, while the archival exemptions of Section 108 (b) and (c) refer to "copies" and "phonorecords" duplicated in "facsimile" form, the user-request exemption of paragraph (d) applies only to "copies" and does not limit itself to "facsimile" reproduction.

Nor does Section 108 generally restrict the nature or subject matter of works subject to reproduction. *All types* of unpublished works are subject to archival reproduction for purposes of preservation, security or deposit; and *all types* of published works are subject to reproduction for purposes of replacement. The "user-request" exemption of Section 108(d) is generally limited to textual books, periodicals and sound recordings; however, there is no limitation on the subject matter of qualifying books, periodicals, and recordings. Thus, novels, plays, poetry, textbooks, technical publications, encyclopedias and reference works, abstracts, etc. are all subject to partial or entire reproduction under the same standards.[11]

Section 108(d) does refer to the reproduction and distribution of "no more than one copy or phonorecord" of a work. However, paragraph (f) makes it clear that this does not preclude multiple reproduction of the same work except where the library "is aware or has substantial reason to believe" that it is engaging in "related" or "concerted" activity. Experience in various areas of law has amply demonstrated the difficulty of imputing knowledge as a basis of liability. Moreover, in many cases there may be no reason for libraries to suspect concerted activity, particularly since they have no duty of inquiry. To a great extent paragraph (f) is an asknowledgment that Section 108 condones on-demand *publishing* of works by persons other than the copyright proprietor.

(vi) In a number of respects, Section 108 is poorly drafted in such manner as to create the potential for unfortunate interpretation or application. For example: The ability of a library to engage in unauthorized reproduction is consistently referred to as a "*right* of reproduction and distribtuion" [§ 108(b) (c) & (d) (1)]. This will invite the courts to resolve issues regarding library photocopying by the traditional judicial practice of "*balancing competing* rights" (herein, "rights" of proprietors and libraries) ; on the contrary we believe that such issues should be resolved by *strict construction* of *limitations* on the *rights of copyright owners.*

§ 108(a)(1) requires that the library's "reproduction *or* distribution" be without purpose of commercial advantage. Where distribution as well as reproduction are involved, such as under the "user-request" exemption or inter-library application of the archival reproduction exemptions, both reproduction *and* distribution should be without such purpose.

---

[10] Nor do we believe the sec. 108(d)(2) condition that the "copy become the property of the user" to bar such uses.

[11] As indicated earlier, we do not believe the reference to the "private study, scholarship or research" purpose of the user to be an effective limitation on users. For similar reasons, we do not believe it offers any meaningful restriction on the nature or subject matter of reproducible works.

§ 108(a), preceding sub-paragraphs (1) and (2), uses the phrase "and if." The "and" is, at the least, superfluous; and more significantly, it may create doubt as to the *cumulative* nature of Section 108.

The foregoing are merely intended as examples of poor draftsmanship having potential substantive effect on the principles embodied in the Section. As noted earlier, we urge that such principles themselves be subjected to examination and evaluation.

IV. CONCLUSION

Title II of the Senate Revision Bill would establish a "National Commission on New Technological Uses of Copyrighted Works." One of the stated purposes of the Commission is to "study and compile data on (1) the reproduction and use of copyrighted works . . . by various forms of machine reproduction . . ." [12] It is surprising that provisions for library copying which will seriously impair proprietary rights would be considered without the proper investigation which the Senate itself called for in appending title II to the Revision Bill.

STATEMENT OF ARTHUR J. ROSENTHAL, ON BEHALF OF THE ASSOCIATION OF AMERICAN UNIVERSITY PRESSES, INC., ON S. 1361

I am Arthur J. Rosenthal, Director of Harvard University Press, a department of Harvard University engaged in not-for-profit publishing of scholarly books and journals. I represent the Association of American University Presses, Inc., in my capacity as Chairman of that organization's Committee on Copyright. With me are Mr. Sanford Thatcher, Social Science Editor of Princeton University Press and a member of AAUP's Copyright Committee, and Mr. John B. Putnam, Executive Director of the Association of American University Presses, Inc.

AAUP is a not-for-profit educational corporation operating in the interests of its membership, comprising 64 scholarly university publishers which are either departments of their respective parent institutions or wholly owned corporations thereof. All are engaged in the not-for-profit publication of works of scholarly distinction. Although AAUP's members together constitute something less than 5% of the dollar volume of books published in the United States, the titles they publish constitute a substantial portion—nearly half—of the serious non-fiction titles published for scholarly readers. This disproportionate balance of income to number of titles published is a measure of the commitment of the university Presses of this country to the dissemination of valuable but economically unprofitable scholarly books.

We appreciate this opportunity to present our views on certain specific aspects of S. 1361 and proposed amendments thereto, particularly since the university press community has not previously participated in the hearings relating to this important piece of legislation. Allow me, therefore, to state our position in brief:

1. We propose a substitute for section 107, as set forth in Exhibit A.
2. We oppose the proposed library amendment to section 108(d)(1).
3. We oppose the proposed "educational exemption" which will be discussed at a later session of these hearings.
4. We wish to associate ourselves, with certain reservations, with the position of the Association of American Publishers in respect of Section 108.
5. We support enactment of S. 1361, with sections 107 and 108 amended as indicated elsewhere in this testimony.

The university press in the United States has traditionally occupied a unique position between the worlds of commerce and scholarship. In fulfilling their responsibility to publish books by and for scholars that would not otherwise be published by reason of their limited marketability, the university presses of this country find themselves actively engaged in the world of business, buying goods and services, selling books and rights thereto, and otherwise fulfilling all the functions of a profit-oriented business, while at the same time maintaining a

paramount interest in the editorial and scholarly integrity of their respective institutional imprints, and, hence, reputations.

It is this unique perspective that allows—or obliges—the university press to view the issue of copyright in general and of library photocopying in particular from the viewpoints of both educator and entrepreneur. The university press has always existed to insure the systematic and orderly transfer of important scholarly information to an appropriate readership, and to act as a faithful steward of its authors' rights and interests in doing so. The scholar is, after all.

[12] S. 644, title II, sec. 201(b)(1)(B).

not only the reader-consumer, but the author-creator as well. Had he the time and resources, he would undertake to transfer his intellectual offerings directly to those who want and need them; since he usually has neither, the publisher—in the case of unprofitable scholarship, the university press—has provided the vital link between producer and user. If the orderly reporting of scholarly research and thought is to continue, the medium through which it occurs must be safeguarded. A vital component of that medium is the traditional privilege and responsibility of registering and protecting an author's claim to copyright in the writings which represent his intellectual achievement, and of exercising and managing all subsidiary rights depending on that copyright in accordance with contractual conditions agreed upon by author and publisher. This component—the responsibility of stewardship—is gravely threatened by the present vagueness of section 107, which is in effect an invitation to undertake unlimited photocopying of copyrighted materials with impunity. Accordingly, we therefore respectfully submit that section 107 be amended as set forth in Exhibit A appended to this testimony, in order to set more specific guidelines for the photocopying of materials in copyright.

It is not, and never has been, the position of the university presses that photocopying for library use is to be prohibited. Indeed, to the contrary, scholarly publishers have long recognized the value, in certain specific circumstances, of the photocopy as a means of assuring further distribution of their works amongst their readerships. Scholarly presses are sympathetic to the growing need for library materials and the shrinking resources with which libraries must seek to satisfy this need. At the same time, it is manifest that the increasingly prevalent practice of systematic library photocopying, in which works are reproduced in their entirety for distribution to multiple users, poses a grave threat both to the integrity of the copyright in the works copied, and to the proprietors—in this case university publishers—who have invested considerable financial and human resources in their production and publication. The present draft of 108 contains the minimum conditions necessary to assure reasonable protection of authors and publishers with regard to copyright; even these minima place strong emphasis on the intent of the library and educational communities to observe them in good faith. Indeed, to invoke the necessary means to assure compliance—particularly in regard to such provisions as 108(d)(1)—would be economically and practically unfeasible. Moreover, these conditions are entirely dependent on the amendment of section 107 I have suggested elsewhere in this testimony, which would give more structure to the circumstances under which limited photocopying of copyrighted materials might be undertaken. Failing such an amendment of 107, AAUP would be forced to argue strongly for revision of section 108 to allow photocopying of archival materials only.

In a field of endeavor where little if any financial reward accrues to the creator, every effort must be made to assure at least that he retains control over the format and content of his creation. Without copyright, this is impossible, and without adequate protection, there is no copyright. Our purpose as stewards of scholarship is to protect the environment in which authorship happens, for without the author, there is nothing to publish, and when nothing is published, there is nothing to read, and when there is nothing to read, the intellectual environment stagnates and ultimately dies.

With regard to the proposed educational exemption, let me once more invoke the dual perspective of the university press, in noting that the long-range interests of scholarship are assuredly ill-served by this proposed amendment. Its provisions are indeed so imprecise and subject to manipulation as to render virtually all copyright material void of any protection against unlimited photocopying.

In the event that S. 1361 cannot be enacted with the changes we have proposed, we would favor the referral of the entire question of library photocopying to the National Commission on New Technological Use of Copyrighted Works proposed in Title II.

[EXHIBIT A]

SUBSTITUTE SECTION 107 TO S. 1361 PROPOSED BY THE ASSOCIATION OF AMERICAN UNIVERSITY PRESSES, INC. JULY 31, 1973

Notwithstanding the provisions of section 106, the fair use of a copyrighted work, including such use by reproduction in copies of phono-records or by any other means specified by that section, for purposes such as criticism, comment, news reporting, display or lecture in teaching, scholarship, or research, is not an infringement of copyright. Fair use does not include the reproduction of a copyrighted work.for its own sake, as in an anthology or book of readings, or as a self-contained unit such as an appendix to another work, or as a substantial part of the text of another work. In determining whether the use of a work in any particular case is a fair use the principal factors to be considered shall be the market value of the use of the copyrighted work and the effect of the use upon the potential market of the work. Factors in making this determination shall include:

(1) the purpose and character of the use;

(2) the nature of the copyrighted work; and

(3) the amount and substantiality of the portion used in relation to the copyrighted work as a whole.

PREPARED STATEMENT ON S. 1361, IN BEHALF OF THE ASSOCIATION OF AMERICAN PUBLISHERS, INC.

I am W. Bradford Wiley, Chairman and Chief Executive of John Wiley & Sons, Inc., publishers. I appear in behalf of the Association of American Publishers, Inc. of which I was formerly Chairman and am now Chairman of its Copyright Committee. With me are Ross Sackett, President of Encyclopedia Britannica Educational Corporation, and present Chairman of AAP; Richard P. Sernett, Secretary and Chief Legal Officer of Scott, Foresman and Company, Vice Chairman of the AAP Copyright Committee; and Charles H. Lieb of the New York Bar, Copyright Counsel to AAP.

AAP is a trade association of book publishers in the United States. Its 260 member companies and subsidiaries are believed to produce 80% or more of the dollar volume of books published in the United States. Some of its members publish scientific and technical journals. Although most of its members are in the private sector, some are religious and educational not-for-profit organizations.

We are grateful for permission to testify at what we understand are limited hearings confined to specific issues, one of which, library photocopying, is the subject of the present discussion.

AAP'S POSITION

We stated our position on library photocopying in response to the Subcommittee's request in our letter of December 5, 1972 to Mr. Thomas C. Brennan, your Chief Counsel, a copy of which marked "Exhibit A" is attached. The library "substitute amendment" to which we referred in that letter is, we believe, the amendment to S. 1361 which the Association of Research Libraries and the American Library Association are presently supporting. The drafting changes to Section 108 of S. 1361 (then S. 644) which we suggested in that letter are those outlined in "Exhibit B" attached hereto.

Our position, in brief, is as follows:

(1) We support Section 107 as a helpful statement of the principles of fair use.

(2) Although in some respects harmful to the interests of copyright proprietors, we support Section 108 but only with drafting changes as outlined in Exhibit B.

(3) We oppose the substitute for Section 108(d)(1) requested by the library associations.

(4) We oppose the overlapping "limited educational exemption" amendment offered by the National Education Association Ad Hoc Committee on Copyright Law Revision which is to be discussed at a later session in these hearings.

(5) We support enactment of S. 1361 in its present form except for the drafting changes to Section 108 referred to above.

The membership of AAP, profit and not-for-profit alike, have a vital interest in protecting their publishing investments against unauthorized library photocopying or periodical articles and contributions to collective works. George D. Cary, then Register of Copyrights, succinctly stated the basis for our objection in a recent address. He said "unlimited copying * * * could well so diminish sales that the journal publisher would have to suspend publication, or increase the cost of the journal in order to make up for the loss in subscriptions caused by the excessive copying." (A.S.I.S. Proceedings, Vol. 9, 1972, at 171.)

AAP does not dispute the need for libraries in given instances to make single photocopies of journal articles. It does dispute that the amendment offered by the library associations provides the proper method.

AAP'S OFFER TO ESTABLISH FAIR USE GUIDELINES

Much of what libraries copy they have the right to copy within the principles of fair use, which would be codified by Section 107. Concededly the line that marks the difference between fair and unfair use in a given case may be difficult to draw. Because we understand the predicament in which this places the librarian we have offered to cooperate with the library associations in establishing quantitative and qualitative guidelines which would eliminate much of the present uncertainty. So far, however, the library associations have not chosen to accept our offer.

GUARANTEED ACCESS TO THE USER

Much also of what libraries copy, clearly not fair use, would be permitted to copy under subsection (b), (c) and (d) of Section 108, both as presently drafted and as amended as suggested in our Exhibit B. These subsections would permit single copying not only for archival purposes but also for the requesting user if he cannot obtain the published work from the publisher or dealer or a reprint or photocopying from an authorized reproducing source. Thus, user access would be guaranteed to any work, whether in or out of print.

AAP'S OFFER TO ESTABLISH CLEARANCE PROCEDURES

We share the view that we understand was stated in the Committee's draft of Report to accompany S. 543 (which was not issued) that the interest of the library community in satisfying existing needs of scholarship and research is adequately provided for in Sections 107 and 108 and that further innovations in reprography policy should await either agreement among the parties or the studies of the National Commission to be appointed under Title II. For our part, we, with the Authors League, members of the Association of American University Presses, several learned societies which publish journals, and the American Business Press, have offered to cooperate with library and other interests to establish workable voluntary arrangements to clear the photocopying of material that would exceed the limits imposed by Section 108 (cf Exhibit A).

The library associations (other than the Special Libraries Association which has recently announced its willingness to work out arrangements to assure access to library resource on reasonable terms) have rejected our proposal, and offer instead a substitute subsection 108(d)(1) which would permit not only the kinds of copying contemplated by Section 108 as presently drafted but also the copying of an entire article in a periodical issue or of an entire contribution to a collective work.

We think this kind of broad-axe indiscriminate treatment of the difficult photocopying issue is a poor substitute for mutually acceptable voluntary arrangements; that it would be ill-advised and counter-productive and, as Mr. Cary noted, could lead to the ultimate disappearance of the very periodicals and collective works which the libraries want to copy.

AAP'S OBJECTIONS TO THE LIBRARY AMENDMENT

We oppose the amendment offered by the library associations. Totally overlooked in their approach are basic differences and distinctions that exist between the kinds of material copied and their varying markets, the kinds of institutions which do the copying and the manner in which they distribute it. Below are a few examples of the distinctions which we have in mind.

(1) The library amendment would ignore the nature and purpose of the work, and would treat in the same manner a work prepared primarily for scientific or educational purposes and an article in a news magazine of current interest only.

(2) It would ignore the cost and effort involved in the creation of the work and the size of its anticipated market and readership.

(3) It would ignore the nature of the library that does the copying, treating in the same manner a small general purpose library with local patronage and a central research library serving a broad geographical area, possibly even crossing national boundaries to form part of a worldwide network.

(4) It draws no distinction between the sporadic over-the-desk delivery of a conventional photocopy and the systematic facsimile transmission of the work by telephone line, cable or over the air.

(5) It takes no account of whether copies of the work are available to the library or the user from the publisher or his authorized reproducing service, and makes no distinction between current and older issues.

NO "NORMAL" FAIR USE

Basically the vice in the library amendment is that it draws no distinction between the kinds of single copying which can be justified under the principles of fair use as stated in Section 107 and the kinds which cannot be so justified. We understand that the draft of the Committee Report which was under consideration in 1969 would have overlooked this distinction and incorrectly, in our opinion, stated that "the making of a single copy of an article or periodical * * * would normally be regarded as fair use." There is no "normal" article, nor "normal" kind of copying or use, and there cannot therefore be an accurate generalization as to what normally would be fair use without at the same time taking into account the nature of the work and its use and the other criteria summarized in Section 107.

Periodical articles and contributions to collective works cannot be treated generically. The library copying of an article translated from the Chinese at a cost of thousands of dollars and with readership limited to a few cannot be fitted into the same pattern as the library copying of an article in a news magazine. Similarly, the systematic distribution of copies through a national or international library network should not be treated in the same manner as the occasional delivery of a copy to a local patron.

SUMMARY AND CONCLUSION

We recognize the need for workable clearance procedures. By their very nature, however, they should be established by mutual agreement, not unilaterally or by statutory fiat. We have offered before and offer again to cooperate with the library associations in working out the necessary arrangements. We hope, in any event, to pursue this path with the Special Libraries Association and with any other group which may wish to participate.

Section 108 with the drafting changes suggested by us goes as far toward compromise in statutory form as publishers can go. The section, from our point of view, is troublesome. With the library amendment it would become intolerable. We urge therefore

(1) that the library substitute amendment be rejected;

(2) that Section 107 and Section 108 with our suggested changes be approved;

(3) and that as presently provided in the bill, the remaining open questions relating to library photocopying be left for study by the National Commission.

Thank you for the opportunity to appear before your subcommittee.

ASSOCIATION OF AMERICAN PUBLISHERS, INC.,
New York, N.Y., December 5, 1972.

Mr. THOMAS C. BRENNAN, Esq.,
Chief Counsel, Committee on Patents, Trademarks, and Copyright, Committee on the Judiciary, U.S. Senate, Washington, D.C.

DEAR MR. BRENNAN : This is in response to your letter of September 19, 1972, in which you invited the views of the Association of American Publishers, Inc., on the library photocopying issue.

As we understand it, Section 108 was added to S. 644 by the subcommittee in an effort "to supplement the general fair use provisions contained in Section 107."[1] This was presumably done in response to library demands for a reproduction privilege including the right to copy an entire journal article on request by a patron.

Section 108 is harmful in some respects to the interests of publishers and their

[1] Your letter of September 19 1972.

authors. In some respects, too, the section has technical flaws. Nevertheless. if the section were acceptable without substantive change to all of the other interested parties, AAP, with appropriate technical clarification, would support it also. We understand, however, that Section 108 in its present form is not acceptable either to the American Library Association or the Association of Research Libraries.

EXHIBIT A

In an effort to reach a fair and reasonable solution, representatives of AAP and the Authors League initiated a series of meetings, to which you referred in your letter. Those attending, in addition to the Authors League and AAP, included representatives of ALA, ARL, the Association of American University Presses, Inc., American Business Press, Inc., of learned societies which publish many scientific and technical journals, and of industry-connected research libraries and information centers.

At the request of the library interests, the group confined its attention to library photocopying of scientific and technical journal articles. In September, 1972, acting upon a proposal by one of the library representatives, a consensus was reached that libraries should have the right to reproduce single copies of articles in such journals but only if copies are not available within a reasonable time and at a reasonable price from the publisher or his authorized reproducing service.

An amendment to the effect was thereupon drafted by the lawyers in the group representing ALA, AAP and the Authors League. Before any of the other groups could take formal action, however, ALA and ARL flatly rejected the draft amendment without identifying in what respects the draft was not acceptable, without offering any changes for terms they might have found objectionable, and without offering any alternative solutions.

We understand that ALA and ARL are unilaterally proposing a "substitute amendment," [3] which we oppose as totally unsatisfactory. We sincerely regret that ALA and ARL apparently have abandoned efforts to achieve a consensus with other interested parties on the library photocopying issue and, instead, have chosen to pursue an adversary position before Congress.

Under these circumstances we respectfully suggest when the Copyright Revision Bill is reintroduced in the 93rd Congress.

A. that apart from technical drafting changes, Section 108 in S. 644 remain unchanged or, in the alternative,

B. that Section 108 in S. 644 be deleted and Section 108 of H.R. 2512 be inserted in its place, and that Section 117 of S. 644 be revised by appropriate amendment so that the remaining library photocopying issues be left for solution by the courts and the proposed National Commission on New Technological Uses of Copyrighted Works.

Section 107 of S. 644, as we understand it, is intended to state without change the principles of fair use as they exist today and, if that understanding of the legislative intent is correct, we support the section.

As always, we support your efforts to bring about the prompt enactment of a sound copyright revision bill.

Sincerely,

CHARLES H. LIEB,
Copyright Counsel, Association of American Publishers, Inc.

ANNEX TO STATEMENT OF AAP ON LIBRARY PHOTOCOPYING, S. 1361

SUGGESTED CHANGES TO SECTION 108

Section 108(a)—Line 7—eliminate "and."

Section 108 (b), (c), (d), (e)(3), (f)—

The phrase "the right" or "the rights" of reproduction and duplication is improperly used in these subsections. The Section should not refer to "rights." Rather, as indicated in the title of Section 108, and of Section 107 as well, the permitted copying and distribution are "limitations" on the exclusive rights of the *owner* of the copyright. These subsections therefore should state that the kinds of reproduction and distribution referred to therein "are not infringements of copyright" and the reference to "rights" should be eliminated.

Section 108 (c), (d)—

---

[3] ARL Newsletter, No. 58, November 14, 1972.

The "availability" portions of 108 (c) and (d) should be amended to read

"* * * that an unused copy cannot be obtained at a *reasonable* price from commonly know trade sources in the United States *or the publisher* or other copyright owner or an authorized reproducing service."

Section 108(e) (3)—Lines 16 and 17—should be changed to read

"* * * assumed *at any time* by the library or archives with respect to any copy or phonorecord of *a work in* its collections."

A new subdivision should be added, possibly as subdivision (3) of Section 108(a) to require that the appropriate copyright notice be included in any copy or phonorecord made in Section 108.

Section 108 and perhaps Section 107 as well should specifically state that the reproduction of copies of consumable works such as work book exercises, problems, or standardized tests and answer sheets and of works used for purpose of compilation are not permitted fair uses.

PHOTOCOPYING AND THE SCIENTIFIC JOURNAL

(A report to the Subcommittee on Patents, Trademarks and Copyrights of the Committee on the Judiciary United States Senate by The Williams & Wilkins Co., Publishers of Medical and Scientific Books and Periodicals July 25, 1973)

THE WILLIAMS & WILKINS' POSITION

Williams & Wilkins publishes 37 medical and scientific periodicals. It believes that the information contained in its journals should be disseminated as widely and as quickly as possible by any method now known, including photocopying, or which may become known. Williams & Wilkins has never so stated nor has any desire to interrupt or halt the process of dissemination through photocopying—but it must be compensated for photocopying of its copyrighted materials so that the journals can remain economically viable and independent of government subsidy.

The journals involved in *Williams & Wilkins* v. *U.S.*, now pending in the U.S. Court of Claims, are universally recognized as leading journals in their fields, but they have extremely limited circulations, e.g. 1,088 to 17,762, which are a function of the relatively limited market potential for the material. If Congress decides that these journals can be photocopied without reasonable compensation to the publisher many will eventually die because it is virtually impossible to increase the number of subscribers to medical and scientific journals beyond those in the discipline served by the particular journal and those relatively few libraries which have chosen to serve such specialists. However, while the number of subscribers remains static, the costs of publication continually increase. At the same time photocopying technology continues to improve, enabling copies to be made more cheaply and efficiently. If subscription prices are raised to cover costs plus a reasonable profit, the point is soon reached where, instead of subscribing, some users of the material will photocopy. And every time there is a subscription price increase and the photocopying technology improves, there is a greater incentive to photocopy. Thus, raising subscription prices does not solve the problem of providing sufficient income to cover cost because it simply encourages fewer subscriptions and more photocopying. Eventually, there will be so few subscribers and the prices will be so high that the journal will cease publication.

The only way to save private limited circulation technical journals from extinction is to broaden the income base. This can only be done by spreading the costs of publication among a greater number of users, including those who use the journal through photocopying. A photocopying license will enable subscription costs to be kept at a reasonable level and place the economic support of the journal more equitably upon those who value its use.

Libraries pay, among others, the Xerox Corporation for the copying equipment, the paper manufacturer for the paper, the utility companies for the electricity to run the equipment, the Post Office for stamps to mail the copies, salaries to the workers who do the copying, and to the librarians who supervise the copying. Yale University, the New York County Medical Society Library, and many other libraries charge a "transactional" charge for photocopying to cover these obvious costs. Someone has to pay for these costs and we see nothing wrong with those libraries which pass these costs on to those who request the photocopies. We also think it entirely appropriate that to these many costs there be added a fair and reasonable royalty to the publisher to ensure that the publisher can continue to make the obviously useful work available in the future.

By means of blanket licenses, clearing houses, or computer accounting a reasonable royalty for copying can be easily paid to the publisher without the need for complicated bookkeeping, interruption or interference in service. These costs can then easily be passed on to the patron who orders the photocopy. We ourselves favor a blanket license plan where the license is incorporated in the subscription price of the journal because it requires no record keeping or accounting on the part of the library.

The doctor in North Dakota or Hawaii who has to obtain a copy of a journal article from Yale University will have to pay a minimum charge of $3.50 plus, perhaps, an additional service charge to his local library. Certainly a slight extra charge by Yale to cover the copyright royalty would not be unfair or interfere with the service. The alternative would be to have no copyright royalties paid by anyone and, thus, eventually destroy the journal when photocopying becomes more and more available through microfiche, computers, lasers, or who know what.

The costs of publication should be equitably divided among those who use the journals by buying printed copies and those who use it by photocopying. If only subscribers to printed copies need pay for their information libraries will cut costs by cancelling subscriptions and servicing their patrons by means of photocopies obtained from other libraries. The library, by charging the patron for the cost of the photocopies, will have serviced the patron, saved the cost of the subscription, and perhaps even received a contribution to its overhead from its charge to the patron. Williams & Wilkins has, of course, no objection to this means of information dissemination—but if it cannot receive a royalty for the copying it will have to raise its prices to those libraries who continue to subscribe and to its individual subscribers. As prices get higher, there will be more incentive to photocopy until the journal is so expensive that it is discontinued.

Furthermore, to put the burden of increased costs on the individual subscriber is, in addition to being self-defeating, simply not equitable. The number of subscribers is decreased because of photocopying. Those who do *not* generally photocopy, i.e. the individual subscribers, should not be required to bear the substantial increased costs per unit created by the decreased circulation which has been caused by the photocopies.

Williams & Wilkins believes that those who use the copyrighted information in its journals by photocopying should contribute to the cost of publication and that copyright is the traditional instrument for insuring this contribution while protecting the public interest in wide distribution. If a new theory, i.e. free indiscriminate and repeated photocopying, is legislated it, in tandem with the new technologies, will destroy the journals and thus create irreparable damage to the public interest.

CHRONOLOGY OF THE DEVELOPMENT OF THE LICENSING/INSTITUTIONAL RATE PLAN

Discussions of a plan to allow libraries to furnish their customers with photocopies of copyrighted articles were begun before the February 16, 1972 decision from Commissioner Davis of the Court of Claims. Above all, the plan was *not* to be a cumbersome administrative or economic burden upon libraries. It was to include a simple system of payment to broaden the income base required to support the journals. This will help offset the loss of income where photocopies will replace the purchase of multiple subscriptions, library and personal subscriptions. Basic ideas about a proposed plan were discussed with several libraries.

When the Davis decision was received, we had a "digest" of the opinion prepared and mailed to more than 8,000 friends and customers of the house, among them some 5,800 libraries. A covering letter (Ex. 1) attempted to allay any concerns that Williams & Wilkins had intentions of curtailing photocopying or of a high-priced and complicated royalty payment system.

Even before a Williams & Wilkins licensing plan was announced, a memorandum (Ex. 2) from L. L. Langley, Ph. D., Associate Director for Extramural Programs at the National Library of Medicine was sent to NLM's Resource Grants grantees stating, "The express purpose of this memorandum is to inform you that grant funds from the National Library of Medicine must not be used for royalty payments to publishers without prior approval from the National

Library of Medicine." (This memo did not come to the attention of Williams & Wilkins until sometime after our plan was formally announced in June 1972.)

Full-page ads (Ex. 3), again stressing that we were developing a simple, workable licensing plan, were purchased for the following journals: "Bulletin of the Medical Library Association" April 1972 issue; "College and Research Libraries" April 1972 issue; "Library Journal" April 15, 1972 issue; and "American Libraries" May 1972 issue.

In June 1972, a letter was sent to our institutional customers formally announcing and describing our licensing plan (Ex. 4) as follows:

1. Beginning 1973, W&W journals would carry an institutional rate, ranging $1–$10 higher than the individual subscription rate.

2. The institutional rate would carry with it an automatic license to make single copy photocopies for patrons in the regular course of library operations.

3. This institutional rate would cover the making of single copy photocopies for the life of the volume and would permit photocopies to be made from all previously published volumes at no additional charge. No additional payments or record keeping would be involved.

4. Multiple copies could be made upon remittance of 5¢ per page per copy, but permission was not granted for copies made for interlibrary loan use.

5. Institutions would be entitled to a refund of the license portion of the subscription rate if no copying of the journal took place.

On June 23, 1972 a personal letter was sent to each Director of the 11 Regional Medical Libraries (Ex. 5) discussing the institutional rate and announcing our intention to license these libraries, which were set up for the purpose of providing interlibrary loan copies, at the rate of 5¢ per page per copy.

BACKGROUND OF THE WILLIAMS & WILKINS LICENSING PLAN

W&W journals would carry an institutional rate, the difference between the individual subscription rate and the institutional rate would constitute the license fee. The fee would be based on the number of text pages published in the journal in 1972, the susceptibility of the journal to be photocopied (based on our experience with reprint requests) multiplied by a ratio no higher than 5¢ per page. (Five cents per page is our average price per page for all printed copies of all our journals.) As a result of using this formula and our desire not to place too great an economic burden upon the library whose practice is not to pass costs on to patrons, the average increase in subscription prices to institutions was $3.65. In all cases the photocopy fees averaged less than one cent per text page published in 1972, however the actual license was to be effective for photocopying materials from Volume 1 through the 1973 volume of the journals. This amounts to thousands of pages for each journal, thus making the average photocopying price per page extraordinarily minimal.

The license fee would apply to single copy photocopying only, as librarians seemed to concede that they do not permit multiple copies. However, to facilitate dissemination where multiple copies were needed, the library was permitted to do so upon remittance of 5¢ per page per copy.

The resulting institutional license fee was too minimal to cover income losses in cases of the interlibrary loan system, which absolutely replaces library subscriptions. To charge a flat rate for every library, great and small, sender or receiver of interlibrary loan copies, would be inequitable. Since the interlibrary loan system already provided for the administration of enumerating individual articles, it seemed reasonable that these "lending or sending" libraries could more equitably be licensed on a pay as you go basis.

On July 31, 1972, Dr. Martin Cummings, Director of the NLM replied to our licensing plan (Ex. 6) with the following: "It is our position that we would accede to a rise in price based on an institutional rate which would be applied 'to all libraries, great and small', but could not accept the implication that a license for photocopying is necessary. We would be pleased to renew our subscriptions at the individual rate, or at an institutional rate which does not include a license for photocopying. If you insist upon tying the renewal of our subscriptions to payment of a license fee, however, we shall have no option other than to let them lapse."

This statement from Dr. Cummings, his similar statement of July 31, 1972 (Ex. 7), along with published statements by the American Library Association, The Special Libraries Association, and the Medical Libraries Association (Ex. 8) in response to our licensing plan, brought forth a deluge of letters from librarians threatening a boycott of W&W journals on the basis that a license for photocopy was not necessary.

WE WITHDRAW OUR LICENSING PLAN

Because such a boycott would affect both The Williams & Wilkins Co. as well as the professional societies of which we publish not only in subscription income but also in the indication by the National Library of Medicine that it would exclude our journals from listing in Index Medicus (Ex. 9), we had no alternative but to accept the position advocated by the NLM.

On October 2, 1972 we again sent letters (Ex. 10) to all of our customers and friends describing our new position as follows: "In order to allow the NLM and all libraries to subscribe to W&W journals at increased rates and include them in Index Medicus, we now accept the NIH-NLM position. Our new institutional rates which we shall continue to request shall have no connection whatever with a license to photocopy, implied or otherwise. In short, libraries may continue to supply their users with royalty free single-copy reproductions of W&W journal articles as they have done in the past. As stated many times, we have no desire to obstruct the dissemination of scientific information between library and scholar, which would certainly be the result of cancellation of subscriptions. Further, in the same spirit we are, again without prejudice, withdrawing our proposal for the five-cents-per-page interlibrary loan fee until the appeal of our case is heard."

A letter of similar content (Ex. 11) was again mailed to all libraries on January 11, 1973.

We stand ready and willing to reinstate the license to photocopy as a part of the institutional subscription price as and when Commissioner Davis' opinion is confirmed in the appeal of our case before the Court of Claims. Furthermore, we have developed a similar type plan to deal with the problems connected with the Interlibrary Loan procedures. The salient points of this plan are described in our letter of April 30, 1973 to Dr. Martin Cummings (Ex. 12). This implementation of the Interlibrary Loan plan also awaits the outcome of our lawsuit in the Court of Claims.

STATISTICAL PROOF OF MARKET LOSS

Although common sense would tell one that the making of photocopies of millions of pages of articles appearing in scientific periodicals would have an adverse effect on the sale of subscriptions, it has been difficult in the past to statistically prove this contention. However, library subscriptions to Williams & Wilkins journals for the past three years now show beyond a reasonable doubt that the Interlibrary Loan procedure is damaging our market.

In 1971 we had 24,217 library subscriptions to our journals; in 1972, 24,502; and as of July 1, 1973, 23,363.

As the figures indicate, there was little library circulation growth in '72 compared to '71, and the current '73 figures indicate our circulation will actually decrease by about 600 subscriptions among libraries.

Several reasons could be offered to explain the decrease. The number of scientific journals continues to grow, while publishers are charging ever-increasing subscription rates. Obviously, if library budgets cannot increase proportionately, some journals must be cut from their lists. Certainly, librarians must be more concerned today about the quality of journals they are purchasing than ever before.

At the same time, however, the number of different libraries purchasing journals is increasing mainly due to the continuing emergence of the Community Hospital Library, but libraries are purchasing smaller numbers of journals, certainly of journals published by Williams & Wilkins. In 1973 we had about 300 more libraries (5,800 total) purchasing our journals than in 1971 but as the figures indicate, fewer journals are being purchased among the total libraries.

Considering the relative quality of W&W journals, the above indicates that the Interlibrary Loan Program is working,[1] but not in the best interests of Williams & Wilkins library circulation. We recently surveyed a random sampling of librarians who had cancelled their subscriptions and asked how they intended to service patrons who might want to use the cancelled journal. Invariably, the replay was, "by means of interlibrary loan," which means one library supplying another with a photocopy. If this trend continues, we could experi-

---

[1] For a description of Interlibrary Loans for Hospital Libraries see Chap. 15 of *Library Practice in Hospitals—A Basic Guide*, edited by Harold Bloomquist, et al, The Press of Western Reserve University, 1972.

ence a 50% decrease in library circulation over the next five years while the number of different libraries served through this well-planned and funded Interlibrary loan network will continue to increase.

There may be no valid argument that the above is not in the best interests of the national library economy, but it is evident that in order to survive, the scientific journals must receive additional income from the libraries engaged in supplying Interlibrary loans.

Other figures which we might sight fail to show the same precise cause and effect relationship as is shown by reduction in library subscriptions. For example, we believe that persons who live in the United States and who do not receive a journal as a part of their membership in a scientific society are the ones most likely to photocopy rather than become or to remain subscribers to the journal. This belief is borne out by the fact that this class of subscribers has actually decreased in 1973 as compared to 1972 with 11 of the journals which we publish and this despite the fact that we have greatly increased our promotional efforts. However, on the other hand, 15 of our journals have responded to our intensified promotion and in these instances the number of domestic non member subscribers has increased.

The following clipping from the July 20, 1973 issue of *Science* points out the economic pressure to photocopy rather than to subscribe.

THE PRICE OF BOOKS

The price of scholarly books has increased drastically in recent years. The books reviewed in *Science* as of 1 June cost 5.0, 5.3, 6.3, 7.2, 7.7, 8.8, 8.9, and an incredible 11.0 cents per page. As the cost of copying has dropped in recent years, one can copy a book at 5 cents a page in most libraries on public copiers and, by copying two pages at a time, reduce the cost to 2.5 cents per page. Of course, this is an infringement of the copyright but, at today's prices, a practice that will become increasingly common. Book publishers appear to be urgently in need of technological advances that will cut the cost of production.

DAVID LESTER,
Psychology Program, Stockton State College, Pomona, N.J., Science, Vol. 181.

We fear that no technological advances can cut the cost of production sufficiently to make up for the fact that the photocopy at present bears no part of the editorial and composition costs which are incurred before a single copy can be reproduced.

New Technological Uses of Copyrighted Works [2][3]

Until the last decade, the vast majority of library resources were in printed form. Library procedures were accomplished using paper products, with an occasional assist from the telephone. The recent proliferation of new media for packages of information has been surpassed only by the rapid birth and growth of technologists concerned with transmission, description, identification and retrieval of these information packages.

Libraries are involved in every phase of information processing from identification and ordering through retrieval and dissemination.

Examples of some current and future library-usable technologies:

1. *Facsimile Transmission*

Facsimile transmission devices can rapidly transmit exact copies of information over long distance network transmission points. While the systems currently on the market are costly and not quite compatible to one another, it is reasonable to believe that problems will be overcome in the future and could provide a working system for the rapid transmission of materials from one library to another.

2. *Satellites*

NASA and HEW are jointly exploring the use of experimental satellites for the exchange of information; one of the tests will involve the exchange of interlibrary loan materials.

3. *Video Telephones*

Video telephones which display pictures from one telephone to another are presently in operation. Certainly future technological improvements will bring about decreased operational costs and hard copy reproductions of video displays.

[2] See "Advanced Technologies/Libraries" published by Knowledge Industries, Inc. 1971-72.

[3] Also see Chap. 16 Health Sciences Information Retrieval Systems Library Practice in Hospital—A Basic Guide Edited by Harold Bloomquist, et al. The Press of Case Western Reserve University, 1972.

We believe that these few examples of new technologies in information dissemination should be the subject matter of study for the National Commission on New Technological Uses of Copyrighted Works proposed in Title II of S. 1361.

We are in favor of Bill S. 1361 as submitted, with some amendments for the sake of clarity. We are opposed to any legislative history which appears to construe fair use so as to permit the photocopying of single copies of entire articles without compensation because fair use is a judicial doctrine and its construction is best left to the flexibility of the Courts. As for guidance, the ultimate decision in *Williams & Wilkins* v. *U.S.* will aid in pointing the way in this area.

THE WILLIAMS & WILKINS CO.,
Baltimore, Md.

EXHIBIT 1

TO OUR FRIENDS AND CUSTOMERS: On February 16, 1972 a Commissioner of the United States Court of Claims issued an opinion sustaining our claim for copyright infringement resulting from the unauthorized reproduction of our copyrighted materials on photocopying machines in certain Government libraries. The Commissioner held that we are entitled to "reasonable and entire compensation." We have prepared a digest of the Commissioner's opinion, a copy of which is enclosed with this letter. We believe that you who are deeply concerned with the health of scientific journals will read this with interest.

Although the Government does have a right to carry the proceedings further, it is, of course, our hope that this will mark the end to four years of litigation to establish the right of medical journals to remain viable so that they might continue to serve the scientific community.

Commissioner Davis' statement, "the plaintiff does not seek to enjoin any photocopying of its journals" should once and forever allay the fears of libraries and their patrons that our suit was aimed at the curtailment of photocopying (see p. 6 of the Report of the Commissioner).

Another concern of the libraries has been that a complicated and costly system of record keeping would be required to handle the payment of royalties to copyright owners. Nothing could be further from the truth. We have developed a simple and workable plan whereby libraries would be permitted to make single photocopies upon payment of a reasonable annual license fee. No record keeping or accounting would be involved. At the same time the plan recognizes that the cost of publication should be spread in a fair manner among the users of medical and scientific publications, including photocopiers, to avoid even higher subscription costs.

We hope that Government libraries as well as other public and private institutions will work with us toward a solution which gives proper balance to the public right to the flow of scientific information and the need of the author or publisher to compensation for having made the information available.

We welcome comments or questions from our many friends in the scientific world in reference to this matter which is of such vital importance to us all.

Most sincerely,

WILLIAM M. PASSANO,
Chairman of the Board.

EXHIBIT 2

DEPARTMENT OF HEALTH, EDUCATION, AND WELFARE,
NATIONAL INSTITUTES OF HEALTH,
March 7, 1972.

To : Resource grants grantees.
From : Associate director for extramural programs, NLM.
Subject : Payment of royalties to publishers.

1. On February 16, 1972, a Commissioner of the United States Court of Claims recommended to that Court that the plaintiff in the case of the Williams & Wilkins Company v. the United States is entitled to recover reasonable compensation for infringement of copyright. The Williams & Wilkins Company publishes 37 medical journals and has sued the United States Government alleging that the National Library of Medicine has infringed the copyright that Williams & Wilkins holds on four of those journals, namely *Medicine, Journal of Immunology, Gastroenterology* and *Pharmacological Reviews.* The alleged copyright infringement is said to have resulted from the practice of the National

Library of Medicine in supplying photocopies of articles from those journals.

2. The recommendation of the Commissioner will now be considered by the full Court of Claims and in all probability will ultimately be carried to the United States Supreme Court. Accordingly, a final decision will not be forthcoming for some time.

3. The Williams & Wilkins Company, following the recommendation of the Commissioner of the United States Court of Claims has approached several libraries requesting royalty payments from the libraries for the right to photocopy articles from the journals. Conceivably, other publishers may do the same.

4. The expressed purpose of this memorandum is to inform you that grant funds from the National Library of Medicine must not be used for royalty payments to publishers without prior approval from the National Library of Medicine. This matter is now under intensive study at various levels and will be considered by the National Library of Medicine's Board of Regents on March 28, 1972. You will be kept informed concerning this matter but until further notice, you are not authorized to utilize grant funds for payment of royalties to any publishers.

L. L. LANGLEY, Ph. D.,
Associate Director for Extramural Programs.

EXHIBIT 3

The Williams & Wilkins Company v. The United States

A STATEMENT OF FACT AND FAITH

We, as a leading publisher of medical books and journals, are dedicated to the concept of the proper dissemination of medical knowledge.

In 1968 we filed suit against the United States Government for infringement of certain copyrights in medical journals resulting from the unauthorized reproduction of our copyrighted materials by photocopying equipment. In the Report of the Commissioner to the Court of Claims (February 16th, 1972), the following facts are reported:

(1) Article 1 of the copyright statute says that the copyright owner ". . . shall have the exclusive right: (a) to print, reprint, publish, copy and vend the copyrighted work . . ."

(2) Each article in a journal is protected from infringement to the same extent as the entire journal issue.

(3) The Williams & Wilkins Company is entitled to recover reasonable and entire compensation for infringement of copyright.

These are the facts of the court case, but the implications may well be causing grave concern to librarians and the users of libraries. Let us make our position clear. We are by no means going to halt the proper dissemination of medical knowledge; our ideals now are the same as formerly—to serve the medical and science communities to the best of our abilities.

There will be no halt to the photocopying of material, as such a halt would indeed be harmful to the dissemination of knowledge. Neither will there be an unmanageable, unwieldy and costly system of record-keeping of photocopied materials as such a system would be detrimental to the library profession.

Instead, we have worked out a simple plan based on the idea of a reasonable annual license fee for the right of copying our materials. In this way, the librarian will be licensed to photocopy copyrighted materials without infringing copyright law, and the publisher will be recompensed for the use of his materials.

We are hopeful that this statement will allay any fears which librarians or library users may be harboring. We welcome your comments and questions, and conclude by assuring you of our good faith and commitment to the medical communities and the library profession.

THE WILLIAMS & WILKINS CO.,
Baltimore, Md.

EXHIBIT 4

A STATEMENT TO LIBRARIANS FROM THE WILLIAMS & WILKINS CO.

The Williams & Wilkins Company has always charged the same subscription price to libraries that it charges to individuals despite the fact that for many years it has been customary for publishers to charge institutional subscribers to journals a higher subscription rate than that paid by individual subscribers. The concept of special institutional rates evolved from the idea that the copy of a journal owned by a library or other institution serves many more readers than does the copy owned by an individual. In light of this, the higher rate is charged to spread fairly the ever-increasing costs of publication among *all* those who *use* the journal and to components for possible loss of individual subscription revenue. If uncompensated, this loss is suffered not only by the publisher, but by those professional societies dependent on income from their journals.

Another aspect of multiple use is the photocopying of material contained in a journal and its subsequent distribution to library users. By allowing the use of photocopying equipment, librarians effect increased use and readership of the journal. The journal paid for by one institutional subscription is thus, through photocopying and multiple exposure, used far more than the journal paid for by an individual.

We have always felt that photocopying without the consent of the copyright owner was against the law. This view has not been confirmed in the first case ever brought on the issue, a suit filed against the United States Government by The Williams & Wilkins Company.

The suit was commenced in 1968 as a test case and has led to a 32 page opinion handed down by Court of Claims Commissioner James F. Davis on February 16, 1972. The opinion held that we are entitled to "reasonable and entire compensation" for library photocopying of our journal articles.

Beginning with 1973 volumes, we have institutional subscription rates which provide for an automatic license to make single-copy photocopies of articles from our journals for your patrons in the regular course of library operations on your premises, but does not include the making of photocopies for other institutions or for fulfilling interlibrary loans. There is no time limit on the exercise of this right and single-copy photocopies may be made throughout the life of the journal volume. The institutional rates are minimal increases of $1 to $10 per journal. No additional payments or any record-keeping procedures will be required. These rights are simply and automatically secured by payment of this institutional rate. Single-copy photocopies may also be made from volumes published prior to 1973 at no charge. Multiple copies of a single article may be made upon remittance of 5¢ per page per copy made to the publisher.

A journal exists to provide wide-spread and quick dissemination of information; its value is to those who subscribe to it or use its information. Subscriptions are the very life blood of a journal, but when *users* do not contribute in any way to its sustenance, the very existence of the journal is jeopardized. In our view, it would not be unreasonable for libraries to pass on to their patrons who request photocopies, a few cents to recover the increase in subscription rates, just as many do to cover charges made by equipment manufacturers.

Beginning with the January issue of each of our journals, there will be an Instruction for Photocopying which advises individuals to patronize their libraries in obtaining photocopies.

As has been documented many times, Williams & Wilkins has no desire to curtail photocopying. We prefer to permit libraries to continue their practices while at the same time insuring that the costs of publishing journals be spread equitably among all users.

The proper dissemination of scientific knowledge is an ideal to which we, as publishers, have always been dedicated. We continue in our dedication to that ideal, and are confident that our solution is fair, reasonable and workable.

You will automatically be billed for the new subscription rate for 1973 volumes via your usual method of ordering (either through your agent or direct from us). In the unlikely event that no photocopies will be made of any articles in one or more of our journals to which you subscribe and you are in a position to assure us of this fact, you may apply for a refund for that portion of the institution rate which covers the license to photocopy. Be sure to make such application directly to The Williams & Wilkins Company and *not* through your agent and then only *after* you have entered your institutional subscription. You should recognize, however, that a license such as that in the institutional subscription rate is a legal requirement in order for you to make photocopies.

We are most willing to communicate directly with our customers. Any inquiries may be directed to Mrs. Andrea Albrecht, 301—727-2870 (collect).

EXHIBIT 5

JUNE 23, 1972.

Dr. MARTIN CUMMINGS,
*Director, National Library of Medicine, Mid-Atlantic Regional Medical Library,
Bethesda, Md.*

DEAR DR. CUMMINGS: The Williams & Wilkins Company publishes 38 scientific journals containing approximately 2,600 articles, 80% of which will appear in journals we publish for societies as their official publications. Net earnings from these journals are shared with the societies. The societies' share is generally 50% (sometimes greater) and it is usually used by them to defray the cost of editing.

In the main our journals are supported by their users. 64% of the journal's income comes from subscribers, 24% from advertiser support, 8½% from the sale of reprints and 3½% from the sale of back issues. Since reprography is another form of use, we continue to reiterate "use all you like, but pay for what you use." Thus, as reprography inevitably grows (and we think it should), this form of use should pay its fair share to help keep the learned periodical afloat. Certainly, without them many publishers and librarians alike would have lesser reasons for being.

So, beginning with the 1973 volumes, each of our journals will be offered to our library subscribers at institutional rates which will average $3.65 per volume higher than the rates to individuals. Such an amount is well below the institutional rates offered by many other publishers with no attending benefits and certainly well below some erroneous forecasts. This modest increase carries with it an automatic license which allows the library to make single-copy photocopies of articles from our journals for their individual patrons in the regular course of library operation on the premises. The institutional rate applies to all libraries, great and small, but it does not include the making of photocopies for other institutions, commercial or noncommercial organizations, or fulfilling interlibrary loans. In the interest of maintaining the principle that scientific journals will be supported by those who use them, it would seem reasonable for libraries to increase their photocopying charge to their patrons by a few pennies which in the course of a year will more than repay the added cost of the institutional rate.

Beginning October 1, 1972, we will license each of the 11 regional libraries engaged in the interlibrary loan program at a rate of 5¢ per page per copy for each photocopy of articles appearing in our journals supplied to other libraries. In connection with this license, we should like to make the following comments:

1. Although we believe that the receipts from interlibrary loan payments will be less than 1% of the journals' total income we nevertheless look upon them as essential to the long-time health of the journals. We can visualize the ultimate case when only the regional libraries will subscribe to some of our journals and if that time should come, the income from library loan photocopies will be vital to the journals' support.

2. As closely as we can estimate we do not expect to receive more than $500 per year per regional library on the average. Even the N.L.M. will probably find the cost in the neighborhood of $1,000 annually which is the cost of 20 average journal subscriptions.

3. We understand that records are currently kept of all interlibrary loan transactions and therefore only a slight additional effort will be required to account for payments to the copyright owner. We propose such payments being made semi-annually.

4. We think it reasonable for regional libraries to add 5¢ per page to the charge which we understand most now make for supplying photocopies on interlibrary loans. Not only will this recover to the library the payments made to us but also will allow the real users of the journals to share in their support.

5. The opinion of Commissioner Davis of the Court of Claims in our suit against the Government is an authoritative judicial interpretation of the Copyright Act as it applies to library photocopying and will remain so unless or until it may be altered on appeal.

This letter is being sent to each of the regional libraries well in advance of our normal billing time so that everyone will have time to digest and discuss our plan. We, of course, welcome the opportunity to discuss any aspect of this plan with you. We hope that by the reasonable nature of our position you will accept our continued affirmation that we are not adversaries but rather concerned public who look upon you as valued customers and colleagues.

Sincerely,

WILLIAM M. PASSANO,
Chairman of the Board.

EXHIBIT 6

DEPARTMENT OF HEALTH, EDUCATION, AND WELFARE,
PUBLIC HEALTH SERVICE,
NATIONAL INSTITUTES OF HEALTH,
Bethesda, Md., July 31, 1972.

Mr. WILLIAM M. PASSANO,
Chairman of the Board,
The Williams & Wilkins Co.,
Baltimore, Md.

DEAR MR. PASSANO: I am writing in response to your letter of June 23, in which you detail the imminent imposition of institutional subscription rates beginning with 1973 volumes, which rates will include payment of licensing fees for photocopying for interlibrary loan purposes, beginning October 1, 1972.

In connection with the institutional subscription rate, your letter indicates that the new rate carries with it an automatic license for making single-copy photocopies for individual patrons in the regular course of operations on the premises. Your recent "Statement to Librarians" states that a *portion* of the institution rate covers this license. However, you have subsequently indicated to us that the *entire* price difference between the institutional rate and the individual rate constitutes payment for this license. It is our position that we would accede to a rise in price based on an institutional rate which would be applied "to all libraries, great and small," but could not accept the implication that a license for photocopying is necessary. We must, therefore, respectfully decline to pay the institutional rate for our subscriptions, at least during the pendency of the litigation between us. We would be pleased to renew our subscriptions at the individual rate, or at an institutional rate which does not include a license for photocopying. If you insist upon tying the renewal of our subscription to the payment of a licensing fee, however, we shall have no option other than to let them lapse.

You also state you plan to charge a fee of 5 cents per page for each photocopy made for purposes of interlibrary loans. On the advice of our counsel, I am instructing my staff, as well as the Regional Medical Libraries, to refuse payment of such a fee based on our position in the case before the Court of Claims. Further, we believe it inappropriate to make any change in acquisition and interlibrary lending practices until that litigation is finally adjudicated.

With respect to the Regional Medical Libraries, our instructions apply, of course, only to those items paid for with contract or grant funds from the National Library of Medicine. Although we have informed them of the action we are taking with regard to the institutional subscription rates, we would not presume to advise them regarding the position to be taken by their parent institution for services they furnish on their own behalf.

Sincerely yours,

MARTIN M. CUMMINGS, M.D.,
Director.

EXHIBIT 7

JULY 31, 1972.

To Regional Medical Library Directors:

As you are aware, on February 16, 1972, Commissioner James F. Davis of the U.S. Court of Claims filed a "Report of Commissioner to the Court" on the copyright infringement suit against the Federal Government by the William & Wilkins Company. This preliminary report holds that the longstanding photocopying practices of NLM and the NIH Library are in violation of the journal publisher's copyright. The Commissioner's Report is not final and the Justice Department has filed an exception to the Report with the Court of Claims.

Despite the fact that the case is still being adjudicated, the Williams and Wilkins Company has informed the National Library of Medicine that beginning October 1, 1972, they plan to license each of the eleven regional medical libraries engaged in interlibrary loans for photocopying articles from their journals at a rate of 5 cents per page per copy. A number of libraries have asked us for clarification of the NLM position on these matters.

Until such time that you are informed otherwise, it remains our policy that no NLM contract or grant funds may be spent for licensure or royalties for photocopying journal articles for interlibrary loan purposes because we believe such payments to be unnecessary. If it should be ultimately decided that such photocopying must be licensed, such costs will then be considered as proper charges against grant and contract funds.

We cannot advise you in your dealings with Williams and Wilkins Company concerning services you provide outside the guidelines of the registered medical library programs. However, it may be of interest to you to know our position concerning Williams and Wilkins Company's new 1973 institutional subscription rates which purportedly provide for an automatic license to make single photocopies of journal articles on the premises. We plan to inform the Company that we will not pay their new institutional subscription price, but will pay whatever subscription rate they may set for institutions that excludes the license fee.

We hope this will assist you in planning for the activities of the NLM component of your library.

MARTIN M. CUMMINGS, M.D.,
Director.

EXHIBIT 8 (A)

The American Library Association (ALA) WASHINGTON NEWSLETTER of August 11, 1972 contained the statement that follows:

Williams & Wilkins has recently published "A Statement to Librarians" which announced the establishment of a "Special Institutional Rate" applicable to library subscribers. Such rate is significantly higher than the regular subscription rate, involving an average increase of approximately 12½ percent.

The Statement further advises that libraries may not make photocopies of Williams & Wilkins' works for purposes of interlibrary loan, even if purchased at the Special Institutional Rate. Moreover, it demands that libraries pay a royalty to William & Wilkins of 5c per page per copy on multiple copies of a single work.

Innumerable libraries, librarians, and library trustees throughout the country have requested advice from ALA as to the response they should make to the demands of Williams & Wilkins.

The American Library Association is not in a position to prescribe the response of libraries and librarians, since that response will necessarily vary on the basis of a variety of local considerations.

However, it should be noted that:

First, a number of leading libraries have individually determined that they will not renew their subscriptions at the Special Institutional Rate;

Second, William & Wilkins' assertion that "a license such as that in the institutional subscription rate is a legal requirement" is based on a Commissioner's Report and is not, to date, the decision of the Court of Claims;

Third, the propriety of the Commissioner's Report is being strenuously contested in the Court of Claims by the Federal Government, the American Library Association, the Association of Research Libraries, the Medical Library Association, and a number of other educational groups and institutions;

Fourth, libraries in which copies are made on coin-operated photocopiers not under library supervision and control, derive substantially no protection which they do not already enjoy under the license granted by the Institutional Subscription Rate;

Fifth, general acceptance of the "use tax" concept of the Williams & Wilkins Institutional Subscription Rate may reasonably be expected to encourage other journal publishers to levy their own "use taxes" at ever-increasing rates;

Sixth, the Institutional Subscription Rate does not authorize copies for interlibrary loans and thus contemplates a continuing and rigorous restriction on access to scholarly materials contained in Williams & Wilkins' publications.

Each library must decide for itself whether it will pay a premium for Williams & Wilkins' works notwithstanding the significant limits imposed on their use, and on the access to them, by the Institutional Subscription Rate.

EXHIBIT 8 (B)

Special Libraries Association (SLA) has issued the following statement to its members which was proposed by the SLA Special Committee for Copyright Law Revision and approved by the SLA Board of Directors.

Through its Special Committee on Copyright Law Revision, the Special Libraries Association has been engaged in the ten-year legislative revision effort that is now before Congress. To special libraries the rights to photocopy research materials under a "fair use" principle has been central to the SLA concern with the revision of the copyright law. Based on a recommendation from its Special Committee, the SLA Board of Directors in 1964 reaffirmed the principle of "fair use" as follows:

"A library owning books or periodical volumes in which copyright still subsists may make and deliver a single photographic reproduction of a part thereof to a scholar representing in writing that he desires such reproduction in lieu of a loan of such publication or in place of manual transcription and solely for the purposes of research."

In view of the recent *Williams & Wilkins* report, it is now deemed desirable that the Association take a position on the photocopying issue for the guidance of the Association's members. Whether adopted or rejected by the U.S. Court of Claims, the *Williams & Wilkins* report implies that libraries will be responsible for reimbursing publishers through a subscription surcharge, a per page licensing fee or a similar royalty arrangement. Increased costs to all special libraries will plainly result. Depending on the basis of reimbursement, any of these schemes will encumber the administration of special libraries and will burden their staff everywhere with unnecessary tasks, thus detracting from important functions. Moreover, an inevitable consequence of the opinion, should it stand, would be the inhibition of the business, education and scientific research communities who are the principal users of special libraries.

Pending final judicial action, the Association advises its members to continue copying practices followed heretofore. In the event that individual libraries are approached by publishers desiring to negotiate licensing agreements, royalty payments or subscription surcharge agreements, such requests should be referred to the legal counsel of their company or library, with advice to SLA's New York office of such actions.

———

EXHIBIT 8 (C)

The following statement was included in the August 1972 issue of MLA NEWS, a publication of the Medical Library Association.

However firmly Williams & Wilkins may be convinced that the Davis report on the copyright suit against NLM and NIH is law, just as firmly the Medical Library Association is convinced that the case is *sub judice*. Williams & Wilkins has demonstrated its conviction by announcing, for the journals that it publishes, special institutional subscription rates, higher than those charged individual subscribers, "which provides for an automatic license to make single-copy photocopies of articles" for library patrons (but not for inter-library loan). *The right of Williams & Wilkins to seek such additional payments is the subject of review by MLA's legal counsel.*

Obviously the Medical Library Association believes that the Williams & Wilkins subscription/photocopy "package" is not in the public interest. Libraries, however, must decide individually whether or not they want to accept this type of proposal. They must weigh the fulfillment of immediate needs against the possibility of weakening the case for legislative provision of single-copy photocopy for medical research and physicians' study. They might also confer with their own institutional counsel.

We are aware that librarians are very conscious of their responsibility for the library's collection. As a means of maintaining the integrity of the collection, they might seek contributions of Williams & Wilkins periodicals to the library by individual subscribers.

Whatever action is decided upon, we suggest that individual institutions and libraries make their opinions known to Williams & Wilkins, to the National Library of Medicine, to the Department of Justice, Civil Division, attention of Thomas J. Byrnes, and to the Medical Library Association.

EXHIBIT 9

DEPARTMENT OF HEALTH, EDUCATION, AND WELFARE,
NATIONAL INSTITUTES OF HEALTH,
Bethesda, Md., September 12, 1972.

EUGENE B. BRODY, M.D.,
Editor, Journal of Nervous and Mental Disease, Institute of Psychiatry and Human Behavior, University of Maryland School of Medicine, Baltimore, Md.

DEAR DR. BRODY: We are addressing this letter to you in your capacity as Editor of the *Journal of Nervous and Mental Disease.* As you probably are aware, your publisher, the Williams and Wilkins Company, has been involved in a copyright infringement suit against the Federal Government. Last February, a report was rendered on the case which was heard before a Commissioner of the U.S. Court of Claims. Subsequently, the Williams and Wilkins Company proposed a new subscription rate schedule for institutional recipients which includes an automatic photocopying license for library patrons and a royalty of five cents per page for articles copied for interlibrary loan.

We have indicated our willingness to pay higher subscription rates; however, we cannot accept the implication that a license for photocopying is necessary. We are therefore faced with the prospect of lapsing the Library's subscription to your journal.

For many years, the National Library of Medicine has indexed the articles contained in your journal and we would be pleased to continue to do so in the future. However, if we are not able to obtain a regular subscription this will no longer be possible unless some other means of acquiring your journal is found.

I thought you should learn in advance why we may no longer be able to index your journal rather than have you discover this after the fact.

Sincerely yours,

MARTIN M. CUMMINGS, M.D.,
Director.

EXHIBIT 10

THE WILLIAMS & WILKINS CO.,
Baltimore, Md., October 2, 1972.

TO OUR CUSTOMERS AND FRIENDS: After many discussions with librarians, administrators, scientists, and scholars, The Williams & Wilkins Co. has arrived at an arrangement concerning the photocopying of copyrighted material which we hope you and the rest of your library staff will find appropriate.

BACKGROUND OF W&W POSITION

First, let us say that we have been publishing medical journals since 1909 and it is our hope and intention to continue doing so for as long as we are able. In most instances, the journals we publish have made modest earnings for their societies as well as a fair margin of profit for The Williams & Wilkins Company. This, we feel, is a reasonable and proper situation. We also feel, and have always felt, that our function as publishers is an important and necessary one to the rapid dissemination of scientific information. Neither the medical society nor The Williams & Wilkins Company is in the publication business to make a quick killing or exorbitant profits. But as publishers and businessmen, we would be remiss if we did not consider all the factors that influence the economic viability of our journals. For when this economic viability is threatened, so too is the very existence of the journals and their role in the spreading of vital medical and scientific information. Over a period of time, an exhaustive analysis of the situation convinced us that uncompensated photocopying could lead to the demise of the scientific journal as we know it. We did not, and do not, wish to discourage scholars and physicians from photocopying journal articles. In fact, we encourage this as a most logical and practical method of disseminating information. It is our contention, however, that the costs of the journal must be spread equitably among all its users to offset the losses in revenue due to dwindling subscriptions.

W&W VERSUS THE UNITED STATES

To establish this principle, we eventually found it necessary to bring suit against the federal government. In February 1972, Commissioner James Davis of the U.S. Court of Claims ruled in favor of The Williams & Wilkins Co., thereby upholding our contention that we are entitled to "reasonable and entire compensation for infringement of copyrights." Our action following this decision has been consistent with our long term objectives, which are to continue publishing journals and thereby serve the scientific community, while earning revenue for their societies and a reasonable profit for ourselves.

W&W'S FIRST PROPOSAL

Instead of resolving the copyright situation, however, Commissioner Davis' ruling seemed only to generate hostility and confusion. Part of this confusion, we must confess, was brought about as a result of our own action. Since we deemed it desirable to implement the ruling as soon as possible, The Williams & Wilkins Co. established a plan that would spread the cost of our journals among all of their users while continuing to allow the unimpeded flow of knowledge. As you know, our plan called for a modest rise in the journal subscription rate to institutions which would include a reproduction license. In return for this license—which, incidentally, averaged less than four dollars for the 56 year term of the copyright—we proposed to allow unlimited single-copy reproduction of all articles, current and past, in journals published by The Williams & Wilkins Co. carrying an institutional rate. (For a complete list of these journals, please see enclosure.) In addition, the plan called for a five-cents-per-page fee for inter-library loan reproductions. Since it is our position that a Commissioner's ruling, unless reversed, has the full weight of law, it seemed logical that we proceed from his decision by requesting that the institutional reproduction fee be paid. Perhaps naively, we did not anticipate the strenuous objections by some segments of your library community. Until the government's appeal has been processed, it is their contention that the ruling does not have the weight of law and that compliance with our new procedures would imply acceptance of our position.

REACTION TO THE PROPOSAL

To further complicate the situation, during the months following our proposed plan announcement, much confusion and conflicting reports circulated as to our intentions. Some exaggerated charges stated that our subscription rates would soar to four or five times what they are at present; it was charged that burdensome bookkeeping would be required by librarians; some claimed that we even wished to curtail the practice of photocopying altogether. As a result of these charges, an atmosphere of distrust was created with both sides maintaining that they could not compromise their legal positions. In a letter to The Williams & Wilkins Co. of July 31, 1972, the National Library of Medicine, stated that it is its position that it would accede to a rise in price based on an institutional rate to all libraries, great and small, but could not accept the implication that a license for photocopying is necessary.

THE SOLUTION

In order to allow the NLM and all libraries to subscribe to W&W journals at increased rates and include them in *Index Medicus*, we now accept the NIH–NLM position. Our new institutional rates, which we shall continue to request, shall have no connection whatever with a license to photocopy, implied or otherwise. In short libraries may continue to supply their uses with royalty-free, single-copy reproductions of W&W journal articles as they have done in the past.

As stated many times, we have no desire to obstruct the dissemination of scientific information between library and scholar, which would certainly be the result of cancellation of subscriptions. Further, in the same spirit, we are, again without prejudice, withdrawing our proposal for the five-cents-per-page inter-library loan fee until the appeal of our case has been heard. In the meantime, we hope to work with libraries in an effort to develop a solution which will be mutually acceptable. Both of these concessions have been made with a sincere desire to see that there is no interruption whatever to the flow of scientific information between you and your patrons which would result from subscription cancellations. We are sure this desire coincides with your own objectives.

To facilitate greater cooperation, please feel free to call Mrs. Andrea Albrecht collect, c/o The Williams & Wilkins Company, with any questions, comments, or suggestions you may have.

Sincerely,

WILLIAM M. PASSANO,
Chairman of the Board.

JOURNALS WHICH CARRY BOTH AN INSTITUTIONAL RATE AND AN INDIVIDUAL RATE [1]

Acta Cytologica ($19.50)
American Journal of Physical Medicine ($14.00)
Current Medical Dialog ($11.00)
Drug Metabolism and Disposition ($42.00)
Fertility and Sterility ($33.00)
Gastroenterology ($35.00)
Investigative Urology ($22.50)
Journal of Criminal Law, Criminology and Police Science ($18.50)
Journal of Histochemistry and Cytochemistry ($33.00)
Journal of Immunology ($58.00)
Journal of Investigative Dermatology $(43.75)
Journal of Nervous and Mental Disease ($23.00)
Journal of Pharmacology and Experimental Therapeutics ($70.00)

Journal of Trauma ($27.00)
Journal of Urology ($40.00)
Laboratory Investigation ($45.00)
Medicine ($15.00)
Obstetrical and Gynecological Survey ($29.00)
Pediatric Research ($32.00)
Pharmacological Reviews ($18.00)
Plastic and Reconstructive Surgery ($30.00)
Radiological Technology ($11.00)
Soil Science ($23.00)
Stain Technology ($12.00)
Survey of Anesthesiology ($13.00)
Survey of Ophthalmology ($26.00)
Transplantation ($43.00)
Urological Survey ($16.00)

NOTE.—Institutional rate in ( )

JOURNALS WHICH CARRY AN INDIVIDUAL RATE ONLY [2]

Cancer Research ($50.00)
International Journal of Gynaecology and Obstetrics ($10.00)
Journal of Neurosurgery ($35.00)
Journal of Biological Chemistry ($120.00)
Applied Spectroscopy ($15.00)
British Journal of Plastic Surgery ($14.00)
British Journal of Surgery ($28.50)
British Journal of Urology ($16.50)

British Veterinary Journal ($20.00)
Clinical Radiology ($18.00)
Community Health ($12.15)
Comparative and General Pharmacology ($40.00)
Dental Practitioner ($12.15)
Injury ($17.85)
Insect Biochemistry ($40.00)
International Journal of Biochemistry ($40.00)
Tubercle ($19.85)

NOTE.—Non-Institutional rate in ( )

EXHIBIT 11

THE WILLIAMS & WILKINS CO.,
Baltimore, Md., Jan. 11, 1973.

DEAR LIBRARIAN: On October 2nd, 1972, we sent you a detailed account of our changed thinking about licensing the photocopying of copyrighted materials, in light of the unfavorable responses generated by our original position. That letter covered the background of our beliefs about photocopying; our suit against the Federal Government; Commissioner Davis's opinion; our first proposal; and the reaction to that proposal from members of your profession. We concluded with a solution to the problem which, to the best of our knowledge, has proved acceptable to the entire library community.

However, we should like to re-state that solution, as there are still some misconceptions about our changed position.

1) We accept the position advocated by the NIH–NLM.

2) Our new institutional rates (see enclosed rate sheet), have no connection with a license to photocopy, implied or otherwise.

---

[1] These journals are published by The Williams & Wilkins Co. and in most cases the copyright is in the name of W&W.

[2] These journals are published by others for which the Williams & Wilkins Co. performs certain services under contract. Policy is set for those journals by their proprietors and is not within the province of W&W. The exception is the International Journal of Gynaecology and Obstetrics which is published by W&W but carries no institutional rate.

3) Libraries may continue to supply their users with royalty-free, single-copy reproductions of our journal articles.

4) We have withdrawn, without prejudice, our proposal for the five-cents-per-page inter-library loan fee for copying.

We hope that this will help clear up any doubts that you may have had about our subscription rates and our attitude toward photocopying.

Sincerely yours,

PATRICIA H. MORRIS,
Subscription Manager.

EXHIBIT 12

APRIL 30, 1973.

Dr. MARTIN CUMMINGS,
Director, National Library of Medicine,
Bethesda, Md.

DEAR DR. CUMMINGS: We at Williams & Wilkins are most anxious to see a solution to the interlibrary loan problem. We realize that the problem must be solved to the satisfaction of the medical libraries as well as to ourselves. Since my last visit with you, I and my colleagues have given much thought to the subject.

Let me tabulate some of the requirements which in our opinion must be met if a plan is to be mutually satisfactory.

1. It should not require record keeping or accounting on the part of the libraries over and above what they are doing at present.

2. It should recognize that photocopying is a valuable library tool which should be utilized whenever the professional librarian believes that it is useful.

3. It should compensate the scientific journals for the loss of subscription income which is the result of the interlibrary loan procedure.

4. Our established institutional rate should include this compensation and our permission for reprography for interlibrary loan and over-the-counter copying.

5. The monies collected under the plan should be built into the subscription price of the journals and should be related to the basic institutional rate so as to assure that future variations will be in direct proportion to changes in that basic rate.

To satisfy these requirements we have developed the following plan:

The subscription price to the 11 Regional Libraries for the 1974 journals will be no greater than twice the institutional rate and for the Medical School Libraries and the 500 ± medical libraries involved in the interlibrary loan operation no greater than one and one half times the institutional rate.

In all instances where libraries of any size subscribe to two or more copies of a journal the additional copies will be billed at the individual subscriber rate. This is with the understanding that the additional copies are for intramural use and are not to be turned over to a branch of the parent library or any other separate institution.

We fully realize that the success of this (or any other) plan is primarily dependent on its meeting with the approval of NLM and upon NLM's willingness to recommend it to the medical libraries throughout the country. The details of the plan (but not its principles) should be subject to adjustment as industry-wide surveys make available additional knowledge of interlibrary loan operation.

It is our firm belief that you and we agree on the realities of this situation and that there is a genuine desire on both sides to arrive at an amicable and satisfactory solution to the problem. We offer this as such a solution and we await with interest your reaction to it.

Most sincerely,

DANIEL H. COYNE,
President, Publishing Services Division.
WILLIAM M. PASSANO, Sr.,
Chairman of the Board.
SUBCOMMITTEE ON PATENTS, TRADEMARKS AND COPYRIGHTS,
COMMITTEE ON THE JUDICIARY, UNITED STATES SENATE,
July 31, 1973.

STATEMENT OF THE AUTHORS LEAGUE OF AMERICA ON "LIBRARY PHOTOCOPYING"
AND S. 1361

Mr. Chairman and Members of the Subcommittee: My name is Jerome Weidman. I am president of The Authors League of America, a national society of professional authors and dramatists. The Authors League appreciates this opportunity to present its views on problems of "library photocopying" related to the Copyright Revision Bill. May I request that this statement be included in the record?

We respectfully recommend to the Subcommittee that:

1. The library associations' proposal for a "library reproduction" exemption should be rejected.

2. The National Commission on New Technological Uses of Copyrighted Works should be established; and it should investigate and make recommendations as to

    (*a*) "workable clearance and licensing conditions" for the library reproduction of copyrighted works, the solution recommended by the House Judiciary Report, in those words; and

    (*b*) "such changes in copyright law or procedures that may be necessary to assure for such purposes access to copyrighted works, and to provide recognition of the rights of copyright owners."

3. Sec. 108 should be revised to eliminate ambiguities which would destroy the rights of authors and publishers.

4. Section 107 should be retained. However the judicial doctrine of fair use (which it simply reaffirms) should not be expanded by interpretation, in the Committee report, to "normally" include so-called "single-copy" reproduction of an entire article.

THE DEMAND FOR A LIBRARY REPRODUCTION EXEMPTION

The Association of Research Libraries and the American Library Association seek an exemption (through a new Sec. 108(d)(1)) permitting libraries or archives (i) to reproduce copies of articles and portions of books and (ii) to reproduce, under loose conditions, copies or phonorecords of entire books or other copyrighted works. Similar exemptions have been proposed in the past and rejected by this Subcommittee and by the House Judiciary Committee. For the reasons discussed below, the Authors League urges the Subcommittee to reject the library associations' current effort to create this damaging limitation on the rights of authors and other copyright owners. "Copyright Owners", it should be noted, include authors, non-profit societies which publish technical and scientific journals (e.g. American Chemical Society), non-profit publishers of books and journals (e.g. the university presses represented by The Association of American University Presses), and for-profit publishers.

The Context of the Issues

Clause (1) of the proposed library exemption would allow libraries to engage in unauthorized, uncompensated "one-at-a-time reprinting" of entire articles, and portions of books and other works.

"One-at-a-time reprinting" is not an argumentative or pejorative term. It is a phrase used by experts to describe the process of disseminating articles, chapters from books, and entire books to readers and users—by reproducing a single reprint to fill each individual order. Each copy, made by Xerox or other process, is an exact reprint of the original—line by line, letter by letter, as originally set in type. The process of one-at-a-time printing is now well-established. It is used by commercial reprint publishers, such as University Microfilms, to supply copies of older books to individual customers,[1] it is used by journal publishers; and it is vigorously employed by several large libraries which serve as reprint centers for the patrons of many other libraries.

The process involves unlimited reproduction of copies of a given article or other work. The reprint publisher produces one copy for each order; but it produces as many copies of a work as there are orders for it. Similarly, under clause (1) of the librarians' proposed exemption, any library could reproduce many copies of an entire article or portion of a book—one copy for each of the several individuals who orders it. And any library could reproduce many "single copies" of each article in a periodical issue, so long as it provided one copy per order.

[1] University Microfilms secures licenses from the copyright owners and pays them royalties.

The Issues—And Positions of the Parties

Copyright owners agree that certain copying of copyrighted works can be done by libraries without permission or compensation—i.e. copying which falls within the scope of fair use. And librarians agree that some library reproduction of copyrighted works is, and should be, copyright infringement.

But there is sharp disagreement over library reproduction of entire articles, and similar portions of entire books. Library spokesmen demand that libraries be permitted to reproduce copies of any article and distribute them, one-at-a-time, to persons who order them, without the copyright owner's permission or compensation. While library spokesmen have focussed their demand on scientific, technical and scholarly articles, their proposed exemption would give libraries the power to reproduce copies of any article or "similarly" sized portion of any book or other work.

Libraries seek power to reproduce these copies without compensation to the copyright owner—even though (1) copies are available from the copyright owner, directly or through its licensed reproduction service, or/and (2) the copyright owner will authorize the libraries to make the copies, provided reasonable compensation is paid to the copyright owner under "workable clearance and licensing conditions."

Copyright owners contended that such unauthorized, uncompensated library reproduction of entire articles and "similarly" sized portions of entire books and other works is not permitted, and should not be permitted, under the Copyright Act. They have made it clear that the only real issue is reasonable compensation to copyright owners for library one-at-a-time reprinting of their articles and other works. Copyright owners have accepted the principle that "workable clearance and licensing conditions" should—and can—be established to authorize libraries to produce copies of these materials, and to provide reasonable compensation to copyright owners.

"Workable clearance and licensing conditions", as the House Judiciary Committee emphasized (Rep. 83, p. 36) are the fair and rational solution to the problem. But library spokesmen have flatly rejected it—in discussions with representatives of copyright owners, and in their current demand for an exemption permitting this type of one-at-a-time reproduction by libraries. Library spokesmen have contended that copyright owners must not be compensated. Their position poses two paradoxes. First, libraries do pay to reproduce copies of entire articles and other works; they pay the Xerox company and other manufacturers of equipment and supplies very handsome compensation for providing the tools of one-at-a-time reprinting; they pay their employees for the work involved in producing the copies; the reprinting libraries often charge substantial amounts to other libraries for reproducing copies for their patrons. Second librarians are deciding that public funds or funds provided by tax-deductible contributions should not be used to compensate those who make their one-at-a-time reprinting possible—the copyright owners who produce the articles and books that are the grist for their reproduction mills. By contrast, librarians have also made the decision that the cost of producing the copies must be absorbed by libraries, and no charge made to the readers and users.

The Proposed Library Exemption Destroys the Balanced Solution Envisioned by Congress

The reports of the House Judiciary Committee, and the draft Report of this Subcommittee, envisioned a 3-part solution to the problems of library copying which would serve the legitimate needs of library patrons, protect the right of copyright owners to reasonable compensation for the use of their property (and for their investment and work in creating it), and preserve the independent, entrepreneurial system of creating and disseminating works of literature, science, technology and art. The solution is based on three components: (1) fair use; (2) "workable clearance and licensing conditions", and (3) the principle of "availability", underlying Sec. 108 of S. 1361. The librarians' proposed library reproduction exemption destroys this balanced solution.

(1) Fair Use

As the House Judiciary Report, and the draft Report of this Subcommittee indicate, the doctrine of fair use applies to libraries; and library copying which is a fair use can be done without the permission or compensation of the copyright owner. The House report said: "Unauthorized library copying, like everything else, must be judged a fair use or an infringement on the basis of all the applicable criteria and the facts of the particular case." (II. Rep. No. 83, p. 36).

A principle purpose of the proposed library reproduction exemption is to alter that concept, and permit all library copying of entire articles and similarly sized parts of books and other works. If the library exemption simply authorized copying which was fair use, it would be unnecessary, and should be rejected to avoid confusion. To the extent that it permits unauthorized, uncompensated library copying which exceeds fair use, the exemption should be rejected because "it is more sweeping than is necessary", and—would wreak great injury on copyright owners, while at the same time destroying the balanced solution that would fairly serve the legitimate rights and needs of all concerned.

The proposed library exemption seeks to legalize the very type of uncompensated library reproduction of entire articles which Commissioner Davis held was infringement, and not fair use, in Williams & Wilkins v. United States. His opinion carefully analyzed—and rejected—the claims of the American Library Association and Association of Research Libraries that such wholesale copying was fair use. His findings and opinion were appealed by the government to the Court of Claims, and its opinion is awaited. But regardless of the outcome, the Authors League contends that such unauthorized, uncompensated one-at-a-time reprinting of entire articles should not be permitted by the Copyright Act, because of its unfair and damaging impact on copyright owners, and the independent, entrepreneurial copyright system of disseminating such works. It is precisely this type of library reproduction which, the House Report emphasized, should be conducted under "workable clearance and licensing conditions"—with payment of reasonable compensation to copyright owners.

(2) *"Workable Clearance and Licensing Conditions"*

The House Judiciary Committee prescribed "workable clearance and licensing conditions" as the second component of a balanced solution. It urged all parties concerned "to resume their efforts to reach an accommodation." Some librarians have recognized that a clearance and licensing system, with reasonable payment to copyright owners, is the rational method permitting library reproduction of copies of entire articles and similarly sized portions of books. Copyright owners have accepted this principle, and have sought to develop such systems in cooperation with library spokesman. The latest effort occurred in March, 1973 when representatives of learned societies, university presses, authors and other journal publishers met in Washington with a large group of library spokesmen, including representatives of The American Library Association and Association of Research Libraries. For two days the group discussed various aspects of clearance and licensing systems for library reproduction of journal articles. Plans were made for a subcommittee to continue the work. But the entire effort collapsed because too many library leaders stubbornly adhered to their earlier position that libraries must have the power to engage in uncompensated reproduction of copies of journal articles—and that copyright owners must be denied compensation. They refused to continue the joint effort.

The stubbornness and unreasonableness of library spokesmen should not be rewarded by giving their constituents, the libraries, the power to engage in uncompensated reproduction of articles and similarly sized portions of books. Such reproduction can be done under fair clearance and licensing systems. And those systems can be developed by the machinery designed by this Subcommittee for that purpose—The National Commission on New Technological Uses of Copyrighted Works.

Moreover, the proposed library exemption is a totally unnecessary abrogation of copyright owners rights, in view of the principle of "availability".

(3) *The Principle of "Availability"*

Section 108(d) permits libraries to reproduce—for their patrons, or patrons of other libraries—single copies of any work that is not "available" from designated sources. As indicated below, The Authors League believes that certain revisions should be made in the section to remove ambiguities that would deprive copyright owners of essential rights. However, the principle of "availability" assures that the patrons of libraries can obtain reprints of entire journal articles and similarly sized portions of books. If the copyright owner will not provide a copy of the article, directly or through its authorized reproduction service; the library may produce a reprint, without permission or compensation.

In a series of meetings held in 1972, representatives of journal and book publisher, and authors, met with library representatives to discuss Sec. 108 and the principle of availability. Library spokesmen indicated that their principal concern was assuring that reprints of scientific, technical and scholarly articles were "available"—i.e. could be provided—to patrons who requested them. Some library spokesmen also recognized that library reproduction of copies of these articles should not be permitted where the journal publisher was making copies available directly, or through its authorized reproduction service. A proposed revision of Sec. 108(d), suggested by a library representative, was drafted. Although it would have increased the obligations of publishers under Sec. 108 to assure "availability" of reprints of articles, it was summarily rejected by The American Library Association and Association of Research Libraries. The reason is simple: their spokesmen insist that libraries must be permitted to reproduce copies of articles without compensation even though the journal publisher is making copies available, directly or through an authorized reprint service. This destruction of the copyright owner's right, and denial of needed income, cannot be justified under the principle of "availability." Where the copyright owner provides copies of the article, as many publishers do, libraries should not be allowed to engage in uncompensated reproduction of these copies. If libraries wish to provide copies to patrons faster than the publisher does, then they should work with copyright owners to establish "workable clearance and licensing conditions."

However, library spokesmen—with some notable dissents—have arbitrarily rejected the 3-part balanced solution. They will have no part of "workable clearance and licensing conditions", or a reasonable concept of "availability" which allows uncompensated library reproduction only when the publisher is not providing copies. They continue to demand the power to engage in uncompensated reproduction of journal articles and similarly sized portions of books, despite the serious injury this would inflict on copyright owners and the copyright system.

The Library Exemption Would Injure Copyright Owners and the Copyright System

(i) Unquestionably, the proposed library reproduction exemption would reduce subscribers to scientific, technical and scholarly journals by libraries, who are their principal subscribers (and by individual subscribers). Librarians have candidly admitted that this is the purpose of library reproduction of journal articles. The attrition occurs at two levels. Some libraries took multiple subscription to heavily used journals so that several patrons could use them at the same time. Now one subscription suffices, since it is used to reproduce copies of articles for each user who wants them.

(ii) On the second level, library reproduction of journal articles allows many libraries to eliminate all subscriptions to many journals. When patrons of these libraries want an article, the library forwards the order to a central library which reproduces a single copy of the article for the patron. Library spokesmen, with a penchant for confusing euphemisms (e.g., they label unlimited library copying of articles as "single copying" because the copies are produced one-for-a-customer) blithely characterize these reprint transactions as "interlibrary loans". In truth, no loan is involved. The reprint is supplied to the patron who ordered, and he keeps it—it is his property. Admittedly, library reproduction of journal articles is designed to permit a few libraries to serve as one-at-a-time reprint services providing copies of articles to many other libraries who will not have to subscribe to these scientific, technical or scholarly journals. The government libraries involved in the Williams and Wilkins case engaged in this "wholesale" one-at-a-time reprinting of journal articles. Each year, their Xerox machines churned out thousands upon thousands of reprints of journal articles—one-at-a-time—to fill the orders of patrons of other libraries as well as their own patrons.

Under these circumstances, the proposed exemption is bound to deprive journal publishers of income from subscriptions that are not renewed, and additional subscriptions that are not placed because of library reproduction of their articles.

(iii) Moreover, the proposed exemption would deprive journal publishers of compensation for uses of their works by audiences reached by the new process of dissemination—one-at-a-time reprinting of articles. Doctors, engineers, scientists in every field and other potential readers can survey the contents of many journals through abstracts—then order reprints of the particular articles that interest them. They are not readers of "journals". They are an audience served directly by reprints of articles. This process of dissemination will continue to expand, for each journal article is a separate (and separately copy-rightable) work, unrelated to the other articles in the issue. One-at-a-time re-printing permits users to acquire copies of only the particular works—i.e. sep-arate articles—they want to read.

Similar developments of new processes for disseminating literary, musical and dramatic works have occurred frequently: e.g., motion pictures and tele-vision (to supplement the stage), the phonograph record, radio and tape record-ings (to supplement sheet music). The paperback book revolution created a process of disseminating books—in low priced editions, through mass distribu-tion—to an audience many times greater than that reached by the convention method of distribution, hard-cover "trade" editions.

Until now, authors and publishers have been compensated for uses of their works by audiences reached through these new processes of dissemination. How-ever library spokesmen now ask Congress to impose an exemption which would deprive journal publishers of payment for uses of their works by the increas-ing audience reached by the one-at-a-time reproduction of their articles. This means that innumerable readers who will benefit from the publisher's work in editing, printing and distributing its journals will not help defray any part of the publisher's cost of doing the work which made the articles "available" in the first place. These costs continue to rise, though subscriptions remain static, or decline. Deprived of income which they need and are entitled to receive, publishers will be obliged to discontinue many scientific, technical and scholarly journals.

(iv) The proposed library exemption would also damage authors of poetry, fiction, and books and articles on current political and social problems, bi-ography, history and a wide range of subjects. After these works first appear in periodicals or books, they are often reprinted—with the author's permission—in anthologies, text books, periodicals and other books (such as collections of an author's poetry, short stories or articles). Many authors earn a substan-tial part of their income from such *reprinting* of their works. Indeed, some earn the major part of their compensation in this manner. Poets and essayists, for example, receive very little when a poem or essay is published in a periodical; but they may license several different publishers to reprint the poem or essay in anthologies or collections. And although each fee is small, the accumula-tion of fees can produce a modest reward for work of substantial literary val-ue. Authors of books also earn a significant part of their compensation, in many instances, from permitting the reprinting of excerpts—of similar size to periodi-cal articles—in anthologies, textbooks and other collections.

Under the proposed exemption, libraries—including college and university libraries—would have the power to reproduce single copies of poems, articles and sections of books, without compensation to the author. The process of supplying these copies—e.g. one to each student in a university class in literature or po-litical science—can replace several copies of an anthology or book in the library, or several copies of a paperback collection or text in the college bookstore. Un-less authors are compensated for uses of their works by audiences reached by the new process of one-at-a-time reprinting, they will be deprived of a sub-stantial portion of their income.

(v) As we have noted, the proposed library exemption would permit an ac-cumulation of uncompensated copies of a given article or similarly sized excerpt from a book. Any one library could reproduce several copies of the work, "one-at-a-time." And many libraries could do the same thing. "Isolated instances of minor infringements," as the Subcommittee's draft report noted, "when multi-plied many times, become in the aggregate a major inroad on copyright that must be prevented." Library spokesmen argue that uncompensated library re-production poses no threat to publishers and authors. But in 1967, according to the *Sophar & Heilpron* report for the Office of Education, "It is estimated that in 1967 one billion copyrighted pages were copied in the U.S."

The library spokesmen can hardly guarantee that the proposed exemption will not seriously injure publishers of journals, or authors. Moreover, the pro-posed exemption does not, and could not, draw a line—limiting the injury a pub-lisher or author would suffer before libraries will cease one-at-a-time reprinting of his articles or portions of his books. And in the light of copyright history, it is dangerous to assume that the process of uncompensated library copying will not inflict substantial damage. Starting with the phonograph record, every new proc-ess of dissemination was greeted initially by the same "it's not a real threat" attitude the library spokesmen have voiced on the techniques of one-at-a-time reprinting.

(vi) One of the gravest dangers of the proposed library exemption is the adverse effect it will have on independent, entrepreneurial system for creating, publishing and disseminating journals, books and other works. The "economic philosophy" underlying the copyright clause was that such a system was preferable to patronage by governments or wealthy institutions. Because the copyright owner was entitled to compensation from users of his work, he could make the expenditures necessary to create, edit, publish and disseminate it. Through the payment of royalties and other compensation, users in effect shared in defraying the costs of producing the materials they desired. But, as we have noted, proposed exemption would deprive journal publishers, and authors, of substantial part of this needed income—compensation for uses of their works by audiences reached by the one-at-a-time production of their articles or portions of their books. It is regrettable that library spokesmen refuse to recognize the serious danger their exemption poses to the independent, entrepreneurial system of publication and dissemination which is essential to them, and—more importantly—to their patrons.

(vii) It should be noted that library reproduction of articles is not merely "note taking", nor a substitute for copying by individual readers. Persons who obtain reprints of articles from a library copying service or the publisher are not taking handwritten notes. They are acquiring reprints of printed articles, 10, 20, 30 or more pages long—just as they buy or acquire other published materials, to avoid the dozens of hours it would take to copy that much by hand. Nor could library patrons reproduce the copies themselves. Many patronize libraries that do not have the journals; the copies are reproduced for them by other libraries dozens or hundred of miles away. And where the patron's own library subscribes to the journal, it will produce and deliver a reprint of the article he wants (rather than lend the journal)—so that it can keep its one issue available to reproduce copies of articles for other patrons, and avoid losing this reprint master through wear and tear, readers' negligence, or theft.

The "Philosophical" Arguments

In the past, the librarians have accompanied their demand for the proposed exemption with an assortment of "philosophical" arguments: e.g., copyright is a monopoly, it is not property but a "privilege." Should it become necessary to respond to these familiar gambits, we respectfully direct the subcommittee's attention to our accompanying statement on the "Educational Exemption," demanded by the National Education Association and other groups.

THE NATIONAL COMMISSION

Although the House Judiciary Committee Report urged the parties to jointly develop "workable clearance and licensing conditions," efforts to do so have collapsed because library spokesmen opposed this phase of a fair and balanced solution to the problem of library photocopying.

It is therefore essential that the National Commission on New Technological Uses of Copyrighted Works be established. And that the Commission proceed, as intended by Title II of S. 1361, to study and make recommendations as to "workable clearance and licensing conditions" for library reproduction of articles and similarly sized portions of books and other works. Much of the information is already available. Practical proposals have been made by various informed individuals, including librarians who favor a licensing system. There are no real obstacles to a reasonable solution—except the position of library spokesmen that authors and publishers are not entitled to any compensation for library one-at-a-time production of their articles and similarly sized portions of their books.

REVISION OF SECTION 108

Sec. 108 (d) would permit uncompensated library reproduction of copies of any work when an unused copy "cannot be obtained at a normal price from commonly known trade sources in the United States including authorized reproducing services." There are certain ambiguities in the section which could seriously damage the rights of authors and publishers. These involve such questions as what "trade sources" are included, what time intervals make the privilege operative, and what is a normal price. A careful and thorough analysis of these ambiguities has been prepared and submitted to the Subcommittee by the firm of Linden and Deutsch. Their memorandum indicates the principal difficulties posed by the section; and we respectfully urge that it be revised to overcome them. We also urge that the revision incorporate the suggestions made by the Association of American Publishers. Finally we urge the revision take account of the difference between various categories of works. Many literary works, for example, are reprinted periodically, as the demand for the work warrants it. If libraries could reproduce copies during these intervals because a copy was not available from trade sources, this could eliminate the possibility of any further reprintings—depriving authors and publishers of income. It would appear that the problems posed by Sec. 108 (c) and (d) could be solved more readily by the Commission; and that it might be preferable to enact Sec. 108, pending the Commission's recommendations, in the form enacted by the House of Representatives.

THE SUBCOMMITTEE'S INTERPRETATION OF FAIR USE

As the Subcommittee's draft report indicates, Sec. 107 of S. 1361 "is intended to restate the present judicial doctrine of fair use, not to change, narrow or enlarge it in any way." We have always supported this interpretation of the section's purpose. The draft report further states "Library copying must be judged a fair use or an infringement on the basis of all the relevant criteria and the facts of a particular situation." This is a correct statement of the application of the fair use doctrine to library copying—paralleling the view of the House Judiciary committee, quoted above. However, the draft report then states: "While it is not possible to formulate rules of general application, the making of a single copy of an article in a periodical or excerpt from a book would normally be regarded as fair use." We believe this sentence is not a correct application of the doctrine of fair use, and contradicts the view of the Subcommittee and the House Judiciary Committee that library copying, like other copying, must be judged for fair use purposes on the basis of all the relevant criteria and the facts of a particular situation. We have discussed the damaging consequences of library reproduction of so-called single copies, which cannot be considered a fair use under all the relevant criteria. Moreover, library reproduction of single copies is, in reality, a process which produces many copies. The crux of Commissioner Davis' opinion in the *William & Wilkins* case was that the copying done by the government libraries—one-at-a-time—"is wholesale copying and meets none of the criteria of fair use." We doubt the sentence in question was intended to condone such copying as fair use. But it may be read that way. We respectfully urge that the senence be deleted. This would be consistent with the fundamental premises adopted by this Subcommittee and The House Judiciary Committee that fair use is a judicial doctrine ("restated" in Sec. 107) and that library copying must be judged, like all other copying, by applying the criteria to the facts of a particular situation.

We thank the Subcommittee for this opportunity to state the views of The Authors League on these vital issues.

JEROME WEIDMAN.

STATEMENT OF AD HOC COMMITTEE (OF EDUCATIONAL INSTITUTIONS AND ORGANIZATIONS) ON COPYRIGHT LAW REVISION BY HAROLD E. WIGREN

Mr. Chairman and Members of the Subcommittee: I am Harold E. Wigren, chairman of the Ad Hoc Committee (of 41 educational organizations) on Copyright Law Revision, a consortium covering a wide spectrum of organizations within the educational community which have joined to protect the public interest in the revision of the copyright law. I am a member of the staff of the National Education Association, and serve as the NEA's Educational Telecommunications Specialist. I appear before you today, however, on behalf of the Ad Hoc Committee on Copyright Law Revision, which represents the interests of teachers, professors, school administrators, subject matter specialists, educational broadcasters, librarians and, most importantly, students themselves. Actually, we represent the only major organized group of copyright users. Our clients are students, and they are completely dependent on the ease with which copyrighted information can be made available to them in reasonable proportions. In an information society, gentlemen, the quality of their education is in your hands. A list of our members is attached to this statement (Exhibit A). For the record, I would like to point out that we support the testimony given by the

---

[1] Other concerns of the Ad Hoc Committee: (a) the expansion of the duration of copyright from 28 year plus 28 years in the present law to life of the author plus 50 years in the proposed law (This we feel is unwarranted and will prevent materials from going into the public domain for at least 75 years and, in some cases, as much as 120 years.); (b) the liability of innocently infringing teachers and the excessive penalties which are possible under the proposed law; (c) the need for "fair use" to apply to instructional broadcasting and to instructional uses of computers and other technology; and (d) concerns as to the composition of the proposed commission on the technological uses of copyrighted works.

library associations this morning. These groups are members of the Ad Hoc Committee on Copyright Law Revision.

Our committee has appeared before you on previous occasions to outline our concerns in the critical matter of copyright law revision. These concerns included the need for a clear delineation of "fair use" so that teachers can know what is permissible and what is not permissible in the uses of materials to stimulate learning. We have still other concerns regarding the copyright legislation now before you. Because of time constraints, we have set forth those concerns in a footnote.[1] We will not, therefore, dwell on any of these matters today but instead will concentrate on the main thrust of this hearing—our proposal that a limited educational exemption be provided for teachers, scholars, and researchers to use materials for nonprofit purposes in carrying out their day-to-day work.

First, we would like to point out to the Subcommittee the rationale for this limited educational exemption. During the past eight years, the Ad Hoc Committee has made every effort to maintain contact and dialogue with publishers, authors, and materials producers to reach some type of accommodation which would take into account the interests of all parties concerned in the revision effort in order to strike a fair balance between the rights of proprietors and the rights of consumers/users of materials.

Our discussions, however, have been frustrated by the impact of the recent ruling by Commissioner Davis of the U.S. Court of Claims in favor of *Williams & Wilkins*, in its copyright infringement suit against the National Library of Medicine. Commissioner Davis' report, in our judgment, has great impact not only on library operations but also on the ability of the educational community to gain access to the intellectual resources of this nation. This ruling, if affirmed by the entire Court of Claims, would seriously limit the scope and meaning of "fair use." The Commissioner's ruling has caused considerable consternation and alarm within the educational community not only because of its effect on libraries but also because it would undercut the accepted and traditional meaning of "fair use" for teachers. The language and rationale are just as applicable against teachers and schools as against libraries.

Because the *Williams & Wilkins* decision proves the unreliability of "fair use" for schools and libraries, the Ad Hoc Committee urges Congress to adopt the concept of a limited educational exemption which would neutralize the harmful effect of the Commissioner's opinion on both schools and libraries and at the same time not be detrimental to publishers or producers of materials. In light of *Williams & Wilkins*, our request for a limited educational exemption is submitted to this committee not in lieu of "fair use" but in addition to "fair use" in the statutes. "Fair use" is generic in nature and is applicable to everyone—commercial and noncommercial user alike. Educational users need special protection over and above that provided commercial users because they have a public responsibility for teaching the children entrusted to them. They work for people—not for profit! They do not use materials for their own gain but for the benefit of the children of all of our citizens, including those of authors and publishers. This is the foundation stone for American education.

THE AD HOC COMMITTEE'S RECOMMENDATION

The Ad Hoc Committee on Copyright Law Revision therefore respectfully asks the Congress to include in its new copyright law the following operative wording of the limited educational exemption:

> "Notwithstanding other provisions of this Act, nonprofit use of a portion of a copyrighted work for noncommercial teaching, scholarship or research is not an infringment of copyright."

The whole proposed language including definitions and limitations is attached to this statement. (See Exhibit B.)

In short, the Ad Hoc Committee's recommendations would enable teachers to make copies or recordings for purely noncommercial classroom teaching purposes of the following, for example:

A short poem.
A short story.
An essay.
A map.
An article from a magazine or newspaper.
Transparency of a chart from a newspaper or from a text for classroom use.

Transparency of a graph or diagram from a book, newspaper or a magazine.

A TV or radio program which is used within 5 school days after the recorder broadcast, then erased.

A rendition of a school orchestra for the purpose of self-evaluation.

A recording of a musical excerpt for the purposes of study.

Excerpts or quotations (such as excerpts from contemporary writings in a duplicated examination).

The Ad Hoc Committee is NOT asking for the right to copy an entire book or novel; a dictionary, reference book, musical score, encyclopedia, magazine, newspaper, pamphlet or monograph; a motion picture or a filmstrip. The Ad Hoc Committee is NOT asking the right to make copies of materials originally consumable upon use, such as workbook exercises, problems, answer sheets for standardized tests; nor is it asking for permission to anthologize.

In conclusion, we would like to point out that the doctrine of "fair use" alone is insufficient to provide the certainty that teachers and other nonprofit educational users of copyrighted materials need for their own protection particularly in light of recent developments in the *Williams & Wilkins* case. Teachers are not interested in mass copying that actually damages authors and publishers, but they need to be free to make creative use of all of the kinds of resources available to them in the classroom, and this necessarily involves some reproduction and distribution of copyrighted works such as contemporaneous material in the press, isolated poems and stories for illustrative purposes, TV or radio materials, and the like. Subjecting the use of modern teaching tools to requirements for advance clearance and payment of fees would inhibit use of teachers' imagination and ingenuity and necessarily restrict students' opportunity to learn. It is imperative, therefore, that a specific limited educational exemption for educational copying or reproduction be granted by the Congress.

In the event that this Subcommittee cannot grant our request, the Ad Hoc Committee will be unable to support the proposed legislation (S. 1361) unless it is changed in two major respects: (1) unless the bill specifically provides adherence to the concepts and meanings of "fair use" which were written into House Report No. 83, 90th Congress, as amended in the following respects:

(*a*) the elimination of the expression "no matter how minor" in reference to the fourth criterion

(*b*) the authorization for classroom purposes for limited multiple copying of short whole works, such as poems, articles, stories, and essays

(*c*) the application of the full impact of "fair use" to instructional television

and (2) unless the decision of the Commissioner in the *Williams & Wilkins* case is specifically rejected to the extent in which it differs from that House Report, as amended.

Accompanying me today are representative members of the Ad Hoc Committee who will speak to the Ad Hoc Committee's request for a limited educational exemption. The 41 organizations represented on the Ad Hoc Committee have thrashed out their differences, and the position we take now at this hearing best states the preponderant view of our Committee.

I turn now to the panel members. In the interest of time, I will ask each panel member to introduce himself to the Subcommittee and indicate the needs and concerns of the organization or organizations he represents relative to the Ad Hoc Committee's recommendation to the Congress.

EXHIBIT A

AD HOC COMMITTEE ON COPYRIGHT LAW REVISION JULY 1973.

American Association for Higher Education
American Association of Colleges for Teacher Education
American Association of Junior Colleges
American Association of Law Libraries
American Association of School Administrators
American Association of School Librarians
American Association of University Women
American Council on Education
American Educational Theatre Association, Inc.
American Library Association
Association for Childhood Education International

Association for Computing Machinery
Association for Educational Communications and Technology
Association of Research Libraries
Baltimore County Schools
College English Association
Corporation for Public Broadcasting
Council on Library Resources
International Reading Association
Joint Council on Educational Telecommunications, Inc.
Medical Library Association
Modern Language Association
Music Educators National Conference
Music Teachers National Association
National Art Education Association
National Association of Educational Broadcasters
National Association of Elementary School Principals
National Association of Schools of Music
National Catholic Educational Association
National Catholic Welfare Conference

National Commission for Libraries and Information Science
National Contemporary Theatre Conference
National Council for the Social Studies
National Council of Teachers of English
National Council of Teachers of Mathematics
National Education Association of the United States
National Instructional Television Center
National Public Radio
National School Boards Association
Public Broadcasting Service
Speech Communication Association

INTERESTED OBSERVERS

American Association of University Professors
American Home Economics Association
American Personnel and Guidance Association
Associated Colleges of the Midwest
Association of American Law Schools
Association for Supervision and Curriculum Development
Federal Communications Commission
National Congress of Parents and Teachers

EXHIBIT B

Section . *Limitations on exclusive rights: Reproduction for teaching, scholarship and research*

Notwithstanding other provisions of this Act, nonprofit use of a portion of a copyrighted work for noncommercial teaching, scholarship or research is not an infringement of copyright.

For purposes of this section,

(1) "use" shall mean reproduction, copying and recording; storage and retrieval by automatic systems capable of storing, processing, retrieving, or transferring information or in conjunction with any similar device, machine or process;

(2) "portion" shall mean brief excerpts (which are not substantial in length in proportion to their source) from certain copyrighted works, except that it shall also include

　(*a*) the whole of short literary, pictorial and graphic works

　(*b*) entire works reproduced for storage in automatic systems capable of storing, processing, retrieving, or transferring information or in conjunction with any similar device, machine or process, *provided* that

　　(i) a method of recording retrieval of the stored information is established at the time of reproduction for storage, and

　　(ii) the rules otherwise applicable under law to copyrighted works shall apply to information retrieved from such systems;

　(*c*) recording and retransmission of broadcasts within five school days after the recorded broadcast; provided that such recording is immediately

destroyed after such 5-day period and that such retransmission is limited
to immediate viewing in schools and colleges.
Provided that "portion" shall not include works which are
> (*a*) originally consumable upon use, such as workbook exercises, problems,
> or standardized tests and the answer sheets for such tests;
> (*b*) used for the purpose of compilation within the provisions of Section
> 103(a).

STATEMENT OF ALFRED CARR, LEGISLATIVE CONSULTANT, NATIONAL EDUCATION
ASSOCIATION

Mr. Chairman and members of the subcommittee, I am Alfred Carr, Legislative
Consultant in the Office of Government Relations of the National Education
Association. I appreciate this opportunity to appear before you this morning on be-
half of the National Education Association of the United States.

Teachers are both authors and consumers of educational materials, many of
which are protected by copyright laws. NEA, representing some 1.4 million teachers and other educators, wants a law which will be equitable to both authors and
consumers. We wish to see proper protection of the interests of those persons
whose creative abilities produce fine instructional materials. At the same time,
we wish to insure that teachers and learners are protected in their creative use
of materials in the classroom. There is an over-riding need to be met in the revision of the copyright law: the need to maintain openness in our society and to
insure reasonable access to information and ideas for all of our citizens. This is
of primary concern in our democracy.

The teacher gives visibility to the author's works and creates markets for
them. One can ask: What good is an author's work if no one is interested in
reading what he has written? In a sense, we promote the works of authors in the
classroom. Teachers have the responsibility of stimulating interest on the part
of learners. This means using a wide variety of materials and resources for
teaching and learning. In the world of information in the 1970s, this imposes
on the teacher a new responsibility to make rapid decisions regarding the use
of materials—decisions which often turn out to be regarded as infringements or
near-infringements of the present archaic copyright law.

Teaching is no longer confined to the use of a single textbook. Creative teachers need bits and pieces of all sorts of written, pictorial, and graphic materials
geared to "the teachable moment" when students are best ready to learn. Requiring a teacher to purchase a large book in order to use a small portion would simply
mean that the teacher would neither buy the book nor use the materials. Teachers
today must work in a world where the very atmosphere is loaded with information which students must learn to sift and evaluate.

What then are education's needs in any new copyright legislation passed by
this Congress?

Immediate access to reasonable portions of printed and non-printed materials
for instructional purposes without payment of royalties. This reasonable access
should be extended to the use of instructional television, computers, automated
systems, and other developments in educational technology.

Certainly that the present law's "not-for-profit" principle be converted into a
limited educational exemption for non-profit uses of copyrighted materials.

Protection for teachers who innocently infringe the law in the performance of
their duties as teachers.

Retention of the same copyright duration period as in present law; i.e., 28
years plus a 28-year renewal period.

The teacher's needs encompass the new teaching-learning processes that are
being stimulated by the enormous amount of new information and the attendant
opportunities afforded by the new educational technology.

New teaching techniques—including the use of computers, closed-circuit television, videotapes, recordings and microfilm, among other forms of communications technology—have been developed to keep pace with the demands of the fast
changing information explosion faced by our schools. They make possible more
learning in less time. Flexible scheduling at the secondary level has been made
possible by computers and has opened a wide choice for learners within the
school day. Computerized scheduling can free students from rigid teaching patterns and enable them to be liberated for a portion of the day for individualized
work, library activities, open laboratory work on a problem or project, or for
individual conferences with teachers.

Schools without walls have opened the parameters of the learner to include attending political conventions, court hearings, sports events, and witnessing moon launches. Tools such as cassettes, videotapes, and cameras can be used to capture these events for sharing with other learners. All of this is to say that the world has changed considerably since 1909 and that this change can be seen in the schools as well as in every other sector of our society. The new copyright law must not freeze education at the 1930 level or even at the 1973 level!

It is important to cite a few teaching practices to illustrate the restrictiveness of S. 1361:

A teacher videotapes a relevant television program off the air for use on the following day with his or her social studies classes in the auditorium or in the classroom.

A teacher reproduces 30 copies of one page out of a copyrighted book.

A teacher puts a chapter from a copyrighted book into a computer in order to make an analysis of the grammatical structure.

A class is having difficulty understanding symbolism in literature, and the class text does not go far enough in its explanation. The teacher therefore makes multiple copies of a poem or a short essay (from another book) that would help the class understand the concept.

All of these practices, according to counsel for some publishers, would constitute infringements under the present law. Likewise, they would be considered infringements under the proposed bill, S. 1361, which is not significantly different from the present law. This again illustrates that the 1909 law is out of joint with present practices in the schools of the '70s.

In our judgment, the proposed copyright law would drastically curtail the use by teachers of various materials for instruction. NEA strongly urges this Committee and this Congress to adopt a revised copyright law that will explicitly provide limited exemptions for teaching, scholarship, or research purposes, and extend "fair use" provisions to new educational technology such as instructional television, computers, and automated systems.

Finally, therefore, we need a new law that will support, rather than thwart, good teaching practices in the 1970s.

Thank you.

STATEMENT BY JOHN C. STEDMAN, THE COPYRIGHT COMMITTEE OF THE ASSOCIATION OF AMERICAN LAW SCHOOLS, THE AMERICAN ASSOCIATION OF UNIVERSITY PROFESSORS AND THE AMERICAN COUNCIL ON EDUCATION

Mr. Chairman and members of the subcommittee, I am John C. Stedman, Professor of Law, the University of Wisconsin. I am a member of the Special Committee on Copyright Law of the Association of American Law Schools. Representatives of the American Association of University Professors and the American Council on Education have joined in the deliberations of that committee. I appear before you today at their request.

This group urges as strongly as it can that the doctrine of fair use not only be preserved, but be given formal recognition by the Congress, both by express statutory provision and by appropriate language in the final committee report, as it has been earlier in this revision and in House Report No. 2237, 89th Congress, Second Session, pages 61 to 66 (1966). This is a modest, but important, recommendation. It merely suggests, after all, that your committee stand by the approach that the House took in 1967 when it passed an earlier version of the Copyright Revision Bill, and the approach your committee takes at the present time, as evidenced by the language of section 107.

Let me emphasize that we do not seek to remove protected material from copyright control. Nor are we adverse or hostile to the basic premise that legitimate rights in intellectual property should be protected. We accept that premise as a matter of principle, as a matter of public policy, and as a matter of self-interest. There are, after all, within our constituent membership many authors whose scholarly works command high prices in the commercial book market and authors whose royalties compare favorably with the royalties of non-academic authors.

Our main concern is to stress before this committee the soundness of the traditional, judicially-constructed doctrine of fair use, and its fundamental importance in the process of higher education. Those among us who are law teachers are moved by an added sense of urgency and concern. Tradition and precedent play an important role in the judicial development of the law. But there is little case precedent to guide the courts with respect to permissible uses by teachers and researchers. Cases simply did not come up in this area. But given this scarcity of cases, if S. 1361, with its present section 107, were enacted without appropriate legislative history—at a time when educational usage *has* become a controversial issue—courts might interpret this silence as indicating a Congressional intent not to go beyond the precedents of the past. You will recall that Congressional silence in the 1909 Act with respect to the protection of phonograph records, despite the fact that phonographic technology existed at that time, resulted in this important area receiving no copyright protection down to the present time. We would not want to see this costly and unfortunate experience repeated in the educational fair use area, because the Congress failed to speak out on the subject. I should add that the dangers that exist here are aggravated by the sweeping language and reasoning contained in Commissioner Davis' opinion in the *Williams and Wilkins* Case.

In seeking to assure the application of traditional fair use doctrine through express statutory recognition coupled with supportive legislative history, we are moved by the essential importance of the availability of copyrighted materials in teaching and research. First and most basic is the fact that the higher education community, college and university administrators and their faculties, are primarily the institutions in which the ultimate task of transmitting and advancing knowledge is reposed. I emphasize that both research and teaching are involved in this process. Each is indispensable to the other. Effective instruction of the next generation of citizens and professionals requires that the current generation of teachers be involved as researchers at the frontiers of their own individual disciplines and specialties. But if the individual teacher is to discharge this duty, he must be current within his own discipline, and this requires that he have access to the work product of allied researchers.

The exponential rate of growth of knowledge in this generation and its expression in written and other forms, underscores the importance to the scholar and teachers of access to this information. As the volume of published material has risen, the library budgets of colleges and universities are increasingly pressed. The typical library of a major law school must spend a substantial portion of its annual budget to acquire the current volumes of the state and federal reports and the current supplements to the vast array of state statutes, treatises, and looseleaf services. It is not possible for every university and law library to acquire one or more copies of every book needed for research and teaching in the institution.

The relevance of this to the fair use doctrine is, I trust, clear, look at it first from the standpoint of the researcher. A teacher at a good private university in the southeastern United States who is interested in research on a particular topic finds that the basic works relating to that topic are available only at one or two distant universities in the northeast. He may want to consult only one chapter in such a work, or a few pages within that chapter to which he has found a citation in a periodical that is available to him. Access to such information is essential to the scholar. Inter-library "lending" has become the means to such access. A definition of fair use that left it uncertain whether such a portion could be photocopied and thus satisfy the researchers' needs, would frustrate the purposes that underlie the fair use doctrine, and would be inimical to the orderly extension of scientific knowledge.

Although the library associations are appearing here on their own behalf, we consider the need to permit restricted photocopying for the individual scholar so basic to the vital inter-library loan process as to warrant emphasis by us as well.

Turning to the teaching function, the need for reasonable photocopying for classroom purposes closely parallels the need of the scholar. Often a current new item will appear first in a newspaper or other periodical. Or it may be a one or two page excerpt from a voluminous book or article. Whatever its source, the quality of teaching is greatly improved by making the excerpt available to students. Denial of the opportunity to do this does not mean that students and teachers will go out and buy the entire book or periodical. They will simply do without. In short, the cause of education will have been disserved, and the copyright owner will be no better off.

In this connection, we reiterate that we do *not* seek the right to reproduce entire books or other publications. We seek only a clear expression of intent that the fair use doctrine, as set forth in section 107, includes classroom use by a teacher, together with a supportive statement in the legislative history to the effect that classroom use by a teacher was intended to be within he ambit of section 107. In urging this statement we accept the limitations cited in House Report No. 2237, 89th Congress, Second Session, at page 62 (1966) that in determining fair use it is appropriate for a trier of fact to consider the non-profit character of a school, the independent volition of the teacher and the spontaneity of the temporary use by the teacher and the students. We accept also the limitation that compilation of anthologies would be outside the ambit of fair use.

We reiterate that we do not seek the right to engage in multiple copying out of the context of research and teaching. We seek only the right of the scholar to have access to knowledge through a single copy of such portion of controlled works as are germane to his established research goals, and, for the classroom teacher, to have the right to use current materials in the non-profit and temporary use context that is his normal classroom situation. In this connection we recognize that the effect on the potential market for the copied work is an appropriate factor to be considered in the determination of fair use, but we also recognize that in the overwhelming proportion of cases, any possible adverse effect will be nil or virtually so. Indeed on balance, access to excerpts appears more likely to stimulate sale of the source product than to discourage it.

Two minor clarifications of points that seem implicit in the existing language of section 107 of S. 1361 would make their meaning explicit. We would like to see the legislative history indicates that none of other sections of the Act limit the force of section 107. We would also like the history to show that the fair use doctrine protects the maker of a copy as fully a sit protects the user of that copy.

We conclude as we began with a request that this committee continue the traditional recognition of fair use in the research and teaching context by the enactment of section 107 coupled with supportive legislative history as outlined above.

STATEMENT OF IRWIN KARP, ESQ., COUNSEL FOR THE AUTHORS LEAGUE OF AMERICA, INC.

Mr. Chairman and members of the subcommittee, my name is Irwin Karp. I am counsel for The Authors League of America, a national society of professional writers and dramatists. I appear to present its views on the amendment to S. 1361 requested by The National Education Association and other groups ("The Ad Hoc Committee on Copyright Law Revision"). I respectfully request that this statement be included in the record.

The Ad Hoc Committee has requested the Subcommittee to add to the Copyright Revision Bill a new section which would create a "general educational exemption" permitting "educators", "scholars" and "researchers" to reproduce, copy and record copyrighted works beyond the limits of fair use; to store and retrieve materials in automatic systems to a greater extent than permitted by fair use or Sec. 117 of the Bill; and to record and retransmit broadcasts for five days to schools and colleges, a practice which constitutes infringement under the present law, and under the Revision Bill.

The Authors League urges the Subcommittee to reject this proposed exemption because (1) it would permit uncompensated educational copying beyond the limits of fair use, and destroy the reasonable, compromise solution to this problem which is reflected in the Report of the House Judiciary Committee and the draft report of this Subcommittee; (2) the exemption would be extremely damaging to authors and publishers; and (3) there is no substance to the educators' claim that the Williams & Wilkins decision is a valid reason for reviving this request for an educational exemption, which had previously been rejected by the House Judiciary Committee and by this Subcommittee.

We focus our discussion on those provisions of the proposed exemption which deal with the reproduction, copying and recording of copyrighted works. However, we should note that authors are as strongly opposed to those provisions of the NEA amendment which would permit the use of copyrighted materials in storage and retrieval systems beyond the limits of fair use, and to the clause which would permit the recording and retransmission of broadcasts.

(1) THE PRIOR REJECTIONS OF THE "EDUCATIONAL EXEMPTIONS"

As the Report of the House Judiciary Committee notes, the NEA and other members of the Ad Hoc Committee had requested Subcommittee No. 3 to insert "a specific, limited exemption for educational copying" into the Revision Bill. As the draft report of this Subcommittee indicates, the Ad Hoc Committee also requested that this educational exemption be included in the Senate version of the Revision Bill. The House Judiciary Committee ·refused the Ad Hoc Committee's request, and their "exemption" was not included in the Bill passed by the House, nor in S. 1361 or the prior Senate revision bills. The reasons why the educational exemption was refused by the House Judiciary Committee are as valid today as they were when the Report was issued in 1967; and nothing in Commissioner Davis' opinion in the William & Wilkins case—the Ad Hoc Committee's stated pretext for reviving its "exemption—affects the validity of the Judiciary Committee's reasoning.

The Committee noted that "photocopying and other reproducing devices were constantly proliferating and becoming easier and cheaper to use." It also took note of the contentions of authors and publishers that "education is the textbook publisher's only market, and that many authors receive their main income from licensing reprints in anthologies and textbooks; if an unlimited number of teachers could prepare and reproduce their own anthologies, the cumulative effect would be disastrous." (H. Rep. No. 83; p. 31). The Committee report noted that "several productive meetings" were held between representatives of authors and publishers and of educators and scholars and that "while no final agreements were reached, the meetings were generally successful in clarifying the issues and in pointing the way to constructive solutions." (Ibid)

Those constructive solutions were reflected in the Judiciary Committee's report, and it is fair to say they were—for a time, at least—accepted by the parties. The solutions were :

(i) The Committee's rejection of the exemption proposed by the NEA and other members of the Ad Hoc Committee: "After full consideration, the committee believes that a specific exemption freeing certain reproductions of copyrighted works for educational and scholarly purposes from copyright control is not justified." (ibid)

(ii) The Committee's explicit recognition and affirmation that "any educational uses that are fair today would be fair use under the bill." (ibid)

(iii) Amendment of Sec. 504(c) to insulate teachers from excessive liability for statutory damages. (ibid)

(iv) Amendment of Sec. 107 to restore a restatement of the criteria of fair use, to indicate it may include reproduction in copies or phonorecords; and "to characterize a fair use as generally being 'for purposes such as criticism, comment, news reporting, *teaching, scholarship or research.*'" (emphasis supplied) (ibid)

(v) A careful analysis by the Committee of the four criteria of fair use "*in the context of typical classroom situations arising today.*" While, as the Committee noted, the analysis had to be broad and illustrative, "it may provide educators with the basis of establishing workable practices and policies." (H. Rep. No. 83, pp 32–36). Actually the Committee was modest in characterizing its analysis—it is an extremely clear and useful set of guidelines for educators, authors and publishers.

Moreover, the Committee's analysis of fair use in the context of typical classroom situations amply supports its judgment that "*the doctrine of fair use, as properly applied is broad enough to permit reasonable educational use,* and education has something to gain in the enactment of a bill which clarifies what may now be a problematical situation."

The House Judiciary Committee also urged educators, authors and publishers to "join together in an effort to establish a continuing understanding as to what constitutes mutually acceptable practices . . ." (H. Rep. 83, p. 33). The Authors League is willing and ready to join in such a continuing, cooperative effort at any time, as is the Association of American Publishers. The Judiciary Committee also urged the parties to join together "to work out means by which permissions for uses beyond fair use can be obtained easily, quickly, and at reasonable fees." Again, the Authors League is willing and ready to join in such an effort. Indeed, the League is willing—alone, or in cooperation with the Association of American Publishers and educational groups—to seek funds from the National Foundation for the Humanities, to establish and operate a pilot information clearing house to receive requests for permissions, process and transmit them to the appropriate licensor (author or publisher), and expedite the copyright owner's reply. As in the case of librarians, the Committee's suggestion for voluntary efforts to "workable clearance and licensing conditions" is anathema to educational spokesmen—they will not even let the phrase cross their lips, no less discuss it seriously. This is regrettable since a voluntary clearing house could well provide the means of establishing a continuing understanding as to what constitutes mutually acceptable practices . . ."

(2) THE PROPOSED EDUCATIONAL EXEMPTION WOULD INJURE AUTHORS AND PUBLISHERS

If the proposed educational exemption is only intended to permit educational copying that would constitute fair use under the Judiciary Committee's analysis of the 4 criteria "in the context of typical classroom situations arising today"— then the proposed exemption is unnecessary. What was fair use under the Committee's analysis is still fair use.

Actually, the educational groups are seeking—via their proposed exemption— to legalize uncompensated, educational copying that goes far beyond the bounds of fair use. The right to quote "excerpts"—i.e. portions of a book or other work which is not substantial in *length*, in proportion to its total size—would be absolute, *regardless* of the circumstances of the reproduction. Thus, an unlimited number of educators or institutions could then reproduce copies of such portions under a variety of circumstances which would make the reproduction an infringement under the Judiciary Committee's analysis of the 4 criteria, in its report. For example, many copies could be produced on an organized basis, rather than by one teacher, spontaneously. For example, multiple copies could be reproduced for many individuals and circulated beyond the classroom. And most important of all, under the proposed exemption copies could be reproduced even though they had a serious adverse effect on the potential market for the work, or its value—and even though they supplanted some part of the normal market for the work.

Similarly, the proposed exemption would permit educators and institutions to reproduce copies of entire *short* works—a 2 page poem? a five page article? a seven page short story? And as with "excerpts", the exemption would allow educators to reproduce these copies under a variety of circumstances that would make the reproduction an infringement under the Judiciary Committee's analysis of the 4 criteria of fair use.

As we noted in our statement on library copying, and in our previous testimony to the Subcommittee, many authors earn a major portion of their income by licensing the reprinting of poems, articles, short stories and other short works—and excerpts from longer works—in anthologies, text books, periodicals and collections. After it is originally published, the same work may be reprinted with the author's permission in many such books. The accumulation of reprint royalties produces a modest income—and for authors of poetry, essays and other works of literary value, it is often the larger part of the compensation they earn from the uses of their writings. Many of these anthologies and other books which reprint the author's short works and excerpts are sold primarily to high schools, colleges, universities and their libraries and book stores—and the student of these institutions are a primary audience for eminent poets, essayists and short story writers. In addition, several courses use articles from journals on various subjects in place of text books.

The proposed educational exemption would allow, educators and educational institutions to produce copies of an author's short works, and excerpts from longer works, thus displacing the sales of anthologies, text books and other collections that formerly reprinted these works. Many authors would thus be deprived of a substantial part of their income—the royalties from the publishers of the anthologies and text books—even though their works would still be widely used by educational audiences, disseminated by uncompensated educational copying.

(3) THERE IS NO JUSTIFICATION FOR REVIVING THE PROPOSED EDUCATIONAL EXEMPTION

The excuse offered by the Ad Hoc Committee for reviving its proposed educational exemption, and thus disrupting the constructive solutions reflected in the House Judiciary Committee's report, is that purportedly Commissioner Davis' opinion in *Williams & Wilkins* created "uncertainties" and indicated "the unreliability of 'fair use' in providing necessary protection for teaching, scholarship and research . . ." (letter from Dr. Wigren of the National Education Association and Chairman of the Ad Hoc Committee, to Mr. Thomas C. Brennan, Chief Counsel of the Subcommittee; Dec. 11, 1972).

In reality, Commissioner Davis' opinion did nothing to change the doctrine of fair use; and it did nothing to change the application of fair use to educational copying, as analyzed in the House Judiciary Report. Educational copying that would constitute fair use under the Judiciary Committee's analysis of the 4 criteria is still fair use.

As the House Judiciary Committee emphasized, "each case raising the question (of fair use) must be decided on its own facts." And the Committee also said that "unauthorized library copying, like everything else, must be judged a fair use or an infringement on the basis of all the applicable criteria *and the facts of the particular case.* (Emphasis supplied.) (H. Rep. No. 83, pp. 29, 36.)

The particular facts of the case Commissioner Davis decided bore no resemblance to the various fact situations involving classroom use or other educational copying which the House Judiciary Committee considered in spelling out its guidelines and analysis of fair use vis-a-vis educational copying. The facts in *Williams & Wilkins* were that two set of government libraries engaged in the systematic reproduction—on a vast scale—of copies of entire articles for their own patrons, and the patrons of other libraries. In his opinion, Commissioner Davis passed no judgment on educational copying in any of the many permuta-

tions analyzed by the House Judiciary Committee. On the contrary, he confined his decision and opinion *"to the facts of (his) particular case"*—to this systematic, large volume reproduction of journal articles. What the Commissioner decided was that *"Defendant's photocopying is wholesale copying and meets none of the criteria for fair use"* (emphasis supplied). He then said:

"The photocopies are exact duplicates of the original articles; are intended to be substitutes for, and serve the same purpose as, the original articles; and serve to diminish plaintiff's potential market for the original articles since the photocopies are made at the request of, and for the benefit of, the very persons who constitute plaintiff's market."

Nothing in the Judiciary Committee's analysis of educational copying and fair use suggested that the systematic process of wholesale copying involved in *Williams & Wilkins* could be condoned as a fair use. Moreover, it should be noted that Commissioner Davis gave examples of photocopying of entire articles that would be fair use and said there are "probably many more which might come to mind on reflection". He then reemphasized that fair use "cannot support wholesale copying of the kind here in suit."

We submit there is nothing in Commissioner Davis' opinion which alters the judicial doctrine of fair use as it applies—according to the Judiciary Committee's analysis—to educational copying, or to library copying. Consequently, there is no justification for the Ad Hoc Committee's effort to revive the educational exemption. Moreover, even if it be assumed that Commissioner Davis' opinion somehow changed the doctrine of fair use as it thus applied to educational copying, that would at most call for an amendment to restore fair use to the contours the Judiciary Committee thought it had. But that is not what the Ad Hoc Committee is asking for—as we noted, it seeks an exemption that would permit educational copying which far exceeds the boundaries of fair use indicated by the analysis of the House Judiciary Committee.

THE "PHILOSOPHICAL" ARGUMENTS

It has become customary for the Ad Hoc Committee to accompany its demands for new limitations on authors' rights with an assortment of "philosophical" arguments—e.g. attacks on the copyright system, suggestions that authors are anti-trust monopolists, and other contentions, including a claim that copyright protection infringes the First Amendment rights of teachers and students. We do not know if the Ad Hoc Committee intends to regale the Subcommittee with this assortment of invalid contentions. Anticipating that it will, we briefly recapitulate our responses, and respectfully refer to our previous testimony for a fuller discussion of these points. Moreover, if the Subcommittee wishes a fuller response to any such contentions which the Ad Hoc Committee may make, we will be pleased to supply it.

These are some of the contentions which have been made by various members of the Ad Hoc Committee, in Copyright Bill hearings and in the Williams & Wilkins case, and summaries of our replies:

(i) Ad Hoc members argue that copyright is a "monopoly" in the anti-trust sense. But an author's copyright does not give him the power to restrain or monopolize the business of book publishing. Copyright is a "monopoly" only in the innocuous sense that all property is—a collection of rights granted by law.

(ii) Ad Hoc members argue that exemptions are justified because a copyright is not property, but "only" rights granted by statute. But all property consists of rights granted by the State, through legislation (e.g. land grant acts) or court decisions. At common law the author's work is his absolute, private property.

(iii) Ad Hoc members argue that copyright is only a "discretionary" grant because Art. I, Sec. 8 says "Congress shall have the power . . ." But the phrase precedes the enumeration of all powers, e.g. to tax, raise armies, borrow money, regulate. The authors of the Constitution did not consider the exercise of these powers, including enactment of copyright laws, as "merely discretionary."

(iv) Ad Hoc members argue that uncompensated library and educational copying must be permitted because they promote the progress of science and art. But the economic philosophy underlying the copyright clause, according to the Supreme Court, was to grant enforceable rights to authors and publishers to encourage individual effort by personal gain; that the independent, entrepreneurial system of creation and dissemination best served the public interest in promoting science and art.

(v) Ad Hoc Committee members argue that exemptions must be granted because library and educational copying is "non-profit." But as the House Judiciary Committee said, "the educational groups are mistaken in their argument that a 'for profit' limitation is applicable to educational copying under the present law."

(vi) Ad Hoc members argue that any copyright limitation on uncompensated library or educational copying restrains "freedom" to read under the First Amendment. But the First Amendment "was fashioned to assure unfettered interchange of ideas (376 U.S. 209) and it is axiomatic that an author's copyright does not prevent anyone from discussing or repeating his ideas (366 F. 2d 303). The Supreme Court has never interpreted "freedom" in the First Amendment to mean "gratis" or "free of charge"; and it has frequently emphasized there is no conflict between publication for profit and the First Amendment.

It is indeed strange that the National Education Association should argue, as it did in *Williams & Wilkins*, that requiring compensation to copyright owners, for library copying that exceeds fair use, violates the First Amendment freedom to read. NEA teachers insist on their right to be adequately compensated for making published materials available to students, and for other teaching services. To obtain what they consider adequate compensation, teachers—by the thousands each year—deny students access to books and other copyrighted materials for prolonged periods of time; their strikes close down schools, school libraries and classrooms. Ironically teachers are thus able to deny students access to copyrighted materials by grace of federal legislation—the exemption of the Clayton Act makes it possible for large groups of teachers to engage in boycotts (strikes) that would otherwise violate Sec. 1 of the Sherman Act; and for these large groups of teachers to combine and fix the prices for their services, which also would otherwise violate the Sherman Act. By contrast, copyright owners do not seek to close down schools or libraries, and do not seek to prevent schools and libraries from making reprints of copyrighted articles; copyright owners simply ask that reasonable compensation be paid them when library or educational copying exceeds the boundaries of fair use.

The Authors League thanks the Subcommittee for this opportunity to present its views on the proposed Educational Copying Exemption.

STATEMENT OF LLOYD OTTERMAN, CHAIRMAN OF THE EDUCATIONAL MEDIA PRODUCERS COUNCIL AND VICE PRESIDENT OF BFA EDUCATIONAL MEDIA; ACCOMPANIED BY DAVID ENGLER, CHAIRMAN, COPYRIGHT COMMITTEE; AND ROBERT FRASE, CONSULTANT

Mr. OTTERMAN. Mr. Chairman, my name is Lloyd Otterman and I am chairman of the Educational Media Producers Council (EMPC) and vice president of BFA Educational Media. I am appearing here today on behalf of EMPC and with me are David Engler, chairman of the EMPC Copyright Committee and Robert W. Frase, economist and consultant on copyright to EMPC.

We have submitted formal testimony to this subcommittee. I ask now that it be included into the record.

Senator BURDICK. Without objection, it will be included.

Mr. OTTERMAN. I will be highlighting those formal remarks in an effort to meet the time constraints we have here today.

We are here to give you our views on S. 1361, and specifically on the issues involved in the educational use of copyrighted audiovisual materials. We support the bill as introduced and oppose amendments which would weaken the protection provided in the bill to those materials.

Let me sketch briefly the economics of producing audiovisual materials for education. This background will be helpful in understanding the importance of appropriate copyright protection in order to insure the continued development of high quality materials for educational use.

EMPC has some 70 members who produce audiovisual materials for use in schools and libraries—materials such as motion pictures, filmstrips, slides, transparencies, and sound recording. We estimate that our members produce 80 percent of these educational audiovisual materials.

In 1972 total sales of educational audiovisual materials amounted to $215 million, produced by some 200 companies; thus the industry is clearly one of active competition among quite small firms.

These materials are designed for instructional purposes, and have no market among consumers in general or for general entertainment.

Because of the way in which audiovisual materials are used in the educational process, the number of copies produced is quite limited. As compared with textbooks, for example, which are generally provided one to a student, one or two copies of a 16-millimeter educational film may serve an entire school system of moderate size; and a single copy of a filmstrip will serve an entire school. A typical audiovisual product will customarily sell in the hundreds or low thousands over 5 to 10 years, as compared with tens or hundreds of thousands of textbooks. Thus the initial investment in editorial work and production, which costs as much for one copy as for thousands, is spread over a relatively limited number of copies. In addition to the substantial initial investments necessary to the production of quality materials there must be added carrying costs for the considerable period of time over which sales are made. The combination of these factors—small editions and sales over an extended period—means that unauthorized duplication of copies has a much greater impact on the economic viability of these products than on some other types of educational materials.

The U.S. Office of Education has granted millions of dollars over the years to educational research laboratories for developing more effective teaching methods and materials. Many good products were developed, but far too few were disseminated to the educational community. Why? Because policies were not developed which allowed companies with marketing expertise to distribute the materials under the protection of copyright. However, recently, USOE revised its policy and provided copyright protection. Now the educational community receives the benefit of the Federal research and development effort.

I think this points out very clearly the need to provide incentives for the production of materials and the need to protect the rights of the copyright holders. The federally funded materials, which under the noncopyright policy were developed and not marketed are now being used by students—because of the incentives given producers to manufacture and distribute the materials. We note that S. 1361 recognizes these realities.

We believe that S. 1361 is a good bill and will provide the necessary incentives to the continued production of quality audiovisual materials for use in the educational system.

We commend the subcommittee in particular for its proposals with respect to fair use and here we have specific reference to section 107 of the bill.

We are pleased that the principal professional organizations of educators directly concerned with the use of audiovisual materials in the educational process, composed of 8,000 members directly concerned with it, has also recently come out in support of section 107 of the bill and in opposition to the so-called educational exemption.

I have here their formal testimony submitted to me this morning. I am reading from page 7, paragraph 2,

Although the AECT's position differs from that of the Ad Hoc Committee on the need for general education exemption, we continue to remain a member of that group.

The statement issued by the executive committee of the Association for Educational Communications and Technology, which is an affiliate of the National Education Association, given on May 31, 1973, is contained in attachment A. I ask now that that statement be placed in the record at this point.

Senator BURDICK. Without objection.

[The statement referred to follows:]

(*Attachment A*)

COPYRIGHT LAW REVISION: A POSITION PAPER

The members of the Association for Educational Communications and Technology (AECT) believe that technology is an integral part of the teaching-learning process and helps to maximize the outcomes of interaction between teacher and pupil.

Regulations governing United States Copyright were originally developed to promote the public welfare and encourage authorship by giving authors certain controls over their work. It follows that revisions in Title 17 of the United States Code (Copyrights) should maintain the balance providing for the compensation of authors and insuring that information remains available to the public. Some of the revisions proposed in S. 1361 lose sight of this balance between user and producer.

AECT endorses the criteria to be used in the determination of "fair use" as contained in Section 107 of the proposed bill:

Section 107.—Limitations on exclusive rights: Fair use . . . the fair use of a copyrighted work, including such use by reproduction in copies or phonorecords or by any other means specified by [Section 106], for purposes such as criticism, comment, news reporting, teaching, scholarship, or research, is not an infringement of copyright. In determining whether the use made of a work in any particular case is a fair use the factors to be considered shall include:

(1) The purpose and character of the use;

(2) The nature of the copyrighted work;

(3) The amount and substantiality of the portion used in relation to the copyrighted work as a whole; and

(4) The effect of the use upon the potential market for or value of the copyrighted work.

Further, we endorse the concepts regarding the intent of these criteria as expanded in the legislative history of the bill as it existed prior to and without regard to the original opinion in the case of Williams and Wilkins v. U.S., for that opinion substantially narrows the scope of "fair use" and irreparably weakens that doctrine.

However, we propose that the concept of "fair use" should apply equally to the classroom teacher and media professional—including specialists in audiovisual and library resources. Media personnel are becoming increasingly important members of educational planning teams and must have the assurance that they may assist classroom teachers in the selection of daily instructional materials as well as with long range curriculum development. Classroom teachers do not always operate "individually and at [their] own volition." The fact that the media professional makes use of advance planning and has knowledge aforethought of the materials he prepares for the teacher should not invalidate the application of the "fair use" principle.

Concerning the use of copyrighted works in conjunction with television, AECT proposes that "fair use," as it has been outlined above, should apply to educational/instructional broadcast or closed-circuit transmission in a nonprofit educational institution, but not to commercial broadcasting.

Once the doctrine of "fair use" has been established in the revised law, negotiations should be conducted between the proprietor and user prior to any use of copyrighted materials that goes beyond that doctrine. We believe that the enactment of the "fair use" concept into law prior to negotiations will guard against the erosion of that concept. Generally, a reasonable fee should be paid for uses that go beyond "fair use," but such fee arrangement should not delay or impede the use of the materials. Producers are urged to give free access (no-cost contracts) whenever possible.

We agree with the Ad Hoc Committee of Educational Organizations and Institutions on Copyright Law Revision that duration of copyright should provide for an initial period of twenty-eight years, followed by a renewal period of forty-eight years, whereas the proposed bill sets duration at the "life of the author plus fifty years." It seems reasonable that provision should be made to permit those materials which the copyright holder has no interest in protecting after the initial period to pass into the public domain.

Regarding the input of copyrighted materials into computers or other storage devices by non-profit educational institutions, we agree with the Ad Hoc Committee that the bill should clearly state that until the proposed National Commission on New Technological Uses of Copyrighted Works has completed its study, such input should not be considered infringement. The proposed bill states only that ". . . [Section 117] does not afford to the owner of copyright in a work any greater or lesser rights with respect to the use of the work in conjunction with any similar device, machine, or process . . ."

A new copyright law that both uses and producers can view as equitable depends upon the mutual understanding of each other's needs and the ability to effectively work out the differences. We will participate in the continuing dialogue with the Educational Media Producers Council and similar interest groups to establish mutually acceptable guidelines regarding the boundaries of "fair use," and reasonable fees to be paid for uses beyond "fair use." This dialogue will be especially important in the area of storage, retrieval, and/or transmission of materials during the time period between the enactment of the law and the issuance of the report of the proposed National Commission on New Technological Uses of Copyrighted Works.

We feel that the above modifications of S. 1361 are needed to insure that the revised law assists rather than hinders teachers and media specialists in their work.

TESTIMONY OF PAUL G. ZURKOWSKI, PRESIDENT AND EXECUTIVE DIRECTOR, INFORMATION INDUSTRY ASSOCIATION

My name is Paul G. Zurkowski. I am President and Executive Director of the Information Industry Association, 4720 Montgomery Lane, Bethesda, Maryland, 20014, (301) 654-4150. I am the first Executive Director of the Association that is now little more than four years old. It has over 60 member firms engaged in a wide variety of commercial information activities. A list of members is attached. Immediately prior to this employment, I served for about five years as legislative assistant to Congressman Bob Kastenmeier, of Wisconsin.

My involvement with the information industry flows directly from that service with Mr. Kastenmeier during the years the Revision Bill was under consideration in the House. My personal interest has always been in the communication of information—documented ideas. Service on Mr. Kastenmeier's staff served to educate me about the important role copyright plays as *the* basic funding mechanism by which the *creative* and *business* activities required to obtain dissemination of information is paid for.

Copyright is a populist monopoly: it assures access for everyone to the ideas of the creative few. It enriches our lives, facilitates our life-long education, and assures the equal availability of information. I left my happy home with Mr. Kastenmeier because I saw the need for a funding mechanism of equal effectiveness in the information technology arena. The practical day-to-day experience of the information industry in creating and marketing information through the application of computers, microfilm and other technologies, new and old, alone or in combination, is that copyright is as valid for this industry as it is for industries which market information as books or journals. Perhaps even more so.

The basic function of this industry is in many respects the other side of the coin of traditional publishing. It is rooted in the abundance of information available to everyone in every discipline. As a general proposition it can be said that information companies identify particular information headaches of very specialized groups of people and seek to pre-process the information of interest to that group in such a way as to facilitate its use.

Another way of describing the mission of the industry is to use the word *Relevance.*

The activities of member firms include, but are not limited to, the following:

(1) *Topical publications*—providing up-to-date information on all facets of a given special interest area, including law, regulations and/or tariffs topically arranged and cross referenced for easy access;

(2) *Current awareness* publications, such as indexes, collected tables of contents, abstracts, citation lists, reports on pending legislation, etc.;

(3) *Catalogs*, including mail-order catalogs, parts lists, price lists, and tables of interchangeable parts;

(4) *Directories*, including those classified by activity, address, etc.;

(5) *Encyclopedias, directories, thesauri*, finding lists and references, aids;

(6) *Files searches*, including computer searches of machine-readable files at the computer site or by remote access terminals;

(7) *Standing order services* ranging from computer search of current publications through news clipping services offering delivery of information on specific interest profile topics;

(8) *Manuals* for operation and repair of equipment;

(9) *Serial reports*, such as court decisions, board rulings, financial reports;

(10) *Periodic publication of related material*, such as journals in hard copy or microform, and voice recordings of talks on related topics;

(11) *Face-to-face meetings*, such as symposia, conferences and conventions;

(12) *Exhibits and demonstrations* for educational, promotional or merchandising purposes; and

(13) *Tours* of plants, facilities, monuments, museums, etc.

Although a variety of communications media are employed, all the above activities have in common the *anticipation* of the need for and the *preprocessing* of *relevant* information. They all involve the expenditure of time, money, and human effort in organizing information materials to meet anticipated needs. They all have a common objective—that of producing economically competitive information products relevant to the addressee's interest, regardless of the media involved.

Many member activities relate to the preparation of what could be classed as "library materials"—materials in printed form for industrial, institutional, agency, business, shop, academic or personal collections. Others reorganize related reference materials for better access. Such products and services require frequent re-organization and amendment to keep them current. Efforts to keep files up-to-date are currently duplicated and re-duplicated in industrial, institutional and personal reference collections. Technologies for economical, rapid, remote access to centrally up-dated information files reduce the need to maintain separate local files. It also reduces the number of copies needed for local files. Costs other than communications charges are involved. The development of such technologies have wide application to society's information problems.

Our basic purpose for appearing here today is to underscore the significance of copyright and to emphasize the need to maintain the integrity of copyright as a funding mechanism for this process. Private risk capital will be applied to this process, and society will have the benefit of continuing advances in the application of these varied technologies, only so long as the investors in this process have a reasonable expectation of receiving a reasonable return on their investment. The only alternative to the investment of private risk capital and the reliance on competition in the marketplace, not only the commercial marketplace, but the marketplace of ideas, is the reliance on the investment of state capital, and its attendant preemption of areas open to competition

Since the Information Industry Association did not exist at the time of the 1967 House Passage and Senate Hearings, we have not previously participated in the revision hearings process. We are, in effect, a new face and one which may not be readily recognized. We feel therefore it is important for us to provide you with detailed information about the activities of the industry.

Information companies create information, refine information, organize information, develop access tools for getting at information. All of these activities add value to information. They make it easier for you to find the information you want. By preparing the tools for you to do this effectively and efficiently they save you time and money. The information industry in authoring these products substitutes the "sweat of its brow" for yours.

The whole information industry process is itself comparable to an individual author's efforts in creating a work. By taking an "exploded" view of the work of information industry company you can see how the efforts it makes relates to the creative efforts of an author.

The steps involved in creating and marketing an information product:

(1) Start with the user. Identify his information problem or need. Spend time with him in his work environment to identify how he uses information, where he is when he needs information, whether he has an immediate need or a need than can be filled subsequently in time.

(2) Gather information from a wide variety of sources and experiences.

(3) Review it, analyze it, organize it, eliminate irrelevancies.

(4) Design a formula for putting it into machine readable form.

(5) Process it into a machine readable form

(6) Design a formula for manipulating the information within the machine to produce the specifically desired end product.

(7) Develop the graphic arts embodiment of that end product, and in other respects design and produce a "human-useable" product.

(8) Educate users to the advantages of the product and in other ways market the product to the group of users for whom the product is designed and developed.

Several points emerge from that list:

(a) Each of these steps, starting with the time spent identifying user needs and continuing through each step of the process to the delivery of the product to the user, is complex and costly.

(b) Many of the products of such efforts qualify for copyright protection as works of authorship.

(c) By virtue of their special design and highly refined specialized markets, they are extremely sensitive to any attrition in the size of their expected market whether through photocopying or other replication methods for by-passing copyright protection. The economic viability of such products, whether they are to be created at all, depends pretty much on each user paying his fair share of the fully amortized cost of creating and delivering the product.

SINGLE COPY LIBRARY PHOTOCOPYING

Before addressing ourselves to the question of the single-copy exemption sought by the libraries, let me state at the outset that the information industry and libraries have many things in common. We are part of the same piece of cloth. Both groups are essentially populist in outlook. We seek to make information as widely available as possible. A major distinction between us is our cost-accounting methods. The industry must operate on a fully allocated cost-accounting basis whereas libraries can and do evaluate services on an incremental cost basis.

The information industry itself represents an attempt by some far-sighted members of the publishing community augmented by people who come at this field from the information technology side to restructure the publishing business to accommodate its skills, and resources to the imperatives of information technologies.

The library community, likewise, is undergoing a major restructuring. Inter-library cooperation, the "mother" library concept, the emergence of some forms of charges for "inter-library" loans and for special research projects are illustrations of ways in which the library community is being restructured to accommodate itself to the fact, costs, and advantages of information technologies. A Presidential Commission on Libraries and Information Science only recently has been established to provide assistance and national perspective to this effort. This restructuring process has been accelerated and aggravated by the serious funding problems facing the library community. We have high regard for the efforts libraries have made and are continuing to make. We also feel libraries have an even greater future as community information centers with immense implications for the educational and cultural as well as economic well-being of us all.

We empathize with the library community and recognize and respect the deeply held motivations which give rise to its request for this single copy exemption. We must, however, oppose the amendment.

Such an exemption would put libraries in the reprint business in direct competition with the information industry. It would give the library an unfair advantage to market reprint materials from its holdings. (Whether it sold these materials or gave them away free, or for the cost of the copying the result would be the same.) It would ironically enable libraries to do so with the products of publishers and information companies without the ultimate users paying a fair share of the costs of the creation and distribution of the information. What looks desirable on an incremental cost analysis to libraries multiplied nationally is a disaster on a fully allocated cost basis for the industry. Such a free information source would lead to more limited circulation of much higher priced products. The paying user will be required in this way to subsidize the non-paying user.

Would there be any basis for a micropublisher to create and market a complete collection of materials in microfilm if a "mother" library could freely copy individual pieces of the collection for its users or the users of its subsidiary libraries?

How would special report information companies which create specialized studies for 75 to 100 customers or less stay in business if some or all of these customers could go to a library and obtain individual copies free of copyright?

How does the information company which authors a machine readable data base market its product when libraries would be able to market access to the same data base free of copyright? A search of such a data base provides a print-out of single articles within the proposed library photocopying language, yet that is in most cases the only way a product of the data base will be generated and used inside or out of a library.

Based on our experience we urge that the library exemption contained in Section 108 be limited to archival copying only. Any additional exemption directly undermines the integrity of the copyright concept and denies the basic principle behind copyright that science and the useful arts will be benefited by providing the author a limited monopoly by which to market the product of his creativity. The library amendment, honoring only the copyright claims of the producers of motion pictures, subjects to the single copy exemption all other categories of information products, whether they be sound recordings, machine readable files or microfilm, in addition to inkprint products such as books and journals. One might just as easily abolish copyright altogether.

Copyright has been the mechanism by which libraries and their suppliers have established working relations. Before you decide to abolish this element in the relationship between libraries and their suppliers, and that is what you would do if you enacted the language sought by libraries, we recommend you defer this language to the Title II National Commission on New Technological Uses of Copyrighted Works.

The library single copy exemption does impact directly on new technological uses of copyrighted works, and adopting the amendment would deprive the Commission of the benefit of continued efforts to develop sound funding mechanisms through the day-to-day interaction in the real world of suppliers and libraries. To the information industry, libraries are established distribution nodes in a national information distribution network serving users. This network has been established working within the framework of copyright and, until it can be shown a better way exists, the basis for that working relationship should be maintained.

We respectfully urge that you defer action on the amendment pending the results of the study of the National Commission to be established by Title II of this bill.

PROPOSED EDUCATION EXEMPTION

We oppose this amendment on economic and technical grounds.

We have a high regard for the educational community as well as the library community. We do, however, have to object to the proposal since it would not only adversely effect the industry but it would have a pervasive effect on many others and on the development of the information service structure of the United States as a whole.

Economically, it would—

(a) Exempt input from copyright protection.

(b) Raise pressures to stretch the Fair Use exemption to cover "small" output.

(c) Put no limit on what could be put into an education computer.

(d) Create unintended and unfair competition for information industry.

(e) Ignore and undermine the business practice of licensing use.

(f) Restructure information services so as to eliminate stimulas and creative force of risk capital and competition.

(a) By implication this amendment acknowledges that to input copyrighted materials into a computer system is an infringement.

The amendment, by exempting input, would strip the author of control over his documented ideas. Without input infringement protection not only can his ideas be used, but they can be re-documented and distorted as to *source, meaning* and *context.*

A search of a data base may produce the fact that there is nothing in the file to print out. That, of itself, is often of great value. That is one of the purposes of investing in the creation of a comprehensive data base. Information that no one has done what you want to do has value. The amendment denies this and would destroy the economic value of that aspect of the author's work.

To search a data base is to "use" the whole file, not just the answer you find. This search capability is a value the amendment denies as well.

(b) The small printouts resulting from most computer searches would by their size alone it will be argued constitute "fair use" of the information. Having inserted in the computer The Encyclopedia Britannica, brief extracts could be printed out. Notwithstanding the fact that that is the only way to use encyclopedia information, many would seek to treat it as fair use. Since there is no provision for any payment system in the proposal, this apparently is the intended result.

(c) Under the language of the proposal "entire works" of any kind could be reproduced for machine processing.

The *Reader's Guide to Periodical Literature,* for example, could be keypunched and installed in a computer system. Encyclopedias and all the other products of the information and publishing industry would be equally exposed to such treatment. Without anything but "fair use" limits on copying and use (how do you apply fair use to the use of a whole file in making a computer search?) and with complete freedom to put entire works into a computer the protection offered by copyright would be minimal.

(d) The result would be the creation of unfair competition for the information industry. Does the educational activity have an iron-willed discipline and a policing procedure by which to assure that its computer information service serves only bonafide students? Many universities now engage in the marketing of information, not only in their city and state, but across the nation. They do so from a tax exempt haven and often without fully allocating to each user the costs of creating and delivering the information. This amendment would create great pressure to market machine readable versions in competition with inkprint and other privately published media. An Association of Scientific Information Dissemination Centers has been created to facilitate the growth of these activities.

(e) In practice few, if any, data bases are marketed exclusively through the author's computer facility. Copyright at input merely provides the author a basis for a licensing agreement by which the users of other computer facilities gain access to his documented ideas. The user is protected in that the integrity of the information and its documentation are subject to continuing contractual relations.

This licensing process facilitates the widest possible sharing in the cost of creating these services. The amendment would not only free a large segment of users from paying its fair share of these costs, but it would also encourage education to engage in the economic replication of already existing and privately funded capabilities.

(f) Competition in the information marketplace in an age of information abundance is essential to competition in the marketplace of ideas. The stress on exemptions would have the effect of eliminating competition in many areas because the basis for private creation and investment, a minimal proprietory position, would be eliminated for many. The result would be a diminished, rather than enhanced, competitive climate in the marketplace of ideas. The information service structure of the U.S. would have to rely primarily on education and government capital resources for its development. The elimination of risk capital in this effort would seriously retard development in this area in the U.S.

On technical grounds the amendment would—

(a) expand its intended objectives by virtue of the proliferation of non-profit uses today.

(b) conflict with the intended purposes of Section 117.

(c) provide only for a method of recording "retrieval" and no for requiring its use, nor for recording "use" itself as distinguished from "retrieval".

(d) make rules otherwise applicable, presumably including "fair use" and the library single copy exemption.

(e) preempt much of the work of the National Commission on New Technological Uses of Copyrighted Works.

(a) The proliferation of non-profit uses, particularly in information, today are legend. Government funding of research in information systems work, for example, is essentially limited to grants to non-profit organizations. This has led to the development of a whole generation of organizations performing this research on a non-profit basis. Separate non-profit groups have grown up to do similar research in education. Public Interest law firms are incorporated in many cases on a non-profit basis. We raise these questions not to challenge the purposes of these groups but to suggest that the amendment is unduly broad as drafted and would serve, if enacted, to stimulate even further the development of subsidy-based activities.

(b) The amendment conflicts with the purpose of Section 117 to maintain the status quo in the law vis a vis copyright at input. The significance of such a development can be seen clearly through a reading of a paper by former Register of Copyrights, George O. Cary, presented at the 1972 meeting of the American Society for Information Science. It appears at pages 169-174 in *The Proceedings of the ASIS Annual Meeting,* Vol. 9, 1972, ASIS, Washington, D.C. We commend it to the attention of the Committee and the Congress.

(c) A method of recording retrieval, as provided for in the amendment, does not require that it be used any more than the seat belt statutes do. Furthermore, retrieval, as noted above, is not a complete measure of the uses made of a copyrighted work in computer form.

(d) The reference to other rules applicable under law apparently refers to "fair use" rules. How reasonable that is for modern information products where the ultimate users should each pay their fair share of the costs is a matter that has not been fully developed and one on which this industry has not yet formulated a position. It is a matter which should be referred to the National Commission.

Furthermore, when it is contemplated that this proposal would be coupled with the library single-copy exemption, there appears to be no copyright protection left.

(e) The proposal if adopted would preempt not only much of the work of the National Commission, but it would also deprive it of the benefit of day-to-day experience developed as suppliers and users seek to work out within existing copyright concepts workable relations for the dissemination of information through these technologies.

This exemption is, in effect, based on the assumption that enough is known today about the effect of the technologies on copyright and the dissemination of copyrighted materials. It may very well be true that this committee could, if it assigned this matter top priority, come to an appropriate determination based on what is known today. That record has not been established here today or in previous hearings. As in other copyright areas, legislation can be based on an extended record of practices developed between conflicting interests. What you are asked to do by this amendment is to enact into law the position of one of the parties and to ignore the practices and positions of the others. We feel it is premature to decide now upon such a major innovation in American Copyright law and that the amendments, both the Library Single-Copy amendment and the Education Exemption should be referred to the Title II National Commission.

As we have argued with the Library exemption, the education exemption in the clearest language is subject matter clearly within the jurisdiction of the National Commission. We respectfully urge that the Commission be established and assigned the fact-gathering function essential to sound legislation. As we have earlier stated, we are ready and willing to be of assistance in working with the Commission in this major undertaking.

CONCLUSION

We wish to draw the Committees attention to the significance of these two amendments in an international sense. What protection U.S. Law provides information will have an effect on how the information products of our technology-based system are treated abroad. Some of our members derive as much as 50% of their revenues from foreign sales, from foreign users seeking to acquire information about the many aspects of the operations of our technologies, etc. The USSR, only recently having joined the Universal Copyright Convention, has also adopted a provision of its copyright law to provide for copyright-free reproduction of printed works for "non-profit scientific, dadactic and educational purposes." Information companies will have little to debate in seeking to receive fair compensation from foreign users for their services if U.S. Law embodies similar provisions.

The domestic effect of the amendments we have described obviously have far-reaching implications internationally, particularly since the U.S. is not only a major producer of copyrighted materials, but it is also a world leader in the development of information technology applications to their distribution. The U.S. must carefully consider major innovations in applying copyright rules to these new media.

We thank you for this opportunity to share our views with you.

CORPORATE MEMBERS

ABC/CLIO, Inc., Santa Barbara, Calif., Richard Abel and Co., Portland, Oreg.; Academic Press, Inc., New York, N.Y.; Aspen Systems Corp., Rockville, Md.; Auerbach Publications Inc., Philadelphia, Pa., Bell & Howell, Wooster, Ohio; Chase Manhattan Corp., New York, N.Y.; Cordura, Los Angeles, Calif.; Congressional Information Service, Washington, D.C.; Data Courier, Inc., Louisville, Ky.; Data Flow Systems, Inc., Bethesda, Md.; Data Search Co., Des Plains, Ill.; Dun & Bradstreet, New York, N.Y.; Encyclopedia Britannica Education Corp., Washington, D.C.; Environment Information Center, Inc., and Frost & Sullivan, New York, N.Y.;

Greenwood Press, a Division of Williamhouse-Regency, Inc., Westport, Conn.; Herner & Co., Washington, D.C.; Information Clearing House, New York, N.Y.; Information Design, Inc., Menlo Park, Calif.; Information Handling Services, Englewood, Colo.; International Data Corp., Newtonville, Mass.; International Development Center, Kensington, Md.; Institute for Scientific Information, Philadelphia, Pa.; Leasco Information Co., Silver Spring, Md.; Leasco Systems & Research Co., Bethesda, Md.; Lockheed Missiles & Space Co., Palo Alto, Calif.; McGraw Hill, Inc., and Macmillan Information Corp., New York, N.Y.; Microforms Intern'l Marketing Corp., Elmsford, N.Y.; Monitor, Inc./Congressional Monitor, and National Congressional Analysis Corp., Washington, D.C.

Jeffrey Norton Publishers, Inc., and New York Times, New York, N.Y.; Pharmaco-Medical Documentation, Inc., Chatham, N.J.; Plenum Publishing Corp., New York, N.Y.; Predicasts, Inc., Cleveland, Ohio; Readex Microprint Corp., New York, N.Y.; Reesarch Publications, Inc., New Haven, Conn.; Time, Inc., New York, N.Y.; U.S. Historical Documents Inst., Inc., Washington, D.C.; John Wiley & Sons, Inc., and Garwood R. Wolff & Co., New York, N.Y.; World Meeting Information Center, Inc., Chestnut Hill, Mass.; and Xerox Corporation, Stanford, Conn.

Almqvist & Wiksell, Uppsala, Sweden; Arrow International, and Fuji Corporation, Tokyo, Japan; Information Retrieval, Ltd., London, England; Opidan Sciences, Inc., Toronto, Canada; Orba Information, Ltd., Montreal Canada; Overseas Data Service, Tokyo, Japan; Thomson Data, Ltd., London, England, and U.S. Asiatic Company, Ltd., Tokyo, Japan.

Composition Technology, Inc., Cambridge, Mass.; Inforonics, Inc., Maynard, Mass.; IBM, Armonk, N.Y.; Multiprint, Inc., New York, N.Y.; Publicate, Inc., Washington, D.C.; Publishers Development Corp., New York, N.Y.; and Rocappi, Inc., Pennsauken, N.J.

STATEMENT OF THE ASSOCIATION OF RESEARCH LIBRARIES, ON THE AMENDMENT RECOMMENDED BY THE LIBRARY ASSOCIATIONS TO S. 1361, GENERAL REVISION OF COPYRIGHT LAW

In order to clarify the proposed amendment and distinguish between it and the language of S. 1361 in its present form, it appears desirable to discuss the sections of the amendment and then to note the difference between these provisions and those of S. 1361.

The initial paragraph of section d reads the same as section d in the printed Bill except that the phrase "but only under the following conditions" is substituted for the word "if" at the end of the paragraph.

Section (1) under d of the proposed amendment refers only to an article or other contribution to a copyrighted collection or periodical issue or to a similar small part of a work. The purpose of this amendment is to enable libraries to continue to supply a photocopy of a small part of a work without being required to do any checking to see whether the issue of the periodical or the book in which the item appears is available for sale. This is particularly important with respect to articles in periodicals, since there is no easy way to determine whether or not a particular issue of a periodical is still available from the publisher or dealer. Even if it should be determined that an issue can be ordered from the publisher, the time required to place the order and receive the issue results in a delay which will probably not meet the need of the user.

Section (2) refers to an "entire work," that is, a book or a major part of a book. In this case the amendment would require that the library determine whether or not the book is still in print before providing a photocopy of it. This can be done with relative ease by checking _Books In Print_.

The distinction may be put in this way: section (1) refers to a periodical article or short excerpt of which a photocopy may be provided without any checking. Section (2) refers to an entire book or a major part of it and in this case a check to see whether the book is still in print is required.

Section (2) of the proposed amendment is similar to section 108(d)(1) in the printed Bill, S. 1361. Section (1) of the proposed amendment is a specific exemption for a periodical article or short excerpt. In this respect, it is an addiction to S. 1361.

"REASONABLE INVESTIGATION"

The phrase "reasonable investigation" is used in the amendment which we are recommending but only in section 108(d)(2). This section refers to books, not to periodical articles. A reasonable investigation of the availability through trade sources of a book can easily be made by checking the annual catalog _Books In Print_. There is no comparable catalog listing all periodical articles.

Section 108(d)(1) of S. 1361 requires the reader to "establish to the satisfaction of the library or archives that an unused copy can not be obtained at a normal price from commonly known trade sources in the United States including authorized reproducing services." This requirement applies both to periodical articles and to books. It can be complied with as regards books through the use of _Books In Print_. There is no feasible way of making a comparable check of the availability of periodicals. _Effects of Library Photocopying on Copyright Proprietors._

Those who oppose the proposed library photocopying amendment take the position that library photocopying eliminates sales and reduces the number of subscriptions to periodicals. The most extreme charge is that library photocopying will result in destroying scientific and technical communication by making it economically impossible to continue the publication of periodicals and books.

The importance of the partnership of libraries with the publishing industry cannot be over-emphasized. The economic viability of this industry is indeed a crucial concern to all involved in the dissemination of information. It is difficult, however, to get precise information regarding the effects of photocopying on publication sales. A most important consideration here is that coin-operated photocopying machines are available to virtually everyone. Thus, a significant and ever-increasing amount of photocopying is unsupervised.

In regard to supervised library photocopying, several studies have been made in the past 12 to 15 years and it is the conclusion of these studies that no evidence of significant economic damage caused by library photocopying could be identified. While the general experience is that the number of subscriptions has increased, there have been exceptions to this but it is by no means clear that the decline in the number of subscriptions have increased very substantially in this period and library budgets, particularly in recent years, have been reduced; thus the canceling of subscriptions cannot be fairly ascribed to library photocopying only.

If it were possible to demonstrate clearly that library photocopying had severely damaged copyright proprietors, it could be expected that publishers would produce this evidence. Since they have not done so, it would appear that the evidence is not persuasive. In the absence of conclusive evidence, it would be most unfortunate if requirements were established for the payment of royalties which would involve "spending dimes to collect pennies."

LIBRARY ASSOCIATIONS SUPPORT THE AMENDMENT RECOMMENDED

The amendment in the form in which it has been recommended to the Subcommittee represents the views and recommendations of the American Library Association, the Association of Research Libraries, and the Medical Library Association. These Associations recommend this amendment on behalf of their readers in order that they may be able to maintain the photocopying services now provided by most libraries of all types. In the aggregate the number of readers who use the libraries represented by these Associations runs to many millions. It is on behalf of these readers that the Library Associations urge the Subcommittee to adopt the amendment which they have recommended.

The statement was made in the course of the hearings that machine-monitoring of materials copied was feasible. However, at the present time there is no practical way that a photocopy machine could differentiate existing copyrighted from uncopyrighted materials.

STEPHEN A. McCARTHY,
Executive Director.

STATEMENT WITH RESPECT TO THE PROPOSED "GENERAL EDUCATIONAL EXEMPTION" AMENDMENT TO THE COPYRIGHT REVISION BILL (S. 1361), SUBMITTED TO THE SUBCOMMITTEE ON PATENTS, TRADEMARKS, AND COPYRIGHTS OF THE SENATE COMMITTEE ON THE JUDICIARY BY THE ASSOCIATION OF AMERICAN PUBLISHERS

The present statement is intended to extend and amplify the necessarily brief oral statement presented to the Subcommittee by Ross Sackett, President of Encyclopaedia Britannica Educational Corporation on behalf of the Association of American Publishers, of which Mr. Sackett is Chairman of the Board of Directors, in opposition to the proposed amendment to the Copyright Revision Bill (S. 1361) granting a general educational exemption.

The Association of American Publishers is the general association of book publishers in the United States, including textbooks and other educational materials. Its more than 260 members, which include many university presses and non-profit religious book publishers, produce the vast majority of all general, educational and religious books and related materials published in the United States.

The Copyright Revision Bill as it stands (S. 1361) provides many limitations on the rights of copyright proprietors that are intended to facilitate the educational use of copyrighted materials. Section 107 for the first time would embody in statute law the judicial doctrine of fair use. It would explicitly define certain uses of copyrighted works in teaching as being fair use if it meets the other specified criteria. Section 108 in certain circumstances would permit copying by a library, including a school or college library, even though it may exceed fair use. Section 108 also exempts school and college libraries from liability for infringements committed on coin-operated copying machines on their premises, provided an appropriate warning has been placed on the machines. Section 110(a) permits the non-profit performance or display of a copyrighted work in the classroom. Section 110(b) permits the broadcast of a nondramatic work in organized instructional programs. Section 112(b) entitles a school to produce and for five years make unlimited use of tapes or other records of live performances of works it broadcasts. Section 504(c)(2) relieves a teacher of liability for statutory damages if he commits an infringement and if he believed on reasonable grounds that the infringing use was a fair use under Section 107 of the act.

These numerous special exemptions for educators reflect the concern that the Judiciary Committees of both Houses and the Copyright Office have consistently shown through the long consideration of copyright revision that no unreasonable impediments should be placed in the way of educational use of copyrighted materials. Publishers share that concern. For that reason, almost all of the special exemptions now in the bill have been not only accepted but supported by publishers. Educators and educational institutions are the sole market for the educational materials produced by publishers, and are by far the most important customers of the industry. The producers and the users of educational materials are hence partners, not opponents. They share a common purpose in achieving the maximum and the most efficient use of educational materials in the actual teaching process.

The provisions of the bill as they affect educators were quite satisfactory to the Ad Hoc Committee when it testified before the Senate Judiciary Subcommittee. (See the testimony of Harry Rosenfield on S. 597, March 1967, Part 1, pp. 187–189.) Now, however the Ad Hoc Committee has revived a proposal for a sweeping exemption.

This exemption would allow anyone to make an unlimited number of copies in any form for the purposes of "noncommercial teaching scholarship or research" of "brief excerpts from literary, pictorial, and graphic works which are not substantial in length in proportion to their source" and also of the "whole of short literary, pictorial and graphic works."

It would also allow an entire copyrighted work to be stored in a computer or other automatic system for storing, processing, retrieving or transferring information, leaving the proprietor with only such control as he can achieve over the retrieval of the information.

Many, perhaps most, of the uses described by the representatives of the Ad Hoc Committee as a justification for this proposed exemption would in any case be lawful under section 107 or other provisions of the bill, particularly the reproduction of brief excerpts in ways that do not reduce the market for the original. Insofar as the proposed general educational exemption relates to uses that would be legal under 107, it is meaningless and unnecessary. The only real purpose sought by the amendment, and indeed the only purpose it can serve, is to legalize uses that a court would otherwise hold to be unfair because they are excessive in quantity or reduce the market for the original work or otherwise exceed "fair use." If no excessive uses or competitive uses are planned, the proposed amendment is simply pointless.

What are some of the uses that would be authorized by the proposed general educational exemption that *would* be likely to be held to exceed fair use today or under Section 107? The most dangerous of those probably relate to the freedom to make and distribute an unlimited number of copies of entire "short" copyrighted works without the proprietor's permission. The only limitation on this freedom would be that the copying must not be for profit, that it must be for "noncommercial teaching, scholarship, and research," that the copies of the separate whole works must not be compiled, as in an anthology, and that the materials copied must not be "consumable."

A "short" whole work is presumably an individual short story, essay, or poem; a map; a transparency; a globe; a wall chart; a slide or photograph; the score of a short music composition. It is difficult to conceive works that are shorter and yet are whole, separately copyrightable "works."

Under the proposed language a city school system, or a state department of education, or the United States Office of Education could, on a nonprofit basis, produce a dozen, or a hundred, or a thousand copies of a slide or of all of the slides a publisher has produced and make them available free, or at the bare reproduction cost, to schools in their jurisdiction for noncommercial teaching activities. Time and time again, a teacher could make multiple copies of a poem or a short story, and hand it out to members of a class or group of classes. A school could reproduce the words and music of a "short" copyrighted song for all the members of a school orchestra and choir. A school system could reproduce for every classroom a copyrighted wall chart or map; the Department of Defense could reproduce a hundred thousand copies of a short copyrighted work to use in training courses. And so through dozens of similar situations in which the uses are clearly not "fair" but would apparently be legal under the proposed language.

We are quite prepared to believe that the sponsors of the general educational exemption had no such sweeping uses in mind; but if that be true, they should not seek legislation that would legalize such abuses.

As we understand it, the sponsors of the general educational exemption assert that they do not wish to cover under the exemption uses that would injure copyright proprietors or that would go beyond what are normal and professionally approved classroom activities now. Their declared purpose is apparently not so much to *enlarge* the area in which copyrighted works may be used without the owner's permission as to define more clearly the present boundaries of that area. They would contend that the uses they envision as actually carried on under the proposed exemption would in almost every case be "fair" uses, but that teachers cannot safely rely on the doctrine of "fair use" because of its vagueness. Teachers may expose themselves to legal peril, the advocates of the exemption say, or more likely they may be deterred from making proper and desirable uses of copyrighted material because they do not know whether or not they are "fair uses" within the meaning of the law.

Admittedly the concept of "fair use", like the concept of "negligence" or of "prudence" in the common law, is one that by its very nature is not susceptible of precise and unvarying definition. But the proposed amendment does not cure this vagueness. It compounds it by introducing a number of terms new to copyright law and uninterpreted by the courts:

How short is a "short" work? Is a 15-page short story "short"? Ten pages? Five pages? Does it depend on the size of the page?

What is "nonprofit" use? Is a professor doing research which he hopes to embody in a textbook from which he hopes to receive substantial royalties engaged in "non profit" research? If he is working on a biography from which he hopes to receive modest royalties? If he is doing an article for a learned journal for which he will receive no payment but hopes for a promotion? Is the Department of Defense engaged in "non-profit" research when it puts the entire content of a highly technical set of copyrighted tables into a computer to use in designing the airfoil of a new plane? Is an aircraft manufacturer engaged in non-profit research when it does the same thing under a contract with the Department of Defense?

The very essence of such legal concepts as "fair use" (or "negligence" or "prudence") is that they *do* avoid rigid *a priori* definitions and permit a judgment of fairness and equity to be made on the basis of the application of common sense and experience to the actual situation in each individual case. To introduce certainty is to introduce rigidity. Any effort to get away from the doctrine of "fair use" and define the area of permissible use in predetermined objective or numerical terms is simply unworkable. Any such inflexible rule, if it is narrow enough to eliminate truly abusive uses of material will eliminate along with them many wholly proper uses. If it is broad enough to include all the uses we all agree are proper, it will open the door to a host of improper uses. There is simply no substitute for the use of informed and impartial judgment in the application of general principles to specific cases.

If the proposed general educational exemption is not intended to legalize sweeping uses of copyrighted material that are clearly beyond the bounds of fair use, and if it is not successful in clearly defining boundaries of use, what is the need for it?

Indeed we believe the needs that have been alleged are hypothetical and illusory. The 1909 Copyright Act under which we now live contains none of the special concessions to education that appear in S. 1361 and that we for the most part support. It is much more restrictive than S. 1361 in its present form. Yet under the present more restrictive law, hundreds of thousands of teachers, scholars, and researchers daily make millions of uses of copyrighted material. No doubt many of those uses may exceed the boundaries of what we would all agree to be fair use. Yet the result when any such well-intentioned excessive use comes to the attention of the publisher is at most a statement of concern followed by discussion and the modification or abandonment of the objection to use or else an agreement that in the circumstance it is proper or, in some cases, a license to continue the use. What are the desirable educational practices that in actual fact go unused for fear of a vaguely defined copyright liability? We have evidence of any. There is simply no reason to believe that under the copyright law as it would be liberalized by S. 1361 without the proposed general educational exemption, as well as under the 1909 law, educators and publishers would not continue to go forward as they have in the past in an easy collaboration, resolving by discussion any occasional differences in the interpretation of fair use that may arise.

But if it is difficult to see any need for or benefits from the proposed exemption, it is only too easy to see the difficulties it would bring to education as well as to authors and publishers:

(1) It would legalize the potential large-scale competitive reproduction for noncommercial teaching use of a host of "small" whole copyrighted works. The limitation of this exemption to "noncommercial teaching" is no protection to the producers of such material, for "noncommercial teaching" is substantially the whole of the market for educational material. Such large-scale reproduction would not only injure authors, producers and publishers; by the lessening of the incentive to produce such works for the educational market, it would injure teachers, students, and the whole educational process as well.

Copyright Law Revision
Report No. 93—983

PURPOSE

The purpose of the proposed legislation, as amended, is to provide in Title I for a general revision of the United States Copyright Law, title 17 of the United States Code. Title II of the bill provides for the establishment in the Library of Congress of a National Commission on New Technological Uses of Copyrighted Works. Title III of the bill creates a new type of protection for ornamental designs of useful articles.

STATEMENT

The present Copyright Law of the United States is essentially that enacted by the Congress in 1909. Many significant developments in technology and communications have rendered that law clearly inadequate to the needs of the country today.

The enactment of legislation "To promote the Progress of Science and useful Arts, by securing for limited Times to Authors and Inventors the exclusive Right to their respective Writings and Discoveries", is one of the powers of the Congress enumerated in Article I, section 8 of the Constitution. Some commentators on the Congress in recent years have expressed concern that the legislative branch has too frequently yielded the initiative in legislative matters to the executive branch. This legislation is exclusively the product of the legislative branch and has received detailed consideration over a period of several years.

The origin of this legislation can ultimately be traced to the Legislative Appropriations Act of 1955 which appropriated funds for a comprehensive program of research and study of copyright law revision by the Copyright Office of the Library of Congress. This committee's Subcommittee on Patents, Trademarks and Copyrights published a series of 34 studies on all aspects of copyright revision, which were prepared under the supervision of the Copyright Office. In 1961 the Congress received the "Report of the Register of Copyrights on the general revision of the U.S. Copyright Law." The Copyright Office subsequently conducted a series of panel meetings on copyright law revision. On July 20, 1964, Senator John L. McClellan, Chairman of the Subcommittee on Patents, Trademarks and Copyrights, introduced, at the request of the Librarian of Congress, S. 3008 of the 88th Congress, for the general revision of the copyright law. No action was taken on this bill prior to the adjournment of the Congress.

In the 1st session of the 89th Congress, Senator McClellan, again introduced at the request of the Librarian of Congress, a general copyright revision bill S. 1006. Hearings on this legislation were commenced by the Subcommittee on August 18, 1965, and continued on August 19 and 20. When the hearings were recessed, a large number of witnesses remained to be heard. During the 2d session of the 89th Congress there were important developments relating to the possible copyright liability of cable television systems under the Copyright Act of 1909. In order to ascertain whether immediate and separate legislative action on the copyright CATV question was necessary and desirable, the Subcommittee commenced hearings on that subject on August 2, 1966. These hearings continued on August 3, 4 and 25. No further action was taken by the Subcommittee during the 89th Congress.

In the 1st session of the 90th Congress Senator McClellan again, at the request of the Librarian of Congress, introduced S. 597, for the general revision of the copyright law. Hearings on this bill commenced on March 15, 1967 and continued on March 16, 17, 20, 21, April 4, 6, 11, 12 and 28. During the Subcommittee hearings more than 100 witnesses were heard and many suggested amendments were submitted for the consideration of the Subcommittee.

On April 11, 1967, the House of Representatives passed H.R. 2512, for the general revision of the copyright law. This bill was subsequently referred to the Subcommittee on Patents, Trademarks and Copyrights. Although the Subcommittee completed the public hearings on copyright revision during the 90th Congress, no further action was taken by the Subcommittee because of problems with certain provisions of the legislation, and because of the pendency of the cable television judicial proceedings.

One of the problems that prevented Subcommittee action during the 90th Congress was uncertainty concerning the impact of the legislation on the use of copyrighted materials in computers and other forms of information storage and retrieval systems. The Subcommittee recommended and the Senate passed on October 12, 1967, S. 2216 to establish in the Library of Congress a National Commission on New Technological Uses of Copyrighted Works. The Commission was authorized to study this subject and recommend any changes in copyright law or procedure. No action was taken on this legislation by the House of Representatives.

On January 22 (legislative day January 10), 1969, Senator McClellan introduced S. 543. Title I of this bill, other than for technical amendments, was identical to S. 597 of the 90th Congress. Title II of the bill incorporated the provisions of S. 2216 providing for the establishment of the National Commission on New Technological Uses of Copyrighted Works.

On December 10, 1969, the Subcommittee favorably reported S. 543, with an amendment in the nature of a substitute. No further action was taken in the Committee on the Judiciary, primarily because of the cable television issue.

On February 18, 1971, Senator McClellan introduced S. 644 for the general revision of the copyright law. Other than for minor amendments, the text of that bill was identical to the revision bill reported by the Subcommittee in the 91st Congress. No action was taken on general revision legislation during the 92nd Congress while the Subcommittee was awaiting the formulation and adoption by the Federal Communications Commission of new cable television rules.

While action on the general revision bill was necessarily delayed, the unauthorized duplication of sound recordings became widespread. It was accordingly determined that the creation of a limited copyright in sound recordings should not await action on the general revision bill. Senator McClellan introduced, for himself and others, S. 644 of the 92nd Congress to amend title 17 of the U.S. Code to provide for the creation of a limited copyright in sound recordings. An amended version of this legislation was enacted as P.L. 92–140.

On March 26, 1973, Senator McClellan introduced S. 1361 for the general revision of the copyright law. Other than for technical amendments, this bill is identical to S. 644 of the 92nd Congress. Additional copyright revision hearings were held on July 31st and August 1, 1973. The Subcommittee conducted a total of 18 days of hearings on copyright law revision.

During the 87th Congress the Senate passed S. 1884 to provide for a new form of protection for original ornamental designs of useful articles by protecting the authors of such designs for a limited time against unauthorized copying. The Senate in the 88th Congress passed S. 776 and, in the 90th Congress S. 1237, bills on the same subject. No final action was taken in the House of Representatives on any of these measures. In the 91st Congress Senator Philip A. Hart introduced a similar bill, S. 1774. The substance of that bill has been incorporated as Title III of this legislation.

SECTION 106. EXCLUSIVE RIGHTS IN COPYRIGHTED WORKS

General scope of copyright

The five fundamental rights that the bill gives to copyright owners—the exclusive rights of reproduction, adaptation, publication, performance, and display—are stated generally in section 106. These exclusive rights, which comprise the so-called "bundle of rights" that is a copyright, are cumulative and may overlap in some cases. Each of the five enumerated rights may be subdivided indefinitely and, as discussed below in connection with section 201, each subdivision of an exclusive right may be owned and enforced separately.

The approach of the bill is to set forth the copyright owner's exclusive rights in broad terms in section 106, and then to provide various limitations, qualifications, or exemptions in the 11 sections that follow. Thus, everything in section 106 is made "subject to sections 107 through 117," and must be read in conjunction with those provisions.

The exclusive rights accorded to a copyright owner under section 106 are "to do and to authorize" any of the activities specified in the five numbered clauses. Use of the phrase "to authorize" is intended to avoid any questions as to the liability of contributory infringers. For example, a person who lawfully acquires an authorized copy of a motion picture would be an infringer if he engages in the business of renting it to others for purposes of unauthorized public performance.

Rights of reproduction, adaptation, and publication

The first three clauses of section 106, which cover all rights under a copyright except those of performance and display, extend to every kind of copyrighted work. The exclusive rights encompassed by these clauses, though closely related, are independent; they can generally be characterized as rights of copying, recording, adaptation, and publishing. A single act of infringement may violate all of these rights at once, as where a publisher reproduces, adapts, and sells copies of a person's copyrighted work as part of a publishing venture. Infringement takes place when any one of the rights is violated: where, for example, a printer reproduces copies without selling them or a retailer sells copies without having anything to do with their reproduction. The references to "copies or phonorecords," although in the plural, are intended here and throughout the bill to include the singular (1 U.S.C. § 1).

Reproduction.—Read together with the relevant definitions in section 101, the right "to reproduce the copyrighted work in copies or phonorecords" means the right to produce a material object in which the work is duplicated, transcribed, imitated, or simulated in a fixed form from which it can be "perceived, reproduced, or otherwise communicated, either directly or with the aid of a machine or device." As under the present law, a copyrighted work would be infringed by reproducing it in whole or in any substantial part, and by duplicating it exactly or by imitation or simulation. Wide departures or variations from the copyrighted works would still be an infringement as long as the author's "expression" rather than merely his "ideas" are taken.

"Reproduction" under clause (1) of section 106 is to be distinguished from "display" under clause (5). For a work to be "reproduced," its fixation in tangible form must be "sufficiently permanent or stable to permit it to be perceived, reproduced, or otherwise communicated for a period of more than transitory duration." Thus, the showing of images on a screen or tube would not be a violation of caluse (1), although it might come within the scope of clause (5).

Preparation of derivative works.—The exclusive right to prepare derivative works, specified separately in clause (2) of section 106, overlaps the exclusive right of reproduction to some extent. It is broader than that right, however, in the sense that reproduction requires fixation in copies or phonorecords, whereas the preparation of a derivative work, such as a ballet, pantomime, or improvised performance, may be an infringement even though nothing is ever fixed in tangible form.

To be an infringement the "derivative work" must be "based upon the copyrighted work," and the definition in section 101 refers to "a translation, musical arrangement, dramatization, fictionalization, motion picture version, sound recording, art reproduction, abridgment, condensation, or any other form in which a work may be recast, transformed, or adapted." Thus, to constitute a violation of section 106(2), the infringing work must incorporate a portion of the copyrighted work in some form; for example, a detailed commentary on a work or a programmatic musical composition inspired by a novel would not normally constitute infringements under this clause.

Use in information storage and retrieval systems—As section 117 declares explicitly, the bill is not intended to alter the present law with respect to the use of copyrighted works in computer systems.

Public distribution.—Clause (3) of section 106 establishes the exclusive right of publication: The right "to distribute copies or phonorecords of the copyrighted work to the public by sale or other transfer of ownership, or by rental, lease, or lending." Under this provision the copyright owner would have the right to control the first public distribution of an authorized copy or phonorecord of his work, whether by sale, gift, loan, or some rental or lease arrangement. Likewise, any unauthorized public distribution of copies or phonorecords that were unlawfully made would be an infringement. As section 109 makes clear, however, the copyright owner's rights under section 106(3) cease with respect to a particular copy or phonorecord once he has parted with ownership of it.

Rights of public performance and display

Performing rights and the "for profit" limitation.—The right of public performance under section 106(4) extends to "literary, musical, dramatic, and choreographic works, pantomimes, and motion pictures and other audiovisual works and sound recordings" and, unlike the equivalent provisions now in effect, is not limited by any "for profit" requirement. The approach of the bill, as in many foreign laws, is first to state the public performance right in broad terms, and then to provide specific exemptions for educational and other nonprofit uses.

This approach is more reasonable than the outright exemption of the 1909 statute. The line between commercial and "nonprofit" organizations is increasingly difficult to draw. Many "nonprofit' organizations are highly subsidized and capable of paying royalties and the widespread public exploitation of copyrighted works by educational broadcasters and other noncommercial organizations is likely to grow. In addition to these trends, it is worth noting that performances and displays are continuing to supplant markets for printed copies and that in the future a broad "not for profit" exemption could not only hurt authors but could dry up their incentive to write.

The exclusive right of public performance is expanded to include not only motion pictures but also audiovisual works such as filmstrips and sets of slides. This provision of section 106(4), which is consistent with the assimilation of motion pictures to audiovisual works throughout the bill, is also related to amendments of the definitions of "display" and "perform" discussed below. The important issue of performing rights in sound recordings is discussed in connection with section 114.

Right of public display. Clause (5) of section 106 represents the first explicit statutory recognition in American copyright law of an exclusive right to show a copyrighted work, or an image of it, to the public. The existence or extent of this right under the present statute is uncertain and subject to challenge. The bill would give the owners of copyright in "literary, musical, dramatic, and choreographic works, pantomimes, and pictorial, graphic, or sculptural works", including the individual images of a motion picture or other audiovisual work, the exclusive right "to display the copyrighted work publicly."

Definitions

Under the definitions of "perform," "display," "publicly," and "transmit" in section 101, the concepts of public performance and public display cover not only the initial rendition or showing, but also any further act by which that rendition or showing is transmitted or communicated to the public. Thus, for example: a singer is performing when he sings a song; a broadcasting network is performing when it transmits his performance (whether simultaneously or from records); a local broadcaster is performing when it transmits the network broadcast; a cable television system is performing when it retransmits the broadcast to its subscribers; and any individual is performing whenever he plays a phonorecord embodying the performance or communicates the performance by turning on a receiving set. Although any act by which the initial performance or display is transmitted, repeated, or made to recur would itself be a "performance" or "display" under the bill, it would not be actionable as an infringement unless it were done "publicly," as defined in section 101. Certain other performances and displays, in addition to those that are "private," are exempted or given qualified copyright control under sections 107 through 117.

To "perform" a work, under the definition in section 101, includes reading a literary work aloud, singing or playing music, dancing a ballet or other choreographic work, and acting out a dramatic work or pantomime. A performance may be accomplished "either directly or by means of any device or process," including all kinds of equipment for reproducing or amplifying sounds or visual images, any sort of transmitting apparatus, any type of electronic retrieval system, and any other techniques and systems not yet in use or even invented.

The definition of "perform" in relation to "a motion picture or other audio visual work" is "to show its images in any sequence or to make the sounds accompanying it audible." The showing of portions of a motion picture, filmstrip, or slide set must therefore be sequential to constitute a "performance" rather than a "display", but no particular order need be maintained. The purely aural performance of a motion picture sound track, or of the sound portions of an audiovisual work, would constitute a performance of the "motion picture or other audiovisual work"; but, where some of the sounds have been reproduced separately on phonorecords, a performance from the phonorecord would not constitute performance of the motion picture or audiovisual work.

The corresponding definition of "display," covers any showing of a "copy" of the work, "either directly or by means of a film, slide, television image, or any other device or process." Since "copies" are defined as including the material object "in which the work is first fixed," the right of public display applies to original works of art as well as to reproductions of them. With respect to motion pictures and other audiovisual works, it is a "display" (rather than a "performance") to show their "individual images nonsequentially." In addition to the direct showings of a copy of a work, "display" would include the projection of an image on a screen or other surface by any method, the transmission of an image by electronic or other means, and the showing of an image on a cathode ray tube, or similar viewing apparatus connected with any sort of information storage and retrieval system.

Under clause (1) of the definition of "publicly", a performance or display is "public" if it takes place "at a place open to the public or at any place where a substantial number of persons outside of a normal circle of a family and its social acquaintances is gathered." One of the principal purposes of the definition was to make clear that, contrary to the decision in *Metro-Goldwyn-Mayer Distributing Corp.* v. *Wyatt*, 21 C.O. Bull. 203 (D. Md. 1932), performances in "semipublic" places such as clubs, lodges, factories, summer camps, and schools are "public performances" subject to copyright control. The term "a family" in this context would include an individual living alone, so that a gathering confined to the individual's social acquaintances would normally be regarded as private. Routine meetings of business and governmental personnel would be excluded because they do not represent the gathering of a "substantial number of persons."

Clause (2) of the definition of "publicly" in section 101 makes clear that the concepts of public performance and public display include not only performances and displays that occur initially in a public place, but also acts that transmit or otherwise communicate a performance or display of the work to the public by means of any device or process. The definition of "transmit"—to communicate a performance or display "by any device or process whereby images or sound are received beyond the place from which they are sent"—is broad enough to include all conceivable forms and combinations of wired or wireless communications media, including but by no means limited to radio and television broadcasting as we know them. Each and every method by which the images or sounds comprising a performance or display are picked up and conveyed is a "transmission," and if the transmission reaches the public in any form, the case comes within the scope of clauses (4) or (5) of section 106.

Under the bill, as under the present law, a performance made available by transmission to the public at large is "public" even though the recipients are not gathered in a single place, and even if there is no direct proof that any of the potential recipients was operating his receiving apparatus at the time of the transmission. The same principles apply whenever the potential recipients of the transmission represent a limited segment of the public, such as the occupants of hotel rooms or the subscribers of a cable television service. Clause (2) of the definition of "publicly" is applicable "whether the members of the public capable of receiving the performance or display receive it in the same place or in separate places and at the same time or at different times."

SECTION 107. FAIR USE

General background of the problem

The judicial doctrine of fair use, one of the most important and well-established limitations on the exclusive right of copyright owners, would be given express statutory recognition for the first time in section 107. The claim that a defendant's acts constituted a fair use rather than an infringement has been raised as a defense in innumerable copyright actions over the years, and there is ample case law recognizing the existence of the doctrine and applying it. The examples enumerated at page 24 of the Register's 1961 Report, while by no means exhaustive, give some idea of the sort of activities the courts might regard as fair use under the circumstances: "quotation of excerpts in a review or criticism for purposes of illustration or comment; quotation of short passages in a scholarly or technical work, for illustration or clarification of the author's observations; use in a parody of some of the content of the work parodied; summary of an address or article, with brief quotations, in a news report; reproduction by a library of a portion of a work to replace part of a damaged copy; reproduction by a teacher or student of a small part of a work to illustrate a lesson; reproduction of a work in legislative or judicial proceedings or reports; incidental and fortuitous reproduction, in a newsreel or broadcast, of a work located at the scene of an event being reported."

Although the courts have considered and ruled upon the fair use doctrine over and over again, no real definition of the concept has ever emerged. Indeed, since the doctrine is an equitable rule of reason, no generally applicable definition is possible, and each case raising the question must be decided on its own facts. On the other hand, the courts have evolved a set of criteria which, though in no sense definitive or determinative, provide some gage for balancing the equities. These criteria have been stated in various ways, but essentially they can all be reduced to the four standards which were stated in the 1964 bill and have been adopted in section 107: "(1) the purpose and character of the use; (2) the nature of the copyrighted work; (3) the amount and substantiality of the portion used in relation to the copyrighted work as a whole; and (4) the effect of the use upon the potential market for or value of the copyrighted work."

The underlying intention of the bill with respect to the application of the fair use doctrine in various situations is discussed below. It should be emphasized again that, in those situations or any others, there is no purpose of either freezing or changing the doctrine. In particular, the reference to fair use "by reproduction in copies or phonorecords or by any other means" should not be interpreted as sanctioning any reproduction beyond the normal and reasonable limits of fair use. In making separate mention of "reproduction in copies or phonorecords" in the section, the provision is not intended to give this kind of use any special or preferred status as compared with other kinds of uses. In any event, whether a use referred to in the first sentence of section 107 is a fair use in a particular case will depend upon the application of the determinative factors, including those mentioned in the second sentence.

Intention behind the provision

In general.—The statement of the fair use doctrine in section 107 offers some guidance to users in determining when the principles of the doctrine apply. However, the endless variety of situations and combinations of circumstances that can rise in particular cases precludes the formulation of exact rules in the statute. The bill endorses the purpose and general scope of the judicial doctrine of fair use, as outlined earlier in this report, but there is no disposition to freeze the doctrine in the statute, especially during a period of rapid technological change. Beyond a very broad statutory explanation of what fair use is and some of the criteria applicable to it, the courts must be free to adapt the doctrine to particular situations on a case-by-case basis.

Section 107 is intended to restate the present judicial doctrine of fair use, not to change, narrow, or enlarge it in any way. However, since this section will represent the first statutory recognition of the doctrine in our copyright law, some explanation of the considerations behind the language used in the list of four criteria is advisable. This is particularly true as to cases of copying by teachers, and by public libraries, since in these areas there are few if any judicial guidelines.

The statements in this report with respect to each of the criteria of fair use are necessarily subject to qualifications, because they must be applied in combination with the circumstances pertaining to other criteria, and because new conditions arising in the future may alter the balance of equities. It is also important to emphasize that the singling out of some instances to discuss in the context of fair use is not intended to indicate that other activities would or would not be beyond fair use.

The purpose and nature of the use

Copyright recognized.—Section 107 makes it clear that, assuming the applicable criteria are met, fair use can extend to the reproduction of copyrighted material for purposes of classroom teaching.

Nonprofit element.—Although it is possible to imagine situations in which use by a teacher in an educational organization operated for profit (day camps, language schools, business schools, dance studios, et cetera) would constitute a fair use, the nonprofit character of the school in which the teacher works should be one factor to consider in determining fair use. Another factor would be whether any charge is made for the copies distributed.

Spontaneity.—The fair use doctrine in the case of classroom copying would apply primarily to the situation of a teacher who, acting individually and at his own volition, makes one or more copies for temporary use by himself or his pupils in the classroom. A different result is indicated where the copying was done by the educational institution, school system, or larger unit or where copying was required or suggested by the school administration, either in special instances or as part of a general plan.

Single and multiple copying.—Depending upon the nature of the work and other criteria, the fair use doctrine should differentiate between the amount of a work that can be reproduced by a teacher for his own classroom use (for example, for reading or projecting a copy or for playing a tape recording), and the amount that can be reproduced for distribution to pupils. In the case of multiple copies, other factors would be whether the number reproduced was limited to the size of the class, whether circulation beyond the classroom was permitted, and whether the copies were recalled or destroyed after temporary use.

Collections and anthologies.—Spontaneous copying of an isolated extract by a teacher, which may be a fair use under appropriate circumstances, could turn into an infringement if the copies were accumulated over a period of time with other parts of the same work, or were collected with other material from various works so as to constitute an anthology.

Special uses.—There are certain classroom uses which, because of their special nature, would not be considered an infringement in the ordinary case. For example, copying of extracts by pupils as exercises in a shorthand or typing class or for foreign language study, or recordings of performances by music students for purposes of analysis and criticism, would normally be regarded as a fair use unless the copies of phonorecords were retained or duplicated.

The nature of the copyrighted work

Character of the work.—The character and purpose of the work will have a lot to do with whether its reproduction for classroom purposes is fair use or infringement. For example, in determining whether a teacher could make one or more copies without permission, a news article from the daily press would be judged differently from a full orchestral score of a musical composition. In general terms it could be expected that the doctrine of fair use would be applied strictly to the classroom reproduction of entire works, such as musical compositions, dramas, and audiovisual works including motion pictures, which by their nature are intended for performance or public exhibition.

Similarly, where the copyrighted work is intended to be "consumable" in the course of classroom activities—workbooks, exercises, standardized tests, and answer sheets are examples—the privilege of fair use by teachers or pupils would have little if any application. Text books and other material prepared primarily for the school markets would be less susceptible to reproduction for classroom use than material prepared for general public distribution. With respect to material in newspapers and periodicals the doctrine of fair use should be liberally applied to allow copying of items of current interest to supplement and update the students' textbooks, but this would not extend to copying from periodicals published primarily for student use.

Availability of the work.—A key, though not necessarily determinative, factor in fair use is whether or not the work is available to the potential user. If the work is "out of print" and unavailable for purchase through normal channels, the user may have more justification for reproducing it than in the ordinary case, but the existence of organizations licensed to provide photocopies of out-of-print works at reasonable cost is a factor to be considered. The applicability of the fair use doctrine to unpublished works is narrowly limited since, although the work is unavailable, this is the result of a deliberate choice on the part of the copyright owner. Under ordinary circumstances the copyright owner's "right of first publication" would outweigh any needs of reproduction for classroom purposes.

The amount and substantiality of the material used

During the consideration of this legislation there has been considerable discussion of the difference between an "entire work" and an "excerpt". The educators have sought a limited right for a teacher to make a single copy of an "entire" work for classroom purposes, but it seems apparent that this was not generally intended to extend beyond a "separately cognizable" or "self-contained" portion (for example, a single poem, story, or article) in a collective work, and that no privilege is sought to reproduce an entire collective work (for example, an encyclopedia volume, a periodical issue) or a sizable integrated work published as an entity (a novel, treatise, monograph, and so forth). With this limitation, and subject to the other relevant criteria, the requested privilege of making a single copy appears appropriately to be within the scope of fair use.

The educators also sought statutory authority for the privilege of making "a reasonable number of copies or phonorecords for excerpts or quotations * * *, provided such excerpts or quotations are not substantial in length in proportion to their source." In general, and assuming the other necessary factors are present, the copying for classroom purposes of extracts or portions, which are not self-contained and which are relatively "not substantial in length" when compared to the larger, self-contained work from which they are taken, should be considered fair use. Depending on the circumstances, the same would also be true of very short self-contained works such as a brief poem, a map in a newspaper, a "vocabulary builder" from a monthly magazine, and so forth. This should not be construed as permitting a teacher to make multiple copies of the same work on a repetitive basis or for continued use.

Effect of use on potential market for or value of work

This factor must almost always be judged in conjunction with the other three criteria. With certain special exceptions (use in parodies or as evidence in court proceedings might be examples) a use that supplants any part of the normal market for a copyrighted work would ordinarily be considered an infringement. As in any other case, whether this would be the result of reproduction by a teacher for classroom purposes requires an evaluation of the nature and purpose of the use, the type of work involved, and the size and relative importance of the portion taken. Fair use is essentially supplementary by nature, and classroom copying that exceeds the legitimate teaching aims such as filling in missing information or bringing a subject up to date would go beyond the proper bounds of fair use. Isolated instances of minor infringements, when multiplied many times, become in the aggregate a major inroad on copyright that must be prevented.

Reproductions and uses for other purposes

The concentrated attention given the fair use provision in the context of classroom teaching activities should not obscure its application in other areas. It must be emphasized again that the same general standards of fair use are applicable to all kinds of uses of copyrighted material, although the relative weight to be given them will differ from case to case.

The fair use doctrine would be relevant to the use of excerpts from copyrighted works in educational broadcasting activities not exempted under sections 110(2) or 112. In these cases the factors to be weighed in applying the criteria of this section would include whether the performers, producers, directors, and others responsible for the broadcast were paid, the size and nature of the audience, the size and number of excerpts taken and, in the case of recordings made for broadcast, the number of copies reproduced and the extent of their reuse or exchange. The availability of the fair use doctrine to educational broadcasters would be narrowly circumscribed in the case of motion pictures and other audiovisual works, but under appropriate circumstances it could apply to the nonsequential showing of an individual still or slide, or to the performance of a short excerpt from a motion picture for criticism or comment.

The committee's attention has been directed to the special problems involved in the reception of instructional television programs in remote areas of the country. In certain areas it is currently impossible to transmit such programs by any means other than communications satellites. A particular difficulty exists when such transmissions extend over several time zones within the same state, such as in Alaska. Unless individual schools in such states may make an off-air recording of such transmissions, the programs may not be received by the students during the school's daily schedule. The committee believes that the making by a school located in such a remote area of an off-the-air recording of an instructional television transmission for the purpose of a delayed viewing of the program by students for the same school constitutes a "fair use". The committee does not intend to suggest however, that off-the-air recording for convenience would under any circumstances, be considered "fair use". To meet the requirement of temporary use the school may retain the recording for only a limited period of time after the broadcast.

Another special instance illustrating the application of the fair use doctrine pertains to the making of copies or phonorecords of works in the special forms needed for the use of blind persons. These special forms, such as copies in braille and phonorecords of oral readings (talking books), are not usually made by the publishers for commercial distribution. For the most part, such copies and phonorecords are made by the Library of Congress' Division for the Blind and Physically Handicapped with permission obtained from the copyright owners, and are circulated to blind persons through regional libraries covering the nation. In addition, such copies and phonorecords are made locally by individual volunteers for the use of blind persons in their communities, and the Library of Congress conducts a program for training such volunteers. While the making of multiple copies or phonorecords of a work for general circulation requires the permission of the copyright owner, the making of a single copy or phonorecord by an individual as a free service for a blind person would properly be considered a fair use under section 107.

A problem of particular urgency is that of preserving for posterity prints of motion pictures made before 1942. Aside from the deplorable fact that in a great many cases the only existing copy of a film has been deliberately destroyed, those that remain are in immediate danger of disintegration; they were printed on film stock with a nitrate base that will inevitably decompose in time. The efforts of the Library of Congress, the American Film Institute, and other organizations to rescue and preserve this irreplaceable contribution to our cultural life are to be applauded, and the making of duplicate copies for purposes of archival preservation certainly falls within the scope of "fair use."

When a copyrighted work contains unfair, inaccurate, or derogatory information concerning an individual or institution, such individual or institution may copy and reproduce such parts of the work as are necessary to permit understandable comment on the statements made in the work.

SECTION 108. REPRODUCTION BY LIBRARIES AND ARCHIVES

Notwithstanding the exclusive rights of the owners of copyright, section 108 provides that under certain conditions it is not an infringement of copyright for a library or archives, or any of their employees acting within the scope of their employment, to reproduce or distribute not more than one copy or phonorecord of a work provided (1) the reproduction or distribution is made without any purpose of direct or indirect commercial advantage and (2) the collections of the library or archives are open to the public or available not only to researchers affiliated with the library or archives, but also to other persons doing research in a specialized field, and (3) the reproduction or distribution of the work includes a notice of copyright.

The rights of reproduction and distribution under section 108 apply in the following circumstances:

Archival reproduction

Subsection (b) authorizes the reproduction and distribution of a copy or phonorecord of an unpublished work duplicated in facsimile form solely for purposes of preservation and security, or for deposit for research use in another library or archives, if the copy or phonorecord reproduced is currently in the collections of the first library or archives. Only unpublished works could be reproduced under this exemption, but the right would extend to any type of work, including photographs, motion pictures and sound recordings. Under this exemption, for example, a repository could make photocopies of manuscripts by microfilm or electrostatic process, but could not reproduce the work in "machine-readable" language for storage in an information system.

Replacement of damaged copy

Subsection (c) authorizes the reproduction of a published work duplicated in facsimile form solely for the purpose of replacement of a copy or phonorecord that is damaged, deteriorating, lost, or stolen, if the library or archives has, after a reasonable effort, determined that an unused replacement cannot be obtained at a fair price. The scope and nature of a reasonable investigation to determine that an unused replacement cannot be obtained will vary according to the circumstances of a particular situation. It will always require recourse to commonly-known trade sources in the United States, and in the normal situation also to the publisher or other copyright owner (if such owner can be located at the address listed in the copyright registration), or an authorized reproducing service.

Articles and small excerpts

Subsection (d) authorizes the reproduction and distribution of a copy of not more than one article or other contribution to a copyrighted collection of a periodical or copy or phonorecord of a small part of any other copyrighted work. The copy may be made by the library where the user makes his request or by another library pursuant to an inter-library loan. It is further required that the copy become the property of the user, that the library or archives have no notice that the copy would be used for any purposes other than private study, scholarship or research, and that the library or archives display prominently at the place where reproduction requests are accepted, and includes in its order form, a warning of copyright in accordance with requirements that the Register of Copyrights shall prescribe by regulation.

Out-of-print works

Subsection (e) authorizes the reproduction and distribution of a copy of a work, with certain exceptions, at the request of the user of the collection if the user has established that an unused copy cannot be obtained at a fair price. The copy may be made by the library where the user makes his request or by another library pursuant to an inter-library loan. The scope and nature of a reasonable investigation to determine that an unused copy cannot be obtained will vary according to the circumstances of a particular situation. It will always require recourse to commonly-known trade sources in the United States, and in the normal situation also to the publisher or other copyright owner (if the owner can be located at the address listed in the copyright registration), or an authorized reproducing service. It is further required that the copy become the property of the user, that the library or archives have no notice that the copy would be used for any purpose other than private study, scholarship, or research, and that the library or archives display prominently at the place where reproduction requests are accepted, and include on its order form, a warning of copyright in accordance with requirements that the Register of Copyrights shall prescribe by regulation.

General Exemptions

Clause (1) of subsection (f) specifically exempts a library or archives or their employees from such liability provided that the reproducing equipment displays a notice that the making of a copy may be subject to the copyright law. Clause (2) of subsection (f) makes clear that this exemption of the library or archives does not extend to the person using such equipment or requesting such copy if the use exceeds fair use. Insofar as such person is concerned the copy made is not considered "lawfully" made for purposes of sections 109, 110 or other provisions of the title. Clause (3) in addition to asserting that nothing contained in section 108 "affects the right of fair use as provided by section 107", also provides that the right of reproduction granted by this section does not override any contractual arrangements assumed by a library or archives when it obtained a work for its collections. For example, if there is an express contractual prohibition against reproduction for any purpose, this legislation shall not be construed as justifying a violation of the contract. This clause is intended to encompass the situation where an individual makes papers, manuscripts or other works available to a library with the understanding that they will not be reproduced.

It is the intent of this legislation that a subsequent unlawful use by a user of a copy of a work lawfully made by a library, shall not make the library liable for such improper use.

Multiple Copies and Systematic Reproduction

Subsection (g) provides that the rights granted by this section extend only to the "isolated and unrelated reproduction of a single copy", but this section does not authorize the related or concerted reproduction of multiple copies of the same material whether made on one occasion or over a period of time, and whether intended for aggregate use by one individual or for separate use by the individual members of a group. For example, if a college professor instructs his class to read an article from a copyrighted journal, the school library would not be permitted, under subsection (g), to reproduce copies of the article for the members of the class.

Subsection (g) also provides that section 108 does not authorize the systematic reproduction or distribution of copies or phonorecords of articles or other contributions to copyrighted collections or periodicals or of small parts of other copyrighted works whether or not multiple copies are reproduced or distributed. Systematic reproduction or distribution occurs when a library makes copies of such materials available to other libraries or to groups of users under formal or informal arrangements whose purpose or effect is to have the reproducing library serve as their source of such material. Such systematic reproduction and distribution, as distinguished from isolated and unrelated reproduction or distribution, may substitute the copies reproduced by the source library for subscriptions or reprints or other copies which the receiving libraries or users might otherwise have purchased for themselves, from the publisher or the licensed reproducing agencies.

While it is not possible to formulate specific definitions of "systematic copying", the following examples serve to illustrate some of the copying prohibited by subsection (g).

(1) A library with a collection of journals in biology informs other libraries with similar collections that it will maintain and build its own collection and will make copies of articles from these journals available to them and their patrons on request. Accordingly, the other libraries discontinue or refrain from purchasing subscriptions to these journals and fulfill their patrons' requests for articles by obtaining photocopies from the source library.

(2) A research center employing a number of scientists and technicians subscribes to one or two copies of needed periodicals. By reproducing photocopies of articles the center is able to make the material in these periodicals available to its staff in the same manner which otherwise would have required multiple subscriptions.

(3) Several branches of a library system agree that one branch will subscribe to particular journals in lieu of each branch purchasing its own subscriptions, and that the one subscribing branch will reproduce copies of articles from the publication for users of the other branches.

The committee believes that section 108 provides an appropriate statutory balancing of the rights of creators, and the needs of users. However, neither a statute nor legislative history can specify precisely which library photocopying practices constitute the making of "single copies" as distinguished from "systematic reproduction". Isolated single spontaneous requests must be distinguished from "systematic reproduction". The photocopying needs of such operations as multi-county regional systems, must be met. The committee therefore recommends that representatives of authors, book, and periodical publishers and other owners of copyrighted material meet with the library community to formulate photocopying guidelines to assist library patrons and employees. Concerning library photocopying practices not authorized by this legislation, the committee recommends that workable clearance and licensing procedures be developed.

In adopting these provisions on library photocopying, the committee is aware that through such programs as those of the National Commission on Libraries and Information Science there will be a significant evolution in the functioning and services of libraries. To consider the possible need for changes in copyright law and procedures as a result of new technology, title II of this legislation establishes a National Commission on New Techonlogical Uses of Copyrighted Works. It is the desire of the committee that the Commission give priority to those aspects of the library-copyright interface which require further study and clarification.

Works excluded

Subsection (h) provides that the rights of reproduction and distribution under this section do not apply to a musical work, a pictorial, graphic or sculptural work, or a motion picture or other audio-visual work. Such limitation does not apply to archival reproduction and replacement of a damaged copy.

ANNUAL REPORT

OF THE LIBRARIAN OF CONGRESS

for the Fiscal Year Ending June 30, 1974

GENERAL REVISION OF THE COPYRIGHT LAW

Just after the fiscal year ended, the bill for general revision of the copyright law passed the 10th anniversary of its original introduction on July 20, 1964. There are some oldtimers in and out of the Copyright Office who remember that the current revision program actually goes back 20 fiscal years, to a special congressional appropriation launching the program in 1955. As fiscal 1974 began there was little optimism about the prospects for prompt enactment of general revision; after passage by the House and active consideration by a Senate Judiciary Subcommittee in 1967, the bill was sidetracked and lost most of its momentum.

As events proved, however, there was still some steam in the boiler; Senator John L. McClellan introduced the basic 1973 version of the bill (S. 1361), and identical versions were introduced in the House by Representatives Bertram L. Podell (H.R. 8186), and Joseph J. Maraziti and Jerome R. Waldie (H.R. 14922 and 15522). The McClellan bill was different in some important respects from both the original 1964 version and the version that passed the House in 1967 but, considering the rapidly changing face of communications technology over the past decade, it was surprising how much of the language survived without change. Some provisions of the McClellan bill were extremely controversial, and it was reasonable to wonder whether the legislative package could continue to hold together much longer.

Hearings on what then seemed to be the most controversial provisions in the bill were held before the Senate Judiciary Committee on July 31 and August 1, 1973. Testimony was limited to five issues: library photocopying, a proposal for a general educational exemption, the cable television royalty schedule, a proposed exemption for recording religious music for authorized broadcasts, and the carriage of sporting events by cable television. Although acknowledged to be

useful, the 1973 hearings did little to make proponents of general revision any more optimistic about the chances of early enactment.

A good many observers had been claiming that the main, if not the only, reason why the general revision bill made little progress for seven years was the controversy over the copyright liability of cable television systems. The assumption was that once the Supreme Court decided the question definitively, the impasse would be broken. Events in the last half of fiscal 1974 tended to bear out this theory; shortly after the Supreme Court's decision in *Teleprompter* v. *Columbia Broadcasting System, Inc.*, 415 U.S. 394 (1974), the Senate Judiciary Subcommittee resumed active consideration of the bill and on April 9, 1974, reported S. 1361, with some amendments, to the full Senate Judiciary Committee. On June 11, 1974, the full committee marked up the bill and ordered it reported with further amendments, which was done just after the close of the fiscal year, on July 3, 1974 (H.R. Rep. No. 93-983). It was passed by the Senate on September 9, 1974, with still further amendments, by a vote of 70 to 1. The 1974 amendments are almost entirely concerned with the scope of certain rights, notably those involving cable television and performances of sound recordings.

THE COPYRIGHT OFFICE

This flurry of activity, and the startling proportions of the final Senate vote, nudged a number of copyright veterans out of their apathy. Plenty of controversy remained, and it was apparent that the bill could not be enacted in any form before the 94th Congress (1975-76), since there was insufficient time for House action in the second session of the 93d. Nevertheless, it is clear that the program for general revision of the copyright law has regained a substantial amount of legislative momentum and that, unless something new comes along to derail it, the chances for enactment before the end of 1976 are fairly good.

Copyright Law Revision
Hearings before the Subcommittee on Courts, Civil Liberties, and the Administration of Justice

STATEMENT OF BARBARA RINGER, REGISTER OF COPYRIGHTS

Mr. Chairman, I am Barbara Ringer, Register of Copyrights in the Copyright Office of the Library of Congress. I appear today in support of H.R. 2223, to review its long and difficult legislative history, and to try to answer any questions you have about its contents, its status, and the issues remaining to be settled.

The Federal copyright law now in effect in the United States was adopted in 1909 and has been amended in only a few relatively minor ways. It is essentially a Nineteenth Century copyright law, based on assumptions concerning the creation and dissemination of author's works that have been completely overturned in the past fifty years. A Twentieth-Century copyright statute is long overdue in the United States, and the present need for a revised law that will anticipate the Twenty-First Century is so obvious as to be undeniable.

It is startling to realize that the program for general revision of the copyright law actually got underway more than 50 years ago, in 1924, and produced four distinct legislative efforts before World War II: The Dallinger, Perkins, and Vestal Bills in 1924–1931, the Sirovich Bill in 1932, the Duffy Bill in 1934–1936, and the "Shotwell" Bill in 1939. One of these measures passed the House, and a later one passed the Senate, but in every case the revision program ultimately failed of enactment because of fierce opposition to particular provisions by certain groups. The history of U.S. copyright law revision in the 1920's and 1930's teaches a basic lesson: the need to work out accommodations on the critical issues in an atmosphere of good will and give and take. It is a great deal easier to recognize the validity of this proposition than to put it into practice.

The failure of the earlier efforts at general revision of the copyright law has been blamed on one group or another, and on the face of it there does appear to be quite a bit of blame to go around. At the same time it is important not to forget that the main purpose behind some of the revision bills was to permit U.S. adherence to the International Convention of Berne. There can be little doubt that some of the Congressional opposition to copyright law revision stemmed from basic objections to U.S. acceptance of foreign principles of copyright jurisprudence and to U.S. assumption of the international obligations involved in becoming a member of the Berne Union.

After World War II the proponents of copyright law reform adopted a new approach. It was assumed, on the basis of past experience, that efforts to revise the copyright law in a way that would permit adherence to the Berne Convention would continue to be futile. It was also recognized that the emergence of the United States as a major exporter of cultural materials made our adherence to a multilateral convention essential. Thus, efforts to secure general revision of the copyright law were temporarily deferred in favor of a major program aimed at developing and implementing a new international copyright convention to which the United States could adhere without major changes in our law. These efforts, under the leadership of Register of Copyrights, Arthur Fisher, achieved success in 1952 with the signing at Geneva of the Universal Copyright Convention, followed in 1954 by the enactment of revisions to the 1909 statute permitting U.S.

adherence to the UCC, and by the coming into force of the Convention in 1955.

Noteworthy as it was, the achievement of bringing the United States into the international copyright community also served to dramatize once more how archaic and inadequate the U.S. copyright statute of 1909 had become. The autumn of 1955, which saw the coming into force of the Universal Copyright Convention and the inauguration of the current program for general revision of the copyright law, marked the end of one epoch and the beginning of another. In August 1955, Congress authorized the formation of a Panel of Consultants on General Revision of the Copyright Law under the chairmanship of the Register of Copyrights, and the Copyright Office undertook a series of basic studies of the major substantive issues involved in revision. At the same time began what has become a seemingly endless series of meetings and discussions with representatives of virtually every interest group affected by the copyright law. By now these discussions, which have been as valuable as they have been time-consuming, must literally run into the thousands.

The study phase of the current revision program began almost exactly 20 years ago, in 1955. It was supposed to take three years, but it took about six. It produced 35 studies covering most of what we thought at the time were the substantive issues in copyright revision. These were published, together with a large body of comments from the Panel of Consultants, and I am proud to say that they are all still in print.

The culmination of this effort was the publication, in 1961, of the 1961 Report of the Register of Copyrights on General Revision of the Copyright Law. The Register's Report was the first of many major contributions to the general revision program by Abraham L. Kaminstein, Mr. Fisher's successor as Register of Copyrights. The purpose of the Reports, as Mr. Kaminstein said in his 1962 Annual Report, "was to furnish a tangible core around which opinions and conclusions could crystalize—to achieve the widest possible agreement on basic principles before proceeding to draft a revised copyright law." The Report attempted to pinpoint the major issues in revision, summarize the present law with respect to each of them, analyze alternative solutions, and present specific recommendations.

The Register's Report succeeded very well in clarifying the issues and in focusing the discussions on them, but some of its most fundamental recommendations proved more controversial than anyone in the Copyright Office had expected. In particular, the Register's proposal for copyright to begin with "public dissemination" and to last for a first term of 28 years, renewable for a second term of 48 years, provoked a flood of opposition; there was strong support for a single Federal copyright system with protection commencing upon the creation of a work and ending 50 years after the author's death. A series of meetings of the Panel of Consultants on General Revision was held between September 1961, and March 1962, at which all of the Report's recommendations were discussed in an increasingly tense atmosphere. The heated arguments at these and other meetings actually stalled the revision program for several months and brought it to a genuine crisis in the later summer and fall of 1962. It became apparent that, if the entire project was not to flounder, some method for advancing and considering alternative recommendations would have to be found.

In November 1962, the Register announced that the Copyright Office was prepared to change its position on some debatable questions and to draft alternative language on others. He indicated that the Office was prepared to revise its recommendations concerning "public dissemination" and the retention of common law protection, and that "at least one alternative version of our draft bill will adopt the life-plus basis for computing the term—in conjunction with a system of notice, deposit, and registration that we consider essential." The Register also announced that he would send preliminary drafts of statutory language to the members of an expanded Panel of Consultants on General Revision for their comments, and that he would convene another series of meetings on the preliminary draft. The process of preparing draft language for circulation occupied practically all of 1963, and included a total of eight meetings of the Panel of Consultants.

The development of this preliminary draft proved to be a difficult but enormously productive phase of the program. The procedure adopted provided a motive and a forum for detailing, critical scrutiny of the language and substance of a new copyright statute by representatives of nearly all of the groups affected. It also created an atmosphere of cooperative effort that has survived various stresses and strains and has continued to grow in breadth and depth.

The preliminary draft of the general revision bill that had reached completion at the beginning of 1964 was never intended to be a final report. The next six months were devoted to compiling, analyzing, and synthesizing all of the comments received on the draft, to making substantive decisions and changes on the basis of these comments, and to preparing a complete, section-by-section revision of the bill. The draft of the bill that emerged from this process was prepared entirely within the Copyright Office without collaboration or consultation with any private groups or individuals. The introduction of the 1964 draft in July 1964 marked the end of the drafting phase of the revision program and the opening of the legislative phase.

Like the preliminary draft on which it was based, the 1964 bill was not intended as a finished product, but as a focal point for further comments and suggestions. In August 1964, a full week of detailed discussions of the bill showed that a great deal of progress had been made, but that still further revisions would be necessary before legislative hearings could profitably begin. During the fall and winter of 1964–1965 the Copyright Office reviewed and analyzed the many oral and written comments on the bill and prepared another complete revision.

At the beginning of the 89th Congress, on February 4, 1965, Representative Celler introduced the 1965 general revision bill and the Copyright Office spent the next three months preparing a supplement to the 1961 Register's Report. The Supplementary Report of the Register of Copyrights on the General Revision of the U.S. Copyright Law: 1965 Revision Bill which was published in May 1965, set forth the reasons for changing a number of recommendations in the 1961 report and clarified the meaning of the provisions of the 1965 bill.

Publication of the Supplementary Report coincided with the opening of Congressional hearings on the bill. Over a period of more than three months, between May 26, 1965 and September 2, 1965, 22 days of public hearings were held before your subcommittee, under the objective and dedicated chairmanship of the man who is still your chairman, Robert W. Kastenmeier. A total of 163 witnesses, representing an extraordinarily wide range of public and private interests, appeared to testify. The record of those 1965 hearings comprises nearly 2,000 pages of printed text, including not only the oral transcript but also more than 150 written statements. The Senate Judiciary Subcommittee under the chairmanship of Senator John McClellan of Arkansas, held brief hearings on the revision bill in August 1965, but delayed a full series pending the conclusion of the intense activity in the House subcommittee.

Several significant factors with respect to the general revision program emerged from the 1965 hearings. Most obvious were the sharp controversies remaining to be settled on some old issues (such as the jukebox exemption, the royalty rate to be paid under the compulsory license for recording music, and the manufacturing requirements with respect to English-language books and periodicals), and on some relatively new issues (such as fair use, and the reproduction of copyrighted works for educational and research purposes, the liability of educational broadcasters and similar transmitters, and the status of community antenna television systems under the copyright law).

Aside from the need to work out further accommodations on several critical issues, the most serious problem arising from the 1965 hearings was now to organize the massive contents of the record in a way that would overlook no significant comment or suggestion but that still would form a comprehensive basis for decision-making. Working in close collaboration, the Copyright Office and the House Judiciary Committee counsel prepared summaries of every statement that had been made, and then divided the entire corpus of the hearings into ten general areas: subject matter of copyright, ownership, duration, notice and registration, manufacturing and importation requirements, community antenna systems and other secondary transmissions, jukebox performances, compulsory license for phonorecords, educational copying and fair use, and educational broadcasting and other performing rights. Each subject was then divided into subtopics, under which were listed every issue raised at the hearings.

This "experiment in legislative technique," as it has been called, proved effective. It enabled the House Judiciary Subcommittee, in its deliberations of the bill, to consider each issue in context, to weigh the arguments for and against it, and to arrive at reasoned decisions. Meeting regularly, usually twice a week, from February through September 1966, the subcommittee held 51 executive sessions, all of which were attended by representatives of the Copyright Office.

Examining each issue in depth and then redrafting the pertinent section of the bill as they went along, the subcommittee produced an entirely revised bill in an atmosphere of informal, bipartisan discussions that could well serve as a model for similar legislative projects.

The bill, as revised by the subcommittee, was reported unanimously to the full House Judiciary Committee on September 21, 1966, and was reported without amendment by the full Judiciary Committee on October 12, 1966. The House Report still remains the basic legislative explanation of the content of the bill, and the reports succeeding it in both Houses have all been drawn from it.

The bill was reported too late in the 89th Congress for further legislative action, and indeed none had been expected in 1966. In the revised form reported by the House, it was introduced by Representative Celler in the 90th Congress, and was considered by the newly-constituted membership of Subcommittee 3, again chaired by Representative Kastenmeier on February 20, 24 and 27, 1967. It was reported to the full Committee on the last of these dates and, after rather heated debates in the full committee on February 28 and March 2, 1967, was again reported to the House. This time, however, the report included minority views by Representatives Byron G. Rogers of Colorado and Basil L. Whitener of North Carolina, devoted to the jukebox issue, and additional dissent by Mr. Whitener on the bill's treatment of CATV.

It was becoming increasingly apparent, as the bill moved toward the House floor, that extremely sharp and unreconciled conflicts on the issues of jukebox performance and CATV transmissions remained, and that there was a serious danger that one or both of these issues could defeat the bill. The bill was considered by the House Rules Committee on March 8, 1967, and the rather acrimonious arguments in the Committee before it took action authorizing full debate on the House floor were another danger signal.

The debates of the bill in the House of Representatives on April 6, 1967, were difficult and protracted. When the House finally recessed after 7:00 p.m., it was apparent that a rescue operation was essential. Over the next four days, in an atmosphere of intense crisis, several crucial compromises were achieved, and on Tuesday, April 11, an amended bill was passed by the House after mild debate with the extraordinary vote of 379 yeas to 29 nays. Fairly radical changes were made in three areas: there were drastic revisions in the provisions establishing copyright liability for jukebox performances; the provisions dealing with community antenna transmission were dropped entirely and the exemptions for instructional broadcasting were considerably broadened. On the other hand, the structure and content of the bill itself has remained substantially intact.

The Senate Judiciary Committee, which had opened hearings in 1965 and had had a short series of hearings on the CATV problem in 1966, resumed full-scale consideration of the bill, under the joint chairmanship of Senators McClellan and Burdick, on March 15, 1967. Indeed, the Senate hearings were in full swing during the crisis in the House, and for a time the general revision program resembled a two-ring circus in more ways than one. To everyone's surprise the record of the Senate hearings, which lasted 10 days and ended on April 28, 1967, very nearly equals that of the House hearings in size and content.

Of the several areas that emerged as fullblown issues at the Senate hearings, by far the most important is the problem of the use of copyrighted works in automated information storage and retrieval systems. This problem was addressed separately in the context of the creation of a National Commission on New Technological Uses which Congress enacted as separate legislation only last year, and which is still awaiting staffing.

Meanwhile, as the 1967 legislative momentum began to slow more and more, it was increasingly apparent that cable television had become the make-or-break issue for copyright revision. Although the Senate Judiciary Subcommittee worked long and hard between 1968 and 1970 to resolve controversies over a number of issues other than cable, and succeeded in reporting the revised bill to the full Senate Judiciary Committee during the 91st Congress, it was not able to push revision any further. An effort spearheaded by the Copyright Office to gain enactment of a "barebones" bill, containing everything except the cable section and other controversial provisions dealing with economic rights, also failed. By 1971 it was apparent that the bill was completely stymied over the CATV issue, and even the issuance of comprehensive FCC rules in 1972, governing the carriage of signals and programming by cable systems, failed to break the impasse.

Because of this long delay, Congress has passed a series of successive bills extending the term of copyright. These now run through the end of the current Congress, and are scheduled to expire on December 31, 1976. The urgent problem of tape piracy was also taken care of through separate legislation. A total of seven years passed between House passage of the bill in 1967 and the resumption of its active consideration in the Senate Subcommittee last year.

There may have been other reasons, but certainly the most immediate cause of the revision bill's new momentum was the Supreme Court decision in *CBS* v. *Teleprompter*, holding that under the 1909 statute cable systems are not liable for copyright infringement when they import distant signals. The decision was followed quickly by favorable actions in the Senate Judiciary Subcommittee and full Committee and, after a brief referral to the Commerce Committee, by passage in the Senate on September 9, 1975, by a vote of 70–1. In late November your Subcommittee held a hearing which, in one respect was a forerunner of these hearings. I testified in an optimistic vein at that time, and I remain hopeful that at long last the entire revision measure will be enacted into law during the current Congress.

STATEMENT OF DR. ROBERT W. CAIRNS, EXECUTIVE DIRECTOR, AMERICAN CHEMICAL SOCIETY

Mr. Chairman and members of the Subcommittee: My name is Robert W. Cairns. I am the Executive Director of the American Chemical Society and, with the authorization of its Board of Directors, I appear before you today to present the Society's statement. I have spent 37 years in industry and retired as Vice President of Hercules Incorporated on July 1, 1971, to accept the position of Deputy Assistant Secretary of Commerce for Science and Technology. I resigned from that position on December 1, 1972, on acceptance of my present appointment. Accompanying me today are Dr. Richard L. Kenyon, Director of the Public, Professional and International Communication Division, Dr. Stephen T. Quigley, Director of the Department of Chemistry and Public Affairs, and Mr. William B. Butler, representing Mr. Arthur B. Hanson, General Counsel of the Society.

We appreciate being given this opportunity to comment on certain features of the Copyright Revision Bill, H.R. 2223. The issues addressed by this legislation are both fundamental to the formulation of national science policy, and of vital significance with respect to the ability of our Society to resolve many of the problems which confront it. These issues have been under discussion for some time now by the Committee on Copyrights of the Board of Directors and Council of the American Chemical Society, as well as by other similar scientific societies, and a general consensus on them has been under development. This consensus has been developed in the context that the protection of copyrighted material will "promote the Progress of Science and Useful Arts", as specified in Article I, Section 8, Clause 8 of the Constitution of the United States. The viewpoint which we attempt to express is that of the chemical, scientific and technological community, as represented by the American Chemical Society.

The American Chemical Society is incorporated by the Federal Congress as a non-profit, membership, scientific, educational society composed of chemists and chemical engineers, and is exempt from the payment of Federal income taxes under section 501(c)(3) of the Internal Revenue Code of 1954, as amended.

The American Chemical Society consists of more than 107,000 such above described members. Its Federal Charter was granted by an Act of the Congress in Public Law 358, 75th Congress, 1st Session, Chapter 762, H.R. 7709, signed into law by President Franklin D. Roosevelt on August 25, 1937, to become effective from the first day of January, 1938.

Section 2 of the Act is as follows:

"Sec. 2. That the objects of the incorporation shall be to encourage in the broadest and most liberal manner the advancement of chemistry in all its branches; the promotion of research in chemical science and industry; the improvement of the qualifications and usefulness of chemists through high standards of professional ethics, education, and attainments; the increase and diffusion of chemical knowledge; and by its meetings, professional contacts, reports, papers, discussions, and publications, to promote scientific interests and inquiry, thereby fostering public welfare and education, aiding the development of our country's industries, and adding to the material prosperity and happiness of our people."

Its Federal incorporation replaced a New York State Charter, which had been effective since November 9, 1877.

One of the principal objects of the Society, as set forth in its Charter, is the dissemination of chemical knowledge through its publications program. The budget for the Society for the year 1975 exceeds $39,000,000 of which more than $30,000,000 is devoted to its publications program.

The Society's publication program now includes three magazines and seventeen journals, largely scholarly journals that contain reports of original research from such fields as medicinal chemistry, biochemistry, and agricultural and food chemistry, as well as a weekly newsmagazine designed to keep chemists and chemical engineers abreast of the latest developments affecting their science and related industries. In addition, the Society is the publisher of Chemical Abstracts, one of the world's most comprehensive abstracting and indexing services. The funds to support these publications are derived chiefly from subscriptions.

The journals and other published writings of the Society serve a very important function, namely: they accomplish the increase and diffusion of chemical knowledge from basic science to applied technology. In so doing, they must generate revenue, without which the Society could not support and continue its publications program in furtherance of its Congressional Charter to serve the science and technology of chemistry. The protection of copyright has proved an essential factor in the growth and development of the scientific-publishing program of the Society.

The twenty periodical publications of the Society produce more than 40,000 pages a year and subscriptions in 1974 totalled 323,000. Chemical Abstracts annually produces more than 140,000 pages which go to 5,500 subscribers. Its

abstracts number in excess of 361,000 yearly and its documents indexed in excess of 425,000. The single greatest source of income for all ACS publications is subscription revenue.

As is indicated by the objectives of the American Chemical Society, we believe that the effective dissemination of scientific and technical information is critical to the development, not only of the society and economy of the U.S.A., but also of modern society worldwide.

These journals provide the knowledge base for technical development of answers to urgent problems facing the United States and the rest of the world, such as the energy crisis, the world food problem, the delivery of adequate health services, and pollution abatement. It is critically important that this system for organizing, evaluating, and providing scientific information remain healthy.

Scholarly journals are the major instruments for dissemination and recording of scientific and technical information. These journals are expensive to produce. If the costs are not supported financially by those who make use of them they cannot continue. There is no adequate substitute in sight.

The scholarly scientific or technical journal is more than merely a repository of information. The scientific paper is the block with which is built our understanding of the workings of the world around us. In his papers, each scientist records his important findings for the permanent record. His successors then have that knowledge precisely recorded and readily available as a base from which they may start. So the process continues in a step-by-step fashion from scientific generation to scientific generation, each worker having available to him or her the totality of the knowledge developed up to that time. Each scientist stands upon the shoulders of his predecessors.

But this analogy of simple physical structure is inadequate, for at least of equal importance is the continuous refinement that takes place. Before new knowledge is added to the record, it is reviewed, criticized and edited by authoritative scholars; then, once published, it is available in the record for continued use, criticism, and refinement. New findings make possible the revelation of weaknesses in the earlier arguments and conclusions, so that as the structure of scientific knowledge is built higher it is also made stronger by the elimination of flaws. While it has been said that mankind is doomed to repeat its mistakes, the system of scientific recording in journals is designed to prevent the repetition of such mistakes and to avoid building upon erroneous conclusions. The scholarly journal record is the instrument for insuring this refining process.

In addition, journal papers form an important part of the basis upon which a scientist's standing among his peers is judged. For this reason, scientific scholars are willing to give their time and effort to help produce these evaluated records and are also willing to leave the management of the copyright on their papers in the hands of the scientific societies. These scholars are rarely concerned with private income from their published papers, but they are vitally concerned with the preservation of the intrinsic value of the scientific publishing system.

Publishing costs have risen and are rising continuously, making the continuation of the scientific-journal system increasingly difficult. This has been recognized by the U.S. Government in acknowledging the philosophy that scientific-research work is not complete until its results are published, and in establishing a policy which makes it proper that money may be used from federal support of research projects to help to pay the cost of journal publication. It is this policy which provides most of the funds for paying page charges, charges originally designed to pay the cost of bringing the research journal through the editing, composition, and other production steps, up to the point of being ready to print. However, publishing costs are now so high that these page charges no longer pay even for these initial parts of the publishing process. American Chemical Society records in 1974 show that page charges supported one-third or more of those costs for fewer than 30% of ACS journals.

Publishing costs *must* be shared by the users. If these users are allowed, without payment to the journal, to make or to receive from others copies of the journal papers they may wish to read, it is not likely they will be willing to pay for subscriptions to these journals. If and as free photocopying of journals proceeds, the number of subscribers will shrink, and subscription prices will have to rise. The reduction of subscription income may continue to the point of financial destruction of these journals.

The problems of the commercial publishers of many good scientific journals are even more severe, because these publishers do not have the moderate assistance of page charges.

The doctrine of fair use, developed judicially but not legislatively, has long been useful to the scholar, for it has allowed him to make excerpts to a limited extent for purposes of the files used in his research. However, the modern technology of reprography has offered such mechanical efficiency and capacity for copying that it is presently endangering the protection given the foundations of the scholarly journal by copyright. "Excerpts," instead of being notes, sentences, or paragraphs, are being interpreted to mean full scientific papers, the aforementioned building blocks.

As the copyrighted journal system developed, it was agreed long ago that the scholar should be allowed to hand-copy excerpts for use as background information. As a further step, authors became accustomed to ordering the reprints of their papers to send to their colleagues as a means of assuring a good record of the progress of work in the field concerned. This was followed, 20-30 years ago, by some minor use of the old "Photostat" machine. While that process strained a little the proprieties of copyright, it was fairly generally agreed that the mechanics of the practice were such as to help the research scientist while difficult and costly enough not to undermine the basic structure of the journal system.

We hold no objection to a scholar himself occasionally making a single copy in a non-systematic fashion for use in his own research. However, in the past decade the techniques of reprography have advanced to such an extent that third parties, human and mechanical, are beginning to be involved in a substantial way. It now is practical to build what amounts to a private library through rapid copying of virtually anything the scholar thinks he might like to have at hand. While this process has obviously personal advantages, it is now being done extensively and increasingly, without any contribution from these scholars—or the libraries which copy for them—to the cost of developing and maintaining the basic information system that makes it possible. Even conservative projections of the development of reprographic techniques within the next decade make it clear that the economic self-destruction of the system within the next decade is a real possibility. Overly permissive legislation could make this destruction a certainty.

Use of a journal by an individual for extracting from it with his own hands, by hand-copying the material specifically needed and directly applicable to his research, is one thing. A practice in which an agent, human or mechanical, acts as copier for an individual or group of individuals wishing to have readily available, without cost, copies of extensive material more or less directly related to his or their studies and research, is quite a different matter. The latter is certainly beyond justification on the mere grounds that technology has made it convenient, or that the purposes are socially beneficial.

Documented evidence of the increase in photocopying is found in "A Study of the Characteristics, Costs, and Magnitude of Inter Library Loans in Academic Libraries," published in 1972 by the Association of Research Libraries. There we find that in 1969–70 the material from periodicals sent out in response to requests for "interlibrary loans" filled by the academic libraries surveyed was 83.2 percent in photocopy form as compared with 15.2 percent in original form and 1.4 percent in microform.

In that same report the volume of interlibrary loan activities from academic libraries is traced. It grew from 859,000 requests received by academic lending libraries in 1965–66 to 1,754,000 in 1969–70, and is projected to reach 2,646,000 in 1974–75.

Much thinking and study are being devoted to systems for improving access to periodicals resources through networks. These networks would make the scientific information available widely and rapidly from a relatively small number of original journal copies. In "Access to Periodical Resources: A National Plan", by Vernon E. Palmour, Marcia C. Bellassai, and Lucy M. Gray, a report prepared at the request of the Association of Research Libraries, it is stated that a number of advantages accrue to the provision of photocopies instead of originals. "Supply of photocopies," the report states, "is more essentially a 'mail order' or merchandising rather than a lending operations." It is also noted that "A single copy, or in some cases a few copies, at a center can meet, without undue delay, the needs of a large number of users."

In viewing the possible growth of service by a National Periodical Resources Center, the authors estimated that from a collection of ten thousand titles, the demand would grow starting in the range of 58,000 to 75,000 in the first year to a range of 2,281,000 to 5,462,000 in the tenth year, with 90 percent of the request being filled by photocopies.

Such estimates as these show expectations of a great growth in use of photocopied material. Obviously the direct uses of the printed journal would be very small.

These data give some indication of the trends in use made of the published literature without contribution of any share of the very considerable cost of evaluating, organizing, and publishing it.

In another report, "Methods of Financing Interlibrary Loan Services," by Vernon E. Palmour, Edwin E. Olson, and Nancy K. Roderer, a fee system is suggested as a practical possibility with the fee initially set at $3.50, about half the full cost recovery, and gradually increasing toward providing the full cost. No consideration is given in this suggestion to payment of a fee to the publishers from whose periodicals the copies are made. An adequate additional fee, paid into a clearinghouse and distributed to the appropriate publishers, could spread the full cost of support of a journals system equitably over the users.

It is desirable that use be made of modern technology in developing optimum dissemination. This technology includes the use of modern reprography, but as technology inherently includes economies the means of financial support of the system must be a part of its design. Therefore, photocopying systems must include an adequate means of control and payment to compensate publishers for their basic editorial and composition costs. Otherwise, "fair use" or library-photocopying loopholes, or any other exemptions from the copyright control for either profit or non-profit use, will ultimately destroy the viability of scientific and technical publications or other elements of information dissemination systems.

The copyright law is directed to the interest of the public welfare. It is not in the interest of the public welfare to modify the copyright laws so as to allow the economic destruction of the scientific and technical information system.

The American Chemical Society is properly concerned with the clarity and vitality of the copyright laws of the United States and of the world. These laws have provided a sound basis for the continuity of scientific communication programs, including at present the primary and secondary journals, microforms, and computerized information systems.

The Society recognizes that its members and others concerned with its publications are both "authors" and "users" of information, and that it is the Society's objective to serve their needs as fully as possible. It recognizes the functions and problems of such vital information channels as libraries, information centers, and information systems and networks. It further recognizes the challenges offered by technological advances in communication techniques.

However, scientific communication programs cannot continue without proper funding, and in the immediate future this funding must continue to come from "authors" and "users." "Page charges" are an acceptance of the philosophy that "authors" (or their employers) must share in the funding of the communication process, and that publication of findings is the final step in the completion of a significant study. "Users" have traditionally paid their share through personal and employer (library) subscriptions to printed publications, but "technology" and "networks" are changing the need for multiple or even local copies, making it all the more vital that revenue be obtained in relation to direct use, wherever and however provided.

Because law is the basis for order among individuals, organizations, and nations, the Society believes that the laws which affect communicaton—information transfer—must be equitable and clear, and that they must be periodically reviewed to maintain these qualities. The copyright law of the United States has not been seriously updated since 1909, and it is badly in need of revision. Its antiquity is the direct cause for present ethical and judicial arguments over what is "fair" or "free" as regards communication—arguments which obscure the basic rights of authorship; the "value added" factors in reviewing, editing, publishing, and information-base creation; and the fact that the real problem seek to avoid coming to its own finite conclusions on key copyright issues, on the ground that such questions could logically be deferred for consideration by the new Commission. In our judgment, such a course would represent a serious abdication of Congressional responsibility, and would increase rather than decrease the ensuing confusion. In a true sense, it would merely shift the debate

to another forum and one not so well placed as the Congress for bringing the controversial questions to clear resolution.

In the nature of things, the ramifications of the copyright issue in the context of rapid technological change will assure that the new Commission has a great many questions to debate and resolve. But the Commission's work will proceed on a far more hopeful basis if the Congress accepts its own responsibility for setting workable guidelines in the new law. In our judgment, Congressional endorsement of the existing language of Sections 107 and 108 constitutes the necessary guidelines for the print media.

STATEMENT OF JULIUS J. MARKE, ON BEHALF OF THE AMERICAN ASSOCIATION OF LAW LIBRARIES

Mr. Chairman, and members of the Committee, I am Julius J. Marke, Law Librarian and Professor of Law, New York University. I am Chairman of the Copyright Committee of the American Association of Law Libraries, and am appearing on its behalf.

The American Association of Law Libraries (A.A.L.L.) was established in 1906 and presently has a membership of approximately 2,000 law librarians servicing University Law School libraries, Bar Association libraries, County Law Libraries, Court libraries, State Law Libraries, and Practitioners Libraries' throughout the nation. Its Headquarters is located at 53 West Jackson Boulevard, Chicago, Illinois, 60604.

The A.A.L.L. is established for educational and scientific purposes and is conducted as a non-profit corporation to promote librarianship, to develop and increase the usefulness of law libraries, to cultivate the science of law librarianship and to foster a spirit of cooperation among the members of the profession. It has twelve regional chapters, known as Association of Law Libraries of Upstate New York, Chicago Association of Law Libraries, Greater Philadelphian Law Library Association, Law Librarians of New England, Law Librarians' Society of Washington, D.C., Law Library Association of Greater New York, Minnesota Chapter of A.A.L.L., Ohio Regional Association of Law Librarians, Southeastern Chapter of AALL, Southern California Association of Law Libraries, Southwestern Chapter of AALL and Western Pacific Chapter of AALL. Foreign Law Librarians, residing in the following countries, are also members of the American Association of Law Libraries: Canada, Australia, Belgium, Colombia, England, Ethiopia, West Germany, Finland, France, Israel, Italy, Jamaica, W.I., Japan, Korea, Netherlands, New Zealand, Nigeria, Northern Ireland, Republic of the Philippines, Singapore, Sudan, Sweden, Switzerland, Tanzania and Turkey.

The American Association of Law Libraries is also a publisher of scholarly and technical publications. It publishes *The Law Library Journal*, The *Index to Foreign Legal Publications*, the *A.A.L.L. Publications Series*, *Current Publications in Legal and Related Fields* and the *A.A.L.L. Newsletter*. In addition the *Index to Legal Publications* is published by the H. W. Wilson Co. with the cooperation of the A.A. L.L.

Although the A.A.L.L. has reservations about. other parts of H.R. 2223, I shall address my comments to those sections of the bill affecting library photocopying.

The A.A.L.L. joins other national library associations in recommending legislative safeguards and exemptions for those library uses of copyrighted works necessary to guarantee the public access to library resources for educational, scientific and scholarly purposes.

The major concern of the A.A.L.L. is that sections 108(g)(1) and 108(g)(2) negate the grant to libraries in section 108 to make single photocopies of copyrighted materials.

I. LEGISLATIVE SAFEGUARDS AND EXEMPTIONS

Section 108(g)(1) limits the right of reproduction and distribution under section 108 only to "the isolated and unrelated reproduction or distribution of a single copy of library materials on "separate occasions". It does not extend, however, to cases where the library, or its employee is "aware or has substantial reason to believe that it is engaging in the related or concerted reproduction or distribution of multiple copies . . . whether made, on one occasion or over a period of time and whether intended for aggregate use by one or more individuals or for separate use by the individual members of a group."

Section 108(g)(2) denies to libraries the "systematic reproduction or distribution of single or multiple copies" of material described in section 108(d).

The AALL is concerned that library systems are evolving in many forms and as a result not even librarians have enough information on library networks all over the country to arrive at an acceptable understanding of the situation. Therefore, it is impracticable at this point of time to define "systematic" with reference to these "systems". Actually, librarians are only attempting to use available resources adequately and maximize their collections rather than economize at the expense of the publishers by promoting photocopying of their library materials. An example of one of these "systems" is multi-county libraries organized to support a single library system. In this context, librarians are concerned about foreclosing interests by definition. Legislative restrictions with reference to "systems" when read into the copyright revision law, could create problems in the future as technological developments in this area are so uncertain and unforeseeable at present. They also are in direct conflict with the express Congressional intent as a matter of public policy to encourage the creation and promotion of such "systems" as set forth in the Higher Education Act referred to under I(d) *supra*.

The AALL also insists that "systematic" library photocopying restrictions under section 108(g)(1) and 108(g)(2) must be relaxed to reflect a recognition of a library's right to make single photocopies of materials in its collection and the applicability of the "fair use" doctrine. Librarians are concerned that "systematic" can be used to whipsaw them. Sections 108(g)(1) and (g)(2) depart from "single" and "multiple". If "systematic" swallows up "single" and the applicability of the Fair Use doctrine then librarians protest. "Systematic" can only refer to "multiple" copying.

The AALL also protests that the concept of library single photocopying as "fair use" is now limited under section 108(g)(1) to "isolated" and "unrelated" single photocopying.

Then again, what is meant by words and phrases in Section 108(g) such as "period of time"? One day, one week, one month, one year? What is meant by the library or its staff "know or has reason to know", of "multiple copying"? At what point and under what circumstances is the library administration put on constructive notice of multiple photocopying? What kind of records must be kept by the library of these activities, or type of consultation required of staff members involved to prevent such "related or concerted" reproduction? What is meant by "distribution" in the section? "What is a branch library? Is the Law Library on a university campus a branch library of the University Library System?

Librarians cannot depend on the courts applying "rule of reason" construction to these nebulous words and phrases in section 108(g). Librarians have serious reservations about this approach and must insist on specific guidelines to prevent "prior restraint".

"Systematic" library photocopying as set forth in section 108(g)(2) allows for a construction depending on "availability" as the key factor in determining when a "system" exists for this purpose. Therefore, any system which provides the comfort of availability of a publication to a library, which therefore does not have to provide for it in its budget, would be "systematic". As a result, a listing of library holdings of serials, such as to be found in the Union List of Serials (which has been on the open market for more than 40 years), even though not prepared for commercial advantage, or for the purpose of interlibrary loan, still provides this availability, and therefore becomes a "system". Hence, any identifiable source of books in print plus knowledge of it by librarians to identify materials they lack for interlibrary loans would amount to a "system". This pervasive effect is considered intolerable by librarians as it could have serious adverse consequences for research and the dissemination and flow of information, especially as services by libraries. Then again, it must be recognized that merely because a library "system" exists, it does not necessarily follow that all photocopying within the system is "systematic".

Is inadequate funding at most stages of the communication process (including libraries).

The Society has repeatedly and clearly stated its need for copyright protection against continuation and growth of "uncontrolled dissemination of scientific information"—the unauthorized regular or systematic or concerted single-copy republishing of Society papers by libraries or networks of libraries. The Society is opposed to copyright-law revisions relating to "copying" that would destroy the copyright protection for its publication programs.

Until communication issues can be further clarified, the Society would prefer that "fair use" remain a judicial rather than a legislative concept. The Society is specifically opposed to any definition of "fair use" that could be further interpreted as permitting unauthorized, concerted "single copying" (photocopying, electronic copying, etc.).

The Society recognizes the need to develop total systems for information transfer; therefore, it specifically opposes any broadening or interpretation of the definition of or the right to prepare a "derivative work" that would reserve to "authors" (primary publications) the right to control the writing of original informative abstracts that are not complete "abridgments" or "condensations." However, the latter are accepted as being fully protected derivative works; they are of significance to the Society's future primary publication of "short papers."

The Society advocates immediate copyright-law revisions that will more completely and explicitly define and continue to protect such technological developments as computerized information bases, computerized data bases, computer programs, and microforms, i.e., that will define and specify these as "Exclusive Rights in Copyrighted Works." Because the scope and importance of these technological developments are already extensive, the Society no longer advocates deferring related copyright-law revisions until after the studies and recommendations of the National Commission on New Technological Uses of Copyrighted Works. In particular, the Society firmly advocates revisions which clarify and continue the protection of copyrighted computer bases at time of input, on the basis that copyright control at output only might be limited severely by broad interpretations of "fair use."

The Society opposes most of the specific additional limitations on the exclusive rights of authors and their publishers to provide copies of copyrighted publications that are contained in recent legislative bills. As proposed, these limitations do not really meet the needs of "users" and libraries for uncomplicated copying.

The Society recognizes that these and other limitations on exclusive rights to provide copies are based on the very real desire of "users," and libraries in their behalf, to avail themselves of such "new technology" as photocopying to prepare or obtain copies of copyrighted documents quickly and easily. The Society has repeatedly declared its readiness to cooperate in the development of a clearinghouse that can grant such permissions in an equitable and simple manner and is presently working actively toward this goal through the Conference on the Resolution of Copyright Issues under the chairmanship of Barbara Ringer, Register of Copyrights, and Fred Burkhardt, Chairman of the National Commission on Libraries and Information Science. The Society also advocates the development of "document-access networks" that will quickly supply actual copies in an equitable manner. The Society therefore advocates copyright-law provisions that will equitably authorize and regulate such important services to "users."

Despite reservations on some segments of this bill, the American Chemical Society recommends passage of the sections of H.R. 2223 related to the library photocopying. This recommendation is made with the belief, based on work with the Conference on the Resolution of Copyright Issues, that a practicable system for licensing and fee collection for photocopies of copyrighted works can be developed which will render fair and equitable charges for systematic photocopying in the interest of an improved and economically viable system for the dissemination of scientific information. Plans now are being developed for testing such a mechanism.

STATEMENT OF TOWNSEND HOOPES, PRESIDENT, THE ASSOCIATION OF AMERICAN PUBLISHERS

Mr. Chairman. My name is Townsend Hoopes. I am President of the Association of American Publishers, the extent and influence of whose membership Mr. Lieb has described. I should add parenthetically that, in addition to representing publishers, I have written two books and intend to write more, so that my convictions about the need for copyright protection are based on authorship as well as publishing. I agree with Ms. Ringer that protection of authors' rights is at the very core of the Constitutional provision for copyright protection, and that the need for such protection is a direct consequence of the need to assure continuance of intellectual creativity, a function which cannot be performed by a committee but only by an individual.

On behalf of the Association, and also speaking to some extent for the other proprietary owners here assembled, my purpose is to reinforce support for the present language of Sections 107 and 108 of H.R. 2223, which Mr. Lieb has addressed in some detail. Mainly I will summarize our recent experience with the library community in seeking to be responsive to pointed suggestions from both the House and Senate Judiciary Committees.

The Senate report accompanying S. 1361 expressed the belief that Section 108 provides "an appropriate balancing of the rights of creators and the needs of users"; at the same time, recognizing the complexities, the report urged the parties—in this instance authors, publishers and librarians—to meet together directly in order to develop more precise photocopying guidelines for "fair use", and also to develop workable clearance and license arrangements for copying beyond fair use. This urging by the Senate Committee repeated a similar proposal by the House Judiciary Committee in 1967. Responsive to that earlier proposal, publishers and authors met with librarians in 1972 and again in 1973 for discussions that became known, somewhat grandiloquently, as the Cosmos Club and Dumbarton Oaks talks. The formula evolved at the Cosmos Club was that, if reprints of a journal article were readily available from the publisher or his agent, the library would refrain from photocopying of its own. The formula evolved at Dumbarton Oaks was that a journal publisher would encode the front page of each journal article with a serial number and a reprint price, and that a library making a copy thereof would so advise a clearinghouse operated by the publishers. At quarterly or semiannual intervals, the clearinghouse would bill the library for the aggregate royalty charges and would then distribute the proceeds to individual publishers. While both the Cosmos and Dumbarton efforts were deemed feasible by the library participants, they were later both shot down by officials of the several library associations.

Since November 1974, the publishers have again been negotiating with the librarians under the joint sponsorship of the Register of Copyrights and the Chairman of the National Commission on Libraries and Information Science. Eight meetings of a twelve-man working group were held between early December 1974 and mid-April of this year. I regret to say, Mr. Chairman, that there has not been much progress to date, chiefly because the librarians have refused to accept either the Senate bill or the guidances suggested by NCLIS and Ms. Ringer as in any way a limiting frame of reference. We have asked them, for example, to join with us in defining typical situations of two kinds: (a) those that would clearly involve fair use copying, and (b) those that would clearly involve systematic copying beyond fair use thereby requiring permission and royalty payment. Their consistent reply has been that they know of no copying done by libraries which extends beyond fair use.

I suggest, Mr. Chairman, there are two possible explanations for this unforthcoming attitude. Either the library community as a whole is still attempting to secure total exemption from copyright, and expects to get its way with the Congress; or the attitude here expressed reflects a minority view within the library community and is not therefore representative of the whole. In this latter connection, I must say that we are struck by the difference in the attitudes we have found among local librarians and those expressed by the official spokesmen of library associations in Washington. In the field, we have encountered widespread sympathy for and understanding of the basic concept of copyright and of the need for copyright protection, accompanied by a felt need for guidelines that will more precisely determine the dividing line between fair use and infringement.

I would like to make brief mention in this same context of the Commission on New Technological Uses of Copyrighted Works which was established by law on December 31, 1974. Our Association has supported and does support this Commission, but we believe it would be a serious mistake if the Congress should

The A.A.L.L. also protests that as there is no objection to interlibrary borrowing of specific hard copy materials under these so-called "systems", why should librarians not be able to make a single photocopy of these materials when randomly requested on interlibrary loan as a substitute for hard copy, especially as permitted in sect. 108(d) of the Copyright Revision Bill.

In a sense these criticisms of section 108 of the revision bill were rejected and implied in the Register of Copyrights' testimony on S. 3976 before this Committee on November 26, 1974 (93rd Cong. 2d Sess, Serial No. 59, 1975) when she stated:

"*Ms. Ringer.*" . . . Section 108 of the revision bill (dealing with the making of single photocopies by libraries) is by no means sufficient to solve the larger problems of reprography, especially in libraries . . . Neither the enactment of the revision bill in the form in which it passed the Senate nor a definitive decision of the Supreme Court in the *Williams and Wilkins* Case is going to settle the larger issues here. . .

"Discussions are under way in the private sector, now on this subject, in recognition that nothing the Congress does . . . is going to solve this issue for the future, and that it is an issue that very desperately needs solving. But both of these important issues, namely, computer uses and reprography urgently need to be studied in depth by recognized experts". (p. 6-7).

The AALL recommends that "these important issues" be submitted for solution to the recently created *National Commission on New Technological Uses of Copyrighted Works* inasmuch as P.L. 93-573, 88 Stat. 1873, enacted into law on December 31, 1974 charges this Commission to study and compile data on the use of copyrighted works" in conjunction with automatic systems capable of storing, processing, retrieving, and transferring information, and . . . by *various forms of machine reproduction* . . .". In the interim period sections 108 should be redrafted to meet the objections set forth above.

II. LIBRARY PHOTOCOPYING ISSUES AND THE COPYRIGHT REVISION BILL

A. *Purpose of copyright protection and the public interest*

Generally, the purpose of copyright protection is to encourage and reward authors of intellectual works and other creative artists to produce such works for the benefit of society, by granting them the exclusive right during a specific period of time to copy, or otherwise multiply, publish, sell or distribute them, as well as to prepare derivative works based upon the copyrighted work. They are also given the exclusive privilege to perform and record these works and to license their production or sale by others during the term of the copyright protection. Basically, the purpose of copyright, as is tested in Article 1, Section 8, Clause 8 of the U.S. Constitution is "to promote the progress of science and the useful arts". This necessarily implies that the copyright holder's rights are never absolute for the monopoly granted serves the added purposes of stimulating the development of scientific and other types of knowledge and to encourage the dissemination of this knowledge to the public. .

To avoid frustrating this purpose, the courts have adopted the concept of a "fair use" doctrine which permits individuals and institutions, other than the copyright owner, to use the copyrighted material in a reasonable manner without the owner's consent. In essence, the "fair use" doctrine attempts to balance the rights of the owners of copyrighted works to their just economic rewards against the rights of scholars and researchers to use these works conveniently in their scholarly endeavors. As the "fair use" doctrine is an equitable rule, each case is determined on its own facts. The courts in the U.S. generally apply the following guidelines laid down initially by Mr. Justice Story in 1841 in *Folsom v. Marsh*, 9 Fed. Cas. 342 (CCD Mass.) in deciding whether an infringement or fair use has occurred : "We must . . . in deciding questions of this sort, look to the nature and objects of the selections made, the quantity and value of the materials used, and the degree in which the use may prejudice the sale, or diminish the profits, or supersede the objects of the original work."

On the issue of public interest, it is relevant to note a question raised by Professor John C. Stedman. What are the rights of an author and those in privity with him? He suggests that it is a policy question of "more or less", not a legal question of what are his rights in the educational process. "How much it is necessary and desirable to give to the author in order to stimulate and encourage him to write and publish in the educational field!" Look at the "effects" of granting or denying copyright protection rather than refer generally to the "interests" of the author. Educational activity, in practical effect and in terms of public interest, must be distinguished from other activities with reference to copyright protection. Consideration must be given to the strong public purpose behind educational activity. "Beware!!" he cautions authors and publishers, if the copyright toll becomes too onerous for educational activities to absorb, the result may be foregoing use of the material completely. (See AAUP Bulletin, 53:129 (June 1967)).

B. Library photocopying and copyright protection

Replication of copyright works is daily taking place in libraries as part of the research and educational process. At present it is primarily reflected in reprographic reproduction (reproduction by photographic methods or processes analogous to photography), and is an established and recognized practice in library administration, teaching and research.

Reprography in libraries and for educational purposes should not be confused, however, with computerized retrieval of data and information, which in its present state of development is hardly a serious threat to owners of intellectual property but which could eventually become so. Researchers, librarians and educators in the future will then become involved with new techniques of electronic document-storage and computerized information-retrieval systems just as they are presently learning about the tremendous potential of miniaturization and remote transmission of data.

Currently, the most pressing problems facing owners and users of copyrighted works lie in the reprography area as distinguished from electronic systems.

Scholars, researchers and librarians, relying on the doctine of fair use, have always felt free to copy by hand the works of others for their own research and study needs. When copying machines become available, it was a simple transition for these scholars, etc., to extend their note-taking to photocopying from copyrighted material. Publishers maintain that the new machine-copiers made replication of their copyrighted materials so easy and inexpensive that their sales are being detrimentally affected to the point that if allowed to continue they will be forced out of business. As a result, the creator of information would lack the income from his ideas to maintain a degree of independence. Educators particularly object to any limitation of their right to make machine-copies on the grounds that they, like librarians, are not doing so for profit; nor for any direct or indirect commercial advantage, but rather to promote the educational process.

The traditional library position on reprography in libraries is to the effect that not only under the Fair Use doctrine, but also as a natural extension of customary library service, a library may make a single copy of copyrighted material it has purchased, for the scholarly use of any of its readers or another library, requesting such service, if done without profit. Such service, employing modern copying methods has become essential. The present demand can be satisfied without inflicting measurable damage on publishers and copyright owners. Improved copying processes will not materially affect the demand for single-copy library duplication for research purposes. Librarians also argue, no matter who is involved, whether it be the librarian, the publisher, or the creator of information, the main concern should be the public interest in access to information. Copyright protection should not be an impediment to transferring information.

C. The economics of library photocopying and the public interest

Publishers allege that although libraries are not in the business of photocopying for profit, still by doing so, they are depriving publishers of the opportunity to sell additional copies and even to maintain their current subscriptions. In the *Williams & Wilkins* case, however, involving a U.S. government library's unauthorized photocopying of copyrighted medical periodicals for and at the request of medical researchers and practitioners, the U.S. Court of Claims not only held this practice constituted "fair use", but that "there is inadequate reason to believe, that it (the publisher) is being or will be harmed substantially by these specific practices." Actually, this conclusion is borne out by the realization that if most of the users in libraries who photocopy copyrighted materials would be deprived of this opportunity, they would not purchase the original material. Then again, researchers, scholars and academicians rarely purchase all or even a few of the books and/or journals they use in their research. They receive complimentary copies and reprints of articles or they borrow library copies. Only if these sources fail to provide the materials sought, do they resort to photocopying. The publishers' complaint that photocopying is depriving them of profits because of lost sales is therefore not a completely valid conclusion. Many of the potential sales the publishers envision are not of the type that ordinarily occur. It appears to be, that the publishers, despite all this library photocopying, are no worse off than before.

While libraries and large industrial organizations are principally involved in replication of copyrighted materials (also there is much private and casual copying by students, faculty and others in college and university libraries) still they continue to purchase many new titles and journal subscriptions, as well as maintaining the older subscriptions. It should be also recognized in this context that these institutions cannot physically shelve more than a few copies of a journal, etc., due to lack of space and therefore would never purchase a great number of subscriptions to a journal merely because at one time there was a demand for additional copies of a given article.

In this context, we should also review the economics of publishing. It is an established fact that publishers of scientific and technical journals, publish limited editions of their issues so that they often are unable to sell additional copies on demand as early as two months after publication. They do not invest in maintaining stock of back issues of their publications, and hardly ever reprint them. Thus, depriving themselves of the opportunity to sell their back issues on demand. Still they are insisting on the payment of fees additional to the subscription price of the publications, for photocopying rights of these back issues. Then again, publishers, especially in the areas of scientific and technical reference works do market research before publishing new titles and publish them only when assured that libraries will purchase them in addition to specialists in the field. When they determine that the sale of a particular work will be limited, the list price established is increased to reflect this in order to insure a profit.

Surveys have also established that as many as 80% of authors of scientific articles are more interested in dissemination of their articles than in receiving royalties. In the scientific field, it should also be noted, authors not only do not receive remuneration for their articles, but often are required to pay for the cost of having them published or absorb the cost by purchasing a stated number of reprints. It has also been noted that subjects dealt with in scientific literature and some of the other disciplines such as law have become so specialized that most researchers in those fields are interested sometimes only in one article out of the many published in a particular journal. Reprography in libraries and documentation centers appears to be the only obvious way today for researchers to have access to the many scholarly resources of their field.

Publishers complain, however, that they are bearing the economic brunt of this development. The hardware and paper used for reprography are bought and paid for by libraries, etc., why shouldn't publishers be given additional income for the right to make copies of their copyrighted works! They also add that even though scientists, etc., etc., pay for publication of their research papers, they should be interested in the survival of the scientific journals which give them an opportunity to disseminate their findings and research reports.

Librarians respond to this copyright confrontation as follows: Non-profit library institutions are not in business and have nothing to gain by photocopying for others. Their purpose is only to promote research in the sciences and humanities in the public interest. They are involved with access to knowledge and its bibliographical control so that scholars, educators, scientists, etc., can use such data in their research and in the process create new information and materials. Why should librarians, under these circumstances be caught in the middle of the conflict between owners and users of copyrighted materials, and be required to take sides? When we become concerned with technology and economics, we must realize that they are not material to the library's ulterior purpose of information dissemination.

Library institutions do have an interest in the reproduction of copyrighted materials for their own internal, nonprofit purposes. They have a vital concern in conserving copies of periodicals and of works in their collection which are out of print, under certain circumstances. They also have an interest in reproducing mutilated or missing pages of works in their collection. Then again, in order to conserve their collection, they recognize the need to photocopy materials in their collection for other libraries, requesting them on inter-library loan. Ground rules should be negotiated for these purposes but not at the expense of limiting the free flow of information, and certainly not with the added cost to libraries for administering a system involving payment of fees, licensing, etc., for the benefit of owners of copyrighted works.

D. *The new technology and the copyright revision bill*

What position should this committee take with reference to computer technology and related copyright problems? When the integrity of a basic collection of materials, copyrighted and otherwise, compacted and stored in electronic information-center computers, will be preserved by Xerographic printers providing facsimile reproduction by remote transmission in hard-copy form, or by video scanning of ephemeral copy on a closed-circuit TV monitor elsewhere; when the library collection will remain intact because the computer, in essence, will assume the role of a duplicating rather than a circulating library; when one copy of a book fed into such a system will service all simultaneous demands for it; when microfiche and computer print-outs will replace copyrighted hard-copy publication of research reports, as well as of scientific and technical materials currently appearing in journals, monographs and books, and when audio-visual dial-access teaching machines, operated by remote control, will provide hundreds and even thousands of students with simultaneous audio and visual access to a journal article or excerpts from a book, it is obvious that the publishers' traditional market will be affected by these developments and the copyright laws will have to respond to this "non-book" production.

Merely on the issue as to when an infringement will occur with reference to input, storage and retrieval of a copyrighted work fed into a computer without permission of the copyright owner remains still to be resolved. Output or retrieval of the copyrighted work may be in the form of abstracts, excerpts, or the work as a whole. It may be delivered to the user in tangible form such as a photo-duplication or in ephemeral form such as the temporary projection of an image on the screen. Should the output of an information storage and retrieval system be considered a copyright infringement or derivative work if such output is an index, abstract, limited quotation or analysis of the copyrighted work? "No," reply some copyright experts, except to the extent that the output is likely to diminish the demand for a copyrighted work, because then the doctrine of fair use should govern. Some experts note that the term "copy" is a word of art construed by the courts in the U.S. to mean a copy which is "visually perceivable" and in "tangible form" and therefore when we are concerned with computer output of punch cards or tape, we are "copying". Thus, the experts cannot agree when a computer system has infringed on a copyright owner's works or for that matter to what extent. Professor Benjamin Kaplan, contends that infringement should not turn on input conversion but rather on output conversion—on what is subsequently done with the stored work.

There are other copyright problems brought out by the new technology, e.g., notice of copyright and deposit, whether doctrine of fair use is applicable. The state of the art today, however, is not sufficient to warrant the acceptance of rules and regulations governing the use of copyrighted materials. When "non-book" production will predominate, the role of the commercial publisher will probably change, especially in his relationship with authors and readers. Publishers may also decide to play a different role with reference to regional, national and international information networks. Libraries will also have to readjust their concepts of reader's services and technical operations and may even become eventually part of projected government information networks. Thus, it is possible that the new technology will change the concept of author protection and that copyright protection will be of little help to the author of scholarly works. Rather than depending on royalties, these authors and/or their publishers will sell directly to the information-system operator either as a complete sale or upon an accounting based on use. The computer could easily be programmed not only to incorporate the new "work" into the existing data but also arrange for accountability of its use in the system. Subscribers to the system will pay for its maintenance.

As a result, many other problems will arise, e.g., the amount of control government will have over these information systems, rates to be established and international agreement and treaties will have to be negotiated to reflect the needs of the system.

In light of all these possibilities, it is my thought that this Committee cannot take a position at present affecting copyright and computer based information storage and retrieval systems. We must await developments in this field to the point where we will be aware of the implications of our decisions.

I would respectfully recommend that this is a problem for the newly created *National Commission on New Technological Uses of Copyrighted Works* to resolve.

The long range problems arising from the effects of this new technology on copyright must first be identified by the Commission and then it should "make recommendations as to such changes in copyright law or procedures that may be necessary to assure for such purposes access to copyrighted works and to provide recognition of the rights of copyrighted owners" as it has been charged by the U.S. Congress to do.

Mr. Chairman, I appreciate the opportunity of appearing here to present the point of view of the American Association of Law Libraries.

STATEMENT OF WILLIAM M. PASSANO, CHAIRMAN OF THE BOARD, WILLIAMS & WILKINS CO.

I thoroughly enjoyed meeting with you on May 13, and I appreciate the opportunity to review with you the subscription figures for the 27 Journals published by The Williams & Wilkins Company. You may recall that a compelling reason given by the four judges of the Court of Claims for finding library photocopying of our Journals to be "fair use" was that we had not convinced them that this practice was doing harm to the financial condition of the Journals. It is true that in 1973, when the Court of Claims decision was handed down, we had no statistical proof of damage.

However, the figures now available, which compare 1973 with 1974 and which I showed you when I was in your office, do to my mind show that the library networks are, in fact, doing just what they were designed to do; namely, reducing the number of Journals which the libraries subscribe to, since the needs of library patrons can be served by obtaining photocopies of requested articles as interlibrary loans through the network systems.

You will notice that the individual subscriptions to the 27 Journals which we publish have increased nearly 17%, comparing 1974 with 1973. Foreign subscriptions of all kinds have increased approximately 13%. Furthermore, there has been a healthy increase in the number of hospital subscriptions, due primarily we believe to the ever-growing number of community hospitals. This record indicates that the Journals as a group are in demand as purveyors of scientific knowledge and are highly respected by the scientific community. Furthermore, we credit much of the increase to the effectiveness of the very substantial direct marketing efforts which we have made during the past year.

The record of individual and foreign subscriptions, however is in sharp contrast with the institutional subscriptions which in the same period of time have fallen off by 3%. I think it is safe to say that this decrease in institutional subscriptions, at a time when individual and foreign subscriptions have substantially increased, is not due to lack of popularity on the part of the Journals in question, but is because of the ease with which interlibrary loans (photocopies) are obtained through membership in library network systems, and that these photocopies can and do replace the necessity for institutions subscribing to the Journals in question. Certainly The American Chemical Society subscription figures confirm this with even larger declines.

We do not quarrel with photocopying, nor do we object to the network systems. They are effective means of efficiently disseminating scientific knowledge. We do believe, however, that those who use the Journals by photocopying them should share in their support and not leave the entire burden on the shoulders of the subscribers, the authors and the advertisers, as is the case at present. It is for this reason that Section 108(g)(2) of the proposed Copyright Bill must be retained if the scientific press is to remain viable and free from governmental subsidy and control.

It should be borne in mind that fully 65% of the cost of producing the typical scientific periodical is incurred before the first copy comes off the press. This means that only a comparatively small erosion of the subscription list can greatly affect the unit cost and therefore jeopardize the financial security of the Journal.

Again, many thanks for permitting me as a member of the Proprietary Rights Committee of the Information Association to place these facts before you.

STATUS OF SUBSCRIBERS TO 27 WILLIAMS & WILKINS JOURNALS COMPARING 1973 WITH 1974

Type of subscriber	Number of subscribers		Change in percent
	1973	1974	
Individual domestic	28,405	33,137	+16.8
Foreign individual and institutional	36,430	41,147	+12.9
Hospitals	8,796	9,562	+8.75
All other domestic institutions	15,369	14,909	−3.0
Breakdown of domestic institutional subscribers:			
Medical schools	3,262	3,361	+3.3
Universities and colleges	5,198	5,149	−.95
Public libraries	489	413	−15.6
Corporations (drug manufacturers)	1,112	1,149	+3.3
U.S. Government libraries and departments	3,644	3,523	−3.3
Associations, foundations, laboratories	1,674	1,314	−21.7

STATEMENT OF HON. DAVID MATHEWS, SECRETARY, DEPARTMENT OF HEALTH, EDUCATION, AND WELFARE

There is now pending before your Committee H.R. 2223, a bill "For the general revision of the Copyright Law, title 17 of the United States Code, and for other purposes."

In brief, the bill as presently worded contains a provision [Subsection 108(g)] which would severely hamper the flow of biomedical information between the National Library of Medicine and the nation's medical libraries and thereby reduce the information available to researchers and practitioners. Deletion of Subsection 108(g) would remove this restriction. However, if deletion of this Subsection is not possible modification of the language contained therein would accomplish the same goal.

We transmit herewith a brief technical report which contains an analysis of select provisions of the bill under consideration and the effects which they might have on the programs of the National Library of Medicine, a bureau of the Department of Health, Education and Welfare.

We are advised by the Office of Management and Budget that there is no objection to the presentation of this legislative proposal from the standpoint of the Administration's program:

AN ANALYSIS OF THE POSSIBLE EFFECTS OF SECTION 108 OF H.R. 2223, GENERAL REVISION OF THE COPYRIGHT LAW

House of Representatives bill, H.R. 2223 "For the general revision of the

Copyright Law, title 17 of the United States Code, and for other purposes," now pending before the Committee on The Judiciary in the House of Representatives, would provide for the first general revision of the copyright law since its passage in 1909. Section 108, "Limitations on exclusive rights: Reproduction by libraries and archives" provides that it is not an infringement of copyright for a library or archives to reproduce no more than one copy of a work for non-commercial purposes in order to preserve deteriorating materials, replace a damaged or lost copy that can not be purchased at a fair price, or provide a copy for the use of an individual library patron for scholarship and research. However, Subsection 108(g) prohibits "the related or concerted reproduction or distribution of multiple copies or phonorecords of the same material, whether made on one occasion or over a period of time" whether intended for the use of one individual or a group. It also prohibits "the systematic reproduction or distribution of single or multiple copies" of a copyrighted work.

Subsection 108(g) in its present form, depending on the interpretation of "systematic reproduction," could possibly make operation of the current interlibrary loan program of the National Library of Medicine and its Regional Medical Library network an infringement of copyright, thereby seriously impairing the nation's health research and scholarship.

The NLM is a "library's library" serving as the back-up source of materials requested by patrons of local medical libraries but which are at that time absent from their collections. There are many reasons for the non-availability of literature which necessitates that a local library request an interlibrary loan; among the common reasons are that the material requested are out of the local library on loan or at the bindery.

To provide more rapid dissemination of biomedical information, the Library has developed a network arrangement through which biomedical literature can be shared more efficiently by medical libraries throughout the nation. Eleven major institutions have been designated Regional Medical Libraries to provide interlibrary loan services to other libraries in their regions.

The interlibrary loan program provides to requestors photocopies of articles from periodicals and brief excerpts from monographs for the purposes of private study, scholarship and research. Single photocopies are provided in lieu of loaning the original literature as a means of safeguarding NLM's archival collection and of assuring uninterrupted availability of the literature of NLM and the resource libraries of the Regional Medical Library network.

The term "systematic reproduction" as used in Section 108(g)(2) is not defined in the bill, but if it is to be used to describe that reproduction carried out in connection with interlibrary cooperation, such as in the Biomedical Library Network, it will mean the end of this orderly and efficient medical literature exchange.

Section 108 in H.R. 2223 is identical to Section 108 of S. 1361 which was passed by the Senate in 1974. It is important to note that the Senate report which accompanied S. 1361 dealt with this issue of systematic reproduction.

The report indicated that Subsection (g)(2) stipulates that Section 108 does not authorize the systematic reproduction or distribution of copies of articles in periodicals or of small parts of other copyrighted works whether or not multiple copies are reproduced or distributed. Systematic reproduction or distribution occurs when a library makes copies of such materials available to other libraries or to groups of users under formal or informal arrangements whose purpose or effect is to have the reproducing library serve as their source of such material. The report states that such systematic reproduction and distribution enable the receiving libraries or users to substitute the copies reproduced by the source library for subscriptions or reprints or other copies which they might otherwise have purchased for themselves, from the publisher or the licensed reproducing agencies.

The potential effects of Section 108(g) are unsure; however, as the Senate Subcommittee interpreted "systematic reproduction" in 1974, NLM's present interlibrary loan program might be found to be an infringement of the copyright law if amended as proposed in this legislation.

Although Section 108(a)–(f) appears to allow for the photocopying of journal articles, Subsection 108(g)(2) threatens to destroy the effectiveness of the biomedical library network and to seriously undermine the ability of local medical libraries to provide medical literature and information requested and needed by the health community. It could in effect eliminate the present practice of interlibrary loans which would seriously impair the dissemination of medical information throughout the nation.

Deletion of Subsection 108(g)(2) would permit the continuation of an unrestricted flow of medical information among libraries. If deletion is not possible, another approach which might accomplish the goal would be to amend Subsection 108(g)(2) by adding the language underlined below:

> (2) engages in the systematic *and unlimited* reproduction or distribution of single or multiple copies or phonorecords of the same material described in Subsection (d) *so as to substantially impair the market for, or value of, the copyrighted work.*

For purposes of avoiding ambiguity the bill should include explicit definitions of "systematic reproduction" and "fair use."

STATEMENT OF KEVIN J. KEANEY, GENERAL COUNSEL FOR THE FEDERAL LIBRARIANS ASSOCIATION

The Federal Librarians Association, incorporated in the District of Columbia, is an organization of professional librarians who work in the libraries and documentation centers of the U.S. Government throughout the world. This statement is submitted to express the view of the association relative to the proposed copyright legislation, particularly Section 108(g)(2).

Section 108 permits the reproduction of single copies of certain materials, in certain circumstances, and under certain conditions, by libraries and archives; but paragraph (g)(2) withholds that permission or right in ". . . cases where the library or archives, or its employee; . . . engages in the systematic reproduction or distribution of single or multiple copies of phonorecords of materials described in subsection (d)."

It is the view of this association that this paragraph will, on the one hand, subject the library and the librarian to a liability so serious as to inhibit the primary purpose of Article 1, Section 8, of the U.S. Constitution, and on the other hand, provoke by the vagueness of the term "systematic" endless and unprofitable litigation.

Federal librarians and Federal libraries have the duty to serve the public by providing whatever documents are available. We contend that the public interest is best served when the documents are provided subject to the primary purpose of the constitutional provision (". . . to promote the progress of Science and the useful Arts. . .") and subject to no more than other parts of Sections 107 and 108. We believe that the "fair use" provisions of Section 107 are sufficient protection to the holder of copyright, buttressed by the more specific provisions of Section 108, but excluding paragraph (g)(2). Librarians do not believe that the public interest is served by unrestricted and unconditional photocopying, but we do believe that the restrictions and conditions contained in other parts of the legislation are sufficient to safeguard the legitimate rights of the holder of copyright. When Congress provided that constitutional protection to holders, we believe Congress intended a "quid pro quo", viz. the fair use of that protected material by the public. We are highly concerned that there seems to be no government defender of that public interest. On the contrary, the National Commission on Libraries and Information Science latest report indicates to us an acceptance of the inevitability of royalties or a licensing agreement. It is no comfort to us that the Register of Copyrights, and the former Register, testified last week before this subcommittee that their first concern is for the "beneficiaries" of the Copyright Office, i.e. authors and publishers. And we are certainly not prepared to agree with the Register that the authors' interest is necessarily the public interest.

Our apprehension about the vagueness of the term "systematic" is confirmed by the report on S. 1361 (no. 93–983) which said ". . . neither a statute nor legislative history can specify precisely which library photocopying practices constitute the making of 'single copies' as distinguished from "systematic reproduction' ". The report's recommendation that meetings of opposing parties be held to resolve the conflict reminds us that these meetings have already been held many times, without success.

But surely, one asks, "systematic" is a term on which reasonable men can reach an understanding? Aside from the fact that one man's reason is another's intransigence, there is the fact that economics is at the root of the matter. Holders of copyright understandably want more money, and libraries are faced with rising costs in serving the public. The economic damage to holders of copyright is at best speculative, in regard to photocopying, and we share the view of the U.S. Court of Claims that, in regard to medical journals at least, the argument is an "untested hypothesis".[1]

Every organization, and hopefully, every library, tries to operate in a "systematic" manner, i.e. according to standard operating principles or uniform principles for each task, and must operate thus out of sheer common sense and business necessity. When your office rents and uses a photocopy machine, you are subscribing to a "system" : even the production of single copies, no less multiple copies, are part of a "system". In this respect, *all* library photocopying is "systematic" and thus subject to the restrictions of paragraph (g) (2).

As members of a profession, and employees of government agencies, devoted to public service and the public interest, we ask you to strike from this proposed legislation paragraph (g) (2) of Section 108, on grounds that this paragraph :

> (a) contains a term so vague as lead to fruitless litigation,
> (b) is against the public interest and the primary purpose of Article I, Section 8, of the U.S. Constitution, and
> (c) is superfluous in the light of the remaining parts of Sections 107 and 108.

TESTIMONY OF SHELDON E. STEINBACH, STAFF COUNSEL, AMERICAN COUNCIL ON EDUCATION; CHAIRMAN, AD HOC COMMITTEE ON COPYRIGHT LAW REVISION

Mr. STEINBACH. Mr. Chairman, members of the subcommittee, I am Sheldon Elliot Steinbach, staff counsel and assistant director of governmental relations of the American Council on Education. I appear before you today, however, representing the Ad Hoc Committee of Education Organizations on Copyright Law Revision, a consortium covering a wide spectrum of 39 organizations within the educational community with interest in the revision of the copyright law. Most especially, we represent the interests of teachers, professors, school and college administrators, subject matter specialists, educational broadcasters, librarians, and indirectly, students themselves. A list of our members is attached to this statement. In addition, we support the testimony given by the library associations yesterday. These groups are also members of the ad hoc committee.

Our testimony today will be presented by four individuals representing several organizations within the ad hoc committee. Although there is a fundamental ad hoc position, the interests of each constituent group varies, and as such, they will emphasize in their testimony today those matters of greatest concern to them. Furthermore, each group under the ad hoc umbrella has reserved the right to determine its own posture with regard to particular issues.

[List of members follows:]

AD HOC COMMITTEE ON COPYRIGHT LAW REVISION

Agency for Instructional Television.
American Association of Colleges for Teacher Education.
American Association of Community and Junior Colleges.
American Association of Law Libraries.
American Association of School Administrators.
American Association of School Librarians.
American Association of University Women.
American Council on Education.
American Educational Theatre Association, Inc.
American Library Association.
Associated Colleges of the Midwest.
Association for Childhood Education International.

Association for Computing Machinery.
Association for Educational Comunications and Technology.
Association of Research Libraries.
Baltimore County Schools.
Corporation for Public Broadcasting.
Council on Library Resources.
International Reading Association.
Joint Council on Educational Telecommunications, Inc.
Medical Library Association.
Modern Language Association.
Music Educators National Conference.
Music Teachers National Association.
National Art Education Association.
National Association of Educational Broadcasters.
National Association of Elementary School Principals.
National Association of Schools of Music.
National Catholic Educational Association.
National Catholic Welfare Conference.
National Commission for Libraries and Information Science.
National Contemporary Theatre Conference.
National Council for the Social Studies.
National Council of Teachers of English.
National Education Association of the United States.
National Public Radio.
National School Boards Association.
Public Broadcasting Service.
Speech Communication Association.

OBSERVERS

American Association of University Professors.
American Home Economics Association.
American Personnel and Guidance Association.
Association of American Law Schools.
Association for Supervision and Curriculum Development.
Federal Communications Commission.
National Congress of Parents and Teachers.

Mr. STEINBACH. I would like to add that the ad 'hoc committee will not address itself today to the question of instructional broadcasting because we have been assured that this matter will be considered at a later date, at which time we will be given an opportunity to speak to those issues.

It is my pleasure now to introduce Prof. Leo J. Raskind, professor of law, University of Minnesota, representing the Association of American Law Schools, the American Association of University Professors, and the American Council on Education—the Joint Copyright Committee for those three organizations.

[The prepared statement of Leo J. Raskind follows:]

STATEMENT OF LEO J. RASKIND, MADE OF BEHALF OF THE ASSOCIATION OF AMERICAN LAW SCHOOLS, AMERICAN ASSOCIATON OF UNIVERSITY PROFESSORS, AND THE AMERICAN COUNCIL ON EDUCATION

Mr. Chairman and members of the subcommittee, I am Leo J. Raskind, professor of law at the University of Minnesota. I am chairman of the Special Committee on Copyright Law of the Association of American Law Schools; I appear here today on behalf of the Association of American Law Schools, the American Association of University Professors, and the American Council on Education. Among these three organizations, we account for some 6,000 law teachers and some 75,000 other university professors. The American Council on Education is an association of national and regional education organizations and nearly 1,400 institutions of higher education.

We strongly urge that the doctrine of fair use be preserved and given formal recognition by Congress, both by express statutory provision and by appropriate language in the final Committee report.

Our position is grounded on the Constitutional directive to Congress contained in Article I, Section 8, Clause 8, which provides:

The Congress shall have Power to promote the Progress of Science and useful Arts, by securing for Limited Times to Authors and Inventors the exclusive Right to their respective Writings and Discoveries.

The higher education community is the principal institution in our society charged with the task of transmitting and advancing knowledge. It is our concern with discharging this basic function of teaching and research that moves us to ask for an effective statutory expression of the doctrine of fair use.

In making this proposal, I wish to emphasize that we do not seek to remove protected material from the ambit of the Copyright statute. We are neither adverse nor hostile to the basic premise that legitimate rights in intellectual property merit protection and compensation. Indeed, we accept this premise as a matter of principle, as a matter of public policy, as well as a matter of self-interest. There are among our membership authors whose works command high prices in the commercial book market; many of our authors write for technical journals without compensation.

Our main concern is to stress before this Committee the soundness of the traditional, judicially constructed doctrine of fair use and to illustrate its instrumental significance in the process of higher education.

As has been recognized throughout this extended process of revising the Copyright Law, a statutory recognition of the doctrine of fair use is preferable to continued reliance upon case law development. As the Senate Report has recently put it, ". . . there are few if any judicial guidelines. . . ." bearing directly on the usage of teachers and libraries in the educational and research context which is our concern. See, S. Rept. No. 93-983, 93rd Cong., 2d Sess. 116 (1974). Given the paucity of decided cases in this area, it is necessary to recognize the difficulty of leaving the resolution of this important problem solely to the limited framework of existing decisions. We urge, therefore, the enactment of § 107, as it now appears in H. 2223, 94th Cong., 1st Sess., as supported by adequate legislative history.

The recent decision of the Court of Claims in *Williams & Wilkins Co.* v. *United States*, 487 F. 2d 1345 (Ct. Cl. 1973), aff'd by an equally divided court, 43 U.S.L.W. 4314 (1975), underscores the significance of the fair use doctrine to the educational and research community. By its affirmance of this Court of Claims opinion, the Supreme Court has left the resolution of this problem to the Congress.

In seeking to have codified the traditional fair use doctrines, adequately supported by legislative history, we are moved by the primary importance of the availability of copyrighted material to our teaching and research duties. First and most basic is the fact that the higher education community on whose behalf we appear today, consists of those institutions in our society charged with the ultimate task of transmitting and advancing knowledge. I emphasize both research and teaching; each function is indispensable to and supportive of the other. Effective instruction of the next generation of citizens and professionals, requires that the current generation of teachers be involved as researchers on the frontiers of their own individual subject areas. If the individual teacher is to discharge this fundamental research obligation, that teacher must be kept abreast of the current developments within a given discipline. This necessarily requires the teacher to have available the work product of allied researchers.

The exponential rate of growth of knowledge expressed in tangible form during this generation, requires that this information be available to the teacher and the scholar. As the volume of published material has risen, the library budgets of colleges and universities are increasingly pressed. The typical library of a law school must expend a substantial portion of its annual budget merely to keep current its holdings of state and federal reports as well as statutes, treatises, and looseleaf services.

In its support of higher education, outside its concern with Copyright Law, the Congress has recognized this basic financial constraint. Thus, in its 1972 amendments to the Higher Education Act of 1965 (and related acts), Congress supported networks for the shared use of library materials (among other facilities). Section 1033(a) of Title 20 U.S.C.A. (1974) provides as follows:

The Commissioner shall carry out a program of encouraging institutions of higher education (including law and other graduate professional schools) to share, to the optimal extent through cooperative arrangements, their technical and other . . . resources. . . .

Subsection (b) designates such authorized projects of shared usages as follows:

(1)(A) joint use of facilities such as . . . libraries, including law libraries . . . including joint use of necessary books. . . .

Against the background of this clear, prior expression favoring shared use, we express our concern that § 108(g) of H.R. 2223 is inconsistent with, and hostile to, this stated desire of Congress.

We therefore urge this Committee to delete § 108(g) (1) and (2) from the present measure because we believe it improperly limits and is inconsistent with, the expression of the fair use doctrine contained in § 107 and the legislative history thereto. It is our recommendation that a period be placed after the phrase, ". . . separate occasions" in the first sentence of § 108(g) and that all language subsequent thereto be deleted.

We oppose the enactment of § 108(g)(1) as presently proposed, because it introduces an inarticulate and troublesome concept of "concerted reproduction"; we consider the reference to "systematic reproduction" in § 108(g)(2) to be equally vague and troublesome.

It is significant that the Senate Report No. 93-983, 93d Cong., 2d Sess. 122 (1974), states of the identical text of § 108(g) which appeared in S. 1361:

However, neither a statute nor legislative history can specify precisely which library photocopying practices constitute the making of "single copies" as distinguished from "systematic reproduction." [At p. 122.]

We urge that the legislative history to § 108 reflect this concern with unduly limiting § 107. We object to the examples of permissible shared library usage under § 108 offered in the above Senate Report, in that they are misleading. To the extent that they would guide a court in the interpretation of the phrase "systematic reproduction," this statement of legislative intent does so without any reflection of the interest of the teacher and scholar to have basic material made available. Moreover, the present expression of legislative purpose underlying § 108 makes no mention of the considerations of the Higher Education Act's stated interest in shared usage.

It would be our preference that the text of the present § 108 be modified as we have indicated above and that the legislative history of this provision reflect the dual concerns of the teacher and scholar's need for the availability of published materials as well as the Education Act's directive for shared usage. It seems to us that the examples in the present Senate Report give little if any weight to these two basic considerations.

From the standpoint of the teacher and the researcher, the doctrine of fair use must be enacted free of effective limitations on library practices. Availability of library materials remains basic both to the teaching and research functions of the higher education community. A teacher in a small private or public university located in the Southeastern part of the United States, may find that a work essential to a current research interest is to be found only at a university at some distance to the Northeast. That teacher may need to obtain only one chapter of a book or a few pages of either a book or a periodical. Having such material available is essential to the scholar. Inter-library lending has become a means of making this information available. A definition of fair use which left uncertain the availability of such material, even if photocopied, would frustrate the purposes underlying both the fair use doctrine and the fundamental commitment to provide and advance knowledge by the university community.

Accordingly we would request that the legislative history of § 108 (a) through (f) clearly state the importance of the availability of library and archival material to the teacher and the scholar.

Turning to the teaching function, the need for reasonable availability of copyrighted material for classroom use is inextricably linked to the needs of the scholar. Often a current news item or periodical article will bear directly and immediately upon a topic scheduled for classroom discussion the next day. The quality of teaching is greatly improved by making available to the students the latest commentary about it while they are studying the topic. Denial of availability of such copyrighted material would not serve the interest of copyright proprietors. Students in the classroom situation are not potential subscribers to the Bureau of National Affairs, Antitrust & Trade Regulation Report, for example, or to the Prentice-Hall multi-volume Federal Income Tax Service, during their tenure as students. Indeed, it is likely that having the benefit of a brief extract from one of these services, complete with its full title, will advertise and acquaint the student with the utility of these loose-leaf services.

To deny the classroom teacher the availability of such material will mean only that the students will be without such current and timely material. Denial of the use of this material will mean simply that the educational process will be less well served and the copyright proprietor will be without even the benefit of having the availability of this material brought to the attention of students.

We reiterate that we do not seek the right to engage in multiple copying out of the context of research and teaching. We seek only the right of the scholar and teacher to have available, subject to the limitations of the statutory fair use doctrine, such copyrighted material as is germane to research and writing. And we seek this availability in the public interest in the promotion and dissemination of education and scholarly pursuits. In taking this position, we recognize that the effect on the potential market for the copyrighted material, is an appropriate factor to be considered in the determination of fair use. We also recognize that in the overwhelming proportion of cases, any possible adverse effect on the economic interest of a proprietor will be nil or virtually so. On balance, such use of excerpts is likely to stimulate the sales of the material in the long run.

We should like to draw the Committee's attention to the forthcoming studies undertaken through the Copyright Office and the National Commission on Libraries and Information Science, of the library usage of copyrighted materials both in the inter-library loan context as well as in meeting requests of scholarly and research users. The feasibility of designing a "payments mechanism" for such library uses is one aspect of this study.

It is our concern that a determination of the feasibility of some means of compensation may serve to vacate the doctrine of fair use. We believe such a conclusion would do great harm to the public interest in the promotion of education and scholarly activities. Moreover, such an outcome would inflict irreparable harm on the educational community without conferring a derivative benefit on copyright proprietors.

We thus advocate that the House Report which accompanies this measure, be drafted to include an express reference to the effect that the doctrine of fair use would be applicable to copyrighted materials which might subsequently be designated as compensable, if photocopied for other uses. By clearly establishing that teaching and research uses are significant to the doctrine of fair use, subsequent uncertainty as to the treatment of library materials which might require compensation if copied for other purposes, would be avoided.

We consider that Chapter 5 of H. 2223 sets out definitions of infringement and remedies therefor, which are unduly restrictive of the doctrine of fair use in the educational context.

Accordingly we urge modification of the present measure, as follows. First, we urge that § 502(a) be modified by the addition of the following sentence, "No temporary or final injunction shall be available against any library or user covered by § 108 or § 110."

In its present form, we believe § 502(a) of the proposed measure would permit the use of the injunction to undercut the effective access by teachers and scholars to the fair use provisions. We would point to the withdrawal by Congress of injunctive relief against collective organizational activity in the labor relations arena by the Norris-LaGuardia Act, 47 Stat. 70 (1932); 29 U.S.C.A. § 101 (1973). It is our position that the parallel should carry over here. The sole statutory framework controlling labor relations is the Labor Relations statutes themselves. We urge that the fair use doctrines of the proposed measure be enacted as the sole framework for governing the use of copyrighted materials in the educational context by teachers and scholars.

Secondly, we consider that the damages provision of § 504(c)(2) also encroaches upon the fair use doctrine of § 107. We urge a change in the last sentence of this provision beginning at line 13 on page 49. In line 18, we would prefer that the reference to § 107 be deleted in favor of the phrase, "§§ 107 through 117." Then we would urge that all language on line 18 after the phrase, "§ 107", in the current version, be deleted. In its place we would urge the following final language as follows: "there shall be neither statutory damages, nor costs, nor attorneys fees."

TESTIMONY OF LEO J. RASKIND, PROFESSOR OF LAW, UNIVERSITY OF MINNESOTA, REPRESENTING THE ASSOCIATION OF AMERI-

CAN LAW SCHOOLS, THE AMERICAN ASSOCIATION OF UNIVERSITY PROFESSORS, AND THE AMERICAN COUNCIL ON EDUCATION

Mr. RASKIND. As Mr. Steinbach has said, Mr. Chairman and members of the subcommittee, I am professor of law at the University of Minnesota. I appear before you today on behalf of these organizations: The Association of American Law Schools, the American Association of University Professors, and the American Council on Education. We account, as a law school association, for some 6,000 law teachers. The American Association of University Professors comprises some 75,000 other university professors. The American Council on Education is an association of national and regional education organizations, and nearly 1,400 institutions of higher education.

We appear before you because of our concern over the revision of the doctrine of fair use in relation to our function. May I draw to your attention, on page 2 of my statement, to the second paragraph; we note above the constitutional directive contained in article I, section 8, clause 8, of Congress' concern in this area of assuring to authors and others the rights to their writings.

As the higher education community, we are the principal institution concerned in this society with the task of transmitting and advancing knowledge. It is for that use that we deem the problem of fair use of copyrighted material as crucial to the discharge of this function.

As a classroom teacher with some 20 years' experience in law schools and departments of economics, I am here to assert to you that without the doctrine of fair use, adequately described in the statute, and supported by articulate legislative history, what we do would be greatly impeded without any derivative benefit to publishers and others.

We use this material—and examples of our use suggests that the students, who are the ultimate consumers of our concern as teachers, are not, at the time that they are students, potential subscribers to the journals for which protection is sought. Many of the journals— Time magazine, for example—recognize the students' status by offering student subscriptions. Many learned journals offer subscriptions. We are only asking through the doctrine of fair use, as researchers and scholars, to advance knowledge by having made available to us, in the library context, materials which our libraries do not have, no matter how good they are. The University of Minnesota has a fine law library, but we do not have everything. On occasion it is necessary for me, if I am writing an article, to have information from other libraries. That is the main nub of our concern with the doctrine of fair use. We think it is crucial for the discharge of our teaching and research. We do not see that it infringes on the economic rights of others.

I draw your attention, on page 2, in the third paragraph, that we expressly recognize that we do not seek to have removed from copyright protection basic material under the statute. We accept this premise as a matter of principle and a matter of public policy and a matter of self-interest. As lawyers, we recognize case law and I draw your attention, now, to the next-to-the-last paragraph on page 2— that the existing state of case law in this area is not articulate, sufficiently articulate, to deal with fair use and describe it.

Therefore, we urge that this revision process produce a statutory doctrine of fair use and it be described by legislative history that will aid the interpretation of it.

I point out to you further—I will not read this statement; I will summarize it and make myself available to your questions—that Congress has, itself, as I point out on the bottom of page 3, enacted legislation suggesting such shared usage and recognizing that, as researchers, our libraries do not have adequate resources and cannot have adequate resources for every library to have a total collection of all the material that is needed for teaching and research.

I draw your attention to Congress' joint- and shared-use provisions in the Higher Education Act, section 1033.

Against this background, we have reviewed the proposed H.R. 2223 and found, as was pointed out to you yesterday, that, for example, section 108(g) trenches and undermines the interpretation of section 107 that we would seek. The details of that, I leave to my statement.

I would draw your attention now to page 6 of my statement, and to the second paragraph; the first and second paragraphs.

Our position is that to deny the classroom teacher the availability of such copyrighted material, in the context of teaching and research, would be to make the teaching and research process less fruitful, less meaningful and less important to scholars; and to do so would not benefit the economic interest of copyrights. We would simply do without, if it were necessary, if we could not have access to this material.

We reiterate, as I say in the second paragraph on page 6, we do not seek the right to engage in multiple copying outside the context of research and teaching. We seek only the right of the scholar and teacher to have available subject matter, subject to the limitations of the statutory doctrine of fair use.

I will close now, and make myself available to your questions.

Mr. Kastenmeier. Unless members are strongly disposed to do so, I would urge they defer questions until each of the witnesses has concluded; then you may ask questions of any of the witnesses who have testified.

Mr. Steinbach. I next would like to introduce Bernard J. Freitag, Council Rock High School, New Town, Pa., on behalf of the National Education Association; accompanied by Dr. Harold E. Wigren.

[The prepared statement of the National Education Association follows:]

Statement of James A. Harris, President, National Education Association

I am James A. Harris, President of the National Education Association. The NEA represents almost 1.7 million teachers in every state across the nation and is the largest professional association in the United States. Its members are active at all levels of education from early childhood through postsecondary and adult. Thus, our interests cover the whole spectrum of educational programs. We appreciate the opportunity to present our views regarding the need to reform copyright law and retain certain positive aspects of the present law, and to comment on H.R. 2223.

The National Education Association is in favor of reform of the U.S. Copyright Law of 1909, but NEA will not support a law which deprives educators of rights derived through long-established practice and which denies teachers and students the right of reasonable access to both print and non-print materials for purposes of teaching, scholarship, and research.

The NEA therefore opposes H.R. 2223 in its present form. It is a regressive bill that curtails or repeals existing rights for education—rights which have been established through the years. We object to H.R. 2223 on a number of grounds.

(A) *The language of H.R. 2223 severely curtails the applicability of the "not-for-profit" concept in the present law and substitutes restrictive language that is not acceptable in meeting the needs of education consumers.* Under the not-for-profit principle, a distinction is made between commercial and noncommercial uses of materials—a distinction which we feel is valid and defensible and which should be preserved in the new law. Educational users need special protection over and above that provided commercial users because they have a public responsibility for teaching the children entrusted to them. They work for people—not for profit. They do not use materials for their own gain but for the benefit of the children of all of our citizens, including those of authors and publishers.

Teachers therefore need the assurance that the present law's not-for-profit principle, granting special exemptions for nonprofit uses of copyrighted materials, will become part of the new law.

Section 110(1) of H.R. 2223 limits permissible uses of copyrighted materials to face-to-face classroom teaching situations and would rule out closed-circuit in-school uses as well as uses over dial- or remote-access system in schools, all of which are designed to bring materials to learners rather than transport learners to materials. Section 110(2) would restrict the transmission of instructional television programs to "reception in classrooms or similar places normally devoted to instruction" and would rule out the use of such programs in open learning situations in community store front learning centers or for high school or postsecondary formal viewing situations in dormitories or at home. Education is rapidly moving in the direction of providing many alternatives and options in learning wherein school is becoming a *concept* rather than a *place*.

(B) *The bill also fails to clarify the meaning of "fair use" as applied to the uses of instructional materials by teachers and students.* The recent Supreme Court decision in the Williams & Wilkins case validates our position that fair use is unreliable at best and is, in the words of the Court of Claims, an "amorphous doctrine." The bill leaves it in that status. If eight Justices of the Supreme Court are unable to reach agreement on whether a given use of a work is a fair use, how can one expect a non-jurist to know? The language and rationale are just as applicable against teachers and schools as against libraries.

The NEA does not condone "under-the-table" uses. It simply wants teachers to have reasonable certainty that a given use of copyrighted work is permissible so that they won't be afraid to use a wide variety of materials and resources in the classroom.

The bill further fails to recognize custom and practice in education as a proper basis for "fair use," as was decided in the Williams & Wilkins case. For many years teachers have been accustomed to certain classroom uses of materials being unchallenged or unquestioned. For example:

A class is having difficulty understanding symbolism in literature, and the class text does not go far enough in its explanation. The teacher therefore makes multiple copies of a short poem or a short essay (from another book) that would help the class understand the concept.

A foreign language teacher tapes a portion of a modern French poem and asks students to verbalize the recorded portion and then tape it so they can see the improvement of their accent.

An economics teacher reproduces 30 copies of graphs and charts from the *Wall Street Journal* to study the stock market.

They consequently have assumed that such uses were legitimate. We argue that custom can become law when it isn't questioned! This is particularly true in cases where the law is ambiguous, as in the case of the fair use doctrine, where long-established and non-contested custom and practice has in fact established a meaning for the statutes.

In this regard, the NEA is also concerned the bill still places the burden of proof on the classroom teacher to prove that he or she has not infringed copyright. The NEA believes strongly that this burden of proof should be shifted to the alleger of the infringement, who has all the data involved in all the criteria for fair use which are specified in Section 107.

(C) *This legislation further reduces accessibility now permitted through the non-renewal of copyrights after 28 years.* It does this by eliminating the renewal requirement and by providing for duration of life plus 50 years. This is a curtailment of education's present rights of access because it unduly extends copyright monopoly from "28 years plus a 28-year renewal period" to approximately 75 years. Copyright Office records show that approximately 85 percent of copyrighted works have not been renewed after the initial 28-year period, but have passed instead into the public domain. The unwarranted extension of copyright in H.R. 2223 would protect the author's or creator's heirs more than it would the author or creator himself or herself. We ask, therefore, why the principle of free access to information so essential to a free society should be sacrificed, especially when the author or creator himself or herself has not seen fit to renew the copyright. Many teachers who are also authors tell us that they are as much—or even more—interested in seeing their works used and their ideas disseminated as they are in receiving remuneration each time their works are used. The profit motive is not the only motive that prompts an author or other creator to produce. There is also the satisfaction that comes from getting one's ideas into the open for discussion and debate, with the hope of finally seeing them adopted and thereby creating a better life for others who follow.

In summary, the NEA will not be able to support a bill unless it—

Retains and clarifies an overall not-for-profit concept for educational, scholarly, and research uses and copying, whether couched as a limited educational exemption or in some other suitable comprehensive form;

Clarifies the meaning of fair use as applied to teachers and learners;

Shifts the burden of proof from the teacher to the alleger of the infringement.

NEA therefore urges the adoption of language by this committee that encompasses the above-stated concepts and makes copyright reform meaningful for the teachers, scholars, researchers, authors, and publishers who create, transmit, and perpetuate our heritage for future generations.

TESTIMONY OF BERNARD J. FREITAG, COUNCIL ROCK HIGH SCHOOL, NEW TOWN, PA., ACCOMPANIED BY HAROLD E. WIGREN, ON BEHALF OF THE NATIONAL EDUCATION ASSOCIATION

Mr. FREITAG. Mr. Chairman, members of the subcommittee, I am Bernard Freitag, teacher of German and foreign language department chairman at the Council Rock High School, New Town, Pa.

I am appearing on behalf of President James A. Harris, President of the National Education Association.

With your approval, I am skipping the first two paragraphs. I now request that the entire statement appear in the record.

The NEA opposes H.R. 2223 in its present form. It is a regressive bill that curtails or repeals existing rights for education—rights which have been established through the years. We object to H.R. 2223 on a number of grounds.

(A) The language of H.R. 2223 severely curtails the applicability of the not-for-profit concept in the present law and substitutes restrictive language that is not acceptable in meeting the needs of educational consumers. Under the not-for-profit principle, a distinction is made between commercial and noncommercial uses of materials—a distinction which we feel is valid and defensible and which should be preserved in the new law. Educational users need special protection over and above that provided commercial users because they have a public responsibility for teaching the children entrusted to them.

They work for people, not for profit. They do not use materials for their own gain, but for the benefit of the children of all of our citizens, including those of authors and publishers. Teachers therefore need the assurance that the present law's not-for-profit principle, granting special exemptions for nonprofit uses of copyrighted materials, will become part of the new law.

Section 110(1) of H.R. 2223 limits permissible uses of copyrighted materials to face-to-face classroom teaching situations and would rule out closed-circuit in-school uses as well as uses over dial- or remote-access systems in schools, all of which are designed to bring materials to learners rather than transport learners to materials. Section 110(2) would restrict the transmission of instructional television programs to reception in classrooms or similar places normally devoted to instruction and would rule out the use of such programs in open learning situations in community storefront learning centers or for high school or postsecondary formal viewing situations in dormitories or at home. Education is rapidly moving in the direction of providing many alternatives and options to learning wherein school is becoming a concept rather than a place.

(B) The bill also fails to clarify the meaning of fair use as applied to the uses of instructional materials by teachers and students. The recent Supreme Court decision in the *Williams & Wilkins* case validates our position that fair use is unreliable at best and is, in the words of the Court of Claims, an amorphous doctrine. The bill leaves it in that status. If eight Justices of the Supreme Court are unable to reach agreement on whether a given use of a work is a fair use, how can one expect a nonjurist to know? The language and rationale are just as applicable against teachers and schools as against libraries.

The NEA does not condone "under the table" uses. It simply wants teachers to have reasonable certainty that a given use of copyrighted work is permissible so that they will not be afraid to use a wide variety of materials and resources in the classroom.

The bill further fails to recognize custom and practice in education as a proper basis for fair use, as was decided in the *Williams & Wilkins* case. For many years, teachers have been accustomed to certain classroom uses of materials being unchallenged or unquestioned. For example: A class is having difficulty understanding symbolism in literature, and the class text does not go far enough in its explanation. The teacher therefore makes multiple copies of a short poem or a short essay—from another book—that would help the class understand the concept.

Allow me to give some personal examples:

Teachers in my department make synchronized tape presentations for classroom use. The basis of those slide tape presentations are, by and large, their own materials: Pictures taken on their own trips. However, some specific items may not be available to the teacher, because you need special permission to get access to the area, or perhaps the pictures taken by the teacher did not turn out quite as well as could be desired. In such an instance, the teacher may prefer to take a picture from the available magazine, make a slide of it, incorporate it right into the slide tape program.

Another example, dealing with foreign exchange values, dealing with the currency of a given country: On the day that that topic may come up, the teacher would perhaps make copies, 30 copies, of the foreign exchange rates of the previous day in order to help the children make the decision on what the daily rate concerning the story at hand, or topic at hand, would be for, say, marks, shillings, or Swiss francs.

Teachers, consequently, have assumed that such uses were legitimate. We argue that custom can become law when it is not questioned. This is particularly true in cases where the law is ambiguous, as in the case of the fair use doctrine, where long-established and noncontested custom and practice has in fact established a meaning for the statutes.

In this regard, the NEA is also concerned that the bill still places the burden of proof on the classroom teacher to prove that he or she has not infringed copyright. The NEA believes strongly that this burden of proof should be shifted to the alleger of the infringement, who has all the data involved in all the criteria for fair use which are specified in section 107.

(C) This legislation further reduces accessibility now permitted through the nonrenewal of copyrights after 28 years. It does this by eliminating the renewal requirement and by providing for duration of life plus 50 years. This is a curtailment of education's present rights of access because it unduly extends copyright monopoly from 28 years plus a 28-year renewal period to approximately 75 years. Copyright Office records show that approximately 85 percent of copyrighted works have not been renewed after the initial 28-year period, but have passed instead into the public domain. The unwarranted extension of copyright in H.R. 2223 would protect the author's or creator's heirs more than it would the author or creator himself or herself. We ask, therefore, why the principle of free access to information so essential to a free society should be sacrificed, especially when the author or creator himself or herself has not seen fit to renew the copyright. Many teachers who are also authors tell us that they are as much—or even more—interested in seeing their works used and their ideas disseminated as they are in receiving remuneration each time their works are used. The profit motive is not the only motive that prompts an author or other creator to produce. There is also the satisfaction that comes from getting one's ideas into the open for discussion and debate, with the hope of finally seeing them adopted and thereby creating a better life for others who follow.

In summary, the NEA will not be able to support a bill unless it (1) retains and clarifies an overall not-for-profit concept for educational, scholarly, and research uses and copying, whether couched as a limited educational exemption or in some other suitable comprehensive form; (2) clarifies the meaning of fair use as applied to teachers and learners; and (3) shifts the burden of proof from the teacher to the alleger of the infringement.

NEA therefore urges the adoption of language by this committee that encompasses the above-stated concepts and makes copyright reform meaningful for the teachers, scholars, researchers, authors, and publishers who create, transmit, and perpetuate our heritage for future generations.

Mr. Chairman, I would like to submit for the record the ad hoc committee's proposal on the exemption.

Mr. KASTENMEIER. Without objection, that proposal will be received and be made part of the record.

[The material referred to follows:]

AD HOC COMMITTEE'S PROPOSAL FOR LIMITED EDUCATIONAL EXEMPTION; LIMITATIONS ON EXCLUSIVE RIGHTS: REPRODUCTION FOR TEACHING, SCHOLARSHIP AND RESEARCH

Notwithstanding other provisions of this Act, nonprofit use of a portion of a copyrighted work for noncommercial teaching, scholarship and research is not an infringement of copyright.

For purposes of this section:

(1) "Use" shall mean reproduction, copying and recording; storage and retrieval by automatic systems capable of storing, processing, retrieving, or transferring information or in conjunction with any similar device, machine or process;

(2) "Portion" shall mean brief excerpts (which are not substantial in length in proportion to their source) from copyrighted works, except that it shall also include (a) the whole of short literary, pictorial and graphic works; (b) entire works reproduced for storage in automatic systems capable of storing, processing, retrieving, or transferring information or in conjunction with any similar device, machine or process, *provided* that

(i) A method of recording retrieval of the stored information is established at the time of reproduction for storage, and

(ii) The rules otherwise applicable under law to copyrighted works shall apply to information retrieved from such systems;

(c) Recording and retransmission of broadcasts within five school days after the recorded broadcast; provided that such recording is immediately destroyed after such 5-day period and that such retransmission is limited to immediate viewing in schools and colleges.

Provided that "portion" shall not include works which are

(a) Originally consumable upon use, such as workbook exercises, problems, or standardized tests and the answer sheets for such tests;

(b) Used for the purpose of compilation within the provisions of Section 103(a).

Mr. STEINBACH. I would next like to introduce Dr. Howard B. Hitchens, executive director, Association for Educational Communications and Technology.

[The prepared statement of Howard B. Hitchens follows:]

STATEMENT OF HOWARD B. HITCHENS, EXECUTIVE DIRECTOR, ASSOCIATION FOR EDUCATIONAL COMMUNICATIONS & TECHNOLOGY

The Association for Educational Communications and Technology represents eight thousand educators whose professional commitment is directed at finding technological solutions for the wide range of educational problems. It is important to note here that we regard technology as far more than a collection of educational machines and materials. Technology represents a systematic approach to practical problems that emphasize the application of relevant research. Professionals in my field occupy any number of roles—whether it's directing media programs; developing specific instructional materials for classroom or individual use; assisting teachers or others in selecting materials to meet a specific educational objective; evaluating materials; identifying long-range educational objectives and developing long-range plans to meet these objectives. Our members with this wide variety of jobs are employed in schools and colleges; in the Armed Forces and industry, and in museums, libraries and hospitals throughout the country.

Because they are so involved in the use of technology and modern communications, AECT members have run head-on into the 1909 copyright law which provides few answers for them in how they can use copyrighted materials. And the problem becomes more difficult as media professionals find themselves placed increasingly in the role of "copyright expert" for their institution. Because media professionals play such a vital role in education planning and materials selection, school administrators are turning to them to answer the complex copyright questions that arise daily in modern educational settings.

So AECT, as an association, is vitally concerned with the future of the bill you are considering today. We have spent much time and energy trying to determine the needs of education in relation to a new copyright law, but have come to realize that we cannot look at the needs of education in isolation. Since we are dependent to a great extent on the output of producers of education materials, we must take their needs into consideration.

There is little doubt that the success of each group—educators and producers—depends upon the support of the other. If the educators do not utilize instructional materials, the producers surely cannot remain in business. The teacher, media professional, and the librarian create markets for an author's work and give them visibility. Likewise, in this day of individualized instruction, the open classroom, ungraded schools, and student self-evaluation, the successful educator—teacher, librarian, curriculum developer—wants to utilize a wide range of learning resources. Certainly, when producers and users can act in concert, the student reaps the benefits.

In considering the needs of both sides—educators and producers—AECT has adopted a position relative to copyright that we feel serves both groups. AECT endorses with one exception the fair use provisions outlined in Section 107 and the accompanying legislative history. The full text of our position paper follows. Particular attention should be paid to the third and fourth paragraphs, which deal with the issue of "fair use."

[H.R. 2223]

COPYRIGHT LAW REVISION: A POSITION PAPER BY THE ASSOCIATION FOR EDUCATIONAL COMMUNICATIONS AND TECHNOLOGY

The members of the Association for Educational Communications and Technology (AECT) believe that technology is an integral part of the teaching-learning process and helps to maximize the outcomes of interaction between teacher and pupil.

Regulations governing United States Copyright were originally developed to promote the public welfare and encourage authorship by giving authors certain controls over their work. It follows that revisions in Title 17 of the United States Code (Copyrights) should maintain the balance between providing for the compensation of authors and insuring that information remains available to the public. Some of the revisions proposed in S. 22 and H.R. 2223 lose sight of this balance between user and producer.

AECT endorses the criteria to be used in the determination of "fair use" as contained in Section 107 of the proposed bill:

Section 107. Limitations on exclusive rights: Fair use

* * * the fair use of a copyrighted work, including such use by reproduction in copies or phonorecords, or by any other means specified by (Section 106), for purposes such as criticism, comment, news reporting, scholarship, or research, is not an infringement of copyright. In determining whether the use made of a work in any particular case is fair use the factors to be considered shall include:

(1) The purpose and character of the use;

(2) The nature of the copyrighted work;

(3) The amount and substantiality of the portion used in relation to the copyrighted work as a whole; and

(4) The effect of the use upon the potential market for or value of the copyrighted work.

However, *we propose that the concept of "fair use" should apply equally to the classroom teacher and media professional—including specialists in audiovisual and library resources.* Media personnel are becoming increasingly important members of educational planning teams and must have the assurance that they may assist classroom teachers in the selection of daily instructional materials as well as with long range curriculum development. Classroom teachers do not always operate "individually and at (their) own volition." The fact that the media professional makes use of advance planning and has knowledge aforethought of the materials he prepares for the teacher should not invalidate the application of the "fair use" principle.

Concerning the use of copyrighted works in conjunction with television, AECT proposes that "fair use," as it has been outlined above, *should apply* to educational/instructional broadcast or closed-circuit transmission in a non-profit educational institution, but not to commercial broadcasting.

Once the doctrine of "fair use" has been established in the revised law, negotiations should be conducted between the proprietor and user prior to any use of copyrighted materials that goes beyond that doctrine. We believe that the enactment of the "fair use" concept into law prior to negotiations will guard against the erosion of the concept. Generally, a reasonable fee should be paid for uses that go beyond "fair use," but such fee arrangement should not delay or impede the use of the materials. Producers are urged to give free access (no-cost contracts) whenever possible.

We agree with the Ad Hoc Committee of Educational Organizations and Institutions on Copyright Law Revision that duration of copyright should provide for an initial period of twenty-eight years, followed by a renewal period of forty-eight years, whereas the proposed bill sets duration at the "life of the author plus fifty years." It seems reasonable that provisions should be made to permit those materials which the copyright holder has no interest in protecting after the initial period to pass into the public domain.

Regarding the input of copyrighted materials into computers or other storage devices by non-profit educational institutions, we agree with the Ad Hoc Committee that the bill should clearly state that until the proposed National Commission on New Technological Uses of Copyrighted Works has completed its study, such input should not be considered infringement. The proposed bill states only that ". . . (Section 117) does not afford to the owner of copyright in a work any greater or lesser rights with respect to the use of the work in conjunction with automatic systems . . ."

A new copyright law that both users and producers can view as equitable depends upon the mutual understanding of each other's needs and the ability to effectively work out the differences. We will participate in the continuing dialogue with the Educational Media Producers Council and similar interest groups to establish mutually acceptable guidelines regarding the boundaries of "fair use," and reasonable fees to be paid for uses beyond "fair use." This dialogue will be especially important in the area of storage, retrieval, and/or transmission of materials during the time period prior to the issuance of the report of the National Commission on New Technological Uses of Copyrighted Works.

We feel that the above modifications of S. 22 and H.R. 2223 are needed to insure that the revised law assists rather than hinders teachers and media specialists in their work.

Our major concern with fair use is that in studying the legislative history of the doctrine, fair use does not seem to apply equally to media professionals as to teachers. The previous House and Senate reports identify "spontaneity" of the use as an important determinant as to whether a use is fair or not. Fair use is extended to a classroom teacher who "*acting individually and at his own volition* makes one or more copies for temporary use by himself or his pupils in the classroom." However, classroom teachers do not always act individually or at their own volition. They are frequently assisted by media professionals with the selection of daily instructional materials as well as long range curriculum development. The fact that a media professional is frequently not classified as a "classroom teacher" and is sometimes even classified as "administration" should not prevent him from continuing his role in the instructional process. *We are not suggesting that any rights beyond "fair use" be extended to media professionals, only that they be allowed as much freedom as other education professionals.* We are currently working with others interested in this problem and will present alternative language to this subcommittee in the near future.

Even though we support the enactment of Section 107 with suggested changes, we realize that it will not solve the daily dilemmas faced by media professionals, teachers, and librarians. AUDIOVISUAL INSTRUCTION, a magazine published by my association, features a monthly column entitled "Copyright Today" that demonstrates the confusion over the bounds of fair use. The column (several reprints are attached) features copyright questions posed by readers with answers suggested by copyright experts, usually including at least one educator and one producer. As you can see from the examples, there are frequently as many answers to a given question as there are copyright experts.

Take the following question from the November 1974 issue of *Audiovisual Instruction:*

Question. Two teachers in this district are preparing audio tutorial packages for the fifth grade botany unit. They found five pictures they need in a color film owned by the district. They want to make slide copies of the five frames. Two copies of each slide is required. Would this be a violation of the copyright law?

There are two opinions as to the legality of this action provided in the article—one by an educator, the other by a representative of the producers. The educator felt the situation cited may be beyond fair use because more than one copy would be made and the copying would be done by someone (the media professional) other than a classroom teacher. The producers' representative states that the situation would fall within "fair use."

As I said we realize the enactment of Section 107 will not solve our problems. Even with the guidelines provided in that Section it is still difficult to determine what is fair use and what is not. And if an educator is not able to determine if the proposed use is fair and feels that permission to copy should be obtained in order to remain safely within the bounds of the law, how does he or she get permission from a publisher or producer to use the material?

Requesting permission to use copyrighted materials is currently a long and frequently tedious process for educators. An attached article entitled "Copyright As It Affects Instructional Development" (Audiovisual Instruction, December 1974) demonstrates the problems of contacting numerous producers with no predetermined procedures. Perhaps this problem could be solved by establishment of a clearinghouse either governmental or privately operated. Certainly this would make it easier for an educator if he or she has to contact only one source for permission rather than trying to deal with numerous producers all with different procedures. But even a clearinghouse arrangement will still result in much time spent in waiting for reply.

We feel this delay, even if it is only (ideally) a week or so, might be detrimental to the teaching/learning process. It doesn't allow the education professional to take advantage of the "teachable moment." For example, on the day following a speech by a noted individual, a teacher may want to use the copy of the speech that appears in the local paper for reproduction and distribution to a speech class for critique. Clearly, if the teacher had to wait several weeks for permission to use the text, the impact of involving students in current events would be lost. So in many instances, some means other than a clearinghouse must be used.

AECT has spent many hours working with producers in an attempt to work out guidelines that would assist educators in upholding the copyright law. We have come increasingly to the conclusion that the best means of solving the problem is by developing voluntary licensing agreements between educators and producers. Such agreements would allow a pre-determined amount of copying, kind of copying, or maybe even unlimited copying either for no charge or for a pre-determined fee. Such an agreement would set the bounds of fair use in advance and would also allow educators to take advantage of the "teachable moment."

We are not asking you, the Congress, to legislate a licensing agreement. It would be almost impossible to include every possible type of necessary agreement in legislation. We think we as educators must take the responsibility to work with producers of materials to develop such agreement. AECT has had and will continue to have dialogue with producers of materials in an attempt to satisfy the needs of both groups. We are asking only support and encouragement from the Congress to both sides to sit down and develop licensing agreements.

The AECT position which has been presented in this testimony has been well received by both educators and materials producers. Representatives of both these communities viewed the position as a realistic step toward resolving the issue of defining the limits of fair use. The statement is viewed by members of each group as offering protection to educators that is not offensive to the producers.

We think the incorporation of the AECT position into H.R. 2223 and its legislative history is essential to the development of a new copyright law that is equitable to educators and creators of materials alike.

I wish to thank the Subcommittee for this opportunity to present our views. I only hope we can impress upon you that we are as concerned as you are with the necessity for a new copyright law that will allow us as education professionals to continue the improvement of education through the application of new technology and communications.

STATEMENT OF BELLA L. LINDEN, ATTORNEY, NEW YORK, N.Y.

Mr. Chairman, I am Bella L. Linden, partner in the law firm of Linden and Deutsch, New York City. I was counsel for many years for the American Textbook Publishers Institute (until its merger with the American Book Publishers Council into the association known as Association of American Publishers), a member of the Panel of Experts appointed by the Register of Copyrights to consider revision of the Copyright Law, and a member of the Committee on Science and Technical Information (COSATI) of the Federal Council for Science and Technology and Chairman of the COSATI sub-panel on rights of access to computerized information systems. My firm represents Harcourt Brace Jovanovich, Inc. and Macmillan, Inc., two of the five largest American educational publishers. However, I appear here today not on behalf of Macmillan or Harcourt alone, nor solely on behalf of educational publishers. Rather, I am here in the interests of our system of educational authorship and publishing, representing the sum total of the combined creative efforts and investments of the authors and publishers of this country's educational materials.

This statement is respectfully submitted in opposition to the proposal for a general educational exemption to the rights of authors and publishers established in H.R. 2223. Eight years ago, in your Committee's analysis of the doctrine of fair use as established in the Revision Bill and, in particular, its application to educational and classroom use, your Committee concluded that " a specific exemption freeing certain reproductions of copyrighted works for educational and scholarly purposes from copyright control is not justified." [H.R. Rep. No. 83, p. 31] At last week's hearings the Register of Copyrights stated that your report "still remains the basic legislative explanation of the content of the Bill, and the [basis from which] the reports succeeding it in both Houses have all been drawn * * *." During the intervening years, the only relevant fact to have changed is the further proliferation of devices for unauthorized, inexpensive and rapid duplication, use and transmission of copyrighted works.

Yet, we find ourselves still debating the request for the so-called "educational exemption."

At bottom, of course, this dispute is based on economic interests. Authors, publishers, educators, librarians, all must live on a budget. I will certainly concede that anything which may be acquired free of charge imposes no burden on a budget, so it is not totally unnatural for users of copyrighted materials to desire unpaid-for duplication privileges. Textbook budgets are extremely low, amounting, on a national average, to between two and three percent of a school's annual budget. Photocopying equipment and other reproduction, storage and retrieval devices are not part of a school's textbook budget, but come under the broad umbrella of "supplies." Thus, the natural and laudable tendency for good teachers is to seek supplementary material via the Xerox and tape machines. Less laudable however, is the insistence of some that authors and publishers should not be paid for such uses of their works.

Throughout the revision program the authors and publishers of educational materials have agreed with the principle of full and prompt access to copyrighted material for educational use. This is the very reason for their creative efforts and existence. Clearly, there is a significant difference between access to educational materials, which we wholeheartedly support, and unpaid-for duplication of these materials.

We have continually offered to work with the proponents of the educational exemption, as urged by your Committee in 1967, "to work out means by which permissions for uses beyond fair use can be obtained easily and quickly and at reasonable fees." [H.R. Rep. No. 83, p. 33] In fact, in my first appearance before your Committee in 1965, I offered a specific proposal for a clearing house system. However, for almost ten years—during which time many educators have loudly and justifiably voiced their demands for adequate compensation for their own services—the proponents of the educational exemption have sought a statutory basis for the replication of copyrighted educational materials without payment. Rather than accept our invitation, those in favor of the educational exemption offer a provision for sweeping appropriation of copyrighted works. They commonly illustrate their so-called plight by referring to the individual school child who wishes to copy an article from a newspaper for a homework assignment. We are, in effect, told that because the patient has a headache, the cure is to chop off his head.

Authorship of an educational work usually entails many thousands of hours over a period of several years doing library and other research, field testing and consulting. The authors of educational works are not highly publicized personalities who write best sellers and appear on television talk shows. Many are practicing teachers. Few become rich as a result of their writings. To the extent that it is possible to describe a typical textbook author, he or she is a member of the faculty of a highly regarded college or university, enjoys an excellent reputation in his or her field, but is little known outside of it and counts on copyright royalties to pay for braces for the children's teeth, a second car for the family or a vacation or study year abroad or some similar expense. More often than not, royalties on educational works are split between several authors.

By and large, it is the publisher who discerns educational needs, searches out and selects the author (or, more commonly, group of authors) to create the books and materials to satisfy the requirements of schools and universities, and directs and supervises the planning, design and creation of the works. The publishing venture generally encompasses continuing review and evaluation by numerous teachers and curriculum specialists, supervisors and consultants and field testing throughout the country. The role of the American educational publisher combines and coordinates various functions of writing, artistic design and technical skills in applied research, packaging, consulting and training as well as manufacturing, marketing and distribution.

Educational materials today are commonly produced in sets or programs integrating various forms and media such as texts, teachers' manuals or editions, filmstrips, slides, sound recordings, cards, charts, puzzles, instructional games, duplicating masters, transparencies, testing materials and the like; similarly, these programs frequently represent the entire range of literary authorship including fiction, non-fiction, prose, poetry, music and drama. It is not at all uncommon for an educational publisher to invest more than one million dollars in pre-development costs alone for the creation of a program which will take five or ten years to reach the market and another three to five years to gain acceptance and even begin to pay off the investment. In the case of one elementary and junior high school science program with which I am familiar, a total of fourteen years elapsed between the time the program was conceived and the first textbooks were published. The program virtually revolutionized the format and content of elementary school science books. The efforts and investments of authors and educational publishers do not stop upon publication, as subsequent editions are continually revised in light of feed-back from the field and changes in publishing techniques.

Commonly, major portions of the expenses of educational publishing are attributable to payments made to other publishers and authors for the use and integration of portions of prior works in new programs. In the case of one recent elementary reading program, permissions fees paid by the publisher exceeded $100,000 and, it is estimated, comprised more than 30,000 permissions granted. The administrative "burden" of clearing the permissions did not impair the development of the program.

We cannot emphasize often enough that many of the products of educational publishing, such as treatises, texts, workbooks, tests, file cards, anthologies, encyclopedias and other reference works, are designed for use in *piecemeal fashion* rather than cover-to-cover reading. To permit unauthorized photo-duplication of copyrighted works for the purposes of teaching, education and research is a request, in unalloyed English, to permit the educational community to engage in on-demand reprinting, on a daily basis, of those portions of copyrighted educational, scientific and technical works which they wish to use and to circumvent payment to authors and publishers whose entire market for such works is that same educational community.

In many respects educational publishing exists apart from other businesses. The authors and publishers of such works are in a very real and essential sense engaged in public service. For education itself to progress, educational authors and publishers must anticipate and effectively serve a broad range of instructional and scholarly needs. To continue to serve this function in today's society, they must be adequately remunerated for the duplication of their work product.

Although on a short term basis an "educational exemption" may appear desirable to some as aiding the budgetary ills of the educational community, it is clear that the longer term consequence would be to discourage authors and publishers from investing in the creation and distribution of educational materials. The only alternative which comes to mind is the nationalization of educational publishing, Among the ways our society has avoided suppression of intellectual work-product, are the system of economic incentive to writers provided by copyright and the free-enterprise publishing system which encompasses multiple outlets for distribution. Thus, authors are encouraged to publish their thoughts, and the views of an author which may be antithetical to one publisher (or be considered by him to be unpublishable for economic, competitive or other reasons) may still receive exposure through publication by another.

If applied to the free storage (input) of copyrighted materials in computerized information systems the proposed exemption would be in complete derogation of the judgment of both Houses of Congress as expressed in the recent passage of a law establishing a National Commission on New Technological Uses of Copyrighted Works. One of the stated purposes of that Commission is to study, compile data on, and make recommendations to Congress concerning "the reproduction and use of copyrighted works of authorship . . . in conjunction with automatic systems capable of storing, processing, retrieving, and transferring information * * *"

Proponents of the educational exemption have repeatedly emphasized their "educational" purpose and its relation to the public welfare. Of course education is in the public interest—but under our system this interest is served by a private and commercial enterprise which requires a profit to survive. The injury to this country's educational system, educators, scholars, and school children will be material under the erosion of copyright which will result from the proposed exemption. This was fully recognized by your Committee in 1967 when, after considering arguments for a specific educational exemption extending beyond fair use, it stated:

"The fullest possible use of the multitude of technical devices now available to education should be encouraged. But, bearing in mind that the basic constitutional purpose of granting copyright protection is the advancement of learning, the committee also recognizes that the potential destruction of incentives to authorship presents a serious danger." [H.R. Rep. No. 83, at p. 31]

STATEMENT OF EDWARD MEELL ON H.R. 2223 ON BEHALF OF THE EDUCATIONAL MEDIA PRODUCERS COUNCIL

My name is Edward Meell and I am Chairman of the Educational Media Producers Council (EMPC) and Editorial Director of the Film Division of McGraw-Hill Book Company. I am appearing here today on behalf of EMPC and with me is Ivan Bender, Chairman of the EMPC Copyright Committee and Assistant Secretary and Legal Counsel of the Encyclopaedia Britannica Educational Corporation.

We are here to present our views on H.R. 2223, the general copyright revision bill, and specifically on the issues involved in the educational use of copyrighted audio-visual materials. We support the bill as introduced and oppose amendments which would weaken the protection provided in the bill for audio-visual materials.

SECTION 107—FAIR USE

We specifically endorse Section 107, which writes into statutory law the main principles of "fair use" as that doctrine has been interpreted by the courts in individual cases over the years. We feel that Section 107 represents a fair compromise between the creators and users of copyrighted educational materials—a compromise which has been carefully negotiated over the past several years.

Our industry is pleased with the recent technological developments which promise to make ideas and information more accessible to scholars, teachers and learners. These developments promise also to expand the role and contribution of educational media producers to the educational process of which we are an integral part. But in order to maintain and increase the incentives for the creation and production of quality materials for our schools, we must not diminish the statutory protection for intellectual products to which any author, creator or artist is entitled.

NO NEED FOR AN "EDUCATIONAL EXEMPTION"

At the time that this testimony was prepared we were uncertain as to whether a broad educational exemption, to be added to the bill as it now stands, would be proposed by one or more organizations in the light of the positions taken by the Association for Educational Communications & Technology (see Attachment A). The language of previously-introduced amendments, however, in our view provided far more than a "limited" exemption. Among other things it would authorize use—for noncommercial teaching, scholarship and research—not only of "brief excerpts" from copyrighted works but also of the whole of short literary, pictorial and graphic works.

Let us take up these two concepts in order, as they would apply to educational audio-visual materials.

The concept of "brief excerpts" (which are not substantial in length in proportion to their source) is very difficult to apply to educational audio-visual materials. A half hour education nature or biology film, for example, may be built around an exceedingly difficult photographic sequence which may take months of work to capture, but may in the final product only take up a minute or two of time in the film. To permit this minute or two to be reproduced freely under an educational exemption would very likely destroy the economic viability of the product.

The concept of exempting use of "the whole of short, literary, pictorial and graphic works" presents difficulties equally great in relation to audio-visual materials. For example, is a short filmstrip a short work? Is a five minute audio cassette a short work? Is an eight minute 16mm film a short work? If so, it would very largely destroy the entire market for short filmstrips, cassettes or films, and they would be produced in extremely small numbers or not at all.

We trust that this subcommittee will not accept the idea of an educational exemption, if such an exemption should continue to be pressed by one or more organizations. If the exemption is adopted, few companies will be able to risk making the capital and time investments needed to produce educational materials and will turn their efforts to other kinds of products and markets. In such a situation, it might well happen that only with government subsidies could the producers in the private sector afford to finance the development and distribution of educational materials.

Such an exemption has no educational rationale. To the extent that school systems wish to reproduce educational audio-visual materials in whole or in part beyond the limits of "fair use," our members stand ready to discuss licensing arrangements which will permit authorized reproduction. Modern methods of reproduction for many types of audio-visual materials are such as to make such reproduction in whole or in part attractive to some school systems and many of our members have already entered into licensing arrangements which would permit duplication under a negotiated compensation formula.

ENDORSEMENT OF SECTION 107 BY AECT

We are pleased that the principal professional organization of educators directly concerned with the use of audio-visual materials in the educational process is also in support of Section 107, without weakening amendments. This support was expressed in a statement issued by the Executive Committee of the Association for Educational Communications and Technology (AECT) in May of 1975. (See Attachment A.) Some of the statements made by the AECT which were of greatest interest to us were the following:

1. "AECT endorses the criteria to be used in the determination of 'fair use' as contained in Section 107 of the proposed bill.

2. "Concerning the use of copyrighted works in conjunction with television, AECT proposes that 'fair use', as it has been outlined above, should apply to educational/instructional broadcast or closed-circuit transmission in a nonprofit educational institution, but not to commercial broadcasting.

3. "Once the doctrine of 'fair use' has been established in the revised law, negotiations should be conducted between the proprietor and user prior to any use of copyrighted materials that goes beyond that doctrine.

4. "A new copyright law that both users and producers can view as equitable depends upon the mutual understanding of each other's needs and the ability to effectively work out the differences. We will participate in the continuing dialogue with the Educational Media Producers Council and similar interest groups to establish mutually acceptable guidelines regarding the boundaries of 'fair use', and reasonable fees to be paid for uses beyond 'fair use.' "

LIMITED LIBRARY REPRODUCTION NOT APPLICABLE

After conducting hearings in 1973, the Senate added subsection (g) to Section 108 (Library Photocopying), to define and place limits on "systematic reproduction" which exceeds "fair use" or permissible use under other subsections of the bill. Subsection (h) was also added, exempting musical works; pictorial, graphic or sculptural works; or motion pictures or other audio-visual works from the reproduction rights granted in Section 108 except for providing archival copies or replacing a damaged work.

We feel both subsections are vitally important—(g) because it defines reasonable parameters for copying; and (h) because it is necessary to ensure the continued creation of the special kinds of works mentioned above. Because of the nature of audio-visual works—that is the manner in which they are used and the fact that one film, filmstrip or recording serves multiple numbers of users during each use—it is manifestly unfair to extend the rationale behind Section 108 to these materials. Each library traditionally buys only one or two copies of a film, filmstrip or sound recording. The library market is an important source of business to producers, though very limited. To permit copying of these audio-visual materials under Section 108 is wholly unnecessary to meet the librarians' need for some freedom to copy some literary works to effectively serve their users. Section 108 would, if extended to audio-visual materials, severely and irrevocably remove the library as a market for audio-visual producers.

LIAISON WITH OTHER EDUCATIONAL ORGANIZATIONS

EMPC has mounted a strong effort to establish and maintain dialogues with users of educational materials over the last three years. We have cosponsored over two dozen panels during state, regional and national meetings of educational groups to explain the producer's point of view and to listen to the educator's needs. Attachment B illustrates the format and content of these discussions. One of the most important results has been the development of licensing plans by major educational media companies to increase school districts' access to materials in an economical fashion.

Members of the Council have also worked with individual school systems to develop guidelines for observing fair copyright practices. Over one dozen short articles on copyright, as it applies to audio-visual media, have been prepared for educational journals. These articles have been reprinted and distributed free of charge by EMPC to all interested individuals, schools and school systems. Several examples are attached as Attachments C, D and E.

In cooperation with AECT, EMPC is now in the process of preparing a booklet explaining the procedures for obtaining permission to duplicate if the need exceeds the limits of "fair use."

We believe all these activities have been helpful to both educators and copyright proprietors in both clarifying general principles and in solving specific problems. EMPC pledges to continue these efforts irrespective of the passage of any revision of the copyright law.

THE EDUCATIONAL AUDIO-VISUAL MATERIALS INDUSTRY

In order to understand fully the unique nature of the educational audio-visual industry, and the importance of copyright protection to the continued development and distribution of high quality materials, a brief description of the industry is in order.

The Educational Media Producers Council (EMPC) is an organization within the National Audio-Visual Association made up of approximately 100 producers and distributors of audio-visual materials for use in schools, colleges and libraries. These member companies create, produce and market items such as motion picture films and video tapes, filmstrips, slides, transparencies, and sound recordings. We estimate that our members account for over 80% of the annual production of audio-visual materials for use in American education.

In 1974 total income from sales and rental of educational audio-visual materials amounted to $277 million. This volume was produced by some 200 companies; and thus, since the 100 EMPC members account for approximately 80% of annual production, the industry is clearly one of active competition among quite small firms. In fact, 50% of our member companies gross less than $1 million per year; 90% gross less than $5 million.

The relative volume of the various products sold in 1974 is shown in the following table:

1974 sales of educational A–V materials

[Millions of dollars]

16 mm. films and videotapes:	
16 mm. films	$63. 3
Videotapes	1. 6
Subtotal	64. 9

Materials acquired for use and storage in individual schools :

8 mm. films (silent)	7. 7
8 mm. films (sound)	. 6
Filmstrips (silent)	15. 3
Filmstrips with records	23. 2
Filmstrips with cassettes	36. 0
Overhead transparencies	11. 1
Slides	2. 1
Records	5. 5
Recorded tapes:	
Reel-to-reel	1. 9
Cassette	15. 6
Study prints	9. 5
Multimedia kits	62. 2
Games, manipulatives and realia	18. 8
Subtotal	209. 3
Grand total	274. 2

It will be noted this list of products is divided into two principal categories: 16 millimeter educational *films and videotapes*, which are comparatively lengthy and expensive and thus usually bought by school district film libraries, stored centrally, and circulated on demand to individual schools; and "building level materials"—*other types of materials* which tend to be used more often and more intensively in the individual schools and therefore are purchased and stored by them rather than by a district library. With the increasing use of audio-visual materials in the educational process, and with the recent trend toward the individualization of instruction, this second category has been growing much more rapidly than the first in the last few years, increasing from 66.5% of total audio-visual sales only six years ago to 75.6% of the total sales in 1974.

USE BY LEVEL OF EDUCATION

Equally important to an understanding of the educational audio-visual industry is the pattern of use at the several levels of education. Sales of 68 representative companies can be broken down as follows:

1974 educational A–V sales by type of institution

	Percent
Public schools	77. 5
Private schools	4. 4
Colleges and universities	7. 6
Public libraries	3. 9
Churches, government, business and industry, etc.	6. 6
Total	100. 0

The percentage in these tables bring out two points quite graphically:

1. The *only market* for those materials is *the educational market*; they have no market among consumers in general or for general entertainment.

2. Sales to schools tend to be concentrated in the lower end of the grade level pyramid, with over 60% of total sales to the elementary schools, less than 30% to high schools, and less than 10% to higher education. Public libraries account for less than 4% of all sales and "all other" for 6.6%. Thus, the kinds of considerations which come into play in discussing library photocopying of highly sophisticated, original research materials are not pertinent here; our companies' materials are used for the instruction of students at *basic levels* of education.

SMALL VOLUME

The vast majority of audio-visual materials are not used in one-to-one situations as are textbooks. They are used generally in groups. This raises two points. First, the number of copies needed is quite limited. One or two copies of a 16 millimeter film may serve an entire school system of moderate size; a single copy of a filmstrip or sound recording will serve an entire school. Second, a typical audio-visual product will customarily sell relatively few copies over a period of five to ten years, as compared to the tens or hundreds of thousands of copies of a textbook. A 16 millimeter film may sell only several hundred copies over its useful life; a $50.00 set of filmstrips does well to sell four thousand. Thus the recapture of initial investment in research, development, editorial and production work—which costs as much for one copy as for thousands—is spread over the sale of a relatively limited number of copies. In addition to the substantial initial investments necessary for production of quality materials, there must be added operational expenses for the considerable period of time over which sales are made before a break-even point is reached. The combination of these factors—*limited market, small volume* and *sales over an extended period*—means that specific broadening of the "fair use" criteria could damage beyond repair the quality and diversity of materials available to our nation's students and teachers.

THE U.S. OFFICE OF EDUCATION EXPERIENCE

The U.S. Office of Education has granted millions of dollars over the years to government-funded educational research laboratories for developing innovative and more effective teaching methods and materials. Many good products were developed, but far too few ever were disseminated to the educational community. As a result, policies were developed by USOE which allowed commercial companies with marketing expertise to distribute the materials under protection of a limited (in time) copyright. Not until then did the educational community receive the benefit of the Federal research effort.

This points out very clearly the need to provide incentive to producers and protection for the rights of copyright holders. The Federally-funded materials which were developed and put on shelves now have a much better chance of being used by, and benefiting, the intended recipients- because those with the expertise necessary to make the materials available are given appropriate incentives.

WILLIAMS & WILKINS CASE

The 4–4 tie vote of the Supreme Court in the Williams & Wilkins case, leaves the issue of "fair use" in an unsettled state. We believe that Congress must act - clearly and explicitly to outline the boundaries of this doctrine for all parties concerned. Once this is accomplished, EMPC commits itself to continue its efforts to work with educational institutions and organizations to establish guidelines to help resolve specific situations within the parameters set by Congress.

SUMMARY AND CONCLUSION

In summary let us repeat that we think that the bill which has been introduced as H.R. 2223 is a good bill and a workable bill, from the point of view both of the creators and the users of educational audio-visual materials, and we urge that it be expeditiously reported to the full House without amendments to Sections 107 and 108. If an educational exemption is added to Section 107, or the provisions of Section 108(g) and (h) are weakened, EMPC could not support the bill. It is universally recognized that revision of the 1909 copyright statute is imperative, and the sooner this is accomplished the better for all concerned.

We appreciate this opportunity to appear before your subcommittee. My colleagues and I will be glad to elaborate on any points in our testimony which the members of the subcommittee may wish to explore further.

ATTACHMENT A

COPYRIGHT LAW REVISION : A POSITION PAPER BY THE ASSOCIATION FOR EDUCATIONAL COMMUNICATIONS AND TECHNOLOGY, MAY 1975

The members of the Association for Educational Communications and Technology (AECT) believe that technology is an integral part of the teaching-learning process and helps to maximize the outcomes of interaction between teacher and pupil.

Regulations governing United States Copyright were originally developed to promote the public welfare and encourage authorship by giving authors certain controls over their work. It follows that revisions in Title 17 of the United States Code (Copyrights) should maintain the balance between providing for the compensation of authors and insuring that information remains available to the public. Some of the revisions proposed in S. 22 and H.R. 2223 lose sight of this balance between user and producer.

AECT endorses the criteria to be used in the determination of "fair use" as contained in Section 107 of the proposed bill:

Section 107. Limitations on exclusive rights: Fair use

. . . the fair use of a copyrighted work, including such use by reproduction in copies or phonorecords, or by any other means specified by (Section 106), for purposes such as criticism, comment, news reporting, teaching, scholarship, or research, is not an infringement of copyright. In determining whether the use made of a work in any particular case is fair use the factors to be considered shall include:

(1) the purpose and character of the use;

(2) the nature of the copyrighted work;

(3) the amount and substantiality of the portion used in relation to the copyrighted work as a whole; and

(4) the effect of the use upon the potential market for or value of the copyrighted work.

However, we propose that the concept of "fair use" should apply equally to the classroom teacher and media professional—including specialists in audiovisual and library resources. Media personnel are becoming increasingly important members of educational planning teams and must have the assurance that they may assist classroom teachers in the selection of daily instructional materials as well as with long range curriculum development. Classroom teachers do not always operate "individually and at (their) own volition." The fact that the media professional makes use of advance planning and has knowledge aforethought of the materials he prepares for the teacher should not invalidate the application of the "fair use" principle.

Concerning the use of copyrighted works in conjunction with television, AECT proposes that "fair use," as it has been outlined above, should apply to educational/instructional broadcast or closed-circuit transmission in a non-profit educational institution, but not to commercial broadcasting.

Once the doctrine of "fair use" has been established in the revised law, negotiations should be conducted between the proprietor and user prior to any use of copyrighted materials that goes beyond that doctrine. We believe that the enactment of the "fair use" concept into law prior to negotiations will guard against the erosion of the concept. Generally, a reasonable fee should be paid for uses that go beyond "fair use," but such fee arrangement should not delay or impede the use of the materials. Producers are urged to give free access (no-cost contracts) whenever possible.

We agree with the Ad Hoc Committee of Educational Organizations and Institutions on Copyright Law Revision that duration of copyright should provide for an initial period of twenty-eight years, followed by a renewal period of forty-eight years, whereas the proposed bill sets duration at the "life of the author plus fifty years." It seems reasonable that provisions should be made to permit those materials which the copyright holder has no interest in protecting after the initial period to pass into the public domain.

Regarding the input of copyrighted materials into computers or other storage devices by non-profit educational institutions, we agree with the Ad Hoc Committee that the bill should clearly state that until the proposed National Commission on New Technological Uses of Copyrighted Works has completed its study, such input should not be considered infringement. The proposed bill states only that ". . . (Section 117) does not afford to the owner of copyright in a work any greater or lesser rights with respect to the use of the work in conjunction with automatic systems . . ."

A new copyright law that both users and producers can view as equitable depends upon the mutual understanding of each other's needs and the ability to effectively work out the differences. We will participate in the continuing dialogue with the Educational Media Producers Council and similar interest groups to establish mutually acceptable guidelines regarding the boundaries of "fair use," and reasonable fees to be paid for uses beyond "fair use." This dialogue will be especially important in the area of storage, retrieval, and/or transmission of materials during the time period prior to the issuance of the report of the National Commission on New Technological Uses of Copyrighted Works.

We feel that the above modifications of S. 22 and H.R. 2223 are needed to insure that the revised law assists rather than hinders teachers and media specialists in their work.

STATEMENT OF PAUL G. ZURKOWSKI, PRESIDENT, INFORMATION INDUSTRY ASSOCIATION

Mr. Chairman, I am Paul G. Zurkowski, President of the Information Industry Association, 4720 Montgomery Lane, Bethesda, Md. 20014. As you know, the information industry has grown up in the years since 1967. The Association was formed in 1968. As an attorney with some publishing experience, I have served since February 1969 as its first principal paid employee. Prior to that time, of course, I served as legislative assistant in your office for approximately five years.

The Association presented testimony to the Senate Committee on these same issues in 1973. I refer you to that testimony for a detailed explanation of the industry. It begins at p. 266 in the July 31, Aug. 1, 1973 Hearings on S1361.

In her testimony last week the Register of Copyrights expressed grave concern about information technologies. She said that because of today's technologies once an author's idea is "out of the cage", he has no way to recapture it. He cannot receive compensation; he cannot control the context, in fact, he has lost his idea. She said that many authors are trying to determine if it is possible not to let their ideas out preferring to keep them to themselves.

In the absence of effective copyright rules for modern information technologies it is possible to devise methods to limit distribution and to limit access to author's ideas and concepts to the elite who can afford it and who will agree to protect it.

The objective of copyright is just the opposite, to encourage the author to permit the wide dissemination of his ideas in return for an exclusive right in the form in which they are expressed.

This is the objective of the information industry as well — to obtain the widest possible dissemination of information, fully utilizing all available information technologies while protecting the rights of authors. This is the industry's central function.

The business of information is a competitive and self-disciplining business. People in the business of information recognize that the materials in which they deal embody human creativity. They recognize that they must deal with it ethically. In addition, from a business standpoint they do not seek for themselves rights in the property of others which they would not be willing to grant to others in their property.

In anticipation of these Hearings, the information industry two years ago, undertook a study of the Revision Bill and the practices that have grown up in industry in dealing with the problems of new technologies.

As in traditional publishing areas the trade practices of the industry are built on the rights granted authors by the Constitution. Wide-spread industry practices were analyzed and recommendations were developed by which the practices that have grown up could be incorporated in the Copyright Revision Bill. Specific language changes were prepared which we submit to you. We choose today to synopsize them so that you will have the benefit of the industry's thinking while you evaluate the major change proposed by the educators.

We urge the Committee to add the issues relating to new technologies to the list of issues prepared by Ms. Ringer and to hold hearings on these issues. Ms. Ringer cited "present need for a revised law that will anticipate the 21st Century". Much of what relates to new technologies can be dealt with in the context of the present Revision Bill. The work of the National Commission on New Technological Uses of Copyrighted Works can be greatly aided by this Committee's serious analysis of the issues to determine what can be resolved now and what needs to be deferred for further study by that Commission.

Before addressing the education amendment the following amendments have been developed by our committee and are offered as detailed suggestions for extending copyright protection to works of authorship in the new information technologies.

Proposed amendments to § 101. Definitions:

Add the following:

A "data base" is a literary work which is a compilation expressed in a form intrinsically intended for use in conjunction with a computer.

A "search" of a data base is the examination or analysis of a data base by a computer for particular information relevant to an inquiry, whether or not the examination or analysis results in any display, copy or performance of all or part of the data base, and whether or not the inquirer received it in the same place or in separate places or at the same or at different times.

A "computer program" is a literary work consisting of a series of instructions or statements which are in a form acceptable to a computer and which are prepared in order to achieve a certain result, regardless of the nature of the material objects, such as documents, punched cards, magnetic tapes or discs, or computer storage elements, in which the works are embodied. A computer program may be a derivative work of a flow chart and either may be a derivative work of a literary work.

A "computer" is any automatic system capable of storing, processing, retrieving or transferring information, or any similar device, machine or process.

A "microform composition" is a literary work that results from the fixation of a series of images regardless of the nature of the material objects, such as fiche, film, opaque or otherwise in which they are embodied.

"Direct or indirect commercial advantage" includes, but is not limited to sale of products or services regardless of the tax status or organizational nature of the vendor, or method of payment be it on a per unit, membership fee or otherwise.

An amendment in the nature of a technical amendment is also offered with regard to the definition for "a work is fixed." To wit:

A work is "fixed" in a tangible medium of expression when its embodiment in a copy or phonorecord, by or under the authority of the author, is non-evanescent and sufficiently permanent or stable to permit it repeatedly to be perceived, reproduced, or otherwise communicated. A work consisting of sounds, images, or both, that are being transmitted, is "fixed" for purposes of this title if a fixation of the work is being made simultaneously with its transmission.

EXPLANATORY LANGUAGE

Because there has been some comment in the literature that the copying of a copyrighted work into the main storage element of a computer might not be an infringement, and because the recorded state of a copyrighted program in main memory (and some other computer storage elements) might only obtain for a few microseconds, it is thought desirable to amend the definition for "a work is fixed". As presently written it is believed that the definition intends, among other things, for an immediately self-decaying embodiment not to be a fixation. Storage in main memory is not self decaying in a whole element sense though the recordings in the components of some computer storage elements are automatically refreshed internally. Storage in main memory is normally erased or replaced on specific instruction only. Such recordation in main memory is, thus, *non-evanescent* and sufficiently permanent or stable to permit it repeatedly to be perceived, reproduced or otherwise communicated. Thus, the definition for "a work is fixed" would be more suitable and accurate if amended. It is believed such amendment does not change the basic intent of the definition while making clear that recordation in the main storage element of a computer would be the making of a copy.

Proposed amendments to § 102. Subject matter of copyright: In general,
Add the following as separate categories of works of authorship:

"(8) Data bases.
"(9) Computer Programs.
"(10) Microform compositions."

EXPLANATORY LANGUAGE

Consistent with the first complete paragraph on page 107 of Senate Report No. 93–083, it is noted in connection with the inclusion of "data bases" and "microform composition" that they may, though not always, involve "authorship" both on the part of those whose ideas and concepts are captured and on the part of the data base and microform composition producers responsible for conceptualizing the data base or microform composition, capturing and processing the data or images, and compiling and editing them to make the final product. There may be cases where the producer's contribution is so minimal that the ideas and concepts embodied in the data base or microform composition are the only copyrightable element in the work and there may be cases (for example, public domain materials) where only the data base or microform composition producer's contribution is copyrightable.

With regard to data bases and microform composition, it is not the intention of this amendment to preclude others from reconstituting the original source materials and ideas into their own independent work, but rather to assure that society has the choice of choosing from amongst a variety of data bases and microform compositions already in being and available readily in the marketplace by virtue of the operation and application of copyright concepts to these intellectual properties.

It is proposed that 102 (b) also be amended, by adding the following:

"However, copyright protection may exist in a collection of ideas or abstractions arbitrarily selected from a plurality of alternative ideas or abstractions or in a discretionary pattern of events or processes."

EXPLANATORY LANGUAGE

This amendment is directed at the copyrightability of computer software. Computer programming is a very flexible art. Given a single problem and a basic plan for its solution, two independent programmers could, and likely would write two different computer programs.

Thus the proposed amendment would ensure that the computer program developer will have copyright protection in the discretionary elements of his sequence of operations and particular processes. Typically, the sequence of operations and particular processes are set forth on a flow chart. A program, as a derivative work of a flow chart, would be protected in that aspect of the developer's creativity effort, too.

Considerable effort is spent in working out the sequence of events or steps (operations) that a program will follow and in selecting the processes to carry out the various individual steps. It is believed that this effort involves the elements of assembly, selecting, arranging, editing, and literary expression, and thus is the work of an author. Section 102(b) appears to be included in the bill to ensure that the copyrighting of programs does not result in the equivalent of patenting its system concepts. As written, Section 102(b) goes further than necessary. Even the Supreme Court in the case of *Baker v. Selden*, 101 U.S. 99, 26 Lawyers Ed 841 (1879) did not go that far. Thus, that decision reads:

"And where the art it teaches cannot be used without employing the methods and diagrams used to illustrate the book, or such as are similar to them, such methods and diagrams are to be considered as necessary incidents to the art, and given therewith the public; not given for purposes of publication in other works explanatory of the art, but for the purpose of practical application."

Therefore, the holding in *Baker v. Selden* is limited to situations where alternative processes and sequences are not available. Where such are available, it would seem that the Copyright Law should apply and the program developer protected against copying of the discretionary elements of his particular development. Others would still be free to use the methods of operation dictated by the results to be accomplished and to flesh out their own versions of how to achieve those results.

It is proposed that § 106, Exclusive Rights in Copyrighted Works be amended as follows:

"(5) in the case of literary, musical, dramatic and choreographic works, pantomimes, and pictorial, graphic, or sculptural works, including the individual images of a motion picture or other audiovisual work, *data bases and computer programs*, to display the copyrighted work publicly."
and add the following:

"(6) to read, to store or to reproduce for storage in a computer;
"(7) to search or use a data base in conjunction with a computer."

It is also proposed that Section 117: scope of exclusive rights: Use in conjunction with computers and similar information systems, *be deleted.*

A concomitant proposed amendment to the amendments to Section 106 is the deletion of Section 117. By specifically addressing the reading into, storage or reproduction for storage in a computer as an exclusive right of the owner of copyright under this title, this language would explicitly resolve a major question left open by the language of Section 117 in favor of the producer of the copyrighted work. Provision of the search and use rights assures the proprietor of a data base copyright with his basic rights and completes resolution of the main question concerning use of copyrighted works in computers. The word search is included among the proposed amendments to the definitions section of the bill. The output of a search of a data base would be protectible as a derivative work.

A new Section is proposed: § 11_. Scope of exclusive rights in computer programs:

NEW section 11.—Scope of exclusive rights: Computer Programs.

"In the case of computer programs, notwithstanding the provisions of sub-sections (a) and (b) of Section 109, it is an infringement of copyright for the possessor of a computer program to make a copy thereof by reproducing it in a computer unless authorized by the copyright owner.

"The copyright status of the result of the execution of a program will be that of a derivative work of the information (which may be a program) processed or modified by the executing program and its ancillary programs."

Explanatory language:

This amendment is necessary if the marketing of programs is to be facilitated by sale and not limited to lease/license arrangements. The amendment would ensure that the repurchaser, or the like, of a machine-readable media copy of a program is not automatically entitled to reproduce the program in his computer. It may be that the first purchaser of a program would have an implied right to reproduce it in his computer. However, if this is an inalienable right of a succeeding holder of a machine-readable media embodying a program, then it may be that the market for the program author is exceedingly limited. This would come about because the first purchaser of a program could read it into his computer, and once having entered it into permanent storage therein, could pass the machine-readable media on to a second computer owner. In this way, the theoretical market for a program might basically be reduced to one. This would not facilitate cost recovery on the part of the author and would undoubtedly, stifle development activity. This amendment would also make clear that it is a copyright infringement where a person borrows a computer storage element (disc machine) containing a program from a friend and transfers the program to another host machine without permission of the copyright owner.

A new Section is proposed: § 11—: Scope of exclusive rights: Microform Compositions.

NEW Section 11—. Scope of exclusive rights: Microform Compositions.

"(a) Limitations on Exclusive Rights. The exclusive rights of the owner of a copyright in a microform composition are limited to the rights specified in clauses (1), (3) and (5) of section 106. The exclusive rights of the owner of copyright in a microform composition to reproduce and display it are limited to the rights to duplicate the microform composition in the form of the microfiche, microfilm, opaques or other microforms that directly or indirectly recapture the actual images in the composition, and to display these actual images. These rights do not extend to the making or duplication of another microform composition that is a fixation of other images, or to the display of other images even though such images derive from the same or similar subject matter to those included in the copyrighted microform composition.

"(b) Right of copy distinct; the exclusive right to copy or to display copyrighted literary or dramatic work, and the right to copy or display a copyrighted microform composition are separate and independent rights under this title."

Explanatory language:

This section is modeled after the language of the tape piracy statute and calls for a recognition of two separate rights.

The intent of this amendment is to create what has been a format copyright in the work of a creator of a microform composition. There are variations in the nature of the contribution different creators will bring to the creation of a microform composition. A simple reproduction of a pre-existing document might not qualify for copyright as a microform composition. The collection, selection, organization, editing and creating of a large set of materials represents a major contribution of the nature copyright protection was intended. This amendment would provide such protection. It should be noted, however, that the protection provided is limited to the specific composition created and does not preclude anyone else, with independent effort and creativity from microfilming those same materials and, perhaps, qualifying for a separate copyright for his efforts.

By way of a technical amendment to § 301. Pre-emption with respect to other laws, the following amendment is proposed:

"§ 301. Pre-emption with respect to other laws.

"(a) On and after January 1, 1977, all legal or equitable rights that are equivalent to any of the exclusive rights within the general scope of copyright as specified by section 106 in works of authorship that are fixed in a tangible medium of expression and come within the subject matter of copyright as specified by sections 102 and 103, whether created before or after that date and whether published or unpublished, are governed exclusively by this title. Thereafter, no person is entitled to any such right or equivalent right in any such work under the common law or statutes of any State.

"(b) Nothing in this title annuls or limits any rights or remedies under the common law or statutes of any State with respect to:

"(1) subject matter that does not come within the subject matter of copyright as specified by Sections 102 and 103, including works of authorship not fixed in any tangible medium of expression; or

"(2) any cause of action arising from undertakings commenced before January 1, 1977; or

"(3) activities violating legal or equitable rights that are not equivalent to any of the exclusive rights within the general scope of copyright as specified by section 106, including rights against misappropriation not equivalent to any of such exclusive rights, breaches of contract, breaches of trust, trespass, conversion, invasion of privacy, defamation, and deceptive trade practices such as passing off and false representation.

"(c) Nothing in this title annuls or limits any rights or remedies under any other Federal Statute.

"(d) Compliance with the deposit requirements of this title shall not be destructive of any such "not equivalent" rights."

An amendment to Section 407. Deposit copies of phonorecords for Library of Congress is offered as follows:

"(b) The required copies or phonorecords shall be deposited in the Copyright Office for the purpose of reference within the Library of Congress. The Register of Copyrights shall, when requested by the depositor and upon payment of the fee prescribed by section 708, issue a receipt for the deposit."

Subsection (b) is amended to limit the use that might be made by the Library of Congress of deposited works. Items such as data bases, computer programs and microform compositions are costly and the use thereof for purposes other than reference within the Library of Congress would substantially impact the opportunities for authors to recover their costs, particularly considering the limited quantities in which they are marketed.

An amendment to Section 408. Copyright Registration in General is offered as follows:

Add a new section (f):

"(f) In the case of microform compositions deposit copies are required only where the retail price of the composition is $1,000 or less. In cases where microform compositions are created in editions, deposit copies are required only when the total number of copies in a particular edition exceeds 200 in number."

The creation of a microform composition often is an expensive process and results in very small unit sales. Many microform compositions sell only 20 or 30 copies and a total sale of 50 is usually considered quite a successful work. To require the creator of a microform composition to deposit two copies out of perhaps a total of 20, represents a disproportionate burden. The manufacture of each copy, in addition, is a costly effort. The purpose of this amendment is to limit the impact of the deposit requirement on the overall objective of the copyright system: to obtain the widest possible dissemination of information useful to science and the useful arts.

An amendment to 704, Retention and Disposition of articles of deposit in Copyright Office is proposed as follows:

"(a) Upon their deposit in the Copyright Office under sections 407 and 408, all copies, phonorecords, and identifying material, including those deposited in connection with claims that have been refused registration, are in the custody of the United States Government."

Subsection (a) would be amended to specify that deposit copies are in the custody of, rather than the property of, the United States Government. Title would thus be left in the author and the Library of Congress' rights of utilization and disposition limited to that of a bailee. Again the intention, in the light of vastly expanded library networking concepts, is to limit the use that may be made of expensive deposit copies by others than the Library of Congress. A replication and redistribution effort by the Library of Congress could severely affect the rights of authors otherwise granted in this legislation.

We believe these amendments deserve consideration in this revision cycle. They represent the results of day-to-day experience of authors, information companies, and users seeking to work out within existing copyright concepts workable relations for the dissemination of information through these technologies. We recognize the great pressure on the Committee to act on this legislation, particularly in view of the immense effort you have already devoted to it. These are no small matters, however: the present and future methods for sharing the works of authors with world-wide audiences are to be found in this complex mix of constitutional, economic and social issues.

Whether you are able to take the time to understand these new technology issues now and to act on those which deserve immediate attention or are constrained to defer to the National Commission on New Technological Uses of Copyrighted Works on all of them, it should be clear that the constitutional rights of authors will not be protected by exemptions that essentially free large computer systems to have free access to all works of authorship.

One of the major features of the computer age is the fact that state after state has created large university-based computer facilities and have given these facilities extensive authority to serve not only educational users, students, but industry, libraries of all kinds and government, state and federal, as well.

The result of granting such facilities an exemption to input into computers copyrighted works of authorship without infringing the copyright would be the creation of a whole new information distribution system in the United States. The system would not be based on author's rights as the present system is based. Rather it would be based on state bureaucratic decisions. Only those authors which the state-owned networks chose to respect would be granted anything approaching the rights of authors enjoyer in inkprint publications. The works of authors could be freely installed in computers without the authors' approval or even knowledge. The authors ideas could be used, re-documented and even distorted as to source, meaning and context. One area served by one system would have access to that systems version of the facts and another area would have access to another state-subsidized version. How would we as a nation sort out the truth without equal access to the same unabridged works of authorship. If the author's control over his work product through copyright is denied him by exemptions which free his works to be input, piecemeal or in total, accurately or inaccurately, it is difficult to see how the nation can stimulate and reward authors for writing the insightful and critical commentaries essential to the functioning of a democracy.

An exemption of input from copyright infringement would have other effects as well:

By implication such an amendment to the present legislation acknowledges that to input copyrighted materials into a computer is an infringement under present law. A need for such a change in the law has not been proved.

The small printouts resulting from most computer searches would by their size alone be argued to constitute "fair use" of the information. Having inserted in the computer the Encyclopaedia Britannica, brief extracts would be printed out. Notwithstanding the fact that this is the only way to use encyclopedic information, many would seek to treat it as fair use. Since there is no provision for any payment system in the proposal, this apparently is the intended result.

If entire works are free to be input, such materials as the *Reader's Guide to Periodical Literature* could be keypunched and installed in a computer system. Such publications are used simply to find a specific article citation. Without specific provision for controlling uses, the protection offered by copyright would be minimal. Little would be published in the open literature and authors would attempt to protect themselves by limiting by contract what uses could be made of their works.

The stress on exemptions would have the effect of eliminating publishing media which did not have exemptions because the basis for creation and investment in dissemination efforts, a minimal proprietary position, would be eliminated. The result would be reduced creation and distribution of works of authorship. The elimination of risk capital and the reliance on state capital would seriously retard development in many areas of science and the useful arts.

The proliferation of non-profit uses, particularly in information, today are legend. Government funding of research in information systems work, for example, is essentially limited to grants to non-profit organizations. This has led to the development of a whole generation of organizations performing this research on a non-profit basis. Separate non-profit groups have grown up to do similar research in education. We raise these questions not to challenge the purposes of these groups, but to suggest that the amendment is unduly broad as drafted and would serve, if enacted, to stimulate even further the development of subsidy-based information dissemination activities.

Finally, we believe there are several basic legislative drafting objections to the exemption proposal:

The amendment conflicts with the purpose of Section 117 to maintain the status quo in the law vis-a-vis copyright at input. If the committee is to consider seriously this exemption, similar serious consideration must be given to the author's-rights-based amendments offered above. It should be clear from a brief reading of the amendments we have suggested that this is an exceedingly complex area and that it cannot be dealt with simplistically.

The amendment, if coupled with the library photocopying exemption, appears to destroy the economic base of publishing. What the education exemption would allow to be input without infringing copyright, the library exemption would permit the copying of. The result would be the elimination of meaningful copyright protection for authors.

The amendment would preempt much of the work of the National Commission on New Technological Uses of Copyrighted Works. By granting such an exemption, the amendment would not only prejudge a large segment of the Commission's responsibilities, but it would also create a situation where there would be no experience for the Commission to draw on in evaluating how authors and users can resolve problems and develop workable relations within an economic framework.

In summary, the information industry position on H.R. 2223 is that, subject to some technical amendments, the bill should be enacted in its present form and that the library and education exemptions should be rejected. In the event that serious consideration is given to any such amendments, of a nature to deprive authors of significant rights in the new information technologies, we respectfully request that the recommendations of our committee be given full and equal consideration including the calling of witnesses with first-hand experience in the day-to-day resolution of the problems encountered. While many of these issues should be referred to the National Commission, some questions could be resolved now on the basis of existing knowledge, expertise and understanding. We, accordingly, urge the Committee to hold hearings with regard to developments in the new technology area. It is in this area of the law that the copyright concept will be most challenged in the months and years immediately ahead. An effective copyright law, "that will anticipate the 21st Century" will need to deal with these issues.

We thank you for your courtesy in providing us this opportunity to share our views with you and we wish you the best of good fortune in this and all other areas requiring your legislative skills.

STATEMENT OF PAUL G. ZURKOWSKI, PRESIDENT, INFORMATION INDUSTRY ASSOCIATION

Mr. Chairman and Members of the Committee. My name is Paul G. Zurkowski, President of the Information Industry Association. I have prepared a formal statement which I will not read but which I ask be submitted for the record.

The Information Industry Association is composed of more than 70 commercial firms. Some create data bases and computer programs. Others specialize in marketing access to such machine readable information sources. Others are microform publishers, traditional book and journal publishers, consultants, information-on-demand companies, suppliers of services to libraries, indexing and abstracting companies, information systems designers, information facilities managers, and others engage in the creation and marketing of information products, services and systems, world-wide.

Many of these companies have a decade or more of experience in disseminating works of authorship through the use of all varieties of advanced information technologies, alone and in combination with traditional ink-print technologies. Our Proprietary Rights Committee spent the past two years matching this practical experience with the provisions of the revision bill. You will find in the statement the results of that effort. We think that before your committee makes or the National Commission on New Technological Uses of Copyrighted Works recommends, any changes in H.R. 2223 affecting the use of works of authorship in these new technologies these recommendations and the experience of this industry should be considered. People in the industry dealing with the opportunities for wider dissemination of information offered by the new technologies are ready and willing to assist you in these matters in any way they can.

The objective of copyright is to encourage the author to permit the wide dissemination of his ideas in return for an exclusive right in the form in which they are expressed. This is the objective of the information industry as well—to obtain the widest possible dissemination of information, fully utilizing all available information technologies while protecting the rights of authors.

We appear to add our support for enactment of H.R. 2223 and to register our opposition to the amendments proposed to sections 107 and 108.

We feel most strongly that a single-copy photocopying exemption combined with an exemption permitting the input of copyrighted works of authorship into a computerized information system would eliminate meaningful copyright for authors. Copyrighted works of authorship which the education exemption would permit to be input without infringing copyright could be copied on a single-copy basis under the library exemption. Stripped of these copyright protections, authors could publish little in the open literature without being subjected to such exempt uses. Authors, in turn, would seek to protect their works, as the Register fears and the Justice Department recommended, by limiting by contract what uses could be made of their works. The end result for both libraries and educators would be less access rather than the free access they initially expect would result from their amendments.

Further objections to the proposals include:

1. No need for such an exemption has been proved. An industry is emerging to provide the widest possible dissemination while respecting the constitutional mandate to protect author's rights.

2. Small printouts from data banks of encyclopedic information would be argued to constitute "fair use", notwithstanding that this is precisely the use intended. These kinds of resources would be denied to research, education and libraries on an open copyrighted basis and would have to be provided under contractual arrangements.

3. By exempting certain activities, and thereby exempting them from costs others have to pay, these exempt activities would tend to replace privately funded publishing and information activities. The elimination of private risk capital from the creation and information distribution functions would seriously retard development in many areas of science and the useful arts.

Finally, the proposal to exempt input conflicts with the provisions of section 117 to maintain the status quo in the law *vis a vis* questions of copyrighted works and computers. This is an exceedingly complex area involving not only author's rights, but also major social policy questions with far-reaching economic implications. Section 117 was originally included in the bill in recognition that neither this Committee nor the Senate Judiciary Committee has explored these issues adequately. The National Commission on New Technological Uses of Copyrighted Works was established to do that investigation for the Congress.

If these exemptions are written into the law the study expected of the Commission would be seriously prejudiced. By granting exemptions at the expense of author's rights and the economic interests of publishers and information companies, the arena within which all parties now are developing workable relations would be destroyed. The Commission would be deprived of the necessary experience in the marketplace on which to base meaningful recommendations for future copyright legislation.

CONCLUSION

While our committee of people who work with these technologies day in and day out were able after lengthy meetings and detailed discussions to agree on some basic definitions and on an approach to the technologies based on author's rights, there also emerged unanimity that these were just the beginning in understanding the whole complex of dynamic technical, esoteric, legal, social and economic relationships which ultimately will form the base for our emerging information society.

It promises to be an exciting and long journey. We recognize as an industry that the serious attention you are giving these matters represents for our society that first step by which any journey must begin.

Mr. Chairman, my name is Irwin Karp. I am counsel for the Authors League of America, the national society of professional writers and dramatists. The League's 6,500 members include authors of biographies, histories and non-fiction books on every subject, novels, plays, poetry, childrens' books, musical plays, magazine articles, textbooks and other works. Several also write for motion pictures, television and radio. And, of course, the works of many members are adapted for use in these media. Copyright is a matter of paramount concern for our members, the full-time professionals and those who also work as teachers or in other fields, for their compensation as writers depends on the Copyright Act, as does their ability to provide for their immediate families after death. I should stress at the outset that most of our members own the copyrights in the works they create.

My testimony this morning addresses two subjects: (1) the "Educational exemption" proposed by members of the Ad Hoc Committee; and (2) demands that your Subcommittee reject the copyright term provided in Sec. 302 (H.R. 2223); i.e. the author's life-plus-50 years after his death. The Authors League supports the term of life-plus 50 years, as it did in previous testimony to your Subcommittee by Rex Stout (then its president), Elizabeth Janeway, John Hersey (its current president), Herman Wouk and myself. [*Hearings Before Subcommittee No. 3;* 89th Cong., 1st Sess.; Part I, Part III]. In the Senate, testimony supporting the life-plus-50 term was given by Mrs. Janeway, Mr. Wouk and the late John Dos Passos. As it has in the past, The Authors League opposes the "educational exemption" which previously has been rejected by both Judiciary Committees and therefore was not included in the Revision Bills passed by the House of Representatives in 1967 and the Senate in 1974.

PRIOR REJECTION OF THE EDUCATIONAL EXEMPTION

As your Committee's Report noted, members of the Ad Hoc Committee had requested the insertion of "a specific, limited exemption for educational copying" into the Revision Bill. The reasons why your Committee and the Senate Committee refused the exemption are as valid today as they were when the Report was issued.

Your Report stated that "photocopying and other reproducing devices were constantly proliferating and becoming easier and cheaper to use" (as indeed they have). It also noted the contentions of authors and publishers that "education is the textbook publisher's only market, and that many authors receive their main income from licensing reprints in anthologies and textbooks; if an unlimited number of teachers could prepare and reproduce their own anthologies, the cumulative effect would be disastrous." (H. Rep. No. 83, p. 31).

THE CONSTRUCTIVE SOLUTIONS ACHIEVED BY THE SUBCOMMITTEE

Your Report noted that "several productive meetings" were held between representatives of authors, publishers and educators, and that "while no final agreements were reached, the meetings were generally successful in clarifying the issues and in pointing the way to constructive solutions." These solutions were reflected in your Committee's Report, and it is fair to say they were—for a time at least—accepted by the parties. The solutions were:

(i) The Committee's rejection of the "educational exemption", because "After full consideration, the committee believes that a specific exemption freeing certain reproductions of copyrighted works for educational and scholarly purposes from copyright control is not justified."

(ii) The Committee's explicit affirmation that "any educational uses that are fair today would be fair use under the bill."

(iii) Amendment of Sec. 504 (c) to insulate teachers from excessive liability for statutory damages.

(iv) Amendment of Sec. 107 to indicate that fair use may include reproductions in copies or phonorecords, and may be for such purposes as "teaching, scholarship or research."

(v) A careful analysis by the Committee of the four criteria of fair use "*in the context of typical classroom situations arising today.*" The Committee noted that although its analysis had to be broad and illustrative, "it may provide educators with the basis of establishing workable practices and policies." (pp 32–36)

Actually, the Committee was modest in characterizing its analysis—it is an extremely clear and useful set of guidelines for educators, authors and publishers. Moreover, the Committee's analysis of fair use amply supported its judgment that "the doctrine of fair use as properly applied is broad enough to permit reasonable educational use, and education has something to gain in the enactment of a bill which clarifies what may now be a problematical situation."

The Committee also urged educators, authors and publishers to "join together in an effort to establish a *continuing* understanding as to what constitutes mutually acceptable practices." The Authors League is willing, as it has stated before, to sit down with educators and publishers periodically to establish and review these practices, to fill out workable guidelines of fair use. This must be done in meetings, with the parties working together. And there should be periodic meetings so that the parties could revise guidelines in light of changing conditions. This would enable them to deal reasonably with current practices, without fear of creating immutable rules that could become damaging if technology or other conditions changed in the future. The Judiciary Committee also urged the parties to join together "to work out means by which permissions for uses beyond fair use can be obtained easily, quickly and at reasonable fees." Again the Authors League is willing, as it stated in the past, to sit down with educators and publishers to work out these methods.

THE PROPOSED EDUCATIONAL EXEMPTION WOULD INJURE AUTHORS

If the proposed exemption, as it bears on copying, is only intended to permit educational copying that would be fair use under this Committee's analysis it would be unnecessary. If the Ad Hoc groups contend that the purpose is to provide clarity then certainly the amendment should be rejected. For as we testified before Senator McClellan, your Committee's analysis of fair use, with its explicit examples and illustrations, is far more precise and instructive to teachers than the completely vague amendment offered by the Ad Hoc groups.

Actually the purpose of the amendment is to legalize uncompensated educational reproduction of copies that goes far beyond the limits of fair use. The privilege of making copies of portions of a work which are not substantial in proportion to its total size would be absolute, regardless of the circumstances of the reproduction; although some of these would clearly involve infringement under your Committee's analysis. Under the Amendment, many copies could be produced on an organized basis, rather than by one teacher acting spontaneously. Multiple copies could be reproduced for many individuals and circulated beyond the classroom. And most important, under the Amendment copies could be reproduced even though they had a serious adverse effect on the work's potential market or value, and even though it would supplant some part of its normal market. Moreover, the proposed exemption would permit educators and institutions to reproduce copies of *entire short* works. How short is short? Would a poem 2 pages long be fair game for educational reprinting? or 4 pages? or 6 pages? Would the Amendment allow a story or article 5 pages long to be reproduced in multiple copies? or 10 pages? or 15 pages? Moreover, as with excerpts, the exemption would allow educators to reproduce these copies under a variety of circumstances that would make them an infringement under your committee's analysis of the four criteria of fair use.

As we noted in our statement on library photocopying yesterday, and in our previous testimony, many authors earn a major portion of their income by licensing the reprinting of poems, articles, short stories and portions of longer works in anthologies, textbooks, collections and similar books. The same poem or story may be reprinted in several of these, and the accumulation of small fees produce a modest income—often the largest part of the income authors of valuable literary works earn from their writings. These anthologies and other collections are sold primarily to high schools, colleges and universities, and their libraries and book stores. Their students are a primary audience for eminent poets, essayists and short story writers.

The proposed educational exemption would allow educators and institutions to produce copies of an author's short works and portions of longer works, thus displacing the sale of the anthologies textbooks and other collections that previously brought these works to educational institutions. Many authors would thus be deprived of a substantial or major portion of their income, even though their works would still be widely used by educational audiences, disseminated by uncompensated educational reproduction that far exceeded the limits of fair use. [Although some educational spokesmen have said they do not intend to "anthologize", it should be noted that the effects are the same whether several short works are provided at one time between covers, or are produced and distributed by the school seriatim.]

THE WILLIAMS & WILKINS DECISION

The Ad Hoc Committee's excuse for requesting the exemption in the Senate was that the Trial Judge's decision in *Williams & Wilkins* created uncertainties as to fair use. As we there pointed out, this was a feeble excuse for disrupting the constructive solutions reflected in your Committee's prior report. It would be an even feebler excuse now, considering the majority opinion in the full Court of Claims. As your report correctly stated, fair use—in the case of library copying as in other instances—depends on the four criteria *"and the facts of the particular case."* (Emphasis ours). The trial judge confined his decision to the facts of that case, stressing that the large scale reproduction of copies involved "was wholesale copying." The facts before him bore no resemblance to the various fact situations involving educational copying and other uses which your Committee considered in spelling out its guidelines and analysis of fair use vis-a-vis educational copying. Nothing in the trial court's opinion cast any doubt on your Report's analysis of guidelines. And there is even less reason for Ad Hoc Committee spokesmen to contend that any doubts have been cast upon them by the majority opinion in the Court of Claims which reversed the judgment below and dismissed Williams & Wilkens complaint. The majority opinion did not imperil fair use in education or detract from your conclusions, nor did the minority opinion.

THE "OTHER" ARGUMENTS

As we noted in our testimony on library photocopying, Ad Hoc Committee spokesmen are wont to accompany their demands for an "educational exemption" with a variety of attacks on copyright. Some of these we discussed yesterday: the "monopoly", "restraint of information" and "mere privilege" claims. As to the others:

Ad Hoc spokesmen contend that uncompensated educational copying beyond the limits of fair use must be legislated because it allegedly "promotes" the progress of science and art. This misses the very point of the Constitution's copyright clause, which intended that authors be granted "valuable, enforceable rights" to encourage them to produce works of lasting value. Granting rights, not destroying them, was how the Constitution intended to promote the progress of science and art. Compensating authors for uses of their work, not depriving them of remuneration, was the method chosen by the Constitution. Authors whose works are used in schools make a positive contribution to the educational process, and for reproduction beyond fair use, they are entitled to compensation.

As your Report noted, "the educational groups are mistaken in their argument that a 'for profit' limitation is applicable to educational copying under the present law."

Ad Hoc Committee spokesmen have argued that any copyright limitation on uncompensated educational copying beyond fair use restrains "freedom" to read under the First Amendment. This utterly fallacious argument was made by them in the Williams & Wilkins case, and was completely ignored by majority and minority opinions. The First Amendment was fashioned to assure unfettered interchange of ideas (Sullivan v. N.Y. Times) and it is axiomatic that an author's copyright does not prevent anyone from discussing or repeating his ideas (Rosemont v. Random House). The Supreme Court has never interpreted the "freedom to read" under the First Amendment to mean that copyrighted works must be provided free of charge; and it has frequently emphasized that there is no conflict between publication for profit and the First Amendment. Under the Ad Hoc theory of "freedom to read", teachers and librarians should work without pay, colleges should cease charging tuition and the Xerox Corporation should be denied copying fees when its machines reproduce "educational" materials.

Our discussion has focused on the copying aspects of the Ad Hoc Committee's proposed exemption, but the Authors League opposes its other provisions as well. It would be highly dangerous to add an "input" exemption with respect to computers. And the educational community is not entitled to further additions to an already too-broad television exemption.

Report by the Subcommittee on Patents, Trademarks, and Copyrights pursuant to S. Res. 255

COPYRIGHT LAW REVISION

During the second session of the 93rd Congress, an historical event occurred in the field of copyright revision legislation. On September 9, 1974, the United States Senate passed S. 1361, a bill introduced by Senator John L. McClellan, Chairman of the Subcommittee, to provide for the first general revision of the copyright laws and procedures since 1909. S. 1361, as amended by the subcommittee, was reported favorably to the Committee on the Judiciary on April 19, 1974. After adopting several amendments to the bill, the Judiciary Committee reported S. 1361 to the Senate on July 8, 1974, with a recommendation that it be approved. It was the view of some members of the Senate that certain provisions of S. 1361, may come within the jurisdiction of the Commerce Committee and that these sections should be considered by that Committee prior to action being taken on the bill by the Senate. Consequently, on July 9, 1974, the measure was removed from the Senate calendar and referred to the Committee on Commerce for a period not to exceed fifteen days. On July 29, 1974, the Commerce Committee reported S. 1361 to the Senate with several amendments.

S. 1361 contains three titles. Title I provides for the general revision of the copyright statutes and procedures. Title II provides for the establishment in the Library of Congress of a National Commisison on New Technological Uses of Copyrighted Works. Title II was later incorporated into S. 3976, a bill which also provided for the temporary extension of copyright protection in certain cases, the removal of the expiration date for a limited copyright in sound recordings and an increase in the criminal penalties for the piracy and counterfeiting of such recordings. Title III provides for protection of Ornamental Designs of Useful Articles. A brief summary of the major provisions of S. 1361 and S. 3976 is included in this section of the report.

TITLE I—GENERAL REVISION OF COPYRIGHT STATUTES AND PROCEDURES

1. Subject Matter of Copyright

The bill provides that the subject matter of copyright is the original works of authorship fixed in any tangible medium of expression, now known or later developed, from which they can be preceived, reproduced, or otherwise communicated, whether directly or with the aid of a machine or device. The measure retains the present categories of copyrightable works, including the protection granted to sound recordings under Public Law 93–573. This law provides that sound recordings as distinguished from phonorecords are copyrightable subject matter. S. 1361 also specifies that the United States Government is prohibited from securing a copyright in any of its publications.

2. Single System of Copyright Protection

S. 1361 abolishes the present duel system of common law protection for unpublished works and the Federal law protection for published works. The bill establishes a single system of Federal statutory protection for all works covered by the bill regardless of whether they are published or unpublished. The bill does not, however, abolish or limit any rights or remedies under the common law or statutes of any State with respect to unpublished works not protected by the bill, or any cause of action arising from undertakings commenced before January 1, 1975, or any activities violating rights that are not equivalent to any of the exclusive rights within the general scope of copyright as specified by the legislation.

3. Duration of Copyright

The present law provides the term of copyright is twenty-eight years from first publication or registration plus another twenty-eight years if the copyright is renewed. S. 1361 changes this term of protection and provides in general that works created after the effective date of the legislation shall endure for a term consisting of the life of the author and fifty years after his death. Regarding joint works, the fifty years is computed from the death of the last surviving author. With respect to anonymous works, pseudonymous works, or works made for hire, the measure specifies that the term shall consist of seventy-five years from the year of its first publication, or a term of one hundred years from the year of its creation, whichever expires first. In the case of works now protected, the legislation provides that copyright subsisting in their first term shall endure for twenty-eight years from the date it was originally secured with renewal rights for a further term of forty-seven years. For copyrights in their renewal term, the bill extends the duration of protection to seventy-five years from the date the copyright was originally secured.

4. Exclusive Rights in Copyrighted Works

The bill provides the owner of a copyrighted work five exclusive rights. Under the measure, a copyright owner is given the exclusive right to, (1) reproduce the work in copies or phonorecords, (2) prepare derivative works based upon the work, (3) distribute copies or phonorecords of the work, (4) perform the work publicly, and (5) display the work publicly. The bill specifies, however, that certain limitations shall apply to these rights.

5. Fair Use

One of the most important limitations on a copyright owner's exclusive rights is the doctrine of fair use. It is a judicially developed doctrine that permits a limited amount of copying without it being an infringement of copyright. The bill provides for the first statutory recognition of the doctrine and specifies that the fair use of a copyrighted work, including the reproduction of copies for purposes of teaching or research is not a copyright infringement. In determining whether the doctrine applies to a particular case, the bill specifies that four factors are to be considered. These factors are the purpose and character of the use, the nature of the work, the amount of the work used and the effect of the use upon the potential market or value of the copyrighted work.

6. Reproduction by Libraries and Archives

Another of the limitations on a copyright owner's exclusive rights is contained in section 108, which provides for the reproduction of copyrighted works by libraries and archives. The bill provides that under certain conditions it is not an infringement of copyright for a library or archives, to reproduce or distribute no more than one copy or phonorecord of a work provided (1) the reproduction or distribution is not made for any commercial gain, (2) the collections of the library or archives are available to the public or to other persons doing research in a specialized field, and (3) the reproduction or distribution of the work includes a notice of copyright.

The bill authorizes archival reproduction, and the replacement of a copy or phonorecord that is damaged, deteriorating, lost or stolen if the library or archives has determined that an unused replacement cannot be obtained at a fair price from commonly-known trade sources in the United States. The bill also provides for the reproduction and distribution of a copy of not more than one article or other contribution to a copyrighted collection of a periodical or copy or phonorecord of a small part of any copyrighted work. The measure requires, however, that the copy become the property of the user, that the library or archives have no notice that the copy would be used for any purpose other than for private study, scholarship or research, and that the library or archives provide to the user a warning of copyright in accordance with regulations prescribed by the Register of Copyrights. The bill further provides for the reproduction and distribution of a copy of an out-of-print work if the user has established that an unused copy cannot be obtained at a fair price from commonly-known trade sources in the United States. As with the reproduction and distribution of a copy of an article and small excerpts, the measure requires that the copy become the property of the user, that the library or archives have no notice that the copy would be used for any purposes other than private study, scholarship or research, and that the library or archives provide to the user a warning of copyright in accordance with regulations prescribed by the Register of Copyrights.

The rights granted by section 108 extend only to "isolated and unrelated reproduction or distribution of a single copy or phonorecord of the same material on separate occasions," but do not authorize the related or concerted reproduction of multiple copies of the same material whether made on one occasion or over a period of time, and whether intended for aggregated use by one or more individuals or for separate use by the individual members of a group. In addition, the section does not authorize the systematic reproduction or distribution of copies or phonorecords of articles or other contributions to copyrighted collections or periodicals or of small parts of other copyrighted works whether or not multiple copies are reproduced or distributed.

The bill further provides, with certain exceptions, that the rights of reproduction and distribution heretofore mentioned do not apply to a musical work, a pictorial, graphic or sculptural work, or a motion picture or other audio-visual work other than an audio-visual work dealing with news.

During Floor consideration of the bill, Senator Howard H. Baker, Jr. of Tennessee, for himself and Senators Bill Brock of Tennessee, Edward J. Gurney of Florida, Barry Goldwater of Arizona and Strom Thurmond of South Carolina introduced and secured approval of an amendment to provide, under certain conditions, that nothing in section 108 shall be construed to limit the reproduction and distribution of a limited number of copies and excerpts by a library or archives of an audiovisual news program. The measure further specifies that rights given to libraries and archives under section 108 are in addition to those granted under section 107, the fair use provisions.

Copyright Law Revision
Report No. 94—473

Mr. McClellan, from the Committee on the Judiciary,
submitted the following

REPORT

together with

ADDITIONAL VIEWS

[To accompany S. 22]

The Committee on the Judiciary, to which was referred the bill (S. 22) for the general revision of the copyright law, title 17 of the United States Code, and for other purposes, having considered the same, reports favorably thereon, with an amendment in the nature of a substitute, and recommends that the bill as amended do pass.

Strike all after the enacting cause and insert in lieu thereof the following:

TITLE I—GENERAL REVISION OF COPYRIGHT LAW

SEC. 101. Title 17 of the United States Code, entitled "Copyrights", is hereby amended in its entirety to read as follows:

TITLE 17—COPYRIGHTS

PURPOSE

The purpose of the proposed legislation, as amended, is to provide in Title I for a general revision of the United States Copyright Law, title 17 of the United States Code, Title II of the bill creates a new type of protection for ornamental designs of useful articles.

STATEMENT

The present Copyright Law of the United States is essentially that enacted by the Congress in 1909. Many significant developments in technology and communications have rendered that law clearly inadequate to the needs of the country today.

The enactment of legislation "To promote the Progress of Science and useful Arts, by securing for limited Times to Authors and Inventors the exclusive Right to their respective Writings and Discoveries", is one of the powers of the Congress enumerated in Article I, section 8 of the Constitution. Some commentators on the Congress in recent years have expressed concern that the legislative branch has too frequently yielded the initiative in legislative matters to the executive branch. This legislation is exclusively the product of the legislative branch and has received detailed consideration over a period of several years.

The origin of this legislation can ultimately be traced to the Legislative Appropriations Act of 1955 which appropriated funds for a comprehensive program of research and study of copyright law revision by the Copyright Office of the Library of Congress. This committee's Subcommittee on Patents, Trademarks and Copyrights published a series of 34 studies on all aspects of copyright revision, which were prepared under the supervision of the Copyright Office. In 1961 the Congress received the "Report of the Register of Copyrights on the general revision of the U.S. Copyright Law." The Copyright Office subsequently conducted a series of panel meetings on copyright law revision. On July 20, 1964, Senator John L. McClellan, Chairman of the Subcommittee on Patents, Trademarks and Copyrights, introduced, at the request of the Librarian of Congress, S. 3008 of the 88th Congress, for the general revision of the copyright law. No action was taken on this bill prior to the adjournment of the Congress.

In the 1st session of the 89th Congress, Senator McClellan, again introduced at the request of the Librarian of Congress, a general copyright revision bill S. 1006. Hearings on this legislation were commenced by the Subcommittee on August 18, 1965, and continued on August 19 and 20. When the hearings were recessed, a large number of witnesses remained to be heard. During the 2d session of the 89th Congress there were important developments relating to the possible copyright liability of cable television systems under the Copyright Act of 1909. In order to ascertain whether immediate and separate legislative action on the copyright CATV question was necessary and desirable, the Subcommittee commenced hearings on that subject on August 2, 1966. These hearings continued on August 3, 4 and 25. No further action was taken by the Subcommittee during the 89th Congress.

In the 1st session of the 90th Congress Senator McClellan again, at the request of the Librarian of Congress, introduced S. 597, for the general revision of the copyright law. Hearings on this bill commenced on March 15, 1967 and continued on March 16, 17, 20, 21, April 4, 6, 11, 12 and 28. During the Subcommittee hearings more than 100 witnesses were heard and many suggested amendments were submitted for the consideration of the Subcommittee.

On April 11, 1967, the House of Representatives passed H.R. 2512, for the general revision of the copyright law. This bill was subsequently referred to the Subcommittee on Patents, Trademarks and Copyrights. Although the Subcommittee completed the public hearings on copyright revision during the 90th Congress, no further action was taken by the Subcommittee because of problems with certain provisions of the legislation, and because of the pendency of the cable television judicial proceedings.

One of the problems that prevented Subcommittee action during the 90th Congress was uncertainty concerning the impact of the legislation on the use of copyrighted materials in computers and other forms of information storage and retrieval systems. The Subcommittee recommended and the Senate passed on October 12, 1976, S. 2216 to establish in the Library of Congress a National Commission on New Technological Uses of Copyrighted Works. The Commission was authorized to study this subject and recommend any changes in copyright law or procedure. No action was taken on this legislation by the House of Representatives.

On January 22 (legislative day January 10), 1969, Senator McClellan introduced S. 543. Title I of this bill, other than for technical amendments, was identical to S. 597 of the 90th Congress. Title II of the bill incorporated the provisions of S. 2216 providing for the establishment of the National Commission on New Technological Uses of Copyrighted Works.

On December 10, 1969, the Subcommittee favorably reported S. 543, with an amendment in the nature of a substitute. No further action was taken in the Committee on the Judiciary, primarily because of the cable television issue.

On February 18, 1971, Senator McClellan introduced S. 644 for the general revision of the copyright law. Other than for minor amendments, the text of that bill was identical to the revision bill reported by the Subcommittee in the 91st Congress. No action was taken on general revision legislation during the 92nd Congress while the subcommittee was awaiting the formulation and adoption by the Federal Communications Commission of new cable television rules.

While action on the general revision bill was necessarily delayed, the unauthorized duplication of sound recordings became widespread. It was accordingly determined that the creation of a limited copyright in sound recordings should not await action on the general revision bill. Senator McClellan introduced, for himself and others, S. 644 of the 92nd Congress to amend title 17 of the U.S. Code to provide for the creation of a limited copyright in sound recordings. An amended version of this legislation was enacted as Public Law 92–140.

On March 26, 1973, Senator McClellan introduced S. 1361 for the general revision of the copyright law. Other than for technical amendments, this bill was identical to S. 644 of the 92d Congress. Additional copyright revision hearings were held on July 31 and August 1, 1973. The subcommittee conducted a total of 18 days of hearings on copyright law revision.

The subcommittee on April 19, 1974 reported S. 1361 with an amendment in the nature of a substitute. After adopting several amendments to the subcommittee bill, the Judiciary Committee reported the legislation on July 8, 1974. On July 9 the measure was removed from the

Senate calendar and referred to the Committee on Commerce. The Commerce Committee reported S. 1361 with additional amendments on July 29. After adopting several amendments the Senate on September 9 passed S. 1361.

Since it was doubtful that adequate time remained in the 93d Congress for consideration in the House of Representatives of S. 1361, on September 9, Senator McClellan introduced and obtained immediate consideration of S. 3976. That bill, passed on September 9, extended the renewal term of expiring copyrights, established on a permanent basis a limited copyright in sound recordings, and created in the Library of Congress a National Commission on New Technological Uses of Copyrighted Works. The House of Representatives passed the measure with amendments on December 19, 1974, and the Senate concurred in the House amendments on the same date. The President approved the bill on December 31, 1974, and it became Public Law 93–573.

On January 15, 1975, Senator McClellan introduced S. 22. Other than for necessary perfecting and technical amendments and changes required by Public Law 93–573, the bill is identical to S. 1361 as passed by the Senate.

During the 94th Congress the Register of Copyrights prepared the Second Supplementary Report of the Register of Copyrights on the General Revision of the U.S. Copyright Law. This report discussed policy and technical issues of the revision legislation. The Register's Report proposed clarification of the legislative intent in several areas, and certain of these recommendations are reflected in this Report.

During the 87th Congress the Senate passed S. 1884 to provide for a new form of protection for original ornamental designs of useful articles by protecting the authors of such designs for a limited time against unauthorized copying. The Senate in the 88th Congress passed S. 776 and, in the 90th Congress, S. 1237, bills on the same subject. No final action was taken in the House of Representatives on any of these measures. In the 81st Congress Senator Philip A. Hart introduced a similar bill, S. 1774. The substance of that bill has been incorporated as Title II of this legislation.

SECTIONAL ANALYSIS AND DISCUSSION

An analysis and discussion of the provisions of S. 22, as amended, follows:

SECTION 101. DEFINITIONS

The significant definitions in this section will be mentioned or summarized in connection with the provisions to which they are most relevant.

SECTION 102. GENERAL SUBJECT MATTER OF COPYRIGHT

"Original works of authorship"

The two fundamental criteria of copyright protection—originality and fixation in tangible form—are restated in the first sentence of this cornerstone provision. The phrase "original works of authorship," which is purposely left undefined, is intended to incorporate without change the standard of originality established by the courts under the present copyright statute. This standard does not include requirements of novelty, ingenuity, or esthetic merit, and there is no intention to enlarge the standard of copyright protection to require them. In using the phrase "original works of authorship," rather than "all the writings of an author" now in section 2 of the statute, the committee's purpose is to avoid exhausting the constitutional power of Congress to legislate in this field, and to eliminate the uncertainties arising from the latter phrase. Since the present statutory language is substantially the same as the empowering language of the Constitution, a recurring question has been whether the statutory and the constitutional provisions are coextensive. If so, the courts would be faced with the alternative of holding copyrightable something that Congress clearly did not intend to protect, or of holding constitutionally incapable of copyright something that Congress might one day want to protect. To avoid these equally undesirable results, the courts have indicated that "all the writings of an author" under the present statute is narrower in scope than the "writings" of "authors" referred to in the Constitution. The bill avoids this dilemma by using a different phrase—"original works of authorship"—in characterizing the general subject matter of statutory copyright protection.

The history of copyright law has been one of gradual expansion in the types of works accorded protection, and the subject matter affected by this expansion has fallen into two general categories. In the first, scientific discoveries and technological developments have made possible new forms of creative expression that never existed before. In some of these cases the new expressive forms—electronic music, filmstrips, and computer programs, for example—could be regarded as an extension of copyrightable subject matter Congress had already intended to protect, and were thus considered copyrightable from the outset without the need of new legislation. In other cases, such as photographs, sound recordings, and motion pictures, statutory enactment was deemed necessary to give them full recognition as copyrightable works.

Authors are continually finding new ways of expressing themselves, but it is impossible to foresee the forms that these new expressive methods will take. The bill does not intend either to freeze the scope of copyrightable subject matter at the present stage of communications technology or to allow unlimited expansion into areas completely outside the present congressional intent. Section 102 implies neither that that subject matter is unlimited nor that new forms of expression within that general area of subject matter would necessarily be unprotected.

The historic expansion of copyright has also applied to forms of expression which, although in existence for generations or centuries, have only gradually come to be recognized as creative and worthy of protection. The first copyright statute in this country, enacted in 1790, designated only "maps, charts, and books"; major forms of expression such as music, drama, and works of art achieved specific statutory recognition only in later enactments. Although the coverage of the present statute is very broad, and would be broadened further by the added recognition of choreography there are unquestionably other areas of existing subject matter that this bill does not propose to protect but that future Congresses may want to.

Fixation in tangible form

As a basic condition of copyright protection, the bill perpetuates the existing requirement that a work be fixed in a "tangible medium of expression," and adds that this medium may be one "now known or later developed," and that the fixation is sufficient if the work "can be perceived, reproduced, or otherwise communicated, either directly or with the aid of a machine or device." This broad language is intended to avoid the artificial and largely unjustifiable distinctions, derived from cases such as *White-Smith Publishing Co.* v. *Apollo Co.*, 209 U.S. 1 (1908), under which statutory copyrightability in certain cases has been made to depend upon the form or medium in which the work is fixed. Under the bill it makes no difference what the form, manner, or medium of fixation may be—whether it is in words, numbers, notes, sounds, pictures, or any other graphic or symbolic indicia, whether embodied in a physical object in written, printed, photographic, sculptural, punched, magnetic, or any other stable form, and whether it is capable of perception directly or by means of any machine or device "now known or later developed."

Under the bill, the concept of fixation is important since it not only determines whether the provisions of the statute apply to a work, but it also represents the dividing line between common law and statutory protection. As will be noted in more detail in connection with section 301, an unfixed work of authorship, such as an improvision or an unrecorded choreographic work, performance, or broadcast, would continue to be subject to protection under State common law or statute, but would not be eligible for Federal statutory protection under section 102.

The definition of "fixed" is contained in section 101. Under the first sentence of this definition a work would be considered "fixed in a tangible medium of expression" if there has been an authorized embodiment in a copy or phonorecord and if that embodiment "is sufficiently permanent or stable" to permit the work "to be perceived, reproduced, or otherwise communicated for a period of more than transitory duration." The second sentence makes clear that, in the case of "a work consisting of sounds, images, or both, that are being transmitted," the work is regarded as "fixed" if a fixation is being made at the same time as the transmission.

Under this new definition "copies" and "phonorecords" together will comprise all of the material objects in which copyrightable works are capable of being fixed. The definitions of these terms in section 101, together with their usage in section 102 and throughout the bill, reflect a fundamental distinction between the "original work" which is the product of "authorship" and the multitude of material objects in which it can be embodied. Thus, in the sense of the bill, a "book" is not a work of authorship, but is a particular kind of "copy." Instead, the author may write a "literary work," which in turn can be embodied in a wide range of "copies" and "phonorecords," including books, periodicals, computer punch cards, microfilm, tape recordings, and so forth. It is possible to have an "original work of authorship" without having a "copy" or "phonorecord" embodying it, and it is also possible to have a "copy" or "phonorecord" embodying something that does not qualify as an "original work of authorship." The two essential elements—original work and tangible object—must merge through fixation in order to produce subject matter copyrightable under the statute.

Categories of copyrightable works

The second sentence of section 102 lists seven broad categories which the concept of "works" of authorship" is said to "include." The use of the word "include," as defined in section 101, makes clear that the listing is "illustrative and not limitative," and that the seven categories do not necessarily exhaust the scope of "original works of authorship" that the bill is intended to protect. Rather, the list sets out the general area of copyrightable subject matter, but with sufficient flexibility to free the courts from rigid or outmoded concepts of the scope of particular categories. The items are also overlapping in the sense that a work falling within one class may encompass works coming within some or all of the other categories. In the aggregate, the list covers all categories of works now copyrightable under title 17; in addition, it specifically enumerates "pantomimes and choreographic works," and it creates a new category of "sound recordings."

Of the seven items listed, four are defined in section 101. The three undefined categories—"musical works," "dramatic works," and "pantomimes and choreographic works"—have fairly settled meanings. There is no need, for example, to specify the copyrightability of electronic or concrete music in the statute since the form of a work would no longer be of any importance, nor is it necessary to specify that "choreographic works" do not include social dance steps and simple routines.

The four items defined in section 101 are "literary works," "pictorial, graphic, and sculptural works," "motion pictures and audiovisual works", and "sound recordings." In each of these cases, definitions are needed not only because the meaning of the term itself is unsettled but also because the distinction between "work" and "material object" requires clarification. The term "literary works" does not connote any criterion of literary merit or qualitative value; it includes catalogs, directories and similar works.

Correspondingly, the definition of "pictorial, graphic, and sculptural works" carries with it no implied criterion of artistic taste, aesthetic value, or intrinsic quality. The term is intended to comprise everything now covered by classes (f) through (k) of section 5 in the present statute, including not only "works of art" in the traditional sense but also works of graphic art and illustration, art reproductions, plans and drawings, photographs and reproductions of them, maps, charts, globes, and other cartographic works, works of these kinds intended for use in advertising and commerce, and work of "applied art." There is no intention whatever to narrow the scope of the subject matter now characterized in section 5(k) as "prints or labels used for articles of merchandise." However, since this terminology suggests the material object in which a work is embodied rather than the work itself, the bill does not mention this category separately.

In accordance with the Supreme Court's decision in *Mazer* v. *Stein*, 347 U.S. 201 (1954), works of "applied art" encompass all original pictorial, graphic, and sculptural works that are intended to be or have been embodied in useful articles, regardless of factors such as mass production, commercial exploitation, and the potential availability of design patent protection. The scope of exclusive rights in these works is given special treatment in section 113, to be discussed below.

Enactment of Public Law 92–140 marked the first recognition in American copyright law of sound recordings as copyrightable works. As defined in section 101, copyrightable "sound recordings" are original works of authorship comprising an aggregate of musical, spoken, or other sounds that have been fixed in tangible form. The copyrightable work comprises the aggregation of sounds and not the tangible medium of fixation. Thus, "sound recordings" as copyrightable subject matter are distinguished from "phonorecords," the latter being physical objects in which sounds are fixed. They are also distinguished from any copyrighted literary, dramatic; or musical works that may be reproduced on a "phonorecord."

As a class of subject matter, sound recordings are clearly within the scope of the "writings of an author" capable of protection under the Constitution, and the extension of limited statutory protection to them too long delayed. Aside from cases in which sounds are fixed by some purely mechanical means without originality of any kind, the copyright protection that would prevent the reproduction and distribution of unauthorized phonorecords of sound recordings is clearly justified.

The copyrightable elements in a sound recording will usually, though not always, involve "authorship" both on the part of the performers whose performance is captured and on the part of the record producer responsible for setting up the recording session, capturing and electronically processing the sounds, and compiling and editing them to make the final sound recording. There may be cases where the record producer's contribution is so minimal that the performance is the only copyrightable element in the work, and there may be cases (for example, recordings of birdcalls, sounds of racing cars, et cetera) where only the record producer's contribution is copyrightable.

Sound tracks of motion pictures, long a nebulous area in American copyright law, are specifically included in the definition of "motion pictures" and excluded in the definition of "sound recordings." "Motion pictures," as defined, requires three elements: (1) a series of images, (2) the capability of showing the images in certain successive order, and (3) an impression of motion when the images are thus shown. Coupled with the basic requirements of original authorship and fixation in tangible form, this definition encompasses a wide range of cinematographic works embodied in films, tapes, and other media. However, it would not include: (1) unauthorized fixations of live performances or telecasts, (2) live telecasts that are not fixed simultaneously with their transmission, or (3) filmstrips and slide sets which, although consisting of a series of images intended to be shown in succession, are not capable of conveying an impression of motion.

On the other hand, the bill also equates audiovisual materials such as filmstrips, slide sets, and sets of transparencies with "motion pictures" rather than with "pictorial, graphic, and sculptural works." Their sequential showing is closer to a "performance" than to a "display," and the definition of "audiovisual works," which applies also to "motion pictures," embraces works consisting of a series of related images that are by their nature, intended for showing by means of projectors or other devices.

Nature of copyright

Copyright does not preclude others from using the ideas or information revealed by the author's work. It pertains to the literary, musical, graphic, or artistic form in which the author expressed intellectual concepts. Section 102(b) makes clear that copyright protection does not extend to any idea, plan, procedure, process, system, method of operation, concept, principle, or discovery, regardless of the form in which it is described explained, illustrated, or embodied in such work. The term "plan" in this context refers to a mental formulation for achieving something, as distinguished from a graphic representation diagramming the mental concept.

Some concern has been expressed lest copyright in computer programs should extend protection to the methodology or processes adopted by the programmer, rather than merely to the "writing" expressing his ideas. Section 102(b) is intended, among other things, to make clear that the expression adopted by the programmer is the copyrightable element in a computer program, and that the actual processes or methods embodied in the program are not within the scope of the copyright law.

Section 102(b) in no way enlarges or contracts the scope of copyright protection under the present law. Its purpose is to restate, in the context of the new single Federal system of copyright, that the basic dichotomy between expression and idea remains unchanged.

SECTION 103. COMPILATIONS AND DERIVATIVE WORKS

Section 103 complements section 102: A compilation or derivative work is copyrightable if it represents an "original work of authorship" and falls within one or more of the categories listed in section 102. Read together, the two sections make plain that the criteria of copyrightable subject matter stated in section 102 apply with full force to works that are entirely original and to those containing preexisting material. Section 103(b) is also intended to define, more sharply and clearly than does section 7 of the present law, the important interrelationship and correlation between protection of preexisting and of "new" material in a particular work. The most important point here is one that is commonly misunderstood today: Copyright in a "new version" covers only the material added by the later author, and has no effect one way or the other on the copyright or public domain status of the preexisting material.

Between them the terms "compilations" and "derivative works" which are defined in section 101, comprehend every copyrightable work that employs preexisting material or data of any kind. There is necessarily some overlapping between the two, but they basically represent different concepts. A "compilation" results from a process of selecting, bringing together, organizing, and arranging previously existing material of all kinds, regardless of whether the individual items in the material have been or ever could have been subject to copyright. A "derivative work," on the other hand, requires a process of recasting, transforming, or adapting "one or more preexisting works"; the "preexisting work" must come within the general subject matter of copyright set forth in section 102, regardless of whether it is or was ever copyrighted.

The second part of the sentence that makes up section 103(a) deals with the status of a compilation or derivative work unlawfully employing preexisting copyrighted material. In providing that protection does not extend to "any part of the work in which such material has been used unlawfully," the bill prevents an infringer from benefiting, through copyright protection, from his unlawful act, but preserves protection for those parts of the work that do not employ the preexisting work. Thus, an unauthorized translation of a novel could not be copyrighted at all, but the owner of copyright in an anthology of poetry could sue someone who infringed the whole anthology, even though the infringer proves that publication of one of the poems was unauthorized. Under this provision, copyright could be obtained as long as the use of the preexisting work was not "unlawful," even though the consent of the copyright owner had not been obtained. For instance, the unauthorized reproduction of a work might be "lawful" under the doctrine of fair use or an applicable foreign law, and if so the work incorporating it could be copyrighted.

SECTION 106. EXCLUSIVE RIGHTS IN COPYRIGHTED WORKS

General scope of copyright

The five fundamental rights that the bill gives to copyright owners—the exclusive rights of reproduction, adaptation, publication, performance, and display—are stated generally in section 106. These exclusive rights, which comprise the so-called "bundle of rights" that is a copyright, are cumulative and may overlap in some cases. Each of the five enumerated rights may be subdivided indefinitely and, as discussed below in connection with section 201, each subdivision of an exclusive right may be owned and enforced separately.

The approach of the bill is to set forth the copyright owner's exclusive rights in broad terms in section 106, and then to provide various limitations, qualifications, or exemptions in the 11 sections that follow. Thus, everything in section 106 is made "subject to sections 107 through 117," and must be read in conjunction with those provisions.

The exclusive rights accorded to a copyright owner under section 106 are "to do and to authorize" any of the activities specified in the five numbered clauses. Use of the phrase "to authorize" is intended to avoid any questions as to the liability of contributory infringers. For example, a person who lawfully acquires an authorized copy of a motion picture would be an infringer if he engages in the business of renting it to others for purposes of unauthorized public performance.

Rights of reproduction, adaptation, and publication

The first three clauses of section 106, which cover all rights under a copyright except those of performance and display, extend to every kind of copyrighted work. The exclusive rights encompassed by these clauses, though closely related, are independent; they can generally be characterized as rights of copying, recording, adaptation, and publishing. A single act of infringement may violate all of these rights at once, as where a published reproduces, adapts, and sells copies of a person's copyrighted work as part of a publishing venture. Infringement takes place when any one of the rights is violated: where, for example, a printer reproduces copies without selling them or a retailer sells copies without having anything to do with their reproduction. The references to "copies or phonorecords," although in the plural, are intended here and throughout the bill to include the singular (1 U.S.C. § 1).

Reproduction.—Read together with the relevant definitions in section 101, the right "to reproduce the copyrighted work in copies or phonorecords" means the right to produce a material object in which the work is duplicated, transcribed, imitiated, or simulated in a fixed form from which it can be "perceived, reproduced, or otherwise communicated, either directly or with the aid of a machine or device." As under the present law, a copyrighted work would be infringed by reproducing it in whole or in any substantial part, and by duplicating it exactly or by imitation or simulation. Wide departures or variations from the copyrighted works would still be an infringement as long as the author's "expression" rather than merely has "ideas" are taken.

"Reproduction" under clause (1) of section 106 is to be distinguished from "display' under clause (5). For a work to be "reproduced," its fixation in tangible form must be "sufficiently permanent or stable to permit it to be perceived, reproduced, or otherwise communicated for a period of more than transitory duration." Thus, the showing of images on a screen or tube would not be a violation of clause (1), although it might come within the scope of clause (5).

Preparation of derivative works.—The exclusive right to prepare derivative works, specified separately in clause (2) of section 106, overlaps the exclusive right of reproduction to some extent. It is broader than that right, however, in the sense that reproduction requires fixation in copies or phonorecords, whereas the preparation of a derivative work, such as a ballet, pantomine, or improvised performance, may be an infringement even though nothing is ever fixed in tangible form.

To be an infringement the "derivative work" must be "based upon the copyrighted work," and the definition in section 101 refers to "a translation, musical arrangement, dramatization, fictionalization motion picture version, sound recording, art reproduction, abridgment, condensation, or any other form in which a work may be recast, transformed, or adapted." Thus, to constitute a violation of section 106(2), the infringing work must incorporate a portion of the copyrighted work in some form; for example, a detailed commentary on a work or a programmatic musical composition inspired by a novel would not normally constitute infringements under this clause.

Use in information storage and retrieval systems.—As section 117 declares explicity, the bill is not intended to alter the present law with respect to the use of copyrighted works in computer systems.

Public distribution.—Clause (3) of section 106 establishes the exclusive right of publication: The right "to distribute copies or phonorecords of the copyrighted work to the public by sale or other transfer of ownership, or by rental, lease, or lending." Under this provision the copyright owner would have the right to control the first public distribution of an authorized copy or phonorecord of his work, whether by sale, gift, loan, or some rental or lease arrangement. Likewise, any unauthorized public distribution of copies or phonorecords that were unlawfully made would be an infringement. As section 109 makes clear, however, the copyright owner's rights under section 106(3) cease with respect to a particular copy or phonorecord once he has parted with ownership of it.

Rights of public performance and display

Performing rights and the "for profit" limitation.—The right of public performance under section 106(4) extends to "literary, musical, dramatic, and choreographic works, pantomimes, and motion pictures and other audiovisual works and sound recordings" and, unlike the equivalent provisions now in effect, is not limited by any "for profit" requirement. The approach of the bill, as in many foreign laws, is first to state the public performance right in broad terms, and then to provide specific exemptions for educational and other nonprofit uses.

This approach is more reasonable than the outright exemption of the 1909 statute. The line between commercial and "nonprofit" organizations is increasingly difficult to draw. Many "nonprofit" organizations are highly subsidized and capable of paying royalties and the widespread public exploitation of copyrighted works by educational broadcasters and other noncommercial organizations is likely to grow. In addition to these trends, it is worth noting that performances and displays are continuing to supplant markets for printed copies and that in the future a broad "not for profit" exemption could not only hurt authors but could dry up their incentive to write.

The exclusive right of public performance is expanded to include not only motion pictures but also audiovisual works such as filmstrips and sets of slides. This provision of section 106(4), which is consistent with the assimilation of motion pictures to audiovisual works throughout the bill, is also related to amendments of the definitions of "display" and "perform" discussed below. The important issue of performing rights in sound recordings is discussed in connection with section 114.

Right of public display.—Clause (5) of section 106 represents the first explicit statutory recognition in American copyright law of an exclusive right to show a copyrighted work, or an image of it, to the public. The existence or extent of this right under the present statute is uncertain and subject to challenge. The bill would give the owners of copyright in "literary, musical, dramatic, and choreographic works, pantomimes, and pictorial, graphic, or sculptural works", including the individual images of a motion picture or other audiovisual work, the exclusive right "to display the copyrighted work publicly."

Definitions

Under the definitions of "perform," "display," "publicly," and "transmit" in section 101, the concepts of public performance and public display cover not only the initial rendition or showing, but also any further act by which that rendition or showing is transmitted or communicated to the public. Thus, for example: a singer is performing when he sings a song; a broadcasting network is performing when it transmits his performance (whether simultaneously or from records); a local broadcaster is performing when it transmits the network broadcast; a cable television system is performing when it retransmits the broadcast to its subscribers; and any individual is performing whenever he plays a phonorecord embodying the performance or communicates the performance by turning on a receiving set. Although any act by which the initial performance or display is transmitted, repeated, or made to recur would itself be a "performance" or "display" under the bill, it would not be actionable as an infringement unless it were done "publicly," as defined in section 101. Certain other performances and displays, in addition to those that are "private," are exempted or given qualified copyright control under sections 107 through 117.

To "perform" a work, under the definition in section 101, includes reading a literary work aloud, singing or playing music, dancing a ballet or other choreographic work, and acting out a dramatic work or pantomime. A performance may be accomplished "either directly or by means of any device or process," including all kinds of equipment for reproducing or amplifying sounds or visual images, any sort of transmitting apparatus, any type of electronic retrieval system, and any other techniques and systems not yet in use or even invented.

The definition of "perform" in relation to "a motion picture or other audio visual work" is "to show its images in any sequence or to make the sounds accompanying it audible." The showing of portions of a motion picture, filmstrip, or slide set must therefore be sequential to constitute a "performance" rather than a "display", but·no particular order need be maintained. The purely aural performance of a motion picture sound track, or of the sound portions of an audiovisual work, would constitute a performance of the "motion picture or other audiovisual work"; but, where some of the sounds have been reproduced separately on phonorecords, a performance from the phonorecord would not constitute performance of the motion picture or audiovisual work.

The corresponding definition of "display" covers any showing of a "copy" of the work, "either directly or by means of a film, slide, television image, or any other device or process." Since "copies" are defined as including the material object "in which the work is first fixed," the right of public display applies to original works of art as well as to reproductions of them. With respect to motion pictures and other audiovisual works, it is a "display" (rather than a "performance") to show their "individual images nonsequentially." In addition to the direct showings of a copy of a work, "display" would include the projection of an image on a screen or other surface by any method, the transmission of an image by electronic or other means, and the showing of an image on a cathode ray tube, or similar viewing apparatus connected with any sort of information storage and retrieval system.

Under clause (1) of the definition of "publicly", a performance or display is "public" if it takes place "at a place open to the public or at any place where a substantial number of persons outside of a normal circle of a family and its social acquaintances is gathered." One of the principal purposes of the definition was to make clear that, contrary to the decision in *Metro-Goldwyn-Mayer Distributing Corp.* v. *Wyatt*, 21 C.O. Bull. 203 (D. Md. 1932), performances in "semipublic" places such as clubs, lodges, factories, summer camps, and schools are "public performances" subject to copyright control. The term "a family" in this context would include an individual living alone, so that a gathering confined to the individual's social acquaintances would normally be regarded as private. Routine meetings of business and governmental personnel would be excluded because they do not represent the gathering of a "substantial number of persons."

Clause (2) of the definition of "publicly" in section 101 makes clear that the concepts of public performance and public display include not only performances and displays that occur initially in a public place, but also acts that transmit or otherwise communicate a performance or display of the work to the public by means of any device or process. The definition of "transmit"—to communicate a performance or display "by any device or process whereby images or sound are received beyond the place from which they are sent"—is broad enough to include all conceivable forms and combinations of wired or wireless communications media, including but by no means limited to radio and television broadcasting as we know them. Each and every method by which the images or sounds comprising a performance or display are picked up and conveyed is a "transmission," and if the transmission reaches the public in any form, the case comes within the scope of clauses (4) or (5) of section 106.

Under the bill, as under the present law, a performance made available by transmission to the public at large is "public" even though the recipients are not gathered in a single place, and even if there is no direct proof that any of the potential recipients was operating his receiving apparatus at the time of the transmission. The same principles apply whenever the potential recipients of the transmission represent a limited segment of the public, such as the occupants of hotel rooms or the subscribers of a cable television service. Clause (2) of the definition of "publicly" is applicable "whether the members of the public capable of receiving the performance or display receive it in the same place or in separate places and at the same time or at different times."

SECTION 107. FAIR USE

General background of the problem

The judicial doctrine of fair use, one of the most important and well-established limitations on the exclusive right of copyright owners, would be given express statutory recognition for the first time in section 107. The claim that a defendant's acts constituted a fair use rather than an infringement has been raised as a defense in innumerable copyright actions over the years, and there is ample case law recognizing the existence of the doctrine and applying it. The examples enumerated at page 24 of the Register's 1961 Report, while by no means exhaustive, give some idea of the sort of activities the courts might regard as fair use under the circumstances: "quotation of excerpts in a review or criticism for purposes of illustration or comment; quotation of short passages in a scholarly or technical work, for illustration or clarification of the author's observations; use in a parody of some of the content of the work parodied; summary of an address or article, with brief quotations, in a news report; reproduction by a library of a portion of a work to replace part of a damaged copy; reproduction by a teacher or student of a small part of a work to illustrate a lesson; reproduction of a work in legislative or judicial proceedings or reports; incidental and fortuitous reproduction, in a newsreel or broadcast, of a work located in the scene of an event being reported."

Although the courts have considered and ruled upon the fair use doctrine over and over again, no real definition of the concept has ever emerged. Indeed, since the doctrine is an equitable rule of reason, no generally applicable definition is possible, and each case raising the question must be decided on its own facts. On the other hand, the courts have evolved a set of criteria which, though in no case definitive or determinative, provide some gage for balancing the equities. These criteria have been stated in various ways, but essentially they can all be reduced to the four standards which were stated in the 1964 bill and have been adopted in section 107: "(1) the purpose and character of the use; (2) the nature of the copyrighted work; (3) the amount and substantially of the portion used in relation to the copyrighted work as a whole; and (4) the effect of the use upon the potential market for or value of the copyrighted work."

The underlying intention of the bill with respect to the application of the fair use doctrine in various situations is discussed below. It should be emphasized again that, in those situations or any others, there is no purpose of either freezing or changing the doctrine. In particular, the reference to fair use "by reproduction in copies or phonorecords or by any other means" should not be interpreted as sanctioning any reproduction beyond the normal and reasonable limits of fair use. In making separate mention of "reproduction in copies or phonorecords" in the section, the provision is not intended to give this kind of use any special or preferred status as compared with other kinds of uses. In any event, whether a use referred to in the first sentence of section 107 is a fair use in a particular case will depend upon the application of the determinative factors, including those mentioned in the second sentence.

Intention behind the provision

In general.—The statement of the fair use doctrine in section 107 offers some guidance to users in determining when the principles of the doctrine apply. However, the endless variety of situations and combinations of circumstances that can rise in particular cases precludes the formulation of exact rules in the statute. The bill endorses the purpose and general scope of the judicial doctrine of fair use, as outlined earlier in this report, but there is no disposition to freeze the doctrine in the statute, especially during a period of rapid technological change. Beyond a very broad statutory explanation of what fair use is and some of the criteria applicable to it, the courts must be free to adapt the doctrine to particular situations on a case-by-case basis.

Section 107 is intended to restate the present judicial doctrine of fair use, not to change, narrow, or enlarge it in any way. However, since this section will represent the first statutory recognition of the doctrine in our copyright law, some explanation of the considerations behind the language used in the list of four criteria is advisable. This is particularly true as to cases of copying by teachers, and by public libraries, since in these areas there are few if any judicial guidelines.

The statements in this report with respect to each of the criteria of fair use are necessarily subject to qualifications, because they must be applied in combination with the circumstances pertaining to other criteria, and because new conditions arising in the future may alter the balance of equities. It is also important to emphasize that the singling out of some instances to discuss in the context of fair use is not intended to indicate that other activities would or would not be beyond fair use.

The purpose and nature of the use

Copyright recognized.—Section 107 makes it clear that, assuming the applicable criteria are met, fair use can extend to the reproduction of copyrighted material for purposes of classroom teaching.

Nonprofit element.—Although it is possible to imagine situations in which use by a teacher in an educational organization operated for profit (day camps, language schools, business schools, dance studios, et cetera) would constitute a fair use, the nonprofit character of the school in which the teacher works should be one factor to consider in determining fair use. Another factor would be whether any charge is made for the copies distributed.

Spontaneity.—The fair use doctrine in the case of classroom copying would apply primarily to the situation of a teacher who, acting individually and at his own volition, makes one or more copies for temporary use by himself or his pupils in the classroom. A different result is indicated where the copying was done by the educational institution, school system, or larger unit or where copying was required or suggested by the school administration, either in special instances or as part of a general plan.

Single and multiple copying.—Depending upon the nature of the work and other criteria, the fair use doctrine should differentiate between the amount of work that can be reproduced by a teacher for his own classroom use (for example, for reading or projecting a copy or for playing a tape recording), and the amount that can be reproduced for distribution to pupils. In the case of multiple copies, other factors would be whether the number reproduced was limited to the size of the class, whether circulation beyond the classroom was permitted, and whether the copies were recalled or destroyed after temporary use.

Collection and anthologies.—Spontaneous copying of an isolated extract by a teacher, which may be a fair use under appropriate circumstances, could turn into an infringement if the copies were accumulated over a period of time with other parts of the same work, or were collected with other material from various works so as to constitute an anthology.

Special uses.—There are certain classroom uses which, because of their special nature, would not be considered an infringement in the ordinary case. For example, copying of extracts by pupils as exercises in a shorthand or typing class or for foreign language study, or recordings of performances by music students for purposes of analysis and criticism, would normally be regarded as a fair use unless the copies of phonorecords were retained or duplicated.

The nature of the copyrighted work

Character of the work.—The character and purpose of the work will have a lot to do with whether its reproduction for classroom purposes is fair use or infringement. For example, in determining whether a teacher could make one or more copies without permission, a news article from the daily press would be judged differently from a full orchestral score of a musical composition. In general terms it could be expected that the doctrine of fair use would be applied strictly to the classroom reproduction of entire works, such as musical compositions, dramas, and audiovisual works including motion pictures, which by their nature are intended for performance or public exhibition.

Similarly, where the copyright work is intended to be "consumable" in the course of classroom activities—workbooks, exercise, standardized tests, and answer sheets are examples—the privilege of fair use by teachers or pupils would have little if any application. Text books and other material prepared primarily for the school markets would be less susceptible to reproduction for classroom use than material prepared for general public distribution. With respect to material in newspapers and periodicals the doctrine of fair use should be liberally applied to allow copying of items of current interest to supplement and update the students' textbooks, but this would not extend to copying from periodicals published primarily for student use.

Availability of the work.—A key, though not necessarily determinative, factor in fair use is whether or not the work is available to the potential user. If the work is "out of print" and unavailable for purchase through normal channels, the user may have more justification for reproducing it than in the ordinary case, but the existence of organizations licensed to provide photocopies of out-of-print works at reasonable cost is a factor to be considered. The applicability of the fair use doctrine to unpublished works is narrowly limited since, although the work is unavailable, this is the result of a deliberate choice on the part of the copyright owner. Under ordinary circumstances the copyright owner's "right of first publication" would outweigh any needs of reproduction for classroom purposes.

The amount and substantiality of the material used

During the consideration of this legislation there has been considerable discussion of the difference between an "entire work" and an "excerpt". The educators have sought a limited right for a teacher to make a single copy of an "entire" work for classroom purposes, but it seems apparent that this was not generally intended to extend beyond a "separately cognizable" or "self-contained" portion (for example a single poem, story, or article) in a collective work, and that no privilege is sought to reproduce an entire collective work (for example, an encyclopedia volume, a periodical issue) or a sizable integrated work published as an entity (a novel, treatise, monograph, and so forth). With this limitation, and subject to the other revelant criteria, the requested privilege of making a single copy appears appropriately to be within the scope of fair use.

The educators also sought statutory authority for the privilege of making "a reasonable number of copies or phonorecords for excerpts or quotations * * *, provided such excerpts or quotations are not substantial in length in proportion to their source." In general, and assuming the other necessary factors are present, the copying for classroom purposes of extracts or portions, which are not self-contained and which are relatively "not substantial in length" when compared to the larger, self-contained work from which they are taken, should be considered fair use. Depending on the circumstances, the same would also be true of very short self-contained works such as a brief poem, a map in a newspaper, a "vocabulary builder" from a monthly magazine, and so forth. This should not be construed as permitting a teacher to make multiple copies of the same work on a repetitive basis or for continued use.

Effect of use on potential market for or value of work

This factor must almost always be judged in conjunction with the other three criteria. With certain special exceptions (use in parodies or as evidence in court proceedings might be examples) a use that supplants any part of the normal market for a copyrighted work would ordinarily be considered an infringement. As in any other case, whether this would be the result of reproduction by a teacher for classroom purposes requires an evaluation of the nature and purpose of the use, the type of work involved, and the size and relative importance of the portion taken. Fair use is essentially supplementary by nature, and classroom copying that exceeds the legitimate teaching aims such as filling in missing information or bringing a subject up to date would go beyond the proper bounds of fair use. Isolated instances of minor infringements, when multiplied many times, become in the aggregate a major inroad on copyright that must be prevented.

Reproduction and uses for other purposes

The concentrated attention given the fair use provision in the context of classroom teaching activities should not obscure its application in other areas. It must be emphasized again that the same general standards of fair use are applicable to all kinds of uses of copyrighted material, although the relative weight to be given them will differ from case to case.

The fair use doctrine would be relevant to the use of excerpts from copyrighted works in educational broadcasting activities not exempted under section 110(2) or 112. In these cases the factors to be weighed in applying the criteria of this section would include whether the performers, producers, directors, and others responsible for the broadcast were paid, the size and nature of the audience, the size and number of excerpts taken and, in the case of recordings made for broadcast, the number of copies reproduced and the extent of their reuse or exchange. The availability of the fair use doctrine to educational broadcasters would be narrowly circumscribed in the case of motion pictures and other audiovisual works, but under appropriate circumstances it could apply to the nonsequential showing of an individual still or slide, or to the performance of a short excerpt from a motion picture for criticism or comment.

The committee's attention has been directed to the special problems involved in the reception of instructional television programs in remote areas of the country. In certain areas it is currently impossible to transmit such programs by any means other than communications satellites. A particular difficulty exists when such transmissions extend over several time zones within the same state, such as in Alaska. Unless individual schools in such states may make an off-air recording of such transmissions, the programs may not be received by the students during the school's daily schedule. The committee believes that the making by a school located in such a remote area of an off-the-air recording of an instructional television transmission for the purpose of a delayed viewing of the program by students for the same school constitutes a "fair use." The committee does not intend to suggest however, that off-the-air recording for convenience would under any circumstances, be considered "fair use." To meet the requirement of temporary use the school may retain the recording for only a limited period of time after the broadcast.

Another special instance illustrating the application of the fair use doctrine pertains to the making of copies or phonorecords of works in the special forms needed for the use of blind persons. These special forms, such as copies in braille and phonorecords of oral readings (talking books), are not usually made by the publishers for commercial distribution. For the most part, such copies and phonorecords are made by the Library of Congress' Division for the Blind and Physically Handicapped with permission obtained from the copyright owners, and are circulated to blind persons through regional libraries covering the nation. In addition, such copies and phonorecords are made locally by individual volunteers for the use of blind persons in their communities, and the Library of Congress conducts a program for training such volunteers. While the making of multiple copies or phonorecords of a work for general circulation requires the permission of the copyright owner, the making of a single copy or phonorecord by an individual as a free service for a blind person would properly be considered a fair use under section 107.

A problem of particular urgency is that of preserving for posterity prints of motion pictures made before 1942. Aside from the deplorable fact that in a great many cases the only existing copy of a film has been deliberately destroyed, those that remain are in immediate danger of disintegration; they were printed on film stock with a nitrate base that will inevitably decompose in time. The efforts of the Library of Congress, the American Film Institute, and other organizations to rescue and preserve this irreplaceable contribution to our cultural life are to be applauded, and the making of duplicate copies for purposes of archival preservation certainly falls within the scope of "fair use".

When a copyrighted work contains unfair, inaccurate, or derogatory information concerning an individual or institution, such individual or institution may copy and reproduce such parts of the work as are necessary to permit understandable comment on the statements made in the work.

During the consideration of the revision bill in the 94th Congress it was proposed that independent newsletters, as distinguished from house organs and publicity or advertising publications, be given separate treatment. It is argued that newsletters are particularly vulnerable to mass photocopying, and that most newsletters have fairly modest circulations. Whether the copying of portions of a newsletter is an act of infringement or a fair use must be judged by the general provisions of this legislation. However, the copying of even a short portion of a newsletter may have a significant impact on the commercial market for the work.

The committee has examined the use of excerpts from copyrighted works in the art work of calligraphers. The committee believes that a single copy reproduction of an excerpt from a copyrighted work by a calligrapher for a single client does not represent an infringement of copyright. Likewise, a single reproduction of excerpts from a copyrighted work by a student calligrapher or teacher in a learning situation would be a fair use of the copyrighted work.

The Register of Copyrights has recommended that the committee report describe the relationship between this section and the provisions of section 108 relating to reproduction by libraries and archives. The doctrine of fair use applies to library photocopying, and nothing contained in section 108 "in any way affects the right of fair use." No provision of section 108 is intended to take away any rights existing under the fair use doctrine. To the contrary, section 108 authorizes certain photocopying practices which may not qualify as a fair use.

The criteria of fair use are necessarily set forth in general terms. In the application of the criteria of fair use to specific photocopying practices of libraries, it is the intent of this legislation to provide an appropriate balancing of the rights of creators, and the needs of users.

SECTION 108. REPRODUCTION BY LIBRARIES AND ARCHIVES

Notwithstanding the exclusive rights of the owners of copyright, section 108 provides that under certain conditions it is not an infringement of copyright for a library or archives, or any of their employees acting within the scope of their employment, to reproduce or distribute not more than one copy of phonorecord of a work provided (1) the reproduction or distribution is made without any purpose of direct or indirect commercial advantage and (2) the collections of the library or archives are open to the public or available not only to researchers affiliated with the library or archives, but also to other persons doing research in a specialized field, and (3) the reproduction or distribution of the work includes a notice of copyright.

The limitation of section 108 to reproduction and distribution by libraries and archives "without any purpose of direct or indirect commercial advantage" is intended to preclude a library or archives in a profit-making organization from providing photocopies of copyrighted materials to employees engaged in furtherance of the organization's commercial enterprise, unless such copying qualifies as a fair use, or the organization has obtained the necessary copyright licenses. A commercial organization should purchase the number of copies of a work that it requires, or obtain the consent of the copyright owner to the making of the photocopies.

The rights of reproduction and distribution under section 108 apply in the following circumstances:

Archival reproduction

Subsection (b) authorizes the reproduction and distribution of a copy or phonorecord of an unpublished work duplicated in facsimile form solely for purposes of preservation and security, or for deposit for research use in another library or archives, if the copy or phonorecord reproduced is currently in the collections of the first library or archives. Only unpublished works could be reproduced under this exemption, but the right would extend to any type of work, including photographs, motion pictures and sound recordings. Under this exemption, for example, a repository could make photocopies of manuscripts by microfilm or electrostatic process, but could not reproduce the work in "machine-readable" language for storage in an information system.

Replacement of damaged copy

Subsection (c) authorizes the reproduction of a published work duplicated in facsimile form solely for the purpose of replacement of a copy or phonorecord that is damaged, deteriorating, lost, or stolen, if the library or archives has, after a reasonable effort, determined that an unused replacement cannot be obtained at a fair price. The scope and nature of a reasonable investigation to determine that an unused replacement cannot be obtained will vary according to the circumstances of a particular situation. It will always require recourse to commonly-known trade sources in the United States, and in the normal situation also to the published or other copyright owner (if such owner can be located at the address listed in the copyright registration), or an authorized reproducing service.

Articles and small excerpts

Subsection (d) authorizes the reproduction and distribution of a copy of not more than one article or other contribution to a copyrighted collection of a periodical or copy or phonocord of a small part of any other copyrighted work. The copy may be made by the library where the user makes his request or by another library pursuant to an inter-library loan. It is further required that the copy become the property of the user, that the library or archives have no notice that the copy would be used for any purposes other than private study, scholarship or research, and that the library or archives display prominently at the place whether reproduction requests are accepted. and includes in its order form, a warning of copyright in accordance with requirements that the Register of Copyrights shall prescribe by regulation.

Out-of-print works

Subsection (e) authorizes the reproduction and distribution of a copy of a work, with certain exceptions, at the request of the user of the collection if the user has established that an unused copy cannot be obtained at a fair price. The copy may be made by the library where the user makes his request or by another library pursuant to an inter-library loan. The scope and nature of a reasonable investigation to determine that an unused copy cannot be obtained will vary according to the circumstances of a particular situation. It will always require recourse to commonly-known trade sources in the United States, and in the normal situation also to the publisher or other copyright owner (if the owner can be located at the address listed in the copyright registration), or an authorized reproducing service. It is further required that the copy become the property of the user, that the library or archives have no notice that the copy would be used for any purpose other than private study, scholarship, or research, and that the library or archives display prominently at the place where reproduction requests are accepted, and include on its order form, a warning of copyright in accordance with requirements that the Register of Copyright shall prescribe by regulation.

General exemptions

Clause (1) of subsection (f) specifically exempts a library or archives or their employees from such liability provided that the reproducing equipment displays a notice that the making of a copy may be subject to the copyright law. Clause (2) of subsection (f) makes clear that this exemption of the library or archives does not extend to the person using such equipment or requesting such copy if the use exceeds fair use. Insofar as such person is concerned the copy made is not considered "lawfully" made for purposes of sections 109, 110 or other provisions of the title. Clause (3) in addition to asserting that nothing contained in section 108 "affects the right of fair use as provided by section 107," also provides that the right of reproduction granted by this section does not override any contractual arrangements assumed by a library or archives when it obtained a work for its collections. For example, if there is an express contractual prohibition against reproduction for any purpose, this legislation shall not be construed as justifying a violation of the contract. This clause is intended to encompass the situation where an individual makes papers, manuscripts or other works available to a library with the understanding that they will not be reproduced.

Clause (4) provides that nothing in section 108 is intended to limit the reproduction and distribution of a limited number of copies and excerpts of an audiovisual news program.

This clause was first added to the revision bill last year by the adoption of an amendment proposed by Senator Baker. It is intended to permit libraries and archives, subject to the general conditions of this section, to make off-the-air videotape recordings of television news programs. Despite the importance of preserving television news, the United States currently has no institution performing this function on a systematic basis.

The purpose of the clause is to prevent the copyright law from precluding such operations as the Vanderbilt University Television News Archive, which makes videotape recordings of television news programs, prepares indexes of the contents, and leases copies of complete broadcasts or compilations of coverage of specified subjects for limited periods upon request from scholars and researchers.

Because of the important copyright policy issues inherent in this issue, the exemption has been narrowly drafted. The Register of Copyrights in 1974 advised that the language of this clause was technically appropriate for its purpose and not "broader than is necessary to validate the Vanderbilt operation."

The Copyright Office recommended that if the Congress desires a news videotape exemption it should be incorporated in section 108. The Copyright Office stated that the inclusion of such a clause in section 108 would be adequate "to enable the Vanderbilt operation to continue."

It is the intent of this legislation that a subsequent unlawful use by a user of a copy of a work lawfully made by a library, shall not make the library liable for such improper use.

Multiple copies and systematic reproduction

Subsection (g) provides that the rights granted by this section extend only to the "isolated and unrelated reproduction of a single copy", but this section does not authorize the related or concerted reproduction of multiple copies of the same material whether made on one occasion or over a period of time, and whether intended for aggregate use by one individual or for separate use by the individual members of a group. For example, if a college professor instructs his class to read an article from a copyrighted journal, the school library would not be permitted, under subsection (g), to reproduce copies of the article for the members of the class.

Subsection (g) also provides that section 108 does not authorize the systematic reproduction or distribution of copies or phonorecords of articles or other contributions to copyrighted collections or periodicals or of small parts of other copyrighted works whether or not multiple copies are reproduced or distributed. Systematic reproduction or distribution occurs when a library makes copies of such materials available to other libraries or to groups of users under formal or informal arrangements whose purpose or effect is to have the reproducing library serve as their source of such material. Such systematic reproduction and distribution, as distinguished from isolated and unrelated reproduction or distribution, may substitute the copies reproduced by the source library for subscriptions or reprints or other copies which the receiving libraries or users might otherwise have purchased for themselves, from the publisher or the licensed reproducing agencies.

While it is not possible to formulate specific definitions of "systematic copying", the following examples serve to illustrate some of the copying prohibited by subsection (g).

(1) A library with a collection of journals in biology informs other libraries with similar collections that it will maintain and build its own collection and will make copies of articles from these journals available to them and their patrons on request. Accordingly, the other libraries discontinue or refrain from purchasing subscriptions to these journals and fulfill their patrons' requests for articles by obtaining photocopies from the source library.

(2) A research center employing a number of scientists and technicians subscribes to one or two copies of needed periodicals. By reproducing photocopies of articles the center is able to make the material in these periodicals available to its staff in the same manner which otherwise would have required multiple subscriptions.

(3) Several branches of a library system agree that one branch will subscribe to particular journals in lieu of each branch purchasing its own subscriptions, and the one subscribing branch will reproduce copies of articles from the publication for users of the other branches.

The committee believes that section 108 provides an appropriate statutory balancing of the rights of creators, and the needs of users. However, neither a statute nor legislative history can specify precisely which library photocopying practices constitute the making of "single copies" as distinguished from "systematic reproduction". Isolated single spontaneous requests must be distinguished from "systematic reproduction". The photocopying needs of such operations as multi-county regional systems must be met. The committee therefore recommends that representatives of authors, book and periodical publishers and other owners of copyrighted material meet with the library community to formulate photocopying guidelines to assist library patrons and employees. Concerning library photocopying practices not authorized by this legislation, the committee recommends that workable clearance and licensing procedures be developed.

It is still uncertain how far a library may go under the Copyright Act of 1909 in supplying a photocopy of copyrighted material in its collection. The recent case of *The Williams and Wilkins Company* v. *The United States* failed to significantly illuminate the application of the fair use doctrine to library photocopying practices. Indeed, the opinion of the Court of Claims said the Court was engaged in "a 'holding operation' in the interim period before Congress enacted its preferred solution."

While the several opinions in the *Wilkins* case have given the Congress little guidance as to the current state of the law on fair use, these opinions provide additional support for the balanced resolution of the photocopying issue adopted by the Senate last year in S. 1361 and preserved in section 108 of this legislation. As the Court of Claims opinion succinctly stated "there is much to be said on all sides."

In adopting these provisions on library photocopying, the committee is aware that through such programs as those of the National Commission on Libraries and Information Science there will be a significant evolution in the functioning and services of libraries. To consider the possible need for changes in copyright law and procedures as a result of new technology, a National Commission on New Technological Uses of Copyrighted Works has been established (Public Law 93–573).

Works excluded

Subsection (h) provides that the rights of reproduction and distribution under this section do not apply to a musical work, a pictorial, graphic or sculptural work, or a motion picture or other audio-visual work. Such limitation does not apply to archival reproduction and replacement of a damaged copy.

SECTION 109. EFFECT OF TRANSFER OF PARTICULAR COPY OR PHONORECORD

Effect on further disposition of copy or phonorecord

Section 109(a) restates and confirms the principle that, where the copyright owner has transferred ownership of a particular copy or phonorecord of his work, the person to whom the copy or phonorecord is transferred is entitled to dispose of it by sale, rental, or any other means. Under this principle, which has been established by the court decisions and section 27 of the present law, the copyright owner's exclusive right of public distribution would have no effect upon anyone who owns "a particular copy or phonorecord lawfully made under this title" and who wishes to transfer it to someone else or to destroy it.

Thus, for example, the outright sale of an authorized copy of a book frees it from any copyright control over its resale price or other conditions of its future disposition. A library that has acquired ownership of a copy is entitled to lend it under any conditions it chooses to impose. This does not mean that conditions on future disposition of copies or phonorecords, imposed by a contract between their buyer and seller, would be unenforceable between the parties as a breach of contract, but it does mean that they could not be enforced by an action for infringement of copyright. Under section 202, however, the owner of the physical copy or phonorecord cannot reproduce or perform the copyrighted work publicly without the copyright owner's consent.

To come within the scope of section 109(a), a copy or phonorecord must have been "lawfully made under this title," though not necessarily with the copyright owner's authorization. For example, any resale of an illegally "counterfeited" phonorecord would be an infringement, but the disposition of a phonorecord made under the compulsory licensing provisions of section 115 would not.

Effect on display of copy

Subsection (b) of section 109 deals with the scope of the copyright owner's exclusive right to control the public display of a particular "copy" of his work (including the original or prototype copy in which the work was first fixed). Assuming, for example, that a painter has sold his only copy of an original work of art without restrictions, would he be able to restrain the new owner from displaying it publicly in galleries, shop windows, on a projector, or on television?

Section 109(b) adopts the general principle that the lawful owner of a copy of a work should be able to put his copy on public display without the consent of the copyright owner. The exclusive right of public display granted by section 106(5) would not apply where the owner of a copy wishes to show it directly to the public, as in a gallery or display case, or indirectly, as through an opaque projector. Where the copy itself is intended for projection, as in the case of a photographic slide, negative, or transparency, the public projection of a single image would be permitted as long as the viewers are "present at the place where the copy is located."

The exemption would extend only to public displays that are made "either directly or by the projection of no more than one image at a time." Thus, even where the copy and the viewers are located at the same place, the simultaneous projection of multiple images of the work would not be exempted. For example, where each person in a lecture hall has his own viewing apparatus in front of him, the copyright owner's permission would generally be required in order to project an image of a work on each individual screen at the same time.

The committee's intention is to preserve the traditional privilege of the owner of a copy to display it directly, but to place reasonable restrictions on his ability to display it indirectly in such a way that the copyright owner's market for reproduction and distribution of copies would be affected. Unless it constitutes a fair use under section 107, or unless one of the special provisions of sections 110 or 111 is applicable, projection of more than one image at a time, or transmission of an image to the public over television or other communications channels, would be an infringement for the same reasons that reproduction in copies would be.

Effect of mere possession of copy or phonorecord

Subsection (c) of section 109 qualifies the privileges specified in subsections (a) and (b) by making clear that they do not apply to someone who merely possesses a copy or phonorecord without having acquired ownership of it. Acquisition of an object embodying a copyrighted work by rental, lease, loan, or bailment carries with it no privileges to dispose of the copy under section 109(a) or to display it publicly under section 109(b). To cite a familiar example, a person who has rented a print of a modern picture from the copyright owner would have no right to rent it to someone else without the owner's permission.

SECTION 110. EXEMPTION OF CERTAIN PERFORMANCES AND DISPLAYS

Clauses (1) through (4) deal with performances and exhibitions that are now generally exempt under the "for profit" limitation or other provisions of the copyright law, and that are specifically exempted from copyright liability under this legislation. Clauses (1) and (2) between them are intended to cover all of the various methods by which systematic instruction takes place.

Face-to-face teaching activities

Clause (1) of section 110 is generally intended to set out the conditions under which performances or displays, in the course of instructional activities other than educational broadcasting, are to be exempted from copyright control. The clause covers all types of copyrighted works, and exempts their performance or display "by instructors or pupils in the course of face-to-face teaching activities of a nonprofit educational institution," where the activities take place "in a classroom or similar place devoted to instruction."

There appears to be no need for a statutory definition of "face-to-face" teaching activities to clarify the scope of the provision. "Face-to-face teaching activities" under clause (1) embraces instructional performances and displays that are not "transmitted." It does not require that the teacher and his student be able to see each other, although it does require their simultaneous presence in the same general place. Use of the phrase "in the course of fact-to-face teaching activities" is intended to exclude broadcasting or other transmissions from an outside location into classroom, whether radio or television and whether open or closed circuit. However, as long as the instructor and pupils are in the same building or general area, the exemption would extend to the use of devices for amplifying or reproducing sound and for projecting visual images. The "teaching activities" exempted by the clause encompass systematic instruction of a very wide variety of subjects, but they do not include performances or displays, whatever their cultural value or intellectual appeal, that are given for the recreation or entertainment of any part of their audience.

Works affected.—Since there is no limitation on the types of works covered by the exemption, a teacher or student would be free to perform or display anything in class as long as the other conditions of the clause are met. He could read aloud from copyrighted text material, act out a drama, play or sing a musical work, perform a motion picture or filmstrip, or display text or pictorial material to the class by means of a projector. However, nothing in this provision is intended to sanction the unauthorized reproduction of copies or phonorecords for the purpose of classroom performance or display, and the amended clause contains a special exception dealing with performances from unlawfully made copies of motion pictures and other audiovisual works, to be discussed below.

Instructors or pupils.—To come within clause (1), the performance or display must be "by instructors or pupils," thus ruling out performances by actors, singers, or instrumentalists brought in from outside the school to put on a program. However, the term "instructors" would be broad enough to include guest lecturers if their instructional activities remain confined to classroom situation. In general, the term "pupils" refers to the enrolled members of a class.

Nonprofit educational institution.—Clause (1) makes clear that it applies only to the teaching activities "of a nonprofit educational institution," thus excluding from the exemption performances or displays in profit-making institutions such as dance studios and language schools.

Classroom or similar place.—The teaching activities exempted by the clause must take place "in a classroom or similar place devoted to instruction." For example, performances in an auditorium or stadium during a school assembly, graduation ceremony, class play, or sporting event, where the audience is not confined to the members of a particular class, would fall outside the scope of clause (1), although in some cases they might be exempted by clause (4) of section 110. The "similar place" referred to in clause (1) is a place which is "devoted to instruction" in the same way a classroom is; common examples would include a studio, a workshop, a gymnasium, a training field, a library, the stage of an auditorium, or the auditorium itself if it is actually used as a classroom for systematic instructional activities.

Motion pictures and other audiovisual works.—The final provision of clause (1) deals with the special problem of performances from unlawfully made copies of motion pictures and other audiovisual works. The exemption is lost where the copy being used for a classroom performance was "not lawfully made under this title" and the person responsible for the performance knew or had reason to suspect as much. This special exception to the exemption would not apply to performances from lawfully made copies, even if the copies were acquired from someone who had stolen or converted them, or if the performances were in violation of an agreement. However, though the performances would be exempt under section 110(a) in such cases, the copyright owner might have a cause of action against the unauthorized distributor under section 106(3), or against the person responsible for the performance for breach of contract.

Projection devices.—As long as there is no transmission beyond the place where the copy is located, both section 109(b) and section 110(1) would permit the classroom display of a work by means of any sort of projection device or process.

Instructional broadcasting

Works affected.—The exemption would apply only to "performance of a nondramatic literary or musical work or of a sound recording, or display of a work." Thus, the copyright owner's permission would be required for the performance on educational television or radio of a dramatic work, of a dramatico-musical work such as an opera or musical comedy, or of a motion picture. Since, as already explained, audiovisual works such as filmstrips are now equated with motion pictures, their sequential showing would be regarded as a performance rather than a display and would not be exempt under section 110(2). The clause is not intended to limit in any way the copyright owner's exclusive right to make dramatizations, adaptations, or other derivative works under section 106(2). Thus, for example, a performer could read a nondramatic literary work aloud under section 110(2), but the copyright owner's permission would be required for him to act it out in dramatic form.

Systematic instructional activities.—Under section 110(2) a transmission must meet three specified conditions in order to be exempted from copyright liability. The first of these, as provided by subclause (A), is that the performance or display must be "a regular part of the systematic instructional activities of a governmental body or a nonprofit educational institution." The concept of "systematic instructional activities" is intended as the general equivalent of "curriculums," but it could be broader in a case such as that of an institution using systematic teaching methods not related to specific course work. A transmission would be a regular part of these activities if it is in accordance with the pattern of teaching established by the governmental body or institution. The use of commercial facilities, such as those of a cable service, to transmit the performance or display, would not affect the exemption as long as the actual performance or display was for nonprofit purposes.

Content of transmissions.—Subclause (B) requires that the performance or display is directly related and of material assistance to the teaching content of the transmission.

Intended recipients.—Subclause (C) requires that the transmission is made primarily for:

   (i) reception in classrooms or similar places normally devoted to instructions, or

   (ii) reception by persons to whom the transmission is directed because their disabilities or other special circumstances prevent their attendance in classrooms or similar places normally devoted to instruction, or

   (iii) reception by officers or employees of governmental bodies as a part of their official duties or employment.

In all three cases, the instructional transmission need only be made "primarily" rather than "solely" to the specified recipients to be exempt. Thus, the transmission could still be exempt even though it is capable of reception by the public at large. Conversely, it would not be regarded as made "primarily" for one of the required groups of recipients if the principal purpose behind the transmission is reception by the public at large, even if it is cast in the form of instruction and is also received in classrooms. Factors to consider in determining the "primary" purpose of a program would include its subject matter, content, and the time of its transmission.

Paragraph (i) of subclause (C) generally covers what are known as "in-school" broadcasts, whether open- or closed-circuit. The reference to "classrooms or similar places" here is intended to have the same meaning as that of the phrase as used in section 110(1). The exemption in paragraph (ii) is intended to exempt transmission providing systematic instruction to individuals who cannot be reached in classrooms because of "their disabilities or other special circumstances." Accordingly, the exemption is confined to instructional broadcasting that is an adjunct to the actual classwork of nonprofit schools or is primarily for people who cannot be brought together in classrooms such as preschool children, displaced workers, illiterates, and shut-ins.

There has been some question as to whether or not the language in this section of the bill is intended to include instructional television college credit courses. These telecourses are aimed at undergraduate and graduate students in earnest pursuit of higher educational degrees who are unable to attend daytime classes due to daytime employment, distance from campus or for some other intervening reason. So long as these broadcasts are aimed at regularly enrolled students and conducted by recognized higher educational institutions, the committee believes that they are clearly within the language of section 110(2) (C)(ii). Like night school and correspondence courses before them, these telecourses are fast becoming a valuable adjunct of the normal college curriculum.

The third exemption in subclause (C) is intended to permit the use of copyrighted material, in accordance with the other conditions of section 110(2), in the course of instructional transmissions of Government personnel who are receiving training "as a part of their official duties or employment."

Religious services

The scope of clause (3) does not cover the sequential showing of motion pictures and other audiovisual works. The exemption, which to some extent has its counterpart in sections 1 and 104 of the present law applies to dramatico-musical works "of a religious nature." The purpose here is to exempt certain performances of sacred music that might be regarded as "dramatic" in nature, such as oratorios, cantatas, musical settings of the mass, choral services, and the like. The exemption is not intended to cover performances of secular operas, musical plays, motion pictures, and the like, even if they have an underlying religious or philosophical theme and take place "in the course of [religious] services."

To be exempted under section 110(3) a performance or display must be "in the course of services," thus excluding activities at a place of worship that are for social, educational, fund raising, or entertainment purposes. Some performances of these kinds could be covered by the exemption in section 110(4), discussed next. Since the performance or display must also occur "at a place of worship or other religious assembly," the exemption would not extend to religious broadcasts or other transmissions to the public at large, even where the transmissions were sent from the place of worship. On the other hand, as long as services are being conducted before a religious gathering, the exemption would apply if they were conducted in places such as auditoriums, outdoor theaters, and the like.

Certain other nonprofit performances

In addition to the educational and religious exemptions provided by clauses (1) through (3) of section 110, clause (4) contains a general exception to the exclusive right of public performance that would cover some, though not all, of the same ground as the present "for profit" limitations.

Scope of exemption.—The exemption in clause (4) applies to the same general activities and subject matter as those covered by the "for profit" limitation today: public performances of nondramatic literary and musical works. However, the exemption would be limited to public performances given directly in the presence of an audience whether by means of living performers, the playing of phonorecords, or the operation of a receiving apparatus, and would not include a "transmission to the public." Unlike the other clauses of section 110, clause (4) applies only to performing rights in certain works and does not affect the exclusive right to display a work in public.

No profit motive.—In addition to the other conditions specified by the clause, the performance must be "without any purpose of direct or indirect commercial advantage." This provision expressly adopts the principle established by the court decisions construing the "for profit" limitation: that public performances given or sponsored in connection with any commercial or profit-making enterprises are subject to the exclusive rights of the copyright owner even though the public is not charged for seeing or hearing the performance.

No payment for performance.—An important condition for this exemption is that the performance be given "without payment of any fee or other compensation for the performance to any of its performers, promoters, or organizers." The basic purpose of this requirement is to prevent the free use of copyrighted material under the guise of charity where fees or percentages are paid to performers, promoters, producers, and the like. However, the exemption would not be lost if the performers, directors, or producers of the performance, instead of being paid directly "for the performance," are paid a salary for duties encompassing the performance. Examples are performances by a school orchestra conducted by a music teacher who receives an annual salary, or by a service band whose members and conductors perform as part of their assigned duties and who receive military pay. The committee believes that performances of this type should be exempt, assuming the other conditions in clause (4) are met, and has not adopted the suggestion that the word "salary" be added to the phrase referring to the "payment of any fee or other compensation."

Admission charge.—Assuming that the performance involves no profit motive and no one responsible for it gets paid a fee, it must still meet one or two alternative conditions to be exempt. As specified in subclauses (A) and (B) of section 110(4), these conditions are: (1) that no direct or indirect admission charge is made, or (2) that the net proceeds are "used exclusively for educational, religious, or charitable purposes and not for private financial gain."

Under the second of these conditions, a performance meeting the other conditions of clause (4) would be exempt even if an admission fee is charged, provided any amounts left "after deducting the reasonable costs of producing the performance" are used solely for bona fide educational, religious, or charitable purposes.

SECTION 117. COMPUTER USES

As the program for general revision of the copyright law has evolved, it has become increasingly apparent that in one major area the problems are not sufficiently developed for a definitive legislative solution. This is the area of computer uses of copyrighted works: the use of a work "in conjunction with automatic systems capable of storing, processing, retrieving, or transferring information." The Commission on New Technological Uses is intended, among other things, to make a thorough study of the emerging patterns in this field and, on the basis of its findings, to recommend definite copyright provisions to deal with the situation.

Since it would be premature to change existing law on computer uses at present, the purpose of section 117 is to preserve the status quo. It is intended neither to cut off any rights that may now exist, nor to create new rights that might be denied under the Act of 1909 or under common law principles currently applicable.

The provision deals only with the exclusive rights of a copyright owner with respect to computer uses, that is, the bundle of rights specified for other types of uses in section 106 and qualified in Sections 107 through 116. With respect to the copyrightability of computer programs, the ownership of copyright in them, the term of protection, and the formal requirements of the remainder of the bill, the new statute would apply.

Under section 117, an action for infringement of a copyrighted work by means of a computer would necessarily be a federal action brought under the new Title 17. The court, in deciding the scope of exclusive rights in the computer area, would first need to determine the applicable law, whether State common law or the Act of 1909. Having determined what law was applicable, its decision would depend upon its interpretation of what that law was on the point on the day before the effective date of the new statute.

Annual Report of the Librarian of Congress for the Fiscal Year Ended June 30, 1975

GENERAL REVISION OF THE COPYRIGHT LAW

The 20th year of the current program for general revision of the copyright law was the most active and significant since 1967, when the bill passed the House of Representatives and was the subject of full hearings in the Senate. During fiscal 1975 the latest version of the revision bill passed the Senate and full hearings in the House got under way. The bill was moving forward rapidly as the year began, and its momentum accelerated as the months passed. By the end of the year the talk about the bill had ceased to be "whether" and was becoming "when."

As noted in last year's annual report, the event that triggered this dramatic legislative revival was the Supreme Court's definitive decision on copyright and cable television in *Teleprompter Corp.* v. *Columbia Broadcasting System, Inc.,* 415 U.S. 394 (1974). Action on the pending revision bill (S. 1361) resumed almost immediately, and fiscal 1975 began with the first of several recent developments in the general revision program. On July 3, 1975, the Senate Judiciary Committee reported the bill favorably, with some amendments and a 228-page report (S. Rept. No. 93-983). By far the most controversial issues in the reported bill involved the provision establishing a royalty for the public performance of sound recordings (section 114), and the provisions on cable television dealing with CATV carriage of broadcasts of sporting events (section 111).

Mainly because of these two issues, which in varying degrees had some implications for communications policy, the Senate Committee on Commerce asked that S. 1361 be referred to it for consideration. In an unusual move, the copyright bill was referred to that committee, but only for 15 days. On July 29, 1974, the Senate Commerce Committee also reported the bill (S. Rept. No. 93-1035), with further amendments and a 92-page report. The amendments proposed by the Commerce Committee not only extended the cable television and performance royalty sections but also deprived the proposed Copyright Royalty Tribunal of the responsibility for periodic review of the annual royalty for jukebox performances.

The Senate debate on the revision bill began on September 6, 1974, and ended with a favorable vote on September 9, 1974. The most controversial issue proved to be section 114, which would have created rights, subject to compulsory licensing, requiring broadcasters, jukebox operators, and music services to pay royalties for playing copyrighted sound recordings. The "sports blackout" provision of the cable television section, and the possibility of tribunal review of the jukebox royalty, also figured prominently in the debate. In the end, the "performance royalty" and "sports blackout" provisions were deleted from the bill, the jukebox royalty was made unreviewable, and some other amendments were added. None of the changes were central to the basic purpose or structure of the bill.

When the final Senate vote came it was overwhelming: 70 ayes and one nay. Although there was no time left in the 93d Congress for the House of Representatives to complete work on S. 1361, the general opinion was that the revision bill had undergone a remarkable recovery and that the state of its health was quite good.

At the beginning of the 94th Congress the revision bill, in the form in which it passed the Senate, was introduced in both Houses. The Senate bill, S. 22, was introduced by Senator John L. McClellan on January 15, 1975, and an identical House version, H.R. 2223, was introduced by Representative Robert W. Kastenmeier on January 28, 1975.

Senate review of the bill by the Subcommittee on Patents, Trademarks, and Copyrights included consideration of a proposal (known informally as the "Mathias amendment") that would create a new compulsory licensing system for performances of nondramatic literary and musical works on public radio and television. On April 13, 1975, the subcommittee reported the bill favorably to the full Senate Judiciary Committee with a number of amendments. Although the "Mathias amendment" was not included in these, it produced, among the interests involved, a number of meetings aimed at resolving the issue through voluntary licensing.

The Senate subcommittee's most controversial amendment was its restoration of the provisions for periodic review of the royalty rate for jukebox performances. Of special interest to the Copyright Office were the amendments it had recommended as separate legislation to raise the fees for registration and other Copyright Office functions and services and to allow authors to group contributions to periodicals in a single application for registration under certain circumstances.

Hearings on the revision bill, the first in the House of Representatives since 1965, began before the House Judiciary Subcommittee on Courts, Civil Liberties, and Administration of Justice on May 7, 1975. Roughly 15 days of House hearings were projected, and eight of these had been held by the end of the fiscal year.

On May 7, 1975, the hearings were opened with testimony from John G. Lorenz, Acting Librarian of Congress, from Abraham L. Kaminstein, former register of copyrights and one of the principal architects of the general revision bill, and from Barbara Ringer, the present register. In her extensive opening testimony, Ms. Ringer sought to put the bill in historical perspective, to pinpoint the major issues remaining to be settled, and to answer the subcommittee's initial questions about the substantive content and status of the legislation. The seven principal issues identified in her testimony were:

Cable television

Library photocopying

Fair use and reproduction for educational and scholarly purposes

Public and nonprofit broadcasting

Royalty for jukebox performance

Mechanical royalty for use of music in sound recordings

Royalty for performance of recordings.

Related issues involved the proposed Copyright Royalty Tribunal, and the register also noted the likelihood of issues arising in connection with the "manufacturing clause" and the rights of graphic artists and designers.

The next day, representatives of the Departments of State, Justice, and Commerce presented the views of their agencies on the bill, and on May 14 and 15 the subcommittee heard testimony on library photocopying, fair use, and proposals for exemptions covering certain educational uses. Hearings were also held on June 3, 5, 11, and 12, 1975, at which the main topics debated were the jukebox royalty review, the entire question of copyright liability of cable television systems, and the Copyright Royalty Tribunal.

Although the subcommittee was presented with a number of interrelated issues and subissues, it was apparent as the 1975 hearings drew to a close that the areas of agreement far exceeded those of disagreement and that the bulk of the bill had remained almost entirely unchanged since it passed the House in 1967. Fundamental provisions such as the establishment of a single federal copyright system, duration based on the life of the author plus 50 years, ownership and transfer of rights, subject matter, and formalities are intact, and they represent the heart of Title I of the legislation.

Title II of the bill consists of what had originally been separate comprehensive legislation for the protection of ornamental designs of useful articles, based on copyright principles. Beginning in the early 1950's, and for more than a decade thereafter, the Copyright Office had worked long and hard for the enactment of this design bill, which has already passed the Senate on three occasions. It is encouraging that this legislation has now been made a part of the program for general revision of the copyright law and shares the momentum of the revision bill itself.

OTHER COPYRIGHT LEGISLATION

In addition to the general revision bill itself, fiscal 1975 saw considerable legislative activity in the copyright area, much of it related, however, to the revision of the copyright law.

The 1975 "Short Bill"

Three matters dealt with in the general revision bill were considered by Congress as too urgent to await final action on the omnibus legislation and were made the subject of a separate measure. This "short bill" was passed by both Houses and, in a real legislative cliffhanger, was signed into law on the last day of calendar 1974.

The first of these matters involved permanent federal legislation to combat record and tape piracy. In 1971, Congress amended the present law to offer federal copyright protection against unauthorized duplication of sound recordings fixed on or after February 15, 1972. However, it did so only on a temporary basis, and the "record piracy" amendment was scheduled to expire on December 31, 1974, unless extended in the meantime. On August 21, 1974, the House Judiciary Subcommittee on Courts, Civil Liberties, and the Administration of Justice reported favorably a bill (H.R. 13364) introduced by its chairman, Representative Kastenmeier, to make the amendment permanent and to increase the criminal penalties for piracy and counterfeiting of copyrighted recordings. The Kastenmeier bill, as amended, was favorably reported by the full House Judiciary Committee on September 30, 1974 (H. Rept. No. 93-1389), and passed the House of Representatives, under suspension of rules, by a two-thirds nonrecord vote on October 7, 1974.

Meanwhile, on September 9, 1974, immediately following Senate passage of the general revision bill, Senator McClellan had introduced S. 3976, an interim package consisting of provisions similar to the Kastenmeier record piracy bill but with somewhat higher criminal penalties; a provision to extend, until December 31, 1976, renewal copyrights otherwise scheduled to expire at the end of 1974; and provisions establishing a National Commission on New Technological Uses of Copyrighted Works. Since all these provisions were covered in the general revision bill, the Senate passed S. 3976 on September 9 within minutes following its introduction.

On November 26, 1974, the House Judiciary Subcommittee, under Representative Kastenmeier's chairmanship, held hearings on S. 3976. The only witness was the register of copyrights, who was asked to testify on the extension of expiring renewals, the National Commission, and the present status of copyright law revision. No testimony was sought with respect to the antipiracy provisions of the bill, since the House had already acted favorably upon the subject. The bill was reported by the subcommittee to the full House Judiciary Committee with some amendments on December 10, 1974, and by the full committee to the House of Representatives on December 12, 1974 (H. Rept. No. 93-1581). On December 19, 1974, the bill passed the House by a vote of 292 to 101, and the bill as amended by the House was accepted by the Senate later the same day, the last day of the 93d Congress. The legislation (Public Law 93-573) was signed by President Ford on December 31, 1974, only a few hours before the record piracy legislation and some 150,000 renewal copyrights were scheduled to expire.

The last-minute legislative action had a further regenerative effect upon the general revision program. Specifically, the two-year extension of expiring renewals (the ninth in a series going back to 1962) was based on the assumption that the omnibus package (which would give all subsisting copyrights a total term of 75 years) could be enacted into law by the end of 1976.

Congressional establishment of CONTU (National Commission on the New Technological Uses of Copyrighted Works) in advance of general revision also reflects a sense of urgency concerning the unsettled copyright questions within the commission's mandate. As stated in the new statute, the purpose of the commission is to study and compile data on:

Reproduction and use of copyrighted works of authorship

(a) in conjunction with automatic systems capable of storing, processing, retrieving, and transferring information, and

(b) by various forms of machine reproduction, not including reproductions by or at the request of instructors for use in face-to-face teaching activities.

Creation of new works by the application or intervention of such automatic systems or machine reproduction.

In addition to conducting studies and compiling data, CONTU is required to make recommendations for legislation. Its first report is due within one year of the commission's first sitting, and the deadline for its final report is December 31, 1977. Although the members of the commission were not appointed until after the end of the fiscal year, Congress appropriated funds to support the commission's work during fiscal 1976.

COPYRIGHT LAW REVISION

SEPTEMBER 3, 1976.—Committed to the Committee of the Whole House on the State of the Union and ordered to be printed

Mr. KASTENMEIER, from the Committee on the Judiciary, submitted the following

REPORT

together with

ADDITIONAL VIEWS

[To accompany S. 22]

The Committee on the Judiciary, to whom was referred the bill (S. 22) for the general revision of the copright law, title 17 of the United States Code, and for other purposes, having considered the same, report favorably thereon with an amendment in the nature of a substitute and recommend that the bill as amended do pass.

The amendments are as follows:

Strike all after the enacting clause and insert in lieu thereof the following:

SEC. 101. Title 17 of the United States Code, entitled "Copyrights", is hereby amended in its entirety to read as follows:

TITLE 17—COPYRIGHTS

Chapter 1.—SUBJECT MATTER AND SCOPE OF COPYRIGHT

CORRECTION OF ERRORS IN PRINTED HOUSE
REPORT ON S.22

CORRECTION OF ERRORS IN PRINTED HOUSE REPORT ON S.22 (H. REP. No. 94-1476, SEPT. 3, 1976)

Page 2: In the definition of "derivative work" following the word "fictionalization" at the end of the 2d line, add: "motion picture version, sound recording, art reproduction, abridgment".

Page 3: In the definition of "pictorial, graphic, and sculptural works", delete "the" at the beginning of the 8th line.

Page 4: In the definition of "work made for hire", in the 11th line of clause (2) of #101 the word "works" should read "work".

Page 4: Delete the last 2 lines at the bottom of the page.

Page 5: Delete the first 6 lines at the top of the page.

Page 10: In #111, in the 14th line of subsection (c) (4) the phrase "the signal or such foreign station" should read "the signal of such foreign station".

Page 10: In #111, in the 12th line of subsection (d) (1), the word "Royalty" should be inserted between the words "Copyright" and "Commission".

Page 11: Following the 1st line at the top of the page insert the following: "subclause (C) or (D), a total royalty fee for the period covered by the".

Page 14: In the 11th line, the phrase "performance and display" should read "performance or display". In the 15th line, the word "as" should be inserted at the beginning of the line and the phrase "year on which" should read "year in which".

Page 15: In #112, in the last line, the last word "programs" should read "program".

Page 15: In #114, in the 12th line of subsection (b), the word "copyright" should read "copyrighted".

Page 20: In #118, in the 4th and 5th lines of subsection (d)(3), delete the repeated phrase "of section 110", and in the 4th line from the bottom of the page the phrase "body of institution" should read "body or institution".

Page 21: In the 4th line from the bottom of the page, "voluntary" should read "voluntarily".

Page 22: In #203, following the 7th line of subsection (a)(1), insert "such author may be exercised as a unit by the".

Page 24: In #301, in the 3d line of subsection (b)(1), the phrase "medium or expression" should read "medium of expression".

Page 25: In #304 (a), in the 3d line, the phrase "Provided, That is the case" should read "Provided, That in the case", and in the 5th line, the phrase "the proprietor thereof, of" should read "the proprietor thereof, or of", and in the 7th line the phrase "employer of whom" should read "employer for whom".

Page 26: In the 11th line, the word "of" should be inserted between "term" and "copyright".

Page 29: In #405, in the 2d line of subsection (a) the word "described" should read "prescribed", and in the 2d line of subsection (c) the word "obligation" should read "obliteration".

Page 29: In the 2d line from the bottom of the page, the word "provision" should read "provisions".

Page 36: In #507, in the 1st line of subsection (a), the word "proceedings" should read "proceeding", and in the 2d line of subsection (b) the word "the" should be inserted between the words "after" and "claim".

Page 37: In #601 (b), at the end of the 4th line of clause (6), insert "or".

Page 39: In #704, in the 4th line of subsection (b), "work" should read "works".

Page 40: In #706, in the 1st line of subsection (b), "reproduction" should read "reproductions".

Page 41: In #710, in the 5th line, "work" should

read "works".

Page 41:   In #801, in the 1st line of subsection (b), "purpose" should read "purposes".

Page 45:   In SEC. 106, in the 3d line, delete "the" between "of" and "title".

Page 45:   In SEC. 110, in the 2d line, "1976" should read "1977".

Page 46:   In SEC. 113, at the end of subclause (B) of subsection (a)(1), add the word "and".

Page 50:   In the 4th line of the 7th full paragraph, the phrase "during the 95th Congress" should read "during the first session of the 95th Congress".

Page 51:   In the 4th line of the 4th full paragraph, the phrase "of copyrightable technology" should read "of copyrightable subject matter at the present stage of communications technology".

Page 52:   At the end of the page, insert "be regarded as fixed and should".

Page 54:   In the 8th line of the 2d full paragraph, "work" should read "works".

Page 55:   In the 7th line of the 1st full paragraph, "statute" should read "statue".

Page 56:   In the 11th line of the 1st full paragraph, "fixation" should read "fixations".

Page 59:   In the 14th line of the 1st full paragraph, delete "is that the public should not be required to pay a 'double subsidy'" and substitute "in this situation, and the basically different policy considerations".

Page 61:   In the 5th line from the bottom of the page, "works" should read "work".

Page 62:   In the 2d line of the 5th paragraph, headed <u>Public distribution</u>, the phrase "right of publications" should read "right of publication".

Page 63:   In the 2d line of the 1st full paragraph, the phrase "works records on film." should read "works recorded on film.".

Page 68:   In the 1st and 2d lines of the 1st paragraph, the phrase "the minimum standards of educational fair use" should read "the minimum and not the maximum standards of educational fair use".

Page 72: In the 2d line of the 2d full paragraph, "kill" should read "will".

Page 73: In the 16th line of the 1st full paragraph, "section 70" should read "section 710".

Page 75: In the 1st full paragraph, beginning "Isolated, spontaneous. . .", in the 7th line the phrase "production or distribution" should read "reproduction or distribution", and in the 9th line the word "advantages" should read "advantage".

Page 76: In the 2d and 3d lines of the 1st full paragraph, the phrase "contribution to copyrighted collection" should read "contribution to a copyrighted collection".

Page 77: In the 5th line of the 4th full paragraph, the word "materials" should read "material".

Page 80: In the 2d line on the page, the word "views" should read "viewers".

Page 81: In the 11th line on the page, the phrase "burden or proving" should read "burden of proving".

Page 84: In the 10th line from the bottom of the page, the reference to "section 1102 (3)" should read "section 110 (3)".

Page 88: In the 6th and 7th lines of the 1st full paragraph, delete "In addition to an installation charge, the subscribers".

Page 90: In the 1st line of the 3d full paragraph, the phrase "their transmission" should read "the retransmission".

Page 91: In the 1st line of the 3d full paragraph, the reference to "Section 11." should read "section 111.".

Purpose

The purpose of the proposed legislation, as amended, is to provide for a general revision of the United States Copyright Law, title 17 of the United States Code.

Statement

The first copyright law of the United States was enacted by the First Congress in 1790, in exercise of the constitutional power "To promote the Progress of Science and useful Arts, by securing for limited Times to Authors and Inventors the exclusive Right to their respective Writings and Discoveries" (U.S. Constitution, Art. I, sec. 8). Comprehensive revisions were enacted, at intervals of about 40 years, in 1831, 1870, and 1909. The present copyright law, title 17 of the United States Code, is basically the same as the act of 1909.

Since that time significant changes in technology have affected the operation of the copyright law. Motion pictures and sound recordings had just made their appearance in 1909, and radio and television were still in the early stages of their development. During the past half century a wide range of new techniques for capturing and communicating printed matter, visual images, and recorded sounds have come into use, and the increasing use of information storage and retrieval devices, communications satellites, and laser technology promises even greater changes in the near future. The technical advances have generated new industries and new methods for the reproduction and dissemination of copyrighted works, and the business relations between authors and users have evolved new patterns.

Between 1924 and 1940 a number of copyright law revision measures were introduced. All these failed of enactment, partly because of controversy among private interests over differences between the Berne Convention and the U.S. law. After World War II, the United States participated in the development of the new Universal Copyright Convention, becoming a party in 1955.

In that year, the movement for general revision of the U.S. copyright law was revived and the legislative appropriations act for the next 3 years provided funds for a comprehensive program of research and studies by the Copyright Office as the groundwork for such revision. There followed a period of study which produced 35 published monographs on most of the major substantive issues in copyright revision, and culminated in 1961 in the "Report of the Register of Copyrights on the General Revision of the U.S. Copyright Law."

Between 1961 and 1964 there were numerous meetings and discussions under the auspices of the Copyright Office, participated in by representatives of a wide range of interests affected by the copyright law. Gradually a draft bill for general revision took shape, and toward the end of the 88th Congress, on July 20, 1964, it was introduced in both Houses. The 1964 revision bill was introduced in the House of Representatives, as H.R. 11947, and in the Senate by request, as S. 3008.

No further legislative action was taken on the revision bill during the 88th Congress, but before the opening of the 89th Congress the Copyright Office completely revised the bill in the light of the many comments that had been received. On February 4, 1965, the revised bill was introduced in both Houses: in the House as H.R. 4347, and in the Senate as S. 1006. The Copyright Office prepared a report to accompany the revised bill, and it was published in May, 1965 as "The Supplementary Report of the Register of Copyrights on the General Revision of the U.S. Copyright Law: 1965 Revision Bill." Extensive hearings on the bill were held in both Houses during 1965, and the Senate hearings continued in 1966. H.R. 4347 was reported by the House Judiciary Committee on October 12, 1966 (H.R. Rep. No. 2237, 89th Cong., 2d Sess.), but the 89th Congress adjourned before further action could be taken.

At the beginning of the 90th Congress the bill, in the form in which it had been reported by the House Judiciary Committee, was again introduced in both Houses: in the House of Representatives on January 17, 1967 as H.R. 2512, and in the Senate on January 23, 1967, as S. 597. H.R. 2512 was reported by the House Judiciary Committee, without further amendment but with dissenting views, on March 8, 1967 (H.R. Rept. No. 83, 90th Cong., 1st Sess.). The bill was passed by the House of Representatives, with several important amendments, on April 11, 1967, by a vote of 379 to 29. The Senate Judiciary Subcommitte conducted further hearings on S. 597 in March and April of 1967. However, it was not possible to complete action on copyright revision in the 90th Congress because of the emergence of certain major problems, notably that of cable television.

On January 22 (legislative day January 10), 1969, S. 543 was introduced in the 91st Congress. Ttitle I of this bill, other than for technical amendments, was identical to S. 597 of the 90th Congress. Title II of the bill incorporated the provisions of S. 2216 providing for the establishment of a National Commission on New Technological Uses of Copyrighted Works. This title was a response to concerns as to the impact of the legislation on the use of copyrighted materials in computers and other forms of information storage and retrieval systems. The Senate had passed, on October 12, 1967, a bill establishing such a Commission for the study of this subject, but there had been no action by the House on this separate legislation.

On December 10, 1969, the Senate Judiciary Subcommittee favorably reported S. 543, with an amendment in the nature of a substitute. No further action was taken in the 91st Congress primarily because of the cable television issue.

On February 18, 1971, S. 644 was introduced in the 92nd Congress. Other than for minor amendments, the text of that bill was identical to the revision bill reported by the Subcommittee in the 91st Congress. No action was taken on general revision legislation during the 92nd Congress, pending the formulation and adoption by the Federal Communications Commission of new cable television rules.

While action on the general revision bill was necessarily delayed the unauthorized duplication of sound recordings became widespread. It was accordingly determined that the creation of a limited copyright in sound recordings should not await action on the general revision bill. S. 646 of the 92nd Congress was introduced to amend title 17 of the U.S. Code to provide for the creation of a limited copyright in sound recordings. This bill passed the Senate on April 29 1971, and, following hearings in June 1971, a companion bill (H.R. 6927) passed the House with amendments on October 4, 1971 and was enacted as Public Law 92–140.

On March 26, 1973 S. 1361, for the general revision of the copyright law, was introduced in the 93rd Congress. Other than for technical amendments, this bill was identical to S. 644 of the 92d Congress. Additional copyright revision hearings were held in the Senate on July 31 and August 1, 1973.

The Senate Judiciary Subcommittee on April 19, 1974 reported S. 1361 with an amendment in the nature of a substitute. After adopting several amendments to the subcommittee bill, the Senate Judiciary Committee reported the legislation on July 8, 1974. On July 9 the measure was removed from the Senate calendar and referred to the Committee on Commerce. The Commerce Committee reported S. 1361 with additional amendments on July 29. After adopting several amendments the Senate on September 9 passed S. 1361 by a vote of 70 to 1.

Since it was doubtful that adequate time remained in the 93d Congress for consideration in the House of Representatives of S. 1361, on September 9, Senator McClellan introduced and obtained immediate consideration of S. 3976. That bill, passed on September 9, extended the renewal term of expiring copyrights, established on a permanent basis a limited copyright in sound recordings, and created in the Library of Congress a National Commission on New Technological Uses of Copyrighted Works. The House of Representatives passed the measure with amendments on December 19, 1974, and the Senate concurred in the House amendments on the same date. The President approved the bill on December 31, 1974, and it became Public Law 93–573.

At the beginning of the 94th Congress the revision bill, substantially identical to S. 1361 as passed by the Senate in 1974, was introduced in both Houses: Senator McClellan introduced S. 22 on January 15, 1975, and Chairman Robert W. Kastenmeier of the House Judiciary Subcommittee on Courts, Civil Liberties, and the Administration of Justice, introduced H.R. 2223 on January 28, 1975. S. 22 was reported, with additional views by the Senate Judiciary Committee on November 20 (legislative day, November 18), 1975, and passed the Senate unanimously, on February 19, 1976, by a vote of 97–0.

During 1975 the House Judiciary Subcommittee conducted extensive hearings on H.R. 2223, at which nearly 100 witnesses were heard. The Register of Copyrights also prepared a "Second Supplementary Report on General Revision of the U.S. Copyright Law," which discussed policy and technical issues of the revision legislation. Following some 22 days of public mark-up sessions in 1976 the House Subcommittee favorably reported S. 22, by a unanimous vote, on August 3, 1976 with an amendment in the nature of a substitute. The Committee on the Judiciary now reports that bill, as amended, without change.

Title II of S. 22, as passed by the Senate, represents a piece of legislation separate from the bill for general legislation. This measure was originally introduced by Chairman Edwin Willis of the House Judiciary Subcommittee in 1957, and received active consideration in both Houses during the early 1960's. It passed the Senate as separate legislation on three occasions, in 1962, 1963, and 1966.

It was reintroduced in the 90th and 91st Congresses, and on December 10, 1969, the Senate Subcommittee conjoined it with the general copyright revision bill, reporting it as Title III of S. 543. As a separate title of S. 1361 of the 93d Congress, and now of S. 22, the design legislation has passed the Senate on two additional occasions.

In reporting S. 22, the House Judiciary Committee has deleted Title II. Until 1954, designs for useful articles were not generally subject to copyright protection. The primary protection available was the design patent, which requires that the design be not only "original", the standard applied in copyright law, but also "novel", meaning that it has never before existed anywhere.

However, in 1954 the Supreme Court decided the case of *Mazer* v. *Stein,* 347 U.S. 201, in which it held that works of art which are incorporated into the design of useful articles, but which are capable of standing by themselves as art works separate from the useful article, are copyrightable. The example used in the *Mazer* case was an ornamental lamp base.

Title II of S. 22 as passed by the Senate would create a new limited form of copyright protection for "original" designs which are clearly a part of a useful article, regardless of whether such designs could stand by themselves, separate from the article itself. Thus designs of useful articles which do not meet the design patent standard of "novelty" would for the first time be protected.

S. 22 is a copyright revision bill. The Committee chose to delete Title II in part because the new form of design protection provided by Title II could not truly be considered copyright protection and therefore appropriately within the scope of copyright revision.

In addition, Title II left unanswered at least two fundamental issues which will require further study by the Congress. These are: first, what agency should administer this new design protection system and, second, should typeface designs be given the protections of the title?

Finally, the Committee will have to examine further the assertion of the Department of Justice, which testified in opposition to the Title, that Title II would create a new monopoly which has not been justified by a showing that its benefits will outweigh the disadvantage of removing such designs from free public use.

The issues raised by Title II have not been resolved by its deletion from the Copyright Revision Bill. Therefore, the Committee believes that it will be necessary to reconsider the question of design protection in new legislation during the 95th Congress. At that time more complete hearings on the subject may be held and, without the encumbrance of a general copyright revision bill, the issues raised in Title II of S. 22 may be resolved.

SECTIONAL ANALYSIS AND DISCUSSION

An analysis and discussion of the provisions of S. 22, as amended, follows:

SECTION 101. DEFINITIONS

The significant definitions in this section will be mentioned or summarized in connection with the provisions to which they are most relevant.

Section 102. General Subject Matter of Copyright

"Original works of authorship"

The two fundamental criteria of copyright protection—originality and fixation in tangible form—are restated in the first sentence of this cornerstone provision. The phrase "original works of authorship," which is purposely left undefined, is intended to incorporate without change the standard of originality established by the courts under the present copyright statute. This standard does not include requirements of novelty, ingenuity, or esthetic merit, and there is no intention to enlarge the standard of copyright protection to require them.

In using the phrase "original works of authorship," rather than "all the writings of an author" now in section 4 of the statute, the committee's purpose is to avoid exhausting the constitutional power of Congress to legislate in this field, and to eliminate the uncertainties arising from the latter phrase. Since the present statutory language is substantially the same as the empowering language of the Constitution, a recurring question has been whether the statutory and the constitutional provisions are coextensive. If so, the courts would be faced with the alternative of holding copyrightable something that Congress clearly did not intend to protect, or of holding constitutionally incapable of copyright something that Congress might one day want to protect. To avoid these equally undesirable results, the courts have indicated that "all the writings of an author" under the present statute is narrower in scope than the "writings" of "authors" referred to in the Constitution. The bill avoids this dilemma by using a different phrase—"original works of authorship"—in characterizing the general subject matter of statutory copyright protection.

The history of copyright law has been one of gradual expansion in the types of works accorded protection, and the subject matter affected by this expansion has fallen into two general categories. In the first, scientific discoveries and technological developments have made possible new forms of creative expression that never existed before. In some of these cases the new expressive forms—electronic music, filmstrips, and computer programs, for example—could be regarded as an extension of copyrightable subject matter Congress had already intended to protect, and were thus considered copyrightable from the outset without the need of new legislation. In other cases, such as photographs, sound recordings, and motion pictures, statutory enactment was deemed necessary to give them full recognition as copyrightable works.

Authors are continually finding new ways of expressing themselves, but it is impossible to foresee the forms that these new expressive methods will take. The bill does not intend either to freeze the scope of copyrightable technology or to allow unlimited expansion into areas completely outside the present congressional intent. Section 102 implies neither that that subject matter is unlimited nor that new forms of expression within that general area of subject matter would necessarily be unprotected.

The historic expansion of copyright has also applied to forms of expression which, although in existence for generations or centuries, have only gradually come to be recognized as creative and worthy of protection. The first copyright statute in this country, enacted in 1790, designated only "maps, charts, and books"; major forms of expression such as music, drama, and works of art achieved specific statutory recognition only in later enactments. Although the coverage of the present statute is very broad, and would be broadened further by the explicit recognition of all forms of choreography, there are unquestionably other areas of existing subject matter that this bill does not propose to protect but that future Congresses may want to.

Fixation in tangible form

As a basic condition of copyright protection, the bill perpetuates the existing requirement that a work be fixed in a "tangible medium of expression," and adds that this medium may be one "now known or later developed," and that the fixation is sufficient if the work "can be perceived, reproduced, or otherwise communicated, either directly or with the aid of a machine or device." This broad language is intended to avoid the artificial and largely unjustifiable distinctions, derived from cases such as *White-Smith Publishing Co.* v. *Apollo Co.*, 209 U.S. 1 (1908), under which statutory copyrightability in certain cases has been made to depend upon the form or medium in which the work is fixed. Under the bill it makes no difference what the form, manner, or medium of fixation may be—whether it is in words, numbers, notes, sounds, pictures, or any other graphic or symbolic indicia, whether embodied in a physical object in written, printed, photographic, sculptural, punched, magnetic, or any other stable form, and whether it is capable of perception directly or by means of any machine or device "now known or later developed."

Under the bill, the concept of fixation is important since it not only determines whether the provisions of the statute apply to a work, but it also represents the dividing line between common law and statutory protection. As will be noted in more detail in connection with section 301, an unfixed work of authorship, such as an improvisation or an unrecorded choreographic work, performance, or broadcast, would continue to be subject to protection under State common law or statute, but would not be eligible for Federal statutory protection under section 102.

The bill seeks to resolve, through the definition of "fixation" in section 101, the status of live broadcasts—sports, news coverage, live performances of music, etc.—that are reaching the public in unfixed form but that are simultaneously being recorded. When a football game is being covered by four television cameras, with a director guiding the activities of the four camermen and choosing which of their electronic images are sent out to the public and in what order. there is little doubt that what the cameramen and the director are doing constitutes "authorship." The further question to be considered is whether there has been a fixation. If the images and sounds to be broadcast are first recorded (on a video tape, film, etc.) and then transmitted, the recorded work would be considered a "motion picture" subject to statutory protection against unauthorized reproduction or retransmission of the broadcast. If the program content is transmitted live to the public while being recorded at the same time, the case would be treated the same; the copyright owner would not be forced to rely on common law rather than statutory rights in proceeding against an infringing user of the live broadcast.

Thus, assuming it is copyrightable—as a "motion picture" or "sound recording," for example—the content of a live transmission should be accorded statutory protection if it is being recorded simultaneously with its transmission. On the other hand, the definition of "fixation" would exclude from the concept purely evanescent or transient reproductions such as those projected briefly on a screen, shown electronically on a television or other cathode ray tube, or captured momentarily in the "memory" of a computer.

Under the first sentence of the definition of "fixed" in section 101, a work would be considered "fixed in a tangible medium of expression" if there has been an authorized embodiment in a copy or phonorecord and if that embodiment "is sufficiently permanent or stable" to permit the work "to be perceived, reproduced, or otherwise communicated for a period of more than transitory duration." The second sentence makes clear that, in the case of "a work consisting of sounds, images, or both, that are being transmitted," the work is regarded as "fixed" if a fixation is being made at the same time as the transmission.

Under this definition "copies" and "phonorecords" together will comprise all of the material objects in which copyrightable works are capable of being fixed. The definitions of these terms in section 101, together with their usage in section 102 and throughout the bill, reflect a fundamental distinction between the "original work" which is the product of "authorship" and the multitude of material objects in which it can be embodied. Thus, in the sense of the bill, a "book" is not a work of authorship, but is a particular kind of "copy." Instead, the author may write a "literary work," which in turn can be embodied in a wide range of "copies" and "phonorecords," including books, periodicals, computer punch cards, microfilm, tape recordings, and so forth. It is possible to have an "original work of authorship" without having a "copy" or "phonorecord" embodying it, and it is also possible to have a "copy" or "phonorecord" embodying something that does not qualify as an "original work of authorship." The two essential elements—original work and tangible object—must merge through fixation in order to produce subject matter copyrightable under the statute.

Categories of copyrightable works

The second sentence of section 102 lists seven broad categories which the concept of "works" of authorship" is said to "include." The use of the word "include," as defined in section 101, makes clear that the listing is "illustrative and not limitative," and that the seven categories do not necessarily exhaust the scope of "original works of authorship" that the bill is intended to protect. Rather, the list sets out the general area of copyrightable subject matter, but with sufficient flexibility to free the courts from rigid or outmoded concepts of the scope of particular caegories. The items are also overlapping in the sense that a work falling within one class may encompass works coming within some or all of the other categories. In the aggregate, the list covers all classes of works now specified in section 5 of title 17; in addition, it specifically enumerates "pantomimes and choreographic works".

Of the seven items listed, four are defined in section 101. The three undefined categories—"musical works," "dramatic works," and "pantomimes and choreographic works"—have fairly settled meanings. There is no need, for example, to specify the copyrightability of electronic or concrete music in the statute since the form of a work would no longer be of any importance, nor is it necessary to specify that "choreographic works" do not include social dance steps and simple routines.

The four items defined in section 101 are "literary works," "pictorial, graphic, and sculptural works," "motion pictures and audiovisual works", and "sound recordings." In each of these cases, definitions are needed not only because the meaning of the term itself is unsettled but also because the distinction between "work" and "material object" requires clarification. The term "literary works" does not connote any criterion of literary merit or qualitative value: it includes catalogs, directories, and similar factual, reference, or instructional works and compilations of data. It also includes computer data bases, and computer programs to the extent that they incorporate authorship in the programmer's expression of original ideas, as distinguished from the ideas themselves.

Correspondingly, the definition of "pictorial, graphic, and sculptural works" carries with it no implied criterion of artistic taste, aesthetic value, or intrinsic quality. The term is intended to comprise not only "works of art" in the traditional sense but also works of graphic art and illustration, art reproductions, plans and drawings, photographs and reproductions of them, maps, charts, globes, and other cartographic works, works of these kinds intended for use in advertising and commerce, and work of "applied art." There is no intention whatever to narrow the scope of the subject matter now characterized in section 5(k) as "prints or labels used for articles of merchandise." However, since this terminology suggests the material object in which a work is embodied rather than the work itself, the bill does not mention this category separately.

In accordance with the Supreme Court's decision in *Mazer* v. *Stein*, 347 U.S. 201 (1954), works of "applied art" encompass all original pictorial, graphic, and sculptural works that are intended to be or have been embodied in useful articles, regardless of factors such as mass production, commercial exploitation, and the potential availability of design patent protection. The scope of exclusive rights in these works is given special treatment in section 113, to be discussed below.

The Committee has added language to the definition of "pictorial, graphic, and sculptural works" in an effort to make clearer the distinction between works of applied art protectable under the bill and industrial designs not subject to copyright protection. The declaration that "pictorial, graphic, and sculptural works" include "works of artistic craftsmanship insofar as their form but not their mechanical or utilitarian aspects are concerned" is classic language: it is drawn from Copyright Office regulations promulgated in the 1940's and expressly endorsed by the Supreme Court in the *Mazer* case.

The second part of the amendment states that "the design of a useful article . . . shall be considered a pictorial, graphic, or sculptural work only if, and only to the extent that, such design incorporates pictorial, graphic, or sculptural features that can be identified separately from, and are capable of existing independently of, the utilitarian aspects of the article." A "useful article" is defined as "an article having an intrinsic utilitarian function that is not merely to portray the appearance of the article or to convey information." This part of the amendment is an adaptation of language added to the Copyright Office Regulations in the mid-1950's in an effort to implement the Supreme Court's decision in the *Mazer* case.

In adopting this amendatory language, the Committee is seeking to draw as clear a line as possible between copyrightable works of applied art and uncopyrighted works of industrial design. A two-dimensional painting, drawing, or graphic work is still capable of being identified as such when it is printed on or applied to utilitarian articles such as textile fabrics, wallpaper, containers, and the like. The same is true when a statute or carving is used to embellish an industrial product or, as in the *Mazer* case, is incorporated into a product without losing its ability to exist independently as a work of art. On the other hand, although the shape of an industrial product may be aesthetically satisfying and valuable, the Committee's intention is not to offer it copyright protection under the bill. Unless the shape of an automobile, airplane, ladies' dress, food processor, television set, or any other industrial product contains some element that, physically or conceptually, can be identified as separable from the utilitarian aspects of that article, the design would not be copyrighted under the bill. The test of separability and independence from "the utilitarian aspects of the article" does not depend upon the nature of the design—that is, even if the appearance of an article is determined by esthetic (as opposed to functional) considerations, only elements, if any, which can be identified separately from the useful article as such are copyrightable. And, even if the three-dimensional design contains some such element (for example, a carving on the back of a chair or a floral relief design on silver flatware), copyright protection would extend only to that element, and would not cover the over-all configuration of the utilitarian article as such.

A special situation is presented by architectural works. An architect's plans and drawings would, of course, be protected by copyright, but the extent to which that protection would extend to the structure depicted would depend on the circumstances. Purely non-functional or monumental structures would be subject to full copyright protection under the bill, and the same would be true of artistic sculpture or decorative ornamentation or embellishment added to a structure. On the other hand, where the only elements of shape in an architectural design are conceptually inseparable from the utilitarian aspects of the structure, copyright protection for the design would not be available.

The Committee has considered, but chosen to defer, the possibility of protecting the design of typefaces. A "typeface" can be defined as a set of letters, numbers, or other symbolic characters, whose forms are related by repeating design elements consistently applied in a notational system and are intended to be embodied in articles whose intrinsic utilitarian function is for use in composing text or other cognizable combinations of characters. The Committee does not regard the design of typeface, as thus defined, to be a copyrightable "pictorial, graphic, or sculptural work" within the meaning of this bill and the application of the dividing line in section 101.

Enactment of Public Law 92–140 in 1971 marked the first recognition in American copyright law of sound recordings as copyrightable works. As defined in section 101, copyrightable "sound recordings" are original works of authorship comprising an aggregate of musical, spoken, or other sounds that have been fixed in tangible form. The copyrightable work comprises the aggregation of sounds and not the tangible medium of fixation. Thus, "sound recordings" as copyrightable subject matter are distinguished from "phonorecords," the latter being physical objects in which sounds are fixed. They are also distinguished from any copyrighted literary, dramatic, or musical works that may be reproduced on a "phonorecord."

As a class of subject matter, sound recordings are clearly within the scope of the "writings of an author" capable of protection under the Constitution, and the extension of limited statutory protection to them was too long delayed. Aside from cases in which sounds are fixed by some purely mechanical means without originality of any kind, the copyright protection that would prevent the reproduction and distribution of unauthorized phonorecords of sound recordings is clearly justified.

The copyrightable elements in a sound recording will usually, though not always, involve "authorship" both on the part of the performers whose performance is captured and on the part of the record producer responsible for setting up the recording session, capturing and electronically processing the sounds, and compiling and editing them to make the final sound recording. There may, however, be cases where the record producer's contribution is so minimal that the performance is the only copyrightable element in the work, and there may be cases (for example, recordings of birdcalls, sounds of racing cars, et cetera) where only the record producer's contribution is copyrightable.

Sound tracks of motion pictures, long a nebulous area in American copyright law, are specifically included in the definition of "motion pictures," and excluded in the definition of "sound recordings." To be a "motion picture," as defined, requires three elements: (1) a series of images, (2) the capability of showing the images in certain successive order, and (3) an impression of motion when the images are thus shown. Coupled with the basic requirements of original authorship and fixation in tangible form, this definition encompasses a wide range of cinematographic works embodied in films, tapes, video disks, and other media. However, it would not include: (1) unauthorized fixation of live performances or telecasts, (2) live telecasts that are not fixed simultaneously with their transmission, or (3) filmstrips and slide sets which, although consisting of a series of images intended to be shown in succession, are not capable of conveying an impression of motion.

On the other hand, the bill equates audiovisual materials such as filmstrips, slide sets, and sets of transparencies with "motion pictures" rather than with "pictorial, graphic, and sculptural works." Their sequential showing is closer to a "performance" than to a "display," and the definition of "audiovisual works," which applies also to "motion pictures," embraces works consisting of a series of related images that are by their nature, intended for showing by means of projectors or other devices.

Nature of copyright

Copyright does not preclude others from using the ideas or information revealed by the author's work. It pertains to the literary musical, graphic, or artistic form in which the author expressed intellectual concepts. Section 102(b) makes clear that copyright protection does not extend to any idea, procedure, process, system, method of operation, concept, principle, or discovery, regardless of the form in which it is described, explained, illustrated, or embodied in such work.

Some concern has been expressed lest copyright in computer programs should extend protection to the methodology or processes adopted by the programmer, rather than merely to the "writing" expressing his ideas. Section 102(b) is intended, among other things, to make clear that the expression adopted by the programmer is the copyrightable element in a computer program, and that the actual processes or methods embodied in the program are not within the scope of the copyright law.

Section 102(b) in no way enlarges or contracts the scope of copyright protection under the present law. Its purpose is to restate, in the context of the new single Federal system of copyright, that the basic dichotomy between expression and idea remains unchanged.

SECTION 103. COMPILATIONS AND DERIVATIVE WORKS

Section 103 complements section 102: A compilation or derivative work is copyrightable if it represents an "original work of authorship" and falls within one or more of the categories listed in section 102. Read together, the two sections make plain that the criteria of copyrightable subject matter stated in section 102 apply with full force to works that are entirely original and to those containing preexisting material. Section 103(b) is also intended to define, more sharply and clearly than does section 7 of the present law, the important interrelationship and correlation between protection of preexisting and of "new" material in a particular work. The most important point here is one that is commonly misunderstood today: copyright in a "new version" covers only the material added by the later author, and has no effect one way or the other on the copyright or public domain status of the preexisting material.

Between them the terms "compilations" and "derivative works" which are defined in section 101, comprehend every copyrightable work that employs preexisting material or data of any kind. There is necessarily some overlapping between the two, but they basically represent different concepts. A "compilation" results from a process of selecting, bringing together, organizing, and arranging previously existing material of all kinds, regardless of whether the individual items in the material have been or ever could have been subject to copyright. A "derivative work," on the other hand, requires a process of recasting, transforming, or adapting "one or more preexisting works"; the "preexisting work" must come within the general subject matter of copyright set forth in section 102, regardless of whether it is or was ever copyrighted.

The second part of the sentence that makes up section 103(a) deals with the status of a compilation or derivative work unlawfully employing preexisting copyrighted material. In providing that protection does not extend to "any part of the work in which such material has been used unlawfully," the bill prevents an infringer from benefiting, through copyright protection, from committing an unlawful act, but preserves protection for those parts of the work that do not employ the preexisting work. Thus, an unauthorized translation of a novel could not be copyrighted at all, but the owner of copyright in an anthology of poetry could sue someone who infringed the whole anthology, even though the infringer proves that publication of one of the poems was unauthorized. Under this provision, copyright could be obtained as long as the use of the preexisting work was not "unlawful," even though the consent of the copyright owner had not been obtained. For instance, the unauthorized reproduction of a work might be "lawful" under the doctrine of fair use or an applicable foreign law, and if so the work incorporating it could be copyrighted.

SECTION 106. EXCLUSIVE RIGHTS IN COPYRIGHTED WORKS

General scope of copyright

The five fundamental rights that the bill gives to copyright owners—the exclusive rights of reproduction, adaptation, publication, performance, and display—are stated generally in section 106. These exclusive rights, which comprise the so-called "bundle of rights" that is a copyright, are cumulative and may overlap in some cases. Each of the five enumerated rights may be subdivided indefinitely and, as discussed below in connection with section 201, each subdivision of an exclusive right may be owned and enforced separately.

The approach of the bill is to set forth the copyright owner's exclusive rights in broad terms in section 106, and then to provide various limitations, qualifications, or exemptions in the 12 sections that follow. Thus, everything in section 106 is made "subject to sections 107 through 118," and must be read in conjunction with those provisions.

The exclusive rights accorded to a copyright owner under section 106 are "to do and to authorize" any of the activities specified in the five numbered clauses. Use of the phrase "to authorize" is intended to avoid any questions as to the liability of contributory infringers. For example, a person who lawfully acquires an authorized copy of a motion picture would be an infringer if he or she engages in the business of renting it to others for purposes of unauthorized public performance.

Rights of reproduction, adaptation, and publication

The first three clauses of section 106, which cover all rights under a copyright except those of performance and display, extend to every kind of copyrighted work. The exclusive rights encompassed by these clauses, though closely related, are independent; they can generally be characterized as rights of copying, recording, adaptation, and publishing. A single act of infringement may violate all of these rights at once, as where a publisher reproduces, adapts, and sells copies of a person's copyrighted work as part of a publishing venture. Infringement takes place when any one of the rights is violated: where, for example, a printer reproduces copies without selling them or a retailer sells copies without having anything to do with their reproduction. The references to "copies or phonorecords," although in the plural, are intended here and throughout the bill to include the singular (1 U.S.C. §1).

Reproduction.—Read together with the relevant definitions in section 101, the right "to reproduce the copyrighted work in copies or phonorecords" means the right to produce a material object in which the work is duplicated, transcribed, imitiated, or simulated in a fixed form from which it can be "perceived, reproduced, or otherwise communicated, either directly or with the aid of a machine or device." As under the present law, a copyrighted work would be infringed by reproducing it in whole or in any substantial part, and by duplicating it exactly or by imitation or simulation. Wide departures or variations from the copyrighted works would still be an infringement as long as the author's "expression" rather than merely the author's "ideas" are taken. An exception to this general principle, applicable to the reproduction of copyrighted sound recordings, is specified in section 114.

"Reproduction" under clause (1) of section 106 is to be distinguished from "display" under clause (5). For a work to be "reproduced," its fixation in tangible form must be "sufficiently permanent or stable to permit it to be perceived, reproduced, or otherwise communicated for a period of more than transitory duration." Thus, the showing of images on a screen or tube would not be a violation of clause (1), although it might come within the scope of clause (5).

Preparation of derivative works.—The exclusive right to prepare derivative works, specified separately in clause (2) of section 106, overlaps the exclusive right of reproduction to some extent. It is broader than that right, however, in the sense that reproduction requires fixation in copies or phonorecords, whereas the preparation of a derivative work, such as a ballet, pantomime, or improvised performance, may be an infringement even though nothing is ever fixed in tangible form.

To be an infringement the "derivative work" must be "based upon the copyrighted work," and the definition in section 101 refers to "a translation, musical arrangement, dramatization, fictionalization, motion picture version, sound recording, art reproduction, abridgment, condensation, or any other form in which a work may be recast, transformed, or adapted." Thus, to constitute a violation of section 106(2), the infringing work must incorporate a portion of the copyrighted work in some form; for example, a detailed commentary on a work or a programmatic musical composition inspired by a novel would not normally constitute infringements under this clause.

Use in information storage and retrieval systems.—As section 117 declares explicitly, the bill is not intended to alter the present law with respect to the use of copyrighted works in computer systems.

Public distribution.—Clause (3) of section 106 establishes the exclusive right of publications: The right "to distribute copies or phonorecords of the copyrighted work to the public by sale or other transfer of ownership, or by rental, lease, or lending." Under this provision the copyright owner would have the right to control the first public distribution of an authorized copy or phonorecord of his work, whether by sale, gift, loan, or some rental or lease arrangement. Likewise, any unauthorized public distribution of copies or phonorecords that were unlawfully made would be an infringement. As section 109 makes clear, however, the copyright owner's rights under section 106(3) cease with respect to a particular copy or phonorecord once he has parted with ownership of it.

Rights of public performance and display.

Performing rights and the "for profit" limitation.—The right of public performance under section 106(4) extends to "literary, musical, dramatic, and choreographic works, pantomimes, and motion pictures and other audiovisual works and sound recordings" and, unlike the equivalent provisions now in effect, is not limited by any "for profit" requirement. The approach of the bill, as in many foreign laws, is first to state the public performance right in broad terms, and then to provide specific exemptions for educational and other nonprofit uses.

This approach is more reasonable than the outright exemption of the 1909 statute. The line between commercial and "nonprofit" organizations is increasingly difficult to draw. Many "non-profit" organizations are highly subsidized and capable of paying royalties, and the widespread public exploitation of copyrighted works by public broadcasters and other noncommercial organizations is likely to grow. In addition to these trends, it is worth noting that performances and displays are continuing to supplant markets for printed copies and that in the future a broad "not for profit" exemption could not only hurt authors but could dry up their incentive to write.

The exclusive right of public performance is expanded to include not only motion pictures, including works records on film, video tape, and video disks, but also audiovisual works such as filmstrips and sets of slides. This provision of section 106(4), which is consistent with the assimilation of motion pictures to audiovisual works throughout the bill, is also related to amendments of the definitions of "display" and "perform" discussed below. The important issue of performing rights in sound recordings is discussed in connection with section 114.

Right of public display.—Clause (5) of section 106 represents the first explicit statutory recognition in American copyright law of an exclusive right to show a copyrighted work, or an image of it, to the public. The existence or extent of this right under the present statute is uncertain and subject to challenge. The bill would give the owners of copyright in "literary, musical, dramatic, and choreographic works, pantomimes, and pictorial, graphic, or sculptural works", including the individual images of a motion picture or other audiovisual work, the exclusive right "to display the copyrighted work publicly."

Definitions

Under the definitions of "perform," "display," "publicly," and "transmit" in section 101, the concepts of public performance and public display cover not only the initial rendition or showing, but also any further act by which that rendition or showing is transmitted or communicated to the public. Thus, for example: a singer is performing when he or she sings a song; a broadcasting network is performing when it transmits his or her performance (whether simultaneously or from records) ; a local broadcaster is performing when it transmits the network broadcast; a cable television system is performing when it retransmits the broadcast to its subscribers; and any individual is performing whenever he or she plays a phonorecord embodying the performance or communicates the performance by turning on a receiving set. Although any act by which the initial performance or display is transmitted, repeated, or made to recur would itself be a "performance" or "display" under the bill, it would not be actionable as an infringement unless it were done "publicly," as defined in section 101. Certain other performances and displays, in addition to those that are "private," are exempted or given qualified copyright control under sections 107 through 118.

To "perform" a work, under the definition in section 101, includes reading a literary work aloud, singing or playing music, dancing a ballet or other choreographic work, and acting out a dramatic work or pantomine. A performance may be accomplished "either directly or by means of any device or process," including all kinds of equipment for reproducing or amplifying sounds or visual images, any sort of transmitting apparatus, any type of electronic retrieval system, and any other techniques and systems not yet in use or even invented.

The definition of "perform" in relation to "a motion picture or other audio visual work" is "to show its images in any sequence or to make the sounds accompanying it audible." The showing of portions of a motion picture, filmstrip, or slide set must therefore be sequential to constitute a "performance" rather than a "display", but no particular order need be maintained. The purely aural performance of a motion picture sound track, or of the sound portions of an audiovisual work, would constitute a performance of the "motion picture or other audiovisual work"; but, where some of the sounds have been reproduced separately on phonorecords, a performance from the phonorecord would not constitute performance of the motion picture or audiovisual work.

The corresponding definition of "display" covers any showing of a "copy" of the work, "either directly or by means of a film, slide, television image, or any other device or process." Since "copies" are defined as including the material object "in which the work is first fixed," the right of public display applies to original works of art as well as to reproductions of them. With respect to motion pictures and other audiovisual works, it is a "display" (rather than a "performance") to show their "individual images nonsequentially." In addition to the direct showings of a copy of a work, "display" would include the projection of an image on a screen or other surface by any method, the transmission of an image by electronic or other means, and the showing of an image on a cathode ray tube, or similar viewing apparatus connected with any sort of information storage and retrieval system.

Under clause (1) of the definition of "publicly" in section 101, a performance or display is "public" if it takes place "at a place open to the public or at any place where a substantial number of persons outside of a normal circle of a family and its social acquaintances is gathered." One of the principal purposes of the definition was to make clear that, contrary to the decision in *Metro-Goldwyn-Mayer Distributing Corp.* v. *Wyatt*, 21 C.O. Bull. 203 (D. Md. 1932), performances in "semipublic" places such as clubs, lodges, factories, summer camps, and schools are "public performances" subject to copyright control. The term "a family" in this context would include an individual living alone, so that a gathering confined to the individual's social acquaintances would normally be regarded as private. Routine meetings of businesses and governmental personnel would be excluded because they do not represent the gathering of a "substantial number of persons."

Clause (2) of the definition of "publicly" in section 101 makes clear that the concepts of public performance and public display include not only performances and displays that occur initially in a public place, but also acts that transmit or otherwise communicate a performance or display of the work to the public by means of any device or process. The definition of "transmit"—to communicate a performance or display "by any device or process whereby images or sound are received beyond the place from which they are sent"—is broad enough to include all conceivable forms and combinations of wired or wireless communications media, including but by no means limited to radio and television broadcasting as we know them. Each and every method by which the images or sounds comprising a performance or display are picked up and conveyed is a "transmission," and if the transmission reaches the public in my form, the case comes within the scope of clauses (4) or (5) of section 106.

Under the bill, as under the present law, a performance made available by transmission to the public at large is "public" even though the recipients are not gathered in a single place, and even if there is no proof that any of the potential recipients was operating his receiving apparatus at the time of the transmission. The same principles apply whenever the potential recipients of the transmission represent a limited segment of the public, such as the occupants of hotel rooms or the subscribers of a cable television service. Clause (2) of the definition of "publicly" is applicable "whether the members of the public capable of receiving the performance or display receive it in the same place or in separate places and at the same time or at different times."

SECTION 107. FAIR USE

General background of the problem

The judicial doctrine of fair use, one of the most important and well-established limitations on the exclusive right of copyright owners, would be given express statutory recognition for the first time in section 107. The claim that a defendant's acts constituted a fair use rather than an infringement has been raised as a defense in innumerable copyright actions over the years, and there is ample case law recognizing the existence of the doctrine and applying it. The examples enumerated at page 24 of the Register's 1961 Report, while by no means exhaustive, give some idea of the sort of activities the courts might regard as fair use under the circumstances: "quotation of excerpts in a review or criticism for purposes of illustration or comment; quotation of short passages in a scholarly or technical work, for illustration or clarification of the author's observations; use in a parody of some of the content of the work parodied; summary of an address or article, with brief quotations, in a news report; reproduction by a library of a portion of a work to replace part of a damaged copy; reproduction by a teacher or student of a small part of a work to illustrate a lesson; reproduction of a work in legislative or judicial proceedings or reports; incidental and fortuitous reproduction, in a newsreel or broadcast, of a work located in the scene of an event being reported."

Although the courts have considered and ruled upon the fair use doctrine over and over again, no real definition of the concept has ever emerged. Indeed, since the doctrine is an equitable rule of reason, no generally applicable definition is possible, and each case raising the question must be decided on its own facts. On the other hand, the courts have evolved a set of criteria which, though in no case definitive or determinative, provide some guage for balancing the equities. These criteria have been stated in various ways, but essentially they can all be reduced to the four standards which have been adopted in section 107: "(1) the purpose and character of the use, including whether such use is of a commercial nature or is for non-profit educational purposes; (2) the nature of the copyrighted work; (3) the amount and substantiality of the portion used in relation to the copyrighted work as a whole; and (4) the effect of the use upon the potential market for or value of the copyrighted work."

These criteria are relevant in determining whether the basic doctrine of fair use, as stated in the first sentence of section 107, applies in a particular case: "Notwithstanding the provisions of section 106, the fair use of a copyrighted work, including such use by reproduction in copies or phonorecords or by any other means specified by that section, **for purposes such as criticism, comment, news reporting, teaching (including multiple copies for classroom use), scholarship, or research, is not an infringement of copyright."**

The specific wording of section 107 as it now stands is the result of a process of accretion, resulting from the long controversy over the related problems of fair use and the reproduction (mostly by photocopying) of copyrighted material for educational and scholarly purposes. For example, the reference to fair use "by reproduction in copies or phonorecords or by any other means" is mainly intended to make clear that the doctrine has as much application to photocopying and taping as to older forms of use; it is not intended to give these kinds of reproduction any special status under the fair use provision or to sanction any reproduction beyond the normal and reasonable limits of fair use. Similarly, the newly-added reference to "multiple copies for classroom use" is a recognition that, under the proper circumstances of fairness, the doctrine can be applied to reproductions of multiple copies for the members of a class.

The Committee has amended the first of the criteria to be considered—"the purpose and character of the use"—to state explicitly that this factor includes a consideration of "whether such use is of a commercial nature or is for non-profit educational purposes." This amendment is not intended to be interpreted as any sort of not-for-profit limitation on educational uses of copyrighted works. It is an express recognition that, as under the present law, the commercial or non-profit character of an activity, while not conclusive with respect to fair use, can and should be weighed along with other factors in fair use decisions.

General intention behind the provision

The statement of the fair use doctrine in section 107 offers some guidance to users in determining when the principles of the doctrine apply. However, the endless variety of situations and combinations of circumstances that can rise in particular cases precludes the formulation of exact rules in the statute. The bill endorses the purpose and general scope of the judicial doctrine of fair use, but there is no disposition to freeze the doctrine in the statute, especially during a period of rapid technological change. Beyond a very broad statutory explanation of what fair use is and some of the criteria applicable to it, the courts must be free to adapt the doctrine to particular situations on a case-by-case basis. Section 107 is intended to restate the present judicial doctrine of fair use, not to change, narrow, or enlarge it in any way.

Intention as to classroom reproduction

Although the works and uses to which the doctrine of fair use is applicable are as broad as the copyright law itself, most of the discussion of section 107 has centered around questions of classroom reproduction, particularly photocopying. The arguments on the question are summarized at pp. 30–31 of this Committee's 1967 report (II.R. Rep. No. 83, 90th Cong., 1st Sess.), and have not changed materially in the intervening years.

The Committee also adheres to its earlier conclusion, that "a specific exemption freeing certain reproductions of copyrighted works for educational and scholarly purposes from copyright control is not justified." At the same time the Committee recognizes, as it did in 1967, that there is a "need for greater certainty and protection for teachers." In an effort to meet this need the Committee has not only adopted further amendments to section 107, but has also amended section 504(c) to provide innocent teachers and other non-profit users of copyrighted material with broad insulation against unwarranted liability for infringement. The latter amendments are discussed below in connection with Chapter 5 of the bill.

In 1967 the Committee also sought to approach this problem by including, in its report, a very thorough discussion of "the considerations lying behind the four criteria listed in the amended section 107, in the context of typical classroom situations arising today." This discussion appeared on pp. 32–35 of the 1967 report, and with some changes has been retained in the Senate report on S. 22 (S. Rep. No. 94–473, pp. 63–65). The Committee has reviewed this discussion, and considers that it still has value as an analysis of various aspects of the problem.

At the Judiciary Subcommittee hearings in June 1975, Chairman Kastenmeier and other members urged the parties to meet together independently in an effort to achieve a meeting of the minds as to permissible educational uses of copyrighted material. The response to these suggestions was positive, and a number of meetings of three groups, dealing respectively with classroom reproduction of printed material, music, and audio-visual material, were held beginning in September 1975.

In a joint letter to Chairman Kastenmeier, dated March 19, 1976, the representatives of the Ad Hoc Committee of Educational Institutions and Organizations on Copyright Law Revision, and of the Authors League of America, Inc., and the Association of American Publishers, Inc., stated:

> You may remember that in our letter of March 8, 1976 we told you that the negotiating teams representing authors and publishers and the Ad Hoc Group had reached tentative agreement on guidelines to insert in the Committee Report covering educational copying from books and periodicals un-

der Section 107 of H.R. 2223 and S. 22, and that as part of that tentative agreement each side would accept the amendments to Sections 107 and 504 which were adopted by your Subcommittee on March 3, 1976.

We are now happy to tell you that the agreement has been approved by the principals and we enclose a copy herewith. We had originally intended to translate the agreement into language suitable for inclusion in the legislative report dealing with Section 107, but we have since been advised by committee staff that this will not be necessary.

As stated above, the agreement refers only to copying from books and periodicals, and it is not intended to apply to musical or audiovisual works.

The full text of the agreement is as follows:

AGREEMENT ON GUIDELINES FOR CLASSROOM COPYING IN NOT-FOR-PROFIT EDUCATIONAL INSTITUTIONS

WITH RESPECT TO BOOKS AND PERIODICALS

The purpose of the following guidelines is to state the minimum standards of educational fair use under Section 107 of H.R, 2223. The parties agree that the conditions determining the extent of permissible copying for educational purposes may change in the future; that certain types of copying permitted under these guidelines may not be permissible in the future; and conversely that in the future other types of copying not permitted under these guidelines may be permissible under revised guidelines.

Moreover, the following statement of guidelines is not intended to limit the types of copying permitted under the standards of fair use under judicial decision and which are stated in Section 107 of the Copyright Revision Bill. There may be instances in which copying which does not fall within the guidelines stated below may nonetheless be permitted under the criteria of fair use.

GUIDELINES

I. *Single Copying for Teachers*

A single copy may be made of any of the following by or for a teacher at his or her individual request for his or her scholarly research or use in teaching or preparation to teach a class:

A. A chapter from a book;

B. An article from a periodical or newspaper;

C. A short story, short essay or short poem, whether or not from a collective work;

D. A chart, graph, diagram, drawing, cartoon or picture from a book, periodical, or newspaper;

II. *Multiple Copies for Classroom Use*

Multiple copies (not to exceed in any event more than one copy per pupil in a course) may be made by or for the teacher giving the course for classroom use or discussion; *provided that:*

A. The copying meets the tests of brevity and spontaneity as defined below; *and,*

B. Meets the cumulative effect test as defined below; *and,*

C. Each copy includes a notice of copyright

Definitions

Brevity

(*i*) Poetry: (a) A complete poem if less than 250 words and if printed on not more than two pages or, (b) from a longer poem, an excerpt of not more than 250 words.

(*ii*) Prose: (a) Either a complete article, story or essay of less than 2,500 words, or (b) an excerpt from any prose work of not more than 1,000 words or 10% of the work, whichever is less, but in any event a minimum of 500 words.

[Each of the numerical limits stated in "i" and "ii" above may be expanded to permit the completion of an unfinished line of a poem or of an unfinished prose paragraph.]

(*iii*) Illustration: One chart, graph, diagram, drawing, cartoon or picture per book or per periodical issue.

(*iv*) "Special" works: Certain works in poetry, prose or in "poetic prose" which often combine language with illustrations and which are intended sometimes for children and at other times for a more general audience fall short of 2,500 words in their entirety. Paragraph "ii" above notwithstanding such "special works" may not be reproduced in their entirety; however, an excerpt comprising not more than two of the published pages of such special work and containing not more than 10% of the words found in the text thereof, may be reproduced.

Spontaneity

(*i*) The copying is at the instance and inspiration of the individual teacher, and

(*ii*) The inspiration and decision to use the work and the moment of its use for maximum teaching effectiveness are so close in time that it would be unreasonable to expect a timely reply to a request for permission.

Cumulative Effect

(*i*) The copying of the material is for only one course in the school in which the copies are made.

(*ii*) Not more than one short poem, article, story, essay or two excerpts may be copied from the same author, nor more than three from the same collective work or periodical volume during one class term.

(*iii*) There shall not be more than nine instances of such multiple copying for one course during one class term.

[The limitations stated in "ii" and "iii" above shall not apply to current news periodicals and newspapers and current news sections of other periodicals.]

III. *Prohibitions as to I and II Above*

Notwithstanding any of the above, the following shall be prohibited:

(A) Copying shall not be used to create or to replace or substitute for anthologies, compilations or collective works. Such replacement or substitution may occur whether copies of various works or excerpts therefrom are accumulated or reproduced and used separately.

(B) There shall be no copying of or from works intended to be "consumable" in the course of study or of teaching. These include workbooks, exercises, standardized tests and test booklets and answer sheets and like consumable material.

(C) Copying shall not:

> (a) substitute for the purchase of books, publishers' reprints or periodicals;
> (b) be directed by higher authority;
> (c) be repeated with respect to the same item by the same teacher from term to term.

(D) No charge shall be made to the student beyond the actual cost of the photocopying.

Agreed MARCH 19, 1976.

Ad Hoc Committee on Copyright Law Revision:

By SHELDON ELLIOTT STEINBACH.

Author-Publisher Group:

Authors League of America:

By IRWIN KARP, Counsel.

Association of American Publishers, Inc.:

By ALEXANDER C. HOFFMAN,
Chairman, Copyright Committee.

In a joint letter dated April 30, 1976, representatives of the Music Publishers' Association of the United States, Inc., the National Music Publishers' Association, Inc., the Music Teachers National Association, the Music Educators National Conference, the National Association of Schools of Music, and the Ad Hoc Committee on Copyright Law Revision, wrote to Chairman Kastenmeier as follows:

> During the hearings on H.R. 2223 in June 1975, you and several of your subcommittee members suggested that concerned groups should work together in developing guidelines which would be helpful to clarify Section 107 of the bill.
>
> Representatives of music educators and music publishers delayed their meetings until guidelines had been developed relative to books and periodicals. Shortly after that work was completed and those guidelines were forwarded to your subcommittee, representatives of the undersigned music organizations met together with representatives of the Ad Hoc Committee on Copyright Law Revision to draft guidelines relative to music.
>
> We are very pleased to inform you that the discussions thus have been fruitful on the guidelines which have been developed. Since private music teachers are an important factor in music education, due consideration has been given to the concerns of that group.
>
> We trust that this will be helpful in the report on the bill to clarify Fair Use as it applies to music.

The text of the guidelines accompanying this letter is as follows:

GUIDELINES FOR EDUCATIONAL USES OF MUSIC

The purpose of the following guidelines is to state the minimum and not the maximum standards of educational fair use under Section 107 of HR 2223. The parties agree that the conditions determining the extent of permissible copying for educational purposes may change in the future; that certain types of copying permitted under these guidelines may not be permissible in the future, and conversely that in the future other types of copying not permitted under these guidelines may be permissible under revised guidelines.

Moreover, the following statement of guidelines is not intended to limit the types of copying permitted under the standards of fair use under judicial decision and which are stated in Section 107 of the Copyright Revision Bill. There may be instances in which copying which does not fall within the guidelines stated below may nonetheless be permitted under the criteria of fair use.

A. Permissible Uses

1. Emergency copying to replace purchased copies which for any reason are not available for an imminent performance provided purchased replacement copies shall be substituted in due course.

2. (a) For academic purposes other than performance, multiple copies of excerpts of works may be made, provided that the excerpts do not comprise a part of the whole which would constitute a performable unit such as a section, movement or aria, but in no case more than (10% of the whole work. The number of copies shall not exceed one copy per pupil

(b) For academic purposes other than performance, a single copy of an entire performable unit (section, movement, aria, etc.) that is, (1) confirmed by the copyright proprietor to be out of print or (2) unavailable except in a larger work, may be made by or for a teacher solely for the purpose of his or her scholarly research or in preparation to teach a class.

3. Printed copies which have been purchased may be edited or simplified provided that the fundamental character of the work is not distorted or the lyrics, if any, altered or lyrics added if none exist.

4. A single copy of recordings of performances by students may be made for evaluation or rehearsal purposes and may be retained by the educational institution or individual teacher.

5. A single copy of a sound recording (such as a tape, disc or cassette) of copyrighted music may be made from sound recordings owned by an educatonal institution or an individual teacher for the purpose of constructing aural exercises or examinations and may be retained by the educational institution or individual teacher. (This pertains only to the copyright of the music itself and not to any copyright which may exist in the sound recording.)

B. Prohibitions

1. Copying to create or replace or substitute for anthologies, compilations or collective works.

2. Copying of or from works intended to be "consumable" in the course of study or of teaching such as workbooks, exercises, standardized tests and answer sheets and like material.

3. Copying for the purpose of performance, except as in A(1) above.

4. Copying for the purpose of substituting for the purchase of music, except as in A(1) and A(2) above.

5. Copying without inclusion of the copyright notice which appears on the printed copy.

The problem of off-the-air taping for nonprofit classroom use of copyrighted audiovisual works incorporated in radio and television broadcasts has proved to be difficult to resolve. The Committee believes that the fair use doctrine has some limited application in this area, but it appears that the development of detailed guidelines will require a more thorough exploration than has so far been possible of the needs and problems of a number of different interests affected, and of the various legal problems presented. Nothing in section 107 or elsewhere in the bill is intended to change or prejudge the law on the point. On the other hand, the Committee is sensitive to the importance of the problem, and urges the representatives of the various interests, if possible under the leadership of the Register of Copyrights, to continue their discussions actively and in a constructive spirit. If it would be helpful to a solution, the Committee is receptive to undertaking further consideration of the problem in a future Congress.

The Committee appreciates and commends the efforts and the cooperative and reasonable spirit of the parties who achieved the agreed guidelines on books and periodicals and on music. Representatives of the American Association of University Professors and of the Association of American Law Schools have written to the Committee strongly criticizing the guidelines, particularly with respect to multiple copying, as being too restrictive with respect to classroom situations at the university and graduate level. However, the Committee notes that the Ad Hoc group did include representatives of higher education, that the stated "purpose of the . . . guidelines is to state the minimum and not the maximum standards of educational fair use" and that the agreement acknowledges "there may be instances in which copying which does not fall within the guidelines . . . may nonetheless be permitted under the criteria of fair use."

The Committee believes the guidelines are a reasonable interpretation of the minimum standards of fair use. Teachers kill know that copying within the guidelines is fair use. Thus, the guidelines serve the purpose of fulfilling the need for greater certainty and protection for teachers. The Committee expresses the hope that if there are areas where standards other than these guidelines may be appropriate, the parties will continue their efforts to provide additional specific guidelines in the same spirit of good will and give and take that has marked the discussion of this subject in recent months.

Reproduction and uses for other purposes

The concentrated attention given the fair use provision in the context of classroom teaching activities should not obscure its application in other areas. It must be emphasized again that the same general standards of fair use are applicable to all kinds of uses of copyrighted material, although the relative weight to be given them will differ from case to case.

The fair use doctrine would be relevant to the use of excerpts from copyrighted works in educational broadcasting activities not exempted under section 110(2) or 112, and not covered by the licensing provisions of section 118. In these cases the factors to be weighed in applying the criteria of this section would include whether the performers, producers, directors, and others responsible for the broadcast were paid, the size and nature of the audience, the size and number of excerpts taken and, in the case of recordings made for broadcast, the number of copies reproduced and the extent of their reuse or exchange. The availability of the fair use doctrine to educational broadcasters would be narrowly circumscribed in the case of motion pictures and other audiovisual works, but under appropriate circumstances it could apply to the nonsequential showing of an individual still or slide, or to the performance of a short excerpt from a motion picture for criticism or comment.

Another special instance illustrating the application of the fair use doctrine pertains to the making of copies or phonorecords of works in the special forms needed for the use of blind persons. These special forms, such as copies in Braille and phonorecords of oral readings (talking books), are not usually made by the publishers for commercial distribution. For the most part, such copies and phonorecords are made by the Library of Congress' Division for the Blind and Physically Handicapped with permission obtained from the copyright owners, and are circulated to blind persons through regional libraries covering the nation. In addition, such copies and phonorecords are made locally by individual volunteers for the use of blind persons in their communities, and the Library of Congress conducts a program for training such volunteers. While the making of multiple copies or phonorecords of a work for general circulation requires the permission of the copyright owner, a problem addressed in section 70 of the bill, the making of a single copy or phonorecord by an individual as a free service for a blind persons would properly be considered a fair use under section 107.

A problem of particular urgency is that of preserving for posterity prints of motion pictures made before 1942. Aside from the deplorable fact that in a great many cases the only existing copy of a film has been deliberately destroyed, those that remain are in immediate danger of disintegration; they were printed on film stock with a nitrate base that will inevitably decompose in time. The efforts of the Library of Congress, the American Film Institute, and other organizations to rescue and preserve this irreplaceable contribution to our cultural life are to be applauded, and the making of duplicate copies for purposes of archival preservation certainly falls within the scope of "fair use."

When a copyrighted work contains unfair, inaccurate, or derogatory information concerning an individual or institution, the individual or institution may copy and reproduce such parts of the work as are necessary to permit understandable comment on the statements made in the work.

The Committee has considered the question of publication, in Congressional hearings and documents, of copyrighted material. Where the length of the work or excerpt published and the number of copies authorized are reasonable under the circumstances, and the work itself is directly relevant to a matter of legitimate legislative concern, the Committee believes that the publication would constitute fair use.

During the consideration of the revision bill in the 94th Congress it was proposed that independent newsletters, as distinguished from house organs and publicity or advertising publications, be given separate treatment. It is argued that newsletters are particularly vulnerable to mass photocopying, and that most newsletters have fairly modest circulations. Whether the copying of portions of a newsletter is an act of infringement or a fair use will necessarily turn on the facts of the individual case. However, as a general principle, it seems clear that the scope of the fair use doctrine should be considerably narrower in the case of newsletters than in that of either mass-circulation periodicals or scientific journals. The commercial nature of the user is a significant factor in such cases: Copying by a profit-making user of even a small portion of a newsletter may have a significant impact on the commercial market for the work.

The Committee has examined the use of excerpts from copyrighted works in the art work of calligraphers. The committee believes that a single copy reproduction of an excerpt from a copyrighted work by a calligrapher for a single client does not represent an infringement of copyright. Likewise, a single reproduction of excerpts from a copyrighted work by a student calligrapher or teacher in a learning situation would be a fair use of the copyrighted work.

The Register of Copyrights has recommended that the committee report describe the relationship between this section and the provisions of section 108 relating to reproduction by libraries and archives. The doctrine of fair use applies to library photocopying, and nothing contained in section 108 "in any way affects the right of fair use." No provision of section 108 is intended to take away any rights existing under the fair use doctrine. To the contrary, section 108 authorizes certain photocopying practices which may not qualify as a fair use.

The criteria of fair use are necessarily set forth in general terms. In the application of the criteria of fair use to specific photocopying practices of libraries, it is the intent of this legislation to provide an appropriate balancing of the rights of creators, and the needs of users.

Section 108. Reproduction by Libraries and Archives

Notwithstanding the exclusive rights of the owners of copyright, section 108 provides that under certain conditions it is not an infringement of copyright for a library or archives, or any of its employees acting within the scope of their employment, to reproduce or distribute not more than one copy or phonorecord of a work, provided (1) the reproduction or distribution is made without any purpose of direct or indirect commercial advantage and (2) the collections of the library or archives are open to the public or available not only to researchers affiliated with the library or archives, but also to other persons doing research in a specialized field, and (3) the reproduction or distribution of the work includes a notice of copyright.

Under this provision, a purely commercial enterprise could not establish a collection of copyrighted works, call itself a library or archive, and engage in for-profit reproduction and distribution of photocopies. Similarly, it would not be possible for a non-profit institution, by means of contractual arrangements with a commercial copying enterprise, to authorize the enterprise to carry out copying and distribution functions that would be exempt if conducted by the non-profit institution itself.

The reference to "indirect commercial advantage" has raised questions as to the status of photocopying done by or for libraries or archival collections within industrial, profitmaking, or proprietary institutions (such as the research and development departments of chemical, pharmaceutical, automobile, and oil corporations, the library of a propritary hospital, the collections owned by a law or medical partnership, etc.).

There is a direct interrelationship between this problem and the prohibitions against "multiple" and "systematic" photocopying in section 108(g) (1) and (2). Under section 108, a library in a profit-making organization would not be authorized to:

(a) use a single subscription or copy to supply its employees with multiple copies of material relevant to their work; or

(b) use a single subscription or copy to supply its employees, on request, with single copies of material relevant to their work, where the arrangement is "systematic" in the sense of deliberately substituting photocopying for subscription or purchase; or

(c) use "interlibrary loan" arrangements for obtaining photocopies in such aggregate quantities as to substitute for subscriptions or purchase of material needed by employees in their work. Moreover, a library in a profit-making organization could not evade these obligations by installing reproducing equipment on its premises for unsupervised use by the organization's staff.

Isolated, spontaneous making of single photocopies by a library in a for-profit organization, without any systematic effort to substitute photocopying for subscriptions or purchases, would be covered by section 108, even though the copies are furnished to the employees of the organization for use in their work. Similarly, for-profit libraries could participate in interlibrary arrangements for exchange of photocopies, as long as the production or distribution was not "systematic." These activities, by themselves, would ordinarily not be considered "for direct or indirect commercial advantages," since the "advantage" referred to in this clause must attach to the immediate commercial motivation behind the reproduction or distribution itself, rather than to the ultimate profit-making motivation behind the enterprise in which the library is located. On the other hand, section 108 would not excuse reproduction or distribution if there were a commercial motive behind the actual making or distributing of the copies, if multiple copies were made or distributed, or if the photocopying activities were "systematic" in the sense that their aim was to substitute for subscriptions or purchases.

The rights of reproduction and distribution under section 108 apply in the following circumstances:

Archival reproduction

Subsection (b) authorizes the reproduction and distribution of a copy or phonorecord of an unpublished work duplicated in facsimile form solely for purposes of preservation and security, or for deposit for research use in another library or archives, if the copy or phonorecord reproduced is currently in the collections of the first library or archives. Only unpublished works could be reproduced under this exemption, but the right would extend to any type of work, including photographs, motion pictures and sound recordings. Under this exemption, for example, a repository could make photocopies of manuscripts by microfilm or electrostatic process, but could not reproduce the work in "machine-readable" language for storage in an information system.

Replacement of damaged copy

Subsection (c) authorizes the reproduction of a published work duplicated in facsimile form solely for the purpose of replacement of a copy or phonorecord that is damaged, deteriorating, lost or stolen, if the library or archives has, after a reasonable effort, determined that an unused replacement cannot be obtained at a fair price. The scope and nature of a reasonable investigation to determine that an unused replacement cannot be obtained will vary according to the circumstances of a particular situation. It will always require recourse to commonly-known trade sources in the United States, and in the normal situation also to the publisher or other copyright owner (if such owner can be located at the address listed in the copyright registration), or an authorized reproducing service.

Articles and small excerpts

Subsection (d) authorizes the reproduction and distribution of a copy of not more than one article or other contribution to copyrighted collection or periodical issue, or of a copy or phonorecord of a small part of any other copyrighted work. The copy or phonorecord may be made by the library where the user makes his request or by another library pursuant to an interlibrary loan. It is further required that the copy become the property of the user, that the library or archives have no notice that the copy would be used for any purposes other than private study, scholarship or research, and that the library or archives display prominently at the place where reproduction requests are accepted, and includes in its order form, a warning of copyright in accordance with requirements that the Register of Copyrights shall prescribe by regulation.

Out-of-print works

Subsection (e) authorizes the reproduction and distribution of a copy or phonorecord of an entire work under certain circumstances, if it has been established that a copy cannot be obtained at a fair price. The copy may be made by the library where the user makes his request or by another library pursuant to an interlibrary loan. The scope and nature of a reasonable investigation to determine that an unused copy cannot be obtained will vary according to the circumstances of a particular situation. It will always require recourse to commonly-known trade sources in the United States, and in the normal situation also to the publisher or other copyright owner (if the owner can be located at the address listed in the copyright registration), or an authorized reproducing service. It is further required that the copy become the property of the user, that the library or archives have no notice that the copy would be used for any purpose other than private study, scholarship, or research, and that the library or archives display prominently at the place where reproduction requests are accepted, and include on its order form, a warning of copyright in accordance with requirements that the Register of Copyrights shall prescribe by regulation.

General exemptions

Clause (1) of subsection (f) specifically exempts a library or archives or its employees from liability for the unsupervised use of reproducing equipment located on its premises, provided that the reproducing equipment displays a notice that the making of a copy may be subject to the copyright law. Clause (2) of subsection (f) makes clear that this exemption of the library or archives does not extend to the person using such equipment or requesting such copy if the use exceeds fair use. Insofar as such person is concerned the copy or phonorecord made is not considered "lawfully" made for purposes of sections 109, 110 or other provisions of the title.

Clause (3) provides that nothing in section 108 is intended to limit the reproduction and distribution by lending of a limited number of copies and excerpts of an audiovisual news program. This exemption is intended to apply to the daily newscasts of the national television networks, which report the major events of the day. It does not apply to documentary (except documentary programs involving news reporting as that term is used in section 107), magazine-format or other public affairs broadcasts dealing with subjects of general interest to the viewing public.

The clause was first added to the revision bill in 1974 by the adoption of an amendment proposed by Senator Baker. It is intended to permit libraries and archives, subject to the general conditions of this section, to make off-the-air videotape recordings of daily network newscasts for limited distribution to scholars and researchers for use in research purposes. As such, it is an adjunct to the American Television and Radio Archive established in Section 113 of the Act which will be the principal repository for television broadcast material, including news broadcasts. The inclusion of language indicating that such material may only be distributed by lending by the library or archive is intended to preclude performance, copying, or sale, whether or not for profit, by the recipient of a copy of a television broadcast taped off-the-air pursuant to this clause.

Clause (4), in addition to asserting that nothing contained in section 108 "affects the right of fair use as provided by section 107," also provides that the right of reproduction granted by this section does not override any contractual arrangements assumed by a library or archives when it obtained a work for its collections. For example, if there is an express contractual prohibition against reproduction for any purpose, this legislation shall not be construed as justifying a violation of the contract. This clause is intended to encompass the situation where an individual makes papers, manuscripts or other works available to a library with the understanding that they will not be reproduced.

It is the intent of this legislation that a subsequent unlawful use by a user of a copy or phonorecord of a work lawfully made by a library, shall not make the library liable for such improper use.

Multiple copies and systematic reproduction

Subsection (g) provides that the rights granted by this section extend only to the "isolated and unrelated reproduction of a single copy or phonorecord of the same material on separate occasions." However, this section does not authorize the related or concerted reproduction of multiple copies or phonorecords of the same materials, whether made on one occasion or over a period of time, and whether intended for aggregate use by one individual or for separate use by the individual members of a group.

With respect to material described in subsection (d)—articles or other contributions to periodicals or collections, and small parts of other copyrighted works—subsection (g) (2) provides that the exemptions of section 108 do not apply if the library or archive engages in "systematic reproduction or distribution of single or multiple copies or phonorecords." This provision in S. 22 provoked a storm of controversy, centering around the extent to which the restrictions on "systematic" activities would prevent the continuation and development of interlibrary networks and other arrangements involving the exchange of photocopies. After thorough consideration, the Committee amended section 108(g) (2) to add the following proviso:

> *Provided*, that nothing in this clause prevents a library or archives from participating in interlibrary arrangements that do not have, as their purpose or effect, that the library or archives receiving such copies or phonorecords for distribution does so in such aggregate quantities as to substitute for a subscription to or purchase of such work.

In addition, the Committee added a new subsection (i) to section 108, requiring the Register of Copyrights, five years from the effective date of the new Act and at five-year intervals thereafter, to report to Congress upon "the extent to which this section has achieved the intended statutory balancing of the rights of creators, and the needs of users," and to make appropriate legislative or other recommendations. As noted in connection with section 107, the Committee also amended section 504(c) in a way that would insulate librarians from unwarranted liability for copyright infringement; this amendment is discussed below.

The key phrases in the Committee's amendment of section 108(g) (2) are "aggregate quantities" and "substitute for a subscription to or purchase of" a work. To be implemented effectively in practice, these provisions will require the development and implementation of more-or-less specific guidelines establishing criteria to govern various situations.

The National Commission on New Technological Uses of Copyrighted Works (CONTU) offered to provide good offices in helping to develop these guidelines. This offer was accepted and, although the final text of guidelines has not yet been achieved, the Committee has reason to hope that, within the next month, some agreement can be reached on an initial set of guidelines covering practices under section 108(g)(2).

Works excluded

Subsection (h) provides that the rights of reproduction and distribution under this section do not apply to a musical work, a pictorial, graphic or sculptural work, or a motion picture or other audiovisual work other than "an audiovisual work dealing with news." The latter term is intended as the equivalent in meaning of the phrase "audiovisual news program" in section 108(f)(3). The exclusions under subsection (h) do not apply to archival reproduction under subsection (b), to replacement of damaged or lost copies or phonorecords under subsection (c), or to "pictorial or graphic works published as illustrations, diagrams, or similar adjuncts to works of which copies are reproduced or distributed in accordance with subsections (d) and (e)."

Although subsection (h) generally removes musical, graphic, and audiovisual works from the specific exemptions of section 108, it is important to recognize that the doctrine of fair use under section 107 remains fully applicable to the photocopying or other reproduction of such works. In the case of music, for example, it would be fair use for a scholar doing musicological research to have a library supply a copy of a portion of a score or to reproduce portions of a phonorecord of a work. Nothing in section 108 impairs the applicability of the fair use doctrine to a wide variety of situations involving photocopying or other reproduction by a library of copyrighted material in its collections, where the user requests the reproduction for legitimate scholarly or research purposes.

SECTION 109. EFFECT OF TRANSFER OF PARTICULAR COPY OR PHONORECORD

Effect on further disposition of copy or phonorecord

Section 109(a) restates and confirms the principle that, where the copyright owner has transferred ownership of a particular copy or phonorecord of a work, the person to whom the copy or phonorecord is transferred is entitled to dispose of it by sale, rental, or any other means. Under this principle, which has been established by the court decisions and section 27 of the present law, the copyright owner's exclusive right of public distribution would have no effect upon anyone who owns "a particular copy or phonorecord lawfully made under this title" and who wishes to transfer it to someone else or to destroy it.

Thus, for example, the outright sale of an authorized copy of a book frees it from any copyright control over its resale price or other conditions of its future disposition. A library that has acquired ownership of a copy is entitled to lend it under any conditions it chooses to impose. This does not mean that conditions on future disposition of copies or phonorecords, imposed by a contract between their buyer and seller, would be unenforceable between the parties as a breach of contract, but it does mean that they could not be enforced by an action for infringement of copyright. Under section 202 however, the owner of the physical copy or phonorecord cannot reproduce or perform the copyrighted work publicly without the copyright owner's consent.

To come within the scope of section 109(a), a copy or phonorecord must have been "lawfully made under this title," though not necessarily with the copyright owner's authorization. For example, any resale of an illegally "pirated" phonorecord would be an infringement, but the disposition of a phonorecord legally made under the compulsory licensing provisions of section 115 would not.

Effect on display of copy

Subsection (b) of section 109 deals with the scope of the copyright owner's exclusive right to control the public display of a particular "copy" of a work (including the original or prototype copy in which the work was first fixed). Assuming, for example, that a painter has sold the only copy of an original work of art without restrictions, would it be possible for him to restrain the new owner from displaying it publicly in galleries, shop windows, on a projector, or on television?

Section 109(b) adopts the general principle that the lawful owner of a copy of a work should be able to put his copy on public display without the consent of the copyright owner. As in cases arising under section 109(a), this does not mean that contractual restrictions on display between a buyer and seller would be unenforceable as a matter of contract law.

The exclusive right of public display granted by section 106(5) would not apply where the owner of a copy wishes to show it directly to the public, as in a gallery or display case, or indirectly, as through an opaque projector. Where the copy itself is intended for projection, as in the case of a photographic slide, negative, or transparency, the public projection of a single image would be permitted as long as the views are "present at the place where the copy is located."

On the other hand, section 109(b) takes account of the potentialities of the new communications media, notably television, cable and optical transmission devices, and information storage and retrieval devices, for replacing printed copies with visual images. First of all, the public display of an image of a copyrighted work would not be exempted from copyright control if the copy from which the image was derived were outside the presence of the viewers. In other words, the display of a visual image of a copyrighted work would be an infringement if the image were transmitted by any method (by closed or open circuit television, for example, or by a computer system) from one place to members of the public located elsewhere.

Moreover, the exemption would extend only to public displays that are made "either directly or by the projection of no more than one image at a time." Thus, even where the copy and the viewers are located at the same place, the simultaneous projection of multiple images of the work would not be exempted. For example, where each person in a lecture hall is supplied with a separate viewing apparatus, the copyright owner's permission would generally be required in order to project an image of a work on each individual screen at the same time.

The committee's intention is to preserve the traditional privilege of the owner of a copy to display it directly, but to place reasonable restrictions on the ability to display it indirectly in such a way that the copyright owner's market for reproduction and distribution of copies would be affected. Unless it constitutes a fair use under section 107, or unless one of the special provisions of section 110 or 11' is applicable, projection of more than one image at a time, or transmission of an image to the public over television or other communication channels, would be an infringement for the same reaso.: that reproduction in copies would be. The concept of "the place where the copy is located" is generally intended to refer to a situation in which the viewers are present in the same physical surroundings as the copy, even though they cannot see the copy directly.

Effect of mere possession of copy or phonorecord

Subsection (c) of section 109 qualifies the privileges specified in subsections (a) and (b) by making clear that they do not apply to someone who merely possesses a copy or phonorecord without having acquired ownership of it. Acquisition of an object embodying a copyrighted work by rental, lease, loan, or bailment carries with it no privilege to dispose of the copy under section 109(a) or to display it publicly under section 109(b). To cite a familiar example, a person who has rented a print of a motion picture from the copyright owner would have no right to rent it to someone else without the owner's permission.

Burden of proof in infringement actions

During the course of its deliberations on this section, the Committee's attention was directed to a recent court decision holding that the plaintiff in an infringement action had the burden of establishing that the allegedly infringing copies in the defendant's possession were not lawfully made or acquired under section 27 of the present law. *American International Pictures, Inc.* v. *Foreman*, 400 F. Supp. 928 (S.D. Alabama 1975). The Committee believes that the court's decision, if followed, would place a virtually impossible burden on copyright owners. The decision is also inconsistent with the established legal principle that the burden of proof should not be placed upon a litigant to establish facts particularly within the knowledge of his adversary. The defendant in such actions clearly has the particular knowledge of how possession of the particular copy was acquired, and should have the burden of providing this evidence to the court. It is the intent of the Committee, therefore, that in an action to determine whether a defendant is entitled to the privilege established by section 109 (a) and (b), the burden or proving whether a particular copy was lawfully made or acquired should rest on the defendant.

SECTION 110. EXEMPTIONS OF CERTAIN PERFORMANCES AND DISPLAYS

Clauses (1) through (4) of section 110 deal with performances and exhibitions that are now generally exempt under the "for profit" limitation or other provisions of the copyright law, and that are specifically exempted from copyright liability under this legislation. Clauses (1) and (2) between them are intended to cover all of the various methods by which performances or displays in the course of systematic instruction take place.

Face-to-face teaching activities

Clause (1) of section 110 is generally intended to set out the conditions under which performances or displays, in the course of instructional activities other than educational broadcasting, are to be exempted from copyright control. The clause covers all types of copyrighted works, and exempts their performance or display "by instructors or pupils in the course of face-to-face teaching activities of a nonprofit educational institution," where the activities take place "in a classroom or similar place devoted to instruction."

There appears to be no need for a statutory definition of "face-to-face" teaching activities to clarify the scope of the provision. "Face-to-face teaching activities" under clause (1) embrace instructional performances and displays that are not "transmitted." The concept does not require that the teacher and students be able to see each other, although it does require their simultaneous presence in the same general place. Use of the phrase "in the course of face-to-face teaching activities" is intended to exclude broadcasting or other transmissions from an outside location into classrooms, whether radio or television and whether open or closed circuit. However, as long as the instructor and pupils are in the same building or general area, the exemption would extend to the use of devices for amplifying or reproducing sound and for projecting visual images. The "teaching activities" exempted by the clause encompass systematic instruction of a very wide variety of subjects, but they do not include performances or displays, whatever their cultural value or intellectual appeal, that are given for the recreation or entertainment of any part of their audience.

Works affected.—Since there is no limitation on the types of works covered by the exemption, teachers or students would be free to perform or display anything in class as long as the other conditions of the clause are met. They could read aloud from copyrighted text material, act out a drama, play or sing a musical work, perform a motion picture or filmstrip, or display text or pictorial material to the class by means of a projector. However, nothing in this provision is intended to sanction the unauthorized reproduction of copies or phonorecords for the purpose of classroom performance or display, and the clause contains a special exception dealing with performances from unlawfully made copies of motion pictures and other audiovisual works, to be discussed below.

Instructors or pupils.—To come within clause (1), the performance or display must be "by instructors or pupils," thus ruling out performances by actors, singers, or instrumentalists brought in from outside the school to put on a program. However, the term "instructors" would be broad enough to include guest lecturers if their instructional activities remain confined to classroom situations. In general, the term "pupils" refers to the enrolled members of a class.

Nonprofit educational institution.—Clause (1) makes clear that it applies only to the teaching activities "of a nonprofit educational institution," thus excluding from the exemption performances or displays in profit-making institutions such as dance studios and language schools.

Classroom or similar place.—The teaching activities exempted by the clause must take place "in a classroom or similar place devoted to instruction." For example, performances in an auditorium or stadium during a school assembly, graduation ceremony, class play, or sporting event, where the audience is not confined to the members of a particular class, would fall outside the scope of clause (1), although in some cases they might be exempted by clause (4) of section 110. The "similar place" referred to in clause (1) is a place which is "devoted to instruction" in the same way a classroom is; common examples would include a studio, a workshop, a gymnasium, a training field, a library, the stage of an auditorium, or the auditorium itself, if it is actually used as a classroom for systematic instructional activities.

Motion pictures and other audiovisual works.—The final provision of clause (1) deals with the special problem of performances from unlawfully-made copies of motion pictures and other audiovisual works. The exemption is lost where the copy being used for a classroom performance was "not lawfully made under this title" and the person responsible for the performance knew or had reason to suspect as much. This special exception to the exemption would not apply to performances from lawfully-made copies, even if the copies were acquired from someone who had stolen or converted them, or if the performances were in violation of an agreement. However, though the performance would be exempt under section 110(1) in such cases, the copyright owner might have a cause of action against the unauthorized distributor under section 106(3), or against the person responsible for the performance, for breach of contract.

Projection devices.—As long as there is no transmission beyond the place where the copy is located, both section 109(b) and section 110(1) would permit the classroom display of a work by means of any sort of projection device or process.

Instructional broadcasting

Works affected. The exemption for instructional broadcasting provided by section 110(2) would apply only to "performance of a nondramatic literary or musical work or display of a work." Thus, the copyright owner's permission would be required for the performance on educational television or radio of a dramatic work, of a dramatico-musical work such as an opera or musical comedy, or of a motion picture. Since, as already explained, audiovisual works such as filmstrips are equated with motion pictures, their sequential showing would be regarded as a performance rather than a display and would not be exempt under section 110(2). The clause is not intended to limit in any way the copyright owner's exclusive right to make dramatizations, adaptations, or other derivative works under section 106(2). Thus, for example, a performer could read a nondramatic literary work aloud under section 110(2), but the copyright owner's permission would be required for him to act it out in dramatic form.

Systematic instructional activities.—Under section 110(2) a transmission must meet three specified conditions in order to be exempted from copyright liability. The first of these, as provided by subclause (A), is that the performance or display must be "a regular part of the systematic instructional activities of a governmental body or a nonprofit educational institution." The concept of "systematic instructional activities" is intended as the general equivalent of "curriculums," but it could be broader in a case such as that of an institution using systematic teaching methods not related to specific course work.

A transmission would be a regular part of these activities if it is in accordance with the pattern of teaching established by the governmental body or institution. The use of commercial facilities, such as those of a cable service, to transmit the performance or display, would not affect the exemption as long as the actual performance or display was for nonprofit purposes.

Content of transmission.—Subclause (B) requires that the performance or display be directly related and of material assistance to the teaching content of the transmission.

Intended recipients.—Subclause (C) requires that the transmission is made primarily for:

(*i*) Reception in classrooms or similar places normally devoted to instruction, or

(*ii*) Reception by persons to whom the transmission is directed because their disabilities or other special circumstances prevent their attendance in classrooms or similar places normally devoted to instruction, or

(*iii*) Reception by officers or employees of governmental bodies as a part of their official duties or employment.

In all three cases, the instructional transmission need only be made "primarily" rather than "solely" to the specified recipients to be exempt. Thus, the transmission could still be exempt even though it is capable of reception by the public at large. Conversely, it would not be regarded as made "primarily" for one of the required groups of recipients if the principal purpose behind the transmission is reception by the public at large, even if it is cast in the form of instruction and is also received in classrooms. Factors to consider in determining the "primary" purpose of a program would include its subject matter, content, and the time of its transmission.

Paragraph (i) of subclause (C) generally covers what are known as "in-school" broadcasts, whether open- or closed-circuit. The reference to "classrooms or similar places" here is intended to have the same meaning as that of the phrase as used in section 110(1). The exemption in paragraph (ii) is intended to exempt transmissions providing systematic instuction to individuals who cannot be reached in classrooms because of "their disabilities or other special circumstances." Accordingly, the exemption is confined to instructional broadcasting that is an adjunct to the actual classwork of nonprofit schools or is primarily for people who cannot be brought together in classrooms such as preschool children, displaced workers, illiterates, and shut-ins.

There has been some question as to whether or not the language in this section of the bill is intended to include instructional television college credit courses. These telecourses are aimed at undergraduate and graduate students in earnest pursuit of higher educational degrees who are unable to attend daytime classes because of daytime employment, distance from campus, or some other intervening reason. So long as these broadcasts are aimed at regularly enrolled students and conducted by recognized higher educational institutions, the committee believes that they are clearly within the language of section 110 (2(C)(ii). Like night school and correspondence courses before them, these telecourses are fast becoming a valuable adjunct of the normal college curriculum.

The third exemption in subclause (C) is intended to permit the use of copyrighted material, in accordance with the other conditions of section 110(2), in the course of instructional transmissions for Government personnel who are receiving training "as a part of their official duties or employment."

Religious services

The exemption in clause (3) of section 110 covers performances of a nondramatic literary or musical work, and also performances "of dramatico-musical works of a religious nature"; in addition, it extends to displays of works of all kinds. The exemption applies where the performance or display is "in the course of services at a place of worship or other religious assembly." The scope of the clause does not cover the sequential showing of motion pictures and other audiovisual works.

The exemption, which to some extent has its counterpart in sections 1 and 104 of the present law, applies to dramatico-musical works "of a religious nature." The purpose here is to exempt certain performances of sacred music that might be regarded as "dramatic" in nature, such as oratorios, cantatas, musical settings of the mass, choral services, and the like. The exemption is not intended to cover performances of secular operas, musical plays, motion pictures, and the like, even if they have an underlying religious or philosophical theme and take place "in the course of [religious] services."

To be exempted under section 1103(3) a performance or display must be "in the course of services," thus excluding activities at a place of worship that are for social, educational, fund raising, or entertainment purposes. Some performances of these kinds could be covered by the exemption in section 110(4), discussed next. Since the performance or display must also occur "at a place of worship or other religious assembly," the exemption would not extend to religious broadcasts or other transmissions to the public at large, even where the transmissions were sent from the place of worship. On the other hand, as long as services are being conducted before a religious gathering, the exemption would apply if they were conducted in places such as auditoriums, outdoor theaters, and the like.

Certain other nonprofit performances

In addition to the educational and religious exemptions provided by clauses (1) through (3) of section 110, clause (4) contains a general exception to the exclusive right of public performance that would cover some, though not all, of the same ground as the present "for profit" limitation.

Scope of exemption.—The exemption in clause (4) applies to the same general activities and subject matter as those covered by the "for profit" limitation today: public performances of nondramatic literary and musical works. However, the exemption would be limited to public performances given directly in the presence of an audience whether by means of living performers, the playing of phonorecords, or the operation of a receiving apparatus, and would not include a "transmission to the public." Unlike the clauses (1) through (3) and (5) of section 110, but like clauses (6) through (8), clause (4) applies only to performing rights in certain works, and does not affect the exclusive right to display a work in public.

No profit motive.—In addition to the other conditions specified by the clause, the performance must be "without any purpose of direct or indirect commercial advantage." This provision expressly adopts the principle established by the court decisions construing the "for profit" limitation: that public performances given or sponsored in connection with any commercial or profit-making enterprises are subject to the exclusive rights of the copyright owner even though the public is not charged for seeing or hearing the performance.

No payment for performance.—An important condition for this exemption is that the performance be given "without payment of any fee or other compensation for the performance to any of its performers, promoters, or organizers." The basic purpose of this requirement is to prevent the free use of copyrighted material under the guise of charity where fees or percentatges are paid to performers, promoters, producers, and the like. However, the exemption would not be lost if the performers, directors, or producers of the performance, instead of being paid directly "for the performance," are paid a salary for duties encompassing the performance. Examples are performances by a school orchestra conducted by a music teacher who receives an annual salary, or by a service band whose members and conductors perform as part of their assigned duties and who receive military pay. The committee believes that performances of this type should be exempt, assuming the other conditions in clause (4) are met, and has not adopted the suggestion that the word "salary" be added to the phrase referring to the "payment of any fee or other compensation."

Admission charge.—Assuming that the performance involves no profit motive and no one responsible for it gets paid a fee, it must still meet one of two alternative conditions to be exempt. As specified in subclauses (A) and (B) of section 110(4), these conditions are: (1) that no direct or indirect admission charge is made, or (2) that the net proceeds are "used exclusively for educational, religious, or charitable purposes and not for private financial gain."

Under the second of these conditions, a performance meeting the other conditions of clause (4) would be exempt even if an admission fee is charged, provided any amounts left "after deducting the reasonable costs of producing the performance" are used solely for bona fide educational, religious, or charitable purposes. In cases arising under this second condition and as provided in subclause (B), where there is an admission charge, the copyright owner is given an opportunity to decide whether and under what conditions the copyrighted work should be performed; otherwise, owners could be compelled to make involuntary donations to the fund-raising activities of causes to which they are opposed. The subclause would thus permit copyright owners to prevent public performances of their works under section 110(4)(B) by serving notice of objection, with the reasons therefor, at least seven days in advance.

Mere reception in public

Unlike the first four clauses of section 110, clause (5) is not to any extent a counterpart of the "for profit" limitation of the present statute. It applies to performances and displays of all types of works, and its purpose is to exempt from copyright liability anyone who merely turns on, in a public place, an ordinary radio or television receiving apparatus of a kind commonly sold to members of the public for private use.

The basic rationale of this clause is that the secondary use of the transmission by turning on an ordinary receiver in public is so remote and minimal that no further liability should be imposed. In the vast majority of these cases no royalties are collected today, and the exemption should be made explicit in the statute. This clause has nothing to do with cable television systems and the exemptions would be denied in any case where the audience is charged directly to see or hear the transmission.

On June 17, 1975, the Supreme Court handed down a decision in *Twentieth Century Music Corp.* v. *Aiken*, 95 S.Ct 2040, that raised fundamental questions about the proper interpretation of section 110(5). The defendant, owner and operator of a fast-service food shop in downtown Pittsburgh, had "a radio with outlets to four speakers in the ceiling," which he apparently turned on and left on throughout the business day. Lacking any performing license, he was sued for copyright infringement by two ASCAP members. He lost in the District Court, won a reversal in the Third Circuit Court of Appeals, and finally prevailed, by a margin of 7–2, in the Supreme Court.

The *Aiken* decision is based squarely on the two Supreme Court decisions dealing with cable television. In *Fortnightly Corp.* v. *United Artists*, 392 U.S. 390, and again in *Teleprompter Corp.* v. *CBS*, 415 U.S. 394, the Supreme Court has held that a CATV operator was not "performing" within the meaning of the 1909 statute, when it picked up broadcast signals off the air and retransmitted them to subscribers by cable. The *Aiken* decision extends this interpretation of the scope of the 1909 statute's right of "public performance for profit" to a situation outside the CATV context and, without expressly overruling the decision in *Buck* v. *Jewell-LaSalle Realty Co.*, 283 U.S. 191 (1931), effectively deprives it of much meaning under the present law. For more than forty years the *Jewell-LaSalle* rule was thought to require a business establishment to obtain copyright licenses before it could legally pick up any broadcasts off the air and retransmit them to its guests and patrons. As reinterpreted by the *Aiken* decision, the rule of *Jewell-LaSalle* applies only if the broadcast being retransmitted was itself unlicensed.

The majority of the Supreme Court in the *Aiken* case based its decision on a narrow construction of the word "perform" in the 1909 statute. This basis for the decision is completely overturned by the present bill and its broad definition of "perform" in section 101. The Committee has adopted the language of section 110(5), with an amendment expressly denying the exemption in situations where "the performance or display is further transmitted beyond the place where the receiving apparatus is located"; in doing so, it accepts the traditional, pre-*Aiken*, interpretation of the *Jewell-LaSalle* decision, under which public communication by means other than a home receiving set, or further transmission of a broadcast to the public, is considered an infringing act.

Under the particular fact situation in the *Aiken* case, assuming a small commercial establishment and the use of a home receiver with four ordinary loudspeakers grouped within a relatively narrow cir-

cumference from the set, it is intended that the performances would
be exempt under clause (5). However, the Committee considers this
fact situation to represent the outer limit of the exemption, and believes that the line should be drawn at that point. Thus, the clause
would exempt small commercial establishments whose proprietors
merely bring onto their premises standard radio or television equipment and turn it on for their customers' enjoyment, but it would
impose liability where the proprietor has a commercial "sound system"
installed or converts a standard home receiving apparatus (by agu-
menting it with sophisticated or extensive amplification equipment)
into the equivalent of a commercial sound system. Factors to consider
in particular cases would include the size, physical arrangement, and
noise level of the areas within the establishment where the transmissions are made audible or visible, and the extent to which the receiving
apparatus is altered or augmented for the purpose of improving the
aural or visual quality of the performance for individual members
of the public using those areas.

Agricultural fairs

The Committee also amended clause (6) of section 110 of S. 22 as
adopted by the Senate. As amended, the provision would exempt "performance of a nondramatic musical work by a governmental body or a
nonprofit agricultural or horticultural organization, in the course of
an annual agricultural or horticultural fair or exhibition conducted
by such body or organization." The exemption extends only to the governmental body or nonprofit organization sponsoring the fair; the
amendment makes clear that, while such a body or organization cannot
itself be held vicariously liable for infringements by concessionaires at
the fair, the concessionaires themselves enjoy no exemption under the
clause.

Retail sale of phonorecords

Clause (7) provides that the performance of a nondramatic musical
work or of a sound recording by a vending establishment open to the
public at large without any direct or indirect admission charge, where
the sole purpose of the performance is to promote the retail sale of
copies or phonorecords of the work, is not an infringement of copyright. This exemption applies only if the performance is not transmitted beyond the place where the establishment is located and is within the immediate area where the sale is occurring.

Transmission to handicapped audiences

The new clause (8) of subsection 110, which had been added to S. 22
by the Senate Judiciary Committee when it reported the bill on November 20, 1975, and had been adopted by the Senate on February 19,
1976, was substantially amended by the Committee. Under the amendment, the exemption would apply only to performances of "nondramatic literary works" by means of "a transmission specifically
designed for and primarily directed to" one or the other of two defined
classes of handicapped persons: (1) "blind or other handicapped persons who are unable to read normal printed material as a result of their
handicap" or (2) "deaf or other handicapped persons who are unable
to hear the aural signals accompanying a transmission." Moreover, the
exemption would be applicable only if the performance is "without

any purpose of direct or indirect commercial advantage," and if the transmission takes place through government facilities or through the facilities of a noncommercial educational broadcast station. a radio subcarrier authorization (SCA), or a cable system.

SECTION 117. COMPUTER USES

As the program for general revision of the copyright law has evolved, it has become increasingly apparent that in one major area the problems are not sufficiently developed for a definitive legislative solution. This is the area of computer uses of copyrighted works: the use of a work "in conjunction with automatic systems capable of storing, processing, retrieving, or transferring information." The Commission on New Technological Uses is, among other things, now engaged in making a thorough study of the emerging patterns in this field and it will, on the basis of its findings, recommend definitive copyright provisions to deal with the situation.

Since it would be premature to change existing law on computer uses at present, the purpose of section 117 is to preserve the status quo. It is intended neither to cut off any rights that may now exist, nor to create new rights that might be denied under the Act of 1909 or under common law principles currently applicable.

The provision deals only with the exclusive rights of a copyright owner with respect to computer uses, that is, the bundle of rights specified for other types of uses in section 106 and qualified in sections 107 through 116 and 118. With respect to the copyright-ability of computer programs, the ownership of copyrights in them, the term of protection, and the formal requirements of the remainder of the bill. the new statute would apply.

Under section 117, an action for infringement of a copyrighted work by means of a computer would necessarily be a federal action brought under the new title 17. The court, in deciding the scope of exclusive rights in the computer area, would first need to determine the applicable law, whether State statutory or common law or the Act of 1909. Having determined what law was applicable, its decision would depend upon its interpretation of what that law was on the point on the day before the effective date of the new statute.

General Revision of the Copyright Law
Title 17 of the United States Code
Report No. 94–1733

The managers on the part of the Senate and the House at the conference on the disagreeing votes of the two Houses on the amendment of the House to the bill (S. 22) for the general revision of the Copyright Law, title 17 of the United States Code, and for other purposes, submit the following joint statement to the House and Senate in explanation of the effect of the action agreed upon by the managers, and recommend in the accompanying conference report:

The House amendment struck out all of the Senate bill after the enacting clause and inserted a substitute text.

The Senate recedes from its disagreement to the amendment of the House with an amendment which is a substitute for the Senate bill and the House amendment. The differences between the Senate bill, the House amendment, and the substitute agreed to in conference are noted below, except for clerical corrections, conforming changes made necessary by agreements reached by the conferees, and minor drafting and clarifying changes.

FAIR USE

Senate bill

The Senate bill, in section 107, embodied express statutory recognition of the judicial doctrine that the fair use of a copyrighted work is not an infringement of copyright. It set forth the fair use doctrine, including four criteria for determining its applicability in particular cases, in general terms.

House bill

The House bill amended section 107 in two respects: in the general statement of the fair use doctrine it added a specific reference to multiple copies for classroom use, and it amplified the statement of the first of the criteria to be used in judging fair use (the purpose and character of the use) by referring to the commercial nature or nonprofit educational purpose of the use.

Conference substitute

The conference substitute adopts the House amendments. The conferees accept as part of their understanding of fair use the Guidelines for Classroom Copying in Not-for-Profit Educational Institutions with respect to books and periodicals appearing at pp. 68–70 of the House Report (H. Rept. No. 94–1476, as corrected at p. H 10727 of the Congressional Record for September 21, 1976), and for educational uses of music appearing at pp. 70–71 of the House report, as amended in the statement appearing at p. H 10875 of the Congressional Record of September 22, 1976. The conferees also endorse the statement concerning the meaning of the word "teacher" in the guidelines for books and periodicals, and the application of fair use in the case of use of television programs within the confines of a nonprofit educational institution for the deaf and hearing impaired, both of which appear on p. H 10875 of the Congressional Record of September 22, 1976.

Reproduction by Libraries and Archives

Senate bill

Section 108 of the Senate bill dealt with a variety of situations involving photocopying and other forms of reproduction by libraries and archives. It specified the conditions under which single copies of copyrighted material can be noncommercially reproduced and distributed, but made clear that the privileges of a library or archives under the section do not apply where the reproduction or distribution is of multiple copies or is "systematic." Under subsection (f), the section was not to be construed as limiting the reproduction and distribution, by a library or archive meeting the basic criteria of the section, of a limited number of copies and excerpts of an audiovisual news program.

House bill

The House bill amended section 108 to make clear that, in cases involving interlibrary arrangements for the exchange of photocopies, the activity would not be considered "systematic" as long as the library or archives receiving the reproductions for distribution does not do so in such aggregate quantities as to substitute for a subscription to or purchase of the work. A new subsection (i) directed the Register of Copyrights, by the end of 1982 and at five-year intervals thereafter, to report on the practical success of the section in balancing the various interests, and to make recommendations for any needed changes. With respect to audiovisual news programs, the House bill limited the scope of the distribution privilege confirmed by section 108(f)(3) to cases where the distribution takes the form of a loan.

Conference substitute

The conference substitute adopts the provisions of section 108 as amended by the House bill. In doing so, the conferees have noted two letters dated September 22, 1976, sent respectively to John L. McClellan, Chairman of the Senate Judiciary Subcommittee on Patents, Trademarks, and Copyrights, and to Robert W. Kastenmeier, Chairman of the House Judiciary Subcommittee on Courts, Civil Liberties, and the Administration of Justice. The letters, from the Chairman of the National Commission on New Technological Uses of Copyrighted Works (CONTU), Stanley H. Fuld, transmitted a document consisting of "guidelines interpreting the provision in subsection 108(g)(2) of S. 22, as approved by the House Committee on the Judiciary." Chairman Fuld's letters explain that, following lengthy consultations with the parties concerned, the Commission adopted these guidelines as fair and workable and with the hope that the conferees on S. 22 may find that they merit inclusion in the conference report. The letters add that, although time did not permit securing signatures of the representatives of the principal library organizations or of the organizations representing publishers and authors on these guidelines, the Commission had received oral assurances from these representatives that the guidelines are acceptable to their organizations.

The conference committee understands that the guidelines are not intended as, and cannot be considered, explicit rules or directions governing any and all cases, now or in the future. It is recognized that their purpose is to provide guidance in the most commonly-encountered interlibrary photocopying situations, that they are not intended to be limiting or determinative in themselves or with respect to other situations, and that they deal with an evolving situation that will undoubtedly require their continuous reevaluation and adjustment. With these qualifications, the conference committee agrees that the guidelines are a reasonable interpretation of the proviso of section 108(g)(2) in the most common situations to which they apply today.

The text of the guidelines follows:

PHOTOCOPYING—INTERLIBRARY ARRANGEMENTS

INTRODUCTION

Subsection 108(g)(2) of the bill deals, among other things, with limits on interlibrary arrangements for photocopying. It prohibits systematic photocopying of copyrighted materials but permits interlibrary arrangements "that do not have, as their purpose or effect, that the library or archives receiving such copies or phonorecords for distribution does so in such aggregate quantities as to substitute for a subscription to or purchase of such work."

The National Commission on New Technological Uses of Copyrighted Works offered its good offices to the House and Senate subcommittees in bringing the interested parties together to see if agreement could be reached on what a realistic definition would be of "such aggregate quantities." The Commission consulted with the parties and suggested the interpretation which follows, on which there has been substantial agreement by the principal library, publisher, and author organizations. The Commission considers the guidelines which follow to be a workable and fair interpretation of the intent of the proviso portion of subsection 108(g)(2).

These guidelines are intended to provide guidance in the application of section 108 to the most frequently encountered interlibrary case: a library's obtaining from another library, in lieu of interlibrary loan, copies of articles from relatively recent issues of periodicals—those published within five years prior to the date of the request. The guidelines do not specify what aggregate quantity of copies of an article or articles published in a periodical, the issue date of which is more than five years prior to the date when the request for the copy thereof is made, constitutes a substitute for a subscription to such periodical. The meaning of the proviso to subsection 108(g)(2) in such case is left to future interpretation.

The point has been made that the present practice on interlibrary loans and use of photocopies in lieu of loans may be supplemented or even largely replaced by a system in which one or more agences or institutions, public or private, exist for the specific purpose of providing a central source for photocopies. Of course, these guidelines would not apply to such a situation.

GUIDELINES FOR THE PROVISO OF SUBSECTION 108(G)(2)

1. As used in the proviso of subsection 108(g)(2), the words ". . . such aggregate quantities as to substitute for a subscription to or purchase of such work" shall mean:

(a) with respect to any given periodical (as opposed to any given issue of a periodical), filled requests of a library or archives (a "requesting entity") within any calendar year for a total of six or more copies of an article or articles published in such periodical within five years prior to the date of the request. These guidelines specifically shall not apply, directly or indirectly, to any request of a requesting entity for a copy or copies of an article or articles published in any issue of a periodical, the publication date of which is more than five years prior to the date when the request is made. These guidelines do not define the meaning, with respect to such a request, of ". . . such aggregate quantities as to substitute for a subscription to [such periodical]".

(b) With respect to any other material described in subsection 108(d), (including fiction and poetry), filled requests of a requesting entity within any calendar year for a total of six or more copies or phonorecords of or from any given work (including a collective work) during the entire period when such material shall be protected by copyright.

2. In the event that a requesting entity—

(a) shall have in force or shall have entered an order for a subscription to a periodical, or

(b) has within its collection, or shall have entered an order for, a copy or phonorecord of any other copyrighted work, material from either category of which it desires to obtain by copy from another library or archives (the "supplying entity"), because the material to be copied is not reasonably available for use by the requesting entity itself, then the fulfillment of such request shall be treated as though the requesting entity made such copy from its own collection. A library or archives may request a copy or phonorecord from a supplying entity only under those circumstances where the requesting entity would have been able, under the other provisions of section 108, to supply such copy from materials in its own collection.

3. No request for a copy or phonorecord of any material to which these guidelines apply may be fulfilled by the supplying entity unless such request is accompanied by a representation by the requesting entity that the request was made in conformity with these guidelines.

4. The requesting entity shall maintain records of all requests made by it for copies or phonorecords of any materials to which these guidelines apply and shall maintain records of the fulfillment of such requests, which records shall be retained until the end of the third

complete calendar year after the end of the calendar year in which the respective request shall have been made.

5. As part of the review provided for in subsection 108(i), these guidelines shall be reviewed not later than five years from the effective date of this bill.

The conference committee is aware that an issue has arisen as to the meaning of the phrase "audiovisual news program" in section 108 (f)(3). The conferees believe that, under the provision as adopted in the conference substitute, a library or archives qualifying under section 108(a) would be free, without regard to the archival activities of the Library of Congress or any other organization, to reproduce, on videotape or any other medium of fixation or reproduction, local, regional, or network newscasts, interviews concerning current news events, and on-the-spot coverage of news events, and to distribute a limited number of reproductions of such a program on a loan basis.

Another point of interpretation involves the meaning of "indirect commercial advantage," as used in section 108(a)(1), in the case of libraries or archival collections within industrial, profit-making, or proprietary institutions. As long as the library or archives meets the criteria in section 108(a) and the other requirements of the section, including the prohibitions against multiple and systematic copying in subsection (g), the conferees consider that the isolated, spontaneous making of single photocopies by a library or archives in a for-profit organization without any commercial motivation, or participation by such a library or archives in interlibrary arrangements, would come within the scope of section 108.

LIMITATIONS ON RIGHTS OF PERFORMANCE AND DISPLAY

Senate bill

Section 110 of the Senate bill set forth eight specific exceptions to the exclusive rights to perform and display copyrighted works. The first four exceptions were roughly the equivalent of the "for profit" limitations on performing rights under the present law. Section 110(5) provided an exemption for public communication of a transmission received on an ordinary receiving set unless a direct charge is made or the transmission "is further transmitted to the public." Section 110(6) exempted performances of nondramatic music at nonprofit annual agricultural or horticultural fairs, and section 110(7) dealt with performances in connection with the retail sale of copies or records of musical works. Clause (8) of section 110 provided an exemption for performances of literary works "in the course of a broadcast service specifically designed for broadcast on noncommercial educational radio and television stations to a print or aural handicapped audience," but did not contain, in section 112 or elsewhere, a provision allowing the making of copies or phonorecords for the purpose of such broadcasts to the blind or deaf.

House bill

The House bill amended the last four clauses of section 110. With respect to clause (5), it made the exemption inapplicable to cases where there is a further transmission "beyond the place where the receiving apparatus is located." Clause (6) was amended to make the exemption applicable only to the governmental body or nonprofit organization sponsoring the fair, and the amendment of clause (7) was merely for purposes of clarification. The House bill amended clause (8) by limiting its application to nondramatic literary works, by clarifying the audiences to which the transmissions are directed, and by more narrowly defining the types of nonprofit transmissions within the exemptions. The House bill also added a new subsection (d) to section 112 to permit the making of ten recordings of performances exempted under section 110(8), their retention for an unlimited period, and their exchange with other nonprofit organizations.

Conference substitute

The conference substitute adopts the House amendments of clauses (6), (7), and (8) of section 110, and of section 112. It adds a new clause (9) to section 110 exempting nonprofit performances of dramatic works transmitted to audiences of the blind by radio subcarrier authorization, but only for a single performance of a dramatic work published at least ten years earlier.

With respect to section 110(5), the conference substitute conforms to the language in the Senate bill. It is the intent of the conferees that a small commercial establishment of the type involved in *Twentieth Century Music Corp.* v. *Aiken*, 422 U.S. 151 (1975), which merely augmented a home-type receiver and which was not of sufficient size to justify, as a practical matter, a subscription to a commercial background music service, would be exempt. However, where the public communication was by means of something other than a home-type receiving apparatus, or where the establishment actually makes a further transmission to the public, the exemption would not apply.

ROBERT W. KASTENMEIER,
GEORGE E. DANIELSON,
ROBERT F. DRINAN,
HERMAN BADILLO,
EDWARD W. PATTISON,
TOM RAILSBACK,
CHARLES E. WIGGINS,
Managers on the Part of the House.

JOHN L. MCCLELLAN,
PHILIP A. HART,
QUENTIN N. BURDICK,
HUGH SCOTT,
HIRAM L. FONG,
Managers on the Part of the Senate.

STATEMENT OF BARBARA RINGER
REGISTER OF COPYRIGHTS
ON H.R. 2223
A BILL FOR GENERAL REVISION OF THE COPYRIGHT LAW

Before the Subcommittee on Courts, Civil Liberties
and Administration of Justice
Committee on the Judiciary
House of Representatives
94th Congress, First Session
October 2, 1975

Mr. Chairman, I am Barbara Ringer, Register of
Copyrights in the Copyright Office of the Library of
Congress. On May 7, the first day of your hearings,
I appeared as one of the opening witnesses on H.R. 2223.
My duty then, as I saw it, was to try to put the bill
in historical perspective, to pinpoint the major issues
remaining to be settled, and to answer your initial
questions about the substantive content and status of
the legislation.

I am returning on the fourteenth day of these
hearings, in response to your letter of September 9, 1975
asking me to "make the final presentation of testimony
reflecting your views with respect to what the hearings
reveal and what changes if any in the bill seem
indicated." I am greatly honored by this request, and I
will do my utmost to fulfill it in a way that will help
the Committee complete the formidable task now
confronting it.

During my testimony on May 7, I sought to
identify what I considered the main issues remaining
after a decade of sporadic legislative consideration of
the general revision bill. The seven principle issues,
more or less in the order of importance as I saw them
then, were:

1) Cable television

2) Library photocopying

3) Fair use and reproduction for educational and scholarly purposes

4) Public and non-profit broadcasting

5) Jukebox

6) Mechanical royalty for use of music in sound recordings

7) Royalty for performance of recordings

Related to several of these issues was the chapter of the bill establishing a Copyright Royalty Tribunal, which also presents some problems on its own. I also mentioned the likelihood of questions arising in connection with the manufacturing clause and with various concerns of graphic artists and designers.

Looking back, I think that most of the testimony you heard during the hearings falls somewhere under one or another of these headings. However, under each one of these big issues there are varying numbers of interrelated sub-issues, and none of them can be approached in isolation. There is a figure in the carpet, but it is hard to find amid all the intricate strands and colors and patterns that go to make it up. I am not going to try to oversimplify something that is inherently complex, but I am going to try to organize the mass of arguments and proposals that have been put forward at these hearings in a way that will make them comprehensible in themselves and as part of a larger whole.

With my testimony on May 7, I submitted seventeen briefing papers covering various aspects of the bill. I also mentioned that I was preparing a Second Supplementary Report of the Register of Copyrights on General Revision, which I hoped to have finished in time for the Subcommittee to be able to use it when it starts its mark-up. I have worked on this report off and on for most of the summer, seeking to incorporate

into it everything that has been raised in these hearings
the changes made by the Senate Subcommittee when it
reported the bill in June, and a very few, mainly
technical, points that I felt I should raise
independently since no one else had mentioned them.

This Supplementary Report is nearing completion
in draft form, and I plan to present it to the Librarian
of Congress for submission to Chairman Rodino of the
House Judiciary Committee and Chairman Eastland of the
Senate Judiciary Committee as soon as possible. In its
final form the report will consist of about fifteen
chapters organized by subject matter in roughly the same
order as the bill. At the beginning of each chapter the
report will identify the sections involved and the
issues remaining to be decided. The body of each chapter will, in varying ways depending upon the nature of
the problem, review the background and content of the
provisions of the bill in question and explain the
nature of the issues raised and the arguments with
respect to them.

The last section in each chapter will consist
of comments and recommendations put forward by me as
Register of Copyrights. In some cases I will put
forward alternatives or suggested possibilities for
methods of compromising disputed issues. My purpose
here is not to add one more burden to the already heavy
load of proposals you need to consider, but to help
you to find ways of deciding among the disputed
proposals and debated points you already have before
you. I have opinions on some of the matters before you
and I will be honest about expressing them when need be
but I have no axes to grind.

You, the members of this Subcommittee, are the only
decision-makers in this room. My aim is not to
influence you; it is to help you, in any way I can
to do your legislative job.

During my scheduled two days of testimony I
will first seek to give you an overview of the bill
and to show how its many parts fit together. I will
then start with Chapter 1 of the new title 17 of the
U.S. Code, as revised by the bill, and proceed by

subject matter through to the end. I am attaching
to this statement the drafts of the first five
chapters of the Supplementary Report, which I will
use as the focal point of my testimony. Next week I
will do my best to give you the draft text of the
remaining chapters.

CHAPTER I

SUBJECT MATTER OF COPYRIGHT

Sections Considered:

> #101 - Definitions ("literary works";
>   "pictorial, graphic and
>   sculptural works"; "work of the
>   United States Government")
>
> #102 - Subject matter of copyright:
>   In general
>
> #104 - Subject matter of copyright:
>   National origin
>
> #105 - Subject matter of copyright:
>   United States Government works

Issues:

> 1. Does the language of sections 101
>   and 102 constitute a satisfactory
>   statement of Congressional intention
>   with respect to federal copyright
>   protection for:
>
>   a) Computer programs?
>
>   b) Type face designs?
>
>   c) Architectural works?

2. Should copyright under section 104
    be extended to published works of
    stateless persons regardless of
    domicile?

3. Should the bill deal with questions
    of expropriation as now proposed in
    section 104(c)?

4. Is the prohibition against copyright
    in U.S. Government works under section
    105 too broad or narrow?

A. DISCUSSION OF IDEAS

1. *SCOPE OF SECTION 102*

a. *In general*

Section 102, the basic provision laying out
what can be copyrighted under the bill, has undergone
only one major change since 1967. This is the
addition of a new subsection (b), reading:

> (b) In no case does copyright
> for an original work of author-
> ship extend to any idea, plan,
> procedure, process, system, method
> of operation, concept, principle,
> or discovery, regardless of the
> form in which it is described,
> explained, illustrated, or embodied
> in such work.

As explained in the 1974 Senate report, the
purpose of this added language was not to enlarge or
contract the scope of copyright protection under the
present law, but rather "to re-state, in the context
of the new single Federal system of copyright, that

the basic dichotomy between expression and idea
remains unchanged." The new provision had been
added in response to the great debate over computers
and copyright, and is intended to disclaim any
intention to protect a programmer's algorithms
under the bill. Beyond this the principle of a
distinction between idea and expression is a fundamental one in traditional copyright law, and extends
to practically all fields of creative endeavor.

The 1974 Senate report also deleted a significant footnote from the 1967 House report, which
has considerable bearing on this question. The
text in the body of the 1967 report, which is unchanged in the 1974 report, reads:

> Although the coverage of the present
> statute is very broad, and would be
> broadened further (under the revsion
> bill)..., there are unquestionably
> other areas of existing subject
> matter that this bill does not propose
> to protect but that future Congresses
> may want to.

The footnote to this statement in the 1967 House
report reads as follows:

> Without implying that they would be
> wholly without protection under one
> or another of the seven categories
> listed in sec. 102, or that they are
> necessarily the "writing" of
> "authors" in the constitutional
> sense, we cite the following as
> examples. These are areas of subject
> matter now on the fringes of
> literary property but not intended,
> solely as such, to come within the
> scope of the bill: typography;
> unfixed performances or broadcast
> emissions; blank forms and calculating
> devices; titles, slogans, and similar
> short expressions; certain three-

> dimensional industrial designs;
> interior decoration; ideas, plans,
> methods, systems, mathematical
> principles; formats and synopses of
> television series and the like;
> color schemes; news and factual
> information considered apart from
> its compilation or expression. Many
> of these kinds of works can be
> clothed in or combined with copy-
> rightable subject matter and thus
> achieve a degree of protection under
> the bill, but any protection for
> them as separate copyrightable works
> is not here intended and will
> require action by a future Congress.

The deletion of this footnote has
acquired even greater significance in light of
the Supreme Court's decision in *Goldstein v.
California* 412 U.S. 546 (1973).

The full import of that decision is subject to debate
but it apparently stands for the proposition that
Federal pre-emption of State copyright protection is
statutory and not consitutional. Thus, a clear-cut
Congressional refusal to protect a certain type of
work at all could be held to mean that the States are
free to give the same kind of work unlimited
protection. This point will be discussed further in
relation to the pre-emption provision, section 301 of
the bill.

b.   *Computer Programs*

Although they are not mentioned as copyrightable
subject matter in section 102 and are not referred to
explicitly in the definition of "literary works" in
section 101, a careful reading of the bill, together
with the 1967 and, especially, the 1974 reports, make
clear an intention to include computer programs or
"software" within the subject matter of copyright.
The definition of "literary works" refers to works
expressed in "words, numbers, or other verbal or

numerical symbols or indicia. This language is
certainly broad enough to cover software, even though
the embodiments mentioned as examples ("books,
periodicals, manuscripts, phono-records or film")
seem limited when it comes to computer programs.
However, the 1974 Senate report expressly limits the
scope of protection to the "writing" expressing the
programmer's ideas, as distinguished from the ideas,
methodology or processes he devises. It states:
"Section 102(b) is intended, among other things, to
make clear that the expression adopted by the
programmer is the copyrightable element in a
computer program are not within the scope of the
copyright law."

     The protection for computer software under
patent, copyright, and trade secret law, or other
theories, has become a burning national and international issue, particularly among members of the
industrial property bar.

Nearly all commentators recognize that
traditional copyright principles are inadequate for
the kind of protection software owners are seeking,
and some of them deplore the failure of the copyright
revision bill to extend rights to original algorithms
and methodology. The bill and the 1974 report have
also been criticized for not making Congressional
intentions clearer, especially since the mandate of
the newly-created National Commission on New
Technological Uses of Copyrighted Works does not
include the question of software protection.

B. COMMENTS AND RECOMMENDATIONS

1. *SCOPE OF SECTION 102*

a. *In general*

     The Copyright Office considers the language and
content of section 102, and the relevant definitions
in section 101, basically satisfactory. The thrust
of the provision, together with the explanatory

material in the report, is not to exhaust completely
the subject matter capable of copyright protection
under the Constitution, leaving it to future
Congresses to expand the subject matter as they see
fit. However, it may be important to express more
clearly, in the report, Congress's intentions with
respect to pre-emption of State common law or statutory
protection. Since section 301 pre-empts only what is
covered by section 102, and since the Supreme Court's
Goldstein decision held that pre-emption is statutory
and not constitutional, the States would presumably
be free to give unlimited protection to any subject
matter outside the scope of section 102. This may be
a desirable result, but Congress should consider the
consequences before adopting it.

b. *Computer Programs*

The Copyright Office favors the result
achieved in the bill: offering copyright protection
to the programmer's original expression of his ideas,
but not to the ideas themselves. It may well be that
the algorithms and methodology embodied in a program
are worthy of protection under other theories of law,
but this is for further judicial or legislative
consideration. The definition of "literary works"
and the explanation in the report could be revised in
minor ways to make the Congressional intention
clearer.

CHAPTER II

FAIR USE AND REPRODUCTION
FOR EDUCATIONAL AND SCHOLARLY PURPOSES

Sections Considered:

#106 - Exclusive rights in copyrighted
works

#107 - Limitations on exclusive rights:
Fair use

#109 - Limitations on exclusive rights:
Effect of transfer of particular
copy or phono-record

#502 - Remedies for infringement:
Injunctions

#504 - Remedies for infringement:
Damages and profits

Issues:

With respect to the reproduction and
distribution of copyrighted works in connection
with teaching and related educational activities,
should the approach of the 1975 bill be changed in
any of the following respects:

a) The fair use provision itself
(#107)?

b) The interpretation of the fair
use provision in the legislative
report?

c) The establishment of evidentiary
presumptions with respect to fair
use?

d) The addition of a specific
exemption for teaching, scholarship, and research?

e) The remedies for copyright
infringement?

f) The re-sale of used textbooks?

g) The addition of a provision
recognizing the special problems
of newsletters?

A. DISCUSSION OF ISSUES

1. SUBSTANTIVE ARGUMENTS

No issue arising under the general revision bill has been hashed over more thoroughly than the extent to which educators can reproduce and distribute copyrighted works outside of copyright control.

The 1973 hearings on this question in the Senate, and the 1975 hearings in the House, produced some changes in position but no new arguments on the substantive issues. These arguments can be summarized very briefly as follows:

    a. Arguments of educational organizations:

    1. It is important that the doctrine of fair use be recognized in the statute, and that its applicability to reproduction for educational and scholarly purposes be made as clear as possible in the statute and report.

    2. A provision on fair use alone is not sufficient to answer the needs of education, since teachers need more certainty about what they can and cannot do than the unpredictable doctrine of fair use can provide.

    3. Teachers actually create a market for authors and publishers, and are not interested in the kind of mass copying that damages copyright owners.

    4. Teachers must be enabled to make creative use of all of the resources available to them in the classroom to supplement textbooks and to seize the "teachable moment," by reproducing a variety of copyrighted materials, such as contemporaneous reports and analyses,

isolated poems, stories, essays, etc., for purposes of emphasis, illustration or bringing a lesson up to date.

5. The "not-for-profit" principle of present law should be applied to restricted educational copying that will not hurt the publishing industry and that will further American education, which is the paramount public interest.

6. Subjecting the use of modern teaching tools to requirements for advance clearance and payment of fees will stifle originality in teaching and inhibit the use of the teacher's imagination and ingenuity.

7. Various proposals for voluntary or compulsory licensing are too complicated and burdensome to be acceptable to teachers, who would be deterred from using valuable works by the necessity for paperwork and payments. Any blanket scheme would imply payment for all uses, even those that would be considered free under the doctrine of fair use.

b. *Arguments of authors and publishers*

1. The doctrine of fair use should be confirmed in the stature, but by its nature it is an equitable rule of reason that must be flexible to avoid a statutory freezing of unintended results. Authors and publishers have no desire to oppress teachers or to stop minor or incidental reproduction of the sort that is

undoubtedly fair use under the
present law; their concern is
with the potential danger of
massive, unreasonable abuse.

2.   Arguments that, since reproductions
     for educational and scholarly
     purposes have become increasingly
     easy and cheap, they should be made
     legal, are unreasonable and un-
     tenable.

3.   The present "for profit"
     limitation has nothing whatever
     to do with copying. The argument
     that education should be exempt
     because it does not make a profit
     overlooks the fact that uncompen-
     sated educational uses, particularly
     in the textbook, reference book and
     scientific publishing areas, result
     in direct and serious loss to copy-
     right owners, and destroy the
     incentives for authorship and
     publication. Education is the text
     -book publisher's only market, and
     the main source of income of many
     authors.

4.   Reproducing devices in educational
     establishments have proliferated
     tremendously, and unit costs
     continue to decrease. It is
     becoming easier and cheaper to make
     a copy than to buy one. Uninhibited
     reproduction of copyrighted material
     by a single educator, taken alone,
     might not do measurable damage to a
     particular author or publisher, but
     uninhibited reproduction of copy-
     righted material by all educators
     and educational establishments will
     literally destroy some important
     forms of authorship and publishing.

5. Workable voluntary licensing systems
    that would place no unwarranted
    budgetary or administrative burdens
    on copyright owners, and that would
    fully recognize the doctrine of fair
    use, are already being worked out,
    and should be expanded and encouraged
    by all concerned.

2. *LEGISLATIVE HISTORY OF SECTION 107*

The 1961 Register's Report concluded that
"the doctrine of fair use is such an important
limitation on the rights of copyright owners, and
occasions to apply that doctrine arise so frequently
that we believe the statute should mention it and
indicate its general scope." This recommendation
was coupled with a proposal for a specific provision
dealing with library photocopying. When these
recommendations were translated into proposals for
statutory language in the 1963 preliminary draft,
the somewhat favorable reaction to the general fair
use provision was drowned out by the strenuous
opposition to the library photocopying section, which
was attacked from all sides. The latter was thus
dropped from the 1964 bill, and attention then focused
on the text of the general fair use provision. The
wording of this provision was closely similar to,
though not identical with, the present text of section
107.

A major part of the discussions of the problem
of reproductions for educational purposes centered on
the wording of the fair use provision, which was
criticized by both sides for quite different reasons.
As stated in the 1965 Supplementary Report of the
Register, it appeared impossible to reach agreement on
a general statement expressing the scope of the fair
use doctrine, and therefore "we decided with some
regret to reduce the fair use section to its barest
essentials." Even in this form, the Supplementary
Report said, section 107 "serves a real purpose and
should be incorporated in the statute":

> Notwithstanding the provisions of
> section 106, the fair use of a copy-
> righted work is not an infringement
> of copyright.

In 1965 there were extensive hearings on this
issue in both Houses.

The 1966 and 1967 House Judiciary Committee reports
noted that the "bare statement" approach had attracted
some support, in preference to an expended definition
of fair use that "could freeze the concept and open the
door to massive, unreasonable abuses." However, it
added that, on the other side, "a number of witnesses
representing various educational and scholarly
organizations criticized the provision as vague and
nebulous, and stressed the need of teachers and scholars
to be certain whether what they were doing constituted
fair use or infringement."

In addition to seeking an expanded statement
of the doctrine of fair use at the 1965 hearings, the
representatives of educators and scholars urged
adoption of an entirely new section specifically
exempting certain non-profit educational uses from
copyright liability. On June 2 and 8, 1966, two
"summit meetings" on "fair use and educational and
scholarly reproductions" were held in the Library of
Congress under the chairmanship of Herbert Fuchs,
then as now Counsel of the House Subcommittee. Every
aspect of the problem was considered; although, as
noted in the 1966 and 1967 reports, no final agreements
were reached, there was evident progress toward
compromise solutions, including the precise wording of
section 107.

The 1967 bill as reported contained a revised
fair use provision, which in its exact language has
remained unchanged up to and including the 1975 bill.
There have been no proposals for amendment of the
wording of section 107 during the most recent hearings.
Although section 107 must, of course, be considered in
the context of the entire problem of educational uses,
the existence of a statutory provision on fair use and

the present language of section 107 both appear to be generally acceptable.

3.   INTERPRETATION OF FAIR USE IN COMMITTEES' REPORTS AND PROPOSALS FOR EDUCATIONAL EXEMPTION

a.   The 1966 report

Much of the June 1966 "summit meetings" consisted of an exploration of actual situations of educational copying and whether or not particular practices should be considered fair use or copyright infringement. A fair amount of agreement was reached in principle on the conditions under which a particular educational practice could be regarded as fair use for copyright purposes.

When it came to mark up of the bill in 1966, the House Subcommittee reviewed not only the testimony and submissions at the 1965 hearings but also the minutes of the June 1966 "summit meetings" reflecting the discussions on specific points. It reached what was, in effect, a compromise consisting of: (1) a provision recognizing the doctrine of fair use as a limitation on the rights of a copyright owner, with statutory language specifically mentioning teaching and intended to offer "some guidance to users in determining when the principles of the doctrine apply"; (2) an amendment to section 504 limiting the liability of teachers who are found to have exceeded the bounds of fair use in good faith; and (3) most important, an extensive section in the Committee report, headed "Intention of the committee," discussing the applicability of the doctrine of fair use to educational photocopying in considerable detail. The purpose of this interpretative passage was to "provide educators with the basis for establishing workable practices and policies" under the fair use doctrine, but without freezing application of the doctrine in the form of outright educational exemptions.

The following excerpt from the House Judiciary Committee reports of 1966 and 1967 indicates the purpose to be achieved by this approach:

... the committee does not favor a
statutory provision specifying educational
uses of copyrighted material that would be
free from copyright control. On the other
hand, the doctrine of fair use, as properly applied, is broad enough to permit
reasonable educational use, and education
has something to gain in the enactment of
a bill that clarifies what may now be a
problematical situation. The committee
sympathizes with the argument that a
teacher should not be prevented by
uncertainty from doing things that he is
legally entitled to do and that improve
the quality of his teaching. It is there
-fore important that some ground rules be
provided for the application of fair use
in particular situations.

b. *The 1967 Senate hearings*

On March 16, 1967, Dr. Harold E. Wigren, on
behalf of an ad hoc committee representing 34
educational institutions and organizations, testified
before the Senate Judiciary Subcommittee on the revised
bill as reported by the House Judiciary Committee on
October 12, 1966. Dr. Wigren's testimony indicated
that, although the groups he represented still preferred
a specific exemption for educational uses, they were
willing to accept the approach reflected in the 1966
House bill and report, subject to certain conditions
and reservations. He made clear that the Ad Hoc
Committee regarded the bill and report "as one piece,"
and stated:

The Ad Hoc Committee regards Section
107 -- the fair use provision of the Bill
and the House Committee Report -- as a
marked improvement for classroom teachers
over the previous draft.

... We are grateful that the House
Committee Report enumerated at some
length examples of reproductions by

teachers for classroom purposes of
single and multiple copying of
materials in the course of teaching
which would be considered as 'fair'
under the provisions of Section 107.
This is in keeping with certain
agreements we reached with the
publishers and authors last June at
the office of the Register of Copyrights.

In our original testimony before
your committee, you will recall we
had requested a statutory limited
copying exemption for education -- a
new Section III -- which we believed
then, and we still believe, provides
the simplest and easiest way to give
the teacher the certainty he needs
in his use of materials. As a result
of the summit conferences held with
the publishing industry representatives at the Register's office, the
present wording of Section 107 was
agreed upon by both groups as a
compromise position, and we are willing to abide by this agreement as a
means of reaching an accommodation
between the two opposing positions.
In so doing, however, we recognize
that we have sacrificed a general
exemption for certain much-needed
educational uses of materials and
have substituted in its stead a
categorical exemption for specific
types of uses which are spelled out
in the House Report.
We must emphasize that our
acceptance of this compromise is
dependent upon retention in the bill
of the words "including its reproduction in copies or phono-records"
and of the full listing of examples
of reproductions which would be

considered "fair" now included in
the Report. Anything less than this
will be totally unacceptable to the
Ad Hoc Committee.

Dr. Wigren went on to urge that the limitation
on the liability of teachers in section 504 be
extended to other educators, and that the bill be
amended with respect to educational broadcasting,
computer uses, and the duration of copyright protection. The Ad Hoc Committee accepted the
language of section 107, but urged two changes in the
commentary in the House report. The first dealt with
fair use in respect to educational broadcasting and
computer uses. The second was described as follows:

> Section 107 sets forth four criteria
> by which teachers may judge whether a
> given use of a work is a fair use.
> The Ad Hoc Committee is greatly con-
> cerned about Criterion No. 4 in this
> section which is "the effect of the
> use on the potential market for or
> value of the work." The House
> Committee Report goes on to explain
> this criterion by stating "where the
> unauthorized copying displaces what
> realistically might have be a sale,
> *no matter how minor the amount of
> money involved,* the interests of the
> copyright owner need protection."
> There are already those who argue
> that *any* given use of a copyrighted
> work would in effect be ruled out by
> this last criterion, particularly
> when followed by the clause "no
> matter how minor the amount of
> money involved." We implore the
> Senate, at the very least, to
> strike this explanation from the
> Report. It will cause appre-
> hension and concern on the part
> of teachers nationwide.

c. *The 1973 Senate hearings*

After a long hiatus, further hearings on this issue were held before the Senate Judiciary Sub-Committee in August, 1973 -- after the ruling by Commissioner Davis of the U.S. Court of Claims in favor of the copyright owner in *Williams & Wilkins, Inc. v. United States*, the famous case involving library photocopying, but before the 4-3 reversal of that ruling by the full Court of Claims and the in-conclusive result in the Supreme Court. The Ad Hoc Committee of Educational Institutions and Organizations, still under the chairmanship of Dr. Wigren put forward the following proposal for specific exemptions covering teaching, scholarship and research:

Section ... *limitations on exclusive rights:*
            Reproduction for teaching,
            scholarship and research

Notwithstanding other provisions of this Act, nonprofit use of a portion of a copyrighted work for noncommercial teaching, scholarship or research is not an infringement of copyright.

For purposes of this section,

(1) "use" shall mean reproduction, copying and recording; storage and retrieval by automatic systems capable of storing, processing, retrieving, or transferring information or in conjunction with any similar device, machine or process;

(2) "portion shall mean brief exerpts (which are not substantial in length in proportion to their source) from certain copyrighted works, except that it shall also include

(a) the whole of short literary,
    pictorial and graphic works

(b) entire works reproduced for
    storage in automatic systems
    capable of storing, processing
    retrieving, or transferring
    information or in conjunction
    with any similar device, machine
    or process, *provided* that

    i) a method of recording
       retrieval of the stored
       information is established
       at the time of reproduction
       for storage, and

    ii) the rules otherwise
       applicable under law to
       copyrighted works shall
       apply to information re-
       trieved from such systems;

(c) recording and retransmission of
    broadcasts within five school
    days after the recorded broadcast;
    provided that such recording is
    immediately destroyed after such
    retransmission is limited to
    immediate viewing in schools and
    colleges.

Provided that "portion" shall not include
works which are

(a) originally consumable upon use, such
    as work-book exercises, problems, or
    standardized tests and the answer
    sheets for such tests;

(b) used for the purpose of compilation
    within the provisions of Section
    103(a).

Dr. Wigren explained this shift in position as follows:

>First, we would like to point out to the
>Subcommittee the rationale for this limited
>educational exemption. During the past
>years, the Ad Hoc Committee has made every
>effort to maintain contact and dialogue
>with publishers, authors, and materials
>producers to reach some type of accommo-
>dation which would take into account the
>interests of all parties concerned in the
>revision effort in order to strike a fair
>balance between the rights of proprietors
>and the rights of consumers/users of
>materials.
>
>Our discussions, however, have been
>frustrated by the impact of the recent
>ruling by Commissioner Davis of the U.S.
>Court of Claims in favor of *Williams &
>Wilkins*, in its copyright infringement
>suit against the National Library of
>Medicine. ... The Commissioner's ruling
>has caused considerable consternation
>and alarm within the educational community
>not only because of its effect on libraries
>but also because it would undercut the
>accepted and traditional meaning of "fair
>use" for teachers. The language and
>rationale are just as applicable against
>teachers and schools as against libraries.
>Because the *Williams & Wilkins* decision
>proves the unreliability of "fair use"
>for schools and libraries, the Ad Hoc
>Committee urges Congress to adopt the
>concept of a limited educational
>exemption which would neutralize the
>harmful effect of the Commissioner's
>opinion on both schools and libraries
>and at the same time not be detrimental
>to publishers or producers of materials.
>In light of *Williams & Wilkins*, our
>request for limited educational exemption
>is submitted to this committee not in

lieu of "fair use" but in addition to
"fair use" in the statute.

At the end of his statement, however, Dr. Wigren set
forth the following fall-back position:

> In the event that this Subcommittee
> cannot grant our request, the Ad Hoc
> Committee will be unable to support the
> proposed legislation (S. 1361) unless it
> is changed in two major respects:
> (1) unless the bill specifically provides
> adherence to the concepts and meanings
> of "fair use" which were written into
> House Report No. 83, 90th Congress, as
> amended in the following respects:
>
>> (a) the elimination of the
>> expression "no matter how
>> minor" in reference to the
>> fourth criterion
>
>> (b) the authorization for classroom
>> purposes for limited multiple
>> copying of short whole works,
>> such as poems, articles,
>> stories and essays
>
>> (c) the application of the full
>> impact of "fair use" to
>> instructional television
>
> and (2) unless the decision of the
> Commissioner in the *Williams & Wilkins*
> case is specifically rejected to the
> extent in which it differs from that
> House Report, as amended.

The 1973 response of authors, publishers,
educational media producers, and representatives of
the information industry was one of concerted opposition
to the new proposal for an educational exemption, and
of support for the approach adopted by the House of
Representatives in 1967.

On July 3, 1974 the Senate Judiciary Committee
reported the revision bill with no change in section
107; the 1974 Senate report retained much of the interpretative language of the 1966 and 1967 House reports,
but with some deletions, additions and revisions. The
proposed educational exemption was not adopted.
During the Senate debates preceding passage of the
revision bill on September 9, 1974, there was no
discussion of this issue.

   d. *The 1975 House hearings*

The draft proposal for an educational exemption
was put forward by the presentative of the National
Education Association during the Ad Hoc Committee's
presentation at the 1975 House Subcommittee hearings,
and its text was identical to that of the 1973 version
except for two words of no real significance. The
opposition from authors and other copyright owners
remained just as strong, and united support was
reconfirmed for the pending bill and the commentary in
the legislative reports.

The witnesses pointed to the extremely broad
language of the proposed amendment and the conflict
between its provisions dealing with computer uses
and section 107 of the bill, which is intended to
preserve the status quo in that field pending the
report of the newly-created National Commission on
New Technological Uses of Copyrighted Works (CONTU).
The representative of the Information Industry
Association submitted a statement indicating that,
if serious consideration were to be given to the
proposed educational exemption, it would be
important to consider rather sweeping proposals
from the IIA to create new rights in connection
with the new information technologies.

Although the thrust of the testimony from the
various witnesses representing educational
organizations belonging to the Ad Hoc Committee was
in the same direction, there were clearly some
differences in emphasis if not in substance. The
witness representing the NEA came closest to re-

stating the Ad Hoc Committee's 1973 position; in
submitting the proposed amendment he said:

> In summary, the NEA will not be able
> to support a bill unless it --
>
> > (a) retains and clarifies an
> > overall not-for-profit
> > concept for educational,
> > scholarly, and research uses
> > and copying, whether couched
> > as a limited educational
> > exemption or in some other
> > suitable comprehensive form;
> >
> > (b) clarifies the meaning of fair
> > use as applied to teachers
> > and learners;
> >
> > (c) shift the burden of proof
> > from the teacher to the
> > alleger of the infringement.
>
> NEA therefore urges the adoption of
> language by this committee that
> encompasses the above-stated concepts
> and makes copyright reform meaningful
> for the teachers, scholars, research-
> ers, authors and publishers who create
> transmit, and perpetuate our heritage
> for future generations.

The witness representing the Association of American
Law Schools, the American Association of University
Professors, and the American Council on Education
did not refer to the proposed new section specifying
educational exemptions, but took a somewhat different
tack. Among other things, he said at various points
in his statement:

> We strongly urge that the doctrine of
> fair use be preserved and given formal
> recognition by Congress, both by

express statutory provision and by
appropriate language in the final
Committee report.

... Given the paucity of decided cases
in this area, it is necessary to
recognize the difficulty of leaving
the resolution of this important
problem solely to the limited framework of existing decisions. We urge,
therefore, the enactment of #107, as
it now appears in H.R. 2223, ... as
supported by adequate legislative
history.

We thus advocate that the House Report
which accompanies this measure, be
drafted to include an express reference to the effect that the doctrine of
fair use would be applicable to copyrighted materials which might
subsequently be designated as compensible
if photocopied for other uses. By
clearly establishing that teaching
and research uses are significant
to the doctrine of fair use,
subsequent uncertainty as to the
treatment of library materials
which might require compensation if
copied for other purposes, would be
avoided.

The representative of the Association for
Educational Communications and Technology (AECT)
likewise made no reference to the proposed
exemption, but endorsed "the criteria to be used
in the determination of 'fair use' as contained
in Section 107 of the proposed bill." He also
recommended that the doctrine of fair use "should
apply equally to the classroom teacher and the
media professional -- including specialists in
audiovisual and library resources." He added:

Media personnel are becoming
increasingly important members
of educational planning teams
and must have the assurance that
they may assist classroom teachers
in the selection of daily instructional materials as well as with
long range curriculum development.
Classroom teachers do not always
operate "individually and at
(their) own volition." The fact
that the media professional makes
use of advance planning and has
knowledge aforethought of the
materials he prepares for the
teacher should not invalidate the
application of the "fair use"
principle.

The AECT representative also stressed the
desirability of voluntary licensing arrangements
covering educational activities beyond the scope of
fair use:

Once the doctrine of "fair use" has
been established in the revised law,
negotiations should be conducted
between the proprietor and user prior
to any use of copyrighted materials
that goes beyond that doctrine. We
believe that the enactment of the
"fair use" concept into law prior to
negotiations will guard against the
erosion of the concept. Generally,
a reasonable fee should be paid for
uses that go beyond "fair use," but
such fee arrangement should not delay
or impede the use of the materials.
Producers are urged to give free
access (no-cost contracts) whenever
possible.

The witness for the National Council of Teachers
of English did not share the AECT's faith in voluntary

licensing arrangements. He strongly urged a change in
one passage in the House Committee's reports dealing
with the length of excerpts that can be copied under
fair use, and summarized his organization's position as
follows:

> What we do seek and need is a clearer
> statement either in the statute or
> in the accompanying report, reassuring
> us that in a spontaneous teaching
> situation, we may make for one-time
> use by our students in our classrooms,
> multiple copies of self-contained
> short works of literature.

Following presentation of the prepared
statements, and in response to a question,
Harry N. Rosenfield, counsel of the Ad Hoc Committee
reviewed very briefly the eight points comprising the
position of the Committee as a whole:

1. The limited educational exemption;

2. The clarification of fair use;

3. Opposition to a copyright term of
    life-plus-fifty years;

4. Waiver of statutory damages for
    innocent infringers;

5. Support of the librarians'
    position on section 108(g);

6. Treatment of instructional
    television as a school activity;

7. Opposition to clearinghouse
    arrangements;

8. "... that input into a computer
    not be infringement for the period
    of the study by the National
    Commission on New Technological

> Uses, ... but that output be paid
> for under the normal rules of the
> game."

At the 1975 hearings the Department of Justice also recommended a specific educational exemption, which it proposed as a proviso to be added at the end of section 107.

A problem related to remedies in this context involves the nature of fair use as either an outright limitation on the rights of the copyright owner or as merely a defense in an infringement action. The 1966 and 1967 House Judiciary Committee reports contained the following comments on this point:

Proposals for presumption as to fair use

The representatives of various educational organizations proposed that, in infringement cases involving nonprofit uses for educational purposes, the use be presumed to be "fair" and the burden of proving otherwise be placed on the copyright owner. The representatives of authors and book publishers objected strenuously to this proposal, arguing that it would transform the doctrine of fair use into a blanket exemption in these cases.

The committee believes that any special statutory provision placing the burden of proving fair use on one side or the other would be unfair and undesirable. It has, however, added a provision to section 504(c), allowing minimum statutory damages to be reduced in these cases if the teacher proves that he acted in the reasonable belief that his reproduction constituted a fair use rather than an infringement.

This passage was deleted in the 1974 Senate report, though its interpretation presumably remains valid.

However, it is clear that the educators have not
dropped their proposal: for example, a shift in
"the burden of proof for the teacher to the alleger
of the infringement" is one of three fundamental
demands listed by the National Education Association
in its 1975 testimony as conditions for support of
the bill.

5. *RE-SALE OF USED TEXTBOOKS*

In his testimony before the House Subcommittee
on June 5, 1975, Professor Rondo Cameron, appearing
as an ordinary citizen as well as a teacher, research
scholar, and author, urged that the bill provide for
the payment of royalties for the commercial re-sale,
through large, organized markets, of "used or 'second
hand' books, especially textbooks." Since section
109(a) specifically excludes the right of re-sale in
this situation, Professor Cameron acknowledged that he
was opposed to this provision.

6. *NEWSLETTERS*

A statement submitted to the House Judiciary
Subcommittee by the Independent Newsletter Association
in connection with the 1975 hearings urges that
independent newsletters, as distinguished from house
organs and publicity or advertising publications, be
given special treatment under the bill. The statement
stresses the vulnerability of newsletters to mass
photocopying because, by their nature, they are
brief and pithy and depend solely on subscriptions for
their existence; the majority of newsletters have less
than 2,000 subscribers at an average annual subscription
fee of $50. It recommends that corporate and business
photocopying of newsletters be expressly excluded from
the fair use doctrine.

B.   COMMENTS AND RECOMMENDATIONS

1. *LANGUAGE OF SECTION 107*

The tortuous history of this provision has finally
produced a text that satisfactorily expresses the

legislative intent and, as far as it goes, is acceptable to the interested parties. Aside from the
Department of Justice, no one has suggested any changes.
It would appear to be unwise and unnecessary to tinker
with the language of section 107 as it stands.

2. *CLARIFICATION OF LEGISLATIVE INTENT*

   a. *Summary of positions*

Upon close analysis the following seems to be a
fair, if somewhat oversimplified, summary of the main
positions with respect to fair use and the problem of
reproduction for educational and scholarly purposes:

1. There is general agreement that,
    because of the importance of the
    problem and the lack of judicial
    precedent, Congress should clarify
    its intentions as to whether certain
    educational practices are or are not
    to be considered fair use, but without
    freezing the application of the doc-
    trine or opening the door to
    widespread abuse.

2. There are essentially two ways of
    accomplishing this: (1) by a
    detailed interpretation of "fair
    use" in the legislative report; or
    (2) by an explicit statutory
    exemption.

3. Following extended discussions, the
    authors and publishers agreed to
    the present wording of section 107
    and to an interpretative commentary
    with respect to educational uses
    along the lines of the 1966, 1967
    and 1974 legislative reports. They
    have consistently and strongly
    opposed any explicit educational
    exemption.

4. Although the educators consistently favored an explicit exemption, they agreed at one point to accept the approach of a legislative interpretation of fair use on certain conditions, including the expanded wording of section 107, certain changes in the language of the commentary, and further insulation from liability for innocent infringement. After the first Commissioner's decision in favor of the copyright owner in the *Williams & Wilkins* litigation, the educators returned to their proposal for an outright exemption, which clearly remains their first choice. However, it also appears that the position of the educators is still flexible enough for them to accept the approach of a legislative interpretation of section 107, provided it is sufficiently clear and reasonable from their point of view, and provided certain changes are made elsewhere in the bill.

b. *General comments*

The Copyright Office adheres to its position favoring the present language of section 107, coupled with a clear legislative interpretation in the Committee reports. The proposed language for an express educational exemption is much too broad, but in any event we seriously doubt whether satisfactory statutory language for this purpose could ever be achieved.

At the same time, we recognize that the interpretative language in the 1974 Senate report consists, with some changes, of a text prepared nearly ten years ago. Given the importance of this section of the Committee reports to an overall solution of this important problem, the Copyright Office

recommends that the commentary be carefully reviewed
and, where necessary, revised to take account of some
of the criticisms leveled at particular statements or
omissions.

Over the years, some of the educators have seemed
to be arguing that, with respect to photocopying, they
enjoy under the present law a "not-for-profit" limitation co-extensive with that applicable to certain
performances, and that somehow this "right" is being
taken away from them.

This line of argument tended to produce a rather testy
reaction, since plainly the only explicit "not-for-
profit" limitations on the copyright owner's exclusive
rights under the present law are with respect to public
performances of nondramatic literary and musical works.
On the other hand, although the commercial or nonprofit
character of a use is not necessarily conclusive with
respect to fair use, in combination with other factors
it can and should weigh heavily in fair use decisions.
It would certainly be appropriate to emphasize this
point in the legislative commentary dealing with fair
use and educational photocopying.

The special situation of newsletters does not
warrant a statutory exclusion from the doctrine of fair
use in section 107, but the problem should be dealt
with in the revised commentary.

A significant letter to Chairman Kastenmeier
dated August 1, 1975 and signed jointly by
Townsend Hoopes, President of the Association of
American Publishers, Inc. and Sheldon Elliot Steinbach,
Chairman of the Ad Hoc Committee on Copyright Law
Revision, states:

> Pursuant to the suggestion made by you
> and several of your Subcommittee members
> during the hearings in June on H.R. 2223
> representatives of publishers, authors,
> and educators have resumed their direct
> discussions of issues relating to the

permissible limits of the photocopying
of copyrighted materials for educational
purposes.

The joint letter expresses the hope that an "agreed
document" will emerge from the discussions "by early
November, which we understand would be a date early
enough to ensure full consideration by your Subcommittee." There is thus some genuine reason to hope
that the interested parties will be able to provide
direct assistance to the Congress in its final review
of this problem in connection with the revision bill.

3.   REMEDIES AND PRESUMPTIONS

a.   *Injunctions, damages, etc.*

The proposals put forward on behalf of educators
at the 1975 hearings, under which the only remedy
available against an innocent educational infringer
would be actual damages, seem to go too far. Certainly
the continuation of an activity after it has been held
an infringement would destroy any argument of innocence
and justify discretionary injunctive relief. On the
other hand, if a defendant can prove complete innocence
in this situation, a mandatory waiver of statutory
(though not actual) damages can be justified.

b.   *Presumptions and burden of proof*

The educators are understandably concerned that,
because the scope of the doctrine of fair use is not
yet clear in this area, an educational defendant would
have the burden not only of proving the facts with
respect to what he or she did, but also of proving why,
as a matter of law, these acts amounted to fair use.
This is a difficult question which should not be
brushed aside lightly. The Copyright Office adheres
to its position that, when it comes to the infinitely
variable questions of fair use, rigid rules involving
legal presumptions and burdens of proof should not be
laid out in the statute. We would have no objection,
however, to an interpretation in the legislative report
making clear that, where a teacher in an infringement

suit proves certain facts and alleges that they
constitute fair use, it is up to the plaintiff to prove
that, as a matter of law, they are beyond the scope of
the fair use doctrine.

4. RE-SALE OF USED TEXTBOOKS

The proposal that royalties be imposed on the
large-scale commercial re-sale of used copies of textbooks and other works received no support; it runs
counter to the traditional "first-sale" doctrine of
copyright law embodied in section 109(a), which has
attracted no opposition.
In fairness, however, it should be noted that, purely
as a legal concept, the idea is not unthinkable. Other
countries are beginning to experiment with analogous
systems, such as the "public lending right," involving
library lending, and the "droit de suite," involving an
artist's participation in the proceeds of later sales
of a work of art. There is little doubt that, as
technology continues to erode authors' ability to
control various uses of their works, additional points
at which control can be exercised will be sought.

5. CONCLUSION

The question of educational photocopying was
expressly excluded from the mandate of the National
Commission on New Technological Uses of Copyrighted
Works, on the assumption that, at the time when the
Commission bill was drafted, the issue was essentially
settled. The immediate key to a reasonable legislative
solution in 1975 appears to lie in a well-drafted
legislative interpretation of section 107, coupled with
some possible changes in the language or interpretation
of the provisions dealing with infringement actions and
remedies.

Beyond this immediate legislative solution,
however, there is a fact that must be faced. Right now
there are activities connected with teaching that
constitute infringement, not fair use, and these are
bound to increase. Everyone seems to assume that they
will somehow be licensed and that royalties will some-

how be paid, but as a practical matter this cannot and will not be done on an individual, item-by-item basis. We are entering an era when blanket licensing and collective payments are essential if the educator is not to be a scofflaw and the author's copyright is not to be a hollow shell. It is not going to be easy, but once the scope of fair use in this field of activity has been clarified by legislative action, immediate efforts to establish workable licensing or clearing-house arrangements will have to begin.

CHAPTER III

REPRODUCTION BY LIBRARIES AND ARCHIVES

Sections Considered:

#106 - Exclusive rights in copyrighted works

#107 - Limitations on exclusive rights: Fair use

#108 - Limitations on exclusive rights: Reproduction by libraries and archives

Issues:

1. How should the legislative report deal with:

   a) the application of the fair use doctrine under section 107 to reproduction by libraries and archives?

   b) the interrelationship between sections 107 and 108 (see #108(f)(3))?

2. Do the provisions of subsections (d) and (e) of section 108, establishing

differing conditions for the reproduction of excerpts and of complete
works, represent a satisfactory
solution to the problem?

3. To what extent should the exemptions
    provided by section 108 apply to:

    a) libraries and archives in profit
       -making business and professional
       organizations (see #108(a))?

    b) music; pictorial, graphic and
       sculptural works; motion
       pictures and other audiovisual
       works (see #108(h))?

    c) making and distribution of video
       -tapes of television news
       programs (see #108 (f)(4) and
       (h))?

4. Is subsection (g)(1), dealing with "one-
    at-a-time multiple copying" an
    appropriate exception to the exemptions
    of section 108?

5. With respect to section 108(g)(2):

    a) Is a provision dealing with
       "systematic reproduction or
       distribution of single or
       multiple copies or phono-
       records" an appropriate
       exception to the exemptions
       of section 108?

    b) Is the wording of the clause
       satisfactory to accomplish its
       purpose?

    c) Is the explanatory commentary
       on the clause in the 1974 Senate
       report a satisfactory statement
       of Congressional intent?

6. Recognizing that the National Commission
    on New Technological Uses is now function-
    ing, and is mandated to study, compile
    data and make recommendations for
    legislation with respect to "various forms
    of machine reproduction," should
    the legislative reports on the
    general revision bills express
    Congressional intent with respect
    to the interrelationship between
    the work of the Commission and the
    effect of sections 107 and 108?

A. DISCUSSION OF ISSUES

1. LEGISLATIVE HISTORY OF SECTION 108

Photocopying as a social phenomenon dates from
the early 1960's, and the earlier copyright problems
that arose from photostating and microfilming by
libraries seem insignificant in comparison to what is
facing us now. Photostats were expensive, microfilm
required special readers which were not widely available, and both were cumbersome, inconvenient and hard
to read.

Yet, as early as the 1930's, the extent to
which a library or other institution could supply
photographic reproductions to scholars had blown up
into a controversy. In 1935 a joint committee of the
American Council of Learned Societies and the Social
Science Research Council entered into the famous
"gentlemen's agreement" with the National Association
of Book Publishers. This agreement had no binding
effect, but it was widely accepted as at least a
norm of conduct for many years. The agreement read in
part as follows:

A library, archives, office, museum, or
similar institution owning books or
periodical volumes in which copyright
still subsists may make and deliver a
single photographic reproduction or
reduction of a part thereof to a scholar
representing in writing that he desires

such reproduction in lieu of loan of such
publication or in place of manual transcription and solely for the purpose of
research; provided (1) that the person
receiving it is given due notice in
writing that he is not exempt from
liability to the copyright proprietor
for any infringement of copyright by
misuse of the reproduction constituting
an infringement under the copyright law;
and (2) that such reproduction is made
and furnished without profit to itself
by the institution making it.

The Copyright Office saw the problem growing in
the 1950's and devoted one of the studies in its
revision series to "Photoduplication of Copyrighted
Material by Libraries." The 1961 Register's Report
analyzed the problem at some length, and made the
following recommendations:

The statute should permit a library,
whose collections are available to the
public without charge, to supply a
single photocopy of copyrighted material
in its collections to any applicant
under the following conditions:

(a) A single photocopy of one
article in any issue of a
periodical, or of a reasonable
part of any other publication,
may be supplied when the
applicant states in writing
that he needs and will use
such material solely for his
own research.

(b) A single photocopy of an
entire publication may be
supplied when the applicant
also states in writing, and
the library is not otherwise
informed, that a copy is not
available from the publisher.

(c) Where the work bears a
copyright notice, the library
should be required to affix
to the photocopy a warning that
the material appears to be copyrighted.

The reaction to these recommendations from copyright
owners ranged from cautious acceptance to strong
opposition, mostly the latter; the few comments
received from librarians were inconclusive. However,
by the time the Copyright Office submitted its 1963
preliminary draft for comment, positions on both sides
had begun to solidify. A joint committee of librarians
agreed upon a policy statement which, as issued in 1961
and revised in 1963, read as follows:

Findings:

1. The making of a single copy by a
    library is a direct and natural
    extension of traditional library
    service.

2. Such service, employing modern
    copying methods, has become
    essential.

3. The present demand can be satisfied
    without inflicting measurable damage
    on publishers and copyright owners.

4. Improved copying processes will not
    materially effect the demand for
    single copy library duplication for
    research purposes.

Recommendations:

The Committee recommends that it be library
policy to fill an order for a single photocopy of any published work or any part
thereof.

Before making a copy of an entire work,
a library should make an effort by
consulting standard sources to determine
whether or not a copy is available
through normal trade channels.

The following is the text of the library photocopying provision in the 1963 preliminary draft:

7.   *LIMITATIONS ON EXCLUSIVE RIGHTS:*
       COPYING AND RECORDING BY LIBRARIES

Notwithstanding the provisions of
section 5, any library whose
collections are available to the
public or to researchers in any
specialized field shall be entitled
to duplicate, by any process
including photocopying and sound
recording, any work in its collections other than a motion picture,
and to supply a single copy of
sound recording upon request, but
only under the following conditions:

(a) The library shall be
    entitled, without further
    investigation, to supply a
    copy of no more than one
    article or other contribution
    to a copyrighted collection
    or periodical issue, or to
    supply a copy or sound
    recording of a similarly
    small part of any other copy-
    righted work.

(b) The library shall be entitled
    to supply a copy or sound
    recording of an entire work,
    or of more than a relatively
    small part of it, if the
    library has first determined,

> on the basis of a
> reasonable investigation
> that a copy or sound
> recording of the copy-
> righted work cannot
> readily be obtained from
> trade sources.
>
> (c) The library shall attach to
> the copy a warning that the
> work appears to be copyrighted.

This modest effort was met with strenuous opposition from all sides. As the 1965 Supplementary Report summed it up:

> Author and publisher groups attacked section 7 as opening the door to wholesale and unrestrained copying by libraries which, as reproduction equipment improves, could supplant the copies offered for sale by publishers and undercut the author's main source of remuneration. Library groups were equally vehement in opposition to the proposals, which they argued would curtail established services and prevent the free utilization of new devices in the interests of research and scholarship.
>
> Opposition to the provision was equally strong on both sides but for exactly opposite reasons, with one side arguing that the provision would permit things that are illegal now and the other side maintaining that it would prevent things that are legal now. Both agreed on one thing: that the section should be dropped entirely.

Having little choice in the matter, the Copyright Office dropped the provision entirely from the 1964 and 1965 bills. At the 1965 House hearings there was very little testimony about library photocopying, and most of it was in the context of fair use.

Lonely support for an explicit exemption came from the
American Council of Learned Societies, which recognized
that the problem was difficult and controversial but
regarded the bill's failure to deal with it a disservice
to scholars. The ACLS felt that a reasonable compromise
could be reached by distinguishing extracts from entire
works: single copies of extracts for research use
would be justified if properly safeguarded, but the
inaccessibility or cost of an entire work would not be
sufficient justification for permitting the copying of
an entire work. The ACLS proposal, which attracted
little attention at the time and is now almost completely forgotten, is worth setting our here:

#__.   *LIMITATIONS ON EXCLUSIVE RIGHTS:*
       COPYING BY LIBRARIES

   (a) Notwithstanding the provisions of
   clauses (1) and (3) of sections 106
   (a), a library of an organization
   operated for scholarly, educational
   or religious purposes and not for
   private gain is entitled, without
   the authority of the copyright owner
   upon the request of any person to
   duplicate by any process and furnish
   to such person a single copy or phonorecord of an extract from a copy or
   phono-record of a copyrighted work
   in its collections other than a
   motion picture, but only under the
   following conditions:

   1.   The extract shall consist of
        no more than one separate
        contribution to any period-
        ical issue or other
        collective work, or no more
        than a relatively small part
        of any other work;

   2.   The library shall furnish
        such copy or phono-record
        without profit to itself,

but shall charge the person
to whom it is furnished an
amount approximately equal
to the cost (including labor
and overhead) of duplicating
and furnishing it;

3.   The library shall furnish
such copy of phono-record
on its premises or by
delivery in the form of a
material object and not by
transmitting the work or the
extract therefrom; and

4.   The library shall by reasonable means inform its patrons
that a person to whom such a
copy or phono-record is
furnished is not exempt from
liability to the copyright
owner for any use of such
copy or phono-record constituting an infringement of
copyright.

The Department of Health, Education and Welfare also
viewed with concern the omission of an exemption for
photocopying and "computerization" by libraries, and
recommended adoption of a somewhat enlarged version of
the Copyright Office's 1963 preliminary draft.

The 1966 and 1967 House Judiciary Committee
reports noted that the position taken at the hearings
by representatives of libraries "that statutory
provisions codifying or limiting present library
practices in this area could crystallize a subject
better left to flexible adjustment," and stated: "the
committee does not favor a specific provision dealing
with library photocopying." It added, however:

Unauthorized library copying, like everything else, must be judged a fair use

or an infringement on the basis of all
of the applicable criteria and the facts
of the particular case. Despite past
efforts, reasonable arrangements
involving a mutual understanding of
what generally constitutes acceptable
library practices, and providing workable clearance and licensing conditions
have not been achieved and are overdue.
The committee urges all concerned to
resume their efforts to reach an
accommodation under which the needs of
scholarship and the rights of authors
would both be respected.

At the same time, however, the House Committee
did accept a proposal by archivists and historians for
a specific exemption permitting facsimile reproduction
of unpublished manuscript collections in archival
institutions under certain conditions and for limited
purposes. This new provision, which was added to the
1966 bill as section 108, turned out to be the seed
from which grew the monster we are now considering.

Library photocopying was not a major issue at the
1967 hearings in the Senate, but there were indications
that the librarians were having second thoughts about
the matter. The chairman of a joint committee of four
major library associations urged that "the facts of
life concerning single copying be recognized in this
bill"; no specific amendment was proposed, but the
joint committee recommended that a provision be added
to the fair use section stating "that making a single
copy within libraries for the use of scholars is within
the concept of fair use."

This shift in position signalled a major policy
reversal by the library community after the 1967
Senate hearings. Specific proposals for a detailed
section dealing with reproductions by libraries and
archives were evolved as the general library position,
and were the subject of various discussions and exchanges
of correspondence.

In gauging these developments it is also important
to recognize that the issue of computer uses of copyrighted works, by networks of academic libraries among
others, had emerged as a major copyright issue at the
1967 Senate hearings, and was the subject of lively
debate during this same period. An approach to that
problem was to establish a National Commission on
New Technological Uses of Copyrighted Works to study
the question of computer uses of copyrighted works and
along the way it was decided to add "various forms of
machine reproduction," including library photocopying,
to the Commission's mandate. A bill to this effect
(S. 2216) was passed by the Senate in 1967, during the
90th Congress, and was added as Title II to S. 543, the
1969 revision bill in its initial Senate version in the
91st Congress.

There was obviously some hope that, if a Commission
could be set up quickly and could take up library photocopying as its first order of business, there might be
no need to grasp the library photocopying nettle in the
general revision bill. The original version of S. 543
contained no library photocopying exemption. However,
as the Commission idea lost momentum and the library
associations pressed harder for an express exemption,
it became apparent that at least some of the recommendations had support on the Senate Judiciary Subcommittee.
No further hearings were held, but on December 10, 1969,
S. 543 was reported by the Subcommittee to the full
Committee with some major amendments. For one thing,
section 108 had grown from an 8-line provision concerning archival collections to a 65-line section with six
subsections dealing fairly comprehensively with
"reproduction by libraries and archives." The new
section as reported was retained verbatim in the 1971
version of the bill (S. 644) and again in the 1973
version as originally introduced in the 93rd Congress
(S. 1361).

The version of section 108 that emerged on
December 10, 1969 and remained a part of the revision
bill until 1974, differed from the 1975 revision bill

now under consideration in several respects, but the
main differences were two:

1. The 1969 bill made no distinction
   between excerpts and short self-
   contained works (like articles) on
   the one hand, and complete works
   on the other. Under the section,
   a library could make a photocopy
   of any work only if "the user has
   established to the satisfaction
   of the library or archives that an
   unused copy cannot be obtained at
   a normal price from commonly known
   trade sources in the United States
   including authorized reproducing
   services." In contrast, the 1975
   bill would allow photocopying of
   a single article or contribution,
   or of a "small part" of a work,
   without further investigation.
   The library would be required to
   "determine, on the basis of a
   reasonable investigation" that a
   copy "cannot be obtained at a
   fair price," only in case the
   material to be photocopied
   constitutes "the entire work, or
   ... a substantial part of it."

2. The 1969 version contained no
   counterpart of the controversial
   subsection (g)(2) of the 1975
   provision, which expressly excludes "systematic" single or
   multiple copying from the scope
   of the exemption.

The 1969 bill fell short of the librarians'
proposal, which would have allowed the making of one
copy of any work, regardless of its length and whether
or not it was "in-print," as long as it was for the
personal use of an individual.

The full sweep of this proposal was vigorously opposed by authors and publishers, who contended that it would authorize virtually unlimited copying and jeopardize scholarship by destroying incentives for creating and publishing many works. Meanwhile, the action of Williams & Wilkins, Inc. against two government medical libraries, alleging copyright infringement on the basis of extensive library photocopying practices, had begun making its way through the U.S. Court of Claims to the Supreme Court. This tended to polarize positions on the issue and to poison the atmosphere for accommodation.

When Senate hearings on this issue were held in August, 1973, the Court of Claims Commissioner had ruled in favor of Williams & Wilkins, and the full Court's reversal of that ruling had not yet occurred. The librarians proposed an amendment that was narrower than their original proposal: in effect it would permit making one copy of a single article or contribution, or of a short excerpt, without further investigation; a library could supply a single copy of an entire work after determining that it was out of print. For their part the authors and publishers in general, appeared willing to accept the approach of section 108 as it then stood, although reluctantly and with some drafting changes. They concentrated their fire upon the librarians' new proposal.

The ground upon which the controversy was based shifted in November, 1973, when the full Court of Claims, in a narrow and split decision, reversed the Commissioner and held in favor of the government libraries. It then shifted again in April, 1974, when the Senate Subcommittee reported the revision bill to the full Judiciary Committee with some striking amendments.

In effect, the 1974 bill accepted the librarians' 1973 proposal but added an entirely new provision stating that "the rights of reproduction and distribut -ion under this section ... do not extend to cases where the library or archives, or its employee: ...

(2) engages in the systematic reproduction or
distribution of single or multiple copies ... ."
The library community greeted this new subsection
(g)(2) and the explanatory commentary accompanying
it with howls of outrage, arguing that its substantive
content had never been discussed at hearings or
elsewhere, and that it took away everything that the
other 1974 amendment had given. Authors and publishers
generally accepted the section with this new provision.
They argued that, as a technical matter, a prohibition
against systematic copying was implicit in the rest of
the section; however, the amendment allowing nearly
unrestricted single copying of journal articles and
similar works made an explicit prohibition against
doing this on a systematic basis essential. The
relevance of this dispute to the *Williams & Wilkins*
case, which was then pending in the Supreme Court, was
not lost on anyone.

The revision bill was reported by the full Senate
Judiciary Committee on July 3, 1974, and was passed by
the Senate on September 9, 1974 with two changes in
section 108 dealing with videotape and new archives.
There was no debate on the fundamental issues underlying
the section. Meanwhile, a great many of the groups and
organizations involved in the dispute were filing briefs
as *amici curiae* in the *Williams & Wilkins* case in the
Supreme Court, and positions on the legislation were
becoming increasingly inflexible and tenacious. During
this difficult period a dialog of sorts was re-estab-
lished through a series of meetings sponsored jointly
by the Copyright Office and the National Commission on
Libraries and Information Science (NCLIS). However, no
consensus concerning the proper interpretation of
"systematic" reproduction or the possibilities of
establishing a practical mechanism for licensing library
photocopying could be achieved under the circumstances.

The *Williams & Wilkins* case was argued before the
Supreme Court in December, 1974. In January, 1975, at
the opening of the 94th Congress, the revision bill was
re-introduced in both Houses.

The Senate version of section 108 was identical with
the version passed by the Senate the previous September.
The House version was identical with the Senate bill.

Then on February 24, 1975, in a spectacular anti-
climax, the Supreme Court split 4-4 on the *Williams &*
Wilkins case, automatically affirming the Court of
Claims decision in favor of the government libraries,
but effectively depriving that decision of any
precendtial weight and wiping out any authority the
Court of Claims majority opinion might otherwise have
carried. In a recent habeas corpus decision *(Neil v.*
Biggers, 409 U.S. 188 (1972)), the U.S. Supreme Court
itself has declared that an equally-divided affirmance
"merely ends the process of direct review but settles
no issue of law." The Court has thus left the issue
squarely up to Congress to settle.

It should also be mentioned that separate
legislation establishing the National Commission on
New Technological Uses of Copyrighted Works (CONTU)
was enacted by Congress late in 1974, and became
effective on the last day of that year. The members
of the Commission were appointed in mid-1975, and
CONTU held its first meeting on October 8, 1975. The
statutory purpose of the Commission is "to study and
compile data on: (1) the reproduction and use of
copyrighted works of authorship ... (b) by various
forms of machine reproduction, not including
reproduction by or at the request of instructors for
use in face-to-face teaching activities." Its mandate
also covers computer uses of copyrighted works. Under
its statute, CONTU must complete its first report by
October 8, 1976, and must conclude its work by the end
of 1977.

2. *ANALYSIS OF 1975 BILL*

Section 108, entitled "Limitations on exclusive
rights: Reproduction by libraries and archives," now
consists of 89 lines divided into eight subsections.

The subsections are currently untitled, but can be summarized under the following headings, most of which are used in the 1974 Senate report:

(a) General scope of single copy exemption

(b) Archival reproduction

(c) Replacement of damaged copy

(d) Articles and small excerpts

(e) Out-of-print works

(f) General exemptions

(g) Multiple copies and systematic reproduction

(h) Works excluded from exemption

(a) Scope of exemption

Subsection (a) lays out the basic conditions under which a library can claim an exemption under the section. These can be summarized very generally as follows:

1. The exemption applies only to a library or archives or their employees acting within the scope of their employment.

2. "No more than one copy or phono-record of a work" can be made under the exemption. This is explained further in subsection (g).

3. No distinction is made between nonprofit libraries and libraries in profit-making institutions, but the reproduction or distribution

itself must be made "without
any purpose of direct or indirect
commercial advantage."

4. The library's collections must
either be open to the public or
to outside persons doing specialised
research.

5. A notice of copyright must accompany
the reproduction.

Note that the conditions set out in subsection
(a) are only a general starting point. For a library
activity to be exempt it must also qualify under one
of the conditions laid out in subsections (b) through
(f), must not run afoul of subsection (g), and must
involve copying of a work that is not mentioned in
subsection (h).

(b) Archival preservation

This exemption applies only to unpublished works
in the current collection of a library or archives.
It allows reproduction only in facsimile form, and only
for "purposes of preservation or security or for
deposit for research use in another library or archives."

(c) Replacement

With respect to published works, a library or
archives can make a facsimile reproduction to replace
material that is "damaged, deteriorating, lost or
stolen, "but only if it finds that an unused replacement copy cannot be obtained at a fair price.

(d) Journal articles, small excerpts, etc.

This subsection applies to "no more than one
article or other contribution to a copyrighted collection or periodical issue, or to ... a small part of any
other copyrighted work." The only conditions for
supplying a reproduction are that "the copy becomes
the property of the user," that there is no reason to

suppose that it "would be used for any purpose other
than private study, scholarship, or research;" and
that warning of copyright be given. The copy must
be "made from the collection of a library or archives
where the user makes his request, or from that of
another library or archives."

(e) Entire works

With one addition the conditions applicable
under subsection (d) apply under subsection (e) to
"the entire work," or "a substantial part of it."
The added condition is that "the library or archives
has first determined, on the basis of a reasonable
investigation, that a copy or phono-record of the
copyrighted work cannot be obtained at a fair price."

(f) General exemptions

This subsection contains four clauses, aimed at
precluding certain interpretations of section 108.
In three of the clauses the effect would be to expand
the scope of permissible copying activity, while in
the fourth the effect would be restrictive.

1. The first clause makes clear that
    no liability attaches to a library
    or its employees for "the unsuper-
    vised use of reproducing equipment
    located on its premises," as long
    as a copyright warning is posted
    on the machine.

2. Conversely, the second clause makes
    clear that the individual user of
    the reproducing equipment is not
    insulated from liability if the
    reproduction exceeds fair use, and
    the same is true if the library is
    asked to make the copy for the
    individual.

3. Clause (3) is important. It
    declares that nothing in section

108 "in any way effects the
right of fair use," or any
contractual obligations the
library has assumed.

4. The fourth clause, which was
    added to the section during the
    floor debates in the Senate in
    September, 1974, reflects the
    controversy over the videotape
    archive of news programs at
    Vanderbilt University. It
    states that nothing in section
    108 "shall be construed to
    limit the reproduction and
    distribution of a limited
    number of copies and excerpts
    by a library or archives of
    an audiovisual news program ..."

(g) *Multiple and systematic copying*

It is hard to tell, from the wording, whether
this controversial subsection is intended as an
exception to the exemptions stated elsewhere in
section 108, or whether its purpose is to offer a
statutory interpretation of their negative effect.
The original intention was probably the latter.

In any event, the subsection starts with a
positive statement: "The rights of reproduction and
distribution under this section extend to the isolated
and unrelated reproduction or distribution of a single
copy or phono-record of the same material on separate
occasions." But, it adds, these "rights" do not
extend to cases where the library knew or should have
known that "one-at-a-time" multiple copying was going
on: where it "is aware or had substantial reason to
believe that it is engaging in the related or concerted
reproduction or distribution of multiple copies or
phono-records of the same material, whether made on one
occasion or over a period of time, and whether intended
for aggregate use by one or more individuals or for
separate use by the individual members of a group."

The first clause of subsection (g), just quoted,
has been in the bill since 1969 and had caused little
comment until clause (2) was joined to it in 1974.
Under the clause, the reproduction and distribution
"rights" of section 108 do not apply where the library
"engages in the systematic reproduction of single or
multiple copies or phono-records of material described
in subsection (d)" (i.e. of articles, contributions and
excerpts).

(h) Works excluded from exemption

Except for situations covered by subsections (b)
and (c) -- archival preservation of unpublished works
and replacement of damaged copies of published material
-- subsection (h) makes the exemptions of section 108
inapplicable to:

1. a musical work;

2. a pictorial, graphic or sculptural
    work;

3. a motion picture or other audio-
    visual work, other than one
    "dealing with news."

3.   1974 SENATE REPORT ON SECTION 108

The 1974 Senate report contains some significant
comments bearing on the purpose and interpretation of
specific provisions of section 108. Where these were
put in issue at the 1975 House hearings, they will be
reviewed below. In addition, the following explanations
deserve note:

(a) "Fair price"

There are some textual differences but, under
both subsections (c), dealing with replacement of
damaged or missing copies, and (e), dealing with what
might be termed "out-of-print works," the library
must, before making a reproduction, have first
determined that a copy "cannot be obtained at a fair

price." In explaining both subsections, the Senate report says:

> The scope and nature of a reasonable
> investigation to determine that an
> unused replacement cannot be obtained
> will vary according to the circumstances
> of a particular situation. It will
> always require recourse to commonly-
> known trade sources in the United States
> and in the normal situation also to the
> publisher or other copyright owner (if
> such owner can be located at the address
> listed in the copyright registration),
> or an authorized reproducing service.

(b) "Lawfully-made" copies and later unlawful use

Clause (2) of subsection (f) confirms the liability of a library patron who, beyond fair use, makes copies on a machine located in the library or has them made by the library for him. The report makes clear that any such copies are not "lawfully made" within the meaning of a number of sections throughout the bill, including sections 109 and 110. This means that, in a variety of situations, that would otherwise be exempted, including cases involving the re-sale, display or importation of the copies or their use for performances, would be considered infringements. Conversely, the report states:

> It is the intent of this legislation that
> a subsequent unlawful use by a user of a
> copy of a work lawfully made by a library
> shall not make the library liable for such
> improper use.

(c) Contractual arrangements

In commenting on subsection (f)(3), providing that section 108 does not override any contractual obligations assumed by a library when it obtained a work for its collections, the report makes the following comments:

For example, if there is an express
contractual prohibition against
reproduction for any purpose, this
legislation shall not be construed
as justifying a violation of the
contract. This clause is intended
to encompass the situation where an
individual makes papers, manuscripts
or other works available to a library
with the understanding that they will
not be reproduced.

4.   *ANALYSIS OF SPECIFIC ISSUES*

   a.   *Interrelationship between fair use and*
        library exemption

The strange eventful history of library
photocopying as a copyright issue has left a major
question unanswered: are the exemptions of section 108
essentially a definitive statement of what Congress
intends fair use to mean in this area? Or are they
supplementary provisions augmenting but not restricting
the present doctrine? Or could it be argued that,
because section 108 says definitively that certain
things can be done and others cannot, the section
prohibits certain activities that might be held fair
use today?

Although section 108(f)(2) says that nothing in
the section "in any way effects the fight of fair use
as provided by section 107," this has been and certainly can be, interpreted in different ways. Suppose, for
example, that the bill were enacted in its present
form and Williams & Wilkins re-instituted suit under
the new law.

The Court of Claims had held that what the National
Library of Medicine was doing constituted fair use
under the 1909 copyright law; would section 108
change that result? The 1974 Senate report offers
no clue to the answer.

b. *Subsections (d) and (e)*

The statement of the Department of Justice recommends that the works "of a small part" be deleted from subsection (d), and that the words "if the library or archives has first determined, on the basis of a reasonable investigation, that a copy or phono-record of the copyrighted work cannot be obtained at a fair price" be deleted from subsection (e). The reason given for the first suggestion was: "Libraries should be able to reproduce entire work for scholarship"; the reason for the second was: "Too difficult and cumbersome to make purchase investigation; discourages use."

c. *Profit-making organizations*

At the 1975 hearings the third of the three specific proposals made by the librarians, through the spokesman for the Special Libraries Association (SLA), involved the interpretation of one of the fundamental conditions of exemption under section 108: that, in the words of section 108(a)(1), "the reproduction is made without any purpose of direct or indirect commercial advantage." The SLA representative urged clarification of this requirement "because the majority of special library operations are conducted for purposes of 'indirect commercial advantage' when the library's parent organization is in the business, industrial or financial communities through its products and services." He suggested that the language might have been intended to refer to "an authorized or unauthorized reprinter or republisher of copyrighted materials." The libraries therefore proposed either that the phrase "to a re-printer or a republisher" be added after the word "advantage" at the end of section 108(a)(1) or, alternatively, that the commentary make this intent clear.

The statement of the Special Libraries Association contains the following justification for this proposal:

Legislation to be enacted must not prevent or penalize the preparation

of photocopies by any library. S.L.A.
is, of course, particularly concerned
about the status of specialized
libraries -- especially those in for-
profit organizations. There will be
immeasurable damage to the total
economy and welfare of the nation if
such intent were to be contained in
the enacted version of H.R. 2223, or
if such interpretation is possible
after enactment of the law. The
rapid transmission of man's knowledge
-- either to not-for-profit or to
for-profit organizations -- must not
be impeded by law. Whether libraries
request or produce photocopies, the
libraries are acting solely as the
agents for the individual and
distinct users of libraries who in
their totality represent *all* strata
of our American society.

d. *Works not covered by exemption*

The broad reproduction privileges provided by
subsections (d) and (e) apply to literary works,
dramatic works, and sound recordings. Under subsection (h) they do not apply to musical works,
pictorial, graphic and sculptural works and
audiovisual works, other than television new
programs. At the 1975 House hearings the librarians
asked that these exclusions from the exemptions be
deleted entirely. Their representative stated:

We are also concerned with Section 108(h)
which would limit the rights otherwise
granted under Section 108 by excluding
a musical work, pictorial, graphic and
other audiovisual works. These
exclusions are illogical. The need of
the scholar doing research in music for
a copy of a portion of a score is as
legitimate and proper as that of the
scholar doing any other kind of

research. Likewise, the copying of one
map from an atlas or a page of diagrams
and plans from a technical journal may
be just as important as any other kind
of material for research.

It seems to us that libraries ought to
be encouraged to collect and preserve
all of the forms in which knowledge is
published and distributed, and that it
should be possible for users of libraries
to have access for their study and
scholarship to all of these forms, not
just some of them. If a student of the
cinema asks a library to make a copy
for him of a few selected frames of some
famous motion picture which is being
studied, so that he may consider at his
leisure a certain key point which is
made in an article he is reading, we
think the library ought to be able to do
that.

This proposal, insofar as it applied to music,
was supported by the Music Library Association, which
stressed the importance of photocopying to serious
music scholarship, it argued that copyright claims are
asserted in edited versions of music in the public
domain, including many works of the great masters, and
that music libraries do not collect the great bulk of
the popular musical ephemera that are copyrighted.

In commenting on the deletion of subsection (h),
the Special Libraries Association apparently assumed
that sound recordings of musical works would be
regarded as "audiovisual works," which is not the
case. However, the SLA's basic point was that printed
music should not be excluded from the over-all
exemptions of section 108:

 # 108(h)

The Association feels that there is a
real need to distinguish between two
formats of "musical works:"

(a) Printed musical works and

(b) Sound reproductions of musical works.

To achieve this distinction, we suggest two possible amendments to # 108(h):

1. Delete the words "a musical work" because performances are included in the subsequent phrase, "or other audiovisual work," or

2. Add a modifying statement so that # 108(h) will read:

> The rights of reproduction and distribution under this section do not apply to a musical work *other than a printed copy* ... (suggested words are in italics.)

It is important that research workers and students of musicology be allowed "fair use" access to portions of printed music just as # 108(a)(2) permits "fair use" access to textual materials. In # 108(h) a clear distinction must be made between performances or sound recordings and music in printed form.

The librarians' proposals on this point were met with strong opposition from book and music publishers, who expressed surprise and dismay that the point was being raised so late in the day. They argued that "the primary purpose of music is performance" and that the overwhelming majority of photocopies that would be made if the exemption applied to music would be precisely for that purpose. They pointed out that fair use would in most cases of real scholarly use, allow all that is needed -- copies of short extracts for illustrative purposes -- and that satisfactory joint arrangements

have already been worked out with respect to obtaining
copies of out-of-print music.

e.   *Videotape archives*

The 1974 amendments offered by Senator Baker
and adopted by the Senate as amendments to subsections
(f) and (h) of section 108, were the subject of 1975
hearings in the House. The amendment was intended to
exempt the Vanderbilt Television News Archive at
Vanderbilt University, and presumably any other library
or archive covered by section 108, from copyright
liability for "the reproduction and distribution of a
limited number of copies and excerpts ... of an audiovisual news program." The correlative amendment in
subsection (h) refers to "an audiovisual work dealing
with news."

At the hearings Robert V. Evans, Vice President
and General Counsel of CBS Inc., urged deletion of the
Baker amendments as being too broad in scope and
unnecessary to accomplish the purpose of establishing
a national repository for television news programs.
Paul C. Simpson, founder of the Vanderbilt Archive
declared that the revision bill should not prohibit
libraries from:

1.   recording news broadcasts from the air;

2.   making them available for viewing at
     the library and copies for viewing
     elsewhere;

3.   making, on specific request, copies
     of single stories or news items from
     the broadcasts available, just as
     such services are rendered by
     libraries from newspaper collections.

He supported the Baker amendments as accomplishing this
result, and argued that national depository and
educational licensing arrangements recently established
by CBS are too restrictive for this purpose.

f. *Multiple copying*

Clause (1) of subparagraph (g) had been included in the librarians' original proposal to the Senate and had apparently been accepted by everyone since its introduction into the bill in December, 1969. The 1974 Senate report contains the following interpretation:

> Subsection (g) provides that the rights granted by this section extend only to the "isolated and unrelated reproduction of a single copy," but this section does not authorize the related or concerted reproduction of multiple copies of the same material whether made on one occasion or over a period of time, and whether intended for aggregate use by one individual or for separate use by the individual members of a group. For example, if a college professor instructs his class to read an article from a copyrighted journal, the school library would not be permitted, under subsection (g), to reproduce copies of the article for the members of the class.

Citing this commentary, the librarians recommended its deletion in their May, 1975, presentation at the House hearings. Professor Low's statement contained the following paragraph:

> Subsection (g)(1) gives us concern because often there is no basis for a library employee to judge whether a request for a copy represents "isolated and unrelated reproduction" as specified in Section 108(g)(1). For example, if a college instructor in a graduate seminar in English were to recommend to his students, some ten men and women sitting around a table, that they read an article on Milton's poetry that appeared ten years ago in *Publications of the Modern Language Association,* and

if two of them over the next week were
to go to that college's library and
look at that article and decide that
they wanted to take copies back to their
dormitory for further study, we don't
see how there is any practical way in
which a library can prevent that kind of
reproduction of a single copy on
separate occasions, and we don't think
they should have to. And yet, the Senate
Committee report S. 1361 (S. Rept. 93-983)
cites such an instance.

As might be expected, the authors and publishers
reacted strongly against this interpretation, arguing,
as they had from the discussions in the early 1960's,
that a limitation of the exemption to single copying
"was meaningless unless it expressly guarded against
the making of multiple copies one at a time."

g. *Systematic reproduction*

By far the most controversial provision of
section 108 is clause (2) of subparagraph (g), and
particularly its use of the undefined but inflammatory
work "systematic." This is an extreme example from the
front page of the Medical Library Association News for
July, 1975:

We have been working very hard for the
deletion of section 108(g)(2) of the
same bill which would not allow us to
photocopy on a "systematic" basis.
This is the same section of the Senate
bill on which the Association passed a
resolution in San Antonio last year.
It is very important that you, as
members, explain to library users that
if HB2223 is passed with Section 108
(g)(2) that all photocopy, especially
interlibrary loan, will be prohibited
and a librarian liable to a very stiff
fine (up to $50,000.)

Almost equally controversial with librarians is the rather long commentary on the clause appearing in the 1974 Senate report:

> Subsection (g) also provides that section 108 does not authorize the systematic reproduction or distribution of copies or phono-records of articles or other contributions to copyrighted collections or periodicals or of small parts of other copyrighted works whether or not multiple copies are reproduced or distributed. Systematic reproduction or distribution occurs when a library makes copies of such materials available to other libraries or to groups of users under formal or informal arrangements whose purpose or effect is to have the reproducing library serve as their source of such material. Such systematic reproduction and distribution, as distinguished from isolated and unrelated reproduction or distribution, may substitute the copies reproduced by the source library for subscriptions or reprints or other copies which the receiving libraries or users might otherwise have purchased for themselves, from the publisher or the licensed reproduction agencies.
>
> While it is not possible to formulate specific definitions of "systematic copying" the following examples serve to illustrate some of the copying prohibited by subsection (g):
>
> 1. A library with a collection of journals in biology informs other libraries with similar collections that it will maintain and build its own collection and will make copies of articles from these journals

available to them and their
patrons on request. Accordingly, the other libraries
discontinue or refrain from
purchasing subscriptions to
these journals and fulfill
their patron's requests for
articles by obtaining photocopies
from the source library.

2. A research center employing a
number of scientists and
technicians subscribes to one
or two copies of needed
periodicals. By reproducing
photocopies of articles the
center is able to make the
material in these periodicals
available to its staff in the
same manner which otherwise
would have required multiple
subscriptions.

3. Several branches of a library
system agree that one branch will
subscribe to particular journals
in lieu of each branch purchasing
its own subscriptions, and that
the one subscribing branch will
reproduce copies of articles from
the publication for users of the
other branches.

The committee believes that section 108
provides an appropriate statutory balancing
of the rights of creators, and the needs
of users. However, neither a statute nor
legislative history can specify precisely
which library photocopying practices
constitute the making of "single copies"
as distinguished from "systematic reproduction". Isolated single spontaneous
requests must be distinguished from
"systematic reproduction." The photo-

copying needs of such operations as
multi-county regional systems, must be
met. The committee therefore recommends
that representatives of authors, book and
periodical publishers and other owners of
copyrighted material meet with the library
community to formulate photocopying
guidelines to assist library patrons and
employees. Concerning library photocopying practices not authorized by this
legislation, the committee recommends
that workable clearance and licensing
procedures be developed.

The following excerpts from a statement submitted
on behalf of the Association of Research Libraries to
the House Judiciary Subcommittee on May 30, 1975 will
serve to summarize the librarians' position on this
subsection, which they are urgently seeking to have
deleted:

At issue, is the making, whether at the
request of a patron or at the request of
another library, of single copies

of copyrighted matter for the private
use of a scholar or other reader. Such
copies may be of articles from law
reviews, medical journals or scientific
or technical periodicals, or they may
be passages from other published works.
They are made in response to *individual*
requests for *single* copies, although
more than one individual may request a
copy of a particular part of a work in
a library's collection. In providing
this service, a library may make a
copy from a work located on its
premises, or in the case of a work not
in its own collection, it may request
the copy from another library, just as
it might obtain the original work
itself on an inter-library loan for a
patron who wished to borrow it ...

Clause (g)(2) excludes from the library
photocopying permitted under Section
108 any instance of "systematic
reproduction and distribution".
Because this restriction was written
into the bill by the Senate Patents,
Trademarks and Copyrights Subcommittee
at the last minute (after public
hearings had been held) and is only
vaguely and confusingly explained in
the committee report, it is impossible
to determine exactly what it means ...
It appears, however, to be potentially
applicable whenever a library makes a
photocopy of an article or other
portion of a published work in the
context of a "system". There are, of
course, many such systems of libraries
from city or county branch library
systems to the university with branch
campuses to regional library consortia.

Where it applies, Section 108(g)(2) would
reach the making of a *single* copy for a
single requester, of any part, however
small, of a copyrighted work. It is
precisely the right to make such copies
which Section 108 was intended to
confirm ...

The sole rationale offered for the new
restrictions is an assertion that they
are necessary in order to prevent present
and potential subscribers from relying
on library photocopying machines in the
place of journal subscriptions. That
assertion is simply and clearly not
valid ...

The question which this Subcommittee is
called upon to answer may be simply put.
Should a library be prohibited from
making, at a user's request, a single
copy of a journal article or of an

excerpt from another published work, or
liable for a royalty fee simply because
it obtains the copy from, or supplies it
to a branch library, a library member
of a county or regional library system,
or other consortium of libraries?
Because it is clear that such customary
copying by libraries is responsive to
specific, specialized needs of library
users, provides the public access to
materials which would otherwise be
unavailable and does not in fact serve
as a substitute for subscription to the
publications concerned, the answer must
be that libraries should not be so
prohibited or so liable.

Of the arguments in favor of retention of subsection (g)(2) put forward by authors and publishers,
the statement on behalf of the Association of American
Publishers will serve as an example:

Systematic copying, in other words,
substitutes the copying for the
original which otherwise would have
been purchased from the publishers.
The library world appears to be
divided on whether or not licensing
procedures should be worked out
for systematic copying. Some insist
that no distinction should be
admitted between unauthorized
systematic copying and copying pursuant to isolated requests, and
that payment should be made for
neither. Others concede the
difference in principle, but say
that the kind of copying that should
be paid for is too imprecisely
defined in Section 108, and that no
practical prodedures have been
established by which clearance can
be obtained and payments made.

We think it unnecessary to belabor
the point that unauthorized
systematic copying -- the kind of
copying that is done at a research
center, or at a central resource
point for use in a library network
-- is the functional equivalent of
piratical reprint publication.
Certainly this kind of copying
must be paid for if, as the National
Commission on Libraries and information Science puts it, "the
economic viability and continuing
creativity of authorship and publishing" are to be protected. (Synopsis
of second draft proposal, June 1974.)

It is equally meretricious to complain
that the "systematic copying" that is
to be paid for is too imprecisely defined
or that payment cannot be made because
payment systems have not been established.

Section 108(g) excludes from library
copying privileges not only "systematic
copying" but also the related or concerted reproduction or distribution of
"multiple" copies. Systematic copying
and multiple copying are general
concepts; both are illustrated by
examples in the Senate committee report
(which closely follows the discussion
of fair use in your 1967 committee
report), and neither is more imprecise
than many other statutory or common
law doctrines with which we are all
familiar. The libraries do not claim
an inability to understand the multiple
copying concept; the systematic copying
concept is no less viable or understandable.

On September 19, 1975, in a letter to

Chairman Rodino of the House Judiciary Committee,
David Mathews, Secretary of the Department of Health,
Education and Welfare, stated:

> In brief, the bill as presently worded
> contains a provision (subsection 108(g))
> which would severely hamper the flow of
> biomedical information between the
> National Library of Medicine and the
> nation's medical libraries and thereby
> reduce the information available to
> researchers and practitioners. Deletion
> of Subsection 108(g) would remove this
> restriction. However, if deletion of
> this Subsection is not possible
> modification of the language contained
> therein would accomplish the same goal.

Attached to Secretary Mathews' letter was a
memorandum which included the following draft revision
of subsection (g)(2):

> ... engages in the systematic *and*
> *unlimited* reproduction or distribution
> of single or multiple copies or phono-
> records of the same material described
> in Subsection (d) *so as to substantially*
> *impair the market for, or value of, the*
> *copyrighted work.*

The memorandum added:

> "For purposes of avoiding ambiguity
> the bill should include explicit
> definitions of 'systematic reproduction'
> and 'fair use'."

h.   Relation to Commission on
*   New Technological Uses (CONTU)*

An immediated question facing the CONTU
commissioners at their first meeting on October 8,
involves the interrelationship between section 108 and
their mandate with respect to studying and making

recommendation on "various forms of machine reproduction."
In connection with section 108 the 1974 Senate report
said:

> In adopting these provisions on
> library photocopying, the committee is
> aware that through such programs as those
> of the National Commission on Libraries
> and Information Science there will be a
> significant evolution in the functioning
> and services of libraries. To consider
> the possible need for changes in copy-
> right law and procedures as a result of
> new technology, title II of this legis-
> lation establishes a National Commission
> on New Technological Uses of Copyrighted
> Works.
>
> It is the desire of the committee that
> the Commission give priority to those
> aspects of the library-copyright
> interface which require further study
> and clarification.

The following statement also appeared in the
section of the report dealing with the Commission itself:

> It is not the intent of the committee that
> the Commission should undertake to re-open
> the examination of those copyright issues
> which have received detailed consideration
> during the current revision effort, and
> concerning which satisfactory solutions
> appear to have been achieved.

5. *COMMENTS AND RECOMMENDATIONS*

    *a. Interrelationship between
       sections 107 and 108*

The librarians finally decided to seek express
photocopying exemptions because the flexible and untested
doctrine of fair use does not provide enough assurance
that some of the things they now want to do are legal.
They object strenuously to the provisions expressly

limiting the scope of those exemptions, because they
fear that these express limitations will also have the
effect of limiting the scope of what a court might hold
to be fair use today. On the other hand, authors and
publishers argue that, if section 108 consists only of
unlimited exemptions, they would be placed in an
impossible situation. To take an extreme example,
suppose that under the new law a library were providing
multiple copies of entire books still in print. This
is clearly not covered by the exemption in section 108.
Should the library be able to argue that, irrespective
of section 108, its activities constitute fair use
under section 107, and support its position with
exactly the same arguments the National Library of
Medicine used in the *Williams & Wilkins* case?

Although it has not been stated, or perhaps
even perceived, in these terms, this is the real crux
of the dispute over subsections (g) and (h). If
section 108 were made to supersede the fair use doctrine completely, no limitations such as those in
subsections (g) and (h) would be necessary; the only
exemptions would be those stated in subsections (a)
through (b). As long as fair use applies to library
photocopying, without much more definitive legal
authority as to its scope than now exists, some limitations are essential if section 108 is to settle
anything.

No one is arguing that the fair use doctrine
should be made inapplicable to library photocopying
and such would be very hard to sustain. The very
amorphousness of fair use provides a needed safety
valve. But as long as the revision bill contains
both a section 107 and a section 108, the latter must
put some express limitations on the express exemptions
it provides. It would be a mistake to delete
subsections (g) and (h) out of hand. What is needed
is a much clearer statement in the report concerning
the interrelationships between sections 107 and 108,
and a careful look at the wording and content of
subsections (g) and (h).

b. *Subsections (d) and (e)*

The deletions suggested by the Justice Department fail to take account of the long history of subsections (d) and (e). They would destroy the entire basis of the 1973 compromise, which was derived from a proposal of the librarians themselves.

Subsections (d) and (e) are the nub of section 108. No one at the 1975 hearings opposed them, and they were praised by representatives from both sides. Under these circumstances there is no convincing reason to change them.

c. *Profit-making organizations*

The language in section 108(a)(1)--"without any purpose of direct or indirect commercial advantage"-- was included in the draft put forward by the librarians and adopted, in part, by the Senate Judiciary Subcommittee in 1969. The question of interpretation was first raised by the librarians at the 1975 hearings, and apparently had not been made an issue earlier. The 1974 Senate report does not provide an explanation of the phrase's meaning in section 108. However, the phrase appears elsewhere in the bill, notably in section 110(4), and in that connection the Senate report has this to say:

> *No profit motive.*--In addition to the other conditions specified by the clause, the performance must be "without any purpose of direct or indirect commercial advantage." This provision expressly adopts the principle established by the court decisions construing the "for profit" limitation: that public performances given or sponsored in connection with any commercial or profit-making enterprises are subject to the exclusive rights of the copyright owner even though the public is not charged for seeing or hearing the performance.

The 1961 Register's Report contained a section

headed "Multiple and commercial photocopying," which
read as follows:

> c. *Multiple and commercial photocopying*
> The question of making photocopies has
> also arisen in the situation where an indus-
> trial concern wishes to provide multiple
> copies of publications, particularly of
> scientific and technical journals, to a
> number of research workers on its staff.
> To permit multiple photocopying may make
> serious inroads on the publisher's potential
> market. We believe that an industrial con-
> cern should be expected to buy the number of
> copies it needs from the publisher, or to
> get the publisher's consent to its making
> of photocopies.
>
> Similarly, any person or organization
> undertaking to supply photocopies to others
> as a commercial venture would be competing
> directly with the publisher, and should be
> expected to get the publisher's consent.
>
> There has been some discussion of the
> possibility of a contractual arrangement
> whereby industrial concerns would be given
> blanket permission to make photocopies for
> which they would pay royalties to the pub-
> lishers. Such an arrangement, which has
> been made in at least one foreign country,
> would seem to offer the best solution for
> the problem of multiple and commercial
> photocopying.

On the other hand, the library photocopying section
of the Copyright Office's 1963 preliminary draft
contained no conditions limiting the exemption to nonprofit libraries or noncommercial motives. This lack
was singled out for severe criticisms by representatives of authors and publishers during the 1963
meetings on the draft.

It should be noted that, as the section is now

written, it makes no difference whether the library
or archive is part of a profit-making organization;
the question is whether "the reproduction is made
without any purpose of direct or indirect commercial
advantage." The legislative history of this provision is sparse and the librarians' 1975 proposal has
not been debated. The point should certainly be
clarified.

On the substance of the question, the Copyright
Office adheres to its 1961 position. We believe that
a library or archives in a profit-making organization
should not, without copyright licenses, be entitled
to go beyond fair use in providing photocopies to
employees engaged in furtherance of the organization's
commercial enterprise. We believe that this was the
meaning intended by the drafters of the language
in question, and that this interpretation should be
reflected in the report.

d. *Works not covered by exemption*

Although the librarians at the 1975 hearings sought
the complete deletion of subsection (h), their proposal seemed to involve music more than the other
categories of works covered by that provision.
The Copyright Office recognizes the concerns of
music librarians, but we believe that--with respect
not only to music but to pictorial graphic, and
sculptural works and motion pictures and other audiovisual works--the needs of scholars can and should
be met through fair use. It is especially important
for the legislative report to make clear the relationship between sections 107 and 108(h).

A point not raised at the hearings but of real
concern in this connection involves pictorial and
graphic works reproduced as illustrations in books,
periodicals, and other literary works. There was
probably no intention to prevent their reproduction as part of works or excerpts covered by subsections (d) and (3), and subsection (h)
should probably be amended to make this clear.

e. *Videotape archives*

At the moment the highly publicized copyright
infringement action of CBS against Vanderbilt University for unauthorized off-the-air taping of copyrighted network newscasts and distribution of the
tapes, in some cases in slightly edited or compiled
form, is in a state of suspension, apparently awaiting a possible agreed settlement, Congressional action,
or some other form of rescue. The public issues underlying the case, and the Baker amendments to section 108,
are important, difficult, fascinating, and in some ways
dangerous.

The Copyright Office cannot support the Baker
amendments as they stand. They go far beyond Senator
Baker's announced purpose of insulating Vanderbilt
from liability under the new law and assuring that it
can continue its valuable work. The language could
be construed to exempt activities that were in no way
contemplated by the sponsors of the legislation, and
that could open the door to completely unjustified
abuses.

The Copyright Office believes strongly that the
fundamental problems addressed in this legislation
should be dealt with by establishing, through the
mandatory copyright deposit system already in the bill,
a national repository of television films, including
but not limited to "hard news" programs, in the Library
of Congress and the National Archives. Recognizing the
commendable initiative Vanderbilt has taken in preserving material of great historic value that was otherwise
threatened with loss, and that other institutions or
individuals might be in the same situation, there
should be no objection to allowing them to continue
on-going activities, at least up to a reasonable point.
We recommend a grandfather clause for this purpose,
coupled with amendments to the current revision bill
establishing a national television repository that
would preserve rather than destroy fully-justified
copyright protection while, at the same time, giving
scholars, the public, and future generations the
real benefits that Mr. Simpson and the Vanderbilt
Archive have been seeking to provide.

This proposal is new to the discussions of the copyright revision bill, but consideration of it, or variations of it, have been going on for several years. Our television heritage is slipping away from us, but agreements on how to save it have been hard to achive. The Baker amendment, and the testimony on it in the 1975 House hearings, reflect a bitter and unproductive controversy in which the public has been the principal loser. We believe that the best answer lies directly in the copyright revision bill, but not by means of the approach accepted by the Senate in section 108. We recommend that the Baker amendment be deleted, and that substitute amendments be drafted along the lines suggested here. The Copyright Office would be proud to play a part in such a program.

f.   *Multiple copying*

The Copyright Office believes that clause (1) of section 108 (g) is reasonable and necessary, and that its language is clear and should not be changed, much less deleted. The legislative report should be revised to make the Congressional intent clearer and to quiet unnecessary fears.

g.   *Systematic reproduction*

As indicated above in paragraph 1 of this section of Chapter III, the Copyright Office believes that it would be a mistake to delete paragraph (g) completely. Instead, the meaning of fair use in the context of library photocopying and section 108 must be clarified. As part of that process, both the language and sub-section (g)(2) and the commentary on it in the report should be carefully reexamined in light of the real concerns of librarians.

A line must be drawn between legitimate interli-brary loans using photocopies instead of bound books, and pre-arranged understandings that result in a par-ticular library agreeing to become the source for an indeterminate number of photcopies. To find that line and draw it clearly is one of the most difficult legis-lative tasks remaining in the revision program.

h. Relation to CONTU

The new National Commission on New Technological Uses of Copyrighted Works has been given very short deadlines, and could benefit from Congressional guidance as to what areas it could most profitably explore with respect to photocopying. Three possibilities have been suggested:

1) Evolution of a more detailed and up-to-date version of the 1935 "gentlemen's agreement" (called by something besides that distasteful term) which would give ordinary librarians daily guidance with respect to practices they could live with;

2) Collection of unimpeachable data concerning library loan and interlibrary loan activities, and development of proposals for voluntary licensing mechanisms;

3) Beyond photocopying by libraries, collection of information about the reprographic reproduction of copyrighted works in large industrial, commercial, and professional profit-making organizations.

CHAPTER IV

LIMITATIONS ON PERFORMING RIGHTS: IN GENERAL*

Sections Considered:

#106 - Exclusive rights in copyrighted works

#110 - Limitations on exclusive rights: Exemption of certain performances and displays.

#501   Infringement of copyright

Issues:

1.   Does the decision of the U.S. Supreme
Court in *Twentieth Century Music Corp.*
v. *Aiken* call for any changes in the
bill itself, in the legislative report,
or both?

2.   Should the bill be amended to absolve
from liability the proprietors of establishments performing copyrighted music,
where the performance is controlled by
an independent contractor?

*   The range of problems arising under sections 110
and 112 with respect to performances and recordings made for nonprofit broadcasting are dealt
with in Chapter V. The questions of cable television and other secondary transmissions is
covered in Chapter VI; that of performing rights
in sound recordings is discussed in Chapter VIII,
and the jukebox provision is the subject of
Chapter X.

A. DISCUSSION OF ISSUES

1. *IN GENERAL*

The general rights of public performance and display, which are enunciated in clauses (4) and (5) of
section 106, are made subject to seven specific limitations in section 110 of the 1975 revision bill.
An eighth limitation, dealing with broadcasts for
blind, deaf, and other handicapped persons, was added
by the Senate Judiciary Subcommittee on June 13, 1975,
when it reported the bill to the full Committee.
Each of the subsections has, at one time or another,
been the focal point of controversy, some of it quite

intense, and issues involving the scope of protection for performances and displays in nonprofit broadcasting still remain to be settled. These issues, and the relevant provisions of clause (2) and the new clause (8) of section 110, will be discussed in the next chapter.

As it has emerged from the legislative process so far, section 110 would exempt the following eight types of public performance and displays from copyright liability under specified conditions:

(1) face-to-face teaching activities;

(2) instructional broadcasting;

(3) religious services;

(4) live performances without commercial advantage to anyone;

(5) mere reception of broadcasts in a public place;

(6) annual agricultural and horticultural fairs;

(7) public performance in connection with sale of records or sheet music;

(8) noncommercial broadcasts to the blind or deaf (added by the Senate Judiciary Subcommittee on June 13, 1975).

At the 1975 hearings the only issues raised in connection with any of these provisions involved clauses (2) and (8). However, as the result of a Supreme Court decision handed down during the course of the hearings, further consideration of clause (5) of section 110 seems necessary. The other issue dealt with in this chapter was raised in connection with section 501, but is probably more germane to the general subject of limitations on performing rights.

Annual Report to the Librarian of Congress by the Register of Copyrights: 1976

DEVELOPMENTS ON COPYRIGHT REVISION

With the passage of the copyright revision bill, S. 22, by the Senate on February 19, 1976, and favorable action on H.R. 2223 by the Subcommittee on Courts, Civil Liberties, and the Administration of Justice of the House Judiciary Committee on August 3, 1976, the revision of the 1909 copyright law made further progress. The register has assisted the subcommittee at its request in the extensive sessions concerned with review and mark-up of the bill, and the Copyright Office's legal staff has been available to the Congress for consultation. In late 1975 and early 1976, the register submitted to the House subcommittee the final portions of the draft "Second Supplementary Report of the Register of Copyrights on Copyright Law Revision." This report, in nineteen chapters, summarizes and discusses the legislative history of the copyright revision bill and identifies its areas of controversy. It is expected that the report will be published by the House Judiciary Committee. If and when the revision becomes a reality, the occasion will represent a historic advance in the story of American copyright and the beginning of a new age in that saga. The delays met by the proposed revision in former years have led to an atmosphere of understandable concern and intense pressures that can only be lifted by enactment of a new law.

The revision bill, to review briefly its general framework, will substitute a single federal system for the present dual common law and federal system divided by the act of publication. This sweeping change means that every work that is eligible for copyright will come within federal statutory copyright from the moment of its fixation. Additionally, an entire new range of unpublished and published materials will be eligible for statutory protection.

The term of copyright protection will be the life of the author plus fifty years—a major breakthrough in American copyright law and one that will not only put the United States in general parity with the rest of the world but may also advance the prospects for our acceding to the Berne Copyright Convention. There will be a reversionary right in the author and his heirs, allowing recapture of the copyright through termination of existing assignments.

Other broad changes involve ownership of copyright, relaxation of many of the rigid rules regarding notice, new deposit and registration requirements that include a radio and television archive, derived through copyright, for the Library of Congress, redrawn infringement remedies, and easing and phasing out of the manufacturing clause. While expected compromises have had to be made—a necessity anticipated because of the pressures from those representing special interests based on modern technology—the basic objective of the bill is protection for the creator of intellectual property.

The major areas of controversy have been discussed in earlier annual reports. Perhaps it is sufficient here simply to list them once again:

Size of the mechanical royalty

Liability for performance of music by coin-operated phonorecord machines (the so-called juke-box exemption)

Compulsory licenses for cable television

Proposals for a royalty upon broadcasting of sound recordings

Exemptions urged for public broadcasting

Photocopying in education and libraries

It is heartening to be able to report that after weeks of deliberation in the House subcommittee these issues, including the difficult questions concerned with compulsory licensing, were settled harmoniously if not to the entire satisfaction of all the special interests. The register, while recognizing the inevitabilty of compromise, took the consistent position that in our rapidly changing technological society extreme care must be taken to ensure that independent, free authorship is preserved as a natural, vital resource.

Every indication is that favorable action by the full House Judiciary Committee on the revision bill will be completed in early September. The necessity for prompt House action and a conference committee to resolve differences between S. 22 and H.R. 2223 placed the revision bill under a tight schedule during this election year. The optimism that the Congress will meet this challenge has been reinforced by the prompt Senate action on S. 22, under the leadership of Senator John L. McClellan, and the remarkably comprehensive and careful work of the House subcommittee, headed by Representative Robert Kastenmeier. At the opening of the subcommittee hearings in May 1975, former register of copyrights Abraham L. Kaminstein (one of the chief architects of revision) alluded to the dedication of the House subcommittee that considered the revision bill in 1965.

The progress of the revision bill has intensified the need for advance planning for new functions and the enormous workload that will accompany implementation, which could be in 1978. A coordinating committee, composed of the general counsel of the Copyright Office, its executive officer, and the chief of the Planning and Technical Office, was organized in April 1976 to begin this task.

The new law, when it finally comes, will augment the work of the Copyright Office in a number of ways. Its protection of a wider variety of creative works will mean a substantial increase in the volume of registrations. Anticipated provisions that require the Copyright Office to collect and distribute royalty fees would be a new function. Secondary transmissions by a cable system of a primary transmission made by a broadcast station licensed by the Federal Communications Commission will be subject to compulsory licensing and the register of copyrights charged with collecting the license fees. Licenses that must be provided by the Copyright Office will also be required for operators of coin-operated phonorecord machines. Guidelines, new procedures, and revised regulations will be required for the administration of each of these new or enlarged functions.

Annual Report to the Librarian of Congress by the Register of Copyrights: 1977

PASSAGE OF THE REVISION BILL

On Tuesday, the nineteenth day of October of America's Bicentennial year, President Gerald R. Ford signed into law the long-awaited bill for the general revision of the copyright law. With this signature the United States took a dramatic step toward a horizon beyond the intellectual property trails worn smooth by copyright practitioners since the inception of a federal literary property statute in 1790, the fourteenth year of our independence. The culmination of many years of sustained effort by its proponents, the new statute, known as Public Law 94-553, an Act for the General Revision of the Copyright Law (title 17 of the United States Code), represents the fourth general revision of that legislation and the first such revision since enactment of the Act of 1909 in the closing hours of the ast term of President Theodore Roosevelt.

The final legislative phase preceding passage of the conference version of the bill by both the Senate and House of Representatives on September 30, 1976, began on February 19, 1976, when the Senate unanimously passed S. 22 by a vote of 97 to 0, a tribute to the patience and leadership of the late Senator John. L. McClellan of Arkansas, chairman of the Subcommittee on Patents, Trademarks, and Copyrights of the Committee on the Judiciary. On August 3, 1976, following twenty-two days of public mark-up sessions, the House Judiciary Subcommittee on Courts, Civil Liberties, and the Administration of Justice favorably reported S. 22 by a unanimous vote, likewise a tribute to the chairmanship and unflagging energy of Representative Robert W. Kastenmeier of Wisconsin. The full Committee on the Judiciary of the House of Representatives reported favorably on S. 22 on August 27, 1976. As so reported, the bill was substantially identical with that reported on August 3 by the subcommittee as an amendment in the nature of a substitute to S. 22. The careful and comprehensive work of the House subcommittee was assisted by the *Second Supplementary Report of the Register of Copyrights on Copyright Law Revision*, an extensive summation of legislative history with an analysis of the technical issues embodied in the revision legislation.

In spite of the press of legislative business in the waning months of a presidential election year, the House of Representatives approved S. 22 on September 22, 1976, by the decisive margin of 316 to 7. A week later the conference report, which reconciled the differences between the Senate version of S. 22 as passed on February 19, 1976, and the House version as passed on September 22, was submitted by the committee of conference to the Congress. The following day, Thursday, September 30, 1976, both the Senate and House of Representatives accepted the conference version of the bill. The die was cast. The presidential signature on October 19, 1976, capped the pyramid inaugurating an unprecedented transformation of laws implementing the Constitutional mandate empowering the Congress "to promote the Progress of Science and useful Arts, by securing for limited Times to Authors . . . the exclusive Right to their respective Writings . . . ."

The new copyright statute that will become fully effective on January 1, 1978, superseding the Copyright Act of 1909, as amended, includes a number of significant innovations. Thus, instead of the present dual system of protecting works under the common law before publication and under the federal statute thereafter, the new law establishes a single unitary system of statutory protection for all copyrightable works, whether published or unpublished.

The term of copyright protection for works created on or after January 1, 1978, will be equal to the life of the author plus an additional fifty years after the author's death. The new term for works made for hire and for anonymous and pseudonymous works will be seventy-five years from publication or one hundred years from creation, whichever is shorter. This same term is also generally applicable to unpublished works already in existence on January 1, 1978, that are not protected by statutory copyright and have not yet entered the public domain.

For works already under statutory protection, the new law retains the present term of copyright of twenty-eight years from first publication (or from registration in some cases), renewable by certain persons for a second period of protection, but increases the length of the second period from twenty-eight to forty-seven years. Copyrights subsisting in their second term at any time between December 31, 1976, and December 31, 1977, inclusive, are automatically extended to last for a total term of seventy-five years from the date they were originally secured, without the need of further renewal. However, copyrights in their first term on January 1, 1978, must still be renewed during the last (twenty-eighth) year of the original copyright term to receive the full new maximum statutory duration of seventy-five years.

The judicial doctrine of "fair use," one of the most important and well-established limitations on the exclusive rights of copyright owners, receives express statutory recognition for the first time in the new law, which provides specific standards for determining whether particular uses fall within this category. In addition to the provisions for fair use, the new law also specifies conditions under which the making or distribution of single copies of works by libraries and archives for noncommercial purposes will not constitute an infringement of copyright.

The new law establishes an independent five-member agency in the legislative branch named the Copyright Royalty Tribunal and entrusts this body with specific regulatory authority governing the procedures and responsibilities for disbursement of funds derived from the use of copyrighted works in cable television transmissions, jukebox performances, and certain other categories where copyright royalty rates are fixed by law.

The limited compulsory license provisions of the present act are extended by the terms of the new act to include the payment of royalties for the secondary transmission of copyrighted works on cable antenna television (CATV) systems, the performance of copyrighted music in jukeboxes, and the noncommercial transmission by public broadcasters of published musical and graphic works. Retained in the new law, with some changes, are the existing provisions in the present law permitting compulsory licensing for the recording of music.

Registration in the Copyright Office under the new law will not be a condition of copyright protection but will be a prerequisite to an infringement suit. Subject to certain exceptions, the remedies of statutory damages and attorney's fees will not be available for infringements occurring before registration. However, if a work has been published in the United States with notice of copyright, copies or phonorecords must be deposited in the Copyright Office for the collections of the Library of Congress, not as a condition of copyright protection, but rather under provisions of the law subjecting the copyright owner to certain penalties for failure to deposit following written demand by the register of copyrights.

REVISION MOVEMENT

The Copyright Act of 1976 embodies essentially the same provisions as its predecessors, H.R. 4347 and S. 1006, introduced in both Houses on February 4, 1965, at the beginning of the 89th Congress, by Senator McClellan, chairman of the Senate Judiciary Subcommittee on Patents, Trademarks, and Copyrights, and Representative Emanuel Celler of New York, chairman of the House Committee on the Judiciary.

These bills represented complete revisions of the original draft bills for revision, H.R. 11947 and S. 3008, which had been introduced in the House and Senate, respectively, on July 20, 1964, during the second session of the 88th Congress. Both earlier versions had taken form as an outgrowth of efforts between 1961 and 1964 to produce a consensus among participating representatives of the many diverse interests affected by the copyright law. Of considerable importance in arriving at these results had been a Panel of Consultants on General Revision, formed under the auspices of the Copyright Office. The 1965 bills represented a complete redraft of their 1964 counterparts, based upon a review and analysis of the many written and oral comments made upon the latter. The publication in May 1965 of the *Supplementary Report of the Register of Copyrights on the General Revision of the U.S. Copyright Law: 1965 Revision Bill,* coincided with the commencement of congressional hearings in the House of Representatives before Subcommittee Number 3 of the Committee on the Judiciary, under the chairmanship of Mr. Kastenmeier and Mr. Celler, respectively.

Between May 26 and September 2, 1965, a total of twenty-two days of public hearings were held which yielded of 1,930 pages of printed text including 150 written statements in addition to the oral transcript, the testimony of 163 witnesses representing the widest spectrum of public and private interests in the proposed legislation. Sharp conflicts on some of the major issues presented by the bill did not prevent a flood of compliments about the remarkable thoroughness of the legislative preparation and the intelligent, germane, and dispassionate statements of the many witnesses. On October 12, 1966, following fifty-one executive sessions of the House Judiciary Subcommittee, Chairman Celler's full Judiciary Committee favorably reported the bill as amended in the 279-page Report 2237 (89th Congress, 2d Session), an unusually valuable addition, at that time, to the legislative history of the general revision bill.

In the meantime, hearings initiated in August 1965, before the Senate Judiciary Subcommittee on S. 1006 temporarily resumed on August 2, 1966, under the acting chairmanship of Senator Quentin N. Burdick of North Dakota, on the specific question of community antenna television systems.

Reintroduced in both Houses at the outset of the 90th Congress as H.R. 2512 and S. 597, the bill was once again, on March 8, 1967, the subject of another Report by the House Judiciary Committee, Number 83 (90th Congress, 1st Session) this time without further amendment but with dissenting views. On April 11, 1967, by a vote of 379 to 29, the measure was passed by the House of Representatives with several important amendments. Although the structure and content of the bill had remained substantially intact, drastic revisions in the compulsory licensing provisions relating to jukebox performances had been made, and the exemptions for instructional television were considerably broadened. Moreover, the provisions dealing with community antenna transmission were dropped entirely, theoretically exposing CATV systems to full liability for copyright infringement under the bill.

On April 28, 1967, the Senate Judiciary Subcommittee, under the joint chairmanship of Senators McClellan and Burdick, completed ten days of hearings on S. 597 begun in mid-March that produced 1,383 pages of printed oral transcript and written statements. Although these hearings did not consider the problem of CATV, which had been the focus of testimony in August of the previous year, other controversial issues emerged, of which probably the most important concerned the use of copyrighted works in automated information storage and retrieval systems. The absence of any ready legislative solution to these questions made it clear that the 90th Congress would not see completed action on copyright revision.

The impact of these emerging controversies slowed the momentum acquired by the revision program after the decisively favorable vote of the House of Representatives in passing H.R. 2512. The midyear landmark Supreme Court decision in *Fortnightly Corp.* v. *United Artists Television, Inc.,* 392 U.S. 390 (1968), gave marked impetus to the same tendency since the affected industries opposed any further legislative action until they had had time enough to absorb and evaluate the results.

The dwindling momentum also aroused concern about the status of copyrights subsisting in their second term but due to expire before December 31, 1967. Anticipating enactment of a general revision bill substantially lengthening the duration of copyrights already in effect, the Congress had adopted in 1962, and again in 1965, two measures extending the term of renewal copyrights otherwise due to expire. In the face of the protracted slowdown in the revision movement, Congress passed the third extension bill, which became Public Law 90-141 on November 16, 1967. Before enactment of the new copyright law was finally achieved in 1976, a total of nine interim extension bills had been passed, automatically extending the duration of copyrights subsisting in their second term to seventy-five years from the date they were originally secured.

In the first month of the 91st Congress, the chairman of the Senate Subcommittee on Patents, Trademarks, and Copyrights introduced a new revision bill, S. 543, which was identical with its predecessor, S. 597, except for technical amendments and the addition of a provision for establishment of a National Commission on New Technological Uses of Copyrighted Works. On December 10, 1969, Senator McClellan's subcommittee favorably reported S. 543, with an amendment in the nature of a substitute, but the cable television issue foreclosed further action in the full Judiciary Committee. Early in the succeeding 92d Congress, Senator McClellan introduced S. 644, which, except for minor amendments, was identical with the revision bill reported by the subcommittee in late 1969. The 92d Congress saw no further action on general revision legislation while proponents awaited formulation and adoption of new cable television rules by the Federal Communications Commission. The delay of revision legislation was also preventing the extension of federal copyright protection to sound recordings. With the unauthorized duplication of sound recordings becoming widespread, the need for special remedial action became apparent. Accordingly, Senator McClellan introduced S. 646 at the outset of the 92d Congress to amend the existing copyright statute to provide for the creation of a limited copyright in sound recordings. Identical with S. 4592, which Mr. McClellan had introduced on December 18, 1970, this bill passed the Senate on April 29, 1971. Following hearings, a companion measure, H.R. 6927, passed the House of Representatives with amendments in early October and was enacted shortly thereafter as Public Law 92-140. By the terms of the act, whose provisions were taken in substance from the general revision bill, statutory copyright protection was made available to sound recordings first fixed on or after February 15, 1972, if the sound recording was published with the prescribed notice of copyright.

On March 26, 1973, Senator McClellan introduced S. 1361 for the general revision of the copyright law. This bill was identical with its predecessor, S. 644, except for technical amendments. On May 29, 1973, Representative Bertram L. Podell of New York introduced H.R. 8186, an identical counterpart to the Senate bill. On July 31 and August 1, 1973, the Senate Subcommittee on Patents, Trademarks, and Copyrights held supplementary hearings on issues affected by current developments relating to library photocopying, general educational exemptions, the cable television royalty schedule, carriage of sporting events by cable television, and an exemption for recording religious music for broadcasts.

Shortly after the Supreme Court's decision of March 4, 1974, in *Teleprompter* v. *Columbia Broadcasting System, Inc.,* 415 U.S. 394, which extended copyright exemption to the importation of distant signal programming by cable antenna television systems, the Senate Judiciary Subcommittee resumed active consideration of the McClellan bill and on April 9, 1974, reported S. 1361 with some amendments to the full Judiciary Committee, which in turn made its favorable report on July 3, 1974, together with a 228-page printed report, Number 93-983.

The most controversial issues in the reported bill involved establishment of a royalty for the public performance of sound recordings and the carriage of broadcasts of sporting events on cable television. Principally because these issues were deemed to hold implications for communications policy, the copyright bill was then referred to the Senate Commerce Committee at its own request. On July 29 that committee also reported the bill with further amendments and a ninety-two page report, Number 93-1035.

Finally on September 9, 1974, by a vote of 70 to 1, the measure passed the Senate with additional amendments. The "performance royalty" for sound recordings and the "sports blackout" provisions were deleted before passage of the bill, whose basic purpose and structure remained unchanged. Although it was apparent that insufficient time remained for House action in the second session of the 93d Congress, the flurry of activity coupled with the decisiveness of the Senate vote showed that the program for general revision of the copyright law had overcome the existing apathy and regained much of its legislative momentum.

However, three matters dealt with in the general revision bill were considered by Congress as too urgent to await final action on the omnibus legislation. The first of these involved making permanent the temporary federal copyright protection against unauthorized duplication of sound recordings fixed on or after February 15, 1972. The so-called "record piracy" law of 1971, Public Law 92-140, was scheduled to expire on December 31, 1974, unless extended in the meantime. The second and third matters, respectively concerned the status of subsisting copyrights in their renewal term which would otherwise expire at the end of 1974 and the establishment of a National Commission on New Technological Uses of Copyrighted Works. Since all three provisions were covered by the general revision bill, the Senate promptly passed S. 3976, an interim bill introduced by Senator McClellan on September 9, 1974.

On August 21, 1974, the House Judiciary Subcommittee on Courts, Civil Liberties, and the Administration of Justice had favorably reported a similar bill, H.R. 13364, which had been introduced by its chairman, Representative Kastenmeier. A favorable report was made on September 30 by the full House Judiciary Committee, accompanied by a printed report, Number 93-1389; thereafter, on October 7, 1974, the House of Representatives cleared the measure, under suspension of rules, by a two-thirds nonrecord vote. At the end of November, Mr. Kastenmeier's Judiciary Subcommittee held hearings on S. 3976, the only witness being the register of copyrights, who was asked to testify on the two issues on which the House was yet to take favorable action, namely, the extension of expiring renewal copyrights and the National Commission.

The subcommittee's favorable report on December 10, 1974, was followed two days later by that of the full Committee, which also issued printed Report 93-1581. The bill passed the House by a vote of 292 to 101 on December 19, 1974, the last day of the 93d Congress, and was accepted later the same day by the Senate. On December 31, 1974, only a few hours before the record piracy legislation and some 150,000 renewal copyrights were scheduled to expire, the legislation was approved by President Ford and became Public Law 93-573.

This last-minute legislative action not only helped regenerate the general revision program but also augured well for tangible progress during the next Congress. Thus, the two-year extension of copyrights in their renewal term was based on the assumption that an omnibus revision bill which would give a total term of seventy-five years to all subsisting copyrights could be enacted before the end of 1976. Establishment of a National Commission in advance of general revision, in order to study and gather information on the reproduction and use of copyrighted works by machine or in conjunction with automatic systems capable of storing, processing, retrieving, and transferring data, likewise showed congressional urgency concerning the unsettled copyright questions within the commission's purview.

Shortly after the convening of the 94th Congress, a new version of the revision bill that was substantially identical with S. 1361 as passed by the Senate the preceding September was introduced in both Houses by the respective chairmen of the concerned subcommittees. On January 15, 1975, Senator McClellan introduced S. 22, and on January 28, 1975, Mr. Kastenmeier introduced H.R. 2223 in the House of Representatives. Senate review of the bill by the Subcommittee on Patents, Trademarks, and Copyrights resulted, on April 13, 1975, in a favorable report to the full Senate Judiciary Committee with, however, a number of amendments, the most controversial of which was the restoration of provisions for periodic review of the royalty rate for jukebox performances.

In the House of Representatives, the first hearings on the revision bill since 1965 began before the Judiciary Subcommittee on Courts, Civil Liberties, and the Administration of Justice on May 7, 1975. Nearly one hundred witnesses appeared during the eighteen days of extensive hearings on H.R. 2223 before their conclusion on December 4, 1975. The resulting 2,240-page record of oral transcripts and written statements covered every important aspect of the proposed legislation, the bulk of whose provisions remained almost entirely unchanged since it passed the House in 1967. The basic features of Title I of the bill—such as the establishment of a single federal copyright system, duration of term based on the life of the author plus fifty years, ownership and transfer of rights, the subject matter of copyright, and the prescribed formalities—were left intact.

Title II of the bill consisted of what had originally been separate comprehensive legislation for the protection of ornamental designs of useful articles, based largely on copyright principles.

Originally introduced in 1957, the design protection measure received active consideration in both Houses during the succeeding decade. As separate legislation, it passed the Senate on three occasions—in 1962, 1963, and 1966. Reintroduced in the 90th and again in the 91st Congress, the Senate Judiciary Subcommittee on Patents, Trademarks, and Copyrights added it to the general copyright revision bill in late 1969, reporting it as Title III of S. 543. Twice thereafter, the design legislation passed the Senate, first as Title III of S. 1361 in the 93d Congress and then finally as Title II of S. 22 in the 94th Congress. Ultimately, the design legislation was deleted before congressional passage of the final conference version of the revision bill lest the unresolved issues it raised cause further delay in acceptance of basic copyright reform.

On November 20, 1975, while hearings in the House of Representatives on H.R. 2223 continued, the Senate Judiciary Committee favorably reported S. 22, accompanied by a 168-page printed report with additional views, Report 94-473. As reported above, soon after the beginning of the second session of the 94th Congress, on February 19, 1976, the Senate passed the bill unanimously by a vote of 97 to 0. Essentially the same as S. 1361, which the Senate had approved in 1974, the 1976 enactment embodied a new provision for the compulsory licensing by noncommercial educational broadcasts of certain works, at royalty fees established by the Copyright Royalty Tribunal. Also included was an amendment designed to ease the burden of copyright liability for smaller CATV systems with annual revenues under $160,000. Except for a number of added provisions, including those relating to cable antenna television, the 1976 Senate version of the revision bill corresponded in its general features with the measure approved by the House of Representatives in 1967.

EARLIER HISTORY

The new statute is the fourth general revision of the U.S. copyright law. Although there have been numerous minor amendments since the enactment of the first federal copyright statute on May 31, 1790, the only earlier general revisions were those of 1831, 1870, and 1909.

The movement for general revision of the copyright law that culminated in the 1976 enactment of Public Law 94-553 owes its modern origin to the Legislative Appropriations Act of 1955, which allocated funds for a comprehensive program of research and study of copyright law revision by the Copyright Office of the Library of Congress. Between 1955 and 1963, a total of thirty-five studies prepared under the supervision of the Copyright Office examined the past, present, and future prospects of the existing law with a view to considering a general revision of the copyright statute. The first thirty-four of these studies were published as committee prints by the Senate Committee on the Judiciary's Subcommittee on Patents, Trademarks, and Copyright (86th Congress, Second Session).

Revival of interest at this time in copyright revision was undoubtedly stimulated in part by the successful efforts to procure U.S. adherence to the text of the Universal Copyright Convention adopted at Geneva, Switzerland, on September 6, 1952. One of the original thirty-six signatories, the United States was also numbered among the first twelve countries whose adherence, under the terms of the convention, ultimately brought it into force on September 16, 1955. On the same date the federal copyright law was modified to comply with the convention in accordance with the provisions of Public Law 743 (68 Stat. 1030) as approved by President Eisenhower on August 31, 1954. By its ratification, the United States had become for the first time a participant in a system of international copyright protection destined to achieve virtually worldwide adoption. It was the most important development of its kind since the Chace Act of 1891 first permitted establishment of copyright relations between the United States and foreign countries.

The series of revision studies sponsored by the Senate subcommittee provided the research and analytical basis for the 1961 *Report of the Register of Copyrights on the General Revision of the U.S. Copyright Law.* This report, which contained detailed recommendations for an omnibus statute, in turn provided a focus for numerous meetings and discussions with a Panel of Consultants on General Revision, held during the following three years under the auspices of the Copyright Office. The resulting suggestions and recommendations, representing the full spectrum of interests affected by the copyright law, enabled the Copyright Office to present a preliminary draft of provisions for a general revision bill in 1963, leading to discussions and comments on that draft. The outcome of all of this sustained effort was the copyright law revision bill of 1964, introduced in the second session of the 88th Congress on July 20, 1964, as H.R. 11947 in the House of Representatives and as S. 3008 in the Senate. Although no legislative action was taken on these measures, the Copyright Office undertook a complete redraft of the bill in the light of the comments received in the wake of its introduction. On February 4, 1965, at the outset of the 89th Congress, the revision movement established itself firmly with the introduction in both Houses of the new and completely revised bill known as H.R. 4347 in the House and S. 1006 in the Senate, which would serve as a basis for extensive hearings soon to begin.

None of the earlier efforts to effect any broad

conform our law to the principles of the Berne Convention.

Nevertheless, the movement for revision continued in the same general direction until deflected by the reappearance in the 73d Congress of a movement to return to the narrower objective of the revision efforts initiated a decade earlier by limiting proposed changes only to those necessary for adherence to the convention. Meanwhile, the 1928 Rome Revision of the Berne Convention added features considered unacceptable by some segments of the American copyright community and no longer permitted adherence with reservations as previously allowed under the 1908 Berlin Revision of the Berne Convention.

The legislative effort continued but seemed to uncover new areas of controversy rather than to produce a consensus. In 1938 the Committee for the Study of Copyright, also called the Shotwell Committee (after its chairman, Prof. James T. Shotwell), arranged a series of conferences with a variety of interested copyright groups. A draft bill for complete revision of the law was prepared and introduced in the Senate of the 76th Congress in January 1940. However, no hearings were held on the so-called Shotwell bill, and no further legislative action was taken on it. After 1940, attempts to alter our law for membership in the Berne Union were abandoned. Following the Second World War, the United States participated actively in the development of the new Universal Copyright Convention, which was essentially consistent with the existing U.S. copyright law. The movement for general copyright revision lay dormant during the intervening years until its revival in 1955, when the new worldwide convention came into force.

revision of the Copyright Act of 1909 had benefited from the sustained and thorough kind of preparation that augured so well for the revision movement that in 1965 stood at the threshold of a strenuous but ultimately triumphant decade of progress. Forty-five years earlier, in the aftermath of the First World War, there were stirrings among publishing and other copyright interests generated by the growing market for American works abroad which attracted attention to shortcomings in our international copyright relations and prompted a desire for adherence to the multilateral treaty arrangement known as the Berne Convention, to which most European countries as well as others of importance subscribed.

Adherence to the Berne Convention would have required many fundamental changes in the U.S. copyright law, a fact that prompted proponents to widen their objectives to cover other issues as well. The first of these broad revision programs was presented to the Congress in 1924. Although no legislative action was taken on this measure, it did give rise to further discussions under congressional auspices that resulted in the emergence of revised proposals, one of which, known as the Vestal bill, was passed by the House of Representatives in early 1931 but failed to come to a vote in the Senate. The near enactment of the Vestal bill in the 71st Congress marked the furthest reach of the efforts to

Mr. MANSFIELD. Mr. President, I suggest the absence of a quorum.

The PRESIDING OFFICER. The clerk will call the roll.

The second assistant legislative clerk proceeded to call the roll.

Mr. McCLELLAN. Mr. President, I ask unanimous consent that the order for the quorum call be rescinded.

The PRESIDING OFFICER. Without objection, it is so ordered.

Mr. McCLELLAN. Mr. President, on September 9, 1974, the Senate by a vote of 70 to 1, passed the legislation for the general revision of the copyright law. It was then anticipated that the House of Representatives would not have time to consider the bill in the remaining weeks of the 93d Congress, and that it would be necessary for the Senate to again consider the copyright legislation in the 94th Congress.

The Committee on the Judiciary has reported by unanimous vote substantially the same bill passed by the Senate in 1974. That is the pending bill. Floor debate focused then on two issues—the creation of a performance right in sound recordings, and the carriage of sporting events by cable television systems. By rollcall votes the Senate decided not to include language on those issues in the bill. No provisions on these subjects are found in the pending bill.

This legislation has been under extensive consideration by the Subcommittee on Copyrights for a number of years. During this period the subcommittee held 19 days of hearings and received testimony from approximately 200 witnesses. Unfortunately, the progress of this legislation was necessarily delayed because of events beyond the control of the subcommittee.

The adoption of copyright legislation is one of the powers of the Congress specifically enumerated in article I of the Constitution. Our first copyright law was enacted in the very first session of the Congress in 1790. Since then it has been generally revised on only three occasions, the last being in 1909.

Although this legislation provides for a complete revision of title 17 of the U.S. Code, only a few sections of S. 22 are still controversial.

While it is understandable that our debate should center on those sections, it should not obscure the many beneficial provisions of this legislation, which are not in dispute.

The Constitution makes clear that the purpose of protecting the rights of an author is to promote the public interest. But, as stated in the committee report on the Act of 1909—

The granting of such exclusive rights, under the proper terms and conditions, confers a benefit upon the public that outweighs the evils of the temporary monopoly.

Some of the most important provisions of this legislation are found in chapter 3 relating to the duration of copyright. The existing statute provides for an initial term of 28 years with the option of a renewal for a second term of the same duration. S. 22 establishes a general copyright term for the life of the author and 50 years after his death. The adoption of this term will bring U.S. law into conformity with the generally recognized international standard. As life expectancy has increased, the existing 56-year term does not insure that an author and his dependents will receive reasonable monetary recognition throughout their life. More and more authors are seeing their works fall into the public domain during their lifetimes. However, even with the revised copyright term, the treatment of authors under this legislation is less favorable than in the copyright legislation of most major nations of the western world.

With respect to the use of copyrighted materials for nonprofit purposes, the bill in the judgment of the committee provides a carefully structure balance be tween the legitimate rights of the creators, and the reasonable needs of users. Particular attention has been given to the concerns of classroom teachers and public libraries. A detailed discussion of these subjects is contained in those portions of the committee report devoted to an explanation of sections 107 and 108 of S. 22. The committee is satisfied that the provisions of this legislation will not interfere with the reasonable needs of education and libraries. I can assure the Senate that the committee carefully considered the scope of all the educational and library exemptions. I hope that the Senate will not disturb the delicate balance achieved on these issues by the committee.

Members of the Senate have received considerable correspondence recommending or opposing changes in section 108 relating to photocopying by public libraries. This section of the bill supplements the doctrine of fair use contained in section 107, and nothing in section 108 is intended in any way to prevent such photocopying as may be permissible under the criteria of section 107. Section 108 contains a series of limitations on the exclusive rights of authors for the benefit of the patrons of public libraries. To protect the rights of authors from gradual erosion by wholesale photocopying, subsection (g) provides that the reproduction rights do not apply to the "concerted" or "systematic" reproductions of certain materials.

In order that the legislative intent of this section may be clear, it may be useful to describe the relationship between the several limitations on exclusive rights and the language of subsection (g). Particular interest has been manifested in the relationship between subsections (d) and (g). During the final subcommittee hearings, the representatives of the library associations proposed the inclusion in section 108 of a specific provision stating that it was not an infringement of copyright for a library to furnish a patron with a single copy of one article from a periodical, or a small part of an entire work. This proposal was considered at great length in the subcommittee markup of this legislation. The subcommittee examined whether particular library photocopying practices could rea-

sonably be considered as the making of a single copy. It was concluded that certain practices did not come within the scope of what is now subsection (d). Illustrative of these practices are the examples of "systematic copying" set forth in the committee report discussion of section 108.

It is thus erroneous to contend that the reference to "systematic" reproduction in subsection (g) takes away reproduction rights intended to be authorized by subsection (d). The inclusion of subsection (g) is appropriate so that the statutory provision provides a reasonable balancing of the rights of authors, and the needs of libraries and their patrons.

Neither a statute nor legislative history can specify exactly which photocopying practices constitute the making of "single copies" as distinguished from "systematic reproduction." The committee has therefore recommended that the representatives of authors, book and peridical publishers and other owners of copyrighted material meet with the library community to formulate photocopying guidelines to assist library patrons and employees. As to library photocopying practices not exempted by this legislation, the committee has recommended that workable clearance and licensing procedures be developed.

The National Commission on Libraries and Information Science has adopted a resolution urging the Congress at the present time to provide only an interim resolution of the photocopying issue, and to require a review of the statutory provisions and related matters in 1980. I not only fully support the objectives of the National Commission on Libraries, but on my initiative, the Congress already has acted to provide the mechanism for the ongoing review desired by the National Commission. When it became apparent that action on the revision project could not be concluded in the 93d Congress, I introduced legislation which became Public Law 93–573 to establish a National Commission on New Technological Uses of Copyrighted Works. The Commission has been given the assignment of studying copyright law and procedures in light of developing technology and to make appropriate recommendations to the Congress. I specifically included in my bill authorization for the Commission to conduct whatever further study of the library photocopying questions that may be necessary. Thus, the Congress already has provided in the National Commission on New

Technological Uses of Copyrighted Works the mechanism for further study of this issue.

Other than for minor clarifying amendments, section 111 of the bill relating to secondary transmissions by cable television systems is identical to the bill passed by the Senate in the 93d Congress. The provisions of section 111 were reviewed in the last Congress by the Committee on Commerce. At the completion of that review, the chairman of the Communications Subcommittee of the Commerce Committee advised the Senate on September 6, 1974, that the Commerce Committee does not have any further reason to deal with that matter and the Judiciary Committee could assume exclusive jurisdiction.

Section 111 undertakes to resolve the coyright liability of cable television systems in a manner consistent with the regulatory scheme adopted by the Federal Communications Commission. This legislation does not determine what signals may be carried by cable television. It grants such systems a copyright compulsory license to carry such signals as are authorized by the Commission. As a condition of the compulsory license, all cable systems would be required to pay a reasonable copyright royalty, the initial schedule of which is established by this legislation.

Section 115 continues the existing compulsory license for the making and distribution of phonorecords. Current law provides a statutory royalty rate, known as the mechanical royalty, of 2 cents for each record manufactured. The bill passed by the Senate in 1974, and the bill reported by the subcommittee in 1975, increased the statutory mechanical royalty to 3 cents. During the consideration of S. 22 in the committee, an amendment was proposed to fix the statutory rate at 2½ cents. I believe that a statutory rate of 3 cents per work is appropriate at the present time, but the committee by majority vote determined on the 2½ cent rate.

Section 118 of S. 22 is entirely new. It is the result of an important amendment proposed by Senator MATHIAS to create a copyright compulsory license for the use by public broadcasting of certain categories of copyrighted works. The subcommittee considered at great length the Mathias amendment and encouraged the interested parties to reach private agreements so as to avoid the difficult policy and procedural issues necessarily presented by a statutory provision. Substantial progress was made on a number of issues and the subcommittee concluded that the issues still in dispute could be resolved if the parties seek reasonable accommodations.

The committee report summarizes the arguments advanced in support and in opposition to the Mathias amendment. I voted against the adoption of this amendment in the committee, but it was approved by a majority vote of the committee. The Register of Copyrights testified in the House of Representatives that the Copyright Office recommends that the Congress reject the entire revision bill if section 118 is retained in its present form. The Register of Copyrights has objected to the loss of control by authors over the use of their work in a major communications medium, and the dangers of State control and loss of freedom of expression implicit in the proposed system.

One of the most significant provisions of this legislation is chapter 8, which I originally proposed, and which was also contained in the bill passed by the Senate in 1974. Chapter 8 establishes the Copyright Royalty Tribunal to provide a mechanism for the periodic review of the statutory royalty rates, and for the resolution of disputes concerning the distribution of royalty fees. Significant changes in this chapter have been made concerning the cable television and jukebox royalty review procedures.

The bill as passed by the Senate in 1974 directed almost immediate review of the royalty rates, and subsequent reviews at 5 year intervals. The committee has amended S. 22 to provide that the initial review of the rates commence 3 years after the effective date, and that the subsequent reviews be at 10 year intervals.

When the copyright bill in the 93d Congress was referred to the Commerce Committee for review of the provisions related to their jurisdiction, the committee adopted, without any study or hearing, an amendment to freeze the royalty rate paid by jukebox operators. Under the rules of the Senate, the copyright status of the jukebox industry comes exclusively within the jurisdiction of the Committee on the Judiciary. Because of the complicated parliamentary situation prevailing in the Senate when the revision bill was considered in 1974, it would have been difficult to obtain a clear expression of the Senate will on this subject. I thus refrained from requesting a rollcall vote on the Commerce Committee jukebox amendment.

Although the Committee on the Judiciary believes there is no justification for the jukebox amendment adopted in the Commerce Committee, our committee has taken this development into account and I believe the provision now in chapter 8 provides a fair compromise. While the jukebox royalty rate will not be exempted from the review procedures of chapter 8, the date of the initial review and any possible adjustment has been delayed for several years so that the Tribunal can give careful consideration to the impact of the copyright payments on the viability of the jukebox industry.

Mr. President, I shall conclude by quoting two paragraphs from my remarks opening the debate on the copyright revision bill in the 93d Congress. I believe these comments are as valid today as when I originally made them:

As one who has struggled with this bill for many years, I can assure my colleagues that it is impossible to satisfy everyone. Whatever we do will disappoint some interest. It would, perhaps, have been more popular for me to have adopted different positions on some issues in this legislation, or to abandon good faith commitments when circumstances changed.

The Judiciary Committee has tried to resolve each issue by applying the standard of what best promotes the constitutional mandate to encourage and reward authorship. Some may disagree with the conclusions we have reached. All that I ask of them is that they also resolve these issues on the basis of what is right for the country, and just for the various interests.

Mr. President, the printed copy of Senate Report 94–473 on S. 22 omits one page of the text which I filed in the Senate on November 20, 1975. In order that the complete report of the committee be available, I ask unanimous consent that the omitted page of the printed report be printed at this point in the RECORD.

There being no objection, the excerpt from the report was ordered to be printed in the RECORD, as follows:

The provision also provides that if there is an admission charge the copyright owner may prevent a public performance of his work under this provision by serving a notice stating his objections at least seven days in advance.

Mere reception in public

Unlike the first four clauses of section 110, clause (5) is not to any extent a counterpart of the "for profit" limitation of the present statute. It applies to performances and displays of all types of works, and its purpose is to exempt from copyright liability anyone who merely turns on, in a public place, an ordinary radio or television receiving apparatus of a kind commonly sold to members of the public for private use.

The basic rationale of this clause is that the secondary use of the transmission by turning on an ordinary receiver in public is so remote and minimal that no further liability should be imposed. In the vast majority of these cases no royalties are collected today, and the exemption should be made explicit in the statute.

While this legislation has been under consideration in the Congress, the Federal courts have considered several issues relevant to this exemption in the context of the Copyright Act of 1909. This clause has nothing to do with cable television systems and is not intended to generally exempt performances or displays in commercial establishments for the benefit of customers or employees. Thus, this exemption would not apply where broadcasts are transmitted by means of loudspeakers or similar devices in such establishments as bus terminals, supermarkets, factories and commercial offices, department and clothing stores, hotels, restaurants and quickservice food shops of the type involved in *Twentieth Century Music Corp. v. Aiken.* The exemption would also be denied in any case where the audience is charged directly to see or hear the transmission.

Agricultural fairs

Clause (6) provides that the performance of a nondramatic musical work or of a sound recording in the course of an annual agricultural or horticultural fair or exhibition conducted by a Government body or a nonprofit organization is not an infringement of copyright. This exemption extends to all activities on the premises of such fairs or exhibitions.

Retail sale of phonorecords

Clause (7) provides that the performance of a nondramatic musical work or of a sound recording by a retail establishment open to the public at large without any direct or indirect admission charge where the sole purpose of the performance is to promote the retail sale of the work is not an infringement of copyright. This exemption applies only if the performance is not transmitted beyond the place where the establishment is located and is within the immediate area where the sale is occurring.

Handicapped audience

Clause (8) was not included in the bill passed by the Senate in 1974. It has been added to facilitate the special services provided by various noncommercial radio and television stations to a print or aural handicapped audience. It provides that it is not an infringement of copyright to perform a literary work in the course of broadcasts "specifically designed" for a print or aural handicapped audience.

Mr. KASTENMEIER. Mr. Speaker, I move that the House resolve itself into the Committee of the Whole House on the State of the Union for the consideration of the Senate bill (S. 22) for the general revision of the copyright law, title 17 of the United States Code, and for other purposes.

The SPEAKER. The question is on the motion offered by the gentleman from Wisconsin (Mr. KASTENMEIER).

IN THE COMMITTEE OF THE WHOLE

Accordingly the House resolved itself into the Committee of the Whole House on the State of the Union for the consideration of the Senate bill, S. 22, with Mr. SMITH of Iowa in the chair.

The Clerk read the title of the Senate bill.

By unanimous consent, the first reading of the bill was dispensed with.

The CHAIRMAN. Under the rule, the gentleman from Wisconsin (Mr. KASTENMEIER) will be recognized for 30 minutes, and the gentleman from Illinois (Mr. RAILSBACK) will be recognized for 30 minutes.

The Chair now recognizes the gentleman from Wisconsin (Mr. KASTENMEIER.)

Mr. KASTENMEIER. Mr. Chairman, I yield such time as he may consume to the distinguished chairman of the Committee on the Judiciary, the gentleman from New Jersey (Mr. RODINO).

(Mr. RODINO asked and was given permission to revise and extend his remarks.)

Mr. RODINO. Mr. Chairman, today is a proud day for the Copyright Subcommittee and for its parent Judiciary Subcommittee as we present to the House—unanimously by the subcommittee and with one sole dissent in the full committee—the bill S. 22 for general revision of the copyright law, with a committee amendment in the nature of a substitute.

When one considers the extended background of this legislation and the difficulties that have been overcome in the process, the reason for our pride is not hard to see. Under the chairmanship and gifted guidance of our colleague BOB KASTENMEIER of Wisconsin and the unflagging cooperation of the ranking minority member of the subcommittee, TOM RAILSBACK of Illinois, our subcommittee undertook and has brilliantly brought to conclusion an enormous task.

The present copyright law is essentially as enacted in 1909. The technological and communications developments since that time have rendered that law obsolete and inadequate. It is the purpose and effect of the copyright bill which we bring you today to provide for a general revision of the copyright law.

The first American copyright law was enacted by the First Congress in 1790, in exercise of the constitutional power:

To promote the Progress of Science and useful Arts, by securing for limited Times to Authors and Inventors the exclusive Right to their respective Writings and Discoveries.

Comprehensive revisions were enacted, at intervals of about 40 years.

Since 1909 significant changes in technology have affected the operation of the copyright law. Motion pictures and sound recordings had just made their appearance in 1909, and radio and television were still in the early stages of their development. During the past half century a wide range of new techniques for capturing and communicating printed matter, visual images, and recorded sounds have come into use, and the increasing use of information storage and retrieval devices, communications satellites, and laser technology promises even greater changes in the near future. The technical advances have generated new industries and new methods for the reproduction nad dissemination of copyrighted works, and the business relations between authors and users have evolved new patterns.

Against this background of need for revision and after extended hearings and study, the committee in 1967 brought forth and the House enacted a comprehensive revision bill. The Senate, however, was unable to enact this measure Not until 1974 did the Senate pass a copyright bill. Reintroduced in 1975, the measure became the basis for S. 22 and the House companion bill, H.R. 2223.

During 1975, the House Judiciary Subcommittee conducted extensive hearings at which nearly 100 witnesses were heard. Following some 22 days of public markup sessions in 1976 the House subcommittee favorably reported S. 22, by a unanimous vote, on August 3, 1976, with an amendment in the nature of a substitute. The Committee on the Judiciary now reports that bill, as amended, without change.

In reporting S. 22, the committee has deleted and held over for further consideration in the 95th Congress title 2 of the bill that would create a new system of protection for ornamental designs of useful articles.

The legislation before us now contains a number of complex and important provisions. These include: Increased term, fair use, exemptions related to the handicapped, royalty fees for cable television systems, mechanical royalties, and compulsory license for public broadcasting. The bill eliminates the so-called manufacturing clause which has performed a tariff function in the guise of copyright.

Mr. Chairman, it is with the most profound respect that I urge my colleagues to vote to enact this monumental revision.

(Mr. KASTENMEIER asked and was given permission to revise and extend his remarks.)

Mr. KASTENMEIER. Mr. Chairman, I yield myself such time as I may consume.

Mr. Chairman, at the outset, I would like to compliment the Members of the subcommittee who worked so hard on this particular legislative endeavor; the gentleman from Illinois (Mr. RAILSBACK); the gentleman from California (Mr. WIGGINS); and on our side, the gentleman from California (Mr. DANIELSON); the gentleman from Massachusetts (Mr. DRINAN); the gentleman from New York (Mr. BADILLO); and the gentleman from New York (Mr. PATTISON); as well as the other gentlemen, the gentleman from California (Mr. EDWARDS); the gentleman from Michigan (Mr. HUTCHINSON); who 10 years ago served on the subcommittee and worked on the project at that time.

Mr. Chairman, the Committee on the Judiciary has reported favorably the bill, S. 22, revising the copyright code of the United States.

The existing Copyright Code was enacted in 1909 and has remained basically unchanged since that time even though the intervening years have witnessed revolutionary technological developments which have totally changed the nineteenth century assumptions upon which that law was based.

Attempts to modernize the law began over 50 years ago, in 1924. Before World War II, revision bills twice passed one House of Congress only to be stymied in the other. The efforts which resulted in the committee bill before you today began in August 1955 when Congress authorized what was to become a 6-year study of needed revisions by a special committee of experts under the supervision of the Register of Copyrights.

On the basis of that study former chairman, Emanuel Celler, in 1965 introduced the general revision which is the forerunner of S. 22. It was my pleasure to chair 22 days of public hearings and 51 days of markup on that bill during the 89th Congress. The result of that effort was successful passage of a revision bill by the House in the 90th Congress in 1967. Because of a controversy over the cable TV provision, however, the bill died in the Senate.

By the 93d Congress the Senate was successful in achieving sufficient agreement to pass the bill. However, our committee received the measure far too late in that session to act, especially given the pressures of the impeachment inquiry.

Near the beginning of the current Congress the Senate quickly passed the bill a second time and our committee began work in earnest to produce a bill that would balance the competing interests of the various affected economic groups and at the same time serve the general public interest. The Subcommittee on Courts, Civil Liberties, and the Administration of Justice held a total of 17 days of hearings at which testimony was received from 99 different witnesses. These hearings were followed by 25 days of markup which resulted in the bill before you this morning.

Much of the bill is merely a restatement of existing law, both statutory law and the judicial doctrines which over the years have grown up around the 1909 code. However, the bill does contain a number of significant changes.

First, copyright protection is changed from the current maximum term of 56 years to the life of the author plus 50 years. This is in keeping with the standard recognized throughout the world, and will enable the United States to more easily reach reciprocal agreeemnts on copyright matters with other nations. All copyrights presently in existence would be valid until 75 years from the date of publication.

Secondly, the bill extends copyright protection to two areas which are not presently covered—performance of copyrighted musical works by jukeboxes and retransmission of copyrighted works by cable television systems. However, the committee has greatly softened the impact of this extended copyright coverage by providing that jukebox operators and cable television systems will be entitled to compulsory licenses at very reasonable fees which are provided in the bill. The bill contains special provisions for small cable systems which require them to make only a nominal payment.

In addition, the bill raises the so-called mechanical royalty from the current 2 cents per pound to 2¾ cents or 6/10 cents per minute of playing time, whichever is greater. The mechanical royalty is the minimum payment which must be made to the copyright owner by record companies for the right to produce a recording of a work which has already been recorded.

In order that Congress itself will not be required to review periodically the rates of the various compulsory licenses established in the bill, a three member Copyright Royalty Commission is established to review royalty rates and settle disputes among parties claiming statutory royalties.

Another important reform contained in S. 22 is the phasing out of the archaic manufacturing requirement, a feature of the 1909 law which requires that virtually all copyrighted books be printed in the United States. The bill provides for the termination of this provision in 1981.

Finally, the legislation establishes for the first time a national television archive in the Library of Congress so that, through the copyright deposit system, a national archive of television programs may be maintained.

Mr. Chairman, although the bill provides for the creation of a copyright royalty commission and a national television archive it is not expected that any additional costs to the United States will be incurred because the revenue from fees authorized under the bill will more than offset costs. As you can see from the cost estimate on p. 184 of the report, revenue from fees during the next 5 years will actually exceed costs.

S. 22 is basically economic legislation which affects a variety of industries and interest groups. Of course, it is impossible to draft a copyright bill which will meet with the approval of every interested party. I believe that we have been successful in writing a bill which resolves the conflicts among the various parties as successfully as is humanly possible.

Three issues in the bill were most troublesome for the committee. These were: Photocopying by public libraries, the copyright liability of cable television systems, and the Senate attempt to create a new type of copyright portection for ornamental design.

I believe that we have successfully balanced the needs of libraries against the rights of copyright proprietors by providing that libraries may photocopy copyrighted material, including for purposes of interlibrary loans, as long as such photocopying is not systematic and a substitute for purchase or subscription.

On the cable TV issue, the Subcommittee had the benfit of an agreement reached by two of the three interested parties, the copyright proprietors and the National Cable Television Association. The third major group is the National Association of Broadcasters. We have endeavored to include in the bill provisions which, short of dictating communications policy, will protect the interest of broadcasters. An example is section 501 which permits local radio and television broadcasters to act as "private attorneys general" by granting them the right to sue cable systems which violate the terms of the compulsory license in the bill even though they have not been directly injured by a cable system's alteration of their own signals. I was disappointed to learn that very recently the Community Antenna Television Association—CATA—has raised several questions about the provisions of the bill dealing with importation of foreign signals from Mexico and Canada, powers of the Copyright Royalty Commission to change cable royalties on the basis of changes in FCC rules governing sports programing, the definition of local service area, and the requirement of the bill that all cable systems, even those retransmitting local signals, pay some copyright royalty.

The Members of the House should know that during the 22 markup sessions on the bill, many of which were attended by representatives of CATA, none of these points was raised. However, the Committee did make special efforts to accommodate the needs of the small cable systems which CATA represents by providing for substantially lower copyright royalty payments for cable systems with gross receipts of less than $160,000. The Senate version had only provided special treatment for systems with gross receipts of less than $80,000. To acquiesce to the further demands of CATA at this time would, in all likelihood, result in a substantial reduction of the total royalty fees available to copyright owners under the bill and; therefore, bring about their opposition to the bill.

The final major area of controversy is title II of the Senate bill which provides for a new form of protection for ornamental designs which cannot be identified separately from the useful articles of which they are part. This "no mans land" between copyright and patent law presents difficult public policy questions. The Department of Justice strongly opposed the creation of this new form of intellectual property on the grounds that no need for it had been demonstrated. Because sufficient information was not available to enable the subcommittee to resolve the issue at this time, we deleted title II from the bill with the understanding that the subject would be considered in depth during the next Congress.

For the most part, affected industries and groups are satisfied with the compromises reached in the bill. I believe that the fact that the bill was approved by the committee on a vote of 27 to 1 testifies vividly to this fact.

Mr. Chairman, before concluding my remarks I would like to discuss several questions which have been raised concerning the meaning of several provisions of S. 22 as reported by the House Judiciary Committee and of statements in the committee's report, No. 94-1476. One of these questions involves the meaning of the concept of "publication" in the case of a work of art, such as a painting or statue, that exists in only one copy. It is not the committee's intention that such a work would be regarded as "published" when the single existing copy is sold or offered for sale in the traditional way—for example, through an art dealer, gallery, or auction house. On the other hand, where the work has been made for reproduction in multiple copies—as in the case of fine prints such as lithographs—or where multiple reproductions of the prototype work are offered for purchase by the public—as in the case of castings from a statue or reproductions made from a photograph of a painting—publication would take place at the point when reproduced copies are publicly distributed or when, even if only one copy exists at that point, reproductions are offered for purchase by multiple members of the public.

Another question involves the reference to "teacher" in the "Agreement on Guidelines for Classroom Copying in Not-for-Profit Educational Institutions" reproduced at pages 68-70 of the committee's report No. 94-1476 in connection with section 107. It has been pointed out that, in planning his or her teaching on a day-to-day basis in a variety of educational situations, an individual teacher will commonly consult with instructional specialists on the staff of the school, such as reading specialists, curriculum specialists, audiovisual directors, guidance counselors, and the like. As long as the copying meets all of the other criteria laid out in the guidelines, including the requirements for spontaneity and the prohibition against the copying being directed by higher authority, the committee regards the concept of "teacher" as broad enough to include instructional specialists working in consultation with actual instructors.

Also in consultation with section 107, the committee's attention has been directed to the unique educational needs and problems of the approximately 50,000 deaf and hearing-impaired students in the United States, and the inadequacy of both public and commercial television to serve their educational needs. It has been suggested that, as long as clear-cut constraints are imposed and enforced, the doctrine of fair use is broad enough to permit the making of an off-the-air fixation of a television program within a nonprofit educational institutional for the deaf and hearing impaired, the reproduction of a master and a work copy of a captioned version of the original fixation, and the performance of the program from the work copy within the confines of the institution. In identifying the constraints that would have to be imposed within an institution in order for these activities to be considered as fair use, it has been suggested that the purpose of the use would have to be noncommercial in every respect, and educational in the sense that it serves as part of a deaf or hearing-impaired student's learning environment within the institution, and that the institution would have to insure that the master and work copy would remain in the hands of a limited number of authorized personnel within the institution, would be responsible for assuring against its unauthorized reproduction or distribution, or its performance or retention for other than educational purposes within the institution. Work copies of captioned programs could be shared among institutions for the deaf abiding by the constraints specified. Assuming that these constraints are both imposed and enforced, and that no other factors intervene to render the use unfair, the committee believes that the activities described could reasonably be considered fair use under section 107.

Further, on pages 70 and 71 of the committee report Guidelines for Educational Uses of Music under section 107 are set forth. Those guidelines represent the understanding of the Music Publishers' Association of the United States, Inc., the National Music Publishers Association, Inc., the Music Teachers National Association, the Music Educators National Conference, the National Association of Schools of Music, and the Ad Hoc Committee on Copyright Law Revision as expressed in a joint letter to me dated April 30, 1976.

The report, as printed, does not reflect a subsequent change in the joint guidelines which was described in a subsequent letter to me from a representative of the above named organizations. Subsection A.2. of the guidelines should be changed to read as follows: "2. For academic purposes other than performance, single or multiple copies of excerpts of works may be made, provided that the excerpts do not comprise a part of the whole which would constitute a performable unit such as a selection, movement or aria, but in no case more than 10 percent of the whole work. The number of copies shall not exceed one copy per pupil."

In addition, Mr. Speaker, the paragraph beginning at the bottom of page 97 and concluding at the top of page 98 is intended to mean that, in one instance, specific additional payments are to be made for carrying specific additional programs. Where a cable system, at its own discretion, deletes certain programs and substitutes other, live, programs, an additional payment is to be made: this identifiable payment is intended to be distributed to the specific program source, that is, owners of live programs.

Finally Mr. Chairman, I would like to observe that the House bill differs from the Senate bill in its treatment of public broadcasting, especially regarding use of nondramatic literary works. We did not feel justified in going as far to guarantee arrangements for public broadcasters as they would have liked. Our preference was to encourage private negotiations, and, particularly in nondramatic literary

works, we established a framework which we believe will be helpful in such private negotiations. We provided for an antitrust exemption so that publishers and authors could get together with public broadcasters in establishing standard terms, rates, and clearance mechanisms without running afoul of the antitrust laws. We also provided for a report to Congress in 2 years so that the outcome of such private arrangements could be made known to us. I am advised that indeed publishers and authors and public broadcasters are talking together this very week in an effort to set up suitable common rates and practices for public broadcasters. I am very encouraged by this report, and I hope they will come to a successful conclusion before our conference on this bill with the Senate.

Mr. Chairman, because of the complexity of this bill and the delicate balances which it creates among competing economic interests, the committee will resist extensive amendment of this bill. On behalf of the committee I would urge all of my colleagues to vote favorably on S. 22.

Mr. SKUBITZ. Mr. Chairman, will the gentleman yield?

Mr. KASTENMEIER. I am happy to yield to my friend, the gentleman from Kansas.

Mr. SKUBITZ. Mr. Chairman, I thank my friend, the gentleman from Wisconsin, for yielding.

Mr. Chairman, I have received a great deal of mail from the schoolteachers in my district who are particularly concerned about section 107—fair use—the fair use of copyrighted material. Having been a former schoolteacher myself, I believe they make a good point and there is a sincere fear on their part that, because of the vagueness or ambiguity in the bill's treatment of the doctrine of fair use, they may subject themselves to liability for an unintentional infringement of copyright when all they were trying to do was the job for which they were trained.

The vast majority of teachers in this country would not knowingly infringe upon a person's copyright, but, as any teacher can appreciate, there are times when information is needed and is available, but may be literally impossible to locate the right person to approve the use of that material and the purchase of such would not be feasible and, in the meantime, the teacher may have lost that "teachable moment."

Did the subcommittee take these problems into consideration and did they do anything to try and help the teachers to better understand section 107?

Have the teachers been protected by this section 107?

Mr. KASTENMEIER. Mr. Chairman, in response to the gentleman's question and his observations preceding the question, I would say, indeed they have.

Over the years this has been one of the most difficult questions. It is a problem that I believe has been very successfully resolved.

Section 107 on "Fair Use" has, of course, restated four standards, and these standards are, namely: The purpose and character of the use of the material; the nature of the copyrighted work; the amount and substantiality of the portion used in relation to the copyrighted work as a whole; and the effect of the use upon the potential market for or value of the copyrighted work.

These are the four "Fair Use" criteria. These alone were not adequate to guide teachers, and I am sure the gentleman from Kansas (Mr. SKUBITZ) understands that as a schoolteacher himself.

Therefore, the educators, the proprietors, and the publishers of educational materials did, at the committee's long insistence, get together. While there were many fruitless meetings, they did finally get together.

Mr. Chairman, I will draw the gentleman's attention to pages 65 through 74 in the report which contain extensive guidelines for teachers. I am very happy to say that there was an agreement reached between teachers and publishers of educational material, and that today the National Education Association supports the bill, and it has, in fact, sent a telegram which at the appropriate time I will make a part of the RECORD and which requests support for the bill in its present form, believing that it has satisfied the needs of the teachers:

NATIONAL EDUCATION ASSOCIATION,
Washington, D.C., September 10, 1976.
National Education Association urgently requests your support of the Copyright Revision bill, H.R. 2223, as reported by the Judiciary Committee. This compromise effort represents a major breakthrough in establishing equitable legal guidelines for the use of copyright materials for instructional and research purposes. We ask your support of the committee bill without amendments.
JAMES W. GREEN.
Assistant Director for Legislation.

Mr. SKUBITZ. Mr. Chairman, if the gentleman will yield further, then the NEA is satisfied with the language in the bill as it now stands; is that correct?

Mr. KASTENMEIER. The gentleman is correct.

Mr. SKUBITZ. Mr. Chairman, I thank the gentleman.

Mr. RAILSBACK. Mr. Chairman, I yield such time as he may consume to the gentleman from Michigan (Mr. HUTCHINSON), the ranking minority member.

(Mr. HUTCHINSON asked and was given permission to revise and extend his remarks.)

Mr. HUTCHINSON. Mr. Chairman, I thank the gentleman for yielding.

Mr. Chairman, I rise in strong support of S. 22, the general revision of the copyright law. Today marks a special day as the House considers and, I am confident, enacts the first general revision of the Nation's copyright laws in over 65 years. I would like to commend the members of the subcommittee who spent just countless hours working on this legislation. I can appreciate what they went through because I had the same experience when this bill went through the House in 1967.

Mr. Chairman, the first chapter of the bill defines the bundle of intangible property rights which inure in an original work of authorship which make up this statutory scope of copyright. That first chapter then proceeds to impose limitations upon those rights.

The second chapter of this bill deals with the ownership of those rights and how they may be transferred.

Now, Mr. Chairman, I propose to take up the consideration of chapter 3, concerned with the duration of those rights. Therefore, I shall be talking about sections 301 through 305 of the bill, sections to be found on pages 125 through 133 thereof.

Mr. Chairman, the constitutional grant of authority under which Congress considers this bill, is to be found in section 8 of article I of the original Constitution, wherein we are charged with the duty "to promote the progress of science and useful arts, by securing for limited times to authors and inventors the exclusive right to their respective writings and discoveries."

Mr. Chairman, for the purposes of chapter 3, the essential phrase in the constitutional grant contains three words—"for limited times."

Mr. Chairman, whatever copyright law

the Congress enacts must limit the duration of the exclusive rights it secures. All works of authorship must eventually fall into the public domain. We are without power to vest those rights in an author in perpetuity.

Still, Mr. Chairman, notwithstanding our inability to create any perpetual exclusive rights in an author, there is another law of copyright—in the common law—and under that law an author's rights in the nature of copyright may be perpetual. These common law rights are unlimited as to time. But the common law must yield to statutory law, wherever statutory law is applicable. So, wherever our statute law reaches, whatever it covers, the common law of rights of unlimited duration in an author is displaced by the congressional law of termination.

Mr. Chairman, our statutory law of copyright draws the line where the common law of unlimited duration ceases, and the present and all prior statutes have drawn that line at the point of publication.

If a work is published, it then loses its common law protections and becomes a subject for copyright. Upon publication, if requisite statutory procedures are followed, the exclusive rights of the author are secured for the statutory time otherwise they fall immediately into the public domain.

Mr. Chairman, under our present statute, the author of a copyrighted work enjoys his exclusive right for a term of 28 years, and he is permitted to renew his copyright for one additional term of 28 years. So, if a valid copyright exists, it is valuable to the author for at least 28 years but never more than 56 years.

At the end of that time, the work falls into the public domain. In all cases, this time is measured from the date of publication under the present law. If the author of a work or his heirs choose not to publish it, they retain it as their exclusive right indefinitely under the common law.

The bill we are now considering will change that law. It will change it by measuring the time of copyright from the time of creation of a work rather than from the time of its publication. The time of creation is determined by the act of fixation of the work in a tangible form. Thus, when an author completes his manuscript the work is fixed in a tangible form, and the copyright term

begins. The effect of this rather far-reaching change in the law is to bring under statutory copyright unpublished as well as published works.

The next important change in the law on the duration of copyright is a longer term. After January 1, 1978, when this bill will go into effect, a work within the copyright statute would be copyrightable for the lifetime of the author plus 50 years. There would be no renewable term available. Thus all the works of an author will fall into the public domain and become public property at the same time. The present complexity where the earlier works of an author become freely available before his later works—that present complexity will be done away with. Present-day records of vital statistics including records of death are now so complete and so available that it will be easy to determine when an author dies and 50 years after that date all of his works will fall at the same time into the free use of the public. Thus, the last works of an author will probably enjoy no longer term of protection that they would under the present law of 56 years. His earlier works may be protected for a longer period of time under the bill than under the present law, but if a man creates something of value, it is his property, and he ought to have the right to enjoy it for his lifetime. In no case would the heirs of an author have any rights beyond 50 years after his death.

The committee was persuaded to make this change in duration from the present maximum of 56 years after publication to the lifetime of the author plus 50 years, measuring the copyright from the creation of the work for the following reasons:

First, life expectancy has increased considerably since the present 56-year maximums were written into law in 1909.

Second, the tremendous growth in communication media has substantially lengthened the commercial life of a great many works. A short term is particularly discriminatory against serious works in music, literature, and art, whose value might not be recognized until after many years.

Next, although limitations on the term of copyright are publicly and constitutionally necessary, too short a term harms the author without giving any special benefit to the public. The public frequently pays the same for works in the public domain as it does for copyrighted works, and the only result is a commercial windfall to certain users at the author's expense.

In some cases the lack of copyright protection actually restricts the dissemination of the work since publishers and other users do not want to risk investing in the work unless they can be assured of some exclusive rights for a limited time.

The present system of measuring copyright from the date of publication is confused by the vagueness of the term "publication". The death of an author is a definite determinable event, and it would be the only date that a potential user would have to be concerned with under this new law.

All of an author's works, including those successively revised by him, would fall into the public domain at the same time, thus avoiding the present problems of determining a multitude of publication dates, and of distinguishing old and new matter in later editions.

The problem of determining when a relatively obscure author died is resolved by establishing a registry of the dates of death of authors in the copyright office. A presumption is written into the law that after 75 years following the first publication of the work or 100 years after its creation, whichever expires first, any person who obtains a certificate from the copyright office that the register has no evidence that the author is living or that he died less than 50 years before, may presume that the author has been dead for at least 50 years so his work has fallen into the public domain.

The committee was also persuaded that the present system requiring renewal of copyright in order to extend its protection beyond the original term of 28 years is a substantial burden and expense. It is highly technical and in a number of cases the renewal requirement has been the cause for the loss of copyright. The life-plus-50-year term provided in the bill provides no renewal term.

The longer term is also justified, we believe, because we subject unpublished works to the copyright law, thus denying them the unlimited exclusive common law rights the author and his heirs have enjoyed in them, including works that have been widely disseminated by means other than publication. It is possible to make a wide dissemination of some kind of works without them ever having been technically or legally published. The life-plus-150-year-term rule in the present bill is fair recompense to authors for the loss of perpetual rights which they have heretofore had in unpublished works.

Lastly, the life-plus-50-year term which authors would have in works created after the effective date of this bill, would conform our law to the copyright law of many foreign countries. In these times of instant communication throughout the world, there is increasing need for some uniformity in the field of copyright. A very large number of countries have already adopted a copyright term of the life of the author and 50 years after his death.

American authors are today frequently protected longer in some foreign countries than in the United States, and some resentment has occasionally been provoked because of this disparity in the duration of the term. Copyrighted materials move across national borders faster than virtually any other economic commodity, and with the techniques now in common use this movement has become instantaneous and effortless in many cases. The need to conform the duration of U.S. copyright to that prevalent throughout the rest of the world is increasingly pressing in order to provide certainty and simplicity in international business dealing.

To this increased term of life plus 50 years, with no renewal term provided, the committee has devised a method by which an author or his heirs may enjoy a right of reverter after 35 years in any copyright sold. This would permit an author to renegotiate with publishers after 35 years in order to protect him against sales which he may have made or some arrangement he could have made with a publisher long before the value of the work was known.

This right of reverter will also afford an author an opportunity to find some other method to exploit his work if during the original 35 years his original publisher has not vigorously promoted the work.

A joint work under the law would enjoy copyright measured by the life plus 50 years of the last survivor of the authors.

If you have more than a single author, several authors joining together in a work, the duration of the copyright would be measured by the death of the last of the surviving authors. An anonymous or pseudonymous work would enjoy copyright for only 75 years from publication or 100 years from creation. A work for hire, where you employ someone to write a literary work for you would be copyrightable for 75 years from publication or 100 years from creation, whichever is earlier. The bill extends existing copyrights so that they may benefit from the longer term. Those in the original 28-year term may at the end of that time be extended for another 47 years, making a total of 75 years. Those in their renewal term will be extended an additional 19 years, to provide the same 75-year coverage.

There is another major provision in chapter 3 which I want to briefly touch upon and that is the doctrine of Federal preemption in the field of copyright. The bill proposes to take under jurisdiction of the Federal law the whole law of copyright. Since the bill would bring within its ken unpublished as well as published works of authorship which have been fixed in tangible form, the area for State regulation in this field will be greatly reduced anyway, and the bill proposes to supersede State law on the subject.

One of the purposes behind the copyright clause in the Constitution was to achieve a uniformity of the copyright law throughout the country and to avoid the difficulty of enforcing an author's rights under the differing laws of the several States.

The intention of section 301, which is the Federal preemption section is to preempt and abolish any rights under the common law or the statutes of a State that are equivalent to copyright and that extend to works coming within the scope of the Federal copyright law.

On the other hand, this bill does not reach works that have not been fixed in any tangible means of expression. Such works would include such things as extemporaneous speeches or original works of authorship communicated solely through conversations or live broadcasts, or a dramatic sketch or a musical composition which has been improvised or developed from memory and without having been recorded or written down. Since these are not subject to copyright, they would continue to be subject to State law and common law until fixed in some tangible form.

In summary, Mr. Chairman, the committee has worked long and hard to bring this piece of legislation before you and the membership of the House and I urge the Members to support the enactment

of S. 22.

Mr. RAILSBACK. Mr. Chairman, I yield myself 5 minutes.

(Mr. RAILSBACK asked and was given permission to revise and extend his remarks.)

Mr. RAILSBACK. Mr. Chairman, I rise in support of Senate bill S. 22. This is the first general copyright revision legislation since 1909.

S. 22 is the first general copyright revision legislation since 1909. I believe it would be appropriate to first pay tribute to the Judiciary Subcommittee members who labored long and hard putting together this rather difficult and complex legislative package. I would especially like to commend our subcommittee chairman for his thoroughness, his fairness and his leadership throughout the consideration of this measure.

I want to pay tribute to the distinguished Register of Copyrights, the Honorable Barbara Ringer and her counsel, John Baumgarten and their staff. In all the rolls of our civil service, I believe, you will find no servants of the public who surpass in knowledge and the talent of these individuals. The Congress and the public are indebted to them for their intellectual labor.

The Congress has been struggling with this legislation for more than 10 years. The concept of general revision has been under study more than 50 years. The present copyright law was enacted in 1909, and, of course, makes no mention of radio, television, cable television, computer information storage, et cetera. It is a credit to what the Congress did in 1909, that such a copyright law has been able to function at all in this day of electronic mass communication.

The courts have pleaded, in case after case, for Congress to reform and update the copyright law. Well, here it is, and it is the closest we have ever come to having a general revision. And what you do here in the next couple of hours will determine whether there will be a new copyright law this year or ever, for that matter.

We have endeavored to balance the many competing interests. Teachers, librarians, and broadcasters, for good reason, are interested in making the most of the latest technologies with the least possible restrictions. Authors, composers, publishers, and the motion picture industries, on the other hand, are interested in protecting their work product. Their livelihood depends on such protection. This bill has more support now, than it has ever had. There is no way to satisfy all the parties who have an interest in this legislation. A good compromise is probably one that satisfies no one, but is acceptable to everyone, and its been said that this bill is a compromise of compromises.

In my opinion, these interests and that of the public have been fairly well balanced. This balance, however, is a delicate one. A change in any one sentence may tilt that balance in such a way so as to unravel the entire bill. For example, one of the most important sections of the bill is section 107, the Fair Use of Copyrighted Works.

Teachers were uncomfortable with this section because of its vagueness. The doctrine of fair use as it has been developed by the courts is purposely vague, since it would be difficult to prescribe precise rules to cover many varied situations. The Judiciary Committee Subcommittee made some slight changes which satisfied the teachers, without unsettling the authors and publishers. In addition, since the subcommittee's action, the two parties have agreed upon guidelines on how this section will work in practice. This agreement, in and of itself, is an amazing development to those of us close to the problem. These parties have rarely agreed upon anything. It is my purpose to support this measure in full and to resist those amendments which I feel, in a substantive way, alter the purpose and intent of this legislation.

This legislation is unlike any processed by the Judiciary Committee. It involves money, big money; it involves special interests, many special interests; and most importantly, it involves the public interest. And the interest best served by the expeditious consideration of S. 22 will be the public's interest.

Copyright involves the process by which one protects his personal, intellectual labor. Copyright has to do with the craft of the author, the craft of the composer and the craft of the artist. The purpose of copyright is to stimulate creativity and by so doing benefit the public. The granting of exclusive rights under the proper terms and conditions confers a public benefit that in my opinion outweighs the evils of this temporary, kind of monopoly. Copyright is not a monopoly in the sense that a patent is a monopoly. Copyright secures only the property right in the manner and content of the expression. Facts and ideas recited or systems

and processes described by the author are freely available to the public at large, and the author has no power under copyright to prescribe their use. For example, a photographer's copyright empowers him to prohibit the copying and use of his original photograph. However, it gives him no power to prevent another photographer from standing on the same spot and taking a picture of the same object with the same lighting, focus, and shutter speed, even if the second picture is identical to the first. Copyright is a constitutional right, even though the word is found nowhere in the U.S. Constitution.

Mr. Chairman, I shall not undertake, except in response to specific questions, to deal at any great length with the technical aspects of the legislation at this time. Rather, I would like to discuss generally an overview of the bill and in particular several of its more controversial provisions.

S. 22 is the complete revision of present copyright law which can be found in title 17, U.S.C., sections 1–201. The legislation is divided into eight chapters with general subject headings. Chapter 1 covers almost all the testimony received by the subcommittee, the vast majority of which covers sections 106 through 118. The subject matter of copyright, that is, the scope of the copyright law in terms of the works it covers, as distinguished from the rights it gives, is covered by chapter 1, sections 102 through 105. Section 106 is a very fundamental provision of the bill in that it lays out the exclusive rights of the copyright owner in general terms. Sections 107 through 118 are the limitations or qualifications on those exclusive rights, and it is these sections which are the ones most talked about.

Section 108 makes clear that the library photocopying exemption applies to the making of a single photocopy by librarians operating without any profit motive, open to the public or to outside researchers. Libraries are subject to the "fair use" doctrine of section 107. Subsection (F)(3) contains the so-called Vanderbilt University exception originally put in the legislation by Senator Baker. For a number of years, Vanderbilt University has been providing a public service by attempting to record for history, major news events, especially the nightly newscast of the major networks. Vanderbilt felt that this was an important part of this country's oral history which, prior to their effort was being lost. S. 22 continues to recognize this special exemption which is intended to cover local, regional, or network newscasts, interviews concerning current news events, and on-the-spot coverage of news events.

Section 110 deals with performances and exhibitions that are now generally exempt under the "for profit" limitation and which are specifically exempted from copyright liability under this legislation. Section 110 is intended to set out the conditions under which performances or displays in the course of instructional activities are to be exempted from copyright. This clause covers all types of works. A teacher or student would be free to perform or display anything in class as long as the conditions are met.

spend the evening at the jukejoint, as it was called, any more. The number of jukeboxes has fallen off tremendously. Although they may have been able to pay a tremendous royalty at one time, it is my opinion the $8 figure which now pertains is probably very appropriate.

We have a provision in the bill that in the future the Copyright Royalty Commission will have the power to review the copyright paid by jukebox operators, but I want the RECORD to reflect the fact that in section 801(b)(1) we put in the caution that such determinations—meaning those of the Copyright Royalty Commission—shall be based upon relevant factors occurring subsequent to the enactment of this act. I think that is a very important caveat and I wish it to appear in the RECORD.

Mr. KASTENMEIER. Mr. Chairman, I yield 2 minutes to the gentleman from Massachusetts (Mr. DRINAN).

Mr. DRINAN asked and was given permission to revise and extend his remarks.)

Mr. DRINAN. Mr. Chairman, I want to pay tribute to the chairman of the subcommittee and the ranking minority member for their patience in the 41 sessions of the subcommittee in hearings and markup.

At this time when one sees the conclusion of a really monumental piece of work, one is troubled by some things. Let me mention only one or two that continue to concern me. One is the right to play certain music under the so-called mechanical rate. The economic data submitted to the committee seemed to justify an increase in that rate but it was not overwhelming. I am pleased that a Copyright Royalty Commission will have the right to reexamine that whole question in the near future.

The performing artists also have for too long been denied the full fruits of their labor. For example, in the manufacture and sale of the average phonograph record every contributor but the performer shares in the royalties. That is not fair and must be remedied. I hope that this subcommittee will in the near future get into those few things which we were not able to complete in this legislation.

Mr. Chairman, the authority to grant copyright is expressly given to the Congress by article I of the Constitution:

To promote the Progress of Science and useful Arts, by securing for limited Times to Authors and Inventors the exclusive Right to their respective Writings and Discoveries.

Because copyright provides exclusive rights to reproduce specific material, it is, by definition, a form of monopoly.

The monopoly is given, because it serves to advance artistic, intellectual, and social development. Without those benefits to society as a whole, granting copyrights would be disadvantageous. In designing a fair copyright law, a proper balance must be struck between these conflicting values. Copyright as a monopolistic practice can only be justified to the extent it serves the public good. That is why the Constitution insists that it be secured only "for limited times."

As one examines this lengthy bill and even longer report, these divergent strains can be seen. The tension between competing values we all share emerges quite clearly. At every intersection the committee sought, with great diligence, to resolve the differences in a manner which would maximize artistic endeavors while protecting the public from unwarranted restrictions on access to the creative works.

Consequently the resulting revision of the copyright law is a series of compromises arrived at after much debate, examination, drafting and redrafting, reconsideration, and confirmation. In my judgment, the compromises in this bill do not represent the kind frequently associated with the legislative process: Cynical political deals worked out behind closed doors. At every step of the way, your committee developed this measure in public sessions, giving every opportunity to competing interests to present their views.

This bill emerged from that free exchange. Of necessity it strikes balances between social goals equally high in value. It is always difficult to legislate on matters in which the opponents have sound arguments. Seeking and finding accommodations of such rational views is a hard task.

In several sections of the bill, the competing interests were particularly difficult to accommodate. In sections 107 and 108, the rights of authors and publishers conflicted with the desire for free access to books and periodicals by teachers, students, and the reading public. In our judgment the Senate version did not strike the proper balance. Consequently the committee modified the Senate-passed bill to provide greater access to published materials by educators, librarians, and the citizenry.

In addition the subcommittee encouraged representatives of the competing interests to negotiate guidelines for the reproduction of copyrighted materials which would be satisfactory to all. While the bill moved forward, the parties met, discussed, and approved the "Guidelines for Classroom Copying in Not-for-Profit Educational Institutions." The Judiciary Committee said in its report that the "guidelines are a reasonable interpretation of the minimum standards of fair use."

I should note, however, that not all the affected parties concurred in the reasonableness of those guidelines. The Association of American Law Schools and the American Association of University Professors were particularly critical of those criteria—see the excerpts from their letters to Chairman KASTENMEIER, which are inserted into the RECORD at the conclusion of these remarks.

In view of the discontent in some areas over these guidelines, I wish to stress that, as the committee report notes, they are "minimum standards." The report also expresses the hope that "if there are areas where standards other than these guidelines may be appropriate, the parties will continue their efforts to provide additional specific guidelines in the same spirit of good will and give and take that has marked the discussion of this subject in recent months." I hope the AAUP and the AALS will continue their efforts to explore additional avenues for the implementation of this critical aspect of the new copyright law.

In view of the monumental task confronting your committee and in light of the exceptional product which resulted, I urge my colleagues to approve the committee amendment in the nature of a substitute to S. 22.

The material follows:

EXCERPTS FROM LETTER OF MAY 25, 1976, TO CHAIRMAN KASTENMEIER FROM THE AMERICAN ASSOCIATION OF UNIVERSITY PROFESSORS

As scholars and teachers who both produce and use copyrighted materials, we appreciate and approve the recognition of the needs of the scholar and university teacher reflected in Sections 107 and 504 of S. 22 as recently amended by your Subcommittee. In Section 504, the mandatory remission of statutory damages for teachers acting in good faith constitutes a recognition of the function of the scholar and teacher. More significantly, by its references to "teaching (including multiple copies for classroom use), scholarship, or research," and in the distinction recognized between commercial and nonprofit uses, Section 107 as presently drafted is an articulate statement of the general principle of fair use on which courts and others may build a comprehensive framework for the educational uses of copyrighted material.

However, these salutary and progressive provisions in the Bill would be undermined by the proposed Guidelines if, as is apparently contemplated by the parties who submitted them to you, they were to become a significant part of the legislative history of Section 107 as a result of incorporation in your Committee Report. We recognize, of course, the right of any given groups mutually to agree upon the terms and conditions by which they, and those they actually represent, will be guided in conforming to a statute such as this. To suggest, however, that such agreements should be binding upon *other* persons or groups or should, through incorporation in a committee report, be given weight in the interpretation of the statute generally, is quite a different matter. Consequently, these Guidelines—agreed to recently by author and publisher representatives and some members of the education community but with no representation from our Association—have caused us deep dismay. They would seriously interfere with the basic mission and effective operation of higher education and with the purpose of the Constitutional grant of copyright protection, which is designed to promote, not hinder, the discovery and dissemination of knowledge. These proposed Guidelines, notwithstanding the insistence that they represent only minimum standards, and despite other disclaimers, ultimately resort to the language of prohibition (see Section III). In so doing, they contradict the basic concept of fair use and threaten the responsible discharge of the functions of teaching and research.

EXCERPTS FROM LETTER TO CHAIRMAN KASTENMEIER FROM THE ASSOCIATION OF AMERICAN LAW SCHOOLS, MAY 26, 1976

Our substantive objections to the guidelines are spelled out in the letters of Professors Raskind and Gorman to you. They are in essence that the guidelines restrict the doctrine of fair use so substantially as to make it almost useless for classroom teaching purposes. Requiring a law school teacher to meet all three tests of brevity, spontaneity and cumulative effect stifles the use of copyrighted material for classroom purposes. The draft guidelines are based on the principle, with which most people would agree, that copying should not substitute generally for purchase of a copyrighted work. The effect of the draft guidelines before you, however, is to stifle dissemination of material rather than encourage purchasing or licensing of it. The realities of classroom teaching and the economics of our students are such that they cannot purchase or pay royalties on works other than the standard text and case books that are used as the major resources in classroom teaching. Thus the teacher's choice is not between purchasing and copying; it is between copying and not using. The vague and restrictive nature of the draft guidelines leaves the teacher with no assurance of safety in the fair-use doctrine and will result in sharply curtailing the use of copyrighted works in the classroom. We would prefer that the courts be allowed to delineate, within the well-phrased current draft of the statute, where to draw the line on abuses of the fair-use doctrine.

The CHAIRMAN. Pursuant to the rule, the Clerk will now read the amendment in the nature of a substitute recommended by the Committee on the Judiciary now printed in the bill as an original bill for the purpose of amendment.

No amendment to the committee amendment is in order except amendments offered by the direction of the Committee of the Judiciary and germane amendments printed in the CONGRESSIONAL RECORD at least 3 calendar days prior to the start of consideration of said bill for amendment, but said amendments shall not be subject to amendment except those offered by direction of the Committee on the Judiciary.

The SPEAKER pro tempore. The question is on the engrossment and third reading of the Senate bill.

The Senate bill was ordered to be engrossed and read a third time, and was read the third time.

The SPEAKER pro tempore. The question is on the passage of the Senate bill.

The question was taken; and the Speaker announced that the ayes appeared to have it.

Mr. ASHBROOK. Mr. Speaker, I object to the vote on the ground that a quorum is not present and make the point of order that a quorum is not present.

The SPEAKER pro tempore. Evidently a quorum is not present.

The Sergeant at Arms will notify absent Members.

The vote was taken by electronic device, and there were—yeas 316, nays 7, answered "present" 3, not voting 104, as follows:

[Roll No. 800]

YEAS—316

Abdnor	Dellums	Kastenmeier
Abzug	Dent	Kazen
Addabbo	Derwinski	Kelly
Alexander	Devine	Kemp
Allen	Dickinson	Ketchum
Ambro	Dodd	Keys
Anderson,	Downey, N.Y.	Kindness
Calif.	Downing, Va.	Koch
Anderson, Ill.	Drinan	Krebs
Andrews, N.C.	Duncan, Oreg.	Lagomarsino
Andrews,	Duncan, Tenn.	Latta
N. Dak.	du Pont	Leggett
Archer	Early	Lehman
Ashbrook	Eckhardt	Lent
Aspin	Edgar	Levitas
AuCoin	Edwards, Ala.	Lloyd, Calif.
Badillo	Edwards, Calif.	Lloyd, Tenn.
Baldus	Eilberg	Long, La.
Baucus	Emery	Long, Md.
Bauman	English	Lott
Beard, Tenn.	Erlenborn	Lujan
Bedell	Evans, Ind.	Lundine
Bennett	Evins, Tenn.	McClory
Bergland	Fary	McCloskey
Bevill	Fascell	McCormack
Biester	Fenwick	McDade
Bingham	Findley	McDonald
Blanchard	Fish	McEwen
Blouin	Fisher	McFall
Boland	Fithian	McHugh
Bolling	Flood	McKay
Bonker	Florio	McKinney
Bowen	Flowers	Madigan
Brademas	Flynt	Maguire
Breaux	Foley	Mahon
Breckinridge	Ford, Mich.	Mann
Brinkley	Ford, Tenn.	Mathis
Brodhead	Fountain	Mazzoli
Brooks	Fraser	Meeds
Brown, Ohio	Frenzel	Melcher
Broyhill	Frey	Metcalfe
Buchanan	Fuqua	Mezvinsky
Burgener	Gaydos	Mikva
Burke, Calif.	Gilman	Milford
Burke, Fla.	Ginn	Miller, Calif.
Burke, Mass.	Grassley	Miller, Ohio
Burleson, Tex.	Hagedorn	Mineta
Burlison, Mo.	Hall, Ill.	Minish
Burton, John	Hall, Tex.	Mitchell, N.Y.
Butler	Hamilton	Moakley
Byron	Hannaford	Montgomery
Carney	Hansen	Moore
Carr	Harkin	Moorhead,
Carter	Harrington	Calif.
Cederberg	Harris	Moorhead, Pa.
Chappell	Harsha	Morgan
Clausen,	Hayes, Ind.	Mosher
Don H.	Hechler, W. Va.	Moss
Clawson, Del	Heckler, Mass.	Mottl
Cleveland	Hefner	Murphy, Ill.
Cochran	Hightower	Murtha
Cohen	Holt	Myers, Ind.
Collins, Ill.	Holtzman	Myers, Pa.
Collins, Tex.	Horton	Natcher

Conable	Hubbard	Nedzi
Conte	Hungate	Nichols
Corman	Hutchinson	Nolan
Cornell	Hyde	Nowak
Cotter	Ichord	Oberstar
Crane	Jacobs	Obey
D'Amours	Jeffords	O'Brien
Daniel, Dan	Jenrette	O'Hara
Daniel, R. W.	Johnson, Calif.	O'Neill
Danielson	Jones, Okla.	Ottinger
Davis	Jones, Tenn.	Patten, N.J.
de la Garza	Jordan	Patterson,
Delaney	Kasten	Calif.
Pattison, N.Y.	Roush	Taylor, N.C.
Perkins	Rousselot	Thone
Pettis	Roybal	Thornton
Pickle	Runnels	Traxler
Pike	Russo	Treen
Poage	Santini	Tsongas
Pressler	Sarasin	Ullman
Preyer	Satterfield	Van Deerlin
Price	Scheuer	Vander Jagt
Pritchard	Schroeder	Vander Veen
Quie	Sebelius	Vanik
Quillen	Seiberling	Vigorito
Railsback	Sharp	Walsh
Randall	Shipley	Wampler
Rangel	Shriver	Waxman
Regula	Simon	Whalen
Reuss	Sisk	White
Rhodes	Skubitz	Whitehurst
Richmond	Smith, Iowa	Wilson, Bob
Rinaldo	Snyder	Winn
Risenhoover	Solarz	Wirth
Roberts	Spence	Wolff
Robinson	Steed	Wydler
Rodino	Steiger, Wis.	Wylie
Roe	Stokes	Yates
Rogers	Studds	Yatron
Roncalio	Symington	Young, Fla.
Rooney	Symms	Young, Ga.
Rose	Talcott	Zablocki
Rostenkowski	Taylor, Mo.	Zeferetti

NAYS—7

Dingell	Mollohan	Stratton
Goldwater	Paul	
Goodling	Staggers	

ANSWERED "PRESENT"—3

Armstrong	Gonzalez	Krueger

NOT VOTING—104

Adams	Hébert	Riegle
Annunzio	Heinz	Rosenthal
Ashley	Helstoski	Ruppe
Bafalis	Henderson	Ryan
Beard, R.I.	Hicks	St Germain
Bell	Hillis	Sarbanes
Biaggi	Hinshaw	Schneebeli
Boggs	Holland	Schulze
Broomfield	Howard	Shuster
Brown, Calif.	Howe	Sikes
Brown, Mich.	Hughes	Slack
Burton, Phillip	Jarman	Smith, Nebr.
Chisholm	Johnson, Colo.	Spellman
Clancy	Johnson, Pa.	Stanton,
Clay	Jones, Ala.	J. William
Conlan	Jones, N.C.	Stanton,
Conyers	Karth	James V.
Coughlin	LaFalce	Stark
Daniels, N.J.	Landrum	Steelman
Derrick	McCollister	Steiger, Ariz.
Diggs	Madden	Stephens
Esch	Martin	Stuckey
Eshleman	Matsunaga	Sullivan
Evans, Colo.	Meyner	Teague
Forsythe	Michel	Thompson
Giaimo	Mills	Udall
Gibbons	Mink	Waggonner
Gradison	Mitchell, Md.	Weaver
Green	Moffett	Whitten
Gude	Murphy, N.Y.	Wiggins
Guyer	Neal	Wilson, C. H.
Haley	Nix	Wilson, Tex.
Hammer-	Passman	Wright
schmidt	Pepper	Young, Alaska
Hanley	Peyser	Young, Tex.
Hawkins	Rees	

The Clerk announced the following pairs:

Mr. Annunzio with Mr. Jarman.

Mr. Murphy of New York with Mr. Gradison.

Mrs. Boggs with Mr. Peyser.

Mr. Nix with Mr. Esch.

Mr. Pepper with Mrs. Smith of Nebraska.

Mr. Matsunaga with Mr. Steelman.

Mr. Giaimo with Mr. Ruppe.

Mr. Hébert with Mr. Steiger of Arizona.

Mr. Helstoski with Mr. Henderson.

Mrs. Mink with Mr. Clancy.

Mr. Neal with Mr. Heinz.

Mr. Charles H. Wilson of California with Mr. McCollister.

Mr. Green with Mr. Bafalis.

Mr. Hawkins with Mr. Eshleman.

Mr. Teague with Mr. Beard of Rhode Island.

Mr. Biaggi with Mr. Derrick.

Mr. Adams with Mr. Brown of Michigan.

Mr. Phillip Burton with Mr. Gude.

Mr. Dominick V. Daniels with Mr. Bell.

Mr. Evans of Colorado with Mr. Hillis.

Mrs. Chisholm with Mr. LaFalce.

Mr. Haley with Mr. Broomfield.

Mr. Gibbons with Mr. Guyer.

Mr. Clay with Mr. Brown of California.

Mr. Hanley with Mr. Hammerschmidt.

Mr. Hicks with Mr. Conlan.

Mrs. Spellman with Mr. Howe.

Mr. Conyers with Mr. Holland.

Mr. Howard with Mr. Johnson of Pennsylvania.

Mr. St Germain with Mr. Karth.

Mr. Diggs with Mr. Hughes.

Mr. Waggonner with Mr. Jones of Alabama.

Mr. Udall with Mr. Landrum.

Mrs. Meyner with Mr. Madden.

Mr. Moffett with Mr. Jones of North Carolina.

Mr. Passman with Mr. Martin.

Mr. Wright with Mr. Mills.

Mr. Sikes with Mr. Riegle.

Mr. Shuster with Mr. Rosenthal.

Mr. Whitten with Mr. Michel.

Mr. Slack with Mr. Mitchell of Maryland.

Mr. Stephens with Mr. Ryan.

Mr. Schulze with Mr. Sarbanes.

Mr. Rees with Mr. Ashley.

Mr. Stark with Mr. James V. Stanton.

Mr. Thompson with Mr. Stuckey.

Mr. J. William Stanton with Mrs. Sullivan.

Mr. Weaver with Mr. Wiggins.

Mr. Young of Alaska with Mr. Charles Wilson of Texas.

Mr. STAGGERS changed his vote from "yea" to "nay."

Messrs. SEBELIUS and BEDELL

changed their vote from "nay" to "yea."

So the Senate bill was passed.

The result of the vote was announced as above recorded.

A motion to reconsider was laid on the table.

GENERAL LEAVE

Mr. KASTENMEIER. Mr. Speaker, I ask unanimous consent that all Members may have 5 legislative days in which to revise and extend their remarks on the Senate bill just passed.

The SPEAKER pro tempore (Mr. McFALL). Is there objection to the request of the gentleman from Wisconsin?

There was no objection.

APPOINTMENT OF CONFEREES ON S. 22 COPYRIGHT LAW REVISION

Mr. KASTENMEIER. Mr. Speaker, I ask unanimous consent to take from the Speaker's table the Senate bill (S. 22) for the general revision of the Copyright Law, title 17 of the United States Code, and for other purposes, with House amendments thereto, insist on the House amendments and request a conference with the Senate thereon.

The SPEAKER pro tempore. Is there objection to the request of the gentleman from Wisconsin? The Chair hears none, and appoints the following conferees: Messrs. KASTENMEIER, DANIELSON, DRINAN BADILLO, PATTISON of New York, RAILSBACK, and WIGGINS.

COPYRIGHT LAW REVISION— CONFERENCE REPORT

Mr. McCLELLAN. Mr. President, I submit a report of the committee of conference on S. 22 and ask for its immediate consideration.

The PRESIDING OFFICER. (Mr. CULVER). The report will be stated by title.

The assistant legislative clerk read as follows:

The committee of conference on the disagreeing votes of the two Houses on the amendment of the House to the bill (S. 22) for the general revision of the copyright law, title 17 of the United States Code, and for other purposes, having met, after full and free conference, have agreed to recommend and do recommend to their respective Houses this report, signed by all of the conferees.

The PRESIDING OFFICER. Without objection, the Senate will proceed to the consideration of the conference report.

The Senate proceeded to consider the report.

(The conference report is printed in the House proceedings of the RECORD of Sept. 30, 1976.)

Mr. McCLELLAN. Mr. President, the conference report has been signed by all the conferees on the part of the Senate and the House of Representatives.

The long journey of this legislation in the Senate began on August 18, 1965, when the Subcommittee on Patents, Trademarks, and Copyrights commenced hearings on a bill for the general revision of the copyright law. I said at that time that my sole objective "was to devise a modern copyright statute that would encourage creativity and protect the interests which the public has in the subject matter of this legislation." I believe these goals have been substantially accomplished in the conference report.

This is not the proper occasion to review the protracted and, at times, acrimonious history of this legislation. Much will be written on that subject in the future. Rather, I believe it is appropriate today to take satisfaction in the successful completion of this monumental legislative project, which is entirely the work product of the legislative branch. Considering the controversies that existed on certain issues in the past, it is gratifying that S. 22 passed the Senate in this Congress by a vote of 97 to 0.

I believe that the final version of this legislation is just and equitable between the creators of copyrighted materials, and the users thereof.

Mr. President, I wish to thank all of my colleagues on the Judiciary Committee and others who have worked with us in developing and processing this legislation. There were many issues that had to be resolved, there were differing opinions that had to be discussed, and a lot of give and take had to occur in order for this bill to emerge; but everyone worked in good faith, with a purpose to revise the copyright laws of this country, which had not been revised since 1909, and we do believe, now, that we have a good bill. In accomplishing that purpose, we were greatly aided by the committee staff; and, Mr. President, I would be greatly remiss in meeting my responsibilities as chairman of the subcommittee that processed this legislation if I did not acknowledge and express deep gratification for the staff assistance we were so fortunate to have throughout our drafting, revising and processing of this measure. The subcommittee staff, under the able direction of Mr. Tom Brennan, gave expert counsel and advice at every stage of work and consideration of this bill—counsel and advice of such quality as guided the committee unerringly to a successful conclusion of the stupendous task that was involved in this important legislative undertaking. We are indeed grateful to Tom and his loyal assistants.

Again, Mr. President, I express my deepest gratitude for the assistance given to me by my colleagues who served on the committee with me.

Mr. President, I move the adoption of the conference report. . . . .

COPYRIGHT LAW REVISION—CON-FERENCE REPORT

The Senate continued with the consideration of the conference report on the bill (S. 22) for the general revision of the Copyright Law, title 17 of the United States Code, and for other purposes.

Mr. GRIFFIN. Mr. President, I ask for the yeas and nays on the adoption of the conference report on the copyright bill.

The PRESIDING OFFICER. Is there a sufficient second? There is a sufficient second.

The yeas and nays were ordered.

The PRESIDING OFFICER. The question is on agreeing to the conference report. On this question the yeas and nays have been ordered, and the clerk will call the roll.

The assistant legislative clerk called the roll.

Mr. ROBERT C. BYRD. I announce that the Senator from Texas (Mr. BENTSEN), the Senator from Florida (Mr. CHILES), the Senator from Idaho (Mr. CHURCH), the Senator from Michigan (Mr. PHILIP A. HART), the Senator from Indiana (Mr. HARTKE), the Senator from Massachusetts (Mr. KENNEDY), the Senator from Wyoming (Mr. McGEE), the Senator from Minnesota (Mr. MONDALE), the Senator from New Mexico (Mr. MONTOYA), the Senator from Louisana (Mr. LONG), the Senator from Connecticut (Mr. RIBICOFF), and the Senator from Alabama (Mr. SPARKMAN) are necessarily absent.

I further announce that the Senator from Ohio (Mr. GLENN), the Senator from Montana (Mr. MANSFIELD), the Senator from South Dakota (Mr. McGOVERN), and the Senator from Hawaii (Mr. INOUYE) are absent on official business.

I further announce that, if present and voting, the Senator from Connecticut (Mr. RIBICOFF) would vote "yea."

Mr. GRIFFIN. I announce that the Senator from Maryland (Mr. BEALL), the Senator from Oklahoma (Mr. BELLMON), the Senator from New York (Mr. BUCKLEY), the Senator from Kansas (Mr. DOLE), the Senator from Vermont (Mr. STAFFORD), the Senator from Alaska (Mr. STEVENS), the Senator from Ohio (Mr. TAFT), and the Senator from South Carolina (Mr. THURMOND) are necessarily absent.

I also announce that the Senator from Virginia (Mr. WILLIAM L. SCOTT) is absent on official business.

I further announce that, if present and voting, the Senator from South Carolina (Mr. THURMOND) would vote "yea."

The result was announced—yeas 75 nays 0, as follows:

[Rollcall Vote No. 681 Leg.]

YEAS—75

Abourezk	Garn	Moss
Allen	Goldwater	Muskie
Baker	Gravel	Nelson
Bartlett	Griffin	Nunn
Bayh	Hansen	Packwood
Biden	Hart, Gary	Pastore
Brock	Haskell	Pearson
Brooke	Hatfield	Pell
Bumpers	Hathaway	Percy
Burdick	Helms	Proxmire
Byrd,	Hollings	Randolph
Harry F., Jr.	Hruska	Roth
Byrd, Robert C.	Huddleston	Schweiker
Cannon	Humphrey	Scott, Hugh
Case	Jackson	Stennis
Clark	Javits	Stevenson
Cranston	Johnston	Stone
Culver	Laxalt	Symington
Curtis	Leahy	Talmadge
Domenici	Magnuson	Tower
Durkin	Mathias	Tunney
Eagleton	McClellan	Weicker
Eastland	McClure	Williams
Fannin	McIntyre	Young
Fong	Metcalf	
Ford	Morgan	

NAYS—0

NOT VOTING—25

Beall	Hartke	Ribicoff
Bellmon	Inouye	Scott,
Bentsen	Kennedy	William L.
Buckley	Long	Sparkman
Chiles	Mansfield	Stafford
Church	McGee	Stevens
Dole	McGovern	Taft
Glenn	Mondale	Thurmond
Hart, Philip A.	Montoya	

So the conference report was agreed to.

Copyright and the Librarian

SECTIONS OF THE NEW COPYRIGHT LAW OF MOST INTEREST TO LIBRARIANS

This circular has been published in an attempt to satisfy many requests by librarians and teachers for information concerning responsibilities, obligations, and limitations under P.L. 94–553 (90 Stat. 2541), the new copyright law. Pertinent sections of the new law, plus minimum standards of educational fair use for books, periodicals, and music, and guidelines on interlibrary arrangements for photocopying adopted by the National Commission on New Technological Uses of Copyrighted Works (CONTU). Additional material from other sources will be added in subsequent revisions of this circular.

SECTION 106: EXCLUSIVE RIGHTS IN COPYRIGHTED WORKS—PUBLIC LAW 94–553

Subject to sections 107 through 118, the owner of copyright under this title has the exclusive rights to do and to authorize any of the following:

(1) to reproduce the copyrighted work in copies or phonorecords;

(2) to prepare derivative works based upon the copyrighted work;

(3) to distribute copies or phonorecords of the copyrighted work to the public by sale or other transfer of ownership, or by rental, lease, or lending;

(4) in the case of literary, musical, dramatic, and choreographic works, pantomimes, and motion pictures and other audiovisual works, to perform the copyrighted work publicly; and

(5) in the case of literary, musical, dramatic, and choreographic works, pantomimes, and pictorial, graphic, or sculptural works, including the individual images of a motion picture or other audiovisual work, to display the copyrighted work publicly.

SECTION 107: LIMITATIONS ON EXCLUSIVE RIGHTS: FAIR USE—PUBLIC LAW 94–553

Notwithstanding the provisions of section 106, the fair use of a copyrighted work, including such use by reproduction in copies or phonorecords or by any other means specified by that section, for purposes such as criticism, comment, news reporting, teaching (including multiple copies for classroom use), scholarship, or research, is not an infringement of copyright. In determining whether the use made of a work in any particular case is a fair use the factors to be considered shall include—

(1) the purpose and character of the use, including whether such use is of a commercial nature or is for nonprofit educational purposes;

(2) the nature of the copyrighted work;

(3) the amount and substantiality of the portion used in relation to the copyrighted work as a whole; and

(4) the effect of the use upon the potential market for or value of the copyrighted work.

CLASSROOM GUIDELINES *

The fair use provision of the new law is, of necessity, general and is not susceptible to either precise definition or automatic application. Each case must be considered and decided on its own merit. To provide more guidance for classroom teachers and other educators, representatives of publishers, authors, and the Ad Hoc Committee of Educational Institutions and Organizations on Copyright Law Revision developed some guidelines.

AGREEMENT ON GUIDELINES FOR CLASSROOM COPYING IN NOT-FOR-PROFIT EDUCATIONAL INSTITUTIONS WITH RESPECT TO BOOKS AND PERIODICALS *

The purpose of the following guidelines is to state the minimum and not the maximum standards of educational fair use under Section 107 of H.R. 2223. The parties agree that the conditions determining the extent of permissible copying for educational purposes may change in the future; that certain types of copying permitted under these guidelines may not be permissible in the future; and conversely that in the future other types of copying not permitted under these guidelines may be permissible under revised guidelines.

Moreover, the following statement of guidelines is not intended to limit the types of copying permitted under the standards of fair use under judicial decision and which are stated in Section 107 of the Copyright Revision Bill. There may be instances in which copying, which does not fall within the guidelines stated below, may nonetheless be permitted under the criteria of fair use.

GUIDELINES

I. Single Copying for Teachers:

A single copy may be made of any of the following by or for a teacher at his or her individual request for his or her scholarly research or use in teaching or preparation to teach a class:

A. A chapter from a book;

B. An article from a periodical or newspaper;

C. A short story, short essay or short poem, whether or not from a collective work;

D. A chart, graph, diagram, drawing, cartoon or picture from a book, periodical, or newspaper.

II. Multiple Copies for Classroom Use:

Multiple copies (not to exceed in any event more than one copy per pupil in a course) may be made by or for the teacher giving the course for classroom use or discussion; **provided that:**

A. The copying meets the tests of brevity and spontaneity as defined below; **and,**

B. Meets the cumulative effect test as defined below; **and,**

C. Each copy includes a notice of copyright.

DEFINITIONS:

Brevity:

1. Poetry: (a) A complete poem if less than 250 words and if printed or not more than two pages or, (b) from a longer poem, an excerpt of not more than 250 words.

2. Prose: (a) Either a complete article, story or essay of less than 2,500 words, or (b) an excerpt from any prose work of not more than 1,000 words or 10% of the work, whichever is less, but in any event a minimum of 500 words.

[Each of the numerical limits stated in "1" and "2" above may be expanded to permit the completion of an unfinished line of a poem or of an unfinished prose paragraph.]

3. Illustration: One chart, graph, diagram, drawing, cartoon or picture per book or per periodical issue.

4. "Special" works: Certain works in poetry, prose or in "poetic prose" which often combine language with illustrations and which are intended sometimes for children and at other times for a more general audience fall short of 2,500 words in their entirety. Paragraph "2" above notwithstanding such "special works" may not be reproduced in their entirety; however, an excerpt comprising not more than two of the published pages of such special work and containing not more than 10% of the words found in the text thereof, may be reproduced.

Spontaneity

1. The copying is at the instance and inspiration of the individual teacher, and

2. The inspiration and decision to use the work and the moment of its use for maximum teaching effectiveness are so close in time that it would be unreasonable to expect a timely reply to a request for permission.

Cumulative Effect

1. The copying of the material is for only one course in the school in which the copies are made.

2. Not more than one short poem, article, story, essay or two excerpts may be copied from the same author, nor more than three from the same collective work or periodical volume during one class term.

3. There shall not be more than nine instances of such multiple copying for one course during one class term.

[The limitations stated in "2" and "3" above shall not apply to current news periodicals and newspapers and current news sections of other periodicals.]

III. Prohibitions as to I. and II. Above

Notwithstanding any of the above, the following shall be prohibited:

A. Copying shall not be used to create or to replace or substitute for anthologies, compilations or collective works. Such replacement or substitution may occur whether copies of various works or excerpts therefrom are accumulated or are reproduced and used separately.

B. There shall be no copying of or from works intended to be "consumable" in the course of study or of teaching. These include workbooks, exercises, standardized tests and test booklets and answer sheets and like consumable material.

C. Copying shall not:

1. substitute for the purchase of books, publisher's reprints or periodicals;

2. be directed by higher authority;

3. be repeated with respect to the same item by the same teacher from term to term.

D. No charge shall be made to the student beyond the actual cost of the photocopying.

GUIDELINES FOR EDUCATIONAL USES OF MUSIC**

Representatives of the Music Publishers' Association of the United States, Inc., the National Music Publishers' Association, Inc., the Music Teachers National Association, the Music Educators National Conference, the National Association of Schools of Music and the Ad Hoc Committee on Copyright Revision developed the following:

The purpose of the following guidelines is to state the minimum and not the maximum standards of educational fair use under Section 107 of H.R. 2223. The parties agree that the conditions determining the extent of permissible copying for educational purpose may change in the future; that certain types of copying permitted under these guidelines may not be permissible in the future; and conversely that in the future other types of copying not permitted under these guidelines may be permissible under revised guidelines.

Moreover, the following statement of guidelines is not intended to limit the types of copying permitted under the standards of fair use under judicial decision and which are stated in Section 107 of the Copyright Revision Bill. There may be instances in which copying which does not fall within the guidelines stated below may nonetheless be permitted under the criteria of fair use.

I. Permissible Uses

A. Emergency copying to replace purchased copies which for any reason are not available for an imminent performance provided purchased replacement copies shall be substituted in due course.

B. For academic purposes other than performance, single or multiple copies of excerpts of works may be made, provided that the excerpts do not comprise a part of the whole which would constitute a performable unit such as a section, movement or aria, but in no case more than (10%) of the whole work. The number of copies shall not exceed one copy per pupil.

C. Printed copies which have been purchased may be edited or simplified provided that the fundamental character of the work is not distorted or the lyrics, if any, altered or lyrics added if none exist.

D. A single copy of recordings of performance by students may be made for evaluation or rehearsal purposes and may be retained by the educational institution or individual teacher.

E. A single copy of a sound recording (such as a tape, disc or cassette) of copyrighted music may be made from sound recordings owned by an educational institution or an individual teacher for the purpose of constructing aural exercises or examinations and may be retained by the educational institution or individual teacher. (This pertains only to the copyright of the music itself and not to any copyright which may exist in the sound recording.)

II. Prohibitions

A. Copying to create or replace or substitute for anthologies, compilations or collective works.

B. Copying of or from works intended to be "consumable" in the course of study or of teaching such as workbooks, exercises, standardized tests and answer sheets and like material.

C. Copying for the purpose of performance, except as in I.A. above.

D. Copying for the purpose of substituting for type purchase of music, except as in I.A. and I.B. above.

E. Copying without inclusion of the copyright notice which appears on the printed copy.

SECTION 108. LIMITATIONS ON EXCLUSIVE RIGHTS: REPRODUCTION BY LIBRARIES AND ARCHIVES—PUBLIC LAW 94-553

(a) Notwithstanding the provisions of section 106, it is not an infringement of copyright for a library or archives, or any of its employees acting within the scope of their employment, to reproduce no more than one copy or phonorecord of a work, or to distribute such copy or phonorecord, under the conditions specified by this section, if—

   (1) the reproduction or distribution is made without any purpose of direct or indirect commercial advantage;

   (2) the collections of the library or archives are (i) open to the public, or (ii) available not only to researchers affiliated with the library or archives or with the institution of which it is a part, but also to other persons doing research in a specialized field; and

   (3) the reproduction or distribution of the work includes a notice of copyright.

(b) The rights of reproduction and distribution under this section apply to a copy or phonorecord of an unpublished work duplicated in facsimile form solely for purposes of preservation and security or for deposit for research use in another library or archives of the type described by clause (2) of subsection (a), if the copy or phonorecord reproduced is currently in the collections of the library or archives.

(c) The right of reproduction under this section applies to a copy or phonorecord of a published work duplicated in facsimile form solely for the purpose of replacement of a copy or phonorecord that is damaged, deteriorating, lost, or stolen, if the library or archives has, after a reasonable effort, determined that an unused replacement cannot be obtained at a fair price.

(d) The rights of reproduction and distribution under this section apply to a copy, made from the collection of a library or archives where the user makes his or her request or from that of another library or archives, of no more than one article or other contribution to a copyrighted collection or periodical issue, or to a copy or phonorecord of a small part of any other copyrighted work, if—

   (1) the copy or phonorecord becomes the property of the user, and the library or archives has had no notice that the copy or phonorecord would be used for any purpose other than private study, scholarship, or research; and

   (2) the library or archives displays prominently, at the place where orders are accepted, and includes on its order form, a warning of copyright in accordance with requirements that the Register of Copyrights shall prescribe by regulation.

(e) The rights of reproduction and distribution under this section apply to the entire work, or to a substantial part of it, made from the collection of a library or archives where the user makes his or her request or from that of another library or archives, if the library or archives has first determined, on the basis of a reasonable investigation, that a copy or phonorecord of the copyrighted work cannot be obtained at a fair price, if—

   (1) the copy or phonorecord becomes the property of the user, and the library or archives has had no notice that the copy or phonorecord would be used for any purpose other than private study, scholarship, or research; and

   (2) the library or archives displays prominently, at the place where orders are accepted, and includes on its order form, a warning of copyright in accordance with requirements that the Register of Copyrights shall prescribe by regulation.

(f) Nothing in this section—

   (1) shall be construed to impose liability for copyright infringement upon a library or archives or its employees for the unsupervised use of reproducing equipment located

on its premises: *Provided,* That such equipment displays a notice that the making of a copy may be subject to the copyright law;

(2) excuses a person who uses such reproducing equipment or who requests a copy or phonorecord under subsection (d) from liability for copyright infringement for any such act, or for any later use of such copy or phonorecord, if it exceeds fair use as provided by section 107;

(3) shall be construed to limit the reproduction and distribution by lending of a limited number of copies and excerpts by a library or archives of an audiovisual news program, subject to clauses (1), (2), and (3) of subsection (a); or

(4) in any way affects the right of fair use as provided by section 107, or any contractual obligations assumed at any time by the library or archives when it obtained a copy or phonorecord of a work in its collections.

(g) The rights of reproduction and distribution under this section extend to the isolated and unrelated reproduction or distribution of a single copy or phonorecord of the same material on separate occasions, but do not extend to cases where the library or archives, or its employee—

(1) is aware or has substantial reason to believe that it is engaging in the related or concerted reproduction or distribution of multiple copies or phonorecords of the same material, whether made on one occasion or over a period of time, and whether intended for aggregate use by one or more individuals or for separate use by the individual members of a group; or

(2) engages in the systematic reproduction or distribution of single or multiple copies or phonorecords of material described in subsection (d): *Provided,* That nothing in this clause prevents a library or archives from participating in interlibrary arrangements that do not have, as their purpose or effect, that the library or archives receiving such copies or phonorecords for distribution does so in such aggregate quantities as to substitute for a subscription to or purchase of such work.

(h) The rights of reproduction and distribution under this section do not apply to a musical work, a pictorial, graphic or sculptural work, or a motion picture or other audiovisual work other than an audiovisual work dealing with news, except that no such limitation shall apply with respect to rights granted by subsections (b) and (c), or with respect to pictorial or graphic works published as illustrations, diagrams, or similar adjuncts to works of which copies are reproduced or distributed in accordance with subsections (d) and (e).

(i) Five years from the effective date of this Act, and at five-year intervals thereafter, the Register of Copyrights, after consulting with representatives of authors, book and periodical publishers, and other owners of copyrighted materials, and with representatives of library users and librarians, shall submit to the Congress a report setting forth the extent to which this section has achieved the intended statutory balancing of the rights of creators, and the needs of users. The report should also describe any problems that may have arisen, and present legislative or other recommendations, if warranted.

CONTU GUIDELINES FOR INTERLIBRARY ARRANGEMENTS—CONFERENCE REPORT, 94–1733, PHOTOCOPYING—INTERLIBRARY ARRANGEMENTS

Introduction

Subsection 108(g) (2) of the bill deals, among other things, with limits on interlibrary arrangements for photocopying. It prohibits systematic photocopying of copyrighted materials but permits interlibrary arrangements "that do not have, as their purpose or effect, that the library or archives receiving such copies or phonorecords for distribution does so in such aggregate quantities as to substitute for a subscription to or purchase of such work."

The National Commission on New Technological Uses of Copyrighted Works offered its good offices to the House and Senate subcommittees in bringing the interested parties together to see if agreement could be reached on what a realistic definition would be of "such aggregate quantities." The Commission consulted with the parties and suggested the interpretation which follows, on which there has been substantial agreement by the principal library, publisher, and author organizations. The Commission considers the guidelines which follow to be a workable and fair interpretation of the intent of the proviso portion of subsection 108(g) (2).

These guidelines are intended to provide guidance in the application of section 108 to the most frequently encountered interlibrary case: a library's obtaining from another library, in lieu of interlibrary loan, copies of articles from relatively recent issues of periodicals—those published within five years prior to the date of the request. The guidelines do not specify what aggregate quantity of copies of an article or articles published in a periodical, the issue date of which is more than five years prior to the date when the request for the copy thereof is made, constitutes a substitute for a subscription to such periodical. The meaning of the proviso to subsection 108(g) (2) in such case is left to future interpretation.

The point has been made that the present practice on interlibrary loans and use of photocopies in lieu of loans may be supplemented or even largely replaced by a system in which one or more agencies or institutions, public or private, exist for the specific purpose of providing a central source for photocopies. Of course, these guidelines would not apply to such a situation.

Guidelines for the Proviso of Subsection 108 (g) (2)—Conference Report, 94–1733

1. As used in the proviso of subsection 108 (g) (2), the words ". . . such aggregate quantities as to substitute for a subscription to or purchase of such work" shall mean:

   (a) with respect to any given periodical (as opposed to any given issue of a periodical), filled requests of a library or archives (a "requesting entity") within any calendar year for a total of six or more copies of an article or articles published in such periodical within five years prior to the date of the request. These guidelines specifically shall not apply, directly or indirectly, to any request of a requesting entity for a copy or copies of an article or articles published in any issue of a periodical, the publication date of which is more than five years prior to the date when the request is made. These guidelines do not define the meaning, with respect to such a request, of ". . . such aggregate quantities as to substitute for a subscription to [such periodical]".

(b) With respect to any other material described in subsection 108(d), (including fiction and poetry), filled requests of a requesting entity within any calendar year for a total of six or more copies or phonorecords of or from any given work (including a collective work) during the entire period when such material shall be protected by copyright.

2. In the event that a requesting entity—

(a) shall have in force or shall have entered an order for a subscription to a periodical, or

(b) has within its collection, or shall have entered an order for, a copy or phonorecord of any other copyrighted work, material from either category of which it desires to obtain by copy from another library or archives (the "supplying entity"), because the material to be copied is not reasonably available for use by the requesting entity itself, then the fulfillment of such request shall be treated as though the requesting entity made such copy from its own collection. A library or archives may request a copy or phonorecord from a supplying entity only under those circumstances where the requesting entity would have been able, under the other provisions of section 108, to supply such copy from materials in its own collection.

3. No request for a copy or phonorecord of any material to which these guidelines apply may be fulfilled by the supplying entity unless such request is accompanied by a representation by the requesting entity that the request was made in conformity with these guidelines.

4. The requesting entity shall maintain records of all requests made by it for copies or phonorecords of any materials to which these guidelines apply and shall maintain records of the fulfillment of such requests, which records shall be retained until the end of the third complete calendar year after the end of the calendar year in which the respective request shall have been made.

5. As part of the review provided for in subsection 108(i), these guidelines shall be reviewed not later than five years from the effective date of this bill.

The conference committee is aware that an issue has arisen as to the meaning of the phrase "audiovisual news program" in section 108(f) (3). The conferees believe that, under the provision as adopted in the conference substitute, a library or ar-

chives qualifying under section 108(a) would be free, without regard to the archival activities of the Library of Congress or any other organization, to reproduce, on videotape or any other medium of fixation or reproduction, local, regional, or network newscasts, interviews concerning current news events, and on-the-spot coverage of news events, and to distribute a limited number of reproductions of such a program on a loan basis.

Another point of interpretation involves the meaning of "indirect commercial advantage," as used in section 108(a) (1), in the case of libraries or archival collections within industrial, profit-making, or proprietary institutions. As long as the library or archives meets the criteria in section 108(a) and the other requirements of the section, including the prohibitions against multiple and systematic copying in subsection (g), the conferees consider that the isolated, spontaneous making of single photocopies by a library or archives in a for-profit organization without any commercial motivation, or participation by such a library or archives in interlibrary arrangements, would come within the scope of section 108.

SECTION 504(c)(2). STATUTORY DAMAGES—PUBLIC LAW 94–553

(2) In a case where the copyright owner sustains the burden of proving, and the court finds, that infringement was committed willfully, the court in its discretion may increase the award of statutory damages to a sum of not more than $50,000. In a case where the infringer sustains the burden of proving, and the court finds, that such infringer was not aware and had no reason to believe that his or her acts constituted an infringement of copyright, the court in its discretion may reduce the award of statutory damages to a sum of not less than $100. The court shall remit statutory damages in any case where an infringer believed and had reasonable grounds for believing that his or her use of the copyrighted work was a fair use under section 107, if the infringer was: (i) an employee or agent of a nonprofit educational institution, library, or archives acting within the scope of his or her employment who, or such institution, library, or archives itself, which infringed by reproducing the work in copies or phonorecords; or (ii) a public broadcasting entity which or a person who, as a regular part of the nonprofit activities of a public broadcasting entity (as defined in subsection (g) of section 118) infringed by performing a published nondramatic literary work or by reproducing a transmission program embodying a performance of such a work.

* As appeared in House Report No. 94–1476, as corrected in the *Congressional Record* (daily edition), Volume 122, Number 143, September 21, 1976, p. H10727.

** As appeared in House Report No. 94–1476, as amended in the *Congressional Record* (daily edition), Volume 122, Number 144, September 22, 1976, p. H10875.

Copyright Revision Bill Becomes Law: Most Provisions To Take Effect January 1, 1978

INTRODUCTION

President Gerald R. Ford signed, on October 19, 1976, the bill for the general revision of the United States copyright law, which became Public Law 94-553 (90 Stat. 2541). The new statute specifies that, with particular exceptions, its provisions are to enter into force on **January 1, 1978.** The new law will supersede the copyright act of 1909, as amended, which will however remain in force until the new enactment takes effect.

HIGHLIGHTS

Some of the highlights of the new statute are listed below. For detailed information about specific changes or new provisions, write to the Copyright Office.

Single National System

Instead of the present dual system of protecting works under the common law before they are published and under the Federal statute after publication, the new law will establish a single system of statutory protection for all copyrightable works, whether published or unpublished.

Duration of Copyright

For works already under statutory protection, the new law retains the present first term of copyright of 28 years from first publication (or from registration in some cases), renewable by certain persons for a second period of protection, but it increases the length of the second period to 47 years. Copyrights in their first term **must still be renewed** to receive the full new maximum term of 75 years, but copyrights in their second term between December 31, 1976 and December 31, 1977, are automatically extended up to the maximum of 75 years without the need for further renewal.

For works created after January 1, 1978, the new law provides a term lasting for the author's life, plus an additional 50 years after the author's death. For works made for hire, and for anonymous and pseudonymous works (unless the author's identity is revealed in Copyright Office records), the new term will be 75 years from publication or 100 years from creation, whichever is shorter.

For unpublished works that are already in existence on January 1, 1978, but that are not protected by statutory copyright and have not yet gone into the public domain, the new Act will generally provide automatic Federal copyright protection for the same life-plus-50 or 75/100-year terms prescribed for new works. Special dates of termination are provided for copyrights in older works of this sort.

The new Act does not restore copyright protection for any work that has gone into the public domain.

Termination of Transfers

Under the present law, after the first term of 28 years the renewal copyright reverts in certain situations to the author or other specified beneficiaries. The new law drops the renewal feature except for works already in their first term of statutory protection when the new law takes effect. Instead, for transfers of rights made by an author or certain of the author's heirs after January 1, 1978, the new Act generally permits the author or certain heirs to terminate the transfer after 35 years by serving written notice on the transferee within specified time limits.

For works already under statutory copyright protection, a similar right of termination is provided with respect to transfers covering the newly-added years extending the present maximum term of the copyright from 56 to 75 years. Within certain time limits, an author or specified heirs of the author are generally entitled to file a notice terminating the author's transfers covering any part of the period (usually 19 years) that has now been added to the end of the second term of copyright in a work already under protection when the new law comes into effect.

Government Publications

The new law continues the prohibition in the present law against copyright in "publications of the United States Government" but clarifies its scope by defining works covered by the prohibition as those prepared by an officer or employee of the U.S. Government as part of that person's official duties.

Fair Use

The new law adds a provision to the statute specifically recognizing the principle of "fair use" as a limitation on the exclusive rights of copyright owners, and indicates factors to be considered in determining whether particular uses fall within this category.

Reproduction by Libraries and Archives

In addition to the provision for "fair use," the new law specifies circumstances under which the making or distribution of single copies of works by libraries and archives for noncommercial purposes do not constitute a copyright infringement.

Copyright Royalty Tribunal

The new law creates a Copyright Royalty Tribunal whose purpose will be to determine whether copyright royalty rates, in certain categories where such rates are established in the law, are reasonable and, if not, to adjust them; it will also in certain circumstances determine the distribution of those statutory royalty fees deposited with the Register of Copyrights.

Sound Recordings

The new law retains the provisions added to the present copyright law in 1972, which accord protection against the unauthorized duplication of sound recordings. The new law does not create a performance right for sound recordings as such.

Recording Rights in Music

The new law makes a number of changes in the present system providing compulsory licensing for the recording of music. Among other things it raises the statutory royalty from the present rate of 2 cents to a rate of 2 and ¾ cents or ½ cent per minute of playing time, whichever amount is larger.

Exempt Performances

The new law removes the present general exemption of public performance of nondramatic literary and musical works where the performance is not "for profit." Instead, it provides several specific exemptions for certain types of nonprofit uses, including performances in classrooms and instructional broadcasting. The law also gives broadcasting organizations a limited privilege of making "ephemeral recordings" of their broadcasts.

Public Broadcasting

Under the new Act, noncommercial transmissions by public broadcasters of published musical and graphic works will be subject to a compulsory license. Copyright owners and public broadcasting entities that do not reach voluntary agreement will be subject to the terms and rates prescribed by the Copyright Royalty Tribunal.

Jukebox Exemption

The new law removes the present exemption for performances of copyrighted music by jukeboxes. It will substitute a system of compulsory licenses based upon the payment by jukebox operators of an annual royalty fee to the Register of Copyrights for later distribution by the Copyright Royalty Tribunal to the copyright owners.

Cable Television

The new law provides for the payment, under a system of compulsory licensing, of certain royalties for the secondary transmission of copyrighted works on cable television systems (CATV). The amounts are to be paid to the Register of Copyrights for later distribution to the copyright owners by the Copyright Royalty Tribunal.

Notice of Copyright

The old law now requires, as a mandatory condition of copyright protection, that the published copies of a work bear a copyright notice. The new enactment calls for a notice on published copies, but omission or errors will not immediately result in forfeiture of the copyright, and can be corrected within certain time limits. Innocent infringers misled by the omission or error will be shielded from liability.

Deposit and Registration

As under the present law, registration will not be a condition of copyright protection but will be a prerequisite to an infringement suit. Subject to certain exceptions, the remedies of statutory damages and attorney's fees will not be available for infringements occurring before registration. Copies or phonorecords of works published with the notice of copyright that are not registered are required to be deposited for the collections of the Library of Congress, not as a condition of copyright protection, but under provisions of the law making the copyright owner subject to certain penalties for failure to deposit after a demand by the Register of Copyrights.

Manufacturing Clause

Certain works must now be manufactured in the United States to have copyright protection here. The new Act would terminate this requirement completely after July 1, 1982. For the period between January 1, 1978 and July 1, 1982, it makes several modifications that will narrow the coverage of the manufacturing clause, will permit the importation of 2,000 copies manufactured abroad instead of the present limit of 1,500 copies, and will equate manufacture in Canada with manufacture in the United States.

BACKGROUND

The present movement for general revision of the copyright law began in 1955 with a program that produced, under the supervision of the Copyright Office, a series of 35 extensive studies of major copyright problems. This was followed by a report of the Register of Copyrights on general revision in 1961, by the preparation in the Copyright Office of a preliminary proposed draft bill, and by a series of meetings with a Panel of Consultants consisting of copyright experts, the majority of them from outside the Government. Following a supplementary report by the Register and a bill introduced in Congress primarily for consideration and comment, the first legislative hearings were held before a subcommittee of the House Judiciary Committee on the basis of a bill introduced in 1965. Also in the same year a companion bill was introduced in the Senate.

In 1967, after the subcommittee had held extensive hearings, the House of Representatives passed a revision bill whose major features were similar to the bill just enacted.

There followed another series of extensive hearings before a subcommittee of the Senate Judiciary Committee but, owing chiefly to an extended impasse on the complex and controversial subject of cable television, the revision bill was prevented from reaching the Senate floor.

Indeed it was not until 1974 that the copyright revision bill was enacted by the Senate. However, that bill, although in its general terms the same as the measure approved by the House in 1967, was different in a number of particulars. In February 1976 the Senate again passed the bill in essentially the same form as the one it had previously passed. Thereafter the House, following further hearings and consideration by the Judiciary subcommittee, passed the bill on September 22, 1976. There followed a meeting of a conference committee of the two Houses, which resolved the differences between the two bills and reported a single version that was enacted by each body and presented to the President.

FURTHER INFORMATION

During the period before January 1, 1978, the Copyright Office will prepare regulations in accordance with the new statute and will also revise its application forms, instructions, and other printed matter to meet the needs under the new law. In addition, the Office plans to hold extensive meetings with interested parties in order to make the transition from the old law to the new as smooth and efficient as possible.

Additional copies of the new statute are available free of charge by writing to the Copyright Office, Library of Congress, Washington, D.C. 20559. You may also have your name added to the Copyright Office Mailing List by sending a written request to the Copyright Office.

Reproduction of Copyrighted Works by Educators and Librarians

A. INTRODUCTORY NOTE

The Subjects Covered in This Booklet

The documentary materials collected in this booklet deal with reproduction of copyrighted works by educators, librarians, and archivists for a variety of uses, including:

- Reproduction for teaching in educational institutions at all levels; and
- Reproduction by libraries and archives for purposes of study, research, interlibrary exchanges, and archival preservation.

The documents reprinted here are limited to materials dealing with **reproduction.** Under the copyright law, reproduction can take either of two forms:

- The making of **copies:** by photocopying, making microform reproductions, videotaping, or any other method of duplicating visually-perceptible material; and
- The making of **phonorecords:** by duplicating sound recordings, taping off the air, or any other method of recapturing sounds.

The new copyright law also contains various provisions dealing with importations, performances, and displays of copyrighted works for educational and other noncommercial purposes, but they are outside the scope of this booklet. You can obtain a copy of the statute and a general summary of its provisions by writing to the Copyright Office.

A Note on the Documents Reprinted

The documentary materials in this booklet are reprints or excerpts from six sources:

1. **The Copyright Act of October 19, 1976.** This is the new copyright law of the United States, effective January 1, 1978 (title 17 of the *United States Code,* Public Law 94–553, 90 Stat. 2541).

2. **The Senate Report.** This is the 1975 report of the Senate Judiciary Committee on S. 22, the Senate version of the bill that became the Copyright Act of 1976 (S. Rep. No. 94–473, 94th Cong., 1st Sess., November 20 (legislative day November 18, 1975).

3. **The House Report.** This is the 1976 report of the House of Representatives Judiciary Committee on the House amendments to the bill that became the Copyright Act of 1976 (H.R. Rep. No. 94–1476, 94th Cong., 2d Sess., September 3, 1976).

4. **The Conference Report.** This is the 1976 report of the "committee of conference on the disagreeing votes of the two Houses on the amendments of the House to the bill (S. 22) for the general revision of the Copyright Law" (H.R. Rep. No. 94–1733, 94th Cong., 2d Sess., September 29, 1976).

5. **The Congressional Debates.** This booklet contains excerpts from the *Congressional Record* of September 22, 1976, reflecting statements on the floor of Congress at the time the bill was passed by the House of Representatives (122 *CONG. REC.* H 10874–76 (daily edition, September 22, 1976).

6. **Copyright Office Regulations.** These are regulations issued by the Copyright Office under section 108 dealing with warnings of copyright for use by libraries and archives (37 *Code of Federal Regulations* §201.14).

Items 2 and 3 on this list—the 1975 Senate Report and the 1976 House Report—present special problems. On many points the language of these two reports is identical or closely similar. However, the two reports were written at different times, by committees of different Houses of Congress, on somewhat different bills. As a result, the discussion on some provisions of the bills vary widely, and on certain points they disagree.

The disagreements between the Senate and House versions of the bill itself were, of course, resolved when the Act of 1976 was finally passed. However, many of the disagreements as to matters of interpretation between statements in the 1975 Senate Report and in the 1976 House Report were left partly or wholly unresolved. It is therefore difficult, in compiling a booklet such as this, to decide in some cases what to include and what to leave out.

The House Report was written later than the Senate Report, and in many cases it adopted the language of the Senate Report, updating it and conforming it to the version of the bill that was finally enacted into law. Thus, where the differences between the two Reports are relatively minor, or where the discussion in the House Report appears to have superseded the discussion of the same point in the Senate Report, we have used the House Report as the source of our documentation. In other cases we have included excerpts from both discussions in an effort to present the legislative history as fully and fairly as possible. Anyone making a thorough study of the Act of 1976 as it affects librarians and educators should not, of course, rely exclusively on the excerpts reprinted here, but should go back to the primary documentary sources.

B. EXCLUSIVE RIGHTS IN COPYRIGHTED WORKS

1. Text of Section 106

> The following is a reprint of the entire text of section 106 of title 17, *United States Code.*

§ 106. Exclusive rights in copyrighted works

Subject to sections 107 through 118, the owner of copyright under this title has the exclusive rights to do and to authorize any of the following:

(1) to reproduce the copyrighted work in copies or phonorecords;

(2) to prepare derivative works based upon the copyrighted work;

(3) to distribute copies or phonorecords of the copyrighted work to the public by sale or other transfer

of ownership, or by rental, lease, or lending;

(4) in the case of literary, musical, dramatic, and choreographic works, pantomimes, and motion pictures and other audiovisual works, to perform the copyrighted work publicly; and

(5) in the case of literary, musical, dramatic, and choreographic works, pantomimes, and pictorial, graphic, or sculptural works, including the individual images of a motion picture or other audiovisual work, to display the copyrighted work publicly.

2. Excerpts From House Report on Section 106

The following excerpts are reprinted from the House Report on the new copyright law (H.R. Rep. No. 94–1476, pages 61–62). The text of the corresponding Senate Report (S. Rep. No. 94–473, pages 57–58) is substantially the same.

SECTION 106. EXCLUSIVE RIGHTS IN COPYRIGHTED WORKS

General scope of copyright

The five fundamental rights that the bill gives to copyright owners—the exclusive rights of reproduction, adaptation, publication, performance, and display—are stated generally in section 106. These exclusive rights, which comprise the so-called "bundle of rights" that is a copyright, are cumulative and may overlap in some cases. Each of the five enumerated rights may be subdivided indefinitely and, as discussed below in connection with section 201, each subdivision of an exclusive right may be owned and enforced separately.

The approach of the bill is to set forth the copyright owner's exclusive rights in broad terms in section 106, and then to provide various limitations, qualifications, or exemptions in the 12 sections that follow. Thus, everything in section 106 is made "subject to sections 107 through 118," and must be read in conjunction with those provisions.

* * *

Rights of reproduction, adaptation, and publication

The first three clauses of section 106, which cover all rights under a copyright except those of performance and display, extend to every kind of copyrighted work. The exclusive rights encompassed by these clauses, though closely related, are independent; they can generally be characterized as rights of copying, recording, adaptation, and publishing. A single act of infringement may violate all of these rights at once, as where a publisher reproduces, adapts, and sells copies of a person's copyrighted work as part of a publishing venture. Infringement takes place when any one of the rights is violated: where, for example, a printer reproduces copies without selling them or a retailer sells copies without having anything to do with their reproduction. The references to "copies or phonorecords," although in the plural, are intended here and throughout the bill to include the singular (1 U.S.C. §1).

Reproduction.—Read together with the relevant definitions in section 101, the right "to reproduce the copyrighted work in copies or phonorecords" means the right to produce a material object in which the work is duplicated, transcribed, imitated, or simulated in a fixed form from which it can be "perceived, reproduced, or otherwise communicated, either directly or with the aid of a machine or device." As under the present law, a copyrighted work would be infringed by reproducing it in whole or in any substantial part, and by duplicating it exactly or by imitation or simulation. Wide departures or variations from the copyrighted work would still be an infringement as long as the author's "expression" rather than merely the author's "ideas" are taken. An exception to this general principle, applicable to the reproduction of copyrighted sound recordings, is specified in section 114.

"Reproduction" under clause (1) of section 106 is to be distinguished from "display" under clause (5). For a work to be "reproduced," its fixation in tangible form must be "sufficiently permanent or stable to permit it to be perceived, reproduced, or otherwise communicated for a period of more than transitory duration." Thus, the showing of images on a screen or tube would not be a violation of clause (1), although it might come within the scope of clause (5).

C. FAIR USE

---

1. Text of Section 107

The following is a reprint of the entire text of section 107 of title 17, *United States Code.*

§ 107. Limitations on exclusive rights: Fair use

Notwithstanding the provisions of section 106, the fair use of a copyrighted work, including such use by reproduction in copies or phonorecords or by any other means specified by that section, for purposes such as criticism, comment, news reporting, teaching (including multiple copies for classroom use), scholarship, or research, is not an infringement of copyright. In determining whether the use made of a work in any particular case is a fair use the factors to be considered shall include—

(1) the purpose and character of the use, including whether such use is of a commercial nature or is for nonprofit educational purposes;

(2) the nature of the copyrighted work;

(3) the amount and substantiality of the portion used in relation to the copyrighted work as a whole; and

(4) the effect of the use upon the potential market for or value of the copyrighted work.

2. Excerpts From House Report on Section 107

The following excerpts are reprinted from the House Report on the new copyright law (H.R. Rep. No. 94–1476, pages 65–74). The discussion of section 107 appears at pages 61–67 of the Senate Report (S. Rep. No. 94–473). The text of this section of the Senate Report is not reprinted in this booklet, but similarities and differences between the House and Senate Reports on particular points will be noted below.

a. House Report: Introductory Discussion on Section 107

The first two paragraphs in this portion of the House Report are closely similar to the Senate Report. The remainder of the passage differs substantially in the two Reports.

SECTION 107. FAIR USE

General background of the problem

The judicial doctrine of fair use, one of the most important and well-established limitations on the exclusive right of copyright owners, would be given express statutory recognition for the first time in section 107. The claim that a defendant's acts constituted a fair use rather than an infringement has been raised as a defense in innumerable copyright actions over the years, and there is ample case law recognizing the existence of the doctrine and applying it. The examples enumerated at page 24 of the Register's 1961 Report, while by no means exhaustive, give some idea of the sort of activities the courts might regard as fair use under the circumstances: "quotation of excerpts in a review or criticism for purposes of illustration or comment; quotation of short passages in a scholarly or technical work, for illustration or clarification of the author's observations; use in a parody of some of the content of the work parodied; summary of an address or article, with brief quotations, in a news report; reproduction by a library of a portion of a work to replace part of a damaged copy; reproduction by a teacher or student of a small part of a work to illustrate a lesson; reproduction of a work in legislative or judicial proceedings or reports; incidental and fortuitous reproduction, in a newsreel or broadcast, of a work located in the scene of an event being reported."

Although the courts have considered and ruled upon

the fair use doctrine over and over again, no real definition of the concept has ever emerged. Indeed, since the doctrine is an equitable rule of reason, no generally applicable definition is possible, and each case raising the question must be decided on its own facts. On the other hand, the courts have evolved a set of criteria which, though in no case definitive or determinative, provide some gauge for balancing the equities. These criteria have been stated in various ways, but essentially they can all be reduced to the four standards which have been adopted in section 107: "(1) the purpose and character of the use, including whether such use is of a commercial nature or is for non-profit educational purposes; (2) the nature of the copyrighted work; (3) the amount and substantiality of the portion used in relation to the copyrighted work as a whole; and (4) the effect of the use upon the potential market for or value of the copyrighted work."

These criteria are relevant in determining whether the basic doctrine of fair use, as stated in the first sentence of section 107, applies in a particular case: "Notwithstanding the provisions of section 106, the fair use of a copyrighted work, including such use by reproduction in copies or phonorecords or by any other means specified by that section, for purposes such as criticism, comment, news reporting, teaching (including multiple copies for classroom use), scholarship, or research, is not an infringement of copyright."

The specific wording of section 107 as it now stands is the result of a process of accretion, resulting from the long controversy over the related problems of fair use and the reproduction (mostly by photocopying) of copyrighted material for educational and scholarly purposes. For example, the reference to fair use "by reproduction in copies or phonorecords or by any other means" is mainly intended to make clear that the doctrine has as much application to photocopying and taping as to older forms of use; it is not intended to give these kinds of reproduction any special status under the fair use provision or to sanction any reproduction beyond the normal and reasonable limits of fair use. Similarly, the newly-added reference to "multiple copies for classroom use" is a recognition that, under the proper circumstances of fairness, the doctrine can be applied to reproductions of multiple copies for the members of a class.

The Committee has amended the first of the criteria to be considered—"the purpose and character of the use"—to state explicitly that this factor includes a consideration of "whether such use is of a commercial nature or is for non-profit educational purposes." This amendment is not intended to be interpreted as any sort of not-for-profit limitation on educational uses of copyrighted works. It is an express recognition that, as under the present law, the commercial or non-profit character of an activity, while not conclusive with respect to fair use, can and should be weighed along with other factors in fair use decisions.

General intention behind the provision

The statement of the fair use doctrine in section 107 offers some guidance to users in determining when the principles of the doctrine apply. However, the endless variety of situations and combinations of circumstances that can rise in particular cases precludes the formulation of exact rules in the statute. The bill endorses the purpose and general scope of the judicial doctrine of fair use, but there is no disposition to freeze the doctrine in the statute, especially during a period of rapid technological change. Beyond a very broad statutory explanation of what fair use is and some of the criteria applicable to it, the courts must be free to adapt the doctrine to particular situations on a case-by-case basis. Section 107 is intended to restate the present judicial doctrine of fair use, not to change, narrow, or enlarge it in any way.

b. House Report: Statement of Intention as to Classroom Reproduction

> The House Report differs substantially from the Senate Report on this point.

(i) Introductory Statement

Intention as to classroom reproduction

Although the works and uses to which the doctrine of fair use is applicable are as broad as the copyright law itself, most of the discussion of section 107 has centered around questions of classroom reproduction, particularly photocopying. The arguments on the question are summarized at pp. 30–31 of this Committee's 1967 report (H.R. Rep. No. 83, 90th Cong., 1st Sess.), and have not changed materially in the intervening years.

The Committee also adheres to its earlier conclusion, that "a specific exemption freeing certain reproductions of copyrighted works for educational and scholarly purposes from copyright control is not justified." At the same time the Committee recognizes, as it did in 1967, that there is a "need for greater certainty and protection for teachers." In an effort to meet this need the Committee has not only adopted further amendments to section 107, but has also amended section 504(c) to provide innocent teachers and other non-profit users of copyrighted material with broad insulation against unwarranted liability for infringement. The latter amendments are discussed below in connection with Chapter 5 of the bill.

In 1967 the Committee also sought to approach this problem by including, in its report, a very thorough discussion of "the considerations lying behind the four criteria listed in the amended section 107, in the context of typical classroom situations arising today." This discussion appeared on pp. 32–35 of the 1967 report, and with some changes has been retained in the Senate report on S. 22 (S. Rep. No. 94–473, pp. 63–65). The Committee has reviewed this discussion, and considers that it still has value as an analysis of various aspects of the problem.

At the Judiciary Subcommittee hearings in June 1975, Chairman Kastenmeier and other members urged the parties to meet together independently in an effort to achieve a meeting of the minds as to permissible educational uses of copyrighted material. The response to these suggestions was positive, and a number of meetings of three groups, dealing respectively with classroom reproduction of printed material, music, and audio-visual material, were held beginning in September 1975.

(ii) Guidelines With Respect to Books and Periodicals

In a joint letter to Chairman Kastenmeier, dated March 19, 1976, the representatives of the Ad Hoc Committee of Educational Institutions and Organizations on Copyright Law Revision, and of the Authors League of America, Inc., and the Association of American Publishers, Inc., stated:

> You may remember that in our letter of March 8, 1976 we told you that the negotiating teams representing authors and publishers and the Ad Hoc Group had reached tentative agreement on guidelines to insert in the Committee Report covering educational copying from books and periodicals under Section 107 of H.R. 2223 and S. 22, and that as part of that tentative agreement each side would accept the amendments to Sections 107 and 504 which were adopted by your Subcommittee on March 3, 1976.
>
> We are now happy to tell you that the agreement has been approved by the principals and we enclose a copy herewith. We had originally intended to translate the agreement into language suitable for inclusion in the legislative report dealing with Section 107, but we have since been advised by committee staff that this will not be necessary.
>
> As stated above, the agreement refers only to copying from books and periodicals, and it is not intended to apply to musical or audiovisual works.

The full text of the agreement is as follows:

AGREEMENT ON GUIDELINES FOR CLASSROOM COPYING IN
NOT-FOR-PROFIT EDUCATIONAL INSTITUTIONS
WITH RESPECT TO BOOKS AND PERIODICALS

The purpose of the following guidelines is to state the minimum and not the maximum standards of educational fair use under Section 107 of H.R. 2223. The parties agree that the conditions determining the extent of permissible copying for educational purposes may change in the future; that certain types of copying permitted under these guidelines may not be permissible in the future; and conversely that in the future other types of copying not permitted under these guidelines may be permissible under revised guidelines.

Moreover, the following statement of guidelines is not intended to limit the types of copying permitted under the standards of fair use under judicial decision and which are stated in Section 107 of the Copyright Revision Bill. There may be instances in which copying which does not fall within the guidelines stated below may nonetheless be permitted under the criteria of fair use.

GUIDELINES

I. *Single Copying for Teachers*

A single copy may be made of any of the following by or for a teacher at his or her individual request for his or her scholarly research or use in teaching or preparation to teach a class:

A. A chapter from a book;
B. An article from a periodical or newspaper;
C. A short story, short essay or short poem, whether or not from a collective work;
D. A chart, graph, diagram, drawing, cartoon or picture from a book, periodical, or newspaper;

II. *Multiple Copies for Classroom Use*

Multiple copies (not to exceed in any event more than one copy per pupil in a course) may be made by or for the teacher giving the course for classroom use or discussion; *provided that:*

A. The copying meets the tests of brevity and spontaneity as defined below; *and,*
B. Meets the cumulative effect test as defined below; *and,*
C. Each copy includes a notice of copyright

Definitions
Brevity
(i) Poetry: (a) A complete poem if less than 250 words and if printed on not more than two pages or, (b) from a longer poem, an excerpt of not more than 250 words.
(ii) Prose: (a) Either a complete article, story or essay of less than 2,500 words, or (b) an excerpt from any prose work of not more than 1,000 words or 10% of the work, whichever is less, but in any event a minimum of 500 words.
[Each of the numerical limits stated in "i" and "ii" above may be expanded to permit the completion of an unfinished line of a poem or of an unfinished prose paragraph.]
(iii) Illustration: One chart, graph, diagram, drawing, cartoon or picture per book or per periodical issue.
(iv) "Special" works: Certain works in poetry, prose or in "poetic prose" which often combine language with illustrations and which are intended sometimes for children and at other times for a more general audience fall short of 2,500 words in their entirety. Paragraph "ii" above notwithstanding such "special works" may not be reproduced in their entirety; however, an excerpt comprising not more than two of the published pages of such special work and containing not more than 10% of the words found in the text thereof, may be reproduced.

Spontaneity
(i) The copying is at the instance and inspiration of the individual teacher, and
(ii) The inspiration and decision to use the work and the moment of its use for maximum teaching effectiveness are so close in time that it would be unreasonable to expect a timely reply to a request for permission.

Cumulative Effect
(i) The copying of the material is for only one course in the school in which the copies are made.
(ii) Not more than one short poem, article, story, essay or two excerpts may be copied from the same author, nor more than three from the same collective work or periodical volume during one class term.
(iii) There shall not be more than nine instances

of such multiple copying for one course during one class term.
[The limitations stated in "ii" and "iii" above shall not apply to current news periodicals and newspapers and current news sections of other periodicals.]

III. *Prohibitions as to I and II Above*

Notwithstanding any of the above, the following shall be prohibited:
(A) Copying shall not be used to create or to replace or substitute for anthologies, compilations or collective works. Such replacement or substitution may occur whether copies of various works or excerpts therefrom are accumulated or reproduced and used separately.
(B) There shall be no copying of or from works intended to be "consumable" in the course of study or of teaching. These include workbooks, exercises, standardized tests and test booklets and answer sheets and like consumable material.
(C) Copying shall not:
(a) substitute for the purchase of books, publishers' reprints or periodicals;
(b) be directed by higher authority;
(c) be repeated with respect to the same item by the same teacher from term to term.
(D) No charge shall be made to the student beyond the actual cost of the photocopying.
Agreed MARCH 19, 1976.
Ad Hoc Committee on Copyright Law Revision:
By SHELDON ELLIOTT STEINBACH.
Author-Publisher Group:
Authors League of America:
By IRWIN KARP, *Counsel.*
Association of American Publishers, Inc.:
By ALEXANDER C. HOFFMAN, *Chairman, Copyright Committee.*

(iii) Guidelines With Respect to Music

In a joint letter dated April 30, 1976, representatives of the Music Publishers' Association of the United States, Inc., the National Music Publishers' Association, Inc., the Music Teachers National Association, the Music Educators National Conference, the National Association of Schools of Music, and the Ad Hoc Committee on Copyright Law Revision, wrote to Chairman Kastenmeier as follows:

During the hearings on H.R. 2223 in June 1975, you and several of your subcommittee members suggested that concerned groups should work together in developing guidelines which would be helpful to clarify Section 107 of the bill.

Representatives of music educators and music publishers delayed their meetings until guidelines had been developed relative to books and periodicals. Shortly after that work was completed and those guidelines were forwarded to your subcommittee, representatives of the undersigned music organizations met together with representatives of the Ad Hoc Committee on Copyright Law Revision to draft guidelines relative to music.

We are very pleased to inform you that the discussions thus have been fruitful on the guidelines which have been developed. Since private music teachers are an important factor in music education, due consideration has been given to the concerns of that group.

We trust that this will be helpful in the report on the bill to clarify Fair Use as it applies to music.
The text of the guidelines accompanying this letter is as follows:

GUIDELINES FOR EDUCATIONAL USES OF MUSIC

The purpose of the following guidelines is to state the minimum and not the maximum standards of educational fair use under Section 107 of HR 2223. The parties agree that the conditions determining the extent of permissible copying for educational purposes may change in the future; that certain types of copying permitted under these guidelines may not be permissible in the future, and conversely that in the future other types of copying not permitted under these guidelines may be permissible under revised guidelines.

Moreover, the following statement of guidelines is not intended to limit the types of copying permitted under the standards of fair use under judicial decision and which are stated in Section 107 of the Copyright Revision Bill. There may be instances in which copying which does not fall within the guidelines stated below may nonetheless be permitted under the criteria of fair use.

A. *Permissible Uses*

1. Emergency copying to replace purchased copies which for any reason are not available for an imminent performance provided purchased replacement copies shall be substituted in due course.

2. For academic purposes other than performance, single or multiple copies of excerpts of works may be made, provided that the excerpts do not comprise a part of the whole which would constitute a performable unit such as a section*, movement or aria, but in no case more than 10 percent of the whole work. The number of copies shall not exceed one copy per pupil.**

3. Printed copies which have been purchased may be edited or simplified provided that the fundamental character of the work is not distorted or the lyrics, if any, altered or lyrics added if none exist.

4. A single copy of recordings of performances by students may be made for evaluation or rehearsal purposes and may be retained by the educational institution or individual teacher.

5. A single copy of a sound recording (such as a tape, disc or cassette) of copyrighted music may be made from sound recordings owned by an educational institution or an individual teacher for the purpose of constructing aural exercises or examinations and may be retained by the educational institution or individual teacher. (This pertains only to the copyright of the music itself and not to any copyright which may exist in the sound recording.)

---
*Corrected from *Congressional Record.*
**Editor's Note:* As reprinted in the House Report, subsection A.2 of the Music Guidelines had consisted of two separate paragraphs, one dealing with multiple copies and a second dealing with single copies. In his introductory remarks during the House debates on S.22, the Chairman of the House Judiciary Subcommittee, Mr. Kastenmeier, announced that "the report, as printed, does not reflect a subsequent change in the joint guidelines which was described in a subsequent letter to me from a representative of [the signatory organizations]," and provided the revised text of subsection A.2. (122 *CONG. REC.* H 10875, Sept. 22, 1976). The text reprinted here is the revised text.

B. *Prohibitions*

1. Copying to create or replace or substitute for anthologies, compilations or collective works.

2. Copying of or from works intended to be "consumable" in the course of study or of teaching such as workbooks, exercises, standardized tests and answer sheets and like material.

3. Copying for the purpose of performance, except as in A (1) above.

4. Copying for the purpose of substituting for the purchase of music, except as in A(1) and A(2) above.

5. Copying without inclusion of the copyright notice which appears on the printed copy.

(iv) Discussion of Off-the-Air Taping

The problem of off-the-air taping for nonprofit classroom uses of copyrighted audiovisual works incorporated in radio and television broadcasts has proved to be difficult to resolve. The Committee believes that the fair use doctrine has some limited application in this area, but it appears that the development of detailed guidelines will require a more thorough exploration than has so far been possible of the needs and problems of a number of different interests affected, and of the various legal problems presented. Nothing in section 107 or elsewhere in the bill is intended to change or prejudge the law on the point. On the other hand, the Committee is sensitive to the importance of the problem, and urges the representatives of the various interests, if possible under the leadership of the Register of Copyrights, to continue their discussions actively and in a constructive spirit. If it would be helpful to a solution, the Committee is receptive to undertaking further consideration of the problem in a future Congress.

(v) Discussion of Guidelines

The Committee appreciates and commends the efforts and the cooperative and reasonable spirit of the parties who achieved the agreed guidelines on books and periodicals and on music. Representatives of the American Association of University Professors and of the Association of American Law Schools have written to the Committee strongly criticizing the guidelines, particularly with respect to multiple copying, as being too restrictive with respect to classroom situations at the university and graduate level. However, the Committee notes that the Ad Hoc group did include representatives of higher education, that the stated "purpose of the . . . guidelines is to state the minimum and not the maximum standards of educational fair use" and that the agreement acknowledges "there may be instances in which copying which does not fall within the guidelines . . . may nonetheless be permitted under the criteria of fair use."

The Committee believes the guidelines are a reasonable interpretation of the minimum standards of fair use. Teachers will know that copying within the guidelines is fair use. Thus, the guidelines serve the purpose of fulfilling the need for greater certainty and protection for teachers. The Committee expresses the hope that if there are areas where standards other than these guidelines may be appropriate, the parties will continue their efforts to provide additional specific guidelines in the same spirit of good will and give and take that has marked the discussion of this subject in recent months.

c. House Report: Additional Excerpts

> Under the heading "Reproduction and uses for other purposes," the House Report, at pages 72-74, parallels much of the material appearing at pages 65-67 of the Senate Report under the same heading, but with some differences.

The concentrated attention given the fair use provision in the context of classroom teaching activities should not obscure its application in other areas. It must be emphasized again that the same general standards of fair use are applicable to all kinds of uses of copyrighted material, although the relative weight to be given them will differ from case to case.

* * *

A problem of particular urgency is that of preserving for posterity prints of motion pictures made before 1942. Aside from the deplorable fact that in a great many cases the only existing copy of a film has been deliberately destroyed, those that remain are in immediate danger of disintegration; they were printed on film stock with a nitrate base that will inevitably decompose in time. The efforts of the Library of Congress, the American Film Institute, and other organizations to rescue and preserve this irreplaceable contribution to our cultural life are to be applauded, and the making of duplicate copies for purposes of archival preservation certainly falls within the scope of "fair use."

* * *

During the consideration of the revision bill in the 94th Congress it was proposed that independent newsletters, as distinguished from house organs and publicity or advertising publications, be given separate treatment. It is argued that newsletters are particularly vulnerable to mass photocopying, and that most newsletters have fairly modest circulations. Whether the copying of portions of a newsletter is an act of infringement or a fair use will necessarily turn on the facts of the individual case. However, as a general principle, it seems clear that the scope of the fair use doctrine should be considerably narrower in the case of newsletters than in that of either mass-circulation periodicals or scientific journals. The commercial nature of the user is a significant factor in such cases: Copying by a profit-making user of even a small portion of a newsletter may have a significant impact on the commercial market for the work.

The Committee has examined the use of excerpts from copyrighted works in the art work of calligraphers. The committee believes that a single copy reproduction of an excerpt from a copyrighted work by a calligrapher for a single client does not represent an infringement of copyright. Likewise, a single reproduction of excerpts from a copyrighted work by a student calligrapher or teacher in a learning situation would be a fair use of the copyrighted work.

The Register of Copyrights has recommended that the committee report describe the relationship between this section and the provisions of section 108 relating to reproduction by libraries and archives. The doctrine of fair use applies to library photocopying, and nothing contained in section 108 "in any way affects the right of fair use." No provision of section 108 is intended to take away any rights existing under the fair use doctrine. To the contrary, section 108 authorizes certain photocopying practices which may not qualify as a fair use.

The criteria of fair use are necessarily set forth in general terms. In the application of the criteria of fair use to specific photocopying practices of libraries, it is the intent of this legislation to provide an appropriate balancing of the rights of creators, and the needs of users.

3. Excerpts From Conference Report on Section 107

> The following excerpt is reprinted from the Report of the Conference Committee on the new copyright law (H.R. Rep. No. 94-1733, page 70).

FAIR USE

Senate bill

The Senate bill, in section 107, embodied express statutory recognition of the judicial doctrine that the fair use of a copyrighted work is not an infringement of copyright. It set forth the fair use doctrine, including four criteria for determining its applicability in particular cases, in general terms.

House bill

The House bill amended section 107 in two respects: in the general statement of the fair use doctrine it added a specific reference to multiple copies for classroom use, and it amplified the statement of the first of the criteria to be used in judging fair use (the purpose and character of the use) by referring to the commercial nature or nonprofit educational purpose of the use.

Conference substitute

The conference substitute adopts the House amendments. The conferees accept as part of their understanding of fair use the Guidelines for Classroom Copying in Not-for-Profit Educational Institutions with respect to books and periodicals appearing at pp. 68-70 of the House Report (H. Rept. No. 94-1476, as corrected at p. H 10727 of the Congressional Record for September 21, 1976), and for educational uses of music appearing at pp. 70-71 of the House report, as amended in the statement appearing at p. H 10875 of the Congressional Record of September 22, 1976. The conferees also endorse the statement concerning the meaning of the word "teacher" in the guidelines for books and periodicals, and the application of fair use in the case of use of television programs within the confines of a nonprofit educational institution for the deaf and hearing impaired, both of which appear on p. H 10875 of the Congressional Record of September 22, 1976.

4. Excerpts From Congressional Debates

> The following excerpts are reprinted from the *Congressional Record* of September 22, 1976, including statements by Mr. Kastenmeier (Chairman of the House Judiciary Subcommittee responsible for the bill) on the floor of the House of Representatives.

MR. KASTENMEIER. * * *

Mr. Chairman, before concluding my remarks I would like to discuss several questions which have been raised concerning the meaning of several provisions of S. 22 as reported by the House Judiciary Committee and of statements in the committee's report, No. 94-1476.

* * *

Another question involves the reference to "teacher" in the "Agreement on Guidelines for Classroom Copying

in Not-for-Profit Educational Institutions" reproduced at pages 68-70 of the committee's report No. 94-1476 in connection with section 107. It has been pointed out that, in planning his or her teaching on a day-to-day basis in a variety of educational situations, an individual teacher will commonly consult with instructional specialists on the staff of the school, such as reading specialists, curriculum specialists, audiovisual directors, guidance counselors, and the like. As long as the copying meets all of the other criteria laid out in the guidelines, including the requirements for spontaneity and the prohibition against the copying being directed by higher authority, the committee regards the concept of "teacher" as broad enough to include instructional specialists working in consultation with actual instructors.

Also in consultation with section 107, the committee's attention has been directed to the unique educational needs and problems of the approximately 50,000 deaf and hearing-impaired students in the United States, and the inadequacy of both public and commercial television to serve their educational needs. It has been suggested that, as long as clear-cut constraints are imposed and enforced, the doctrine of fair use is broad enough to permit the making of an off-the-air fixation of a television program within a nonprofit educational institution for the deaf and hearing impaired, the reproduction of a master and a work copy of a captioned version of the original fixation, and the performance of the program from the work copy within the confines of the institution. In identifying the constraints that would have to be imposed within an institution in order for these activities to be considered as fair use, it has been suggested that the purpose of the use would have to be noncommercial in every respect, and educational in the sense that it serves as part of a deaf or hearing-impaired student's learning environment within the institution, and that the institution would have to insure that the master and work copy would remain in the hands of a limited number of authorized personnel within the institution, would be responsible for assuring against its unauthorized reproduction or distribution, or its performance or retention for other than educational purposes within the institution. Work copies of captioned programs could be shared among institutions for the deaf abiding by the constraints specified. Assuming that these constraints are both imposed and enforced, and that no other factors intervene to render the use unfair, the committee believes that the activities described could reasonably be considered fair use under section 107.

* * *

Mr. Chairman, because of the complexity of this bill and the delicate balances which it creates among competing economic interests, the committee will resist extensive amendment of this bill. On behalf of the committee I would urge all of my colleagues to vote favorably on S. 22.

Mr. SKUBITZ. Mr. Chairman, will the gentleman yield?

Mr. KASTENMEIER. I am happy to yield to my friend, the gentleman from Kansas.

Mr. SKUBITZ. Mr. Chairman, I thank my friend, the gentleman from Wisconsin, for yielding.

Mr. Chairman, I have received a great deal of mail from the schoolteachers in my district who are particularly concerned about section 107—fair use—the fair use of copyrighted material. Having been a former schoolteacher myself, I believe they make a good point and there is a sincere fear on their part that, because of the vagueness or ambiguity in the bill's treatment of the doctrine of fair use, they may subject themselves to liability for an unintentional infringement of copyright when all they were trying to do was the job for which they were trained.

The vast majority of teachers in this country would not knowingly infringe upon a person's copyright, but, as any teacher can appreciate, there are times when information is needed and is available, but may be literally impossible to locate the right person to approve the use of that material and the purchase of such would not be feasible and, in the meantime, the teacher may have lost that "teachable moment."

Did the subcommittee take these problems into consideration and did they do anything to try and help the teachers to better understand section 107?

Have the teachers been protected by this section 107?

Mr. KASTENMEIER. Mr. Chairman, in response to the gentleman's question and his observations preceding the question, I would say, indeed they have.

Over the years this has been one of the most difficult questions. It is a problem that I believe has been very successfully resolved.

Section 107 on "Fair Use" has of course, restated four standards, and these standards are, namely: The purpose and character of the use of the material; the nature of the copyrighted work; the amount and substantiality of the portion used in relation to the copyrighted work as a whole; and the effect of the use upon the potential market for or value of the copyrighted work.

These are the four "Fair Use" criteria. These alone were not adequate to guide teachers, and I am sure the gentleman from Kansas (Mr. SKUBITZ) understands that as a schoolteacher himself.

Therefore, the educators, the proprietors, and the publishers of educational materials did, at the committee's long insistence, get together. While there were many fruitless meetings, they did finally get together.

Mr. Chairman, I will draw the gentleman's attention to pages 65 through 74 in the report which contain extensive guidelines for teachers. I am very happy to say that there was an agreement reached between teachers and publishers of educational material, and that today the National Education Association supports the bill, and it has, in fact, sent a telegram which at the appropriate time I will make a part of the RECORD and which requests support for the bill in its present form, believing that it has satisfied the needs of the teachers:

NATIONAL EDUCATION ASSOCIATION,
Washington, D.C., September 10, 1976.
National Education Association urgently requests your support of the Copyright Revision bill, H.R. 2223, as reported by the Judiciary Committee. This compromise effort represents a major breakthrough in establishing equitable legal guidelines for the use of copyright materials for instructional and research purposes. We ask your support of the committee bill without amendments.
JAMES W. GREEN,
Assistant Director for Legislation.

Mr. SKUBITZ. Mr. Chairman, if the gentleman will yield further, then the NEA is satisfied with the language in the bill as it now stands; is that correct?

Mr. KASTENMEIER. The gentleman is correct.

Mr. SKUBITZ. Mr. Chairman, I thank the gentleman.

D. REPRODUCTION BY LIBRARIES AND ARCHIVES

1. Text of Section 108

The following is a reprint of the entire text of section 108 of title 17, *United States Code.*

§ 108. **Limitations on exclusive rights: Reproduction by libraries and archives**

(a) Notwithstanding the provisions of section 106, it is not an infringement of copyright for a library or archives, or any of its employees acting within the scope of their employment, to reproduce no more than one copy or phonorecord of a work, or to distribute such copy or phonorecord, under the conditions specified by this section, if—

(1) the reproduction or distribution is made without any purpose of direct or indirect commercial advantage;

(2) the collections of the library or archives are (i) open to the public, or (ii) available not only to researchers affiliated with the library or archives or with the institution of which it is a part, but also to other persons doing research in a specialized field; and

(3) the reproduction or distribution of the work includes a notice of copyright.

(b) The rights of reproduction and distribution under this section apply to a copy or phonorecord of an unpublished work duplicated in facsimile form solely for purposes of preservation and security or for deposit for research use in another library or archives of the type described by clause (2) of subsection (a), if the copy or phonorecord reproduced is currently in the collections of the library or archives.

(c) The right of reproduction under this section applies to a copy or phonorecord of a published work duplicated in facsimile form solely for the purpose of replacement of a copy or phonorecord that is damaged, deteriorating, lost, or stolen, if the library or archives has, after a reasonable effort, determined that an unused replacement cannot be obtained at a fair price.

(d) The rights of reproduction and distribution under this section apply to a copy, made from the collection of a library or archives where the user makes his or her request or from that of another library or archives, of no more than one article or other contribution to a copyrighted collection or periodical issue, or to a copy or phonorecord of a small part of any other copyrighted work, if—

(1) the copy or phonorecord becomes the property of the user, and the library or archives has had no notice that the copy or phonorecord would be used for any purpose other than private study, scholarship, or research; and

(2) the library or archives displays prominently, at the place where orders are accepted, and includes on its order form, a warning of copyright in accordance with requirements that the Register of Copyrights shall prescribe by regulation.

(e) The rights of reproduction and distribution under this section apply to the entire work, or to a substantial part of it, made from the collection of a library or archives where the user makes his or her request or from that of another library or archives, if the library or archives has first determined, on the basis of a reasonable investigation, that a copy or phonorecord of the copyrighted work cannot be obtained at a fair price, if—

(1) the copy or phonorecord becomes the property of the user, and the library or archives has had no notice that the copy or phonorecord would be used for any purpose other than private study, scholarship, or research; and

(2) the library or archives displays prominently, at the place where orders are accepted, and includes on its order form, a warning of copyright in accordance with requirements that the Register of Copyrights shall prescribe by regulation.

(f) Nothing in this section—

(1) shall be construed to impose liability for copyright infringement upon a library or archives or its employees for the unsupervised use of reproducing equipment located on its premises: *Provided,* That such equipment displays a notice that the making of a copy may be subject to the copyright law;

(2) excuses a person who uses such reproducing equipment or who requests a copy or phonorecord under subsection (d) from liability for copyright infringement for any such act, or for any later use of such copy or phonorecord, if it exceeds fair use as provided by section 107;

(3) shall be construed to limit the reproduction and distribution by lending of a limited number of copies and excerpts by a library or archives of an audiovisual news program, subject to clauses (1), (2), and (3) of subsection (a); or

(4) in any way affects the right of fair use as provided by section 107, or any contractual obligations assumed at any time by the library or archives when it obtained a copy or phonorecord of a work in its collections.

(g) The rights of reproduction and distribution under this section extend to the isolated and unrelated reproduction or distribution of a single copy or phonorecord of the same material on separate occasions, but do not extend to cases where the library or archives, or its employee—

(1) is aware or has substantial reason to believe that it is engaging in the related or concerted reproduction or distribution of multiple copies or

phonorecords of the same material, whether made on one occasion or over a period of time, and whether intended for aggregate use by one or more individuals or for separate use by the individual members of a group; or

(2) engages in the systematic reproduction or distribution of single or multiple copies or phonorecords of material described in subsection (d): *Provided,* That nothing in this clause prevents a library or archives from participating in interlibrary arrangements that do not have, as their purpose or effect, that the library or archives receiving such copies or phonorecords for distribution does so in such aggregate quantities as to substitute for a subscription to or purchase of such work.

(h) The rights of reproduction and distribution under this section do not apply to a musical work, a pictorial, graphic or sculptural work, or a motion picture or other audiovisual work other than an audiovisual work dealing with news, except that no such limitation shall apply with respect to rights granted by subsections (b) and (c), or with respect to pictorial or graphic works published as illustrations, diagrams, or similar adjuncts to works of which copies are reproduced or distributed in accordance with subsections (d) and (e).

(i) Five years from the effective date of this Act, and at five-year intervals thereafter, the Register of Copyrights, after consulting with representatives of authors, book and periodical publishers, and other owners of copyrighted materials, and with representatives of library users and librarians, shall submit to the Congress a report setting forth the extent to which this section has achieved the intended statutory balancing of the rights of creators, and the needs of users. The report should also describe any problems that may have arisen, and present legislative or other recommendations, if warranted.

2. Excerpts From Senate Report on Section 108

The following excerpts are reprinted from the 1975 Senate Report on the new copyright law (S. Rep. No. 94-473, pages 67-71). Where the discussions of particular points are generally similar in the two Reports, the passages from the later House Report are reprinted in this booklet. Where the discussion of particular points is substantially different, passages from both Reports are reprinted.

a. Senate Report: Discussion of Libraries and Archives in Profit-Making Institutions

The limitation of section 108 to reproduction and distribution by libraries and archives "without any purpose of direct or indirect commercial advantage" is intended to preclude a library or archives in a profit-making organization from providing photocopies of copyrighted materials to employees engaged in furtherance of the organization's commercial enterprise, unless such copying qualifies as a fair use, or the organization has obtained the necessary copyright licenses. A commercial organization should purchase the number of copies of a work that it requires, or obtain the consent of the copyright owner to the making of the photocopies.

b. Senate Report: Discussion of Multiple Copies and Systematic Reproduction

Multiple copies and systematic reproduction

Subsection (g) provides that the rights granted by this section extend only to the "isolated and unrelated reproduction of a single copy", but this section does not authorize the related or concerted reproduction of multiple copies of the same material whether made on one occasion or over a period of time, and whether intended for aggregate use by one individual or for separate use by the individual members of a group. For example, if a college professor instructs his class to read an article from a copyrighted journal, the school library would not be permitted, under subsection (g), to reproduce copies of the article for the members of the class.

Subsection (g) also provides that section 108 does not authorize the systematic reproduction or distribution of copies or phonorecords of articles or other contributions

to copyrighted collections or periodicals or of small parts of other copyrighted works whether or not multiple copies are reproduced or distributed. Systematic reproduction or distribution occurs when a library makes copies of such materials available to other libraries or to groups of users under formal or informal arrangements whose purpose or effect is to have the reproducing library serve as their source of such material. Such systematic reproduction and distribution, as distinguished from isolated and unrelated reproduction or distribution, may substitute the copies reproduced by the source library for subscriptions or reprints or other copies which the receiving libraries or users might otherwise have purchased for themselves, from the publisher or the licensed reproducing agencies.

While it is not possible to formulate specific definitions of "systematic copying", the following examples serve to illustrate some of the copying prohibited by subsection (g).

(1) A library with a collection of journals in biology informs other libraries with similar collections that it will maintain and build its own collection and will make copies of articles from these journals available to them and their patrons on request. Accordingly, the other libraries discontinue or refrain from purchasing subscriptions to these journals and fulfill their patrons' requests for articles by obtaining photocopies from the source library.

(2) A research center employing a number of scientists and technicians subscribes to one or two copies of needed periodicals. By reproducing photocopies of articles the center is able to make the material in these periodicals available to its staff in the same manner which otherwise would have required multiple subscriptions.

(3) Several branches of a library system agree that one branch will subscribe to particular journals in lieu of each branch purchasing its own subscriptions, and the one subscribing branch will reproduce copies of articles from the publication for users of the other branches.

The committee believes that section 108 provides an appropriate statutory balancing of the rights of creators, and the needs of users. However, neither a statute nor legislative history can specify precisely which library photocopying practices constitute the making of "single copies" as distinguished from "systematic reproduction". Isolated single spontaneous requests must be distinguished from "systematic reproduction". The photocopying needs of such operations as multi-county regional systems must be met. The committee therefore recommends that representatives of authors, book and periodical publishers and other owners of copyrighted material meet with the library community to formulate photocopying guidelines to assist library patrons and employees. Concerning library photocopying practices not authorized by this legislation, the committee recommends that workable clearance and licensing procedures be developed.

It is still uncertain how far a library may go under the Copyright Act of 1909 in supplying a photocopy of copyrighted material in its collection. The recent case of *The Williams and Wilkins Company* v. *The United States* failed to significantly illuminate the application of the fair use doctrine to library photocopying practices. Indeed, the opinion of the Court of Claims said the Court was engaged in "a 'holding operation' in the interim period before Congress enacted its preferred solution."

While the several opinions in the *Wilkins* case have given the Congress little guidance as to the current state of the law on fair use, these opinions provide additional support for the balanced resolution of the photocopying issue adopted by the Senate last year in S. 1361 and preserved in section 108 of this legislation. As the Court of Claims opinion succinctly stated "there is much to be said on all sides."

In adopting these provisions on library photocopying, the committee is aware that through such programs as those of the National Commission on Libraries and Information Science there will be a significant evolution in the functioning and services of libraries. To consider the possible need for changes in copyright law and procedures as a result of new technology, a National Commission on New Technological Uses of Copyrighted Works has been established (Public Law 93-573).

3. Excerpts From House Report on Section 108

a. House Report: Introductory Statement

Notwithstanding the exclusive rights of the owners of copyright, section 108 provides that under certain conditions it is not an infringement of copyright for a library or archives, or any of its employees acting within the scope of their employment, to reproduce or distribute not more than one copy or phonorecord of a work, provided (1) the reproduction or distribution is made without any purpose of direct or indirect commercial advantage and (2) the collections of the library or archives are open to the public or available not only to researchers affiliated with the library or archives, but also to other persons doing research in a specialized field, and (3) the reproduction or distribution of the work includes a notice of copyright.

b. House Report: Discussion of Libraries and Archives in Profit-Making Institutions

Under this provision, a purely commercial enterprise could not establish a collection of copyrighted works, call itself a library or archive, and engage in for-profit reproduction and distribution of photocopies. Similarly, it would not be possible for a non-profit institution, by means of contractual arrangements with a commercial copying enterprise, to authorize the enterprise to carry out copying and distribution functions that would be exempt if conducted by the non-profit institution itself.

The reference to "indirect commercial advantage" has raised questions as to the status of photocopying done by or for libraries or archival collections within industrial, profitmaking, or proprietary institutions (such as the research and development departments of chemical, pharmaceutical, automobile, and oil corporations, the library of a proprietary hospital, the collections owned by a law or medical partnership, etc.).

There is a direct interrelationship between this problem and the prohibitions against "multiple" and "systematic" photocopying in section 108 (g) (1) and (2). Under section 108, a library in a profit-making organization would not be authorized to:

(a) use a single subscription or copy to supply its employees with multiple copies of material relevant to their work; or

(b) use a single subscription or copy to supply its employees, on request, with single copies of material relevant to their work, where the arrangement is "systematic" in the sense of deliberately substituting photocopying for subscription or purchase; or

(c) use "interlibrary loan" arrangements for obtaining photocopies in such aggregate quantities as to substitute for subscriptions or purchase of material needed by employees in their work.

Moreover, a library in a profit-making organization could not evade these obligations by installing reproducing equipment on its premises for unsupervised use by the organization's staff.

Isolated, spontaneous making of single photocopies by a library in a for-profit organization, without any systematic effort to substitute photocopying for subscriptions or purchases, would be covered by section 108, even though the copies are furnished to the employees of the organization for use in their work. Similarly, for-profit libraries could participate in interlibrary arrangements for exchange of photocopies, as long as the reproduction or distribution was not "systematic." These activities, by themselves, would ordinarily not be con-

sidered "for direct or indirect commercial advantage," since the "advantage" referred to in this clause must attach to the immediate commercial motivation behind the reproduction or distribution itself, rather than to the ultimate profit-making motivation behind the enterprise in which the library is located. On the other hand, section 108 would not excuse reproduction or distribution if there were a commercial motive behind the actual making or distributing of the copies, if multiple copies were made or distributed, or. if the photocopying activities were "systematic" in the sense that their aim was to substitute for subscriptions or purchases.

c. House Report: Rights of Reproduction and Distribution Under Section 108

The rights of reproduction and distribution under section 108 apply in the following circumstances:

Archival reproduction

Subsection (b) authorizes the reproduction and distribution of a copy or phonorecord of an unpublished work duplicated in facsimile form solely for purposes of preservation and security, or for deposit for research use in another library or archives, if the copy or phonorecord reproduced is currently in the collections of the first library or archives. Only unpublished works could be reproduced under this exemption, but the right would extend to any type of work, including photographs, motion pictures and sound recordings. Under this exemption, for example, a repository could make photocopies of manuscripts by microfilm or electrostatic process, but could not reproduce the work in "machine-readable" language for storage in an information system.

Replacement of damaged copy

Subsection (c) authorizes the reproduction of a published work duplicated in facsimile form solely for the purpose of replacement of a copy or phonorecord that is damaged, deteriorating, lost or stolen, if the library or archives has, after a reasonable effort, determined that an unused replacement cannot be obtained at a fair price. The scope and nature of a reasonable investigation to determine that an unused replacement cannot be obtained will vary according to the circumstances of a particular situation. It will always require recourse to commonly-known trade sources in the United States, and in the normal situation also to the publisher or other copyright owner (if such owner can be located at the address listed in the copyright registration), or an authorized reproducing service.

Articles and small excerpts

Subsection (d) authorizes the reproduction and distribution of a copy of not more than one article or other contribution to a copyrighted collection or periodical issue, or of a copy or phonorecord of a small part of any other copyrighted work. The copy or phonorecord may be made by the library where the user makes his request or by another library pursuant to an interlibrary loan. It is further required that the copy become the property of the user, that the library or archives have no notice that the copy would be used for any purposes other than private study, scholarship or research, and that the library or archives display prominently at the place where reproduction requests are accepted, and includes in its order form, a warning of copyright in accordance with requirements that the Register of Copyrights shall prescribe by regulation.

Out-of-print works

Subsection (e) authorizes the reproduction and distribution of a copy or phonorecord of an entire work under certain circumstances, if it has been established that a copy cannot be obtained at a fair price. The copy may be made by the library where the user makes his request or by another library pursuant to an interlibrary loan. The scope and nature of a reasonable investigation to determine that an unused copy cannot be obtained will vary according to the circumstances of a particular situation. It will always require recourse to commonly-known trade sources in the United States, and in the normal situation also to the publisher or other copyright owner (if the owner can be located at the address listed in the copyright registration), or an authorized reproducing service. It is further required that the copy become the property of the user, that the library or archives have no notice that the copy would be used for any purpose other than private study, scholarship, or research, and that the library or archives display prominently at the place where reproduction requests are accepted, and include on its order form, a warning of copyright in accordance with requirements that the Register of Copyrights shall prescribe by regulation.

d. House Report: General Exemptions for Libraries and Archives

> Parts of the following paragraphs are substantially similar in the Senate and House Reports. Differences in the House Report on certain points reflect certain amendments in section 108(f) and elsewhere in the Copyright Act.

General exemptions

Clause (1) of subsection (f) specifically exempts a library or archives or its employees from liability for the unsupervised use of reproducing equipment located on its premises, provided that the reproducing equipment displays a notice that the making of a copy may be subject to the copyright law. Clause (2) of subsection (f) makes clear that this exemption of the library or archives does not extend to the person using such equipment or requesting such copy if the use exceeds fair use. Insofar as such person is concerned the copy or phonorecord made is not considered "lawfully" made for purposes of sections 109, 110 or other provisions of the title.

Clause (3) provides that nothing in section 108 is intended to limit the reproduction and distribution by lending of a limited number of copies and excerpts of an audiovisual news program. This exemption is intended to apply to the daily newscasts of the national television networks, which report the major events of the day. It does not apply to documentary (except documentary programs involving news reporting as that term is used in section 107), magazine-format or other public affairs broadcasts dealing with subjects of general interest to the viewing public.

The clause was first added to the revision bill in 1974 by the adoption of an amendment proposed by Senator Baker. It is intended to permit libraries and archives, subject to the general conditions of this section, to make off-the-air videotape recordings of daily network newscasts for limited distribution to scholars and researchers for use in research purposes. As such, it is an adjunct to the American Television and Radio Archive established in Section 113 of the Act which will be the principal repository for television broadcast material, including news broadcasts. The inclusion of language indicating that such material may only be distributed by lending by the library or archive is intended to preclude performance, copying, or sale, whether or not for profit, by the recipient of a copy of a television broadcast taped off-the-air pursuant to this clause.

Clause (4), in addition to asserting that nothing contained in section 108 "affects the right of fair use as provided by section 107," also provides that the right of reproduction granted by this section does not override any contractual arrangements assumed by a library or archives when it obtained a work for its collections. For example, if there is an express contractual prohibition against reproduction for any purpose, this legislation shall not be construed as justifying a violation of the contract. This clause is intended to encompass the situation where an individual makes papers, manuscripts or other works available to a library with the understanding that they will not be reproduced.

It is the intent of this legislation that a subsequent unlawful use by a user of a copy or phonorecord of a work lawfully made by a library, shall not make the library liable for such improper use.

e. House Report: Discussion of Multiple Copies and Systematic Reproduction

> The Senate and House Reports differ substantially on this point. The Senate Report's discussion is reprinted at page 17, above.

Multiple copies and systematic reproduction

Subsection (g) provides that the rights granted by this section extend only to the "isolated and unrelated reproduction of a single copy or phonorecord of the same material on separate occasions." However, this section does not authorize the related or concerted reproduction of multiple copies or phonorecords of the same material, whether made on one occasion or over a period of time, and whether intended for aggregate use by one individual or for separate use by the individual members of a group.

With respect to material described in subsection (d)—articles or other contributions to periodicals or collections, and small parts of other copyrighted works—subsection (g) (2) provides that the exemptions of section 108 do not apply if the library or archive engages in "systematic reproduction or distribution of single or multiple copies or phonorecords." This provision in S.22 provoked a storm of controversy, centering around the extent to which the restrictions on "systematic" activities would prevent the continuation and development of interlibrary networks and other arrangements involving the exchange of photocopies. After thorough consideration, the Committee amended section 108 (g) (2) to add the following proviso:

> *Provided*, that nothing in this clause prevents a library or archives from participating in interlibrary arrangements that do not have, as their purpose or effect, that the library or archives receiving such copies or phonorecords for distribution does so in such aggregate quantities as to substitute for a subscription to or purchase of such work.

In addition, the Committee added a new subsection (i) to section 108, requiring the Register of Copyrights, five years from the effective date of the new Act and at five-year intervals thereafter, to report to Congress upon "the extent to which this section has achieved the intended statutory balancing of the rights of creators, and the needs of users," and to make appropriate legislative or other recommendations. As noted in connection with section 107, the Committee also amended section 504(c) in a way that would insulate librarians from unwarranted liability for copyright infringement; this amendment is discussed below.

The key phrases in the Committee's amendment of section 108(g) (2) are "aggregate quantities" and "substitute for a subscription to or purchase of" a work. To be implemented effectively in practice, these provisions will require the development and implementation of more-or-less specific guidelines establishing criteria to govern various situations.

The National Commission on New Technological Uses of Copyrighted Works (CONTU) offered to provide good offices in helping to develop these guidelines. This offer was accepted and, although the final text of guidelines has not yet been achieved, the Committee has reason to hope that, within the next month, some agreement can be reached on an initial set of guidelines covering practices under section 108(g) (2).

f. House Report: Discussion of Works Excluded

> The House Report's discussion of section 108(h) is longer than the corresponding paragraph in the Senate Report, and reflects certain amendments in the subsection.

Works excluded

Subsection (h) provides that the rights of reproduction and distribution under this section do not apply to a musical work, a pictorial, graphic or sculptural work, or a motion picture or other audiovisual work other than "an audiovisual work dealing with news." The latter term is intended as the equivalent in meaning of the phrase "audiovisual news program" in section 108 (f) (3). The exclusions under subsection (h) do not apply to archival reproduction under subsection (b), to replacement of damaged or lost copies or phonorecords under subsection (c), or to "pictorial or graphic works published as illustrations, diagrams, or similar adjuncts to works of which copies are reproduced or distributed in accordance with subsections (d) and (e)."

Although subsection (h) generally removes musical, graphic, and audiovisual works from the specific exemptions of section 108, it is important to recognize that the doctrine of fair use under section 107 remains fully applicable to the photocopying or other reproduction of such works. In the case of music, for example, it would be fair use for a scholar doing musicological research to have a library supply a copy of a portion of a score or to reproduce portions of a phonorecord of a work. Nothing in section 108 impairs the applicability of the fair use doctrine to a wide variety of situations involving photocopying or other reproduction by a library of copyrighted material in its collections, where the user requests the reproduction for legitimate scholarly or research purposes.

4. Excerpts From Conference Report

The following excerpt is reprinted from the Report of the Conference Committee on the new copyright law (H.R. Rep. No. 94-1733, pages 70–74).

a. Conference Report: Introductory Discussion of Section 108

REPRODUCTION BY LIBRARIES AND ARCHIVES

Senate bill

Section 108 of the Senate bill dealt with a variety of situations involving photocopying and other forms of reproduction by libraries and archives. It specified the conditions under which single copies of copyrighted material can be noncommercially reproduced and distributed, but made clear that the privileges of a library or archives under the section do not apply where the reproduction or distribution is of multiple copies or is "systematic." Under subsection (f), the section was not to be construed as limiting the reproduction and distribution, by a library or archive meeting the basic criteria of the section, of a limited number of copies and excerpts of an audiovisual news program.

House bill

The House bill amended section 108 to make clear that, in cases involving interlibrary arrangements for the exchange of photocopies, the activity would not be considered "systematic" as long as the library or archives receiving the reproductions for distribution does not do so in such aggregate quantities as to substitute for a subscription to or purchase of the work. A new subsection (i) directed the Register of Copyrights, by the end of 1982 and at five-year intervals thereafter, to report on the practical success of the section in balancing the various interests, and to make recommendations for any needed changes. With respect to audiovisual news programs, the House bill limited the scope of the distribution privilege confirmed by section 108 (f) (3) to cases where the distribution takes the form of a loan.

b. Conference Report: Conference Committee Discussion of CONTU Guidelines on Photocopying and Interlibrary Arrangements

Conference substitute

The conference substitute adopts the provisions of section 108 as amended by the House bill. In doing so, the conferees have noted two letters dated September 22, 1976, sent respectively to John L. McClellan, Chairman of the Senate Judiciary Subcommittee on Patents, Trademarks, and Copyrights, and to Robert W. Kastenmeier, Chairman of the House Judiciary Subcommittee on Courts, Civil Liberties, and the Administration of Justice. The letters, from the Chairman of the National Commission on New Technological Uses of Copyrighted Works (CONTU), Stanley H. Fuld, transmitted a document consisting of "guidelines interpreting the provision in subsection 108 (g) (2) of S. 22, as approved by the House Committee on the Judiciary." Chairman Fuld's letters explain that, following lengthy consultations with the parties concerned, the Commission adopted these guidelines as fair and workable and with the hope that the conferees on S. 22 may find that they merit inclusion in the conference report. The letters add that, although time did not permit securing signatures of the represen-

tatives of the principal library organizations or of the organizations representing publishers and authors on these guidelines, the Commission had received oral assurances from these representatives that the guidelines are acceptable to their organizations.

The conference committee understands that the guidelines are not intended as, and cannot be considered, explicit rules or directions governing any and all cases, now or in the future. It is recognized that their purpose is to provide guidance in the most commonly-encountered interlibrary photocopying situations, that they are not intended to be limiting or determinative in themselves or with respect to other situations, and that they deal with an evolving situation that will undoubtedly require their continuous reevaluation and adjustment. With these qualifications, the conference committee agrees that the guidelines are a reasonable interpretation of the proviso of section 108 (g) (2) in the most common situations to which they apply today.

c. Conference Report: Reprint of CONTU Guidelines on Photocopying and Interlibrary Arrangements

The text of the guidelines follows:

PHOTOCOPYING—INTERLIBRARY ARRANGEMENTS

INTRODUCTION

Subsection 108 (g) (2) of the bill deals, among other things, with limits on interlibrary arrangements for photocopying. It prohibits systematic photocopying of copyrighted materials but permits interlibrary arrangements "that do not have, as their purpose or effect, that the library or archives receiving such copies or phonorecords for distribution does so in such aggregate quantities as to substitute for a subscription to or purchase of such work."

The National Commission on New Technological Uses of Copyrighted Works offered its good offices to the House and Senate subcommittees in bringing the interested parties together to see if agreement could be reached on what a realistic definition would be of "such aggregate quantities." The Commission consulted with the parties and suggested the interpretation which follows, on which there has been substantial agreement by the principal library, publisher, and author organizations. The Commission considers the guidelines which follow to be a workable and fair interpretation of the intent of the proviso portion of subsection 108 (g) (2).

These guidelines are intended to provide guidance in the application of section 108 to the most frequently encountered interlibrary case: a library's obtaining from another library, in lieu of interlibrary loan, copies of articles from relatively recent issues of periodicals—those published within five years prior to the date of the request. The guidelines do not specify what aggregate quantity of copies of an article or articles published in a periodical, the issue date of which is more than five years prior to the date when the request for the copy thereof is made, constitutes a substitute for a subscription to such periodical. The meaning of the proviso to subsection 108 (g) (2) in such case is left to future interpretation.

The point has been made that the present practice on interlibrary loans and use of photocopies in lieu of loans may be supplemented or even largely replaced by a system in which one or more agencies or institutions, public or private, exist for the specific purpose of providing a central source for photocopies. Of course, these guidelines would not apply to such a situation.

GUIDELINES FOR THE PROVISO OF SUBSECTION 108 (G) (2)

1. As used in the proviso of subsection 108 (g) (2), the words " . . . such aggregate quantities as to substitute for a subscription to or purchase of such work" shall mean:

(a) with respect to any given periodical (as opposed to any given issue of a periodical), filled requests of a library or archives (a "requesting entity") within any calendar year for a total of six or more copies of an article or articles published in such periodical within five years prior to the date of the request. These guidelines specifically shall not apply, directly or indirectly, to any request of a requesting entity for a copy or copies of an article or articles published in any issue of a periodical, the publication date of which is more than five years prior to the date when the request is made. These guidelines do not define the meaning, with respect to such a request, of " . . . such aggregate quantities as to substitute for a subscription to [such periodical]".

(b) With respect to any other material described in subsection 108 (d), (including fiction and poetry), filled requests of a requesting entity within any calendar year for a total of six or more copies or phonorecords of or from any given work (including a collective work) during the entire period when such material shall be protected by copyright.

2. In the event that a requesting entity—

(a) shall have in force or shall have entered an order for a subscription to a periodical, or

(b) has within its collection, or shall have entered an order for, a copy or phonorecord of any other copyrighted work, material from either category of which it desires to obtain by copy from another library or archives (the "supplying entity"), because the material to be copied is not reasonably available for use by the requesting entity itself, then the fulfillment of such request shall be treated as though the requesting entity made such copy from its own collection. A library or archives may request a copy or phonorecord from a supplying entity only under those circumstances where the requesting entity would have been able, under the other provisions of section 108, to supply such copy from materials in its own collection.

3. No request for a copy or phonorecord of any material to which these guidelines apply may be fulfilled by the supplying entity unless such request is accompanied by a representation by the requesting entity that the request was made in conformity with these guidelines.

4. The requesting entity shall maintain records of all requests made by it for copies or phonorecords of any materials to which these guidelines apply and shall maintain records of the fulfillment of such requests, which records shall be retained until the end of the third complete calendar year after the end of the calendar year in which the respective request shall have been made.

5. As part of the review provided for in subsection 108 (i), these guidelines shall be reviewed not later than five years from the effective date of this bill.

d. Conference Report: Discussion of "Audiovisual News Program"

The conference committee is aware that an issue has arisen as to the meaning of the phrase "audiovisual news program" in section 108 (f) (3). The conferees believe that, under the provision as adopted in the conference substitute, a library or archives qualifying under section 108 (a) would be free, without regard to the archival activities of the Library of Congress or any other organization, to reproduce, on videotape or any other medium of fixation or reproduction, local, regional, or network newscasts, interviews concerning current news events, and on-the-spot coverage of news events, and to distribute a limited number of reproductions of such a program on a loan basis.

e. Conference Report: Discussion of Libraries and Archives in Profit-Making Institutions

Another point of interpretation involves the meaning of "indirect commercial advantage," as used in section 108 (a) (1), in the case of libraries or archival collections within industrial, profit-making, or proprietary institutions. As long as the library or archives meets the criteria in section 108 (a) and the other requirements of the section, including the prohibitions against multiple and systematic copying in subsection (g), the conferees consider that the isolated, spontaneous making of single photocopies by a library or archives in a for-profit organization without any commercial motivation, or participation by such a library or archives in interlibrary arrangements, would come within the scope of section 108.

5. Copyright Office Regulations Under Section 108

> The following is the text of regulations adopted by the Copyright Office to implement sections 108 (d) (2) and 108 (e) of the new copyright law (37 *Code of Federal Regulations* § 201.14).

§ 201.14 Warnings of copyright for use by certain libraries and archives.

(a) *Definitions.* (1) A "Display Warning of Copyright" is a notice under paragraphs (d) (2) and (e) (2) of section 108 of Title 17 of the United States Code as amended by Pub. L. 94–553. As required by those sections the "Display Warning of Copyright" is to be displayed at the place where orders for copies or phonorecords are accepted by certain libraries and archives.

(2) An "Order Warning of Copyright" is a notice under paragraphs (d) (2) and (e) (2) of section 108 of Title 17 of the United States Code as amended by Pub. L. 94–553. As required by those sections the "Order Warning of Copyright" is to be included on printed forms supplied by certain libraries and archives and used by their patrons for ordering copies or phonorecords.

(b) *Contents.* A Display Warning of Copyright and an Order Warning of Copyright shall consist of a verbatim reproduction of the following notice, printed in such size and form and displayed in such manner as to comply with paragraph (c) of this section:

NOTICE

WARNING CONCERNING COPYRIGHT RESTRICTIONS

The copyright law of the United States (Title 17, United States Code) governs the making of photocopies or other reproductions of copyrighted material.

Under certain conditions specified in the law, libraries and archives are authorized to furnish a photocopy or other reproduction. One of these specified conditions is that the photocopy or reproduction is not to be "used for any purpose other than private study, scholarship, or research." If a user makes a request for, or later uses, a photocopy or reproduction for purposes in excess of "fair use," that user may be liable for copyright infringement.

This institution reserves the right to refuse to accept a copying order if, in its judgment, fulfillment of the order would involve violation of copyright law.

(c) *Form and Manner of Use.* (1) A Display Warning of Copyright shall be printed on heavy paper or other durable material in type at least 18 points in size, and shall be displayed prominently, in such manner and location as to be clearly visible, legible, and comprehensible to a casual observer within the immediate vicinity of the place where orders are accepted.

(2) An Order Warning of Copyright shall be printed within a box located prominently on the order form itself, either on the front side of the form or immediately adjacent to the space calling for the name or signature of the person using the form. The notice shall be printed in type size no smaller than that used predominantly throughout the form, and in no case shall the type size be smaller than 8 points. The notice shall be printed in such manner as to be clearly legible, comprehensible, and readily apparent to a casual reader of the form.

E. LIABILITY FOR INFRINGEMENT

1. Text of Section 504

> The following is a reprint of the entire text of section 504 of title 17, *United States Code*. The special provisions affecting librarians and educators are in subsection (c) (2).

§ 504. Remedies for infringement: Damages and profits.

(a) In General. — Except as otherwise provided by this title, an infringer of copyright is liable for either—

(1) The copyright owner's actual damages and any additional profits of the infringer, as provided by subsection (b); or

(2) statutory damages, as provided by subsection (c).

(b) Actual Damages and Profits. — The copyright owner is entitled to recover the actual damages suffered by him or her as a result of the infringement, and any profits of the infringer that are attributable to the infringement and are not taken into account in computing the actual damages. In establishing the infringer's profits, the copyright owner is required to present proof only of the infringer's gross revenue, and the infringer is required to prove his or her deductible expenses and the elements of profit attributable to factors other than the copyrighted work.

(c) STATUTORY DAMAGES.—

(1) Except as provided by clause (2) of this subsection, the copyright owner may elect, at any time before final judgment is rendered, to recover, instead of actual damages and profits, an award of statutory damages for all infringements involved in the action, with respect to any one work, for which any one infringer is liable individually, or for which any two or more infringers are liable jointly and severally, in a sum of not less than $250 or more than $10,000 as the court considers just. For the purposes of this subsection, all the parts of a compilation or derivative work constitute one work.

(2) In a case where the copyright owner sustains the burden of proving, and the court finds, that infringement was committed willfully, the court in its discretion may increase the award of statutory damages to a sum of not more than $50,000. In a case where the infringer sustains the burden of proving, and the court finds, that such infringer was not aware and had no reason to believe that his or her acts constituted an infringement of copyright, the court in its discretion may reduce the award of statutory damages to a sum of not less than $100. The court shall remit statutory damages in any case where an infringer believed and had reasonable grounds for believing that his or her use of the copyrighted work was a fair use under section 107, if the infringer was: (i) an employee or agent of a nonprofit educational institution, library, or archives acting within the scope of his or her employment who, or such institution, library, or archives itself, which infringed by reproducing the work in copies or phonorecords; or (ii) a public broadcasting entity which or a person who, as a regular part of the nonprofit activities of a public broadcasting entity (as defined in subsection (g) of section 118) infringed by performing a published nondramatic literary work or by reproducing a transmission program embodying a performance of such a work.

2. Excerpts From House Report on Section 504

The following excerpts are reprinted from the House Report on the new copyright law (H.R. Rep. No. 94-1476, pages 161-163). Material not of immediate interest to librarians and educators has been omitted. Much of the corresponding discussion in the Senate Report (S. Rep. No. 94-473, pages 143-145) is substantially the same; the House Report's discussion of statutory damages applicable to librarians and educators is new.

IN GENERAL

A cornerstone of the remedies sections and of the bill as a whole is section 504, the provision dealing with recovery of actual damages, profits, and statutory damages. The two basic aims of this section are reciprocal and correlative: (1) to give the courts specific unambiguous directions concerning monetary awards, thus avoiding the confusion and uncertainty that have marked the present law on the subject, and, at the same time, (2) to provide the courts with reasonable latitude to adjust recovery to the circumstances of the case, thus avoiding some of the artificial or overly technical awards resulting from the language of the existing statute.

Subsection (a) lays the groundwork for the more detailed provisions of the section by establishing the liability of a copyright infringer for either "the copyright owner's actual damages and any additional profits of the infringer," or statutory damages. Recovery of actual damages and profits under section 504 (b) or of statutory damages under section 504 (c) is alternative and for the copyright owner to elect; as under the present law, the plaintiff in an infringement suit is not obliged to submit proof of damages and profits and may choose to rely on the provision for minimum statutory damages. However, there is nothing in section 504 to prevent a court from taking account of evidence concerning actual damages and profits in making an award of statutory damages within the range set out in subsection (c).

Actual damages and profits

In allowing the plaintiff to recover "the actual damages suffered by him or her as a result of the infringement," plus any of the infringer's profits "that are attributable to the infringement and are not taken into

account in computing the actual damages," section 504 (b) recognizes the different purposes served by awards of damages and profits. Damages are awarded to compensate the copyright owner for losses from the infringement, and profits are awarded to prevent the infringer from unfairly benefiting from a wrongful act.***

Statutory damages

Subsection (c) of section 504 makes clear that the plaintiff's election to recover statutory damages may take place at any time during the trial before the court has rendered its final judgment. The remainder of clause (1) of the subsection represents a statement of the general rates applicable to awards of statutory damages.

Clause (2) of section 504 (c) provides for exceptional cases in which the maximum award of statutory damages could be raised from $10,000 to $50,000, and in which the minimum recovery could be reduced from $250 to $100. The basic principle underlying this provision is that the courts should be given discretion to increase statutory damages in cases of willful infringement and to lower the minimum where the infringer is innocent. The language of the clause makes clear that in these situations the burden of proving willfulness rests on the copyright owner and that of proving innocence rests on the infringer, and that the court must make a finding of either willfulness or innocence in order to award the exceptional amounts.

The "innocent infringer" provision of section 504 (c) (2) has been the subject of extensive discussion. The exception, which would allow reduction of minimum statutory damages to $100 where the infringer "was not aware and had no reason to believe that his or her acts constituted an infringement of copyright," is sufficient to protect against unwarranted liability in cases of occasional or isolated innocent infringement, and it offers adequate insulation to users, such as broadcasters and newspaper publishers, who are particularly vulnerable to this type of infringement suit. On the other hand, by establishing a realistic floor for liability, the provision preserves its intended deterrent effect; and it would not allow an infringer to escape simply because the plaintiff failed to disprove the defendant's claim of innocence.

In addition to the general "innocent infringer" provision clause (2) deals with the special situation of teachers, librarians, archivists, and public broadcasters, and the nonprofit institutions of which they are a part. Section 504 (c) (2) provides that, where such a person or institution infringes copyrighted material in the honest belief that what they were doing constituted fair use, the court is precluded from awarding any statutory damages. It is intended that, in cases involving this provision, the burden of proof with respect to the defendant's good faith should rest on the plaintiff.

3. Excerpts From Conference Report on Section 504

The following excerpts are reprinted from the Report of the Conference Committee on the new copyright law (H.R. Rep. No. 94-1733, pages 79-80).

REMEDIES FOR COPYRIGHT INFRINGEMENT

Senate bill

Chapter 5 of the Senate bill dealt with civil and criminal infringement of copyright and the remedies for both. Subsection (c) of section 504 allowed statutory damages within a stated dollar range, and clause (2) of that subsection provided for situations in which the maximum could be exceeded and the minimum lowered; the court was given discretion to reduce or remit statutory damages entirely where a teacher, librarian, or archivist believed that the infringing activity constituted fair use.***

House bill

Section 504 (c) (2) of the House bill required the court to remit statutory damages entirely in cases where a teacher, librarian, archivist, or public broadcaster, or the institution to which they belong, infringed in the honest belief that what they were doing constituted fair use.***

Conference substitute

The conference substitute adopts the House amendments with respect to statutory damages in section 504 c) (2)***

Computer Science and Technology:
Copyright in Computer–Readable Works

1. EXECUTIVE SUMMARY AND CONCLUSIONS

1.1 ORIGIN OF THIS STUDY

This study began in October, 1974, and has been sponsored by the Division of Science Information of the National Science Foundation. The problem seen at that time was that copyrighted works were being fixed in computer-readable media and the copyright law concerning the use of such works was unclear. The copyright law had not been fully revised since 1909, a time when the possibility of copies of literature fixed in media that would make the copies invisible to the unaided eye was unthinkable.

A major issue in 1974 and for several previous years was whether a copyright owner deserved compensation when his work was first encoded into electronic form, or for the time it continued to be stored, or only upon each instance of a hard-copy being created. In addition, a sense of urgency had been created at Congressional hearings in 1967 with predictions that in the near future, hard copy distribution of technical books and scientific journals would be replaced by a single copy, converted into computerized form, being replicated at hundreds, perhaps thousands of remote terminals. The implications for copyright owners were severe. As a result of those conditions, what was desired was a multi-disciplinary, "policy-oriented" study which would clarify the issues, including the issue of economically-sound, technical mechanisms in such automated systems that would enable reporting of the data on which royalties could be based.

However, the National Commission on New Technological Uses of Copyrighted Works (CONTU) was established at the very end of 1974, with the function of recommending to Congress changes in the copyright law with respect to uses of copyrighted works in conjunction with computers. In October, 1976, the General Revision of Copyright Law was enacted, which did much to clarify the rights of copyright owners to their works when fixed in any tangible medium, but did not finally resolve the issues of computer-readable works.

CONTU has not yet submitted its recommendations to Congress, and the copyright laws with respect to computer-readable works will remain ambiguous until Congress acts on those forthcoming recommendations.

This study analyzes the issues of copyright in computer-readable works and is pertinent to current policy considerations.

1.2 CONTENT OF THIS REPORT

The purpose of this report is to present the results of the study, and to recommend mechanisms that will maximize the long-term availability of computer-based information.

The subject of this study does not concern an activity in which there is a comprehensive or coordinated investment program aimed at achieving a specific goal. Consequently, recommendations are not based on a quantification of benefits and a resulting cost-benefit comparison. In order to establish a firm basis for recommendations, basic principles of copyright have been surveyed; and an analysis has been made of the impact of information technology on copyright law as that technology has advanced during the twentieth century. In addition, fundamental concepts of economics have been reviewed to assure that recommendations are well-grounded in that discipline.

As an outcome of the evaluation of fundamentals, and of the historical analyses, it has been possible to enumerate a set of basic principles that are employed as the foundation of the recommendations. In addition, insights have been developed and conclusions drawn about the reduction of transaction costs, the impact of technological change and about the existing and expected mechanisms of policymaking in copyright. It is hoped that the recommendations and conclusions will be of value to decision-makers, as well as to policy analysts and researchers. Certainly the findings, conclusions and recommendations of this report are not to be taken as the final, definitive view. Other analyses of the legal and historical precedents may reveal different interpretations and consequently different conclusions and recommendations. Additional contributions to the literature are welcomed.

1.3 FINDINGS OF BASIC PRINCIPLES

1. The concept of common law copyright conforms to the philosophy of the Enlightenment, enunciated by Locke, that each person has the right to the fruits of his creations.

2. Due to the inherent rights in the copy, an intrinsic market failure results from the ease of copying or plagiarism of intellectual property. Correction of the failure requires the public good of statutory copyright protection.

3. The principle of inherent ownership and consequent statutory protection do not imply a value judgment as to the relative merit of an individual work or the inherent right to financial remuneration. The economic value of a work is to be determined in the marketplace where copyright protects the distributors of intellectual works as well as the creators.

4. If free economic competition is possible, opportunities for it should be maximized, including opportunities for entry of new products and new competitors.

5. Copyright protection assumes the concept of the *quid pro quo* of a social contract. The application of this concept requires that in return for protection of law, the copyright holder makes a public disclosure of his work.

6. The dissemination of scientific and technical information should be maximized, subject to resource constraints, excepting where such principles as personal privacy, trade secrecy and national security take precedence.

7. There would be transaction costs attached to any market, including the market for intellectual property, even if there were no copyright protection. The trade-off in structuring a market is in the kinds of transaction costs a society is willing to tolerate, as well as in the size of such costs. All other things being equal, the size of transaction costs should be minimized.

8. Decisionmaking on copyright involves the achievement of a balance of equities between user needs and owner rights that should include consideration of the general public as well.

1.4 RECOMMENDATIONS FOR IMPLEMENTATION

1.4.1 Computer-Readable Data Bases

1. Computer-readable data bases, whether compilations, collective works, or reference works of a single author should be copyrightable in any tangible medium of expression.

2. Complete disclosure of the contents of the data base to the Copyright Office should be required, in some tangible medium, when the data base is initially registered.

3. Deposit requirements for data-base updating should be satisfied by a yearly submission of a complete list of additions and deletions. At some multi-year interval, e.g. ten years, a complete re-disclosure should be made if the data base has been frequently updated.

4. Clarification of what constitutes publication of a data base is needed when a data base is distributed only in computer-readable form via a terminal query system through one or a very few specifically-licensed computer systems.

1.4.2 Computer Programs

1. A computer program written by a person in a source language, with or without the assistance of a computer, generically qualifies as a work of authorship. An original computer program should be copyrightable in source language in any tangible medium of expression. Machine (object) code should not qualify as a source language.

2. Disclosure of the computer program upon copyright registration should be accompanied by definition and usage manuals for the computer language and dialect in which the program is written, if such information is not on file already with the Copyright Office.

3. The transformation of a copyrighted computer program into object code from source language should be considered to be the making of a copy, even if the translation requires the imple-

mentation of some housekeeping functions such as the selection of peripheral units, storage allocation and the assignment of absolute addresses.

4. The translation of a copyrighted computer program into a completely different source language (not just a dialect or variant) should constitute the authorship of a derivative work.

5. The duration of copyright protection for computer programs should be no less than the duration of protection of other original works of authorship, in order to promote the use of computer languages that can be expected to endure regardless of changes in hardware technology.

6. Decisionmakers should be aware that assignment of computer programs to a particular category of copyrighted work forces the adoption of the limitations on exclusive rights already inherent in that category. For example, categorization of a computer program as a "literary work", rather than as a separate copyrightable category assigns to computer program users the exemptions to exclusive rights granted to users of literary works in Section 110 of the 1976 General Revision of Copyright Law.

7. The flowchart of a computer program ought to be separately copyrightable as a pictorial work, but it ought not to be able to employed to support an infringement charge against another program that employs the same flowchart unless the flowchart is sufficiently detailed so as to mirror the specific expression of the original program.

1.4.3 Transfer of Ownership of Copies of Computer-Readable Works

1. Outright sale of computer-readable works, i.e. transfer of ownership of copies as distinguished from lease or rental with permissions, should be promoted so as to reduce transaction costs.

2. In order to effectively use a copyrighted computer-readable work, an owner of a copy should have the right to make and retain additional copies for his internal use (which would have to be destroyed when and if he resold the work), and should have the right to use a copy in a computer. The right of internal use should not include the right to make the work available to outsiders via a computer network or otherwise. The assignment of usage rights to purchasers should not prevent

copyright owners from retaining all exclusive rights in situations not involving transfer of ownership of copies.

1.5 CONCLUSIONS

1.5.1 Technological Change and Copyright

1. An essential point at issue, as seen by decisionmakers in copyright policymaking, is the definition of the boundaries of the property right, regardless of the specific technologies involved.

2. A major effect of technological change is that it causes ambiguities in some of the definitions of property rights that may have seemed perfectly clear before the change.

3. An effect of successful technological change is a multiplication of interest groups organized around the new technologies. The increase in number of interest groups causes an increased incidence of inter-group conflict. This often results in additional rules as well as more complex rules regulating group interactions.

4. It seems inescapable that "a complex civilization necessarily develops complex political arrangements" if each interest group is granted a certain legitimacy through a democratic process.

1.5.2 Judicial Decisionmaking Under Technological Change

1. One viewpoint taken by the Federal Courts in copyright litigation is that if the general concept of the law then in effect can be extended to the new situation without stretching the law's meaning too far, it should be done. This interpretation is more likely to be employed when the decision so taken will not extend much beyond the boundaries of the specific case at hand, that is, will not affect the balance among interest groups.

2. A second viewpoint is that stretching the law's meaning (or specifically defining the ambiguous) beyond a certain point would be for the Federal Courts to take on a responsibility better left to Congress. This viewpoint is more likely to be taken in a situation in which a decision has ramifications beyond the particular litigants, i.e., affects the balance among interest groups.

3. In taking the second viewpoint, the Courts apparently recognize that Congress is much more capable of implementing a flexible solution involving give and take among interest groups, while the Courts are simply required to give a right-wrong solution. Therefore, it appears that the Courts have decided these cases in favor of the side upholding the status quo, so that Congress can receive the situation without the effect of an unbalancing Court decision.

1.5.3 Models of Copyright Policymaking

1. Decisionmaking in copyright in the twentieth century has been essentially a pluralist process, that is, has consisted of compromises among various interest groups gathered around different functions related to copyrighted works.

2. The power arena model of Theodore Lowi which assigns decisions to the distributional, regulatory or redistributional arenas is a useful vehicle with which to examine copyright policymaking.

3. Individual copyrights may be the ultimate distributional good, since they can be dispensed in small units, and since registra-

tion of copyrights does not reduce the stock of unregistered or uncopyrighted works waiting for claimants. Originality is an unlimited resource, although nurturing and institutionalizing originality may not be.

4. The effect of technological change has been, in Lowi's terms, to move copyright policymaking from the distributional arena (in the nineteenth century) to the regulatory arena (primarily in the twentieth century). The regulatory arena is very close in concept to the pluralist model of policymaking.

5. As long as copyright continues to be seen mainly as a problem of "balancing the equities" (i.e., in the regulatory arena), Congress will retain the major role vis-a-vis the Executive Branch.

6. Increasing concern for consumer welfare and for prevention of monopoly are indicative of redistributional concern and with the potential for increased Executive Branch involvement.

7. While not apparent at present, it is conceivable that changes in prices of raw materials (such as paper) and other resources, as well as technological change, may serve to bring copyright more significantly into the redistributive arena; but probably as part of a more encompassing and consumer-related issue, such as "public access to information."

1.5.4 Economic Efficiency

1. Clearinghouses are useful multi-producer organizations for reducing the transaction costs of information and communication in the collection and payment of royalties for a permission system, but there may be a blurring of individual proprietor considerations.

2. The selection of blanket or per-use licenses on a least-cost basis in a permissions system may be technologically determined. For example, a computerized system of data base access is likely to develop usage information at low cost. In that situation, per-use calculation of royalties is not difficult.

3. With high data-collection costs of usage information, a blanket license is likely to result in lower overhead costs than a per-use license, provided the less-precise information available from the reduced data collection does not result in inequitable treatment of some of the concerned parties.

4. Price differentials in subscription charges between individual purchasers of journals and institutional purchasers are economically justified on efficiency criteria. This concept can be applied to computer-readable works that are sold, as it has been to journals.

5. The exemption from royalty payments for "worthy" users is inefficient because it forces the "less worthy" users to carry more than their share. On efficiency criteria, "worthy" use is public good which should be paid for by everyone.

6. Whether a copyright is an exercisable economic monopoly depends on the substitutability of other copyrighted works as determined by the actions of consumers of such works.

7. Since a researcher must be comprehensive in the literature of his field, there may be very little substitutability among works he must have.

8. The possibility exists that in some field of research, by virtue of economy of scale, an established system of suppliers and customers and already amortized costs of market entry, a single organization may achieve a virtual market monopoly over a class of nonsubstitutable computer-readable data bases.

9. If there were no copyright protection at all, there would still be the transaction costs of increased secrecy, cut-throat competition, and lowered opportunity for recognition of creative talents.

1.6 RECOMMENDATIONS FOR FURTHER INVESTIGATIONS

1. The potential for monopoly in the delivery of computer-readable data-base access services, as discussed above and in Section 5.6.3, may be an area of useful additional investigation. There is a need to consider the fostering of useful innovations as well as the potential for monopoly pricing.

2. The effectiveness of discovery of infringements in the copying and unauthorized sale and use of computer-readable works may need study. The question of the practical value of copyright protection can be raised if significant infringements can be shown to be occurring without discovery, prosecution and conviction.

3. New types of technologically-based intellectual property may be invented and new copyright problems may arise. Continuing review of inventions and innovations might be undertaken to examine the possibility of the need for further changes in the copyright statute.

4. The electronic journal, while strongly forecasted by some, has not materialized. A useful study would be a consumer-oriented (user-pull) survey, determining to what extent such a product would be acceptable and purchased by potential users.

5. The "worthy use" exemption from copyright royalty payments has been suggested to be economically inefficient. It could be hypothesized that innovations of intellectual products serving the market in which there is a worthy-use exemption would be stifled because of the potential for lesser returns. It would be useful to examine this hypothesis in a research project.

6. Additional examination of whether it would serve the public interest if computer programs were protected under a more-encompassing concept than copyright appears to be worthwhile.

7. While the concept of price descrimination between individual

and institutional purchasers of scientific and technical information has been shown to be economically efficient, the
legal ramifications controlling its use have not been examined
in this report. Such an examination may prove valuable.

2.   THE FOUNDATIONS OF COPYRIGHT

2.1 COMMON LAW AND THE PRINCIPLE OF NATURAL EQUITY

Article I, Section 8 of our Constitution gives to Congress the power

"To promote the progress of science and the useful arts,
by securing for limited times to authors and inventors the
exclusive right to their respective writings and discoveries;..."

The extant documents that might describe for us the original basis used
by the framers of the Constitution for inclusion of this clause are
very limited. The Federalist, written in 1787 and 1788 by Alexander
Hamilton, James Madison, and John Jay in an effort to explain, defend
and obtain support for the ratification by the States of the then-pend-
ing Constitution devotes just five sentences to the clause. In
Federalist No. 43, James Madison wrote:

"The utility of this power /¯of Congress ¯/ will scarcely be
questioned. The copyright of authors has been solemnly adjudged in Great Britain to be a right of common law. The
right to useful inventions seems with equal reason to belong
to the inventors. The public good fully coincides in both
cases with the claims of individuals. The States cannot
make effectual provision for either of the cases, and most
of them have anticipated the decision of this point by laws
passed at the instance of Congress."

Into Madison's short sentences are packed a wealth of social, economic
and political philosophy. In his statement that "copyright of authors
has been solemnly adjudged in Great Britain to be a right of common law,"
Madison implied that basic principles of British common law were valuable, and in addition, continued in effect in the United States; at
that time newly-formed out of British colonies. Walter Pforzheimer, in
a scholarly historical review of copyright law, has similarly quoted an
1807 Massachusetts decision as stating:

"Our ancestors, when they came into this new world, claimed
the common law as their birth-right, and brought it with them,
except such parts as were judged inapplicable to their new
state and condition."[1]

Professor Emmette Redford, in describing our legal and ideological
heritage, has noted that "...early English judges looked not alone to
custom, but also to reason and natural equity for their decisions."[2]
Thus, by citing British common law, Madison implied principles of natural justice which included the concept that each person has an inherent
right to control of the products of his own creation.

The philosopher most associated with this principle and whose writings

would have been known to Madison was Englishman John Locke (1632-1704).
Locke has been called "first advocate of the modern conception of civil
liberties and definer of the limitations of property and the powers of
the common wealth...the formulator of constitutional law and the democratic processes as we know them."[3]   Locke had written, in his Second
Treatise on Civil Government, (Chapter V, para. 27):

> "...every man has a property in his own person...The labor
> of his body and the work of his hands we may say are properly
> his...It being by him removed from the common state nature
> placed it in, it hath by his labor something annexed to it
> that excludes the common right of other men..."

It is useful to note at this point that common law copyright in all unpublished works (with its basis in the British common law to which
Madison referred) will continue to be in force in the United States
through December 31, 1977. Pforzheimer notes that a principle of British common law that has been carried down to us, and is in effect at
this time, is that the author has complete dominion over his work until publication, after which his rights conform to the statute then in
effect. The case of Donaldson v. Becket decided in 1774 in Great Britain confirmed this situation.[4]

However, on January 1, 1978, the 1976 General Revision of Copyright Law
takes effect, and under this new statute, common law copyright is ended
for all unpublished works fixed in any tangible medium of expression.
As of that date, such works will be covered by the Federal copyright
statute and will not be subject to the common law or statutes of any
State.[5] Works not fixed in any tangible medium such as unscripted
utterances or performances will continue to be subject to common law
as interpreted by the Judiciary.

2.2 NATIONAL UNIFORMITY IN THE FACE OF MOBILITY

In calling in The Federalist for a Federal copyright law, as opposed
to a set of State laws, Madison recognized the natural mobility of information (recently proclaimed by some to a 20th century concept) and
the inefficiency of different requirements for intellectual property
rights in the separate States. Professor Redford has noted that this
attempt at uniformity was part of an overall pattern of Constitutional
provisions that had a strong economic impact. As Redford states:

> "/The framers of the Constitution 7 made certain decisions
> that were necessary to allow the free flow of persons, in-
> vestment money, and commerce over the nation as a whole,
> thus opening a vast area and a vast market to the entre-
> preneurial genius of Americans, wherever located . . .
> / The framers 7 made possible national uniformity in cer-
> tain facilities for commerce, such as coinage, patents
> and copyrights, uniform weights and measures, and a post-
> al system."[6]

2.3 PRIVATE ACTIONS IN THE PUBLIC INTEREST

Finally, in asserting in <u>The Federalist</u> that "the public good fully co-incides . . . with the claims of individuals / for copyright and patent protection 7" Madison made a bold statement with profound economic as well as political implications. The statement implies, first, that there exists a "public good" that is distinct and separate from individual or private goods. Second, it is implied that the Government may grant incentive benefits or remuneration to individuals for private and voluntary activities that are consistent with the public good. Third, in the cases of patents and copyrights, the private benefits to be granted by the Government will have no public effects except good effects; and fourth, the value of benefits granted is equivalent to the public good thereby obtained.

These implications raise issues that even today, have not been fully analyzed and may never be fully resolved. They are in the arena of what has been referred to as the theory of public goods or public expenditure analysis, but which Professor Peter Steiner has broadened to call "the theory of the public interest."[7] These economic theories "concern the way in which demands for public activity arise, are articulated, and are legitimatized."[8] The theories include the definition and classification of public goods and the mechanisms of their creation, financing, and distribution. In the case of intellectual property, the specific public good is the protection offered to copyright proprietors by the Government through its registration and enforcement mechanisms. Note that the Government protection is the public good; the individually-held copyright is a private asset.

2.4 MARKET FAILURES AND PUBLIC GOODS

Public goods may be differentiated in general from private goods and from collective goods. The necessity for public provision of a good may arise because the technical nature of the good is such that a private market, however perfectly competitive, would not be able to provide it.

The need for a public good may arise also if the imperfections of a real market create public "bads" (e.g., an externality, for example, pollution) which only Government action can cause to correct. In either case, "market failure" is said to occur. If some group of persons acting together take cognizance of the inability of the market to supply the good and provide the good for themselves outside of the free market activity, a collective good results. "Any publicly-induced or provided collective good is a public good,"[9] according to Steiner.

In the case of copyright protection, a conventional economic analysis would state that the need for a public good arises because intrinsic technical characteristics of an intellectual work prevents the operation of the perfectly competitive market for such works without Government intervention. One technical characteristic is simply that an original authored work fixed in any tangible medium of expression (i.e., a copyrightable work) is typically reproducible at a very low cost in the same or similar medium. The work is also subject to plagiarism. In the presence of these technical facts, and with the condition that the author or his assignees have a property right in the work, a market failure would result without the protection and enforcement power of the

Government. The market failure is that without copyright protection
the author or rights proprietor would not be able to fully appropriate
the economic value of originality through sale.

2.5 PROTECTION FOR PUBLICATION AS WELL AS CREATION

The conventional economic analysis given above has been discussed in a
perceptive paper on "The Economic Rationale of Copyright" [10] by Professors Robert M. Hurt and Robert M. Schuchman. One question these authors
ask is: "Does the copyright system induce the creation of new goods
which would not have been created in the absence of copyrights?"[11] The
authors answer that "copyright does lead to the creation of new goods by
encouraging the assumption of greater risks."[12]

It is necessary to comment, however, (as Hurt and Schuchman imply) that
many kinds of works are subject to copyright, and the importance of
copyright for the creation of new works varies with the type of work.
In particular, for scientific and technical research papers, copyright
is typically of minor importance to the authors of such papers even
though publication is very important to them. The remuneration to authors of research papers occurs indirectly through increased salary,
improved job security, prizes, travel opportunities and prestige, but
not typically from the sale of papers.

However, copyright is extremely important to the publishers of such papers because (as is pointed out in Appendix B of this report), copyright protects the publishers' opportunities to cover their fixed costs.
Thus in the case of research papers, copyright does not lead directly
to the creation of new goods, but rather to the direct protection of
channels of publication for already-existing goods. (This may lead, as
a secondary effect, to the further creation of new goods of a similar
type for distribution through the protected publication channels.)

2.6 THE VALUE JUDGMENT OF COPYRIGHT

Under the assumption, then, that copyright increases the creation and/or
publication of some original works of authorship, Hurt and Schuchman
then inquire "whether the reallocation of resources induced thereby is
conducive to general welfare."[13] One argument is that copyright encourages literature, which like education, has greater intrinsic merit than
its alternative product. Thus social welfare in enhanced. Hurt and
Schuchman state that this assumption is in the nature of a value judgment. This is undeniable. It may be noted, in addition, that such a
judgment was conceivably in the minds of the Constitution ratifiers who
voted "to promote the progress of science and the useful arts" without
conclusive proof that copyright protection (along with patent protection)
was the most economically efficient or socially equitable method of
pursuing that goal.

However, the Judiciary has held that this Constitutional qualification
is explanatory and not prescriptive; and that a copyrighted work need
not specifically promote anything as publicly valuable as science or the
useful arts, however those terms might have been defined in the 18th
century or are defined in the 20th. At present, the judgment of (U.S.)
society is, as expressed in law, that any "original works of authorship
fixed in any tangible medium of expression "[14] that are accepted for
copyright protection are more valuable than the alternatives, whatever
they might be.

Furthermore, copyright protection provides society with no comparative value judgment as to the inherent worth of a particular work of authorship; although the availability of copyright may be a Lockean/Madisonian judgment that all such works are qualitatively worth something. Copyright protection is primarily a mechanism designed to correct a flaw or failure in the competitive economic market. As such, it carries no intrinsic predetermined dollar value for any work so protected. It may be, therefore, that "copyright seems to be an inefficient device for simply rewarding authors"[15] as Hurt and Schuchman suggest, but specific financial reward for an individual never has been shown to be the function of copyright. Copyright is directly pertinent to the market for works, and certainly pertinent to the rights of authors, but secondary to authors' specific income. Although copyright protection makes possible a certain monetary compensation for all those involved on the producer side of the economic market for works of authorship, remuneration occurs only to the extent of the revenue that can be obtained from the set of costs, prices, and quantities of sale that market conditions permit. As persons of uncommon taste or strongly-held belief can attest, market prices and revenues rarely reflect an individual's sense of basic priorities or fundamental values. The just rewards to the creators of intellectual works of lasting value that advance the state of civilization will not be through the market mechanism, however protected, by copyright or otherwise.

2.7 SUMMARY

This chapter has provided a background in the foundations of copyright, both ideological and economic. It has considered the question of who gains from copyright protection and the extent, if any, of value judgment in copyright.

The ideological basis for copyright has been shown to be closely related to the concept that each person has the right to control the products of his own creation. This natural right evolved into common law copyright in Great Britain; and the limitations of the protection inherent there was part of the rationale for the Copyright Clause in the Constitution.

Because of the rights of the creator or his assignees, a technical failure exists in the market for intellectual property. The technical failure, which is the ease of misappropriation through copying or plagiarism, is corrected through a public good, the Government protection of copyright. Note that if there were no inherent right in the copy, there could be no misappropriation, and consequently no implicit market failure. Thus, there would be no reason for Government intervention in the free market.

Copyright is of importance to the publisher as well as the author. This is particularly true in the case of scientific journals. However, the fact of copyright carries with it no comparative value judgment of works so protected. The economic worth of a work is determined in the marketplace where remuneration for the author and/or publisher may (or may not) be obtained. Copyright is not a financial subsidy for authors nor was it ever meant to be. It is a tool through which an author or his assignees may earn an income in the marketplace, if they so choose to use the tool in that manner.

3. SOME LANDMARKS OF TECHNOLOGY-CONDITIONED COPYRIGHT POLICYMAKING

3.1 EARLY HISTORICAL ACTIVITIES

The Constitution was declared in effect on March 4, 1789, having been ratified by the minimum nine States and two others by that time. The first U.S. Congress began regular sessions on April 6, 1789 and the Copyright Act of 1790 was adopted on May 31 of that year.[16] Maps, charts, and books were covered by the first Act. The very early adoption of a Copyright Act may be indicative of the general inclinations of the members of our first Federal government towards the pursuit of knowledge for its practical implications. A less practical, more esthetic class of work, prints, were protected in 1802, although Taubman states that the art of the engraver had been protected in England by 1735.[17] Musical compositions embodied as sheet music were added as a protected class in the general copyright revision of 1831. Photographs were added by the Act of 1865 and works of fine arts were enumerated in the second general copyright revision in 1870.

The adaption of the copyright laws to the technologies of the twentieth century (except for computer technology) is detailed in Appendix A, Chapter A.2 of this report. Much of the following part of this chapter is essentially a summary of that material. Special organization and additional information and interpretation have been added to clarify and elucidate certain concepts.

3.2 COPYRIGHT IN SOUND RECORDINGS

This technology is considered first because of the early consideration by the Supreme Court of a principle that was to have effect on thinking about copyright, even with respect to other technologies, until 1976.

The essential question at issue before the Supreme Court in the 1908 case of White-Smith Music Publishing Co. v. Apollo Co. was whether a perforated piano roll constituted a "copy" of sheet music. Now a piano roll, which is simply a cylinder of hard material with holes in it, is a sound recording, as that term is understood today. True, music is only heard when the piano roll is used together with a properly-instrumented piano, but the analogy with a phonograph record or magnetic tape is clear. Neither of those latter recording media contain sounds either; they contain grooves or altered magnetic domains. When a record or tape is used together with properly-instrumented equipment, the intended music is heard; and it cannot be heard from the recording without that equipment or other equipment performing the same function. In effect, the piano used with the piano roll is the playback equipment.

However, sound recordings were not a protected class in 1908 and the Supreme Court decided in White-Smith that the definition of a copy of a musical composition was "a written or printed record of it in intelligible notation." To the Supreme Court in 1908, a piano roll, or for that matter a phonograph record, was not a copy (because it was not humanly intelligible through the sense of sight) and therefore, in the Court's opinion, was not covered by the copyright statute.

Furthermore, the Court said, in keeping with its narrow construction of the word "copy", that issues of a new technology not specifically covered in the current statute "properly address themselves to the legislative and not to the judicial branch of the Government." However, it was clear from other Court statements that the Court was sympathetic to sound recording protection, despite its contrary ruling on the basis of its interpretation of the law as written.

At the time of the White-Smith ruling, Congress was working on the prospective Copyright Act of 1909, and one issue was whether copyright owners should have a new exclusive right to make recordings of their music. During hearings, Congress was told that one company had contracted with most of the major music publishers for exclusive licenses under the anticipated new law to record all the music controlled by those publishers for many years to come. The result was that Congress, in the 1909 Act, established a compulsory license for musical recording, requiring that once an owner of a musical copyright had permitted his work to be recorded by one company, any other company could record it similarly, upon payment of 2 cents for each reproduction of the composition manufactured. This step prevented the anticipated recording monopoly.

However, this did not mean, necessarily, that recordings of musical compositions were copyrightable. They were not, strictly speaking, even though no one could lawfully manufacture records of copyrighted music without paying the compulsory license fee. Nevertheless, Congress provided for the copyright owner of a dramatic work to have exclusive rights in "any transcription or record thereof" in the 1909 Act, and extended this right this right to nondramatic literary works in 1952. The question whether, under the Constitutional clause on copyright, a recorded performance could be considered the "writing" of an "author" and therefore eligible for copyright protection if Congress so chose to grant it, was apparently disposed of in the affirmative in the case of Capitol Records, Inc. v. Mercury Records Corp., heard by the 2nd Circuit Court in 1955. However, it was not until 1971 that Congress passed a law naming "sound recordings" as a category of copyrightable works, when it became evident that "record piracy" had become rampant and was growing. In the 1976 General Revision, Congress provided for copyright of works "fixed in any tangible medium of expression" and defined "sound recordings" as "works that result from the fixation of a series of musical, spoken, or other sounds, but not including the sounds accompanying a motion picture or other audiovisual work, regardless of the nature of the material objects such as disks, tapes, or other phonorecords in which they are embodied" (Section 101). Thus motion picture sound tracks are not covered as "sound recordings," although they are covered elsewhere. This is due to their judicial history and their closer connection with motion pictures as an industry.

3.2.1 Copyrighted Music in Sound Tracks

In 1946, the question arose whether a producer of motion pictures was entitled to a compulsory license for 2 cents per recording for use of a performance of copyrighted music in a sound track of a motion picture. Clearly, in 1909, when the compulsory license for music recordings became law, sound tracks in motion pictures were unknown. Consequently, this was a clear case for judicial interpretation. That the Court decided in the negative on purely economic grounds may be noted from the following quotes from the Court decision on this case, Jerome v. Twentieth Century - Fox Film Corp:

"Counsel assert that no more than 500 positive prints of a

film of a musical motion picture are made to supply the demands for exhibition purposes. If Section 1(e) /‾ the compulsory license provision of the 1909 Copyright Act‾/ applied to a motion picture use of a musical composition, then
and producer could appropriate a copyrighted musical composition for use in a motion picture for a total sum of
about $10.00, at the rate of 2¢ for each positive print...
The result would be destructive of valuable rights of composers and publishers, which the Act was intended to secure and protect."

In the 1976 Act, the view that the compulsory license provision did not
apply to sound tracks was stated explicitly. Owners of copyrights in music retained the exclusive rights to record on sound tracks and the compulsory license to record was confined to the making of "phonorecords"
which excludes sound tracks as a subset.

3.2.2 Educational and Library Reproduction of Phonorecords

In the 1976 General Revision of Copyright Law, sections 107 and 108 and
related pages of House Reports 94-1476 and 94-1733 concern the concepts
of fair use and permitted educational and library reproduction of works.
The content of this material is discussed in Section 3.6.2 below in the
context of photocopying because the problems addressed by that material
arose primarily from that cause. However, a review of the documents
shows that the solutions applied to photocopies also apply, in general,
to phonorecords.

3.3 COPYRIGHT IN MOTION PICTURES

With this technology, as with others, the Federal Courts struggled with
the question of whether new technology not specifically provided for by
Congress is protected by virtue of extension of concept or is not protected by virtue of strict literal interpretation.

The problem arose in 1903 in the question whether a sequence of photographs telling a story could be protected with the affixation of a single copyright notice or whether each photograph had to have its own
notice, as literally intended when Congress protected (individual)
photographs in 1870. This was the situation in Edison v. Lubin. In
that case, the District Court said:

"...if...the law is defective, it should be altered by Congress, not strained by the courts."

On the other hand, the Circuit Court of Appeals, in reversing the District Court, said:

"When Congress...saw fit...to extend copyright protection to
a photograph...it is not to be presumed it thought such art
could not progress, and that no protection was to be afforded
such progress. It must be recognized there would be change
and advance..."

In 1912, Congress amended the copyright statutes to include "motion-
picture photoplays" and "motion pictures other than photoplays" as protected classes of works. The 1909 revision had made no mention of these

concepts, although they were well-known at the time. After 1912, then, there was protection for motion pictures against unauthorized copying, but due to the specific language of the statute, it was clear that there was protection against unauthorized "public performances" (as distinguished from copying) <u>only</u> for dramatic and musical works. The question whether a motion picture photoplay was a dramatic work arose therefore through litigation.

Specifically, this question arose in <u>Tiffany Productions</u> v. <u>Dewing</u>, (1931), and in <u>M. G. M.</u> v. <u>Bijou Theatre</u>, (1933). The effect of both cases was to insure that a motion picture photoplay was legally defined as a type of dramatic work and that the protection of copyright was accorded to public performances or exhibitions of this type of motion picture.

In the <u>Tiffany Productions</u> case, the Court (holding that a motion picture photoplay was a form of a dramatic work) said that:

> "The statute must be given a sensible meaning in its application to modern invention, expressly within the scope of the statute."

In the <u>M. G. M.</u> case, the District Court, in a decision later countermanded, had said:

> "...the effect of a new invention in any given field seems to be a matter for legislative consideration, rather than for the extension of existing statutes by judicial construction."

3.3.1 Sound Tracks in Motion Pictures

"Talking motion pictures began to be produced about 1924, some 12 years after motion pictures were added to the copyright statutes as a protected class of work. Despite the lack of explicit copyright protection, the industry groups concerned tacitly accepted and operated on the premise that the sound track is protected as an integral part of the motion picture; and this premise appeared then and continues to appear to be logically valid since the pictures and sound together are necessary to constitute the complete work and to convey its artistic effect. This concept was given some judicial validity in the case of <u>L. C. Page & Co.</u> <u>v. Fox Film Corp.</u>, (1936); in which the Court stated that "as the plaintiff well says, 'talkies' are but a species of the genus motion pictures."

In 1971, in the House Report on the amendment to the copyright statute which extended protection to sound recordings excepting those sounds accompanying a motion picture, a statement on sound tracks was made. The House Report stated:

> "The exclusion /‾of sound tracks from the protection accorded sound recordings‾/ reflects the...opinion that sound tracks or audio tracks are an integral part of the "motion pictures" already accorded protection...and that the reproduction of the sound accompanying a motion picture is an infringement of copyright in the motion picture."

Finally in the 1976 General Revision, it was clearly stated that the definition of motion picture included accompanying sounds, and that the copyright in a motion picture included the right to perform it publicly by making its images visible or its sounds audible.

Thus, from 1924 until 1976, more by general unstated agreement than by actual law or judicial interpretation, sound tracks were accepted as an integral part of motion pictures.

3.4 RADIO AND TELEVISION BROADCASTING

In 1909, radio and television broadcasting were unknown and a public performance was thought of as a performance given in the presence of a group of persons assembled within sight or hearing of the performers. When the use of the copyrighted music and plays in radio broadcasts became common in the early 1920's, the question arose whether broadcasts of copyrighted works were public performances within the scope of the 1909 Statute.

This question was considered in the case of Jerome H. Remick & Co. v. American Automobile Accessories Co. in 1925 with respect to a radio broadcast of a musical work. The court held that the broadcast did constitute a public performance, stating:

"While the fact that the radio was not developed at the time the Copyright Act...was enacted may raise some question as to whether it comes within the purview of the statute, it is not by that fact alone excluded....The statute may be applied to new situations not anticipated by Congress, if, fairly construed, such situations come within its intent and meaning.... While statutes should not be stretched to apply to new situations not fairly within their scope, they should not be so narrowly construed as to permit their evasion because of changing habits due to new inventions and discoveries....The artist / in a radio broadcast / is consciously addressing a great, though unseen and widely scattered audience, and is therefore participating in a public performance."

The ruling in this case was generally accepted in practice by broadcasters and other concerned parties. In addition, the ruling in this case determined that the public performance was "for profit" if the broadcast was over a commercial station that was used as a medium for advertising, regardless of the fact that the broadcast listeners did not pay an admission fee.

A similar result ensued in the case of Leo Feist, Inc. v. Lew Tendler Tavern in 1958, which extended the public performance concept from broadcasting to wire transmissions. In this case, music transmitted over wire from a central location to a restaurant and then made audible there for the benefit of restaurant patrons was found to be a public performance for profit.

The 1976 Act codified these results by assigning the copyright owner the exclusive right (with certain exemptions) of public performance and display; and by including in the definition of public performance and display transmission or communication to the public "by means of any device or process, whether the members of the public capable of receiving the performance or display receive it in the same place or in separate places and at the same time or at different times" (Section 101).

3.4.1 Retransmissions of Broadcasts

A question that was to have very important ramifications 35 years later for cable television retransmissions was raised in the case of Buck v. Jewell-La Salle Realty Co. in 1931 before the U.S. Supreme Court. In that case, a hotel maintained a master radio set which was wired to loud speakers from which the radio programs could be heard in all of the public and private rooms of the hotel. The Court held that the hotel's reproduction of the broadcast performance, through its receiving set and loudspeakers, for the entertainment of its guests, was itself a public performance under the 1909 Statute and therefore not exempt from the implications of the Statute for royalty payment. The opinion in this case by Justice Brandeis for the Court is quoted from extensively in Section A.2.4.2 of Appendix A of this report and is a prime example of reasoning by analogy in determining the law with respect to new technological devices not previously considered by Congress.

Another similar case which confirmed the copyright owners' rights to retransmissions in a hotel situation was SESAC v. New York Hotel Statler Co. decided in 1937.

3.5 COPYRIGHT IN CABLE TELEVISION RETRANSMISSIONS

By the middle of the 1960s, commercial enterprises had sprung up whose functions were to provide TV viewers with programs that the viewers were unable to receive satisfactorily with standard antennae. This industry, because it serviced subscribers via cable, a non-broadcast mode, became known as CATV, community antenna television, or cable television. The industry obtained much of its program material from broadcasted TV which it acquired with more sensitive receiving equipment and more sophisticated or better situated antennae than its subscribers were capable of providing for themselves individually.

In the opinion of copyright owners, significant copyright problems existed. The primary over-the-air boardcasters obtained licenses from copyright owners for the motion pictures, plays, music, and other works that they broadcast. Was the retransmission of the broadcasted programs by the cable system to its subscribers to be treated as a further public performance of the copyrighted works which infringed the copyright owners exclusive rights?

This question came before the courts in 1966 through 1968 in the case of United Artists Television, Inc. v. Fortnightly Corp. The District and Circuit Courts held for the copyright owners, relying on the previous decisions described above, i.e. Remick, Jewell-LaSalle, and SESAC, that the retransmission, as a public performance for profit, was covered by the Copyright Act then in force. It is not surprising, in light of previous decisions quoted, that the District Court in this case spoke about "accomodating the statute to the realities of modern science and technology."

However, to the surprise of many, the Supreme Court reversed the lower court findings by essentially determining that cable television program providers were acting as viewers' agents rather than as secondary producers. The Court reasoned that:

"...while both broadcasters and viewers play crucial roles in the total television process, a line is drawn between them. One is treated as active performer; the other as passive beneficiary.

"When CATV is considered in this framework, we conclude that it falls on the viewer's side of the line...."

The Court carried forward this precedent-breaking decision and similarly found no infringement in the 1974 case of CBS v. Teleprompter. The issue in the latter case was a possible distinction between the retransmission over cable of local signals that could have been received over the air by cable subscribers and the retransmission of far distant signals not originally intended for the cabled locale. The Supreme Court found no distinction and determined that there was no infringement in either case.

The more complete discussion of Section A.2.6 of Appendix A provides some rationales for these Supreme Court decisions. As noted there, a major element in the decisionmaking appeared to be a desire to prevent the CATV industry from being retroactively liable for royalties and infringement damages. The majority opinion in the Fortnightly decision had said in a footnote, that a decision consistent with Jewell-La Salle would be such "as retroactively to impose copyright liability where it has never been acknowledged to exist before." Here the Court is implying that a judicial decision for the copyright owners (unlike a legislated decision) could not cause royalties to flow from that time on, but would be forced to require that the CATV industry be responsible for all past royalties it should have paid. These back royalties might be large enough to destroy many of these small operations.

The fact that Congress was considering major revisions to the Copyright Act during the times of the Fortnightly and Teleprompter litigations cannot be ignored as a factor in the Supreme Court's decisionmaking. As noted in Section A.2.6, both the majority and dissenting opinions in Fortnightly, as well as in the lower court decisions, in both Fortnightly and Teleprompter, took cognizance of the on-going considerations by Congress of the copyright problem of cable retransmissions in the context of the general revision of copyright law. Justice Fortas, in his dissent in Fortnightly had commented:

"Our major object, I suggest, should be to do as little damage as possible to traditional copyright principles and to business relationships, until the Congress legislates and relieves the embarrassment which we and the interested parties face."

Similarly, the Circuit Court of Appeals noted in Teleprompter:

"The complex problems represented by the issues in this case are not readily amenable to judicial resolution....We hope that the Congress will in due course legislate a fuller and more flexible accomodation of competing copyright, anti-trust, and communications policy considerations, consistent with the challenge of modern CATV technology."

Thus the judiciary in general, saw the issues as more complex than a simple extension of principle as embodied in Buck v. Jewell-La Salle. The interaction of basic communications policy in the public interest and the economic interests of the concerned parties demanded a legislative solution. Ultimately, the approximately ten years of negotiation among the various concerned parties resulted in the provisions of Section 111 of the 1976 General Revision of Copyright Law.

This 1976 General Revision makes cable retransmissions subject to the restrictions of copyright, thereby validating at least the principle of the dissent in Teleprompter which was based on the precedent of Buck v. Jewell-La Salle. However, a cable company now may obtain a compulsory license for retransmission of programs from those stations whose signals the system is authorized to carry by the Federal Communications Commission, and it is not liable for any royalties before the effective date of the new Act.

3.6 COPYRIGHT IN PHOTOCOPIES

The issue of photocopying as a serious concern to copyright proprietors of printed matter dates from the 1930s. During that period, microphotography came to be extensively used, because it was a process that enabled printed matter to be reproduced at a reasonable cost.

In the 1930s, discussions took place between the predecessor to the Association of American Publishers and organizations of scholarly users such as the American Council of Learned Societies and the Social Science Research Council in order to define the boundaries of acceptable non-infringing photocopying. These discussions resulted in the "Gentlemen's Agreement" of 1935 which, although not binding, provided guidelines that were followed by many libraries and which stood as a basis governing library photocopying for a generation.

The significant paragraphs of the Gentlemen's Agreement are as follows:

"A library, archives, office, museum, or similar institution owning books or periodical volumes in which copyright still subsists may make and deliver a single photographic reproduction or reduction of a part thereof to a scholar representing in writing that he desires such reproduction in lieu of loan of such publication or in place of manual transcription and solely for the purpose of research; provided

(1) that the person receiving it is given due notice in writing that he is not exempt from liability to the copyright proprietor for any infringement of copyright by misuse of the reproduction constituting an infringement under the copyright law;

(2) that such reproduction is made and furnished without profit to itself by the institution making it."

This was an important effort on the part of opposing interest groups to solve a national copyright problem among themselves without recourse to Government instrumentalities.

From the 1960s onward, the photocopying problem became progressively more acute as new photocopying technologies and improved mechanical paper-handling systems combined to reduce significantly the cost per copy and to increase significantly the speed of multi-copying. Publishers, especially of scientific and technical journals and of educational

texts, expressed fears that loss of sales due to photocopying might force
them to discontinue certain publications. However, the several opposing
interests groups agreed that in the revision bills Congress considered
in the late 1960s, the doctrine of fair use would be incorporated rather
than any specific rules for photocopying. The groups hoped to work out
the details of an agreement among themselves using the fair use doctrine
as a basis. This doctrine, as it had been developed by the courts, was
contained in Section 107 of the copyright bill passed by the House of
Representatives in 1966 but never enacted into law. Section 107 of the
1966 bill included the following:

> "...the fair use of a copyrighted work such as criticism,
> comment, news reporting, teaching, scholarship or research,
> is not an infringement of copyright. In determining whether
> the use made of a work in any particular case is a fair use,
> the factors to be considered shall include--
>
> (1) the purpose and character of the use;
> (2) the nature of the copyrighted work;
> (3) the amount and substantiality of the portion used in
>   relation to the copyrighted work as a whole; and
> (4) the effect of the use upon the potential market for or
>   value of the copyrighted work."

However, final agreement between librarians and publishers was not able
to be worked out at that time. It foundered on the essential question
of the specific boundary between fair use and infringement, and the
quantity and purposes of copying which crossed the boundary.

3.6.1 Williams & Wilkins v. United States

In 1971, a suit was instituted in the U.S. Court of Claims in which the
plaintiff, a publisher of medical journals and books, charged that two
Government libraries, The National Institutes of Health library and the
National Library of Medicine, had infringed the copyright in several of
its medical journals. The plaintiff claimed that the copying done by
those institutions in supplying journal articles to other medical libraries, research institutes, individual researchers, and practitioners
exceeded fair use.

This case was Williams & Wilkins Co. v. United States. The initial
opinion of the Commissioner hearing the case (1972) held that photocopying practices of the two Government libraries exceeded fair use.
The full Court (1973) reversed this decision, 4 to 3, basing its majority opinion on essentially three criteria:

> "First, plaintiff has not in our view shown, and there is in-
> adequate reason to believe that it is being or will be harmed
> substantially by these specific practices of NIH and NLM;
>
> "second, we are convinced that medicine and medical research
> will be injured by holding these particular practices to be an
> infringement; and
>
> "third, since the problem of accomodating the interests of
> science with those of the publishers (and authors) calls
> fundamentally for legislative solution or guidance, which

has not yet been given, we should not, during the period before congressional action is forthcoming, place such a risk
of harm upon science and medicine."[18]

The three dissenting judges of the Court of Claims noted, in opposition:

"What we have before us is a case of wholesale copying, and
distribution of copyrighted material by defendant's libraries
on a scale so vast that it dwarfs the output of many small
publishing companies...This is the very essence of wholesale
copying and, without more, defeats the defense of fair use."

Thus, the two sides differed materially on the interpretation of the
facts. The situation is reminiscent of the cable TV cases, Fortnightly
and Teleprompter, where Court majorities were of the opinion that the
situation demanded a legislative answer that was more flexible, involving components of right from both sides, rather than the limited yes-no
answer of a judicial decision. As in those cases, the Court refrains
here from providing the decision that would tend more to permanently
end the controversy and would tend to end it with a greater detriment to
one side than the Court feels that the losing side deserves. This interpretation may be supported with this quote from the majority opinion in
Williams & Wilkins:

"The Courts are now precluded, both by the Act and by the nature of the judicial process, from contriving pragmatic or
compromise solutions which would reflect the legislature's
choice of policy and its mediation among the competing interests...Hopefully, the result in the present case will be but
a 'holding operation' in the interim period before Congress
enacts its preferred solutions."

The Williams & Wilkins case was accepted for review by the Supreme Court,
where, after the arguments were heard, the Court split 4 to 4 without an
exposition of the reasoning on the two sides. This had the effect of
affirming the decision of the full Court of Claims.

3.6.2 The 1976 General Revision

Certain provisions included in the 1976 General Revision of Copyright
Law were the result of hard bargaining among authors, publishers, educators, and librarians. Section 107 of the 1976 Act contains the fair
use concept essentially as reproduced above (in Section 3.6) except for
the addition of two phrases as concessions to educators. A purpose of
use for which fair use is allowable is now teaching "(including multiple
copies for classroom use)." In addition, a factor to be considered in
determining whether a particular use is a fair use is "whether such use
is of a commercial nature or is for nonprofit educational purposes."
The House of Representatives report on the proposed 1976 Act (Report No.
94-1476 at pages 67-71) includes the texts of agreements between educators on one side and authors and publishers on the other establishing
standards of fair use for educational purposes. These agreements were
reached at the urging of the Congressional committees, after a series of
meetings between the opposing parties.

The problem of library photocopying for scholars and researchers is
dealt with in Section 108 of the 1976 Act. The language of Section 108

makes it clear that library rights do not extend to "the related or concerted reproductions...of multiple copies...of the same material," or
"the systematic reproduction...of single or multiple copies." In addition, the Conference Report on the proposed 1976 General Revision (House
Report No. 94-1733 at pages 71-73) contains a set of guidelines agreed
to by the opposing parties that define the extent of loans permitted in
interlibrary arrangements. These guidelines were developed with the
assistance of the National Commission on New Technological Uses of
Copyrighted Works (see Section 3.8, below).

3.6.3 Current Situation

Despite the successful negotiations that resulted in the provisions of
the 1976 General Revision, the photocopying problem is not fully solved.
There does not exist at this time any fully-established clearinghouse
or other mechanism for payment of royalties for photocopying beyond the
guidelines established, nor is it clear that the current guidelines can
be enforced. At present, an effort is underway through the auspices of
the Association of American Publishers to establish a clearinghouse
system.[19]

3.7 COPYRIGHT IN MICROMEDIA AND VIDEOTAPE

The decision to accept for copyright registration a work on a micromedi-
um that would otherwise be copyrightable if intelligible to the unaided
eye was made independently by the Copyright Office through its regulations. It was believed by that office that the 1908 Supreme Court decision in the White-Smith case, which had never been overturned, would
not prevent the registration of a work on micromedia since that Court
ruling concerned a piano roll which was not intended to be made visually
intelligible in its normal use. Since a work on any type of micromedia
was intended to be made visually intelligible (with the aid of devices)
when communicating information to people, the Copyright Office did not
believe that the White-Smith ruling took precedence. The same reasoning
was applied in the later acceptance for copyright of works on videotape.

These regulations of the Copyright Office were generally accepted and
not challenged in the Courts. The 1976 General Revision of Copyright
Law removed any lingering doubts about these regulations by making copyrightability independent of the medium in which a work is fixed.

3.8 THE ESTABLISHMENT OF CONTU

Significant recognition of the need for the National Commission on New
Technological Uses of Copyrighted Works (CONTU) dates from 1967. It
became clear at that time that the lack of adequate study of the problem
of the impact of computers and information storage and retrieval systems
on copyright would conflict with efforts to enact a general revision of
copyright law.

The question of how the law would view computer uses of copyrightable
works during the time that CONTU was deliberating and before Congress
acted on CONTU's recommendations prevented quick agreement on the formation of CONTU and delayed its establishment. Ultimately, agreement
was achieved among opposing interest groups on inserting a section in
the proposed general revision of copyright law that provided that the
law on the use of copyrighted works in computer systems was to be unaffected by enactment of the general revision. This paved the way for

establishment of CONTU on Dec. 31, 1974 as P.L. 93-573.[20]

In addition, the "hold constant" section, Section 117, was enacted as a part of the 1976 General Revision of Copyright Law, P.L 94-553 on Oct. 19, 1976. The new Act takes effect on January 1, 1978. Section 117 states that:

> "...this title does not afford to the owner of copyright in a work any greater or lesser rights with respect to the use of the work in conjunction with automatic systems capable of storing, processing, retrieving, or transferring information... than those afforded to works under the law...in effect on December 31, 1977..."

The function of CONTU (according to P.L. 93-573, Section 201) is to study and make recommendations to Congress on legislation or procedures concerning:

> "(1) the reproduction and use of copyrighted works of author-
> ship--
> (A) in conjunction with automatic systems capable of storing, processing, retrieving, and transferring in-
> formation, and
> (B) by various forms of machine reproduction, not in-
> cluding reproduction by or at the request or instructors for use in face-to-face teaching activities; and
> (2) the creation of new works by the application or inter-
> vention of such automatic systems of machine reproduc-
> tion."

It may be noted also that CONTU is to be concerned with:

> "Changes in copyright law or procedures that may be necessary to assure...access to copyrighted works, and to provide recog-
> nition of the rights of copyright owners" (Section 201 (c)).

In the above, the balancing of the needs of users and producers may be seen. Similarly, the balancing of several interest groups may be noted in the establishment of the requirements for memberships on the Commission (Section 202 (a)):

> "The Commission shall be composed of thirteen voting members, appointed as follows:
>
> (1) Four members, to be appointed by the President, selected from authors and other copyright owners;
> (2) Four members, to be appointed by the President, selected from users of copyright works;
> (3) Four nongovernmental members to be appointed by the President, selected from the public generally, with at least one member selected from among experts in consumer protection affairs;
> (4) The Librarian of Congress."

CONTU must present its final report to Congress by July, 1978, if the extension of time it has requested is enacted by Congress. Otherwise its final report is due in December, 1977.

3.9 SUMMARY

This chapter has examined policymaking about copyright through a review of some important litigations and some aspects of enacted law and regulation which have concerned the impact of technological change. The review appears to show that some significant litigations in this field have concerned the boundaries of property rights left ambiguous because of the occurrence of technological change unforseen by Congress in previous revisions of law or the occurrence of specific situations not definable in legislation.

In general, the Federal Courts have approached the question of ambiguities due to technological change from two distinct points of view. The first viewpoint is that, if the general concept of current law can be easily extended to new situations without stretching the law's meaning too far, it should be done. The second viewpoint is that stretching the law's meaning (or specifically defining the ambiguous) beyond a certain point would be to take on a responsibility better left to Congress, particularly if a judicial decision would be precedent setting, involving relations between interest groups, not just the particular litigants.

The first viewpoint may be seen in the final decisions of the cases described involving broadcasting, motion pictures, and sound recordings except for White-Smith. The second viewpoint was taken in the prevailing decisions in White-Smith, the cable TV cases Fortnightly and Teleprompter, and in Williams & Wilkins.

Significantly, during all the cases above involving the second viewpoint, Congress was in the process of actively revising the copyright statute. Such statutory revision often involves representation of many opposing interest groups and the ultimate statutory language may involve interest group compromise setting forth obligations and responsibilities and establishing new institutions in a manner completely impossible to accomplish through a judicial decision. In fact, in the 1976 General Revision, the new statutory language and associated legislative documentations involving cable TV and educational and library copying are examples of such a complex balancing of interests.

Furthermore, in the more recent situation described above, a new balancing of interests may be seen which is not apparent in the earlier cases. If persons concerned with copyrighted works may be considered either producers or users, the earlier cases described are all essentially conflicts between original producers and secondary producers. (The enactment of the compulsory license for phonorecord manufacturing in 1909 could be viewed as expression of user concern, however).

In the Fortnightly decision (1968), the view was taken that the cable TV company was the viewer's (i.e. user's) agent. In photocopying, the conflict between authors and publishers on one side and librarians and educators on the other is essentially a user-producer conflict (although some educators are also producers). This increasing concern with the user in the copyright field has been carried forward in the establishment of CONTU where both representatives of users and producers and "at least one member selected from among experts in consumer protection affairs" are included in the membership of the Commission by statutory requirement.

Finally, it seems clear from the above that, in this field, administrative regulation plays a relatively small role in contrast with some other Federal domestic responsibilities. Nevertheless, the Copyright Office has played a role in technological change by agreeing to accept for copyright registration, works in micromedia and videotape by its interpretation of existing law rather than through explicit congressional action or judicial orders. However, see Section 5.5.1 and 5.5.2 for an important policy-impacting function of the Register of Copyrights.

4.   TOWARDS AN EFFICIENT MARKETPLACE FOR COPYRIGHTED WORKS

The previous chapter considered the legal framework for copyright. This chapter is concerned with economic questions relevant to the market for copyrighted works. Clearly, an effective legal structure and an efficient marketplace for copyrighted works are both necessary and mutually supportive.

In this chapter, the fundamental question of transaction costs is considered. The question of exclusion and enforcement is discussed in light of the ease of modern technology to permit easily available and low-cost duplication of works. Mechanisms for the minimization of transaction costs are described including types of efficient pricing schedules. In addition, fair use is considered from an economic viewpoint. Lastly, the question of monopoly is discussed and government remedies are described.

4.1 THE PROBLEM OF TRANSACTION COSTS

The view of Professor Kenneth Arrow is that transaction costs are more fundamental than market failure as a basic problem pertinent to the choice of whether a particular good should be provided through the market mechanism or through some form of collective action. He states that:

> "...transaction costs....are attached to any market and indeed to any mode of resource allocation. Market failure is the particular case where transaction costs are so high that the existence of a market is no longer worthwhile."[21]

Two major sources of transaction costs, according to Arrow, are:

> "(1) exclusion costs /̲ and ̲/ (2) costs of communication and information, including both the supplying and the learning of the terms on which transactions are carried out."[22]

Steiner sees transaction costs specifically involved when there is an

> "inability of the market to translate potential willingness to pay into revenues /̲ and ̲/ where the private market is technically able to collect revenues, but at a high cost."[23]

Hurt and Schuchman are, to a large extent, considering transaction costs when they ask:

> "If there is a benefit from the copyright system, is it offset, at least in part, by various administrative costs and frictions inherent in the system?"[24]

Specifically, transaction costs play a large role in copyright problems, and overcoming high transaction costs plays a large role in the solution of copyright problems.

4.2 THE QUESTION OF ENFORCEMENT

There are situations involving copyright that concern the fundamental issue of what Arrow referred to as "exclusion." At the present time, some of these situations are occurring because of the availability of the technologies of high-speed photocopying and of copying digitized information by computer.

Persons with easy access to machines employing these technologies can become low-cost publishers, legalities aside. Thus, these persons are not easily "excluded" from ownership of copies upon their failure to pay a royalty. The question of enforcement then arises, and the cost of enforcement must become an issue. Concern with efficient allocation of resources as well as the deleterious effects of easy evasion of law must prompt the question of whether there is any value in issuing copyrights that cannot be enforced with any reasonable allocation of effort.

Hurt and Schuchman have theorized about strategies an original book publisher might employ in the absence of any copyright at all.[25] According to one scenario, the original publisher must produce enough books in his first edition to saturate the market. If a copying publisher enters the market (probably with a similar number of copies), the first publisher must be prepared to compete by lowering his prices. Many unsold books can be expected in this situation. A second strategy is for the first publisher to be prepared with an extremely low-cost edition as a retaliatory measure.

Similarly, in a 1970 article in the Harvard Law Review opposing copyright protection for computer programs at that time, Professor Stephen Breyer proposed a strategy that could be employed by program developers in the absence of such protection.[26]

> "One may wonder, for example, whether, without protection, smaller hardware or software firms would not find it easier to use parts of IBM programs in their efforts to compete with IBM,"

Professor Breyer wrote.[27]

Although Professor Breyer did not extend his scenario, it is possible to theorize about protective behaviors available to the originators of computer programs to protect themselves in such a hypothetical situation. One such strategy could be for an originator to produce programs for sale in object code only, with minimum documentation, thereby making it very difficult for a potential copier to know exactly what he had in hand. In fact a proposal for "sealed-in software" that might be protectable by either trade secret or copyright has been made recently by Calvin Mooers.[28]

4.2.1 Transaction Costs Even If No Copyright

A conclusion that can be drawn from both these examples is that there are transaction costs regardless of whether the imperfect protection of law exists or does not exist. To repeat from Arrow, "transaction costs ....are attached to any market and indeed to any mode of resource allocation." In the Hurt and Schuchman example, among the transaction costs that might be expected are the extra books left over, the poor quality of merchandise required to prevent financial losses, the extra secrecy required to prevent future plans and the first copies from being prematurely revealed, and the extra efforts that would be needed in merchandizing strategems to thwart a competitor's sales outlet possibilities. In the Breyer example, assuming the protective strategy of object code dissemination only with minimal documentation, among the transaction costs to be expected are the reduction in information dissemination about program content to everyone including disinterested observers who might benefit in another context, the reduction in ability to recognize mistakes in programs and to correct them, and the lowering of incentives to produce new programs that are genuinely novel or original.

Thus, in both examples which assume no Government copyright protection, we have postulated that cut-throat competition, losses in information flow and increases in secrecy would result. In a society in which the market protection of copyright is available, Government regulation has its cost and some infringement from imperfect exclusion can be expected to result, but we suggest that in addition, a more open society with greater opportunities for creativity exists. Thus, the choice is not just between the size of transaction costs inherent in the alternatives, but in the kinds of costs and their effects which a society is willing to tolerate.

4.2.2 The Optimal Level of Enforcement and Its Consequences

Hopefully, a society will select that set of resource allocation mechanisms that maximizes its satisfactions. However, a difficult state of affairs for a society to accept is that it cannot achieve the complete maximization of its satisfactions with any set of mechanisms because of the limited resources it can apply. A reasonable strategy is to achieve an optimum level of satisfaction from resources available, permitting a certain amount of dissatisfaction to remain. Professor Edwin Mansfield has demonstrated that there is an optimum level of crime whose cost ought to be tolerated, based on the finite resources of enforcement which a society is willing to allocate.[29] This concept can be easily adapted to copyright infringement.

As shown in Fig. 1, the probability of apprehension and conviction of infringers increases with increasing expenditure of resources devoted to enforcement; but the costs to society of infringements increase as fewer resources are devoted to enforcement and the probability of conviction goes down. A minimum total cost results from the sum of infringement and enforcement costs, at a particular probability less than 1.0 of apprehension and conviction. This leaves some infringers unapprehended or unconvicted.

If a society is unhappy with this level of infringement, it can raise the resources allocated to enforcement. However, it might take unrealistically large resources to guarantee conviction of all infringers. On the other hand, abolishment of enforcement on the grounds of its ineffectiveness and the consequent large increase in what was formerly called crime might create new, unanticipated kinds of dissatisfactions which society is unprepared to accept.

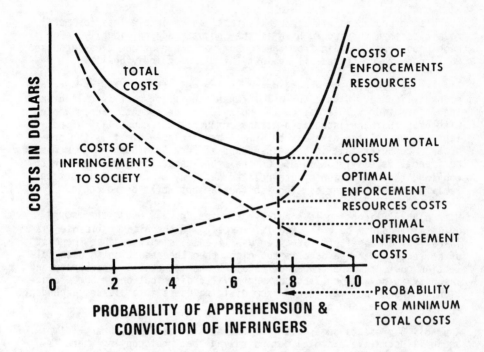

Figure 1. The "Optimal" Level of Copyright Enforcement

4.3 THE DESIGN OF ROYALTY COLLECTION SYSTEMS

Under the assumption that the benefits to a society of providing copyright protection and enforcement outweigh the costs, a question that arises is how the market for intellectual property should be structured to minimize transaction costs and to promote efficient pricing. The transaction costs considered here are Arrow's "costs of communication and information." A situation requiring special consideration for reduction of transaction costs is that which exists when there are a large number of users and a large number of producers. In this case, one of a number of different licensing schemes may be most effective.

4.3.1 A Comparison of Types of Licenses

Clearinghouse licensing and direct licensing are examples of licensing types that may be employed. With either of these situations, there is the possibility of a blanket license or a per-use license.

A clearinghouse is simply a multi-producer organization established for royalty collection. The advantage of a clearinghouse over direct licensing is that the user has a single point of negotiation, a single place to send royalty payments; and there is likely to be a reduction in the number of payments having to be made. The producer similarly has a reduction in transaction costs because he obtains his royalties from one place and with one payment. On the other hand, with a clearinghouse, there may be a blurring of individual producer considerations. The necessity of simple, all-encompassing contractual provisions may cause some producers with special situations to obtain less (or more) royalties than they would have if they negotiated individually. For each producer, the gain from the economy of scale of the clearinghouse would need to be traded-off against this loss of individuality.

Similar problems must be considered in the selection of the per-use or blanket license. With a per-use license, the major cost is collecting the information. This may be technologically dependent. For example, with uses that are associated with a computer, the capability of collecting use-related data may be high, particularly if it is the producer's computer that is being used and if "use," as opposed to memory-residence, is easily defined. On the other hand, for mechanical photocopying, the collection of use-related data may be difficult, particularly data which might distinguish the various works being copied.

With blanket licensing (a single yearly fee for all use), the amount of data needed to be collected is reduced. If the blanket license is in reality a substitute for a per-use license, simply because the cost of collecting per-use data is too high, then the reduction in data collection costs must be traded-off against the increase in inaccuracy and inequity in royalty collections and royalty distributions. Some reduction in inaccuracy may result from dividing users into classes dependent on expected use; and by sampling uses.

Appendix B presents some data from the British Lending Library (simply as an illustrative example) demonstrating that photocopying there is heavily skewed in terms of the frequency of photocopying from various journal titles. A survey indicates that of approximately 15,000 serial titles held by the British Lending Library, the top 200 titles accounted for 20% of the photocopying demand and the 6000 least-requested titles accounted for the last 10% of the demand. U.S. data will likely show a similar skewness.

As noted in Appendix B, this skewness can lead either to lower or higher payments to individual copyright proprietors, depending on the payment algorithm employed. In addition, for those journal titles little used, a larger amount of sampling conceivably coupled with more sophisticated sampling methods might be needed to accurately determine the true extent of photocopying.

At a time a new licensing scheme is to be established, producers may find it important to consider these various trade-offs so that the mechanism with the lowest transaction costs can be adopted. From the user's viewpoint, transaction costs include the value of time and effort as well as the dollar amount of royalties. That mechanism that is easiest to use, i.e. least costly in time and effort, all other things being equal, will probably generate the least amount of deliberate evasions and therefore the lowest enforcement costs as well.

4.3.2 Examples of Existing Clearinghouses

The Harry Fox Office is the mechanism through which many of the music publishers have issued licenses for the recording of individual compositions on phonorecords. (See Appendix A, Section A.4.6.3). Despite the availability, since the passage of the 1909 Act, of a compulsory license with the Copyright Office serving as a repository of ownership information[30], licensees may find that better terms are available from the Harry Fox Office in return for greater assurance of precise information about numbers of records manufactured and delivered. Royalties owed are computed from this information.

Three clearinghouses now exist for the collecting royalty payments for public performances of musical works. These are the American Society of Composers, Authors and Publishers, Inc. (ASCAP), Broadcast Music, Inc. (BMI) and SESAC, Inc. The combined membership of ASCAP, BMI and SESAC comprise the copyright owners of virtually all music copyrighted in the United States. Licensees are required to pay only a lump-sum royalty annually in a predetermined amount (a blanket license). However, many broadcasters maintain logs as a matter of standard practice, and these are made available to the clearinghouses if required. These logs, plus a limited amount of sampling of performances, provide sufficient information for proportioned distribution among the individual copyright owners of the fees collected. The distribution is made approximately according to the estimated number of performances of each work. The cost of operating ASCAP is said to run about 19% to 20% of its gross revenues.

4.4 ROYALTY PRICING SCHEMES

This section considers pricing rules that can be employed to differentiate different classes of users and to cover different types of costs. It is assumed that all users in a particular class are treated identically, and that the purpose of the pricing rules is not for anticompetitive reasons, but to efficiently maximize income.

4.4.1 Individual and Institutional Users

A theory which justifies price differentials between individual and institutional users is described in Appendices C1 and C2 of this report. Here, an institutional user is one that serves to further distribute the work among individuals served by the institution. It is noted in Appendix C1 that, for a product distributed to classified users who do not move from class to class, an existing theory states that the prices among the classes should be inversely proportional to those classes' respective price elasticities, provided that marginal costs are the same for each class. However, in the provision of certain copyrightable works, e.g. scientific journals, users may obtain their copies either as the result of individual subscription or through use of an institutional copy. Thus, there are "cross-market" effects as users move between the classes. In this case, the work of Appendix C2 employs a variable called "the average number of potential subscribers" which measures the number of additional individual uses that would result from discontinued institutional use due to increased prices to the latter class. The value of this variable determines the price differential that should be offered. Tests that producers can make about the potential market can determine the value of this variable.

A second issue raised in these Appendices is whether the users of the institutionally-obtained work should pay per-use fees to the institution to defray the cost of the institutional subscription. In general, to the extent that the individual uses via the institutional subscription are private appropriations, these uses should be paid for by the users unless there are valid countermanding reasons. One such reason might be that it is in the public interest (or in the interest of the

institution's owner) to encourage such individual use; and a second reason might be that the costs of collection are high relative to the
revenue gained.

4.4.2 Services With High Fixed Costs

A pricing system often used for the provision of services that have a
high fixed-cost element is the combination entry fee and per-use charge.
Utilities often have connection charges as well as per-use charges.
Some computerized, on-line, bibliographic or full-text search services
are now using this type of pricing. Typically, there is a monthly or
yearly use fee or entry charge, a time-on-line charge, and a "hit"
charge for retrieval.

It is possible, also, to offer a user a choice between two charge plans.
For example, a user might be offered either (a) a higher connect (entry)
charge and a very low per-use charge or (b) a very low entry charge and
a higher per-use charge. Depending on the break point, the high volume
user will probably select (a), the plan with the low per-use charge,
whereas the casual user probably will select (b), the plan with the low
entry charge. The offering of two such plans may prevent either type
of user, casual or high volume, from subsidizing the other type.

4.5 FAIR USE AS AN ECONOMIC CONCEPT

"Fair use" was originally a judicially-developed concept that can be
conceived as a method of reducing certain kinds of transaction costs.
It is now embodied in Section 107 of the 1976 General Revision of Copyright Law, as described in Section 3.6 above. The "fair use" concept
historically recognized and attempted to allow for two basic principles
that can be counterposed to the principle of copyright in a potential
infringement situation. A third principle of "fair use" was added in
the 1976 General Revision.

The first principle is that of the freedom of communication of ideas,
derived from First Amendment considerations. (Professor Melville Nimmer
has delineated the balance point in this potential conflict.[31]) Where
First Amendment principles have dominance, there can be no exclusion.
Thus, under "fair use", purposes of use such as "criticism, comment,
news reporting, teaching..scholarship or research" are permitted, subject to limiting factors such as the amount of the work used. "Fair
use" may be viewed as a method of reducing the cost inherent in a conflict between Article 1, Section 8 of the Constitution and the First
Amendment.

The second principle allowed for under "fair use" is lack of marketplace impact. In the consideration of whether a particular use is a
"fair use," a factor to be taken into account is "the effect of the use
upon the potential market or value of the copyrighted work." Thus, it
is recognized to be uneconomical and therefore inappropriate for resources to be expended in contractual efforts to obtain permission for
usage of little or no market impact.

The third principle now added to "fair use" is indicated by the phrases
in Section 107 of the 1976 General Revision relating to education.
These phrases, concerning allowable purposes of fair use, are "(....
multiple copies for classroom use)" and "for nonprofit educational pur-

poses."

The exemption of royalty payments for worthy uses has been criticized by economists on principles of economic efficiency. The argument is that if a use is genuinely worthy, it is a public good whose cost ought to be spread over all the population and paid for through taxes. Otherwise, allowing an exemption for some uses and not for others has the effect of imposing the costs of worthy use exemptions on the "less-worthy users" as a specific class. This argument was similarly expressed by Professor Paul Goldstein in a criticism of the full Court of Claims decision in the Williams & Wilkins case[32]. In that case, the worthy use of medical research was given as a reason for rejecting the plaintiff's claim of infringement in a wholesale copying situation.

4.6 PRICE SETTING FOR COMPULSORY LICENSES

Compulsory licenses have been established in statute by Congress for certain categories of intellectual property; and in one case, a compulsory license is being enforced by Court order. In general, royalty prices in these situations have been (or will be) established by adversary proceedings involving producers and users and their supporters testifying before some institutional group empowered to set the figures.

4.6.1 The Phonorecord Manufacturing License, 1976 Act

An example of the procedure is the establishment of the compulsory license royalty fee for phonorecord manufacturing as a statutory matter in the 1976 General Revision. A summary of the testimony on this subject and the conclusion of the Senate Committee on the Judiciary is given on pages 91 through 94 of Senate Report No. 94-473.

Among the subjects of the testimony were (1) the need for an increase in the fee by copyright holders, (2) the potential impact of an increase on the record industry, and (3) the potential impact of an increase on the consuming public. Songwriters and publishers testified in favor of an increase over the 2¢ per each recording manufactured that was provided for in the 1909 Statute. They were supported by music consumers represented by the National Federation of Music Clubs who preferred a higher (royalty) ceiling "as a means of encouraging the writing of more and better music." The record companies testified in opposition to any increase in the 2¢ figure. They were supported by the Consumer Federation of America who wrote to the Committee agreeing that if the statutory fee were raised, record manufacturers would have to avoid risks on new and unusual compositions, reduce the number and length of selections, record fewer serious works and rely more on the public domain for popular material.

Some of the factors discussed in testimony included the royalty as a percent of list price per song; the royalty as a percent of manufacturer's wholesale selling price; record company sales and profits; organization of the record industry; changes in income of copyright owners as a function of time, inflation rate, and royalty fee; and the effect of royalty fee on incentives for quality and quantity of products.

The Senate Committee concluded that the royalty fee per work embodied in each phonorecord manufactured and distributed should be 2 1/2 cents or one-half cent per minute of playing time, whichever is greater.

The House Committee on the Judiciary, on the basis of essentially the same testimony, concluded that the royalty fee per each work embodied in a phonorecord that is made and distributed should be "2 3/4 cents or 0.6 of one cent per minute of playing time or fraction thereof which-ever amount is larger." (See House Report No. 94-1476 at pages 16 and 111).

The Conference Report (House Report No. 94-1733 at page 77) adopted the House fixed rate and the Senate per minute rate. This was ultimately enacted. Therefore the royalty is "either two and three-fourths cents or one-half of one cent per minute of playing time or fraction thereof, whichever is larger." (Section 115(c)(2), P.L. 94-553).

4.6.2 Jukebox Performance Royalty, 1976 Act

Under the 1909 statute, renditions of musical compositions through re-cordings in coin-operated machines (jukeboxes) were not classified as public performances for profit unless an admission fee to the location of the performance was also charged. Thus, most jukebox renditions were exempted from royalty payments. As both the Senate and House Re-ports on the 1976 Copyright Law Revision state, efforts to remove this exemption have persisted for 40 years. It is believed by some observers that in 1909, the extent of the jukebox industry could not be forecast and that this exemption was an historical accident. Testimony by copy-right owners in congressional hearings on copyright revision strongly urged the imposition of a royalty fee on jukebox renditions of copy-righted works. Testimony by jukebox operators and manufacturers sup-ported the retention of the present exemption. (See House Report No. 94-1476 at pages 111 to 115, and Senate Report No. 94-473 at pages 95 to 99.)

In the 1976 General Revision, Congress ended the exemption and imposed a yearly compulsory blanket license of $8 per jukebox (Section 116(b)(1), P.L. 94-553). In general the reasons given for ending the exemption were that the exemption was unfair to music producers; and also unfair to those other users who paid royalties and therefore were also paying the jukebox operators' share.

4.6.3 New Statutory Compulsory Licenses

The 1976 General Revision established two other compulsory licenses in addition to the jukebox performance license, all three of which joined the previously-established phonorecord manufacturing license. The new licenses are for cable-assisted television (CATV) retransmission of broadcasted programs (Section 111(c) and 111(d), and for the use of cer-tain copyrighted works in non-commercial broadcasting (Section 118).

As stated in Appendix A, Section A.4.6.3 "the purpose of the compulsory license in these three instances...is to avoid the difficulties that the user groups would encounter if they had to obtain licenses from and pay fees to the individual copyright holders." In other words, transaction costs are lessened under the compulsory license system.

4.6.4 The Copyright Royalty Tribunal

The 1976 Act establishes a Copyright Royalty Tribunal as an independent agency in the legislative branch (See Chapter 8 of the Act). The Tribunal's function is to periodically and equitably adjust the statutory blanket license fees for jukebox operation, to distribute equitably to copyright holders the statutory royalty proceeds collected from CATV operators, and to determine the terms and conditions of the compulsory license for non-commercial broadcasting of certain copyrighted works, but in the latter case, only if the interested parties fail to negotiate their own arrangements. The Tribunal determines, also, the royalty rates for CATV retransmissions under certain conditions.

4.7 COPYRIGHT AND MONOPOLY

It is common understanding that copyright is a monopoly, although limited to some degree. Walter Pforzheimer has quoted Judge Learned Hand on this point:

> "Copyright in any form, whether statutory or at common law, is a monopoly;...Congress has created the monopoly in exchange for a dedication, and when the monopoly expires the dedication must be complete."[33]

Similarly, the House Committee on Patents in their report accompanying the bill that became the 1909 Copyright Act stated:

> "The granting of such exclusive rights, under the proper terms and conditions, confers a benefit upon the public that out-weighs the evils of the temporary monopoly."[34]

The appellation of "monopoly" can have several implications. A question that can be asked is: to what extent does the exclusive right granted to an author and his assignees constitute an exercisable economic monopoly in a market sense, thereby requiring Government regulation or other collective action as an antidote? The answer to this question may also provide an answer to an issue raised by Hurt and Schuchman which is: whether "copyright protection artificially enhances the private returns on /¯some_/ ventures and leads to the distortions of monopoly pricing."[35]

The answer depends, to some extent, on the nature of the copyrighted work and whether other works can be considered substitutable and therefore competing.

If the copyrighted work is a book, musical performance or film produced for a general audience, there may very well be high substitutability among individual works as far as the ultimate consumer is concerned. In this situation, one author's exclusive right must compete with other exclusive rights in the marketplace to be selected or rejected by a typical consumer. However, since the competing works have a certain individuality about them, by the fact of their having the requisite originality for copyright protection, pure competition in a classical sense cannot exist. Nevertheless, the "monopolistic competition" which exists among the works may be very close to pure competition in the absence of externalities, collusion or restraints of trade by competitors. As Professor Mansfield states about competition in general, "...most firms face relatively close substitutes and most commodities are not completely homogeneous from one producer to another....In other words, there is no single homogeneous commodity called an automobile; instead, each producer differentiates its product from that of the next producer. This, of course, is a prevalent case in the modern economy."[36]

Thus, among certain classes of copyrighted works, there may be as much or more competition for consumer interest as exists among competitive hard goods or other "non-intellectual" properties. Competition among copyrighted works is assisted by the fact that although protection covers the author's specific expression, it does not extend "to any idea, procedure, process, system, method of operation, concept, principle, or discovery, regardless of the form in which it is described, explained, illustrated, or embodied...."[37] Although a copyrighted work must be "original," it need not be novel or non-obvious, which are requirements for patent protection.

4.7.1 Government Remedies for Market Monopoly

The problem of monopoly has arisen in the music and motion picture industries on several occasions but not in the context of control exercised by virtue of an exclusive right in a single property. The problem in these industries has invariably related to attempted control over a market due to exclusive rights in at least several properties, and in some cases, exclusive rights in very many properties. The example of the potential monopoly over phonorecord recording which resulted in the compulsory license provision of the 1909 Act has been mentioned previously and is also described in Appendix A, Section A.4.6.3.

A number of monopoly-related cases in the performing rights area are mentioned by Taubman.[38] ASCAP consented to an anti-trust decree of the U.S. Dept. of Justice in 1941 and the decree was further modified in 1950.[39] In the 1948 decision, (Alden-Rochelle v. ASCAP) "ASCAP was declared to have achieved monopolistic domination of the music integrated in sound films, in violation of Section 2 of the Sherman Act."[40] As a result, ASCAP "must license all qualified applicants, all licensees of the same class are charged the same fees, and any licensee or applicant may request the Court / the U.S. District Court for the Southern District of New York / to review the fees charged." (See Appendix A, Section A.4.6.2.1.)

In general, the result of a threat of market monopoly is additional Government intervention and regulation. Both the phonorecord manufacturing and ASCAP situations have resulted in compulsory licensing requirements. In one case, the royalty fee was fixed in law by Congress; and in the other case, the Federal Judiciary, although not fixing the royalty payment, required that ASCAP must license all qualified applicants and must provide equitable treatment to all licensees, with Court jurisdiction retained as a place of recourse.

4.8 SUMMARY

Problems in the development and maintenance of an efficient market for copyrighted works have been considered and some remedies have been discussed. Problems considered have included exclusion costs, the costs of information and communication, trade-offs in the design of royalty collection systems, royalty pricing schemes, economic implications in the "fair use" doctrine, price setting for compulsory licenses, and economic monopoly.

The presence of transaction costs is not necessarily a reason for abolishing copyright, despite the cost of Government regulation. There are transaction costs in any market. Without copyright, it is postulated

that there would be cut-throat competition, increased secrecy and a reduced flow of information. A society must select which set of dissatisfactions it finds less onerous or more contributing to its overall
goals.

Clearinghouses are one method of reducing the costs of communication and
information. Blanket licenses assist similarly, but there are costs to
the use of these systems as well. That payment mechanism that is least
costly in time and effort to users, all other things being equal, will
probably generate the least amount of deliberate evasions.

There are efficient royalty pricing schemes that distinguish different
classes of users and which account for both fixed and marginal costs.
Pricing may usefully distinguish institutions from individuals and may
usefully offer a choice of schedules to suit both the heavy user and
the casual user.

Fair use may be treated as a mechanism for the reduction of certain
transaction costs. However, the doctrine of permitting an exemption
from royalty fees for "worthy" uses that do not come under First Amendment or "lack of market impact" considerations can be criticized on
efficiency criteria.

Compulsory licenses have been established in three new areas under the
1976 Act. Price-setting of royalty fees for compulsory licenses is
essentially an adversary proceding between producers and users before
an impartial panel empowered to set rates.

Copyright is a limited monopoly over a single work. In the markets for
works of general interest (e.g. phonorecords, musical performances)
anti-trust problems have concerned, in general, attempted control over
many works. The results have been imposition of a compulsory license or
judicial intervention.

5. COPYRIGHT IN COMPUTER-READABLE WORKS

Following the development in the preceding chapters, the questions of
copyrightability in computer-readable data bases, full text, and computer programs may be considered. First some of the issues raised in
1967 hearings are reviewed, so that some of the arguments can be aired
and the situation can be placed in context. Then, the current situation resulting from the passage of the 1976 General Revision is described.
The issue of registration and disclosure is then considered in the context of public policy about information transfer.

The technical issues of copyrightability are then pursued, with the
economic aspects of data base uniqueness and computer network distribution of copyrighted works considered. The conditions of sale of
computer-readable works which need to be different than works in hard
copy are discussed.

5.1 TECHNOLOGY FORECASTING, 1967 STYLE

The questions of copyright in literary works entered into a computer
and of copyright in computer software were raised substantially in
testimony before the Senate Committee on the Judiciary concerning

revision bill S.597 in March 1967.[41] Authors and publishers appeared concerned by the possibility that, in the near future, a significant amount of publishing would be done in machine-readable format with extensive distribution of works accomplished by computer networks without hard copy. Clearly, there were serious copyright implications in this concept. Professor Jesse Markham, speaking on behalf of the American Book Publishers Council and American Text Publishers Institute stated that:

> "The present state of technology suggests that the computer will affect conventional publishing in two distinct ways: (1) The initial versions of some types of information that are reduced to writing, copyrighted and published, will very likely be computerized, thus by-passing conventional publishing altogether; and (2) The contents of published works will be stored in computers and, once stored, serve as a substitute for additional printed copies . . ."[42]

Similarly, Mr. Lee C. Deighton, also appearing on behalf of the American Textbook Publishers Institute, stated that:

> "The same kind of transmission [as closed-circuit television] is now technologically possible in computer network systems. It is contemplated that in these systems, a central computer will store copyrighted works, and that they will be transmitted by wire to hundreds of individual console screens upon demand. It is merely displayed on the console screen to be read at leisure by the user. The computer in effect becomes the library."[43]

Ms. Elizabeth Janeway, appearing on behalf of the Authors League of America, was more certain of the arrival of electronic publishing. "It is clear that computers and computer networks will soon become a principal means of disseminating much that authors write," she stated.[44] As a reference, Ms. Janeway cited a study Copyright and Intellectual Property published (in paper) by the Fund for the Advancement of Education.[45] This study was cited also by another testifier, Mr. Charles Gosnell, chairman of the Committee on Copyright Issues of the American Library Association and director of the libraries of New York University.[45] The cited study included the following quotes:

> "The library of the future will be unrecognizable to the librarian of today; it will be so dependent on the hardware of the new technology, that apocryphally speaking, the librarian of the future will be a mechanic with a screwdriver, ever alert to repair breakdowns in the service."[47]

> "Audio-visual dial-access teaching machines, operated by remote control, will provide hundreds and even thousands of students with simultaneous audio and visual access to a journal article or excerpts from a book."[48]

> ". . . the computer, in essence, assumes the role of a duplicating rather than a circulating library. One copy of a book fed into such a system can service all simultaneous demands for it; of course this substitution for

additional copies will vitally affect the publishers'
traditional market."[49]

"The information world of the future will revolve around
information systems, educational programs, and library
complexes in which the complete documentation of the
system concerned will be equivalent to a computer memory.
In a sense, therefore, by providing copies of works
stored in the computer, these systems become publishers.
Traditional publications will also be available from
commercial publishers, but it would seem that 'nonbook'
production will predominate."[50]

The cited study quoted an article from the New York Times which was
mentioned also by Professor Jesse Markham.[51] This article had reported that:

"The medical libraries of three major eastern universities
will be tied together in a network of computers and telephone lines to give scholars virtually instant access to
their pooled resources . . . the three libraries will
then contain 1,025,000 items. These can be searched by
computers in seconds . . . When telecommunication and
photographic reproducing devices are added to the network
system . . . pages from a book in New York could be
flashed to a user in another city and even reproduced
for him in take-home form."[52]

The time scale in which these changes would come about was unfortunately
not reported. The relative economics of the situation, such as the
development and implementing costs as well as the operating costs
relative to current systems, were similarly not reported. As of 1977,
some publishing in electronic media is being done, particularly with
data bases of various types. In addition, computers are now heavily
used in the publishing process, e.g., typesetting and line justification. However, the vast changes contemplated by the above quotes have
not materialized, although they might occur in the future. Certainly,
the bulkiness of paper-based systems and library labor-intensivity are
forcing functions. The costs of paper, of data and postal communications, and of computer programming, the sunk costs (economic and social)
in current systems, and the psychological needs of readers to prefer
one kind of media to another will be factors in the rate of change.

Not everything that is technically feasible is economically feasible
or even desirable. As was reported by the National Academy of Sciences
in 1971:

"The primary bar to development of national computer-based
library and information systems is no longer basically a
technology-feasibility problem. Rather it is the combination of complex institutional and organizational human-
related problems and the inadequate economic/value system
associated with these activities."[53]

This means, in plain text, that decisionmakers didn't want it strongly
enough to put up the money at that time.

5.1.1 Technology of the Future, Updated

Although the time scale implied by the predictions of 1967 was incorrect, the technological feasibility of what was described cannot be denied. Changes in prices among various elements of current and future systems plus additional technological breakthroughs may yet cause more electronic publishing than can be envisioned currently.

At present, the development of large-scale integration of logic elements and improvements in mass production technology have brought down the prices of central processor units of computers enormously. The capabilities of peripheral units have similarly been improved. The result is that the prices of some mini-computers of substantial capability are now equivalent to the prices of some automobiles. The sale of electronic home entertainment centers that involve substantial logic capability and which plug into TV sets have burgeoned. This is one step short of the home computer.

It may be that books will be sold on video disks the way phonograph records are sold, to be viewed on a TV screen controlled by a home computer. It may be that libraries will store many books in memory, and that hundreds of terminals will permit simultaneous reading by patrons on TV screens (with optional printout) of anything in the memory. The current uses of computer-assisted instruction and of computerized data bases may set the example.

However, the cost of computer software to accomplish the desired functions cannot be ignored, and it is not decreasing in cost. The cost of operating any computer system today is fast approaching a 90%-10% split in software and personnel versus hardware. In addition, it is likely that social, institutional, and psychological factors will have as much if not more control over the future in this area than technological and economic factors.

5.2 SOME TECHNICAL ISSUES IN THE HEARINGS, 1967

The issues raised in the Senate hearings in 1967 on computer-related works can be indicated in part, with reference to two points raised by EDUCOM (the Interuniversity Communications Council) in its statement entitled The Copyright Revision Bill In Relation to Computers.[54]

First, the EDUCOM statement opposed granting copyright protection to computer programs except in a very narrow sense. The statement said that "as the programs represent algorithmic plans for using machines to achieve practical results, they are poles apart from the conventional subject matter of copyright . . ."[55] Furthermore, the statement said that if a copyright were granted to a program, this should "in no event" bar an outsider from replicating the program exactly and using it "in order to carry out the process or practice the art."[56]

Second, the statement called for an educational exemption from infringement for entering copyrighted material into a computer, noting that there will be cases where the proprietor is not interested in making the needed transformation (to machine-readable form) and the institutions must have access to the work.[57]

The EDUCOM statement also called for retaining "traditional exemptions" in educational use of copyrighted works and suggested that the Revision Bill then being considered had provisions which "seem to eliminate virtually all preference for educational and related institutions utilizing copyrighted works by means of computers."[58]

The General Counsel to the Electronic Industries Association, Mr. Graham W. McGowan, also testified at this hearing.[59] Mr. McGowan testified that his organization favored exemption from infringement for computer input of copyrighted works (as distinguished from computer output). Among the bases of the argument were: (a) the author's reward should be based on demand for his work and that entering a work into a computer "is not attributed to the demand for the copyrighted work"; (b) "when in a computer, a copyrighted work is not intelligible to any human being. Therefore, there is no harm to any copyright owner to put works in storage . . ."; (c) "to be required to seek permission to only store the work in a computer is time-consuming and expensive in and of itself. Having to deal with every copyright owner would be overly burdensome and highly impractical . . ."

The publishers point of view was perhaps summed up by this statement of Mr. Lee Deighton:

> "We have looked at copyright legislation not only as
> publishers but as citizens of a free economic society.
> We have observed a central thread running through the
> dialogue of the past three years. It is quite simply a
> demand for free use of copyrighted materials through the
> grant of special exemptions. It is our position equally
> with authors, composers, artists and other creative talents
> that the product of a man's mind and imagination is
> property just as much as the product of his hands or
> machines. Every exemption granted is an abridgment
> of the creator's rights to enjoy the fruits of his labor.
> As citizens, we are concerned lest the granting of exemp-
> tions proceed so far as to hinder the flow of creative
> materials."[60]

5.3   CURRENT STATUS, 1976 GENERAL REVISION

Several additional Congressional hearings and debates have been held since 1967. An analysis of the issues of copyright and the computer as seen in 1973 is available in a publication of the American Society for Information Science.[61] The recent history of copyright legislation may be obtained from the Copyright Law Revision Reports of the Congress (Senate Report No. 94-473 at pages 47-50 and House Report 94-1476 at pages 47-50). The net results of those hearings and debates at this time are embodied in the new statute P.L. 94-553, enacted October 19, 1976, to take effect January 1, 1978.

The law with respect to the use of copyrighted works in conjunction with computers would be considerably clearer at this time if it were not for the provisions of Section 117. That section says that the new Act has no effect on the use of copyrighted works in connection with computers. That means, in effect, that copyright law on computer use remains in doubt.

Section 117 was inserted because of the existence of CONTU, and the

section is expected to be altered or eliminated as a result of eventual
Congressional action on CONTU recommendations.

In any event, the new Act states, in Section 102, that "copyright protection subsists . . . in original works of authorship fixed in any
tangible means of expression," and states, in Section 106 that "the
owner of copyright....has the exclusive rights....(1) to reproduce the
copyrighted work in copies or phonorecords [and] (2) to prepare derivative works based upon the copyrighted work...."

That means that the right of conversion of a copyrighted work from one
medium to another is reserved to the proprietor, excluding specific exemptions given elsewhere in the Act. It seems clear, then, if a copyrighted work can be converted to a computer-readable format without
actually using a computer to do it, the converted work is protected.
The law with respect to the use of the work in a computer or the conversion of a work to computer-readable format using a computer is not
clear at present because of Section 117. Thus, if it were not for Section 117, the debate over infringement at input or output would be over.
The copyright holders in the absence of Section 117 have control of
their works in any medium (excluding specific exemptions) and therefore
at input.

On the subject of the copyrightability of computer programs, the Copyright Office has been accepting programs for registration since 1964;
although its Circular 61, Computer Programs, of latest date March 1975,
states that certain issues about the copyrightability of programs are
"doubtful." The two issues asked in Circular 61 are these:

> "(1) Is a program the 'writing of an author' and thus copy-
>   rightable, and
> (2) Can a reproduction of the program in a form actually
>   used to operate or be 'read' by a machine be considered
>   an acceptable 'copy' for copyright registration?"

The first question above references the Copyright Clause in the Constitution, not any particular Act of Congress. If computer programs are
Constitutionally copyrightable, it seems clear at least that the human-
written hard-copy form of an "original" computer program is copyrightable, barring specific denial by Congress, regardless of question (2)
above.

Furthermore, if (1) above is answered in the affirmative, then in the
absence of Section 117 of the new Act, the computer-readable version
most likely would be considered a valid copy. However, because of Section 117, if the computer-readable version had been made with the aid
of a computer, its copyrightability is clearly in doubt.

5.4 THE IMPLICATIONS OF ABOLISHMENT OF COMMON LAW PROTECTION

It was made clear in Section 2.1 above that common law copyright is ended in the United States as of the effective date of the 1976 General
Revision. The concept now ending, dating back to Donaldson v. Becket,
1774, is that the author has complete dominion over his work with common law copyright protection before publication, but he must rely on
statutory copyright following publication. Despite the fact that this
"dual system" was unique among nations, it originally had considerable

appeal.

Specifically, the line of demarcation between works intended for general public distribution and those intended to be kept private was publication. Those works intended to be distributed publicly could be disclosed and given statutory copyright protection. Those works intended to be kept private were, at the option of the owner, not disclosed and not copyrighted under statute. Thus, for disclosure and publication, activities which made the work more susceptible to infringement, the copyright owner obtained the protection of the Federal Government. Without publication or disclosure, a proprietor could still make lease agreements with specific users involving nondisclosure which were enforceable in State courts under common law copyright (as well as under other types of protection).

Under the 1976 General Revision of Copyright Law, the legal distinction based on publication is ended. All works, "whether published or unpublished" are governed as of January 1, 1978 by the Federal copyright statute with regard to "all legal or equitable rights that are equivalent to any of the exclusive rights within the general scope of copyright" (Section 301(a)). On and after the effective date, "no person is entitled to any such right or equivalent right in any such work under the common law or statutes of any State" (Section 301(a)).

Thus, common law copyright protection in unpublished works is ended. However, unlawful activities "violating legal or equitable rights that are not equivalent to any of the exclusive rights within the general scope of copyright . . ." are still subject to the available "remedies under the common law or statutes of any State . . ." (Section 301(b)). The bill that passed the Senate, S.22, gave examples of unlawful activities against which remedies are still available. These included nonequivalent misappropriation, breaches of contract, breaches of trust, trespass, conversion, invasion of privacy, defamation and deceptive trade practices such as false representation. However, these examples were eliminated from the final bill as enacted. Therefore, the totality of exactly what remedies would qualify may be in doubt.

Since unpublished works are now copyrightable, a new definition was needed to define the onset of copyright. Now copyright in a work "subsists" (begins) at "its creation" (Section 302(a)) which essentially means from the moment that the last finishing stroke of creation is completed. Thus, even if the author does not wish copyright, his work has it from the moment of its completion if it is in a category of copyrightable works and the work is not otherwise exempted from copyright.

5.5 REGISTRATION AND DISCLOSURE

A copyright owner need not take advantage of copyright. He need not register his work with the Copyright Office if he does not wish to disclose his work publicly. Under the 1976 General Revision, registration is optional; but agreement to register involves deposit of the work with the Copyright Office and therefore a certain public disclosure (Section 408). For works that have been published with a notice of copyright, there is the additional requirement at the option of the Register of Copyrights, of deposit of two copies for the Library of Congress (Section 407(a)). Unpublished works and works published without copyright notice are exempt from this latter requirement. Even if copies for the

Library of Congress are demanded, this requirement may be circumvented by payment of a fine of $250 plus the retail price of two copies of the work (Section 407(d)).

The advantage of registration, under the 1976 General Revision, is that it is a prerequistie to an infringement suit (Section 411); and furthermore, awards of statutory damages are permitted _only_ for infringements occurring _after_ the date of registration of an unpublished or a published work; or for infringements occurring after the date of publication of a work and before the date of its registration if and only if the work is registered within three months of its date of first publication (Section 412).

Thus, the copyright owner has a trade-off. If he wants the maximum Government legal protection, he must register his work and disclose it to the extent of Government requirements. If he does not wish to register and disclose it, he need not; but in that case he must depend for protection, to a large extent, on lesser remedies or on remedies available through State courts that are not equivalent to copyright protection.

5.5.1 The Extent of Disclosure Requirements

The maximum statutory requirements for registration (of a literary work) must include, in the case of an unpublished work, one complete copy, and in the case of a published work, two complete copies (Section 408(b)).

However, the Register of Copyrights is authorized to permit, for particular classes of works (with classes defined by the Register), "the deposit of identifying material instead of copies . . ." (Section 408(c)(1)). Furthermore, "the Register of Copyrights may by regulation exempt any categories of material from the deposit requirements [for the Library of Congress]." (Section 407(c)).

Thus, the Register has been assigned regulatory authority which has very important public policy implications.

5.5.2 The Policy Implications of Disclosure Rules

There is in this nation an underlying philosophy that information transfer should be maximized, subject to certain restraints, such as those due to personal privacy, trade secrecy, and national security. In the area of scientific and technical information, Federal responsibilities are quite clear.
The National Science Foundation Act of 1950 authorized and directed NSF to "foster the interchange of scientific information among scientists in the United States and foreign countries."[62] In the same Act, NSF was given the authority "to publish or arrange for the publication of scientific and technical information so as to further the full dissemination of information of scientific value consistent with the national interest."[63]

In a report of the President's Science Advisory Committee, 1963, known as the Weinberg Panel Report, it was concluded that "transfer of information is an inseparable part of research and development."[64] In a report of the National Academy of Sciences, the SATCOM report, 1969, rec-

ommendations were made to insure effective communication of scientific
and technical information;[65] and in the "Greenberger Report" of the NSF
and the Federal Council for Science and Technology, 1972, technical information was referred to as "a vital national resource."[66]

The importance of information flow to modern society has been noted by
important observers such as Daniel Bell and Peter Drucker. Bell has
written that the United States is the first postindustrial nation and
that "a postindustrial society is organized around information and
utilization of information in complex systems, and the use of that information as a way of guiding the society."[67] Drucker has concluded
that "knowledge, during the last few decades has become the central
capital, the cost center, and the critical resource of the economy. . .
Free trade in goods . . . is important. But free movement of capital
and free movement of knowledge may be more important still."[68]

It would seem, therefore, that there is a strong public interest in
maximizing disclosure on two counts: first, for the maximization of
information transfer about original works, with all the implications for
additional creativity that this implies; and second, to make meaningful
the exchange of full protection of copyright for disclosure through
registration. If registration is to imply a minimal disclosure, then
the proprietor is capable of obtaining two opposite types of protection,
surely not the intent of Congress. A permission for minimal disclosure
would give full copyright protection; but, would permit the proprietor
to maintain his work essentially secret, particularly if he makes it
available through lease agreements only with restrictive disclosure
clauses.

It is hoped that provisions for maximum disclosure in the public interest can be worked out without imposing difficult or costly tasks on
copyrighted proprietors. This subject is further discussed below in
connection with the characteristics of specific kinds of computer-readable works.

5.6 COPYRIGHT IN COMPUTER-READABLE DATA BASES

A data base, in many cases, is a "compilation." In copyright terminology, a compilation "is a work formed by the collection and assembling
of preexisting materials or of data that are selected, coordinated, or
arranged in such a way that the resulting work as a whole constitutes
an original work of authorship" (Section 101, (Definitions), 1976 General Revision). Compilations are copyrightable under Section 103 of
the 1976 General Revision, but the copyright is in the organization of
the materials and not in any used materials that are in the public domain or are already copyrighted. Copyright in the compilation does not
imply any exclusive right in the preexisting used materials. As examples, a telephone book, a gazetteer, and an almanac are all compilations in which copyright subsists primarily in the organization of the
materials and not in the individual materials contained therein.

This type of work has been given copyright protection in human-readable
form as a type of literary work, one of the categories of protectable
subject matter.

As the House Report 94-1476 makes clear (on page 54),

"The term 'literary works' does not connote any criterion of
literary merit or qualitative value: it includes catalogs,
dictionaries, and similar factual, reference, or instructional
works and compilations of data . . ."

The House Report goes on to state that "computer data bases" are also
literary works with the implication that they are copyrightable, but
for certainty about that question, the caveat "in the absence of Section
117" should be added. In the long run, however, Section 117 is certain
to be excised or significantly altered, and therefore the caveat will be
rendered moot. There seems to be no serious opposition to the copyrightability of compilations in computer-readable form.

Other literary works of a factual nature for example, encyclopedias and
other reference works, may be used and treated as data bases even though
copyright may subsist in the literary expressions in the entire works.
A work of this type may be either a "collective work" like an encyclopedia, or a reference work on a specialized subject by a single author,
e.g. Nimmer on Copyright. Copyrightability in the computer-readable
form of the work is just as clear for these works as it is for compilations. The following discussion will concern computer-readable data
bases in general without regard to their subcategory as either compilations, collective works, or literary works of a single author. The
important connecting element of all of them is how they are used.

5.6.1 Publication Only in Computer-Readable Form

There may be some question as to what constitutes publication of a
computer-readable data base that has not been published previously in
a paper edition. It is assumed that the date of publication of a computer-readable data base that has been published previously in a paper
edition without any change in content is the same date as that for the
paper edition.

5.6.1.1 Display Only, Single Licensee:

The particular situation of
interest here is that in which the data base is made available only
through user terminals attached to a central computer. This is a typical method of permitting accessibility. It is assumed that the central
computer is owned either by the copyright proprietor or by a distributor
who has obtained the data base from the proprietor under an exclusive
license.

Now, if either the proprietor or the exclusive licensee make the data
base available by display only at the terminals and do not permit
printouts to change hands, no publication has occurred. The basis of
this statement is the definition of "publication," in Section 101, and
the explanatory material in House Report 94-1476 at page 138 and Senate
Report 94-473 at page 121. (The pertinent sentences from both reports
beginning "Under the definition in Section 101. . ." are identical):

First, the definition states that "display of a work does not of itself
constitute publication." Thus the proprietor's display is not publication. However, the definition also states that "the offering to distribute copies . . . to a group of persons for purposes of further distribution . . . or public display, constitutes publication." Thus,
distribution to a single exclusive licensee for display purposes only
is not publication (since a single individual is not a group).

Suppose the proprietor distributed the data base to two or more licensees for display only. Whether this constitutes publication depends on how many licensees constitutes "a group " The answer to this question had best be left to the Judiciary or to further Congressional interpretation.

5.6.1.2 <u>Printouts at Terminals</u>: If users at terminals are permitted to make printouts of retrieved material, without any "explicit or implicit restrictions with respect to disclosure of the contents," then publication has occurred. The argument could be made that if restrictions are placed on disclosure or distribution of the printouts, then no publication has occurred. However, since the concept of "publication" is no longer central to copyright, extended analysis of particular situations is unwarrented at this point. In any event, it would be expected, if there is a likelihood that a printout would be considered "published," that a proprietor or a licensee would be sure to have the computer mark each printout with a complete notice of copyright to insure that proprietary rights were protected under Chapter 4 of the 1976 General Revision.

5.6.1.3 <u>Identity of the Publication</u>: The question of exactly what has been published remains to be discussed. The printouts, if provided under no restriction, are published material. The physical printout belongs to the user who paid for it. The copyright ownership of the printouts belongs to the proprietor of the data base. This is not unusual. When a book is purchased at retail, the buyer owns the book and the publisher continues to own the copyright in the content.

The argument could be made that only the printouts have been published and the data base has not been published. After all, only the printouts have changed hands; and it is assumed here that the proprietor or his exclusive licensee have retained control of the full data base. In the manner in which data base systems are operated, a user identifies a particular set of categories of information in which he is interested and queries the data base. The data base system responds with the number of items in the set, and on command, the text retrieved is shown on a CRT terminal. If the user is satisfied with the text retrieved, he requests a printout. It would seem that the printout is a "derivative work," similar to an abridgment or condensation (see Section 101 for definition), and there appears to be no requirement that a published derivative work be based on a <u>published</u> preexisting work. On the other hand, each printout may be different, depending on the specific query which the user has entered into the computer. Thus, the published "derivative works" may be one of a kind.

5.6.1.4 <u>Needed Clarification</u>: It seems reasonable to suggest that a clarification of what constitutes publication of a computer-readable data base is in order. For example, a reasonable understanding is that a computer-readable data base is to be considered "published" in its entirety if it is offered to the public on a query basis such that any item in the data base is capable of being retrieved and printed out and the printouts become the physical property of the users on the basis of unrestricted disclosure. Furthermore, "publication" occurs in this situation whether the offering to users is made by the proprietor or his licensee.

Additional clarification appears to be needed, also, in the definition

of how many persons constitute "a group of persons" as the number of
distributors to whom a work has to be offered in order to be published.
Furthermore, it does not seem to be clear if a work is "published" if
it is offered to a group of persons on a restricted-disclosure basis
for further distribution on a restricted-disclosure basis.

5.6.2 Statutory Deposit to the Library of Congress

As was indicated in Section 5.5 above, there are valid public policy
considerations that suggest the maximum disclosure of copyrighted works
in return for copyright protection. There is no reason to exempt computer-readable data bases from these considerations.

The Library of Congress could be viewed in this connection as an archival location where anyone could view and peruse nearly any computer-
readable work published with copyright notice. This would be an immense
aid to scholarship, to historical review, and to the generation of new
ideas for the future, as it has been with works in the older technological media.

The issue, then, is the form in which computer-readable data bases
should be deposited under Section 407 in order to maximize their
availability, minimize storage and handling problems for the Library,
not provide a hardship of supply to the proprietors and not strain fair
use.

It is not immediately clear, on these criteria, whether the initial
deposit should be a printout or a magnetic tape, but it seems reasonable to suggest that it should be the complete data base, not just
identifying descriptions, regardless of which medium is chosen. The
advantage of the printout is that any reader could peruse it without
straining fair use. Microfilm could be used to reduce size and bulkiness. The advantage of the magnetic tape is that the data base is published in that medium; and it is a medium in which it is available for
a scholar's manipulation and use, assuming it were an outdated tape
that the proprietor no longer saw as an immediately marketable product
that the scholar ought to buy by signing on the proprietor's computer
system.

Many data bases are updated frequently, and it seems reasonable to
suggest that a yearly update, containing only the new material added
during the preceding year and the old material dropped, is not a burdensome requirement. The deposit of a complete data base, under the
circumstances of continuous updating, could conceivably be required at
least once in a period of several years, for example, ten.

5.6.3 The Question of Monopoly

In Section 4.7 of this report, the question of monopoly was discussed,
and it was noted that the existence of an economic monopoly depends on
the availability of substitutable works. In works produced for the
general consumer, there may be high substitutability among individual
works.

However, an important distinction must be noted between the respective
market behaviors of the general consumer and the researcher-consumer of
copyrighted works. The general consumer typically selects competitively

for purchase or use one (or a few) of a class of relatively substitutable works while rejecting all others. The researcher in any professional field desires to be comprehensive in the full-text as well as in the data base literature of his field. Thus, the researcher (or his library surrogate) cannot reject totally anything pertinent, and his marketplace behavior with respect to competitive producers cannot be analogous to the general consumer. The question may be asked whether there is a greater potential for a market monopoly in this situation. If such is the case, a question that may be asked is what form of intervention should be pursued by consumers collectively or by the Government

With respect to scientific journal articles, the situation is ameliorated through the formation of professional societies which serve as the collective good to circumvent the implicit market failure. Furthermore, the social ethic of research is that all those involved, even in different organizations, benefit from the unimpeded flow of information.

This ethic may tend to lower the prices of journals produced by scientific societies rather than raise them. Therefore, any independent entrepreneur of a proprietary journal may find that the subscription prices that can be charged are limited by competition from journals of non-profit societies. The fact that the primary producer community and the final user community of scientific journal articles are essentially the same population may be a key factor in preventing monopoly pricing.

With respect to bibliographic and other specialized data bases, a different situation exists. In contrast to the situation with scientific journal articles, there is very little in the publication of continual updates of a data base that can be translated by a professional researcher into either financial or symbolic remuneration unless the work is a full-time business. Thus the producer and consumer communities need not be the same population and this particular negative feedback restraint on the subscription price of journals need not hold for data bases. It is not surprising, therefore, to find that (excluding Government production) a significant fraction of data bases used for research purposes are produced and distributed for profit as proprietary products.

The development of computer-based information retrieval systems based on machine-readable data bases has added an additional complicating factor. First, the development of a computer-readable data base (with continual updating to insure an indefinite life) requires a certain investment in data collection, organization, manipulation, and digital conversion. Clearly, those organizations that already have computer-aided publishing systems to help produce hard-copy informational products may be able to generate computer-readable data bases as relatively inexpensive by-products. Secondly, a parameter of usefulness of a data base is the comprehensiveness of its coverage of a specific field; and conceivably, only the largest organization with well-established lines of data supply and customer acceptance may be able to satisfy this need.

Thus, the possibility exists that in some field of research, by virtue of economy of scale, an established system of suppliers and customers and already amortized costs of entry in the market, a single organization may achieve a virtual market monopoly over a class of nonsubstitutable computer-readable data bases. An anti-trust suit concerning this very problem is now under litigation in the field of computer-based legal information retrieval.

Additional sources of monopoly control and a potential solution are described in Appendix A, Section A.4.4.5 of this report. The following is excerpted from that Section:

"In some instances, publishers of data bases have leased them exclusively for use in one computerized information service system . . . Exclusive licensing of data bases may tend to foster the monopolization of data base search services by one or two giant systems. Whether the prevention of such a monopoly or the regulatory control of a permitted monopoly as a public service organization would be preferable is an open question.

"From the standpoint of providing maximum service for researchers, and at the same time preventing the development of a monopoly . . ., the ideal situation might be the development of a number of competing systems, each of which can offer comprehensive coverage of any subject area. One way of encouraging such a development would be to provide for a compulsory licensing scheme under which a data base made available for use in any one system would thereupon become available for use in all other systems.

"Whether a compulsory licensing scheme . . . is needed and whether is would be desirable, are debatable issues . . ."

It seems reasonable to suggest that a valid research subject at this time is the economics of provision of data base information in computerized form, considering both the incentives for innovation and the potential for monopoly pricing.

5.7 COPYRIGHT IN COMPUTER PROGRAMS

Some of the questions concerning the copyrightability of computer programs are first listed below and then are considered individually in some detail. These questions are:

(a) Is a computer program a writing of an author and thus eligible for copyright protection under the Constitution?

(b) Is a computer program a "literary work"?

(c) Can a computer program be sufficiently "original" that it meets the requirements for a copyrighted work?

(d) Should a program in object code be treated any differently under copyright than a program in a source language?

(e) Is protection of the specific expression of a program but not the underlying conception sufficient protection to be valuable?

(f) Should copyright protection be denied computer programs on the basis of the strength of the software industry?

(g) How long should protection last, if a program is copyrightable?

(h) What should be a buyer's usage rights in a program?

5.7.1 The Program as the Writing of an Author

In general, a computer program is written by a human being, and is written in a specific formal language. Those persons engaged in the occupational specialty of writing programs are known as programmers. Others engaged in the tasks of determining requirements for and blocking out the logical flow of programs may be known as systems analysts. However, engineers, scientists, and others may write programs in the course of using a computer to assist them in solving problems in which they are engaged. In the United States today, there are probably several million persons who can comprehend at least superficially a computer program written in FORTRAN, a widely-used programming language.

In opposition to the copyrightability of computer programs, the point has been made that a computer program is a set of instructions for a machine, and in fact, according to this view, since the machine cannot operate without the program, the program is really part of the machine. Thus, programmers are really engaged in machine design, according to this argument, and the output of their work is more appropriately protected under a different legal mechanism than copyright.

Several points can be made in rebuttal to this line of reasoning. First, there is nothing inherent in a computer program that cannot be carried out by human labor, given either enough time or enough people to undertake the work. That is, the computer program written by a programmer is a set of instructions understandable by other persons; and it consists of individual steps that are possible to accomplish by humans, if time restraints are relaxed. The only capabilities needed to carry out the instructions of a program written in a typical source language, besides an understanding of the language, are (a) the ability to distinguish negative, zero and positive numbers, (b) the ability to perform arithmetic and elementary Boolean algebra, and (c), the ability to correctly select the next instruction, given explicit and unambiguous directions as to where to find it. It hardly seems fair to the author of such a set of instructions or to the public interest in economic efficiency to deny Government protection to the author's expression simply because, for purposes of speed and accuracy, the instructions are to be carried out by machine instead of by human labor.

If it is to be put forward that computer programs are not in a language in which humans speak to each other, that point can be accepted without damaging the case for copyrightability. Categories of works now copyrightable include musical works (that is, sheet music not necessarily including any accompanying words); pantomimes and choreographic works; and pictorial, graphic and sculptural works. None of these communicate to humans in natural language. Certainly included in the category of pictorial and graphic works are engineering and architectural drawings and schematic diagrams, all of which can be employed as instructions to those persons engaged in the construction of machines, devices, and structures.

Close to the concept of the computer program is musical notation and similar notations for sequences of choreographic motions. Musical notation is, in essence, a set of instructions for the operation of mechanical devices so as to produce a particular sequence of sounds, each

with a particular pitch held for a particular length of time. It
follows that the question whether a computer without its program is
still a computer is analogous to the question whether a piano without
someone playing it is still a piano. Discussion of such a question is
not likely to be fruitful in the present context.

It may be helpful to point out, however, that a computer program is
more than simply a set of instructions used to operate a machine. Computer programs are involved, in their operational use, in a variety of
real human purposes. Some of those purposes involve research and other
professional activities, while other purposes may appear to be mundane.
However, the development of a computer program that will be used in
connection with any real human purpose must include an understanding
of the human and physical systems with which the program will be associated. Implicit in any set of calculations that represent the real
world is a model of that portion of the real world. Clearly, the computer programs now in use throughout the United States that assist
physicians in the diagnosis of heart ailments on the basis of an analysis of electrocardiogram signals constitute models of the heart's operation. Similarly, but perhaps not so obviously, accountants have begun to realize that the system of financial records of an organization
including the records of collections, inventory, and disbursements is
nothing less than a financial model of the organization.

In effect, the computer program is an implementation of the view that
the physical world and at least part of the human world is amenable to
rational analysis and quantification, and to understanding deduced from
these processes. Scientists, engineers, economists and statisticians
must be listed among those whose core of professional work conforms to
this view. No person need accept this view either in its entirety or
uncritically. In fact, a world run solely on the basis of this view
might very well lack fundamental and essential value judgments that
cannot be deduced or quantified. Copyright protection, however, as
discussed in Section 2.6, requires no value judgment as to the individual merit of a particular writing of an author; and it is clear that the
source code written by a programmer is such a writing.

While the most fundamental statutory test of copyrightability is whether
the category in question constitutes a writing of an author, it is useful to consider the basic principle enumerated in Section 1.3 of this
report. Under these principles, this study finds that the author of a
computer program is entitled to the fruits of his creation; and that
the ease of copying of this form of intellectual property constitutes
an intrinsic market failure requiring the public good of statutory
copyright protection. In addition, this study finds that without copyright protection for computer programs, losses in information flow, increased procedures for secrecy and less opportunity for creativity
would result.

5.7.2 Computer Programs and Literary Works

Seven categories of works are now granted protection under Section 102
of the 1976 General Revision of Copyright Law. While the definition of
"literary works" given in Section 101 of the new Act is broad enough to
include computer programs, it is not necessary that computer programs
be defined for purposes of the statute as literary works. An alternative is a new category of copyrightable work to be enumerated in Sec-

tion 102, namely "computer programs."

One reason for consideration of this question is that computer programs are used in different ways than prose or poetry. The limitations on exclusive rights granted to users of literary works, for example, as specified in Section 110 of the 1976 General Revision, may or may not be appropriate for computer programs. In particular, the applicability of the limitations of Section 110 to computer programs used for computer-assisted instructional purposes is worthy of examination.

Similarly, as the uses to which computer programs are put or the manner in which they are used differ from more standard literary works, additional modifications of the copyright statute may be appropriate to specify the assignment of property rights with respect to each type of work. Categorization of computer programs separately from literary works might assist the process of specifying these differences.

5.7.3 Originality of Computer Programs

While no specific research study can be identified yielding definitive results that computer programs can be "original", as the meaning of that term is understood in copyright law, experience and knowledge of the field make possible an unequivocal affirmative response.

Many books have been written on the subject of how to write programs and how to write better programs. If originality were not possible, it would have been difficult if not impossible for Gerald M. Weinberg to have written the book The Psychology of Computer Programming[69] including sections on "Programming as Human Performance" and Programming as an Individual Activity." Similarly, it would have been far less likely for Dennie Van Tassel to have written on "Program Style" in his book on Program Style, Design, Efficiency, Debugging, and Testing[70] or for Frederick P. Brooks, Jr. to have written of "the joys of the craft" or of "craftsmanship" in his book on The Mythical Man-Month, Essays on Software Engineering.[71]

Of course, the more complex a program's function, the greater the variety of unique ways of expressing the steps in the performance. On the other hand, it is questionable whether a program carrying out an elementary and well-defined function such as the calculation of the roots of a second-order polynomial could be considered "original." It may be within the discretionary power of the Register of Copyrights to deny copyright to such a program on that basis. It is likely, however, that the copyrighting process will be self-regulating. Only programs having an intrinsic originality are likely to be submitted for registration.

5.7.4 Protection of Object Code as a Computer Program

The object code is the conversion into symbols usable directly by the computer of the source program written by the programmer. The basic question with respect to object code is whether it should be able to be copyrighted independently of the source code. If it were independently copyrightable as a computer program, a programmer could submit the object code to the Copyright Office for registration and never disclose the source code at all.

The point has been raised that, very likely, the sequence of ones and zeros in hard-copy form constituting the object code is, in the abstract, already copyrightable as a literary work under present law. Analogously, the sequence of numbers in a data base are clearly copyrightable and similarly, original sequences of nonsense syllables are acceptable for registration since no value judgment need be made as to literary merit.

However, the concept of a "computer program" implies a sequence of instructions involving a solution to a quantifiable problem. The granting of the protection of copyright implies the right to prevent infringements and imposes responsibilities on the Government. Yet the object code (except for a program of very short length) is unreadable as a computer program by a person. It would be exceedingly difficult for the Copyright Office to assure that the object code was "original" for registration purposes and similarly difficult for the facts to be determined in an infringement action.

The registration of the sequence of ones and zeros constituting the object code could be used, certainly, to prevent unauthorized copying and use of exactly that sequence. However, many infringements of the underlying program could occur without the use of the exact sequence. For example, it would be extremely easy to shift the specific sequence while still plagiarizing the program through the insertion of a single instruction not changing the logic of the sequence, or to change the encoded addresses of operands, or to use different encodings for the machine commands. A copyright registrant might find that object code registration actually provided, as a practical matter, very little real protection.

In addition, copyright registration of object code as a computer program discloses almost nothing in return for the protection of law. Information transfer about the program is deliberately minimized, not maximized. Thus, this study finds that the independent copyrightability of object code as a computer program is not in accord with the basic principles on which its recommendations are based.

On the other hand, the above should not be understood as implying the finding that object code is not protectable at all. The copyrightability of programs in source language would have very little value if the object code could be produced or copied with impunity. It is concluded, therefore, that the conversion of a source program into object code, which implies no addition to the logic of the program and therefore no value added, constitutes the making of a copy.

Thus, object code should be protected by virtue of the copyright in the source program. It may be noted that in the process of producing object code from a source program, the usual procedure is to combine certain necessary operating parameters into the object code. These parameters often select the specific peripheral units that will be used with the program when the program is run and also select the location of the program in the computer storage units. In the view of this study, these additions to the object code constitute almost nothing that could be classed as original works of authorship. Thus, the generation of object code, even with the addition of these housekeeping functions, cannot be classed as the preparation of a derivative work.

5.7.5 Translation To a New Source Language

The translation of a source program from one source language to another source language should be considered the preparation of a derivative work. The translation makes possible the understanding of the program by an additional group of persons and provides for wider dissemination and use.

5.7.6 Value of Copyright Protection

It is clear from the concept of copyright and from Section 102(b) of the 1976 General Revision that only the "expression" of a program can be protected. As stated in Section 102(b):

> "In no case does copyright protection for an original work of authorship extend to any idea, procedure, process, system, method of operation, concept, principle, or discovery, regardless of the form in which it is described, explained, illustrated, or embodied in such work."

The question may be asked, whether protecting the expression only, rather than the concept is valuable. An answer is that copyright protection hopes to prevent a major type of market failure with regard to computer programs, but does not claim to protect against all types of market failure. Therefore, copyright is valuable, but not valuable for every purpose.

It is important to note that unauthorized copying of computer programs, even without any further use or dissemination of the concepts of the program, is a major type of market failure. The reason this is true is that examination of the program code to determine any unique concepts contained therein requires the expenditure of significant resources, while copying by itself requires only a bare minimum of resources. A copier who is assured that the program in question performs the functions he desires in an error-free manner has obtained something of considerable value, at minimum expense. The added effort of understanding any unique procedures contained in the program is not likely to yield a corresponding advantage for a pragmatic user.

The disclosure of unique concepts, certainly, will assist competitors in the development of competing programs, but whether a particular unique or innovative design concept is protectable would depend on how a statute (such as the patent law) protecting such concepts might be written or might be interpreted. This report is not the proper vehicle for a detailed discussion of this matter; but it can be pointed out that very few programs contain (or need to contain) new concepts as unique as the simplex method for the solution of linear programming problems or the fast fourier transform algorithm, both outstanding advances in computational procedures. For the most part, what is required of programs is that they carry out their intended functions with precision and in an error-free manner. Performance is improved if in addition, programs minimize execution time and use of storage space to the extent practicable. For most applications, unique concepts are not required, and for these programs, copyright protection should be sufficient. Clearly, there appears to be room for further study on the possible protection of unique and innovative programming concepts.

5.7.7 Copyright and Software Industry Strength

One argument against copyrightability of computer programs is that the industry is burgeoning and therefore copyright is unnecessary. It must be noted, however, that copyright does not specifically protect an industry, but rather a particular work in the marketplace. The protection is particularly important for the smaller entrepreneur who does not have the resources to engage in the kind of retaliatory measures suggested by Hurt and Schuchman or to protect himself against the predatory practice proposed by Breyer and described in Section 4.2 above. Copyrightability promotes competition and innovations by the small competitor. These aspects of the marketplace are important criteria for public policy towards an industry, as are growth and size of the industry.

5.7.8 Duration of Copyright Protection

It seems reasonable to propose that the author of a computer program should not be treated any differently than the author of any other type of copyrightable work. Therefore, the duration of copyright in computer programs should be the same as the duration of copyright in other works.

A reason that has been given for proposing a shorter duration of copyright is that with changing technology, computer programs would become valueless after several years. However, if the proposal of this report is adopted, that an original computer program copyright should be obtainable only in the source program, and not in the object code, then a separation of the programmer's expression from the hardware technology is promoted. Furthermore, even if popular source languages are altered or improved, the copyright proprietor retains the right to prepare derivative works, permitting him to update the program as required.

5.7.9 User Rights in Computer-Readable Works

A computer program, and a computerized data base as well, are intended for use in conjunction with a computer. That is, a computer-readable work is used by entering it into a computer system and manipulating it through the logic of a computer. It seems reasonable to propose that the copyright proprietor should retain the exclusive right to the use of a computer-readable work in a computer.

However, this study proposes a limitation on the exclusive right of use, in order to reduce transaction costs in connection with the transfer of ownership of copies of computer-readable works. This limitation is intended to operate through improved salability of computer programs and computerized data bases, considered immediately below.

5.8 IMPROVING SALABILITY OF COMPUTER-READABLE WORKS

Several kinds of copyrighted works are offered for sale at retail. Books, maps, and sound recordings are typical of this class. The advantage of sale over lease or rental is that transaction costs are minimized. No agreement, except to pay the retail price, need be made. The buyer obtains ownership over the copy or phonorecord he has purchased, including the right to resell that copy, except for certain rights retained by the copyright owner. The retained rights include the rights to make and sell copies (with exemption for fair use, compulsory licenses, etc.), the right to prepare derivative works, and the rights to perform and display the work publicly.

If the rights to computer-readable works could be defined in such a way as to promote the sale rather than lease of such works, transaction costs might be similarly minimized. This would be, certainly, in the public interest.

5.8.1 The Right to Ephemeral Recordings

One of the problems in the sale of computer-readable works is the right of the buyer to copy for his own use. Here, "buyer" means the purchaser of a copy where ownership of the copy is transferred. For works published in paper, "use" simple means "reading" and no copying is required. For sound recordings, "use" means "playing" the recording on a playback mechanism, but again, no copying is required. For computer-readable works, copying into the computer is required in order to use, and in addition, archival copies are made in normal practice in case a copy in use is destroyed inadvertently.

In Section 112 of the 1976 General Revision, the right to ephemeral recordings is recognized for a "transmitting organization." This means that a radio station or TV station has the right to record a performance that it is transmitting for its own internal purposes, for example, "for purposes of archival preservation or security."

It seems reasonable to suggest that buyers of computer-readable works ought to have similar statutory rights of ephemeral recording in order to be able to effectively use what they have bought. It seems reasonable to suggest, also, that restrictions on the use of such ephemeral recordings ought to be imposed. For example, if a buyer resells the copy of the computer-readable work that he has bought, he ought to be required to destroy all ephemeral copies. The buyer ought to be able to resell no more than one copy of a computer-readable work if he had bought only one copy. Furthermore, the right of internal use should be distinguished from network use. The usage rights of a buyer should not include the right to make the work available to outsiders through a computer network or otherwise.

The effect of the allowance for free internal use in situations of transfer of ownership means that there could be no performance royalty charged. If the seller wants the buyer to pay for each individual use of the computer-readable work, the seller would have to negotiate a lease or rental agreement with the buyer. For lease with per-use charges, the transaction costs are probably higher than for outright sale.

5.8.2 The Right to Make and Use Machine Code

Similarly, the need of a buyer to copy a computer-readable work into a computer in order to use it requires that the buyer make object code out of the work. It seems reasonable to suggest, in order to promote the sale of computer-readable works and thereby reduce transaction costs, that a buyer be permitted, for his own use, to convert a computer-readable work to object code and to use the code in his own computer.

5.8.3 Differential Pricing

Another concept which might induce an increase in sales rather than

leases is differential pricing between individual buyers and institutional buyers. This concept has been described in Chapter 4 of this
report as having a theoretical economic basis, and the concept is further described in Appendices C1 and C2. The concept, in general, has
been described in terms of the sale of scientific journals, but there
is no reason why the concept could not be adapted and utilized for the
sale of computer-readable works, as proposed in Appendix D.

In general, an individual buyer would be one with a single computer
system and a small number of terminals. For the sale of computer programs, that is, computer-readable works that are typically manipulated
by the arithmetic units of computer systems, an institutional buyer
could be defined as one with a large number of computer systems on
which the program might run or as one who could be expected to use the
program to benefit many individuals. For the sale of computer-readable
data bases or textual works, that is, works that are typically viewed
at terminals with subsets being retrieved by users, an institutional
buyer could be defined as one with a large number of internal (user)
terminals attached to his system.

5.8.4 Data Base Access Services

A special type of institutional buyer must be noted. The independent
data-base access service employs a computer-readable data base, and for
a use-dependent fee, permits outsiders to obtain printouts of subsets
of the data base at external user terminals.

The data base access service is providing derivative works to outsiders
through the printouts, as well as displaying the work publicly, two
rights which are reserved to the copyright holder under Section 106.

In order to make the concept of outright sale useful to independent
data base access services, these services would have to be given statutory permission to display computer-readable works publicly and to prepare derivative works. It is not clear that copyright proprietors
would want to give up these rights in this situation.

5.9 SUMMARY

The issue of computer-readable works was raised significantly in Senate
hearings in 1967. Predictions of vast changes in methods of production
and distribution of works alerted publishers and authors to the need
for language in the copyright law which protected their works in computers. The predictions were premature, but technically feasible, and
within the realm of possibility, depending on many social, economic,
and psychological factors.

The 1976 General Revision clarified rights in works fixed in any tangible medium, but the insertion of Section 117, because of the establishment of CONTU, continued certain ambiguities. The 1976 Act abolishes
common law protection for fixed, but unpublished works and provides
statutory protection instead.

The most important act assuring maximum Federal protection is registration of the copyright and deposit of the necessary copy. Disclosure
through this act is an important *quid pro quo* for Federal protection.

The Register of Copyrights is entitled to make rules allowing the deposit of identifying information instead of complete copies for certain classes of work. The principle of maximum information transfer would seem to demand complete disclosure for scientific and technical information.

Data bases should be copyrightable in any medium of expression. Clarification is needed as to what constitutes publication for a data base distributed only in computer-readable form to one or a small number of computer systems that provide user-access via a terminal query.

There is a need to review the possibility of monopoly pricing in computer-readable, data-base access services. Some of these data bases are relatively nonsubstitutable, and competitive entry in the field may be difficult. Compulsory licensing may be a remedy but innovation should not be stifled.

Computer programs should be copyrightable in human-readable form (source language) in any tangible medium of expression. The object code should be protectable as a copy of a computer program, but not as an original copyrightable computer program by itself, because it fails to disclose anything substantial. Material defining the language of a computer program should be disclosed at time of registration. For most computer programs, copyright protection is sufficient because the programs contain no innovative concepts. Further study may be worthwhile to determine the value of protecting the innovative concepts that might be contained. The duration of copyright for computer programs should be no less than the duration of protection of other works. This should promote the writing of programs in enduring languages. The definition of a program converted to a new source language as a derivative work will help extend the life of programs.

There is a need to insure a user's rights in computer-readable works if the user has purchased the work in outright sale. The sale of copyrighted works rather than lease or rental should be promoted as being lower in transaction costs. A buyer needs the right to make source-language copies for his internal use and the right to make and use object code. The buyer would not be permitted to resell more than the number of copies he had purchased nor make the work available externally to others on a computer network without permission. At the time of resale, extra copies would have to be destroyed.

6. POLICYMAKING FOR COPYRIGHT

In the course of this project, it was recognized that if conclusions were to be drawn about the applicability of copyright to computer-readable works, then decisionmaking with respect to other kinds of copyrightable works ought to be researched. Therefore, an historical analysis was undertaken, and the fundamental principles and concepts underlying copyright were reviewed.

This historical and conceptual study has been found to be extremely useful. It has elucidated the principles of political philosophy and economics on which copyright is based. It has clarified the roles of the separate branches of the Federal Government in copyright policymaking and demonstrated their interactions. It has identified the impact of incremental technological change, thereby showing decisionmaking under increasing complexity. Finally, it has enabled copyright policymaking to be placed in the matrix of decisionmaking in general, thereby making possible an identification of the political system models with which it is most closely associated.

6.1 COPYRIGHT AND OTHER PROPERTY RIGHTS

The history of copyright presents evidence that an essential point at issue, regardless of the technology involved, is the definition of the boundaries of the property right. In this, copyright is not much different than other kinds of property, tangible or intangible. In addition, with the property right is typically associated reciprocal responsibilities. An example of the conception of property rights in this manner is presented by Walter Lippmann in The Public Philosophy; in which the concept of *quid pro quo* is stated to be fundamental to our system of government:

> "Early in the history of Western society, political thinkers in Rome hit upon the idea that the concepts of the public philosophy - particularly the idea of reciprocal rights and duties under law - could be given concreteness by treating them as contracts. In this way, freedom emanating from a constitutional order has been advocated....by establishing the presumption that civilized society is founded on a public social contract.
>
> "A contract is an agreement reached voluntarily, *quid quo pro* and likely, therefore, to be observed - in any event, rightfully enforceable..."[72]

Copyright appears at first glance to be encumbered with many kinds of conditional rights and complexities, whereas other property rights may appear to be relatively clean and easily defined. Actually, this is not so. A farmer may be restrained from using insecticides if his neighbor is a beekeeper and may be induced by Government to plant or not to plant certain crops. A builder may be restrained from constructing a factory in a residential neighborhood. Airplanes may be confined to certain corridors for purposes of noise abatement and places of business must meet many standards of safety and occupancy.

In general, the rights of property are the creation of law. Lippmann has quoted Blackstone's Commentaries on this question:

> "The original of private property is probably founded in nature....but certainly the modifications under which we at present find it, the method of conserving it in its present owner, and of translating it from man to man, are entirely derived from society, and are some of those civil advantages in exchange for which every individual has resigned a part of his natural liberty."[73]

Thus, people may act from a foundation of what they believe to be naturally right, but one view is that enforcement of those rights is derived from the public social contract, through which some liberty is exchanged for some protection of law. Copyright appears to assume such a social contract.

6.2 APPLICABLE DECISIONMAKING MODELS

6.2.1 Pluralism

It seems clear that decisionmaking on copyright questions has been very much in the pluralist mode in the twentieth century. That is, conflict has been among contending factions (interest groups) gathered around different functions related to copyrighted works. For the most part, the contenders have been the primary producers, i.e., authors and their original publishers, against secondary producers, that is, those who would use copyrighted works to provide ultimate consumers with additional products and services. In general, the Congress refers to the secondary producers as "users" although they are not the ultimate consumers. The secondary producers have included phonorecord manufacturers, jukebox owners, movie makers (in the use of copyrighted music in sound tracks), over-the-air broadcasters, cable TV broadcasters, educational photocopiers (for further distribution to students), and Government librarians (for further distribution to researchers).

The ultimate consumers are usually not involved, although users of computer programs and researchers in educational institutions who use photocopies have been involved. Neither of these groups can be identified with the general public consumer of copyrighted works, e.g., the general buyers of books, records, movie tickets, concert tickets, etc.

The governmental role envisioned by the pluralist model is:

> "(1) establishing rules of the game in the group struggle, (2) arranging compromises and balancing interests, (3) enacting compromises in the form of public policy, and (4) enforcing these compromises."[74]

There is no question that Congress and the Judiciary have served these purposes in copyright decisionmaking. In fact, the idea of group compromise is no secret in this field. The 1976 General Revision of Copyright Law calls upon the Register of Copyrights to submit a report to Congress "setting forth the extent to which this section $/\overline{\ }108\overline{\ }/$ has achieved the intended statutory balancing of the rights of creators, and the needs of users." Thus, the balancing concept is specifically written into law in the photocopying area. Similarly, House Report 94-1476 on page 65 speaks of the definition of "fair use" $/\overline{\ }$Section 107$\overline{\ }/$ as "balancing the equities."

The setting of the royalty rate for the phonorecord manufacturing license between the 3¢ per musical piece manufactured asked by some representatives of the publishers and writers and the 2¢ requested to be retained by representatives of the record manufacturers, and the further compromise between the Senate-passed royalty fee and the House-passed royalty fee is an additional example. The statutory balancing of the membership of the National Commission on New Technological Uses of Copyrighted Works is another example; and in the statement contained within House Report 94-1476 on page 360, the Hon. George E. Danielson states (about Section 111) that:

> "....the committee has arrived at a solution which I submit is fair and equitable to both the owners and the users of copyrighted materials...."

It can be reasonably expected that decisionmaking will continue in a primarily pluralist mode for the foreseeable future in order to resolve disputes in which a balance of equities is the primary consideration. Probably, the Copyright Royalty Tribunal will be aided in its efforts by a rational analysis of economic issues.

6.2.2 The Power Arena Model

Professor Theodore J. Lowi has defined domestic policies as falling into one of three arenas of power: distribution, regulation, or redistribution. Lowi states that:

> "distribution /̄was_7 almost the exclusive type of national domestic policy from 1789 until virtually 1890. Agitation for regulatory and redistributive policies began at about the same time, but regulation had become an established fact before any headway at all was made in redistribution."[75]

Distributive policies are those decisions that can be made in the short run without regard to limited resources. The standard example is 19th century land policy. Distributive policies are typically capable of disaggregation so that what is being distributed can be dispensed in small units. Under distribution, indulged and deprived may be members of the same group (i.e. the winner and loser of a Government contract or grant).

Regulatory decisions normally affect an entire industry and often concern the ability of that industry to do business in the long term. Within the context of the regulatory structure, there may be distributive decisionmaking (e.g. assignment of a TV channel or an airline route), but regulatory decisions typically affect all industry members in a similar manner. Often, the regulatory policies affecting one industry are of little concern to other industries.

The redistributive arena, according to Lowi, involves issues that concern "haves and have-nots, bigness and smallness....."[76] Typical issues that appear in the redistributive arena are overall tax policy and policies on unemployment and retirement income. Industry groups concerned with separated regulatory policies are likely to find a common ground in the redistributive arena.

The importance of the power arena model is in what it says about the changing nature of copyright decisionmaking. In 1790 and until about the time that Lowi dates the beginning of regulatory policies, copyright fitted neatly into the distributive arena. The contention among factions was not a primary factor. Clearly, individual copyrights have been and will continue to be dispensed in small units in the short run without regard to limited resources. In fact, copyrights (and patents) may be the ultimate distributive good since originality and creativity are essentially independent of resource constraints (although nurturing these qualities may not be). The increase in registered copyrights and patents does not diminish the stock of un-issued copyrights and patents waiting for new claimants.

While the distribution of copyrights continues, it seems clear that much copyright policymaking since the turn of the century has been in the regulatory arena, and is increasingly so. This has been due to the increasing number of secondary producer groups ("users") who have been contending the boundaries of intellectual property rights with primary producers. Each field of copyright has its own contenders, and major decisions in each field treat all producers in the same way, as the regulatory arena requires. Not surprisingly, Lowi recognizes that his regulatory arena is very close in concept to the pluralist model of policymaking.

Another factor causing an increase in regulatory policymaking in copyright is the increase in the sensitivity of public decisionmakers to monopoly and other forms of market failure such as high transaction costs; and the consequent increase in public institutions and mechanisms involved in correcting these market problems. Thus, there are now four compulsory license types within the copyright domain, a Copyright Royalty Tribunal to oversee certain aspects of these licenses, and a Federal court supervising the performing rights area. It remains to be seen if the photocopying problem can be successfully concluded with a collective mechanism that does not involve additional, permanent Federal intervention; and final Congressional action in the area of computer-readable works is yet to come.

Very little about copyright is directly in the redistributive arena unless the truism is cited that, in the long run, all policies are redistributive. It could be said, however, that activities that prevent monopoly pricing of copyrighted works are redistributive since prices affect the ultimate consumer. At the same time, it may be noted that, except for anti-monopoly and infringement prosecution activities in the Department of Justice, the only Executive Branch concern with copyright is as a peripheral policy issue that may affect research through the availability of data and scientific journals, and may affect TV viewers in the quality of available programs. There is no administrative "program" about which one could make cost-benefit calculations with concern for objectives achieved in relation to funds spent. Copyright is now primarily a regulatory balancing issue involving producer interests and special classes of users, and is likely to remain so. Congress appears to regard the balancing of equities in copyright as a distinct function reserved to itself.

The future cannot be predicted with any certainty but it is possible that additional technological change, coupled with increases in the costs of resources such as raw materials, may bring copyright policymaking more into the redistributive arena. If that occurs, it is likely to be in a context in which copyright is an element of a more consumer-oriented issue, such as "public access to information."

6.3 THE IMPACT OF TECHNOLOGICAL CHANGE

It is most interesting that Lowi dates the beginning of the regulatory policy era at approximately the start of growth in innovations of information technology. The effect of new innovations is to make available new opportunities, which means in economic terms, new industries and increases in investment and employment; but which means in political terms, increases in the number of interest groups and the consequences of their activities.

Furthermore, another effect of new innovations is to make ambiguous the definitions of property rights that were perfectly clear before the innovations. As John Dewey stated many years ago,

> "Every thinker puts some portion of an apparently stable
> world in peril and no one can predict what will emerge in
> its place."[77]

Thus, "public performance for profit" has an entirely different meaning
after the commencement of commercial broadcasting than before. "Fair
use" has an entirely different meaning after the diffusion of high speed
photocopying than before; "copy" a different meaning after the invention
of punch cards and magnetic tape than before.

It seems completely in the spirit of free enterprise for an innovator
to attempt to combine a new technology with the new ambiguity or uncertainty it raises in order to develop a new market and a new industry.
Should the innovator succeed, a new interest group is formed around the
successful technology, but the proliferation of interest groups must
generate additional conflict in the contention for the same property
right.

Consequently, the nearly inevitable result of the successful introduction of new technology is increased regulation as contenders pursue
their rights through the Judiciary and Congress. This is happening with
information technology and copyright as it has in other fields. To
quote from Professor David Truman in The Governmental Process:

> "The causes of this growth /¯in organized interest groups_7
> lie in the increased complexity of techniques for dealing
> with the environment, in the specializations that these in-
> volve, and in associated disturbances of the manifold expec-
> tations that guide individual behavior in a complex and in-
> terdependent society. Complexity of technique, broadly con-
> ceived, is inseparable from complexity of social structure.."[78]

Thus, complex ways of using information technology, for example by amplifying distant TV signals and distributing them by cable to viewers,
or by abstracting scientific articles, combining them with key words
and distributing them to researchers via terminals attached to a computer with a logical query system, must involve complex rules of property rights in a society where such things are important.

By setting priorities that establish the importance of a balance of
property rights, rational decisionmakers must then establish a working
regulatory system that minimizes transaction costs but allows for the
balance of rights established. This may be a complex system of rules,
and if the rules appear to be difficult to follow or enforce, perhaps
the priorities must be reviewed. Care must be exercised, however, so
as not to throw out basic principles simply for the sake of simplifica-
tion.

6.4 THE PUBLIC INTEREST AND COMPUTER-READABLE WORKS

In proposing recommendations for the application of copyright to computer-readable works, a set of criteria must be used. It seems reasonable to suggest that the overriding criterion must be "the public interest," however, that may be defined.

One aspect of the public interest is how decisionmaking affects the individual citizen. It has been pointed out earlier in this chapter that in the twentieth century, copyright decisionmaking has involved contending interests groups gathered around different functions related to copyrighted works. The individual citizen, in general, has not been directly involved. Such decisionmaking, not involving the public directly but having an ultimate impact, has concerned some observers. The following statement of concern is by Victor Ferkiss in *Technological Man: The Myth and the Reality*:

> "The danger is not that industrialism has destroyed the intermediate group in modern democratic society but that the group is so strong that the individual, instead of finding freedom in the interstices created by group competition, may be crushed between the contending parties, or that instead of a dominant total government riding roughshod over an inert society, public purposes will be lost sight of in the feudalistic struggle of competing special interests."[79]

Professor David Truman considered the question raised above and concluded that "multiple memberships in potential groups based on widely held and accepted interests"[80] prevents the culmination of a situation such as that suggested by Ferkiss. That is, while groups may contend over specific property rights, the members of the groups share common fundamental views that prevent the erosion of individual rights that would have the effect of hurting everyone. Truman calls these shared attituded the "rules of the game" and quotes others as describing them as a "general ideological consensus" and as "a broad body of attitudes and understandings regarding the nature and limits of authority." As a further description, Truman states that "....the 'rules' would include the value generally attached to the dignity of the individual human being, loosely expressed in terms of 'fair dealing'...."[81]

For the purposes of proposing recommendations on computer-readable works, this study has enumerated in Section 1.3 those "Findings of Basic Principles" which it conceives to be the applicable "shared attitudes" and "rules of the game." As stated in Section 1.2, these findings are not be be taken as the final, definitive view. Other analyses may reveal different interpretations. Additional contributions to the literature are welcomed.

REFERENCES

[1] Walter L. Pforzheimer, "Historical Perspective on Copyright Law and Fair Use" in Lowell H. Hattery and George P. Bush, (eds.) *Reprography and Copyright Law*, Washington, D.C., American Institute of Biological Sciences, 1964, p. 25.

[2] Emmette S. Redford, *American Government and the Economy*, New York, The Macmillan Co., 1965, p. 13.

[3] Saxe Commins and Robert N. Linscott (eds.) *Man and the State: The Political Philosophers*, New York, Random House, Inc., 1947, p. 56.

[4] Walter L. Pforzheimer, op. cit., p.24.

[5] P. L. 94-553, Section 301, 94th Congress, October 19, 1976.

[6] Emmette S. Redford, op. cit., pp. 6, 7.

[7] Peter O. Steiner, "The Public Sector and The Public Interest" in Robert H. Haveman and Julius Margolis (eds.), <u>Public Expenditures and Policy Analysis</u>, Chicago, Rand McNally Publishing Co., 1970, p.21.

[8] ibid,. p. 21.

[9] ibid,. p. 25.

[10] Robert M. Hurt and Robert M. Schuchman, "The Economic Rationale of Copyright" in <u>The Economics of Publishing</u>, American Economic Rev., May 1966, pp. <u>421-432</u>.

[11] ibid., p. 425.

[12] ibid., p. 429.

[13] ibid., p. 429.

[14] P. L. 94-553, Section 102(a)

[15] Hurt and Schuchman, op. cit., p. 424.

[16] Joseph Taubman, "Creation, Copyright and the Constitutional Clause," <u>Bulletin. Copyright Society of the U.S.A.</u> (1959), vol. 6, pp. 163-164.

[17] ibid.

[18] Paul Goldstein, "The Private Consumption of Public Goods: A Comment on <u>Williams & Wilkins Co. v. United States</u>," <u>Bulletin. Copyright Society of the U.S.A.</u> (1974), vol. 21, p. 204.

[19] Association of American Publishers, Inc., "Program for the Provision of Copies of Technical-Scientific-Medical Journal Articles and for Related Information Service Copies," March 17, 1977, One Park Avenue, New York, N.Y. 10016

[20] National Commission on New Technological Uses of Copyrighted Works Preliminary Report, Oct. 1976, National Technical Information Service, Springfield, Va. 22161, Report No. PB 260373.

[21] Kenneth J. Arrow, "The Organization of Economic Activity: Issues Pertinent to the Choice of Market Versus Non-Market Allocation," in Robert H. Haveman and Julius Margolis (eds.), op. cit., p. 68.

[22] ibid.

[23] Peter O. Steiner, op. cit., p. 30.

[24] Hurt and Schuchman, op. cit., p. 425.

[25] ibid., p. 428.

[26] Stephen Breyer, "The Uneasy Case for Copyright: A Study of Copyright in Books, Photocopies and Computer Programs" <u>Harvard Law Review</u>, vol. 84, no. 2, Dec. 1970, pp. 281-351.

[27] ibid., p. 348.

[28] Calvin Mooers, "Preventing Software Piracy" <u>COMPUTER</u>, March, 1977, p. 30.

[29] Edwin Mansfield, <u>Microeconomics: Theory and Applications</u>, Second Edition, New York, Norton, 1975, p. 164.

[30] P. L. 94-553, Section 115.

[31] Melville Nimmer, "Copyright vs. The First Amendment" <u>Bulletin. Copyright Society of the U.S.A.</u> (1970), pp. 255-279.

[32] Paul Goldstein, op. cit., pp. 206-208.

[33] Walter L. Pforzheimer, op. cit., p. 28.

[34] ibid., p. 29.

[35] Hurt and Schuchman, op. cit., p. 429-430.

[36] Edwin Mansfield, op. cit., p. 302.

[37] P. L. 94-553, Section 102(b).

[38] Joseph Taubman, op. cit.

[39] ibid., p. 154.

[40] Hurt and Schuchman, op. cit., p. 431

[41] Copyright Law Revision (1967), Hearings before the Subcommittee on Patents, Trademarks and Copyrights of the Committee on the Judiciary, United States Senate, Ninetieth Congress, First Session, Part 1, March 15, 16, and 17, 1967.

[42] ibid., p. 71.

[43] ibid., p. 85.

[44] ibid., p. 53.

[45] Julius J. Marke, <u>Copyright and Intellectual Property</u>, New York, Fund for the Advancement of Education, 1967.

[46] Copyright Law Revision (1967), op. cit., p. 609.

[47] Julius J. Marke, op. cit., p. 89.

[48] ibid., p. 93.

[49] ibid., p. 92, 93.

[50] ibid., p. 103.

[51] Copyright Law Revision (1967), op. cit., p. 71.

[52] Julius J. Marke, op. cit., p. 91.

[53] National Academy of Sciences, Information Systems Panel, Computer Science and Engineering Board, <u>Libraries and Information Technology: A National System Challenge</u>. Report to the Council on Library Resources, Inc. Washington, D.C., 1971, p. 10.

[54] Copyright Law Revision (1967), op. cit., pp. 570-578.

[55] ibid., p. 571.

[56] ibid., p. 573.

[57] ibid., p. 576-577.

[58] ibid., p. 575.

[59] ibid., pp. 969-974.

[60] ibid., p. 83.

[61] Cambridge Research Institute, <u>Omnibus Copyright Revision, Comparative Analysis of the Issues</u>, Washington, D.C. American Society for Information Science, 1973, pp. 87-100.

[62] <u>Federal Management of Scientific and Technical Performation (STINFO) Activities: The Role of the National Science Foundation</u>, Special Subcommittee on the National Science Foundation of the Committee on Labor and Public Welfare, United States Senate, July, 1975, p. 22.

[63] ibid., pp. 22, 23.

[64] ibid., p. 75.

[65] ibid., p. 78.

[66] ibid., p. 79.

[67] Daniel Bell, "Remarks of the Moderator," in <u>The Management of Information and Knowledge</u>, Committee on Science and Astronautics, U.S. House of Representatives, 1970, p. 14.

[68] Peter F. Drucker, <u>The Age of Discontinuity-Guidelines to our Changing Society</u>, New York, Harper & Row, 1968.

[69] Gerald M. Weinberg, <u>The Psychology of Computer Programming</u>, New York, Van Nostrand Reinhold Co., 1971.

[70] Dennie Van Tassel, <u>Program Style, Design, Efficiency, Debugging, and Testing</u>, Englewood Cliffs, N.J., Prentice-Hall, Inc., 1974.

[71] Frederick P. Brooks, Jr., <u>The Mythical Man-Month, Essays on Software Engineering</u>, Reading, Mass., Addison-Wesley Pub. Co., 1975.

[72] Walter Lippmann, The Public Philosophy, New York, Mentor Books, 1956, p. 127.

[73] Walter Lippmann, op. cit., p. 92.

[74] Thomas R. Dye, Understanding Public Policy, Englewood Cliffs, N.J., Prentice-Hall, 1972, p. 23.

[75] Theodore J. Lowi, "American Business, Public Policy, Case Studies, and Political Theory," World Politics, vol. 16, n.4, July 1964, p. 689.

[76] ibid., p. 691.

[77] quoted in Joseph Weizenbaum, Computer Power and Human Reason, San Francisco, W. H. Freeman and Co., 1976, p. 26.

[78] David B. Truman, The Governmental Process. New York, Knopf, 1951, p. 502.

[79] Victor Ferkiss, Technological Man: The Myth and the Reality, New York, George Braziller, 1969, p. 163.

[80] David B. Truman, op. cit., p. 514.

[81] ibid., p. 512.

S. 22

IN THE HOUSE OF REPRESENTATIVES

FEBRUARY 23, 1976

Referred to to Committee on the Judiciary

AN ACT

For the general revision of the Copyright Law, title 17 of the United States
Code, and for other purposes.

1   *Be it enacted by the Senate and House of Representatives of the*

2   *United States of America in Congress assembled,*

3   TITLE I—GENERAL REVISION OF COPYRIGHT LAW

4   SEC. 101. Title 17 of the United States Code, entitled "Copyrights",

5   is hereby amended in its entirety to read as follows:

6   ## TITLE 17—COPYRIGHTS

Chapter	Sec.
1. SUBJECT MATTER AND SCOPE OF COPYRIGHT	101
2. COPYRIGHT OWNERSHIP AND TRANSFER	201
3. DURATION OF COPYRIGHT	301
4. COPYRIGHT NOTICE, DEPOSIT, AND REGISTRATION	401
5. COPYRIGHT INFRINGEMENT AND REMEDIES	501
6. MANUFACTURING REQUIREMENT AND IMPORTATION	601
7. COPYRIGHT OFFICE	701
8. COPYRIGHT ROYALTY TRIBUNAL	801

7   ## Chapter 1.—SUBJECT MATTER AND SCOPE OF COPYRIGHT

Sec.
101. Definitions.
102. Subject matter of copyright: In general.
103. Subject matter of copyright: Compilations and derivative works.
104. Subject matter of copyright: National origin.
105. Subject matter of copyright: United States Government works.
106. Exclusive rights in copyrighted works.

1   # TITLE 17—COPYRIGHTS—Continued

2   ## Chapter 1.—SUBJECT MATTER AND SCOPE OF

3   ## COPYRIGHT—Continued

4   ## § 101. Definitions

5   As used in this title, the following terms and their variant forms

6   mean the following:

7   An "anonymous work" is a work on the copies or phonorecords

8   of which no natural person is identified as author.

9   "Audiovisual works" are works that consist of a series of related

10   images which are intrinsically intended to be shown by the use of

11   machines or devices such as projectors, viewers, or electronic

12   equipment, together with accompanying sounds, if any, regardless

13   of the nature of the material objects, such as films or tapes, in

14   which the works are embodied.

15   The "best edition" of a work is the edition, published in the

16   United States at any time before the date of deposit, that the Li-

17   brary of Congress determines to be most suitable for its purposes.

18   A person's "children" are his immediate offspring, whether

19   legitimate or not, and any children legally adopted by him.

20   A "collective work" is a work, such as a periodical issue, an-

21   thology, or encyclopedia, in which a number of contributions,
22   constituting separate and independent works in themselves, are
23   assembled into a collective whole.

24   A "compilation" is a work formed by the collection and assem-
25   bling of pre-existing materials or of data that are selected, coordi-
26   nated, or arranged in such a way that the resulting work as a
27   whole constitutes an original work of authorship. The term "com-
28   pilation" includes collective works.

1   "Copies" are material objects, other than phonorecords, in which
2   a work is fixed by any method now known or later developed, and
3   from which the work can be perceived, reproduced, or otherwise
4   communicated, either directly or with the aid of a machine or
5   device. The term "copies" includes the material object, other than
6   a phonorecord, in which the work is first fixed.

7   "Copyright owner", with respect to any one of the exclusive
8   rights comprised in a copyright, refers to the owner of that par-
9   ticular right.

10   A work is "created" when it is fixed in a copy or phonorecord
11   for the first time; where a work is prepared over a period of time,
12   the portion of it that has been fixed at any particular time con-
13   stitutes the work as of that time, and where the work has been
14   prepared in different versions, each version constitutes a separate
15   work.

16   A "derivative work" is a work based upon one or more pre-
17   existing works, such as a translation, musical arrangement, dram-
18   atization, fictionalization, motion picture version, sound record-
19   ing, art reproduction, abridgment, condensation, or any other
20   form in which a work may be recast, transformed, or adapted. A
21   work consisting of editorial revisions, annotations, elaborations,
22   or other modifications which, as a whole, represent an original
23   work of authorship, is a "derivative work".

24   A "device", "machine", or "process" is one now known or later
25   developed.

26 To "display" a work means to show a copy of it, either directly
27 or by means of a film, slide, television image, or any other device
28 or process or, in the case of a motion picture or other audiovisual
29 work, to show individual images nonsequentially.

30 A work is "fixed" in a tangible medium of expression when its
31 embodiment in a copy or phonorecord, by or under the authority
32 of the author, is sufficiently permanent or stable to permit it to
33 be perceived, reproduced, or otherwise communicated for a period
34 of more than transitory duration. A work consisting of sounds,
35 images, or both, that are being transmitted, is "fixed" for pur-
36 poses of this title if a fixation of the work is being made simultane-
37 ously with its transmission.

38 The terms "including" and "such as" are illustrative and not
39 limitative.

1 A "joint work" is a work prepared by two or more authors
2 with the intention that their contributions be merged into insepa-
3 rable or interdependent parts of a unitary whole.

4 "Literary works" are works, other than audiovisual works,
5 expressed in words, numbers, or other verbal or numerical sym-
6 bols or indicia, regardless of the nature of the material objects,
7 such as books, periodicals, manuscripts, phonorecords, or film, in
8 which they are embodied.

9 "Motion pictures" are audiovisual works consisting of a series
10 of related images which, when shown in succession, impart an
11 impression of motion, together with accompanying sounds, if any.

12 To "perform" a work means to recite, render, play, dance, or
13 act it, either directly or by means of any device or process or, in
14 the case of a motion picture or other audiovisual work, to show its
15 images in any sequence or to make the sounds accompanying it
16 audible.

17 "Phonorecords" are material objects in which sounds, other than
18 those accompanying a motion picture or other audiovisual work,
19 are fixed by any method now known or later developed, and from

which the sounds can be perceived, reproduced, or otherwise communicated, either directly or with the aid of a machine or device. The term "phonorecords" includes the material object in which the sounds are first fixed.

"Pictorial, graphic, and sculptural works" include two-dimensional and three-dimensional works of fine, graphic, and applied art, photographs, prints and art reproductions, maps, globes, charts, plans, diagrams, and models.

A "pseudonymous work" is a work on the copies or phonorecords, of which the author is identified under a fictitious name.

"Publication" is the distribution of copies or phonorecords of a work to the public by sale or other transfer of ownership, or by rental, lease, or lending. The offering to distribute copies or phonorecords to a group of persons for purposes of further distribution, public performance, or public display, constitutes publication. A public performance or display of a work does not of itself constitute publication.

To perform or display a work "publicly" means:

(1) to perform or display it at a place open to the public or at any place where a substantial number of persons outside of a normal circle of a family and its social acquaintances is gathered; or

(2) to transmit or otherwise communicate a performance or display of the work to a place specified by clause (1) or to the public, by means of any device or process, whether the members of the public capable of receiving the performance or display receive it in the same place or in separate places and at the same time or at different times.

"Sound recordings" are works that result from the fixation of a series of musical, spoken, or other sounds, but not including the sounds accompanying a motion picture or other audiovisual work, regardless of the nature of the material objects, such as disks, tapes, or other phonorecords, in which they are embodied.

14   "State" includes the District of Columbia and the Common-
15   wealth of Puerto Rico, and any territories to which this title is
16   made applicable by an act of Congress.

17   A "transfer of copyright ownership" is an assignment, mort-
18   gage, exclusive license, or any other conveyance, alienation, or
19   hypothecation of a copyright or of any of the exclusive rights
20   comprised in a copyright, whether or not it is limited in time or
21   place of effect, but not including a nonexclusive license.

22   A "transmission program" is a body of material that, as an
23   aggregate, has been produced for the sole purpose of transmission
24   to the public in sequence and as a unit.

25   To "transmit" a performance or display is to communicate it
26   by any device or process whereby images or sounds are received
27   beyond the place from which they are sent.

28   The "United States", when used in a geographical sense, com-
29   prises the several States, the District of Columbia and the Com-
30   monwealth of Puerto Rico, and the organized territories under
31   the jurisdiction of the United States Government.

32   A "useful article" is an article having an intrinsic utilitarian
33   function that is not merely to portray the appearance of the
34   article or to convey information. An article that is normally a part
35   of a useful article is considered a "useful article".

36   The author's "widow" or "widower" is the author's surviving
37   spouse under the law of his domicile at the time of his death,
38   whether or not the spouse has later remarried.

39   A "work of the United States Government" is a work prepared
1   by an officer or employee of the United States Government as part
2   of his official duties.

3   A "work made for hire" is:

4   (1) a work prepared by an employee within the scope of
5   his employment; or

6   (2) a work specially ordered or commissioned for use as
7   a contribution to a collective work, as a part of a motion pic-
8   ture or other audiovisual work, as a translation, as a supple-

mentary work, as a compilation, as an instructional text, as a test, as answer material for a test, as a photographic or other portrait of one or more persons, or as an atlas, if the parties expressly agree in a written instrument signed by them that the work shall be considered a work made for hire. A "supplementary work" is a work prepared for publication as a secondary adjunct to a work by another author for the purpose of introducing, concluding, illustrating, explaining, revising, commenting upon, or assisting in the use of the other work, such as forewords, afterwords, pictorial illustrations, maps, charts, tables, editorial notes, musical arrangements, answer material for tests, bibliographies, appendixes, and indexes. An "instructional text" is a literary, pictorial, or graphic work prepared for publication with the purpose of use in systematic instructional activities.

§ 102. Subject matter of copyright: In general

(a) Copyright protection subsists, in accordance with this title, in original works of authorship fixed in any tangible medium of expression, now known or later developed, from which they can be perceived, reproduced, or otherwise communicated, either directly or with the aid of a machine or device. Works of authorship include the following categories:

> (1) literary works;
>
> (2) musical works, including any accompanying words;
>
> (3) dramatic works, including any accompanying music;
>
> (4) pantomimes and choreographic works;
>
> (5) pictorial, graphic, and sculptural works;
>
> (6) motion pictures and other audiovisual works; and
>
> (7) sound recordings.

(b) In no case does copyright protection for an original work of authorship extend to any idea, plan, procedure, process, system, method of operation, concept, principle, or discovery, regardless of the form in which it is described, explained, illustrated, or embodied in such work.

3   **§ 103. Subject matter of copyright: Compilations and derivative**

4   **works**

5   (a) The subject matter of copyright as specified by section 102 in-

6   cludes compilations and derivative works, but protection for a work

7   employing pre-existing material in which copyright subsists does not

8   extend to any part of the work in which such material has been used

9   unlawfully.

10   (b) The copyright in a compilation or derivative work extends only

11   to the material contributed by the author of such work, as dis-

12   tinguished from the pre-existing material employed in the work,

13   and does not imply any exclusive right in the pre-existing material.

14   The copyright in such work is independent of, and does not affect

15   or enlarge the scope, duration, ownership, or subsistence of, any copy-

16   right protection in the pre-existing material.

17   **§ 104. Subject matter of copyright: National origin**

18   (a) UNPUBLISHED WORKS.—The works specified by sections 102 and

19   103, while unpublished, are subject to protection under this title with-

20   out regard to the nationality or domicile of the author.

21   (b) PUBLISHED WORKS.—The works specified by sections 102 and

22   103, when published, are subject to protection under this title if—

23   (1) on the date of first publication, one or more of the authors

24   is a national or domiciliary of the United States, or is a national,

25   domiciliary, or sovereign authority of a foreign nation that is a

26   party to a copyright treaty to which the United States is also a

27   party; or

28   (2) the work is first published in the United States or in a for-

29   eign nation that, on the date of first publication, is a party to the

30   Universal Copyright Convention of 1952; or

31   (3) the work is first published by the United Nations or any

32   of its specialized agencies, or by the Organization of American

33   States; or

34   (4) the work comes within the scope of a Presidential procla-

35   mation. Whenever the President finds that a particular foreign

36   nation extends, to works by authors who are nationals or domicili-

37   aries of the United States or to works that are first published in
38   the United States, copyright protection on substantially the same
39   basis as that on which the foreign nation extends protection to
40   works of its own nationals and domiciliaries and works first pub-
1   lished in that nation, he may by proclamation extend protection
2   under this title to works of which one or more of the authors is,
3   on the date of first publication, a national, domiciliary, or sov-
4   ereign authority of that nation, or which was first published in
5   that nation. The President may revise, suspend, or revoke any
6   such proclamation or impose any conditions or limitations on
7   protection under a proclamation.

8   **§ 105. Subject matter of copyright: United States Government**
9   **works**

10   Copyright protection under this title is not available for any work
11   of the United States Government, but the United States Government
12   is not precluded from receiving and holding copyrights transferred
13   to it by assignment, bequest, or otherwise.

14   **§ 106. Exclusive rights in copyrighted works**

15   Subject to sections 107 through 118, the owner of copyright under
16   this title has the exclusive rights to do and to authorize any of the
17   following:

18   (1) to reproduce the copyrighted work in copies or phono-
19   records;

20   (2) to prepare derivative works based upon the copyrighted
21   work;

22   (3) to distribute copies or phonorecords of the copyrighted
23   work to the public by sale or other transfer of ownership, or by
24   rental, lease, or lending;

25   (4) in the case of literary, musical, dramatic, and choreographic
26   works, pantomimes, and motion pictures and other audiovisual
27   works, to perform the copyrighted work publicly; and

28   (5) in the case of literary, musical, dramatic, and choreographic
29   works, pantomimes, and pictorial, graphic, or sculptural works,
30   including the individual images of a motion picture or other

31   audiovisual work, to display the copyrighted work publicly.

32   **§ 107. Limitations on exclusive rights: Fair use**

33   Notwithstanding the provisions of section 106, the fair use of a

34   copyrighted work, including such use by reproduction in copies or

35   phonorecords or by any other means specified by that section, for pur-

36   poses such as criticism, comment, news reporting, teaching, scholar-

37   ship, or research, is not an infringement of copyright. In determining

38   whether the use made of a work in any particular case is a fair use

39   the factors to be considered shall include:

40   (1) the purpose and character of the use;

1   (2) the nature of the copyrighted work;

2   (3) the amount and substantiality of the portion used in re-

3   lation to the copyrighted work as a whole; and

4   (4) the effect of the use upon the potential market for or value

5   of the copyrighted work.

6   **§ 108. Limitations on exclusive rights: Reproduction by libraries**

7   **and archives**

8   (a) Notwithstanding the provisions of section 106, it is not an in-

9   fringement of copyright for a library or archives, or any of its em-

10   ployees acting within the scope of their employment, to reproduce no

11   more than one copy or phonorecord of a work, or to distribute such copy

12   or phonorecord, under the conditions specified by this section, if:

13   (1) the reproduction or distribution is made without any pur-

14   pose of direct or indirect commercial advantage;

15   (2) the collections of the library or archives are (i)' open to the

16   public, or (ii) available not only to researchers affiliated with the

17   library or archives or with the institution of which it is a part, but

18   also to other persons doing research in a specialized field; and

19   (3) the reproduction or distribution of the work includes a

20   notice of copyright.

21   (b) The rights of reproduction and distribution under this section

22   apply to a copy or phonorecord of an unpublished work duplicated in

23   facsimile form solely for purposes of preservation and security or for

24   deposit for research use in another library or achives of the type de-

25 scribed by clause (2) of subsection (a), if the copy or phonorecord
26 reproduced is currently in the collections of the library or archives.
27   (c) The right of reproduction under this section applies to a copy
28 or phonorecord of a published work duplicated in facsimile form solely
29 for the purpose of replacement of a copy or phonorecord that is dam-
30 aged, deteriorating, lost, or stolen, if the library or archives has, after
31 a reasonable effort, determined that an unused replacement cannot be
32 obtained at a fair price.
33   (d) The rights of reproduction and distribution under this section
34 apply to a copy, made from the collection of a library or archives
35 where the user makes his request or from that of another library or
36 archives, of no more than one article or other contribution to a copy-
37 righted collection or periodical issue, or to a copy or phonorecord of a
38 small part of any other copyrighted work, if:
1   (1) the copy becomes the property of the user, and the library
2   or archives has had no notice that the copy would be used for any
3   purpose other than private study, scholarship, or research; and
4   (2) the library or archives displays prominently, at the place
5   where orders are accepted, and includes on its order form, a warn-
6   ing of copyright in accordance with requirements that the Reg-
7   ister of Copyrights shall prescribe by regulation.
8   (e) The rights of reproduction and distribution under this section
9   apply to the entire work, or to a substantial part of it, made from the
10 collection of a library or archives where the user makes his request or
11 from that of another library or archives, if the library or archives has
12 first determined, on the basis of a reasonable investigation, that a copy
13 or phonorecord of the copyrighted work cannot be obtained at a fair
14 price, if:
15   (1) the copy becomes the property of the user, and the library
16   or archives has had no notice that the copy would be used for any
17   purpose other than private study, scholarship, or research; and
18   (2) the library or archives displays prominently, at the place
19   where orders are accepted, and includes on its order form, a warn-
20   ing of copyright in accordance with requirements that the Register

21 of Copyrights shall prescribe by regulation.

22 (f) Nothing in this section—

23 (1) shall be construed to impose liability for copyright in-
24 fringement upon a library or archives or its employees for the un-
25 supervised use of reproducing equipment located on its premises,
26 provided that such equipment displays a notice that the making
27 of a copy may be subject to the copyright law;

28 (2) excuses a person who uses such reproducing equipment or
29 who requests a copy under subsection (d) from liability for copy-
30 right infringement for any such act, or for any later use of such
31 copy, if it exceeds fair use as provided by section 107;

32 (3) in any way affects the right of fair use as provided by sec-
33 tion 107, or any contractual obligations assumed at any time by
34 the library or archives when it obtained a copy or phonorecord of
35 a work in its collections; or

36 (4) shall be construed to limit the reproduction and distribu-
37 tion of a limited number of copies and excerpts by a library or
38 archives of an audiovisual news program subject to clauses (1),
39 (2), and (3) of subsection (a).

1 (g) The rights of reproduction and distribution under this section
2 extend to the isolated and unrelated reproduction or distribution of a
3 single copy or phonorecord of the same material on separate occasions,
4 but do not extend to cases where the library or archives, or its
5 employee:

6 (1) is aware or has substantial reason to believe that it is
7 engaging in the related or concerted reproduction or distribution
8 of multiple copies or phonorecords of the same material, whether
9 made on one occasion or over a period of time, and whether
10 intended for aggregate use by one or more individuals or for sepa-
11 rate use by the individual members of a group; or

12 (2) engages in the systematic reproduction or distribution of
13 single or multiple copies or phonorecords of material described
14 in subsection (d).

15 (h) The rights of reproduction and distribution under this section

16 do not apply to a musical work, a pictorial, graphic or sculptural work,
17 or a motion picture or other audiovisual work other than an audio-
18 visual work dealing with news, except that no such limitation shall
19 apply with respect to rights granted by subsections (b) and (c).

20 **§ 109. Limitations on exclusive rights: Effect of transfer of par-**
21   **ticular copy or phonorecord**

22   (a) Notwithstanding the provisions of section 106(3), the owner of
23 a particular copy or phonorecord lawfully made under this title, or any
24 person authorized by him, is entitled, without the authority of the
25 copyright owner, to sell or otherwise dispose of the possession of that
26 copy or phonorecord.

27   (b) Notwithstanding the provisions of section 106(5), the owner
28 of a particular copy lawfully made under this title, or any person
29 authorized by him, is entitled, without the authority of the copyright
30 owner, to display that copy publicly, either directly or by the projec-
31 tion of no more than one image at a time, to viewers present at the
32 place where the copy is located.

33   (c) The privileges prescribed by subsections (a) and (b) do not,
34 unless authorized by the copyright owner, extend to any person who
35 has acquired possession of the copy or phonorecord from the copy-
36 right owner, by rental, lease, loan, or otherwise, without acquiring
37 ownership of it.

38 **§ 110. Limitations on exclusive rights: Exemption of certain per-**
39   **formances and displays**

1   Notwithstanding the provisions of section 106, the following are not
2   infringements of copyright:

3   (1) performance or display of a work by instructors or pupils
4   in the course of face-to-face teaching activities of a nonprofit
5   educational institution, in a classroom or similar place devoted
6   to instruction, unless, in the case of a motion picture or other
7   audiovisual work, the performance, or the display of individual
8   images, is given by means of a copy that was not lawfully made
9   under this title, and that the person responsible for the perform-
10   ance knew or had reason to believe was not lawfully made;

11 (2) performance of a nondramatic literary or musicial work
12 or display of a work, by or in the course of a transmission, if:
13 (A) the performance or display is a regular part of the
14 systematic instructional activities of a governmental body or
15 a nonprofit educational institution; and
16 (B) the performance or display is directly related and of
17 material assistance to the teaching content of the transmis-
18 sion; and
19 (C) the transmission is made primarily for:
20   (i) reception in classrooms or similar places normally
21 devoted to instruction, or
22   (ii) reception by persons to whom the transmission is
23 directed because their disabilities or other special circum-
24 stances prevent their attendance in classrooms or similar
25 places normally devoted to instruction, or
26   (iii) reception by officers or employees of governmen-
27 tal bodies as a part of their official duties or employ-
28 ment;
29 (3) performance of a nondramatic literary or musical work
30 or of a dramatico-musical work of a religious nature, or display of
31 a work, in the course of services at a place of worship or other
32 religious assembly;
33 (4) performance of a nondramatic literary or musical work
34 otherwise than in a transmission to the public, without any pur-
35 pose of direct or indirect commercial advantage and without
36 payment of any fee or other compensation for the performance
37 to any of its performers, promoters, or organizers, if:
38 (A) there is no direct or indirect admission charge, or
39 (B) the proceeds, after deducting the reasonable costs of
40 producing the performance, are used exclusively for educa-
1 tional, religious, or charitable purposes and not for private
2 financial gain, except where the copyright owner has served
3 notice of his objections to the performance under the follow-
4 ing conditions:

5
6

(i) the notice shall be in writing and signed by the copyright owner or his duly authorized agent; and

7
8
9
10

(ii) the notice shall be served on the person responsible for the performance at least seven days before the date of the performance, and shall state the reasons for his objections; and

11
12
13

(iii) the notice shall comply, in form, content, and manner of service, with requirements that the Register of Copyrights shall prescribe by regulation;

14
15
16
17

(5) communication of a transmission embodying a performance or display of a work by the public reception of the transmission on a single receiving apparatus of a kind commonly used in private homes, unless:

18
19

(A) a direct charge is made to see or hear the transmission; or

20
21

(B) the transmission thus received is further transmitted to the public;

22
23
24
25

(6) performance of a nondramatic musical work in the course of an annual agricultural or horticultural fair or exhibition conducted by a governmental body or a nonprofit agricultural or horticultural organization;

26
27
28
29
30
31

(7) performance of a nondramatic musical work by a vending establishment open to the public at large without any direct or indirect admission charge, where the sole purpose of the performance is to promote the retail sale of copies or phonorecords of the work and the performance is not transmitted beyond the place where the establishment is located; and

32
33
34
35

(8) performance of a literary work in the course of a broadcast service specifically designed for broadcast on noncommercial educational radio and television stations to a print or aural handicapped audience.

36

§ 111. Limitations on exclusive rights: Secondary transmissions

37

(a) CERTAIN SECONDARY TRANSMISSIONS EXEMPTED.—The second-

38

ary transmission of a primary transmission embodying a performance

39   or display of a work is not an infringement of copyright if:

1   (1) the secondary transmission is not made by a cable system,
2   and consists entirely of the relaying, by the management of a
3   hotel, apartment house, or similar establishment, of signals trans-
4   mitted by a broadcast station licensed by the Federal Communica-
5   tions Commission, within the local service area of such station, to
6   the private lodgings of guests or residents of such establishment,
7   and no direct charge is made to see or hear the secondary trans-
8   mission; or

9   (2) the secondary transmission is made solely for the purpose
10   and under the conditions specified by clause (2) of section 110; or

11   (3) the secondary transmission is made by any carrier who
12   has no direct or indirect control over the content or selection of
13   the primary transmission or over the particular recipients of the
14   secondary transmission, and whose activities with respect to the
15   secondary transmission consist solely of providing wires, cables,
16   or other communications channels for the use of others: *Provided*,
17   That the provisions of this clause extend only to the activities of
18   said carrier with respect to secondary transmissions and do not
19   exempt from liability the activities of others with respect to their
20   own primary or secondary transmission; or

21   (4) the secondary transmission is not made by a cable system but
22   is made by a governmental body, or other nonprofit organization,
23   without any purpose of direct or indirect commercial advantage,
24   and without charge to the recipients of the secondary transmission
25   other than assessments necessary to defray the actual and reason-
26   able costs of maintaining and operating the secondary transmis-
27   sion service.

28   (b) SECONDARY TRANSMISSION OF PRIMARY TRANSMISSION TO CON-
29   TROLLED GROUP.—Except as provided by subsections (a) and (c), the
30   secondary transmission to the public of a primary transmission
31   embodying a performance or display of a work is actionable as an
32   act of infringement under section 501, and is fully subject to the
33   remedies provided by sections 502 through 506, if the primary trans-

34 mission is not made for reception by the public at large but is con-
35 trolled and limited to reception by particular members of the public:
36 *Provided, however,* That such secondary transmission is not action-
37 able as an act of infringement if the carriage of the signals com-
38 prising the secondary transmission is required under the rules, regula-
39 tions, or authorizations of the Federal Communications Commission.

1   (c) SECONDARY TRANSMISSIONS BY CABLE SYSTEMS.—

2   (1) Subject to the provisions of clause (2) of this subsection, sec-
3   ondary transmissions to the public by a cable system of a primary
4   transmission made by a broadcast station licensed by the Federal
5   Communications Commission and embodying a performance or dis-
6   play of a work shall be subject to compulsory licensing upon compli-
7   ance with the requirements of subsection (d) in the following cases:

8   (A) Where the signals comprising the primary transmission
9   are exclusively aural and the secondary transmission is permis-
10   sible under the rules, regulations or authorizations of the Federal
11   Communications Commission; or

12   (B) Where the community of the cable system is in whole or
13   in part within the local service area of the primary transmitter;
14   or

15   (C) Where the carriage of the signals comprising the second-
16   ary transmission is permissible under the rules, regulations or
17   authorizations of the Federal Communications Commission.

18 (2) Notwithstanding the provisions of clause (1) of this subsection,
19 the willful or repeated secondary transmission to the public by a cable
20 system of a primary transmission made by a broadcast station licensed
21 by the Federal Communications Commission and embodying a per-
22 formance or display of a work is actionable as an act of infringement
23 under section 501, and is fully subject to the remedies provided by
24 sections 502 through 506, in the following cases:

25   (A) Where the carriage of the signals comprising the second-
26   ary transmission is not permissible under the rules, regulations
27   or authorizations of the Federal Communications Commission; or

28   (B) Where the cable system, at least one month before the date

29 of the secondary transmission, has not recorded the notice speci-
30 fied by subsection (d).

31 (d) COMPULSORY LICENSE FOR SECONDARY TRANSMISSIONS BY CABLE
32 SYSTEMS.—

33 (1) For any secondary transmission to be subject to compulsory
34 licensing under subsection (c), the cable system shall at least one month
35 before the date of the secondary transmission or within 30 days after
36 the enactment of this Act, whichever date is later, record in the Copy-
37 right Office a notice including a statement of the identity and address
38 of the person who owns or operates the secondary transmission service
39 or has power to exercise primary control over it, together with the
1 name and location of the primary transmitter or primary transmit-
2 ters, and thereafter, from time to time, such further information as the
3 Register of Copyrights shall prescribe by regulation to carry out the
4 purposes of this clause.

5 (2) A cable system whose secondary transmissions have been subject
6 to compulsory licensing under subsection (c) shall, during the months
7 of January, April, July, and October, deposit with the Register of
8 Copyrights, in accordance with requirements that the Register shall
9 prescribe by regulation—

10 (A) a statement of account, covering the three months next
11 preceding, specifying the number of channels on which the cable
12 system made secondary transmissions to its subscribers, the names
13 and locations of all primary transmitters whose transmissions
14 were further transmitted by the cable system, the total number
15 of subscribers to the cable system, the gross amounts paid to the
16 cable system irrespective of source, and separate statements of
17 the gross revenues paid to the cable system for advertising, leased
18 channels, and cable-casting for which a per-program or per-
19 channel charge is made, and by subscribers for the basic service of
20 providing secondary transmissions of primary broadcast trans-
21 mitters; and

22 (B) a total royalty fee for the period covered by the state-
23 ment, computed on the basis of specified percentages of the gross

24 receipts from subscribers to the cable service during said period
25 for the basic service of providing secondary transmissions of
26 primary broadcast transmitters, as follows:

27   (i) ½ percent of any gross receipts up to $40,000;

28   (ii) 1 percent of any gross receipts totalling more than
29 $40,000 but not more than $80,000;

30   (iii) 1½ percent of any gross receipts totalling more than
31 $80,000, but not more than $120,000;

32   (iv) 2 percent of any gross receipts totalling more than
33 $120,000, but not more than $160,000; and

34   (v) 2½ percent of any gross receipts totalling more than
35 $160,000.

36 Where actual gross receipts paid by subscribers to a cable serv-
37 ice total less than $40,000, gross receipts for the purpose of this
38 subparagraph shall be computed by subtracting from such actual
39 gross receipts the amount by which $40,000 exceeds such actual
1 gross receipts, except that in no case shall a cable system's gross
2 receipts be reduced to less than $1,500.

3 (3) The royalty fees thus deposited shall be distributed in accord-
4 ance with the following procedures:

5 (A) During the month of July in each year, every person claim-
6 ing to be entitled to compulsory license fees for secondary trans-
7 missions made during the preceding twelve-month period shall
8 file a claim with the Register of Copyrights, in accordance with
9 requirements that the Register shall prescribe by regulation. Not-
10 withstanding any provisions of the antitrust laws (as designated
11 in section 1 of the Act of October 15, 1914, 38 Stat. 730, title 15,
12 U.S.C., section 12, and any amendments of such laws), for pur-
13 poses of this clause any claimants may agree among themselves
14 as to the proportionate division of compulsory licensing fees
15 among them, may lump their claims together and file them
16 jointly or as a single claim, or may designate a common agent to
17 receive payment on their behalf.

18 (B) After the first day of August of each year, the Register of

19 Copyrights shall determine whether there exists a controversy
20 concerning the statement of account or the distribution of royalty
21 fees. If he determines that no such controversy exists, he shall,
22 after deducting his reasonable administrative costs under this
23 section, distribute such fees to the copyright owners entitled, or
24 to their designated agents. If he finds the existence of a contro-
25 versy he shall certify to that fact and proceed to constitute a
26 panel of the Copyright Royalty Tribunal in accordance with
27 section 803. In such cases the reasonable administrative costs of
28 the Register under this section shall be deducted prior to distribu-
29 tion of the royalty fee by the Tribunal.

30   (C) During the pendency of any proceeding under this sub-
31 section, the Register of Copyrights or the Copyright Royalty Tri-
32 bunal shall withhold from distribution an amount sufficient to
33 satisfy all claims with respect to which a controversy exists, but
34 shall have discretion to proceed to distribute any amounts that
35 are not in controversy.

36 (e) DEFINITIONS.—

37 As used in this section, the following terms and their variant forms
38 mean the following:

1   A "primary transmission" is a transmission made to the public
2 by the transmitting facility whose signals are being received and
3 further transmitted by the secondary transmission service, regard-
4 less of where or when the performance or display was first
5 transmitted.

6   A "secondary transmission" is the further transmitting of a
7 primary transmission simultaneously with the primary trans-
8 mission, or nonsimultaneously with the primary transmission if by
9 a "cable system" not located in whole or in part within the bound-
10 ary of the forty-eight contiguous States, Hawaii, or Puerto Rico:
11 *Provided, however*, That a nonsimultaneous further transmission
12 by a cable system located in a television market in Hawaii of a
13 primary transmission shall be deemed to be a secondary trans-
14 mission if such further transmission is necessary to enable the

15   cable system to carry the full complement of signals allowed it
16   under the rules and regulations of the Federal Communciations
17   Commission.

18   A "cable system" is a facility, located in any State, Territory,
19   Trust Territory or Possession, that in whole or in part receives
20   signals transmitted or programs broadcast by one or more tele-
21   vision broadcast stations licensed by the Federal Communications
22   Commission, and makes secondary transmissions of such signals
23   or programs by wires, cables, or other communications channels
24   to subscribing members of the public who pay for such service.
25   For purposes of determining the royalty fee under subsection
26   (d)(2)(B), two or more cable systems in contiguous communi-
27   ties under common ownership or control or operating from one
28   headend shall be considered as one system.

29   The "local service area of a primary transmitter" comprises
30   the area in which a television broadcast station is entitled to
31   insist upon its signal being retransmitted by a cable system
32   pursuant to the rules and regulations of the Federal Communica-
33   tions Commission.

34   ## § 112. Limitations on exclusive rights: Ephemeral recordings

35   (a) Notwithstanding the provisions of section 106, and except in the
36   case of a motion picture or other audiovisual work, it is not an
37   infringement of copyright for a transmitting organization entitled to
38   transmit to the public a performance or display of a work, under a
39   license or transfer of the copyright or under the limitations on exclu-
40   sive rights in sound recordings specified by section 114(a), to make
1   no more than one copy or phonorecord of a particular transmission
2   program embodying the performance or display, if—

3   (1) the copy or phonorecord is retained and used solely by the
4   transmitting organization that made it, and no further copies or
5   phonorecords are reproduced from it; and

6   (2) the copy or phonorecord is used solely for the transmitting
7   organization's own transmissions within its local service area, or
8   for purposes of archival preservation or security; and

9   (3) unless preserved exclusively for archival purposes, the copy

10   or phonorecord is destroyed within six months from the date the

11   transmission program was first transmitted to the public.

12   (b) Notwithstanding the provisions of section 106, it is not an in-

13   fringement of copyright for a governmental body or other nonprofit

14   organization entitled to transmit a performance or display of a work,

15   under section 110(2) or under the limitations on exclusive rights in

16   sound recordings specified by section 114(a), to make no more than

17   thirty copies or phonorecords of a particular transmission program

18   embodying the performance or display, if—

19   (1) no further copies or phonorecords are reproduced from the

20   copies or phonorecords made under this clause; and

21   (2) except for one copy or phonorecord that may be preserved

22   exclusively for archival purposes, the copies or phonorecords are

23   destroyed within seven years from the date the transmission pro-

24   gram was first transmitted to the public.

25   (c) Notwithstanding the provisions of section 106, it is not an in-

26   fringement of copyright for a governmental body or other nonprofit

27   organization to make for distribution no more than one copy or phono-

28   record, for each transmitting organization specified in clause (2) of

29   this subsection, of a particular transmission program embodying a

30   performance of a nondramatic musical work of a religious nature, or

31   of a sound recording of such a musical work, if—

32   (1) there is no direct or indirect charge for making or dis-

33   tributing any such copies or phonorecords; and

34   (2) none of such copies or phonorecords is used for any per-

35   formance other than a single transmission to the public by a trans-

36   mitting organization entitled to transmit to the public a perform-

37   ance of the work under a license or transfer of the copyright; and

38   (3) except for one copy or phonorecord that may be preserved

39   exclusively for archival purposes, the copies or phonorecords are

1   all destroyed within one year from the date the transmission pro-

2   gram was first transmitted to the public.

3   (d) The transmission program embodied in a copy or phonorecord

4   made under this section is not subject to protection as a derivative
5   work under this title except with the express consent of the owners
6   of copyright in the pre-existing works employed in the program.

7   **§ 113. Scope of exclusive rights in pictorial, graphic, and sculp-**
8   **tural works**

9   (a) Subject to the provisions of clauses (1) and (2) of this subsec-
10 tion, the exclusive right to reproduce a copyrighted pictorial, graphic,
11 or sculptural work in copies under section 106 includes the right to
12 reproduce the work in or on any kind of article, whether useful or
13 otherwise.

14   (1) This title does not afford, to the owner of copyright in a
15   work that portrays a useful article as such, any greater or lesser
16   rights with respect to the making, distribution, or display of the
17   useful article so portrayed than those afforded to such works
18   under the law, whether title 17 or the common law or statutes of
19   a State, in effect on December 31, 1976, as held applicable and
20   construed by a court in an action brought under this title.

21   (2) In the case of a work lawfully reproduced in useful articles
22   that have been offered for sale or other distribution to the public,
23   copyright does not include any right to prevent the making, dis-
24   tribution, or display of pictures or photographs of such articles
25   in connection with advertisements or commentaries related to the
26   distribution or display of such articles, or in connection with news
27   reports.

28 (b) When a pictorial, graphic, or sculptural work in which copy-
29 right subsists under this title is utilized in an original ornamental
30 design of a useful article, by the copyright proprietor or under an
31 express license from him, the design shall be eligible for protection
32 under the provisions of title II of this Act.

33 (c) Protection under this title of a work in which copyright subsists
34 shall terminate with respect to its utilization in useful articles when-
35 ever the copyright proprietor has obtained registration of an orna-
36 mental design of a useful article embodying said work under the pro-
37 visions of title II of this Act. Unless and until the copyright proprietor

38 has obtained such registration, the copyrighted pictorial, graphic,
39 or sculptural work shall continue in all respects to be covered by and
40 subject to the protection afforded by the copyright subsisting under
1   this title. Nothing in this section shall be deemed to create any addi-
2   tional rights or protection under this title.

3   (d) Nothing in this section shall affect any right or remedy held
4   by any person under this title in a work in which copyright was sub-
5   sisting on the effective date of title II of this Act, or with respect to
6   any utilization of a copyrighted work other than in the design of a
7   useful article.

8   **§ 114. Scope of exclusive rights in sound recordings**

9   (a) The exclusive rights of the owner of copyright in a sound record-
10 ing are limited to the rights specified by clauses (1), (2), and (3) of
11 section 106, and do not include any right of performance under
12 section 106(4).

13   (b) The exclusive right of the owner of copyright in a sound record-
14 ing to reproduce it under section 106(1) is limited to the right to
15 duplicate the sound recording in the form of phonorecords that directly
16 or indirectly recapture the actual sounds fixed in the recording. This
17 right does not extend to the making or duplication of another sound
18 recording that is an independent fixation of other sounds, even though
19 such sounds imitate or simulate those in the copyrighted sound
20 recording.

21   (c) This section does not limit or impair the exclusive right to per-
22 form publicly, by means of a phonorecord, any of the works specified
23 by section 106(4).

24 **§ 115. Scope of exclusive rights in nondramatic musical works:**
25   **Compulsory license for making and distributing phono-**
26   **records**

27   In the case of nondramatic musical works, the exclusive rights pro-
28 vided by clauses (1) and (3) of section 106, to make and to distribute
29 phonorecords of such works, are subject to compulsory licensing under
30 the conditions specified by this section.

31   (a) AVAILABILITY AND SCOPE OF COMPULSORY LICENSE.—

32   (1) When phonorecords of a nondramatic musical work have
33   been distributed to the public under the authority of the copyright
34   owner, any other person may, by complying with the provisions
35   of this section, obtain a compulsory license to make and distribute
36   phonorecords of the work. A person may obtain a compulsory
37   license only if his primary purpose in making phonorecords is to
38   distribute them to the public for private use. A person may not
39   obtain a compulsory license for use of the work in the duplication
1   of a sound recording made by another, unless he has first obtained
2   the consent of the owner of that sound recording.

3   (2) A compulsory license includes the privilege of making a
4   musical arrangement of the work to the extent necessary to con-
5   form it to the style or manner of interpretation of the perform-
6   ance involved, but the arrangement shall not change the basic
7   melody or fundamental character of the work, and shall not be
8   subject to protection as a derivative work under this title, except
9   with the express consent of the copyright owner.

10 (b) NOTICE OF INTENTION TO OBTAIN COMPULSORY LICENSE; DES-
11 IGNATION OF OWNER OF PERFORMANCE RIGHT.—

12   (1) Any person who wishes to obtain a compulsory license
13   under this section shall, before or within thirty days after making,
14   and before distributing any phonorecords of the work, serve notice
15   of his intention to do so on the copyright owner. If the registra-
16   tion or other public records of the Copyright Office do not identify
17   the copyright owner and include an address at which notice can
18   be served on him, it shall be sufficient to file the notice of intention
19   in the Copyright Office. The notice shall comply, in form, con-
20   tent, and manner of service, with requirements that the Register
21   of Copyrights shall prescribe by regulation.

22   (2) If the copyright owner so requests in writing not later than
23   ten days after service or filing of the notice required by clause (1),
24   the person exercising the compulsory license shall designate, on
25   a label or container accompanying each phonorecord of the work
26   distributed by him, and in the form and manner that the Register

27 of Copyrights shall prescribe by regulation, the name of the
28 copyright owner or his agent to whom royalties for public per-
29 formance of the work are to be paid.

30   (3) Failure to serve or file the notice required by clause (1), or
31 to designate the name of the owner or agent as required by clause
32 (2), forecloses the possibility of a compulsory license and, in the
33 absence of a negotiated license, renders the making and distribu-
34 tion of phonorecords actionable as acts of infringement under
35 section 501 and fully subject to the remedies provided by sections
36 502 through 506.

37 (c) ROYALTY PAYABLE UNDER COMPULSORY LICENSE.—

38   (1) To be entitled to receive royalties under a compulsory
39 license, the copyright owner must be identified in the registration
40 or other public records of the Copyright Office. The owner is
1 entitled to royalties for phonorecords manufactured and distrib-
2 uted after he is so identified but he is not entitled to recover for
3 any phonorecords previously manufactured and distributed.

4   (2) Except as provided by clause (1), the royalty under a
5 compulsory license shall be payable for every phonorecord manu-
6 factured and distributed in accordance with the license. With
7 respect to each work embodied in the phonorecord, the royalty
8 shall be either two and one-half cents, or one-half cent per minute
9 of playing time or fraction thereof, whichever amount is larger.

10   (3) Royalty payments shall be made on or before the twentieth
11 day of each month and shall include all royalties for the month
12 next preceding. Each monthly payment shall be accompanied
13 by a detailed statement of account, which shall be certified by a
14 certified public accountant and comply in form, content, and
15 manner of certification with requirements that the Register of
16 Copyrights shall prescribe by regulation.

17   (4) If the copyright owner does not receive the monthly pay-
18 ment and statement of account when due, he may give written
19 notice to the licensee that, unless the default is remedied within
20 thirty days from the date of the notice, the compulsory license

21   will be automatically terminated. Such termination renders the
22   making and distribution of all phonorecords, for which the roy-
23   alty had not been paid, actionable as acts of infringement under
24   section 501 and fully subject to the remedies provided by sections
25   502 through 506.

26   **§ 116. Scope of exclusive rights in nondramatic musical works:**
27   **Public performances by means of coin-operated phono-**
28   **record players**

29   (a) LIMITATION ON EXCLUSIVE RIGHT.—In the case of a non-
30   dramatic musical work embodied in a phonorecord, the exclusive right
31   under clause (4) of section 106 to perform the work publicly by means
32   of a coin-operated phonorecord player is limited as follows:

33   (1) The proprietor of the establishment in which the public
34   performance takes place is not liable for infringement with re-
35   spect to such public performance unless:

36   (A) he is the operator of the phonorecord player; or

37   (B) he refuses or fails, within one month after receipt by
38   registered or certified mail of a request, at a time during
39   which the certificate required by subclause (1)(C) of sub-
40   section (b) is not affixed to the phonorecord player, by the
1   copyright owner, to make full disclosure, by registered or
2   certified mail, of the identity of the operator of the phono-
3   record player.

4   (2) The operator of the coin-operated phonorecord player may
5   obtain a compulsory license to perform the work publicly on that
6   phonorecord player by filing the application, affixing the certifi-
7   cate, and paying the royalties provided by subsection (b).

8   (b) RECORDATION OF COIN-OPERATED PHONORECORD PLAYER, AFFIXA-
9   TION OF CERTIFICATE, AND ROYALTY PAYABLE UNDER COMPULSORY
10   LICENSE.—

11   (1) Any operator who wishes to obtain a compulsory license
12   for the public performance of works on a coin-operated phono-
13   record player shall fulfill the following requirements:

14   (A) Before or within one month after such performances

15   are made available on a particular phonorecord player, and
16   during the month of January in each succeeding year that
17   such performances are made available in that particular
18   phonorecord player, he shall file in the Copyright Office, in
19   accordance with requirements that the Register of Copyrights
20   shall prescribe by regulation, an application containing the
21   name and address of the operator of the phonorecord player
22   and the manufacturer and serial number or other explicit
23   identification of the phonorecord player, and he shall deposit
24   with the Register of Copyrights a royalty fee for the current
25   calendar year of $8 for that particular phonorecord player.
26   If such performances are made available on a particular
27   phonorecord player for the first time after July 1 of any
28   year, the royalty fee to be deposited for the remainder of
29   that year shall be $4.00.

30   (B) Within twenty days of receipt of an application and a
31   royalty fee pursuant to subclause (A), the Register of Copy-
32   rights shall issue to the applicant a certificate for the phono-
33   record player.

34   (C) On or before March 1 of the year in which the certifi-
35   cate prescribed by subclause (B) of this clause is issued, or
36   within ten days after the date of issue of the certificate, the
37   operator shall affix to the particular phonorecord player, in a
38   position where it can be readily examined by the public, the
39   certificate, issued by the Register of Copyrights under sub-
40   clause (B), of the latest application made by him under sub-
1   clause (A) of this clause with respect to that phonorecord
2   player.

3   (2) Failure to file the application, to affix the certificate, or to
4   pay the royalty required by clause (1) of this subsection renders
5   the public performance actionable as an act of infringement under
6   section 501 and fully subject to the remedies provided by section
7   502 through 506.

8 (c) DISTRIBUTION OF ROYALTIES.—

9   (1) During the month of January in each year, every person
10   claiming to be entitled to compulsory license fees under this section
11   for performances during the preceding twelve-month period shall
12   file a claim with the Register of Copyrights, in accordance with
13   requirements that the Register shall prescribe by regulation.
14   Such claim shall include an agreement to accept as final, except as
15   provided in section 809 of this title, the determination of the Copy-
16   right Royalty Tribunal in any controversy concerning the distri-
17   bution of royalty fees deposited under subclause (A) of subsec-
18   tion (b)(1) of this section to which the claimant is a party. Not-
19   withstanding any provisions of the antitrust laws (the Act of
20   October 15, 1914, 38 Stat. 730, title 15, U.S.C., section 12, and any
21   amendments of any such laws), for purposes of this subsection
22   any claimants may agree among themselves as to the proportion-
23   ate division of compulsory licensing fees among them, may lump
24   their claims together and file them jointly or as a single claim, or
25   may designate a common agent to receive payment on their behalf.

26   (2) After the first day of October of each year, the Register of
27   Copyrights shall determine whether there exists a controversy
28   concerning the distribution of royalty fees deposited under sub-
29   clause (A) of subsection (b)(1). If he determines that no such
30   controversy exists, he shall, after deducting his reasonable ad-
31   ministrative costs under this section, distribute such fees to the
32   copyright owners and performers entitled, or to their designated
33   agents. If he finds that such a controversy exists, he shall certify
34   to that fact and proceed to constitute a panel of the Copyright
35   Royalty Tribunal in accordance with section 803. In such cases the
36   reasonable administrative costs of the Register under this section
37   shall be deducted prior to distribution of the royalty fee by the
38   Tribunal.

39   (3) The fees to be distributed shall be divided as follows:

1   (A) To every copyright owner not affiliated with a perform-
2   ing rights society the pro rata share of the fees to be dis-
3   tributed to which such copyright owner proves his entitle-

4   ment.

5   (B) To the performing rights societies the remainder of
6   the fees to be distributed in such pro rata shares as they shall
7   by agreement stipulate among themselves, or, if they fail to
8   agree, the pro rata share to which such performing rights
9   societies prove their entitlement.

10   (C) During the pendency of any proceeding under this
11   section, the Register of Copyrights or the Copyright Royalty
12   Tribunal shall withhold from distribution an amount suffi-
13   cient to satisfy all claims with respect to which a controversy
14   exists, but shall have discretion to proceed to distribute any
15   amounts that are not in controversy.

16   (4) The Register of Copyrights shall promulgate regulations
17 under which persons who can reasonably be expected to have
18 claims may, during the year in which performances take place,
19 without expense to or harassment of operators or proprietors of
20 establishments in which phonorecord players are located, have
21 such access to such establishments and to the phonorecord players
22 located therein and such opportunity to obtain information with
23 respect thereto as may be reasonably necessary to determine, by
24 sampling procedures or otherwise, the proportion of contribution
25 of the musical works of each such person to the earnings of the
26 phonorecord players for which fees shall·have been deposited.
27 Any person who alleges that he has been denied the access per-
28 mitted under the regulations prescribed by the Register of Copy-
29 rights may bring an action in the United States District Court
30 for the District of Columbia for the cancellation of the compul-
31 sory license of the phonorecord player to which such access has
32 been denied, and the court shall have the power to declare the
33 compulsory license thereof invalid from the date of issue thereof.

34   (d) CRIMINAL PENALTIES.—Any person who knowingly makes a
35 false representation of a material fact in an application filed under
36 clause (1)(A) of subsection (b), or who knowingly alters a certificate
37 issued under clause (1)(B) of subsection (b) or knowingly affixes

38 such a certificate to a phonorecord player other than the one it covers,
39 shall be fined not more than $2,500.

1   (e) DEFINITIONS.—As used in this section, the following terms and
2   their variant forms mean the following:

3   (1) A "coin-operated phonorecord player" is a machine or
4   device that:

5   (A) is employed solely for the performance of non-
6   dramatic musical works by means of phonorecords upon being
7   activated by insertion of a coin;

8   (B) is located in an establishment making no direct or
9   indirect charge for admission;

10   (C) is accompanied by a list of the titles of all the musical
11   works available for performance on it, which list is affixed to
12   the phonorecord player or posted in the establishment in a
13   prominent position where it can be readily examined by the
14   public; and

15   (D) affords a choice of works available for performance
16   and permits the choice to be made by the patrons of the
17   establishment in which it is located.

18   (2) An "operator" is any person who, alone or jointly with
19 others:

20   (A) owns a coin-operated phonorecord player; or

21   (B) has the power to make a coin-operated phonorecord
22   player available for placement in an establishment for pur-
23   poses of public performance; or

24   (C) has the power to exercise primary control over the
25   selection of the musical works made available for public
26   performance in a coin-operated phonorecord player.

27   (3) A "performing rights society" is an association or corpora-
28 tion that licenses the public performance of nondramatic musical
29 works on behalf of the copyright owners, such as the American
30 Society of Composers, Authors and Publishers, Broadcast Music,
31 Inc., and SESAC, Inc.

§ 117. Scope of exclusive rights: Use in conjunction with computers and similar information systems

Notwithstanding the provisions of sections 106 through 116 and 118, this title does not afford to the owner of copyright in a work any greater or lesser rights with respect to the use of the work in conjunction with automatic systems capable of storing, processing, retrieving, or transferring information, or in conjunction with any similar device, machine, or process, than those afforded to works under the law, whether title 17 or the common law or statutes of a State, in effect on December 31, 1976, as held applicable and construed by a court in an action brought under this title.

§ 118. Limitations on exclusive rights: Public broadcasting of non-dramatic literary and musical works, pictorial, graphic, and sculptural works

(a) Notwithstanding the provisions of section 106, it is not an infringement of copyright for a public broadcasting entity to broadcast any nondramatic literary or musical work, pictorial, graphic, or sculptural work under the provisions of this section.

(b) Public broadcasting of nondramatic literary and musical works, pictorial, graphic, and sculptural works by a public broadcasting entity shall be subject to compulsory licensing upon compliance with the requirements of this section. The public broadcasting entity shall—

(1) record in the Copyright Office, at intervals and in accordance with requirements prescribed by the Register of Copyrights, a notice stating its identity, address and intention to obtain a license under this section; and

(2) deposit with the Register of Copyrights, at intervals and in accordance with requirements prescribed by the Register, a statement of account and the total royalty fees for the period covered by the statement based on the royalty rates provided for in subsection (c).

(c) Reasonable royalty fees for public broadcasting shall be estab-

26   lished by the Copyright Royalty Tribunal. Such royalty fees may be
27   calculated on a per-use, per-program, prorated or annual basis as the
28   Copyright Royalty Tribunal finds appropriate with respect to the type
29   of the copyrighted work and the nature of broadcast use. A par-
30   ticular or general license agreement between one or more public broad-
31   casting entities and one or more copyright owners prior or subsequent
32   to determination of applicable rates determined by the Copyright
33   Royalty Tribunal may be substituted for a compulsory license pro-
34   vided in this section. Public broadcasting entities and copyright own-
35   ers shall negotiate in good faith and cooperate fully with the Copy-
36   right Royalty Tribunal in establishing reasonable royalty fees in an
37   expeditious manner.

38   (d) The royalty fees deposited with the Register of Copyrights
39   under this section shall be distributed in accordance with the follow-
40   ing procedures:

1   (1) During the month of July of each year, every person claim-
2   ing to be entitled to compulsory license fees for public broadcast-
3   ing during the preceding twelve-month period shall file a claim
4   with the Register of Copyrights in accordance with the require-
5   ments that the Register shall prescribe by regulation. Notwith-
6   standing any provision of the antitrust laws (as defined in section
7   1 of the Act of October 15, 1914, 38 Stat. 730; 15 U.S.C. 12, and
8   any amendments of such laws), for purposes of this paragraph
9   any claimants may agree among themselves as to the proportion-
10   ate division of compulsory license fees among them, may lump
11   their claims together, and may designate a common agent to
12   receive payments on their behalf.

13   (2) On the first day of August of each year, the Register of
14   Copyrights shall determine whether there exists a controversy
15   regarding the statement of account or distribution of royalty fees.
16   If the Register determines that no such controversy exists, the
17   Register shall, after deducting reasonable administrative costs
18   under this section, distribute such fees to the copyright owners
19   entitled, or to their designated agents. If the Register finds the

20   existence of a controversy, the Register shall certify to such effect
21   and proceed to constitute a panel of the Copyright Royalty Tri-
22   bunal in accordance with section 803. In such cases, the reasonable
23   administrative costs of the Register under this section shall be
24   deducted prior to distribution of the royalty fees by the Tribunal.

25   (3) During the pendency of any proceeding under this subsec-
26   tion, the Register of Copyrights or the Copyright Royalty Tri-
27   bunal shall withhold from distribution, an amount sufficient to
28   satisfy all claims with respect to which a controversy exists, but
29   shall have discretion to proceed to distribute any amounts that are
30   not in controversy.

31   (e) The compulsory license provided in this section shall not apply
32 to unpublished nondramatic literary or musical works or to dramatiza-
33 tion rights for nondramatic literary or musical works.

34   (f) As used in this section, the term "public broadcasting" means
35 the transmission over noncommercial educational broadcast stations
36 (as defined in section 397 of the Federal Communications Act of 1934
37 (47 U.S.C. 397)) and the following activities incidental thereto; pro-
38 duction and recording by, or solely for use by, distribution, sale or li-
39 censing solely to, and acquisition by, noncommercial educational broad-
40 cast stations of educational television or radio programs (as defined in
1   section 397 of the Federal Communications Act of 1934 (47 U.S.C.
2   397)); and recording by, or solely for use by a nonprofit educational
3   institution of any educational television or radio program off the air
4   from a transmission by an educational broadcast station, provided
5   such recording is used only by such institution as a regular part of its
6   instructional activities for a period of one week from the date of the
7   broadcast from which such off the air recording was made and that
8   each such recording shall be destroyed or erased upon the expiration
9   of such one week period. No person supplying a recording to an educa-
10 tional institution under this subsection shall have any liability as a
11 result of failure of such institution to destroy or erase such recording
12 provided it shall have notified such institution of the requirement for
13 such destruction or erasure pursuant to this subsection.

14   **Chapter 2.—COPYRIGHT OWNERSHIP AND TRANSFER**

Sec.
201. Ownership of copyright.
202. Ownership of copyright as distinct from ownership of material object.
203. Termination of transfers and licenses granted by the author.
204. Execution of transfers of copyright ownership.
205. Recordation of transfers and other documents.

§ 201. Ownership of copyright

15   (a) INITIAL OWNERSHIP.—Copyright in work protected under this

16   title vests initially in the author or authors of the work. The authors

17   of a joint work are co-owners of copyright in the work.

18   (b) WORKS MADE FOR HIRE.—In the case of a work made for hire,

19   the employer or other person for whom the work was prepared is

20   considered the author for purposes of this title, and, unless the parties

21   have expressly agreed otherwise in a written instrument signed by

22   them, owns all of the rights comprised in the copyright.

23   (c) CONTRIBUTIONS TO COLLECTIVE WORKS.—Copyright in each sep-

24   arate contribution to a collective work is distinct from copyright in

25   the collective work as a whole, and vests initially in the author of the

26   contribution. In the absence of an express transfer of the copyright

27   or of any rights under it, the owner of copyright in the collective

28   work is presumed to have acquired only the privilege of reproducing

29   and distributing the contribution as part of that particular collective

30   work, any revision of that collective work, and any later collective

31   work in the same series.

32   (d) TRANSFER OF OWNERSHIP.—

33   (1) The ownership of a copyright may be transferred in whole

34   or in part by any means of conveyance or by operation of law, and

1   may be bequeathed by will or pass as personal property by the

2   applicable laws of intestate succession.

3   (2) Any of the exclusive rights comprised in a copyright,

4   including any subdivision of any of the rights specified by section

5   106, may be transferred as provided by clause (1) and owned sepa-

6   rately. The owner of any particular exclusive right is entitled, to

7   the extent of that right, to all of the protection and remedies

8   accorded to the copyright owner by this title.

9   (e) INVOLUNTARY TRANSFER.—When an individual author's owner-
10 ship of a copyright, or of any of the exclusive rights under a copy-
11 right, has not previously been transferred voluntarily by him, no
12 action by any governmental body or other official or organization
13 purporting to seize, expropriate, transfer, or exercise rights of owner-
14 ship with respect to the copyright, or any of the exclusive rights under
15 a copyright, shall be given effect under this title.

16 **§ 202. Ownership of copyright as distinct from ownership of**
17   **material object**

18 Ownership of a copyright, or of any of the exclusive rights under
19 a copyright, is distinct from ownership of any material object in
20 which the work is embodied. Transfer of ownership of any material
21 object, including the copy or phonorecord in which the work is first
22 fixed, does not of itself convey any rights in the copyrighted work
23 embodied in the object; nor, in the absence of an agreement, does
24 transfer of ownership of a copyright or of any exclusive rights under
25 a copyright convey property rights in any material object.

26 **§ 203. Termination of transfers and licenses granted by the author**

27 (a) CONDITIONS FOR TERMINATION.—In the case of any work other
28 than a work made for hire, the exclusive or nonexclusive grant of a
29 transfer or license of copyright or of any right under a copyright,
30 executed by the author on or after January 1, 1977, otherwise than
31 by will, is subject to termination under the following conditions:

32   (1) In the case of a grant executed by one author, termination
33   of the grant may be effected by that author or, if he is dead, by
34   the person or persons who, under clause (2) of this subsection,
35   own and are entitled to exercise a total of more than one half of
36   that author's termination interest. In the case of a grant executed
37   by two or more authors of a joint work, termination of the grant
38   may be effected by a majority of the authors who executed it;
39   if any of such authors is dead, his termination interest may be
40   exercised as a unit by the person or persons who, under clause (2)
1   of this subsection, own and are entitled to exercise a total of more
2   than one half of his interest.

(2) Where an author is dead, his or her termination interest is owned, and may be exercised, by his widow (or her widower) and children or grandchildren as follows:

(A) the widow (or widower) owns the author's entire termination interest unless there are any surviving children or grandchildren of the author, in which case the widow (or widower) owns one half of the author's interest;

(B) the author's surviving children, and the surviving children of any dead child of the author, own the author's entire termination interest unless there is a widow (or widower), in which case the ownership of one half of the author's interest is divided among them;

(C) the rights of the author's children and grandchildren are in all cases divided among them and exercised on a per stirpes basis according to the number of his children represented; the share of the children of a dead child in a termination interest can be exercised only by the action of a majority of them.

(3) Termination of the grant may be effected at any time during a period of five years beginning at the end of thirty-five years from the date of execution of the grant; or, if the grant covers the right of publication of the work, the period begins at the end of thirty-five years from the date of publication of the work under the grant or at the end of forty years from the date of execution of the grant, whichever term ends earlier.

(4) The termination shall be effected by serving an advance notice in writing, signed by the number and proportion of owners of termination interests required under clauses (1) and (2) of this subsection, or by their duly authorized agents, upon the grantee or his successor in title.

(A) The notice shall state the effective date of the termination, which shall fall within the five-year period specified by clause (3) of this subsection, and the notice shall be served not less than two or more than ten years before that date. A

37 copy of the notice shall be recorded in the Copyright Office
38 before the effective date of termination, as a condition to its
39 taking effect.

1 (B) The notice shall comply, in form, content, and man-
2 ner of service, with requirements that the Register of Copy-
3 rights shall prescribe by regulation.

4 (5) Termination of the grant may be effected notwithstand-
5 ing any agreement to the contrary, including an agreement to
6 make a will or to make any future grant.

7 (b) EFFECT OF TERMINATION.—Upon the effective date of termina-
8 tion, all rights under this title that were covered by the terminated
9 grant revert to the author, authors, and other persons owning termi-
10 nation interests under clauses (1) and (2) of subsection (a), includ-
11 ing those owners who did not join in signing the notice of termination
12 under clause (4) of subsection (a), but with the following limitations:

13 (1) A derivative work prepared under authority of the grant
14 before its termination may continue to be utilized under the terms
15 of the grant after its termination, but this privilege does not ex-
16 tend to the preparation after the termination of other derivative
17 works based upon the copyrighted work covered by the terminated
18 grant.

19 (2) The future rights that will revert upon termination of the
20 grant become vested on the date the notice of termination has
21 been served as provided by clause (4) of subsection (a). The
22 rights vest in the author, authors, and other persons named in,
23 and in the proportionate shares provided by, clauses (1) and (2)
24 of subsection (a).

25 (3) Subject to the provisions of clause (4) of this subsection,
26 a further grant, or agreement to make a further grant, of any
27 right covered by a terminated grant is valid only if it is signed
28 by the same number and proportion of the owners, in whom the
29 right has vested under clause (2) of this subsection, as are re-
30 quired to terminate the grant under clauses (1) and (2) of sub-
31 section (a). Such further grant or agreement is effective with

32   respect to all of the persons in whom the right it covers has vested
33   under clause (2) of this subsection, including those who did not
34   join in signing it. If any person dies after rights under a ter-
35   minated grant have vested in him, his legal representatives,
36   legatees, or heirs at law represent him for purposes of this clause.

37   (4) A further grant, or agreement to make a further grant, of
38   any right covered by a terminated grant is valid only if it is made
39   after the effective date of the termination. As an exception, how-
1   ever, an agreement for such a further grant may be made between
2   the persons provided by clause (3) of this subsection and the
3   original grantee or his successor in title, after the notice of termi-
4   nation has been served as provided by clause (4) of subsection (a).

5   (5) Termination of a grant under this section affects only those
6   rights covered by the grant that arise under this title, and in no
7   way affects rights arising under any other Federal, State, or for-
8   eign laws.

9   (6) Unless and until termination is effected under this section,
10   the grant, if it does not provide otherwise, continues in effect for
11   the term of copyright provided by this title.

§ 204. Execution of transfers of copyright ownership

13   (a) A transfer of copyright ownership, other than by operation of
14   law, is not valid unless an instrument of conveyance, or a note or
15   memorandum of the transfer, is in writing and signed by the owner
16   of the rights conveyed or his duly authorized agent.

17   (b) A certificate of acknowledgement is not required for the valid-
18   ity of a transfer, but is prima facie evidence of the execution of the
19   transfer if:

20   (1) in the case of a transfer executed in the United States, the
21   certificate is issued by a person authorized to administer oaths
22   within the United States; or

23   (2) in the case of a transfer executed in a foreign country, the
24   certificate is issued by a diplomatic or consular officer of the
25   United States, or by a person authorized to administer oaths
26   whose authority is proved by a certificate of such an officer.

27   **§ 205. Recordation of transfers and other documents**

28   (a) CONDITIONS FOR RECORDATION.—Any transfer of copyright own-
29   ership or other document pertaining to a copyright may be recorded
30   in the Copyright Office if the document filed for recordation bears the
31   actual signature of the person who executed it, or if it is accompanied
32   by a sworn or official certification that it is a true copy of the original,
33   signed document.

34   (b) CERTIFICATE OF RECORDATION.—The Register of Copyrights
35   shall, upon receipt of a document as provided by subsection (a) and
36   of the fee provided by section 708, record the document and return it
37   with a certificate of recordation.

38   (c) RECORDATION AS CONSTRUCTIVE NOTICE.—Recordation of a docu-
39   ment in the Copyright Office gives all persons constructive notice of the
40   facts stated in the recorded document, but only if:

1   (1) the document, or material attached to it, specifically identi-
2   fies the work to which it pertains so that, after the document is
3   indexed by the Register of Copyrights, it would be revealed by a
4   reasonable search under the title or registration number of the
5   work; and

6   (2) registration has been made for the work.

7   (d) RECORDATION AS PREREQUISITE TO INFRINGEMENT SUIT.—No per-
8   son claiming by virtue of a transfer to the owner of copyright or of
9   any exclusive right under a copyright is entitled to institute an in-
10   fringement action under this title until the instrument of transfer
11   under which he claims has been recorded in the Copyright Office, but
12   suit may be instituted after such recordation on a cause of action that
13   arose before recordation.

14   (e) PRIORITY BETWEEN CONFLICTING TRANSFERS.—As between two
15   conflicting transfers, the one executed first prevails if it is recorded, in
16   the manner required to give constructive notice under subsection (c),
17   within one month after its execution in the United States or within two
18   months after its execution abroad, or at any time before recordation in
19   such manner of the later transfer. Otherwise the later transfer prevails
20   if recorded first in such manner, and if taken in good faith, for valu-

21 able consideration or on the basis of a binding promise to pay royal-
22 ties, and without notice of the earlier transfer.

23   (f) PRIORITY BETWEEN CONFLICTING TRANSFER OF OWNERSHIP AND
24 NONEXCLUSIVE LICENSE.—A nonexclusive license, whether recorded or
25 not, prevails over a conflicting transfer of copyright ownership if the
26 license is evidenced by a written instrument signed by the owner of the
27 rights licensed or his duly authorized agent, and if:

28   (1) the license was taken before execution of the transfer; or
29   (2) the license was taken in good faith before recordation of
30   the transfer and without notice of it.

31   **Chapter 3.—DURATION OF COPYRIGHT**

Sec.

32 **§ 301. Pre-emption with respect to other laws**

33   (a) On and after January 1, 1977, all legal or equitable rights that
34 are equivalent to any of the exclusive rights within the general
35 scope of copyright as specified by section 106 in works of authorship
36 that are fixed in a tangible medium of expression and come within
1 the subject matter of copyright as specified by sections 102 and 103,
2 whether created before or after that date and whether published or
3 unpublished, are governed exclusively by this title. Thereafter, no
4 person is entitled to any such right or equivalent right in any such
5 work under the common law or statutes of any State.

6   (b) Nothing in this title annuls or limits any rights or remedies
7 under the common law or statutes of any State with respect to:

8   (1) subject matter that does not come within the subject mat-
9   ter of copyright as specified by sections 102 and 103, including
10   works of authorship not fixed in any tangible medium of expres-
11   sion; or

12   (2) any cause of action arising from undertakings commenced
13   before January 1, 1977; or

14   (3) activities violating legal or equitable rights that are not
15   equivalent to any of the exclusive rights within the general scope
16   of copyright as specified by section 106, including rights against
17   misappropriation not equivalent to any of such exclusive rights,
18   breaches of contract, breaches of trust, trespass, conversion,
19   invasion of privacy, defamation, and deceptive trade practices
20   such as passing off and false representation; or

21   (4) sound recordings fixed prior to February 15, 1972.

22   (c) Nothing in this title annuls or limits any rights or remedies
23 under any other Federal statute.

24 **§ 302. Duration of copyright: Works created on or after Janu-**
25   **ary 1, 1977**

26   (a) IN GENERAL.—Copyright in a work created on or after January
27 1, 1977, subsists from its creation and, except as provided by the
28 following subsections, endures for a term consisting of the life of the
29 author and fifty years after his death.

30   (b) JOINT WORKS.—In the case of a joint work prepared by two
31 or more authors who did not work for hire, the copyright endures for
32 a term consisting of the life of the last surviving author and fifty
33 years after his death.

34   (c) ANONYMOUS WORKS, PSEUDONYMOUS WORKS, AND WORKS MADE
35 FOR HIRE.—In the case of an anonymous work, a pseudonymous work,
36 or a work made for hire, the copyright endures for a term of seventy-
37 five years from the year of its first publication, or a term of one
38 hundred years from the year of its creation, whichever expires first.
39 If, before the end of such term, the identity of one or more of the
40 authors of an anonymous or pseudonymous work is revealed in the
1 records of a registration made for that work under subsection (a)
2 or (d) of section 407, or in the records provided by this subsection,
3 the copyright in the work endures for the term specified by subsection
4 (a) or (b), based on the life of the author or authors whose identity
5 has been revealed. Any person having an interest in the copyright in
6 an anonymous or pseudonymous work may at any time record, in
7 records to be maintained by the Copyright Office for that purpose, a

8 statement identifying one or more authors of the work; the statement
9 shall also identify the person filing it, the nature of his interest, the
10 source of his information, and the particular work affected, and shall
11 comply in form and content with requirements that the Register of
12 Copyrights shall prescribe by regulation.

13   (d) RECORDS RELATING TO DEATH OF AUTHORS.—Any person having
14 an interest in a copyright may at any time record in the Copyright
15 Office a statement of the date of death of the author of the copy-
16 righted work, or a statement that the author is still living on a par-
17 ticular date. The statement shall identify the person filing it, the
18 nature of his interest, and the source of his information, and shall
19 comply in form and content with requirements that the Register
20 of Copyrights shall prescribe by regulation. The Register shall main-
21 tain current records of information relating to the death of authors
22 of copyrighted works, based on such recorded statements and, to the
23 extent he considers practicable, on data contained in any of the records
24 of the Copyright Office or in other reference sources.

25   (e) PRESUMPTION AS TO AUTHOR'S DEATH.—After a period of seventy-
26 five years from the year of first publication of a work, or a period
27 of one hundred years from the year of its creation, whichever expires
28 first, any person who obtains from the Copyright Office a certified re-
29 port that the records provided by subsection (d) disclose nothing to
30 indicate that the author of the work is living, or died less than fifty
31 years before, is entitled to the benefit of a presumption that the author
32 has been dead for at least fifty years. Reliance in good faith upon this
33 presumption shall be a complete defense to any action for infringe-
34 ment under this title.

35 **§ 303. Duration of copyright: Works created but not published**
36 **or copyrighted before January 1, 1977**

37   Copyright in a work created before January 1, 1977, but not thereto-
38 fore in the public domain or copyrighted, subsists from January 1,
39 1977, and endures for the term provided by section 302. In no case,
1 however, shall the term of copyright in such a work expire before

2   December 31, 2001 ; and, if the work is published on or before December

3   31, 2001, the term of copyright shall not expire before December 31,

4   2026.

5   **§ 304. Duration of copyright : Subsisting copyrights**

6   (a) COPYRIGHTS IN THEIR FIRST TERM ON JANUARY 1, 1977.—Any

7   copyright, the first term of which is subsisting on January 1, 1977,

8   shall endure for twenty-eight years from the date it was originally

9   secured : *Provided,* That in the case of any posthumous work or of any

10   periodical, cyclopedic, or other composite work upon which the copy-

11   right was originally secured by the proprietor thereof, or of any work

12   copyrighted by a corporate body (otherwise than as assignee or li-

13   censee of the individual author) or by an employer for whom such

14   work is made for hire, the proprietor of such copyright shall be en-

15   titled to a renewal and extension of the copyright in such work for the

16   further term of forty-seven years when application for such renewal

17   and extension shall have been made to the Copyright Office and duly

18   registered therein within one year prior to the expiration of the origi-

19   nal term of copyright : *And provided further,* That in the case of any

20   other copyrighted work, including a contribution by an individual

21   author to a periodical or to a cyclopedic or other composite work, the

22   author of such work, if still living, or the widow, widower, or children

23   of the author, if the author be not living, or if such author, widow,

24   widower, or children be not living, then the author's executors, or in

25   the absence of a will, his next of kin shall be entitled to a renewal and

26   extension of the copyright in such work for a further term of forty-

27   seven years when application for such renewal and extension shall

28   have been made to the Copyright Office and duly registered therein

29   within one year prior to the expiration of the original term of copy-

30   right : *And provided further,* That in default of the registration of

31   such application for renewal and extension, the copyright in any work

32   shall terminate at the expiration of twenty-eight years from the date

33   copyright was originally secured.

34   (b) COPYRIGHTS IN THEIR RENEWAL TERM OR REGISTERED FOR RE-

35   NEWAL BEFORE JANUARY 1, 1977.—The duration of any copyright, the
36   renewal term of which is subsisting at any time between December 31,
37   1975, and December 31, 1976, inclusive, or for which renewal registra-
38   tion is made between December 31, 1975, and December 31, 1976,
39   inclusive, is extended to endure for a term of seventy-five years from
40   the date copyright was originally secured.

1   (c) TERMINATION OF TRANSFERS AND LICENSES COVERING EXTENDED
2   RENEWAL TERM.—In the case of any copyright subsisting in either
3   its first or renewal term on January 1, 1977, other than a copyright
4   in a work made for hire, the exclusive or nonexclusive grant of a trans-
5   fer or license of the renewal copyright or of any right under it,
6   executed before January 1, 1977, by any of the persons designated by
7   the second proviso of subsection (a) of this section, otherwise than by
8   will, is subject to termination under the following conditions:

9   (1) In the case of a grant executed by a person or persons other
10   than the author, termination of the grant may be effected by the
11   surviving person or persons who executed it. In the case of a
12   grant executed by one or more of the authors of the work, termina-
13   tion of the grant may be effected, to the extent of a particular
14   author's share in the ownership of the renewal copyright, by the
15   author who executed it or, if such author is dead, by the person or
16   persons who, under clause (2) of this subsection, own and are
17   entitled to exercise a total of more than one half of that author's
18   termination interest.

19   (2) Where an author is dead, his or her termination interest is
20   owned, and may be exercised, by his widow (or her widower) and
21   children or grandchildren as follows:

22   (A) the widow (or widower) owns the author's entire
23   termination interest unless there are any surviving children
24   or grandchildren of the author, in which case the widow (or
25   widower) owns one half of the author's interest;

26   (B) the author's surviving children, and the surviving
27   children of any dead child of the author, own the author's
28   entire termination interest unless there is a widow (or wid-

29   ower), in which case the ownership of one half of the author's

30   interest is divided among them;

31   (C) the rights of the author's children and grandchildren

32   are in all cases divided among them and exercised on a per

33   stirpes basis according to the number of his children repre-

34   sented; the share of the children of a dead child in a termina-

35   tion interest can be exercised only by the action of a major-

36   ity of them.

37   (3) Termination of the grant may be effected at any time dur-

38   ing a period of five years beginning at the end of fifty-six years

39   from the date copyright was originally secured, or beginning on

40   January 1, 1977, whichever is later.

1   (4) The termination shall be effected by serving an advance

2   notice in writing upon the grantee or his successor in title. In the

3   case of a grant executed by a person or persons other than the

4   author, the notice shall be signed by all of those entitled to termi-

5   nate the grant under clause (1) of this subsection, or by their duly

6   authorized agents. In the case of a grant executed by one or more

7   of the authors of the work, the notice as to any one author's share

8   shall be signed by him or his duly authorized agent or, if he is

9   dead, by the number and proportion of the owners of his termina-

10   tion interest required under clauses (1) and (2) of this subsection,

11   or by their duly authorized agents.

12   (A) The notice shall state the effective date of the termi-

13   nation, which shall fall within the five-year period specified

14   by clause (3) of this subsection, and the notice shall be served

15   not less than two or more than ten years before that date. A

16   copy of the notice shall be recorded in the Copyright Office

17   before the effective date of termination, as a condition to its

18   taking effect.

19   (B) The notice shall comply, in form, content, and manner

20   of service, with requirements that the Register of Copyrights

21   shall prescribe by regulation.

22   (5) Termination of the grant may be effected notwithstanding

23   any agreement to the contrary, including an agreement to make
24   a will or to make any future grant.

25   (6) In the case of a grant executed by a person or persons other
26   than the author, all rights under this title that were covered by
27   the terminated grant revert, upon the effective date of termination,
28   to all of those entitled to terminate the grant under clause (1) of
29   this subsection. In the case of a grant executed by one or more
30   of the authors of the work, all of a particular author's rights
31   under this title that were covered by the terminated grant revert,
32   upon the effective date of termination, to that author or, if he is
33   dead, to the persons owning his termination interest under clause
34   (2) of this subsection, including those owners who did not join
35   in signing the notice of termination under clause (4) of this sub-
36   section. In all cases the reversion of rights is subject to the follow-
37   ing limitations:

38   (A) A derivative work prepared under authority of the
39   grant before its termination may continue to be utilized under
1   the terms of the grant after its termination, but this privilege
2   does not extend to the preparation after the termination of
3   other derivative works based upon the copyrighted work cov-
4   ered by the terminated grant.

5   (B) The future rights that will revert upon termination
6   of the grant become vested on the date the notice of termi-
7   nation has been served as provided by clause (4) of this
8   subsection.

9   (C) Where an author's rights revert to two or more per-
10   sons under clause (2) of this subsection, they shall vest in
11   those persons in the proportionate shares provided by that
12   clause. In such a case, and subject to the provisions of sub-
13   clause (D) of this clause, a further grant, or agreement to
14   make a further grant, of a particular author's share with
15   respect to any right covered by a terminated grant is valid
16   only if it is signed by the same number and proportion of
17   the owners, in whom the right has vested under this clause,

18 as are required to terminate the grant under clause (2) of
19 this subsection. Such further grant or agreement is effective
20 with respect to all of the persons in whom the right it
21 covers has vested under this subclause, including those who
22 did not join in signing it. If any person dies after rights
23 under a terminated grant have vested in him, his legal repre-
24 sentatives, legatees, or heirs at law represent him for purposes
25 of this subclause.

26 (D) A further grant, or agreement to make a further
27 grant, of any right covered by a terminated grant is valid
28 only if it is made after the effective date of the termination.
29 As an exception, however, an agreement for such a further
30 grant may be made between the author or any of the per-
31 sons provided by the first sentence of clause (6) of this
32 subsection, or between the persons provided by subclause
33 (C) of this clause, and the original grantee or his successor
34 in title, after the notice of termination has been served as
35 provided by clause (4) of this subsection.

36 (E) Termination of a grant under this subsection affects
37 only those rights covered by the grant that arise under this
38 title, and in no way affects rights arising under any other
39 Federal, State, or foreign laws.

1 (F) Unless and until termination is effected under this
2 section, the grant, if it does not provide otherwise, continues
3 in effect for the remainder of the extended renewal term.

4 **§ 305. Duration of copyright: Terminal date**

5 All terms of copyright provided by sections 302 through 304 run to
6 the end of the calendar year in which they would otherwise expire.

7 **Chapter 4.—COPYRIGHT NOTICE, DEPOSIT, AND**
8 **REGISTRATION**

9   ## § 401. Notice of copyright: Visually perceptible copies

10   (a) GENERAL REQUIREMENT.—Whenever a work protected under
11   this title is published in the United States or elsewhere by authority
12   of the copyright owner, a notice of copyright as provided by this sec-
13   tion shall be placed on all publicly distributed copies from which the
14   work can be visually perceived, either directly or with the aid of a
15   machine or device.

16   (b) FORM OF NOTICE.—The notice appearing on the copies shall con-
17   sist of the following three elements:

18   (1) the symbol © (the letter C in a circle), the word "Copy-
19   right", or the abbreviation "Copr.";

20   (2) the year of first publication of the work; in the case of
21   compilations or derivative works incorporating previously pub-
22   lished material, the year date of first publication of the compila-
23   tion or derivative work is sufficient. The year date may be omitted
24   where a pictorial, graphic, or sculptural work, with accompanying
25   text matter, if any, is reproduced in or on greeting cards, post-
26   cards, stationery, jewelry, dolls, toys, or any useful articles;

27   (3) the name of the owner of copyright in the work, or an ab-
28   breviation by which the name can be recognized, or a generally
29   known alternative designation of the owner.

30   (c) POSITION OF NOTICE.—The notice shall be affixed to the copies in
31   such manner and location as to give reasonable notice of the claim
1   of copyright The Register of Copyrights shall prescribe by regula
2   tion, as examples, specific methods of affixation and positions of the
3   notice on various types of works that will satisfy this requirement, but
4   these specifications shall not be considered exhaustive.

5   ## § 402. Notice of copyright: Phonorecords of sound recordings

6   (a) GENERAL REQUIREMENT.—Whenever a sound recording pro-

7 tected under this title is published in the United States or elsewhere by
8 authority of the copyright owner, a notice of copyright as provided
9 by this section shall be placed on all publicly distributed phonorecords
10 of the sound recording.

11 (b) FORM OF NOTICE.—The notice appearing on the phonorecords
12 shall consist of the following three elements:

13 (1) the symbol ℗ (the letter P in a circle) ;

14 (2) the year of first publication of the sound recording; and

15 (3) the name of the owner of copyright in the sound record-
16 ing, or an abbreviation by which the name can be recognized, or a
17 generally known alternative designation of the owner; if the
18 producer of the sound recording is named on the phonorecord
19 labels or containers, and if no other name appears in conjunction
20 with the notice, his name shall be considered a part of the notice.

21 (c) POSITION OF NOTICE.—The notice shall be placed on the surface
22 of the phonorecord, or on the phonorecord label or container, in such
23 manner and location as to give reasonable notice of the claim of copy-
24 right.

25 **§ 403. Notice of copyright: Publications incorporating United**
26 **States Government works**

27 Whenever a work is published in copies or phonorecords consisting
28 preponderantly of one or more works of the United States Govern-
29 ment, the notice of copyright provided by section 401 or 402 shall
30 also include a statement identifying, either affirmatively or negatively,
31 those portions of the copies or phonorecords embodying any work or
32 works protected under this title.

33 **§ 404. Notice of copyright: Contributions to collective works**

34 (a) A separate contribution to a collective work may bear its own
35 notice of copyright, as provided by sections 401 through 403. How-
36 ever, a single notice applicable to the collective work as a whole is
37 sufficient to satisfy the requirements of sections 401 through 403 with
38 respect to the separate contributions it contains (not including adver-
39 tisements inserted on behalf of persons other than the owner of copy-
40 right in the collective work), regardless of the ownership of copyright

1   in the contributions and whether or not they have been previously
2   published.

3   (b) Where the person named in a single notice applicable to a
4   collective work as a whole is not the owner of copyright in a separate
5   contribution that does not bear its own notice, the case is governed
6   by the provisions of section 406(a).

7   **§ 405. Notice of copyright: Omission of notice**

8   (a) EFFECT OF OMISSION ON COPYRIGHT.—The omission of the copy-
9   right notice described by sections 401 through 403 from copies or
10   phonorecords publicly distributed by authority of the copyright
11   owner does not invalidate the copyright in a work if:

12   (1) the notice has been omitted from no more than a relatively
13   small number of copies or phonorecords distributed to the public;
14   or

15   (2) registration for the work has been made before or is made
16   within five years after the publication without notice, and a
17   reasonable effort is made to add notice to all copies or phono-
18   records that are distributed to the public in the United States
19   after the omission has been discovered; or

20   (3) the notice has been omitted in violation of an express re-
21   quirement in writing that, as a condition of the copyright owner's
22   authorization of the public distribution of copies or phonorecords,
23   they bear the prescribed notice.

24   (b) EFFECT OF OMISSION ON INNOCENT INFRINGERS.—Any person
25   who innocently infringes a copyright, in reliance upon an authorized
26   copy or phonorecord from which the copyright notice has been
27   omitted, incurs no liability for actual or statutory damages under sec-
28   tion 504 for any infringing acts committed before receiving actual
29   notice that registration for the work has been made under section 408,
30   if he proves that he was misled by the omission of notice. In a suit
31   for infringement in such a case the court may allow or disallow re-
32   covery of any of the infringer's profits attributable to the infringe-
33   ment, and may enjoin the continuation of the infringing undertaking
34   or may require, as a condition for permitting the infringer to con-

35 tinue his undertaking, that he pay the copyright owner a reason-
36 able license fee in an amount and on terms fixed by the court.

37   (c) REMOVAL OF NOTICE.—Protection under this title is not affected
38 by the removal, destruction, or obliteration of the notice, without
39 the authorization of the copyright owner, from any publicly distrib-
40 uted copies or phonorecords.

1   **§ 406. Notice of copyright: Error in name or date**

2   (a) ERROR IN NAME.—Where the person named in the copyright
3   notice on copies or phonorecords publicly distributed by authority of
4   the copyright owner is not the owner of copyright, the validity and
5   ownership of the copyright are not affected. In such a case, however,
6   any person who innocently begins an undertaking that infringes the
7   copyright has a complete defense to any action for such infringement
8   if he proves that he was misled by the notice and began the undertak-
9   ing in good faith under a purported transfer or license from the person
10 named therein, unless before the undertaking was begun:

11   (1) registration for the work had been made in the name of
12   the owner of copyright; or

13   (2) a document executed by the person named in the notice
14   and showing the ownership of the copyright had been recorded.
15 The person named in the notice is liable to account to the copyright
16 owner for all receipts from purported transfers or licenses made by
17 him under the copyright.

18   (b) ERROR IN DATE.—When the year date in the notice on copies or
19 phonorecords distributed by authority of the copyright owner is
20 earlier than the year in which publication first occurred, any period
21 computed from the year of first publication under section 302 is to be
22 computed from the year in the notice. Where the year date is more
23 than one year later than the year in which publication first occurred,
24 the work is considered to have been published without any notice and
25 is governed by the provisions of section 405.

26   (c) OMISSION OF NAME OR DATE.—Where copies or phonorecords
27 publicly distributed by authority of the copyright owner contain no
28 name or no date that could reasonably be considered a part of the

29   notice, the work is considered to have been published without any
30   notice and is governed by the provisions of section 405.

31   **§ 407. Deposit of copies or phonorecords for Library of Congress**

32   (a) Except as provided by subsection (c), the owner of copyright
33   or of the exclusive right of publication in a work published with no-
34   tice of copyright in the United States shall deposit, within three
35   months after the date of such publication:

36   (1) two complete copies of the best edition; or

37   (2) if the work is a sound recording, two complete phono-
38   records of the best edition, together with any printed or other
39   visually perceptible material published with such phonorecords.

40   This deposit is not a condition of copyright protection.

1   (b) The required copies or phonorecords shall be deposited in the
2   Copyright Office for the use or disposition of the Library of Congress.
3   The Register of Copyrights shall, when requested by the depositor
4   and upon payment of the fee prescribed by section 708, issue a receipt
5   for the deposit.

6   (c) The Register of Copyrights may by regulation exempt any
7   categories of material from the deposit requirements of this section,
8   or require deposit of only one copy or phonorecord with respect to
9   any categories.

10   (d) At any time after publication of a work as provided by sub-
11   section (a), the Register of Copyrights may make written demand
12   for the required deposit on any of the persons obligated to make the
13   deposit under subsection (a). Unless deposit is made within three
14   months after the demand is received, the person or persons on whom
15   the demand was made are liable:

16   (1) to a fine of not more than $250 for each work; and

17   (2) to pay to the Library of Congress the total retail price of
18   the copies or phonorecords demanded, or, if no retail price has
19   been fixed, the reasonable cost to the Library of Congress of
20   acquiring them.

21   **§ 408. Copyright registration in general**

22   (a) REGISTRATION PERMISSIVE.—At any time during the subsistence
23 of copyright in any published or unpublished work, the owner of
24 copyright or of any exclusive right in the work may obtain registration
25 of the copyright claim by delivering to the Copyright Office the deposit
26 specified by this section, together with the application and fee specified
27 by sections 409 and 708. Subject to the provisions of section 405(a),
28 such registration is not a condition of copyright protection.

29   (b) DEPOSIT FOR COPYRIGHT REGISTRATION.—Except as provided by
30 subsection (c), the material deposited for registration shall include:

31   (1) in the case of an unpublished work, one complete copy or
32   phonorecord;

33   (2) in the case of a published work, two complete copies or
34   phonorecords of the best edition;

35   (3) in the case of a work first published abroad, one complete
36   copy or phonorecord as so published;

37   (4) in the case of a contribution to a collective work, one com-
38   plete copy or phonorecord of the best edition of the collective
39   work.

1 Copies or phonorecords deposited for the Library of Congress under
2 section 407 may be used to satisfy the deposit provisions of this section,
3 if they are accompanied by the prescribed application and fee, and by
4 any additional identifying material that the Register may, by regula-
5 tion, require.

6   (c) ADMINISTRATIVE CLASSIFICATION AND OPTIONAL DEPOSIT.—

7   (1) The Register of Copyrights is authorized to specify by regu-
8   lation the administrative classes into which works are to be placed
9   for purposes of deposit and registration, and the nature of the
10   copies or phonorecords to be deposited in the various classes speci-
11   fied. The regulations may require or permit, for particular classes,
12   the deposit of identifying material instead of copies or phono-
13   records, the deposit of only one copy or phonorecord where two
14   would normally be required, or a single registration for a group
15   of related works. This administrative classification of works has
16   no significance with respect to the subject matter of copyright or

17   the exclusive rights provided by this title.

18   (2) Without prejudice to his general authority under clause
19   (1), the Register of Copyrights shall establish regulations specifi-
20   cally permitting a single registration for a group of works by the
21   same individual author, all first published as contributions to
22   periodicals, including newspapers, within a twelve-month period,
23   on the basis of a single deposit, application, and registration fee,
24   under all of the following conditions:

25   (A) if each of the works as first published bore a separate
26   copyright notice, and the name of the owner of copyright in
27   the work, or an abbreviation by which the name can be recog-
28   nized, or a generally known alternative designation of the
29   owner was the same in each notice; and

30   (B) if the deposit consists of one copy of the entire issue
31   of the periodical, or of the entire section in the case of a news-
32   paper, in which each contribution was first published; and

33   (C) if the application identifies each work separately, in-
34   cluding the periodical containing it and its date of first
35   publication.

36   (3) As an alternative to separate renewal registrations under
37   subsection (a) of section 304, a single renewal registration may be
38   made for a group of works by the same individual author, all first
39   published as contributions to periodicals, including newspapers,
1   upon the filing of a single application and fee, under all of the
2   following conditions:

3   (A) the renewal claimant or claimants, and the basis of
4   claim or claims under section 304(a), is the same for each of
5   the works; and

6   (B) the works were all copyrighted upon their first publi-
7   cation, either through separate copyright notice and registra-
8   tion or by virtue of a general copyright notice in the peri-
9   odical issue as a whole; and

10   (C) all of the works were first published not more than
11   twenty-eight or less than twenty-seven years before the date

12   of receipt of the renewal application and fee; and

13   (D) the renewal application identifies each work sepa-
14   rately, including the periodical containing it and its date of
15   first publication.

16   (d) CORRECTIONS AND AMPLIFICATIONS.—The Register may also
17   establish, by regulation, formal procedures for the filing of an applica-
18   tion for supplementary registration, to correct an error in a copyright
19   registration or to amplify the information given in a registration.
20   Such application shall be accompanied by the fee provided by sec-
21   tion 708, and shall clearly identify the registration to be corrected
22   or amplified. The information contained in a supplementary registra-
23   tion augments but does not supersede that contained in the earlier
24   registration.

25   (e) PUBLISHED EDITION OF PREVIOUSLY REGISTERED WORK.—Regis-
26   tration for the first published edition of a work previously registered
27   in unpublished form may be made even though the work as published
28   is substantially the same as the unpublished version.

29   § 409. **Application for registration**

30   The application for copyright registration shall be made on a form
31   prescribed by the Register of Copyrights and shall include:

32   (1) the name and address of the copyright claimant;

33   (2) in the case of a work other than an anonymous or pseudony-
34   mous work, the name and nationality or domicile of the author or
35   authors and, if one or more of the authors is dead, the dates of
36   their deaths;

37   (3) if the work is anonymous or pseudonymous, the nationality
38   or domicile of the author or authors;

39   (4) in the case of a work made for hire, a statement to this
40   effect;

1   (5) if the copyright claimant is not the author, a brief state-
2   ment of how the claimant obtained ownership of the copyright;

3   (6) the title of the work, together with any previous or alterna-
4   tive titles under which the work can be identified;

5   (7) the year in which creation of the work was completed;

6 (8) if the work has been published, the date and nation of its
7 first publication;

8 (9) in the case of a compilation or derivative work, an identi-
9 fication of any pre-existing work or works that it is based on or
10 incorporates, and a brief, general statement of the additional
11 material covered by the copyright claim being registered;

12 (10) in the case of a published work containing material of
13 which copies are required by section 601 to be manufactured in
14 the United States, the names of the persons or organizations
15 who performed the processes specified by subsection (c) of sec-
16 tion 601 with respect to that material, and the places where those
17 processes were performed; and

18 (11) any other information regarded by the Register of Copy-
19 rights as bearing upon the preparation or identification of the
20 work or the existence, ownership, or duration of the copyright.

21 **§ 410. Registration of claim and issuance of certificate**

22 (a) When, after examination, the Register of Copyrights deter-
23 mines that, in accordance with the provisions of this title, the material
24 deposited constitutes copyrightable subject matter and that the other
25 legal and formal requirements of this title have been met, he shall reg-
26 ister the claim and issue to the applicant a certificate of registration
27 under the seal of the Copyright Office. The certificate shall contain
28 the information given in the application, together with the number
29 and effective date of the registration.

30 (b) In any case in which the Register of Copyrights determines
31 that, in accordance with the provisions of this title, the material de-
32 posited does not constitute copyrightable subject matter or that the
33 claim is invalid for any other reason, he shall refuse registration and
34 shall notify the applicant in writing of the reasons for his action.

35 (c) In any judicial proceedings the certificate of a registration made
36 before or within five years after first publication of the work shall
37 constitute prima facie evidence of the validity of the copyright and
38 of the facts stated in the certificate. The evidentiary weight to be
39 accorded the certificate of a registration made thereafter shall be

40   within the discretion of the court.

1   (d) The effective date of a copyright registration is the day on
2   which an application, deposit, and fee, which are later determined by
3   the Register of Copyrights or by a court of competent jurisdiction to
4   be acceptable for registration, have all been received in the Copyright
5   Office.

6   **§ 411. Registration as prerequisite to infringement suit**

7   (a) Subject to the provisions of subsection (b), no action for in-
8   fringement of the copyright in any work shall be instituted until
9   registration of the copyright claim has been made in accordance with
10   this title. In any case, however, where the deposit, application, and fee
11   required for registration have been delivered to the Copyright Office
12   in proper form and registration has been refused, the applicant is
13   entitled to institute an action for infringement if notice thereof, with
14   a copy of the complaint, is served on the Register of Copyrights. The
15   Register may, at his option, become a party to the action with respect
16   to the issue of registrability of the copyright claim by entering his
17   appearance within sixty days after such service, but his failure to do
18   so shall not deprive the court of jurisdiction to determine that issue.

19   (b) In the case of a work consisting of sounds, images, or both, the
20   first fixation of which is made simultaneously with its transmission,
21   the copyright owner may, either before or after such fixation takes
22   place, institute an action for infringement under section 501, fully
23   subject to the remedies provided by sections 502 through 506, if, in
24   accordance with requirements that the Register of Copyrights shall
25   prescribe by regulation, the copyright owner—

26   (1) serves notice upon the infringer, not less than ten or more
27   than thirty days before such fixation, identifying the work and
28   the specific time and source of its first transmission, and declar-
29   ing an intention to secure copyright in the work; and

30   (2) makes registration for the work within three months after
31   its first transmission.

32   **§ 412. Registration as prerequisite to certain remedies for**
33   **infringement**

34   In any action under this title, other than an action instituted under
35   section 411(b), no award of statutory damages or of attorney's fees, as
36   provided by sections 504 and 505, shall be made for:

37   (1) any infringement of copyright in an unpublished work
38   commenced before the effective date of its registration; or

39   (2) any infringement of copyright commenced after first pub-
40   lication of the work and before the effective date of its registra-
1   tion, unless such registration is made within three months after
2   its first publication.

3   ## Chapter 5.—COPYRIGHT INFRINGEMENT AND REMEDIES

Sec.
501. Infringement of copyright.
502. Remedies for infringement: Injunctions.
503. Remedies for infringement: Impounding and disposition of infringing
      articles.
504. Remedies for infringement: Damages and profits.
505. Remedies for infringement: Costs and attorney's fees.
506. Criminal offenses.
507. Limitations on actions.
508. Notification of filing and determination of actions.
509. Seizure and forfeiture.

4   ## § 501. Infringement of copyright

5   (a) Anyone who violates any of the exclusive rights of the copy-
6   right owner as provided by sections 106 through 118, or who imports
7   copies or phonorecords into the United States in violation of section
8   602, is an infringer of the copyright.

9   (b) The legal or beneficial owner of an exclusive right under a
10   copyright is entitled, subject to the requirements of sections 205(d)
11   and 411, to institute an action for any infringement of that particular
12   right committed while he is the owner of it. The court may require
13   him to serve written notice of the action with a copy of the complaint
14   upon any person shown, by the records of the Copyright Office or
15   otherwise, to have or claim an interest in the copyright, and shall re-
16   quire that such notice be served upon any person whose interest is
17   likely to be affected by a decision in the case. The court may require
18   the joinder, and shall permit the intervention, of any person having
19   or claiming an interest in the copyright.

20   (c) For any secondary transmission by a cable system that em-

21 bodies a performance or a display of a work which is actionable as an
22 act of infringement under subsection (c) of section 111, a television
23 broadcast station holding a copyright or other license to transmit or
24 perform the same version of that work shall, for purposes of subsection
25 (b) of this section, be treated as a legal or beneficial owner if such
26 secondary transmission occurs within the local service area of that
27 television station.

28 **§ 502. Remedies for infringement: Injunctions**

29 (a) Any court having jurisdiction of a civil action arising under
30 this title may, subject to the provisions of section 1498 of title 28,
31 grant temporary and final injunctions on such terms as it may deem
32 reasonable to prevent or restrain infringement of a copyright.

33 (b) Any such injunction may be served anywhere in the United
1 States on the person enjoined; it shall be operative throughout the
2 United States and shall be enforceable, by proceedings in contempt or
3 otherwise, by any United States court having jurisdiction of that per-
4 son. The clerk of the court granting the injunction shall, when re-
5 quested by any other court in which enforcement of the injunction is
6 sought, transmit promptly to the other court a certified copy of all
7 the papers in the case on file in his office.

8 **§ 503. Remedies for infringement: Impounding and disposition of**
9 **infringing articles**

10 (a) At any time while an action under this title is pending, the court
11 may order the impounding, on such terms as it may deem reasonable,
12 of all copies or phonorecords claimed to have been made or used in vio-
13 lation of the copyright owner's exclusive rights, and of all plates,
14 molds, matrices, masters, tapes, film negatives, or other articles by
15 means of which such copies or phonorecords may be reproduced.

16 (b) As part of a final judgment or decree, the court may order the
17 destruction or other reasonable disposition of all copies or phonorec-
18 ords found to have been made or used in violation of the copyright
19 owner's exclusive rights, and of all plates, molds, matrices, masters,
20 tapes, film negatives, or other articles by means of which such copies
21 or phonorecords may be reproduced.

22   **§ 504. Remedies for infringement: Damages and profits**

23   (a) IN GENERAL.—Except as otherwise provided by this title, an in-
24   fringer of copyright is liable for either:

25   (1) the copyright owner's actual damages and any additional
26   profits of the infringer, as provided by subsection (b) ; or

27   (2) statutory damages, as provided by subsection (c).

28   (b) ACTUAL DAMAGES AND PROFITS.—The copyright owner is en-
29   titled to recover the actual damages suffered by him as a result of the
30   infringement, and any profits of the infringer that are attributable to
31   the infringement and are not taken into account in computing the
32   actual damages. In establishing the infringer's profits, the copyright
33   owner is required to present proof only of the infringer's gross revenue,
34   and the infringer is required to prove his deductible expenses and the
35   elements of profit attributable to factors other than the copyrighted
36   work.

37   (c) STATUTORY DAMAGES.—

38   (1) Except as provided by clause (2) of this subsection, the
39   copyright owner may elect, at any time before final judgment is
40   rendered, to recover, instead of actual damages and profits, an
1   award of statutory damages for all infringements involved in
2   the action, with respect to any one work, for which any one
3   infringer is liable individually, or for which any two or more
4   infringers are liable jointly and severally, in a sum of not less
5   than $250 or more than $10,000 as the court considers just. For
6   the purposes of this subsection, all the parts of a compilation or
7   derivative work constitute one work.

8   (2) In a case where the copyright owner sustains the burden
9   of proving, and the court finds, that infringement was committed
10   willfully, the court in its discretion may increase the award of
11   statutory damages to a sum of not more than $50,000. In a case
12   where the infringer sustains the burden of proving, and the court
13   finds, that he was not aware and had no reason to believe that his
14   acts constituted an infringement of copyright, the court in its
15   discretion may reduce the award of statutory damages to a sum

16   of not less than $100. In a case where an instructor, librarian or
17   archivist in a nonprofit educational institution, library, or ar-
18   chives, who infringed by reproducing a copyrighted work in copies
19   or phonorecords, sustains the burden of proving that he believed
20   and had reasonable grounds for believing that the reproduction
21   was a fair use under section 107, the court in its discretion may
22   remit statutory damages in whole or in part.

23   § 505. Remedies for infringement: Costs and attorney's fees

24   In any civil action under this title, the court in its discretion may
25   allow the recovery of full costs by or against any party other than
26   the United States or an officer thereof. Except as otherwise provided
27   by this title, the court may also award a reasonable attorney's fee to
28   the prevailing party as part of the costs.

29   § 506. Criminal offenses

30   (a) CRIMINAL INFRINGEMENT.—Any person who infringes a
31   copyright willfully and for purposes of commercial advantage or pri-
32   vate financial gain shall be fined not more than $2,500 or imprisoned
33   not more than one year, or both, for the first such offense, and shall
34   be fined not more than $10,000 or imprisoned not more than three
35   years, or both, for any subsequent offense: *Provided, however*, That
36   any person who infringes willfully and for purposes of commercial
37   advantage or private financial gain the copyright in a sound recording
38   afforded by subsections (1), (2), and (3) of section 106 or the copy-
39   right in a motion picture afforded by subsections (1), (3), and (4) of
40   section 106 shall be fined not more than $25,000 or imprisoned for not
1   more than three years, or both, for the first such offense and shall be
2   fined not more than $50,000 or imprisoned not more than seven years,
3   or both, for any subsequent offense.

4   (b) FORFEITURE AND DESTRUCTION.—When any person is convicted
5   of any violation of subsection (a), the court in its judgment of con-
6   viction shall, in addition to the penalty therein prescribed, order the
7   forfeiture and destruction or other disposition of all infringing copies
8   or phonorecords and all implements, devices, or equipment used or
9   intended to be used in the manufacture, use, or sale of such infringing

10   copies or phonorecords.

11   (c) FRAUDULENT COPYRIGHT NOTICE.—Any person who, with fraud-
12   ulent intent, places on any article a notice of copyright or words of
13   the same purport that he knows to be false, or who, with fraudulent
14   intent, publicly distributes or imports for public distribution any
15   article bearing such notice or words that he knows to be false, shall be
16   fined not more than $2,500.

17   (d) FRAUDULENT REMOVAL OF COPYRIGHT NOTICE.—Any person who,
18   with fraudulent intent, removes or alters any notice of copyright
19   appearing on a copy of a copyrighted work shall be fined not more
20   than $2,500.

21   (e) FALSE REPRESENTATION.—Any person who knowingly makes a
22   false representation of a material fact in the application for copyright
23   registration provided for by section 409, or in any written statement
24   filed in connection with the application, shall be fined not more than
25    $2,500.

§ 507. Limitations on actions

27   (a) CRIMINAL PROCEEDINGS.—No criminal proceeding shall be main-
28   tained under the provisions of this title unless it is commenced within
29   three years after the cause of action arose.

30   (b) CIVIL ACTIONS.—No civil action shall be maintained under the
31   provisions of this title unless it is commenced within three years after
32   the claim accrued.

§ 508. Notification of filing and determination of actions

34   (a) Within one month after the filing of any action under this title,
35   the clerks of the courts of the United States shall send written notifica-
36   tion to the Register of Copyrights setting forth, as far as is shown
37   by the papers filed in the court, the names and addresses of the parties
38   and the title, author, and registration number of each work involved
39   in the action. If any other copyrighted work is later included in the
40   action by amendment, answer, or other pleading, the clerk shall also
1   send a notification concerning it to the Register within one month
2   after the pleading is filed.

3   (b) Within one month after any final order or judgment is issued

4 in the case, the clerk of the court shall notify the Register of it,
5 sending him a copy of the order or judgment together with the written
6 opinion, if any, of the court.

7   (c) Upon receiving the notifications specified in this section, the
8 Register shall make them a part of the public records of the Copyright
9 Office.

10 **§ 509. Seizure and forfeiture**

11   (a) All copies or phonorecords manufactured, reproduced, distrib-
12 uted, sold, or otherwise used, intended for use, or possessed with intent
13 to use in violation of section 506(a), and all plates, molds, matrices,
14 masters, tapes, film negatives, or other articles by means of which such
15 copies or phonorecords may be reproduced, and all electronic, mechani-
16 cal, or other devices for manufacturing, reproducing, assembling, us-
17 ing, transporting, distributing, or selling such copies or phonorecords
18 may be seized and forfeited to the United States.

19   (b) All provisions of law relating to (1) the seizure, summary and
20 judicial forfeiture, and condemnation of vessels, vehicles, merchandise,
21 and baggage for violations of the customs laws contained in title 19,
22 United States Code, (2) the disposition of such vessels, vehicles,
23 merchandise, and baggage or the proceeds from the sale thereof, (3)
24 the remission or mitigation of such forfeiture, (4) the compromise of
25 claims, and (5) the award of compensation to informers in respect of
26 such forfeitures, shall apply to seizures and forfeitures incurred, or
27 alleged to have been incurred, under the provisions of this section,
28 insofar as applicable and not inconsistent with the provisions of
29 this section; except that such duties as are imposed upon the collector
30 of customs or any other person with respect to the seizure and forfeiture
31 of vessels, vehicles, merchandise, and baggage under the provisions of
32 the customs laws contained in title 19 of the United States Code shall
33 be performed with respect to seizure and forfeiture of all articles de-
34 scribed in subsection (a) by such officers, agents, or other persons as
35 may be authorized or designated for that purpose by the Attorney
36 General.

37   **Chapter 6.—MANUFACTURING REQUIREMENT AND**
38   **IMPORTATION**

Sec.
601. Manufacture, importation, and public distribution of certain copies.
602. Infringing importation of copies or phonorecords.
603. Importation prohibitions: Enforcement and disposition of excluded articles.

1   **§ 601. Manufacture, importation, and public distribution of cer-**
2   **tain copies**

3   (a) Except as provided by subsection (b), the importation into or
4   public distribution in the United States of copies of a work consisting
5   preponderantly of nondramatic literary material that is in the English
6   language and is protected under this title is prohibited unless the
7   portions consisting of such material have been manufactured in the
8   United States or Canada.

9   (b) The provisions of subsection (a) do not apply:

10   (1) where, on the date when importation is sought or public
11   distribution in the United States is made, the author of any sub-
12   stantial part of such material is neither a national nor a domicil-
13   iary of the United States or, if he is a national of the United
14   States, has been domiciled outside of the United States for a
15   continuous period of at least one year immediately preceding that
16   date; in the case of a work made for hire, the exemption provided
17   by this clause does not apply unless a substantial part of the work
18   was prepared for an employer or other person who is not a na-
19   tional or domiciliary of the United States or a domestic corpora-
20   tion or enterprise;

21   (2) where the United States Customs Service is presented with
22   an import statement issued under the seal of the Copyright Office,
23   in which case a total of no more than two thousand copies of any
24   one such work shall be allowed entry; the import statement shall
25   be issued upon request to the copyright owner or to a person
26   designated by him at the time of registration for the work under
27   section 408 or at any time thereafter;

28   (3) where importation is sought under the authority or for the
29   use, other than in schools, of the Government of the United States

30   or of any State or political subdivision of a State;

31   (4) where importation, for use and not for sale, is sought:

32   (A) by any person with respect to no more than one copy

33   of any one work at any one time;

34   (B) by any person arriving from abroad, with respect to

35   copies forming part of his personal baggage; or

36   (C) by an organization operated for scholarly, educa-

37   tional, or religious purposes and not for private gain, with

38   respect to copies intended to form a part of its library;

39   (5) where the copies are reproduced in raised characters for

40   the use of the blind; or

1   (6) where, in addition to copies imported under clauses (3)

2   and (4) of this subsection, no more than two thousand copies of

3   any one such work, which have not been manufactured in the

4   United States or Canada, are publicly distributed in the United

5   States.

6   (c) The requirement of this section that copies be manufactured in

7   the United States or Canada is satisfied if:

8   (1) in the case where the copies are printed directly from type

9   that has been set, or directly from plates made from such type,

10   the setting of the type and the making of the plates have been

11   performed in the United States or Canada; or

12   (2) in the case where the making of plates by a lithographic

13   or photoengraving process is a final or intermediate step preceding

14   the printing of the copies, the making of the plates has been per-

15   formed in the United States or Canada; and

16   (3) in any case, the printing or other final process of producing

17   multiple copies and any binding of the copies have been performed

18   in the United States or Canada.

19   (d) Importation or public distribution of copies in violation of

20   this section does not invalidate protection for a work under this title.

21   However, in any civil action or criminal proceeding for infringement

22   of the exclusive rights to reproduce and distribute copies of the work,

23   the infringer has a complete defense with respect to all of the non-

24   dramatic literary material comprised in the work and any other parts
25   of the work in which the exclusive rights to reproduce and distribute
26   copies are owned by the same person who owns such exclusive rights
27   in the nondramatic literary material, if he proves:

28   (1) that copies of the work have been imported into or publicly
29   distributed in the United States in violation of this section by or
30   with the authority of the owner of such exclusive rights; and

31   (2) that the infringing copies were manufactured in the United
32   States or Canada in accordance with the provisions of subsection
33   (c); and

34   (3) that the infringement was commenced before the effective
35   date of registration for an authorized edition of the work, the
36   copies of which have been manufactured in the United States or
37   Canada in accordance with the provisions of subsection (c).

38   (e) In any action for infringement of the exclusive rights to repro-
39   duce and distribute copies of a work containing material required by
1   this section to be manufactured in the United States or Canada, the
2   copyright owner shall set forth in the complaint the names of the per-
3   sons or organizations who performed the processes specified by subsec-
4   tion (c) with respect to that material, and the places where those
5   processes were performed.

6   **§ 602. Infringing importation of copies or phonorecords**

7   (a) Importation into the United States, without the authority of
8   the owner of copyright under this title, of copies or phonorecords of
9   a work that have been acquired abroad is an infringement of the
10   exclusive right to distribute copies or phonorecords under section 106,
11   actionable under section 501. This subsection does not apply to:

12   (1) importation of copies or phonorecords under the authority
13   or for the use of the Government of the United States or of any
14   State or political subdivision of a State but not including copies
15   or phonorecords for use in schools, or copies of any audiovisual
16   work imported for purposes other than archival use;

17   (2) importation, for the private use of the importer and not
18   for distribution, by any person with respect to no more than one

19 copy or phonorecord of any one work at any one time, or by any
20 person arriving from abroad with respect to copies or phono-
21 records forming part of his personal baggage; or

22   (3) importation by or for an organization operated for schol-
23 arly, educational, or religious purposes and not for private gain,
24 with respect to no more than one copy of an audiovisual work
25 solely for its archival purposes, and no more than five copies or
26 phonorecords of any other work for its library lending or archival
27 purposes.

28   (b) In a case where the making of the copies or phonorecords would
29 have constituted an infringement of copyright if this title had been
30 applicable, their importation is prohibited. In a case where the copies
31 or phonorecords were lawfully made, the United States Customs Serv-
32 ice has no authority to prevent their importation unless the provisions
33 of section 601 are applicable. In either case, the Secretary of the Treas-
34 ury is authorized to prescribe, by regulation, a procedure under which
35 any person claiming an interest in the copyright in a particular work
36 may, upon payment of a specified fee, be entitled to notification by
37 the Customs Service of the importation of articles that appear to be
38 copies or phonorecords of the work.

1 **§ 603. Importation prohibitions: Enforcement and disposition of**
2   **excluded articles**

3   (a) The Secretary of the Treasury and the United States Postal
4 Service shall separately or jointly make regulations for the enforce-
5 ment of the provisions of this title prohibiting importation.

6   (b) These regulations may require, as a condition for the exclusion
7 of articles under section 602:

8   (1) that the person seeking exclusion obtain a court order
9   enjoining importation of the articles; or

10   (2) that he furnish proof, of a specified nature and in accord-
11   ance with prescribed procedures, that the copyright in which he
12   claims an interest is valid and that the importation would violate
13   the prohibition in section 602; he may also be required to post a

14   surety bond for any injury that may result if the detention or
15   exclusion of the articles proves to be unjustified.

16   (c) Articles imported in violation of the importation prohibitions
17   of this title are subject to seizure and forfeiture in the same manner
18   as property imported in violation of the customs revenue laws. For-
19   feited articles shall be destroyed as directed by the Secretary of the
20   Treasury or the court, as the case may be; however, the articles may be
21   returned to the country of export whenever it is shown to the satisfac-
22   tion of the Secretary of the Treasury that the importer had no reason-
23   able grounds for believing that his acts constituted a violation of law.

24   Chapter 7.—COPYRIGHT OFFICE

25   **§ 701. The Copyright Office: General responsibilities and organi-**
26   **zation**

27   (a) All administrative functions and duties under this title, ex-
28   cept as otherwise specified, are the responsibility of the Register of
29   Copyrights as director of the Copyright Office of the Library of Con-
30   gress. The Register of Copyrights, together with the subordinate
1   officers and employees of the Copyright Office, shall be appointed by
2   the Librarian of Congress, and shall act under his general direction
3   and supervision.

4   (b) The Register of Copyrights shall adopt a seal to be used on
5   and after January 1, 1977, to authenticate all certified documents
6   issued by the Copyright Office.

7   (c) The Register of Copyrights shall make an annual report to
8   the Librarian of Congress of the work and accomplishments of the

9   Copyright Office during the previous fiscal year. The annual report
10   of the Register of Copyrights shall be published separately and as
11   a part of the annual report of the Librarian of Congress.

12 **§ 702. Copyright Office regulations**

13   The Register of Copyrights is authorized to establish regulations
14   not inconsistent with law for the administration of the functions and
15   duties made his responsibility under this title. All regulations estab-
16   lished by the Register under this title are subject to the approval of
17   the Librarian of Congress.

18 **§ 703. Effective date of actions in Copyright Office**

19   In any case in which time limits are prescribed under this title
20   for the performance of an action in the Copyright Office, and in
21   which the last day of the prescribed period falls on a Saturday, Sun-
22   day, holiday or other non-business day within the District of Colum-
23   bia or the Federal Government, the action may be taken on the next
24   succeeding business day, and is effective as of the date when the
25   period expired.

26 **§ 704. Retention and disposition of articles deposited in Copyright**
27   **Office**

28   (a) Upon their deposit in the Copyright Office under sections 407
29   and 408, all copies, phonorecords, and identifying material, including
30   those deposited in connection with claims that have been refused
31   registration, are the property of the United States Government.

32   (b) In the case of published works, all copies, phonorecords, and
33   identifying material deposited are available to the Library of Con-
34   gress for its collections, or for exchange or transfer to any other
35   library. In the case of unpublished works, the Library is entitled to
36   select any deposits for its collections.

37   (c) Deposits as selected by the Library under subsection (b), or
38   identifying portions or reproductions of them, shall be retained under
39   the control of the Copyright Office, including retention in Govern-
1   ment storage facilities, for the longest period considered practicable
2   and desirable by the Register of Copyrights and the Librarian of
3   Congress. After that period it is within the joint discretion of the

4   Register and the Librarian to order their destruction or other disposi-
5   tion; but, in the case of unpublished works, no deposit shall be de-
6   stroyed or otherwise disposed of during its term of copyright.

7   (d) The depositor of copies, phonorecords, or identifying material
8   under section 408, or the copyright owner of record, may request
9   retention, under the control of the Copyright Office, of one or more
10   of such articles for the full term of copyright in the work. The Regis-
11   ter of Copyright shall prescribe, by regulation, the conditions under
12   which such requests are to be made and granted, and shall fix the
13   fee to be charged under section 708(a)(11) if the request is granted.

14   **§ 705. Copyright Office records: Preparation, maintenance, public**
15   **inspection, and searching**

16   (a) The Register of Copyrights shall provide and keep in the Copy-
17   right Office records of all deposits, registrations, recordations, and
18   other actions taken under this title, and shall prepare indexes of all
19   such records.

20   (b) Such records and indexes, as well as the articles deposited in
21   connection with completed copyright registrations and retained under
22   the control of the Copyright Office, shall be open to public inspection.

23   (c) Upon request and payment of the fee specified by section 708,
24   the Copyright Office shall make a search of its public records, indexes,
25   and deposits, and shall furnish a report of the information they dis-
26   close with respect to any particular deposits, registrations, or recorded
27   documents.

28   **§ 706. Copies of Copyright Office records**

29   (a) Copies may be made of any public records or indexes of the
30   Copyright Office; additional certificates of copyright registration and
31   copies of any public records or indexes may be furnished upon request
32   and payment of the fees specified by section 708.

33   (b) Copies or reproductions of deposited articles retained under
34   the control of the Copyright Office shall be authorized or furnished
35   only under the conditions specified by the Copyright Office regulations.

36   **§ 707. Copyright Office forms and publications**

37　　(a) CATALOG OF COPYRIGHT ENTRIES.—The Register of Copyrights
38　shall compile and publish at periodic intervals catalogs of all copy-
39　right registrations. These catalogs shall be divided into parts in
1　accordance with the various classes of works, and the Register has
2　discretion to determine, on the basis of practicability and usefulness,
3　the form and frequency of publication of each particular part.

4　　(b) OTHER PUBLICATIONS.—The Register shall furnish, free of
5　charge upon request, application forms for copyright registration and
6　general informational material in connection with the functions of the
7　Copyright Office. He also has authority to publish compilations of
8　information, bibliographies, and other material he considers to be
9　of value to the public.

10　　(c) DISTRIBUTION OF PUBLICATIONS.—All publications of the Copy-
11　right Office shall be furnished to depository libraries as specified under
12　section 1905 of title 44, United States Code, and, aside from those fur-
13　nished free of charge, shall be offered for sale to the public at prices
14　based on the cost of reproduction and distribution.

15　**§ 708. Copyright Office fees**

16　　(a) The following fees shall be paid to the Register of Copyrights:

17　　　(1) for the registration of a copyright claim or a supplementary
18　　registration under section 408, including the issuance of a certifi-
19　　cate of registration, $10;

20　　　(2) for the registration of a claim to renewal of a subsisting
21　　copyright in its first term under section 304(a), including the
22　　issuance of a certificate of registration, $6;

23　　　(3) for the issuance of a receipt for a deposit under section
24　　407, $2;

25　　　(4) for the recordation, as provided by section 205, of a transfer
26　　of copyright ownership or other document of six pages or less,
27　　covering no more than one title, $10; for each page over six and
28　　for each title over one, 50 cents additional;

29　　　(5) for the filing, under section 115(b), of a notice of intention
30　　to make phonorecords, $6;

31   (6) for the recordation, under section 302(c), of a statement

32   revealing the identity of an author of an anonymous or pseu-

33   donymous work, or for the recordation, under section 302(d), of a

34   statement relating to the death of an author, $10 for a document of

35   six pages or less, covering no more than one title; for each page

36   over six and for each title over one, $1 additional;

37   (7) for the issuance, under section 601, of an import state-

38   ment, $3;

39   (8) for the issuance, under section 706, of an additional certifi-

40   cate of registration, $4;

1   (9) for the issuance of any other certification, $4; the Register

2   of Copyrights has discretion, on the basis of their cost, to fix the

3   fees for preparing copies of Copyright Office records, whether

4   they are to be certified or not;

5   (10) for the making and reporting of a search as provided by

6   section 705, and for any related services, $10 for each hour or frac-

7   tion of an hour consumed;

8   (11) for any other special services requiring a substantial

9   amount of time or expense, such fees as the Register of Copyrights

10   may fix on the basis of the cost of providing the service.

11   (b) The fees prescribed by or under this section are applicable to the

12 United States Government and any of its agencies, employees, or

13 officers, but the Register of Copyrights has discretion to waive the

14 requirement of this subsection in occasional or isolated cases involving

15 relatively small amounts.

16 **§ 709. Delay in delivery caused by disruption of postal or other**

17   **services**

18   In any case in which the Register of Copyrights determines, on the

19 basis of such evidence as he may by regulation require, that a deposit,

20 application, fee, or any other material to be delivered to the Copyright

21 Office by a particular date, would have been received in the Copyright

22 Office in due time except for a general disruption or suspension of

23 postal or other transportation or communications services, the actual

24 receipt of such material in the Copyright Office within one month after

25 the date on which the Register determines that the disruption or sus-
26 pension of such services has terminated, shall be considered timely.

27 **§ 710. Reproductions for use of the blind and physically handi-**
28 **capped: Voluntary licensing forms and procedures**

29 The Register of Copyrights shall, after consultation with the Chief
30 of the Division for the Blind and Physically Handicapped and other
31 appropriate officials of the Library of Congress, establish by regula-
32 tion standardized forms and procedures by which, at the time applica-
33 tions covering certain specified categories of nondramatic literary
34 works are submitted for registration under section 408 of this title, the
35 copyright owner may voluntarily grant to the Library of Congress a
36 license to reproduce the copyrighted work by means of Braille or
37 similar tactile symbols, or by fixation of a reading of the work in a
38 phonorecord, or both, and to distribute the resulting copies or phono-
39 record solely for the use of the blind and physically handicapped and
40 under limited conditions to be specified in the standardized forms.

1 **Chapter 8.—COPYRIGHT ROYALTY TRIBUNAL**

2 **§ 801. Copyright Royalty Tribunal: Establishment and purpose**

3 (a) There is hereby created in the Library of Congress a Copyright
4 Royalty Tribunal.

5 (b) Subject to the provisions of this chapter, the purpose of the
6 Tribunal shall be: (1) to make determinations concerning the adjust-
7 ment of the copyright royalty rates as provided in sections 111, 115,
8 116, and 118 so as to assure that such rates are reasonable and, in the
9 event that the Tribunal shall determine that the statutory rate, or a
10 rate previously established by the Tribunal, or the basis in respect to
11 such rates, does not provide a reasonable royalty fee for the basic

12   service of providing secondary transmissions of the primary broad-
13   cast transmitter or is otherwise unreasonable, the Tribunal may change
14   the royalty rate or the basis on which the royalty fee shall be
15   assessed or both so as to assure a reasonable royalty fee; and (2) to
16   determine in certain circumstances the distribution of the royalty fees
17   deposited with the Register of Copyrights under sections 111, 116,
18   and 118.

19   **§ 802. Petitions for the adjustment of royalty rates**

20   (a) On January 1, 1980, the Register of Copyrights shall cause to be
21   published in the Federal Register notice of the commencement of pro-
22   ceedings with respect to the royalty rates as provided in sections 111,
23   115, 116, and 118.

24   (b) During the calendar year 1990, and in each subsequent tenth
25   calendar year, any owner or user of a copyrighted work whose royalty
26   rates are specified by this title, or by a rate established by the Tri-
27   bunal, may file a petition with the Register of Copyrights declaring
28   that the petitioner requests an adjustment of the rate. The Register
29   shall make a determination as to whether the applicant has a signifi-
30   cant interest in the royalty rate in which an adjustment is requested.
31   If the Register determines that the petitioner has a significant interest,
32   he shall cause notice of his decision to be published in the Federal
33   Register.

1   **§ 803. Membership of the Tribunal**

2·   (a) In accordance with section 802, or upon certifying the existence
3   of a controversy concerning the distribution of royalty fees deposited
4   pursuant to sections 111, 116, and 118, the Register shall request the
5   American Arbitration Association or any similar successor organiza-
6   tion to furnish a list of three members of said Association. The Regis-
7   ter shall communicate the names together with such information as
8   may be appropriate to all parties of interest. Any such party, within
9   twenty days from the date said communication is sent, may submit to
10   the Register written objections to any or all of the proposed names. If
11   no such objections are received, or if the Register determines that said

12 objections are not well founded, he shall certify the appointment of the
13 three designated individuals to constitute a panel of the Tribunal for
14 the consideration of the specified rate or royalty distribution. Such
15 panel shall function as the Tribunal established in section 801. If the
16 Register determines that the objections to the designation of one or
17 more of the proposed individuals are well founded, the Register shall
18 request the American Arbitration Association or any similar successor
19 organization to propose the necessary number of substitute individ-
20 uals. Upon receiving such additional names the Register shall consti-
21 tute the panel. The Register shall designate one member of the panel
22 as Chairman.

23 (b) If any member of a panel becomes unable to perform his duties,
24 the Register, after consultation with the parties, may provide for the
25 selection of a successor in the manner prescribed in subsection (a).

26 **§ 804. Procedures of the Tribunal**

27 (a) The Tribunal shall fix a time and place for its proceedings and
28 shall cause notice to be given to the parties.

29 (b) Any organization or person entitled to participate in the pro-
30 ceedings may appear directly or be represented by counsel.

31 (c) Except as otherwise provided by law, the Tribunal shall deter-
32 mine its own procedure. For the purpose of carrying out the provisions
33 of this chapter, the Tribunal may hold hearings, administer oaths,
34 and require, by subpoena or otherwise, the attendance and testimony
35 of witnesses and the production of documents.

36 (d) Every final decision of the Tribunal shall be in writing and
37 shall state the reasons therefor.

38 (e) The Tribunal shall render a final decision in each proceeding
39 within one year from the certification of the panel. Upon a showing
1 of good cause, the Senate Committee on the Judiciary and the House of
2 Representatives Committee on the Judiciary may waive this require-
3 ment in a particular proceeding.

4 **§ 805. Compensation of members of the Tribunal: Expenses of the**
5   **Tribunal**

6   (a) In proceedings for the distribution of royalty fees, the compen-
7   sation of members of the Tribunal and other expenses of the Tribunal
8   shall be deducted prior to the distribution of the funds.

9   (b) In proceedings for the determination of royalty rates, there is
10   hereby authorized to be appropriated such sums as may be necessary.

11   (c) The Library of Congress is authorized to furnish facilities and
12   incidental services to the Tribunal.

13   (d) The Tribunal is authorized to procure temporary and inter-
14   mittent services to the same extent as is authorized by section 3109 of
15   title 5, United States Code.

16   **§ 806. Reports to the Congress**

17   The Tribunal, immediately upon making a final determination
18   in any proceeding with respect to royalty rates, shall transmit its
19   decision, together with the reasons therefor, to the Secretary of the
20   Senate and the Clerk of the House of Representatives for reference
21   to the Judiciary Committees of the Senate and the House of
22   Representatives.

23   **§ 807. Effective date of royalty adjustment**

24   (a) Prior to the expiration of the first period of ninety calendar
25   days of continuous session of the Congress, following the transmittal
26   of the report specified in section 806, either House of the Congress may
27   adopt a resolution stating in substance that the House does not favor
28   the recommended royalty determination, and such determination,
29   therefore, shall not become effective.

30   (b) For the purposes of subsection (a) of this section—

31   (1) continuity of session shall be considered as broken only by
32   an adjournment of the Congress sine die, and

33   (2) in the computation of the ninety-day period there shall be
34   excluded the days on which either House is not in session because
35   of an adjournment of more than three days to a day certain.

36   (c) In the absence of the passage of such a resolution by either
37   House during said ninety-day period, the final determination of roy-
38   alty rates by the Tribunal shall take effect on the first day following
39   ninety calendar days after the expiration of the period specified by

40   subsection (a).

1   (d) The Register of Copyrights shall give notice of such effective
2 date by publication in the Federal Register not less than sixty days
3 before said date.

4 **§ 808. Effective date of royalty distribution**

5   A final determination of the Tribunal concerning the distribution
6 of royalty fees deposited with the Register of Copyrights pursuant to
7 sections 111 and 116 shall become effective thirty days following such
8 determination unless, prior to that time, an application has been filed
9 pursuant to section 809 to vacate, modify or correct the determination,
10 and notice of such application has been served upon the Register of
11 Copyrights. The Register upon the expiration of thirty days shall dis-
12 tribute such royalty fees not subject to any application filed pursuant
13 to section 809.

14 **§ 809. Judicial review**

15   In any of the following cases the United States District Court for
16 the District of Columbia may make an order vacating, modifying or
17 correcting a final determination of the Tribunal concerning the distri-
18 bution of royalty fees—

19   (a) where the determination was procured by corruption, fraud,
20   or undue means; or

21   (b) where there was evident partiality or corruption in any
22   member of the panel; or

23   (c) where any member of the panel was guilty of any miscon-
24   duct by which the rights of any party have been prejudiced.

25   TRANSITIONAL AND SUPPLEMENTARY PROVISIONS

26   SEC. 102. This title becomes effective on January 1, 1977, except as
27 otherwise provided by section 304(b) of title 17 as amended by this
28 title.

29   SEC. 103. This title does not provide copyright protection for any
30 work that goes into the public domain before January 1, 1977. The
31 exclusive rights, as provided by section 106 of title 17 as amended
32 by this title, to reproduce a work in phonorecords and to distribute
33 phonorecords of the work, do not extend to any nondramatic musical

34   work copyrighted before July 1, 1909.

35   SEC. 104. All proclamations issued by the President under section
36   1(e) or 9(b) of title 17 as it existed on December 31, 1976, or under
37   previous copyright statutes of the United States shall continue in
38   force until terminated, suspended, or revised by the President.

39   SEC. 105. (a)(1) Section 505 of title 44, United States Code, Sup-
40   plement IV, is amended to read as follows:

1   **"§ 505. Sale of duplicate plates**

2   "The Public Printer shall sell, under regulations of the Joint Com-
3   mittee on Printing to persons who may apply, additional or duplicate
4   stereotype or electrotype plates from which a Government publication
5   is printed, at a price not to exceed the cost of composition, the metal,
6   and making to the Government, plus 10 per centum, and the full
7   amount of the price shall be paid when the order is filed.".

8   (2) The item relating to section 505 in the sectional analysis at the
9   beginning of chapter 5 of title 44, United States Code, is amended to
10   read as follows:

"505. Sale of duplicate plates.".

11   (b) Section 2113 of title 44, United States Code, is amended to read
12   as follows:

13   **"§ 2113. Limitation on liability**

14   "When letters and other intellectual productions (exclusive of
15   patented material, published works under copyright protection, and
16   unpublished works for which copyright registration has been made)
17   come into the custody or possession of the Administrator of General
18   Services, the United States or its agents are not liable for infringe-
19   ment of copyright or analogous rights arising out of use of the mate-
20   rials for display, inspection, research, reproduction, or other
21   purposes.".

22   (c) In section 1498(b) of title 28 of the United States Code, the
23   phrase "section 101(b) of title 17" is amended to read "section 504(c)
24   of title 17".

25   (d) Section 543(a)(4) of the Internal Revenue Code of 1954, as
26   amended, is amended by striking out "(other than by reason of sec-

27 tion 2 or 6 thereof)".

28 (e) Section 3202(a) of title 39 of the United States Code is
29 amended by striking out clause (5). Section 3206(c) of title 39 of the
30 United States Code is amended by striking out clause (c). Section
31 3206(d) is renumbered (c).

32 (f) Subsection (a) of section 290(e) of title 15 of the United States
33 Code is amended by deleting the phrase "section 8" and inserting in
34 lieu thereof, the phrase "section 105".

35 SEC. 106. In any case where, before January 1, 1977, a person has
36 lawfully made parts of instruments serving to reproduce mechani-
37 cally a copyrighted work under the compulsory license provisions of
38 section 1(e) of title 17 as it existed on December 31, 1976, he may
39 continue to make and distribute such parts embodying the same me-
1   chanical reproduction without obtaining a new compulsory license
2   under the terms of section 115 of title 17 as amended by this title.
3   However, such parts made on or after January 1, 1977, constitute
4   phonorecords and are otherwise subject to the provisions of said
5   section 115.

6   SEC. 107. In the case of any work in which an ad interim copyright
7   is subsisting or is capable of being secured on December 31, 1976,
8   under section 22 of title 17 as it existed on that date, copyright pro-
9   tection is hereby extended to endure for the term or terms provided
10 by section 304 of title 17 as amended by this title.

11 SEC. 108. The notice provisions of sections 401 through 403 of title
12 17 as amended by this title apply to all copies or phonorecords publicly
13 distributed on or after January 1, 1977. However, in the case of a work
14 published before January 1, 1977, compliance with the notice provi-
15 sions of title 17 either as it existed on December 31, 1976, or as amended
16 by this title, is adequate with respect to copies publicly distributed
17 after December 31, 1976.

18 SEC. 109. The registration of claims to copyright for which the
19 required deposit, application, and fee were received in the Copyright
20 Office before January 1, 1977, and the recordation of assignments of
21 copyright or other instruments received in the Copyright Office before

22   January 1, 1977, shall be made in accordance with title 17 as it existed
23   on December 31, 1976.

24   SEC. 110. The demand and penalty provisions of section 14 of title 17
25   as it existed on December 31, 1976, apply to any work in which copy-
26   right has been secured by publication with notice of copyright on or
27   before that date, but any deposit and registration made after that date
28   in response to a demand under that section shall be made in accordance
29   with the provisions of title 17 as amended by this title.

30   SEC. 111. Section 2318 of title 18 of the United States Code is
31   amended to read as follows:

32   **"§ 2318. Transportation, sale or receipt of phonograph records**
33   **bearing forged or counterfeit labels**

34   "(a) Whoever knowingly and with fraudulent intent transports,
35   causes to be transported, receives, sells, or offers for sale in interstate or
36   foreign commerce any phonograph record, disk, wire, tape, film, or
37   other article on which sounds are recorded, to which or upon which is
38   stamped, pasted, or affixed any forged or counterfeited label, knowing
39   the label to have been falsely made, forged, or counterfeited shall be
40   fined not more than $25,000 or imprisoned for not more than three
1   years, or both, for the first such offense and shall be fined not more than
2    $50,000 or imprisoned for not more than seven years or both, for any
3   subsequent offense.

4   "(b) When any person is convicted of any violation of subsection
5   (a), the court in its judgment of conviction shall, in addition to the
6   penalty therein prescribed, order the forfeiture and destruction or
7   other disposition of all counterfeit labels and all articles to which
8   counterfeit labels have been affixed or which were intended to have
9   had such labels affixed.

10   "(c) Except to the extent they are inconsistent with the provisions
11   of this title, all provisions of section 509, title 17, United States Code,
12   are applicable to violations of subsection (a).".

13   SEC. 112. All causes of action that arose under title 17 before Jan-
14   uary 1, 1977, shall be governed by title 17 as it existed when the cause

15   of action arose.

16   SEC. 113. Notwithstanding section 802 of title 17, as amended by

17 this title, not later than thirty days following the date of enactment

18 of this Act, the Register of Copyrights shall cause notice to be pub-

19 lished in the Federal Register to convene the Copyright Royalty

20 Tribunal established under section 801 of such title 17, to establish

21 initial royalty rates under section 118 (of such title 17, as amended by

22 this title). The royalty rates so established shall apply to compulsory

23 licensing under such section 118, except that payment of any royalty

24 due during the period between the effective date of this Act and the

25 date on which such rates become effective shall not be required until

26 sixty days after such rates become effective.

27   SEC. 114. If any provision of title 17, as amended by this title, is

28 declared unconstitutional, the validity of the remainder of the title

29 is not affected.

30   TITLE II—PROTECTION OF ORNAMENTAL DESIGNS

31   OF USEFUL ARTICLES

32   DESIGNS PROTECTED

33   SEC. 201. (a) The author or other proprietor of an original orna-

34 mental design of a useful article may secure the protection provided

35 by this title upon complying with and subject to the provisions hereof.

36   (b) For the purposes of this title—

37   (1) A "useful article" is an article which in normal use has an

38   intrinsic utilitarian function that is not merely to portray the

39   appearance of the article or to convey information. An article

1   which normally is a part of a useful article shall be deemed to be

2   a useful article.

3   (2) The "design of a useful article", hereinafter referred to as

4   a "design", consists of those aspects or elements of the article,

5   including its two-dimensional or three-dimensional features of

6   shape and surface, which make up the appearance of the article.

7   (3) A design is "ornamental" if it is intended to make the

8   article attractive or distinct in appearance.

9   (4) A design is "original" if it is the independent creation of an

10   author who did not copy it from another source.

11   DESIGNS NOT SUBJECT TO PROTECTION

12   SEC. 202. Protection under this title shall not be available for a

13   design that is—

14   (a) not original;

15   (b) staple or commonplace, such as a standard geometric figure,

16   familiar symbol, emblem, or motif, or other shape, pattern, or con-

17   figuration which has become common, prevalent, or ordinary;

18   (c) different from a design excluded by subparagraph (b) above

19   only in insignificant details or in elements which are variants com-

20   monly used in the relevant trades;

21   (d) dictated solely by a utilitarian function of the article that

22   embodies it; or

23   (e) composed of three-dimensional features of shape and sur-

24   face with respect to men's, women's, and children's apparel, in-

25   cluding undergarments and outerwear.

26   REVISIONS, ADAPTATIONS, AND REARRANGEMENTS

27   SEC. 203. Protection for a design under this title shall be available

28   notwithstanding the employment in the design of subject matter ex-

29   cluded from protection under section 202 (b) through (d), if the

30   design is a substantial revision, adaptation, or rearrangement of said

31   subject matter: *Provided*, That such protection shall be available to a

32   design employing subject matter protected under title I of this Act,

33   or title 35 of the United States Code or this title, only if such pro-

34   tected subject matter is employed with the consent of the proprietor

35   thereof. Such protection shall be independent of any subsisting pro-

36   tection in subject matter employed in the design, and shall not be

37   construed as securing any right to subject matter excluded from pro-

38   tection or as extending any subsisting protection.

1   COMMENCEMENT OF PROTECTION

2   SEC. 204. The protection provided for a design under this title shall

3   commence upon the date of publication of the registration pursuant to

4   section 212(a).

TERM OF PROTECTION

6 SEC. 205. (a) Subject to the provisions of this title, the protection
7 herein provided for a design shall continue for a term of five years
8 from the date of the commencement of protection as provided in sec-
9 tion 204, but if a proper application for renewal is received by
10 the Administrator during the year prior to the expiration of the five-
11 year term, the protection herein provided shall be extended for an
12 additional period of five years from the date of expiration of the first
13 five years.

14 (b) Upon expiration or termination of protection in a particular
15 design as provided in this title all rights under this title in said design
16 shall terminate, regardless of the number of different articles in which
17 the design may have been utilized during the term of its protection.

18 **THE DESIGN NOTICE**

19 SEC. 206. (a) Whenever any design for which protection is sought
20 under this title is made public as provided in section 209(b), the
21 proprietor shall, subject to the provisions of section 207, mark it or
22 have it marked legibly with a design notice consisting of the following
23 three elements:

24 (1) the words "Protected Design", the abbreviation "Prot'd
25 Des." or the letter "D" within a circle thus Ⓓ;

26 (2) the year of the date on which the design was registered;
27 and

28 (3) the name of the proprietor, an abbreviation by which the
29 name can be recognized, or a generally accepted alternative desig-
30 nation of the proprietor; any distinctive identification of the
31 proprietor may be used if it has been approved and recorded by
32 the Administrator before the design marked with such identifica-
33 tion is registered.

34 After registration the registration number may be used instead of
35 the elements specified in (2) and (3) hereof.

36 (b) The notice shall be so located and applied as to give reasonable
37 notice of design protection while the useful article embodying the

38 design is passing through its normal channels of commerce. This re-
39 quirement may be fulfilled, in the case of sheetlike or strip materials
1   bearing repetitive or continuous designs, by application of the notice
2   to each repetition, or to the margin, selvage, or reverse side of the ma-
3   terial at reasonably frequent intervals, or to tags or labels affixed to
4   the material at such intervals.

5   (c) When the proprietor of a design has complied with the provi-
6   sions of this section, protection under this title shall not be affected
7   by the removal, destruction, or obliteration by others of the design
8   notice on an article.

9   EFFECT OF OMISSION OF NOTICE

10   SEC. 207. The omission of the notice prescribed in section 206 shall
11 not cause loss of the protection or prevent recovery for infringement
12 against any person who, after written notice of the design protection,
13 begins an undertaking leading to infringement: *Provided*, That such
14 omission shall prevent any recovery under section 222 against a person
15 who began an undertaking leading to infringement before receiving
16 written notice of the design protection, and no injunction shall be
17 had unless the proprietor of the design shall reimburse said person
18 for any reasonable expenditure or contractual obligation in connection
19 with such undertaking incurred before written notice of design protec-
20 tion, as the court in its discretion shall direct. The burden of proving
21 written notice shall be on the proprietor.

22   INFRINGEMENT

23   SEC. 208. (a) It shall be infringement of a design protected under
24 this title for any person, without the consent of the proprietor of
25 the design, within the United States or its territories or possessions
26 and during the term of such protection, to—

27   (1) make, have made, or import, for sale or for use in trade,
28   any infringing article as defined in subsection (d) hereof; or
29   (2) sell or distribute for sale or for use in trade any such
30   infringing article: *Provided, however*, That a seller or distributor
31   of any such article who did not make or import the same shall be
32   deemed to be an infringer only if—

33 (i) he induced or acted in collusion with a manufacturer to
34 make, or an importer to import such article (merely purchas-
35 ing or giving an order to purchase in the ordinary course of
36 business shall not of itself constitute such inducement or
37 collusion) ; or

38 (ii) he refuses or fails upon the request of the proprietor
39 of the design to make a prompt and full disclosure of his
1 source of such article, and he orders or reorders such article
2 after having received notice by registered or certified mail
3 of the protection subsisting in the design.

4 (b) It shall be not infringement to make, have made, import, sell,
5 or distribute, any article embodying a design created without knowl-
6 edge of, and copying from, a protected design.

7 (c) A person who incorporates into his own product of manufacture
8 an infringing article acquired from others in the ordinary course of
9 business, or who, without knowledge of the protected design, makes or
10 processes an infringing article for the account of another person in the
11 ordinary course of business, shall not be deemed an infringer except
12 under the conditions of clauses (i) and (ii) of paragraph (a)(2) of
13 this section. Accepting an order or reorder from the source of the in-
14 fringing article shall be deemed ordering or reordering within the
15 meaning of clause (ii) of paragraph (a)(2) of this section.

16 (d) An "infringing article" as used herein is any article, the design
17 of which has been copied from the protected design, without the con-
18 sent of the proprietor: *Provided, however,* That an illustration or
19 picture of a protected design in an advertisement, book, periodical,
20 newspaper, photograph, broadcast, motion picture, or similar medium
21 shall not be deemed to be an infringing article. An article is not an
22 infringing article if it embodies, in common with the protected design,
23 only elements described in subsections (a) through (d) of section 202.

24 (e) The party alleging rights in a design in any action or proceed-
25 ing shall have the burden of affirmatively establishing its originality
26 whenever the opposing party introduces an earlier work which is
27 identical to such design, or so similar as to make a prima facie show-

28   ing that such design was copied from such work.

29   <center>APPLICATION FOR REGISTRATION</center>

30   SEC. 209. (a) Protection under this title shall be lost if application
31   for registration of the design is not made within six months after the
32   date on which the design was first made public.

33   (b) A design is made public when, by the proprietor of the design
34   or with his consent, an existing useful article embodying the design is
35   anywhere publicly exhibited, publicly distributed, or offered for sale or
36   sold to the public.

37   (c) Application for registration or renewal may be made by the
38   proprietor of the design.

39   (d) The application for registration shall be made to the Adminis-
40   trator and shall state (1) the name and address of the author or
1   authors of the design; (2) the name and address of the proprietor
2   if different from the author; (3) the specific name of the article,
3   indicating its utility; and (4) such other information as may be
4   required by the Administrator. The application for registration may
5   include a description setting forth the salient features of the design,
6   but the absence of such a description shall not prevent registration
7   under this title.

8   (e) The application for registration shall be accompanied by a
9   statement under oath by the applicant or his duly authorized agent or
10   representative, setting forth that, to the best of his knowledge and be-
11   lief (1) the design is original and was created by the author or authors
12   named in the application; (2) the design has not previously been regis-
13   tered on behalf of the applicant or his predecessor in title; and (3) the
14   applicant is the person entitled to protection and to registration under
15   this title. If the design has been made public with the design notice
16   prescribed in section 206, the statement shall also describe the exact
17   form and position of the design notice.

18   (f) Error in any statement or assertion as to the utility of the article
19   named in the application, the design of which is sought to be regis-
20   tered, shall not affect the protection secured under this title.

21 (g) Errors in omitting a joint author or in naming an alleged joint
22 author shall not affect the validity of the registration, or the actual
23 ownership or the protection of the design: *Provided*, That the name of
24 one individual who was in fact an author is stated in the application.
25 Where the design was made within the regular scope of the author's
26 employment and individual authorship of the design is difficult or im-
27 possible to ascribe and the application so states, the name and address
28 of the employer for whom the design was made may be stated instead
29 of that of the individual author.

30 (h) The application for registration shall be accompanied by two
31 copies of a drawing or other pictorial representation of the useful
32 article having one or more views, adequate to show the design, in a
33 form and style suitable for reproduction, which shall be deemed a
34 part of the application.

35 (i) Where the distinguishing elements of a design are in substan-
36 tially the same form in a number of different useful articles, the design
37 shall be protected as to all such articles when protected as to one of
38 them, but not more than one registration shall be required.

39 (j) More than one design may be included in the same application
40 under such conditions as may be prescribed by the Administrator. For
1 each design included in an application the fee prescribed for a single
2 design shall be paid.

3 BENEFIT OF EARLIER FILING DATE IN FOREIGN COUNTRY

4 SEC. 210. An application for registration of a design filed in this
5 country by any person who has, or whose legal representative or pred-
6 ecessor or successor in title has previously regularly filed an applica-
7 tion for registration of the same design in a foreign country which af-
8 fords similar privileges in the case of applications filed in the United
9 States or to citizens of the United States shall have the same effect
10 as if filed in this country on the date on which the application was
11 first filed in any such foreign country, if the application in this country
12 is filed within six months from the earliest date on which any such
13 foreign application was filed.

14   OATHS AND ACKNOWLEDGMENTS

15   SEC. 211. (a) Oaths and acknowledgments required by this title may
16   be made before any person in the United States authorized by law to
17   administer oaths, or, when made in a foreign country, before any
18   diplomatic or consular officer of the United States authorized to ad-
19   minister oaths, or before any official authorized to administer oaths in
20   the foreign country concerned, whose authority shall be proved by a
21   certificate of a diplomatic or consular officer of the United States, and
22   shall be valid if they comply with the laws of the state or country
23   where made.

24   (b) The Administrator may by rule prescribe that any document to
25   be filed in the Office of the Administrator and which is required by any
26   law, rule, or other regulation to be under oath may be subscribed to by
27   a written declaration in such form as the Administrator may pre-
28   scribe, such declaration to be in lieu of the oath otherwise required.

29   (c) Whenever a written declaration as permitted in subsection (b)
30   is used, the document must warn the declarant that willful false state-
31   ments and the like are punishable by fine or imprisonment, or both
32   (18 U.S.C. 1001) and may jeopardize the validity of the application
33   or document or a registration resulting therefrom.

34   EXAMINATION OF APPLICATION AND ISSUE OR REFUSAL OF REGISTRATION

35   SEC. 212. (a) Upon the filing of an application for registration in
36   proper form as provided in section 209, and upon payment of the fee
37   provided in section 215, the Administrator shall determine whether
38   or not the application relates to a design which on its face appears to
39   be subject to protection under this title, and if so, he shall register the
1   design. Registration under this subsection shall be announced by
2   publication. The date of registration shall be the date of publication.

3   (b) If, in his judgment, the application for registration relates to
4   a design which on its face is not subject to protection under this title,
5   the Administrator shall send the applicant a notice of his refusal to
6   register and the grounds therefor. Within three months from the date
7   the notice of refusal is sent, the applicant may request, in writing, re-
8   consideration of his application. After consideration of such a request,

9   the Administrator shall either register the design or send the applicant

10   a notice of his final refusal to register.

11   (c) Any person who believes he is or will be damaged by a registra-

12   tion under this title may, upon payment of the prescribed fee, apply

13   to the Administrator at any time to cancel the registration on the

14   ground that the design is not subject to protection under the provisions

15   of this title, stating the reasons therefor. Upon receipt of an applica-

16   tion for cancellation, the Administrator shall send the proprietor of

17   the design, as shown in the records of the Office of the Administrator, a

18   notice of said application, and the proprietor shall have a period of

19   three months from the date such notice was mailed in which to present

20   arguments in support of the validity of the registration. It shall also

21   be within the authority of the Administrator to establish, by regula-

22   tion, conditions under which the opposing parties may appear and be

23   heard in support of their arguments. If, after the periods provided for

24   the presentation of arguments have expired, the Administrator deter-

25   mines that the applicant for cancellation has established that the de-

26   sign is not subject to protection under the provisions of this title, he

27   shall order the registration stricken from the record. Cancellation

28   under this subsection shall be announced by publication, and notice of

29   the Administrator's final determination with respect to any application

30   for cancellation shall be sent to the applicant and to the proprietor

31   of record.

32   (d) Remedy against a final adverse determination under subpara-

33   graphs (b) and (c) above may be had by means of a civil action

34   against the Administrator pursuant to the provision of section 1361 of

35   title 28, United States Code, if commenced within such time after such

36   decision, not less than sixty days, as the Administrator appoints.

37   (e) When a design has been registered under this section, the lack

38   of utility of any article in which it has been embodied shall be no

39   defense to an infringement action under section 220, and no ground

1   for cancellation under subsection (c) of this section or under sec-

2   tion 223.

3   CERTIFICATION OF REGISTRATION

4   SEC. 213. Certificates of registration shall be issued in the name of
5   the United States under the seal of the Office of the Administrator and
6   shall be recorded in the official records of that Office. The certificate
7   shall state the name of the useful article, the date of filing of the appli-
8   cation, the date of registration, and shall contain a reproduction of
9   the drawing or other pictorial representation showing the design.
10   Where a description of the salient features of the design appears in the
11   application, this description shall also appear in the certificate. A
12   renewal certificate shall contain the date of renewal registration in
13   addition to the foregoing. A certificate of initial or renewal registra-
14   tion shall be admitted in any court as prima facie evidence of the
15   facts stated therein.

16   PUBLICATION OF ANNOUNCEMENTS AND INDEXES

17   SEC. 214. (a) The Administrator shall publish lists and indexes of
18   registered designs and cancellations thereof and may also publish the
19   drawing or other pictorial representations of registered designs for
20   sale or other distribution.

21   (b) The Administrator shall establish and maintain a file of the
22   drawings or other pictorial representations of registered designs,
23   which file shall be available for use by the public under such condi-
24   tions as the Administrator may prescribe.

25   FEES

26   SEC. 215. (a) There shall be paid to the Administrator the follow-
27   ing fees:

28   (1) On filing each application for registration or for renewal
29   of registration of a design, $15.

30   (2) For each additional related article included in one applica-
31   tion, $10.

32   (3) For recording an assignment, $3 for the first six pages, and
33   for each additional two pages or less, $1.

34   (4) For a certificate of correction of an error not the fault of
35   the Office, $10.

36   (5) For certification of copies of records, $1.

37   (6) On filing each application for cancellation of a registra-
38   tion, $15.

39   (b) The Administrator may establish charges for materials or serv-
40   ices furnished by the Office, not specified above, reasonably related to
41   the cost thereof.

1   REGULATIONS
2   SEC. 216. The Administrator may establish regulations not incon-
3   sistent with law for the administration of this title.

4   COPIES OF RECORDS
5   SEC. 217. Upon payment of the prescribed fee, any person may
6   obtain a certified copy of any official record of the Office of the Admin-
7   istrator, which copy shall be admissible in evidence with the same effect
8   as the original.

9   CORRECTION OF ERRORS IN CERTIFICATES
10   SEC. 218. The Administrator may correct any error in a registration
11   incurred through the fault of the Office, or, upon payment of the re-
12   quired fee, any error of a clerical or typographical nature not the fault
13   of the Office occurring in good faith, by a certificate of correction under
14   seal. Such registration, together with the certificate, shall thereafter
15   have the same effect as if the same had been originally issued in such
16   corrected form.

17   OWNERSHIP AND TRANSFER
18   SEC. 219. (a) The property right in a design subject to protection
19   under this title shall vest in the author, the legal representatives of a
20   deceased author or of one under legal incapacity, the employer for
21   whom the author created the design in the case of a design made
22   within the regular scope of the author's employment, or a person to
23   whom the rights of the author or of such employer have been trans-
24   ferred. The person or persons in whom the property right is vested
25   shall be considered the proprietor of the design.

26   (b) The property right in a registered design, or a design for which
27   an application for registration has been or may be filed, may be as-
28   signed, granted, conveyed, or mortgaged by an instrument in writing,
29   signed by the proprietor, or may be bequeathed by will.

30   (c) An acknowledgment as provided in section 211 shall be prima
31 facie evidence of the execution of an assignment, grant, conveyance,
32 or mortgage.

33   (d) An assignment, grant, conveyance, or mortgage shall be void
34 as against any subsequent purchaser or mortgagee for a valuable con-
35 sideration, without notice, unless it is recorded in the Office of the
36 Administrator within three months from its date of execution or prior
37 to the date of such subsequent purchase or mortgage.

38   REMEDY FOR INFRINGEMENT

39   SEC. 220. (a) The proprietor of a design shall have remedy for in-
40 fringement by civil action instituted after issuance of a certificate of
41 registration of the design.

1   (b) The proprietor of a design may have judicial review of a final
2 refusal of the Administrator to register the design, by a civil action
3 brought as for infringement if commenced within the time specified
4 in section 212(d), and shall have remedy for infringement by the same
5 action if the court adjudges the design subject to protection under this
6 title: *Provided,* That (1) he has previously duly filed and duly pros-
7 ecuted to such final refusal an application in proper form for regis-
8 tration of the design, and (2) he causes a copy of the complaint in
9 action to be delivered to the Administrator within ten days after the
10 commencement of the action, and (3) the defendant has committed acts
11 in respect to the design which would constitute infringement with
12 respect to a design protected under this title.

13   INJUNCTION

14   SEC. 221. The several courts having jurisdiction of actions under
15 this title may grant injunctions in accordance with the principles of
16 equity to prevent infringement, including, in their discretion, prompt
17 relief by temporary restraining orders and preliminary injunctions.

18   RECOVERY FOR INFRINGEMENT, AND SO FORTH

19   SEC. 222. (a) Upon finding for the claimant the court shall award
20 him damages adequate to compensate for the infringement, but in
21 no event less than the reasonable value the court shall assess them.

22 In either event the court may increase the damages to such amount,
23 not exceeding $5,000 or $1 per copy, whichever is greater, as to the
24 court shall appear to be just. The damages awarded in any of the
25 above circumstances shall constitute compensation and not a penalty.
26 The court may receive expert testimony as an aid to the determination
27 of damages.

28   (b) No recovery under paragraph (a) shall be had for any infringe-
29 ment committed more than three years prior to the filing of the
30 complaint.

31   (c) The court may award reasonable attorney's fees to the prevail-
32 ing party. The court may also award other expenses of suit to a
33 defendant prevailing in an action brought under section 220(b).

34   (d) The court may order that all infringing articles, and any plates,
35 molds, patterns, models, or other means specifically adapted for mak-
36 ing the same be delivered up for destruction or other disposition as
37 the court may direct.

POWER OF COURT OVER REGISTRATION

39   SEC. 223. In any action involving a design for which protection is
40 sought under this title, the court when appropriate may order registra-
41 tion of a design or the cancellation of a registration. Any such order
1 shall be certified by the court to the Administrator, who shall make
2 appropriate entry upon the records of his Office.

LIABILITY FOR ACTION ON REGISTRATION FRAUDULENTLY OBTAINED

4   SEC. 224. Any person who shall bring an action for infringement
5 knowing that registration of the design was obtained by a false or
6 fraudulent representation materially affecting the rights under this
7 title, shall be liable in the sum of $1,000, or such part thereof as the
8 court may determine, as compensation to the defendant, to be charged
9 against the plaintiff and paid to the defendant, in addition to such
10 costs and attorney's fees of the defendant as may be assessed by the
11 court.

PENALTY FOR FALSE MARKING

13   SEC. 225. (a) Whoever, for the purpose of deceiving the public,

14   marks upon, or applies to, or uses in advertising in connection with any
15   article made, used, distributed, or sold by him, the design of which
16   is not protected under this title, a design notice as specified in section
17   206 or any other words or symbols importing that the design is pro-
18   tected under this title, knowing that the design is not so protected,
19   shall be fined not more than $500 for every such offense.

20   (b) Any person may sue for the penalty, in which event, one-half
21   shall go to the person suing and the other to the use of the United
22   States.

23   PENALTY FOR FALSE REPRESENTATION

24   SEC. 226. Whoever knowingly makes a false representation mate-
25   rially affecting the rights obtainable under this title for the purpose
26   of obtaining registration of a design under this title shall be fined
27   not less than $500 and not more than $1,000, and any rights or privi-
28   leges he may have in the design under this title shall be forfeited.

29   RELATION TO COPYRIGHT LAW

30   SEC. 227. (a) Nothing in this title shall affect any right or remedy
31   now or hereafter held by any person under title I of this Act, subject
32   to the provisions of section 113(c) of title I.

33   (b) When a pictorial, graphic, or sculptural work in which copy-
34   right subsists under title I of this Act is utilized in an original orna-
35   mental design of a useful article, by the copyright proprietor or under
36   an express license from him, the design shall be eligible for protection
37   under the provisions of this title.

38   RELATION TO PATENT LAW

39   SEC. 228. (a) Nothing in this title shall affect any right or remedy
40   available to or held by any person under title 35 of the United States
41   Code.

1   (b) The issuance of a design patent for an ornamental design for
2   an article of manufacture under said title 35 shall terminate any pro-
3   tection of the design under this title.

4   COMMON LAW AND OTHER RIGHTS UNAFFECTED

5   SEC. 229. Nothing in this title shall annul or limit (1) common law
6   or other rights or remedies, if any, available to or held by any person

7   with respect to a design which has not been registered under this title,
8   or (2) any trademark right or right to be protected against unfair
9   competition.

10   ADMINISTRATOR

11   Sec. 230. The Administrator and Office of the Administrator re-
12   ferred to in this title shall be such officer and office as the President
13   may designate.

14   SEVERABILITY CLAUSE

15   Sec. 231. If any provision of this title or the application of such
16   provision to any person or circumstance is held invalid, the remainder
17   of the title or the application to other persons or circumstances shall
18   not be affected thereby.

19   AMENDMENT OF OTHER STATUTES

20   Sec. 232. (a) Subdivision (a)(2) of section 70 of the Bankruptcy
21   Act of July 1, 1898, as amended (11 U.S.C. 110(a)), is amended
22   by inserting "designs," after "patent rights,".

23   (b) Title 28 of the United States Code is amended—
24   (1) by inserting "designs," after "patents," in the first sentence
25   of section 1338(a);
26   (2) by inserting ", design," after "patent" in the second sen-
27   tence of section 1338(a);
28   (3) by inserting "design," after "copyright," in section 1338
29   (b);
30   (4) by inserting "and registered designs" after "copyrights" in
31   section 1400; and
32   (5) by revising section 1498(a) to read as follows:

33   "(a) Whenever a registered design or invention is used or manu-
34   factured by or for the United States without license of the owner
35   thereof or lawful right to use or manufacture the same, the owner's
36   remedy shall be by action against the United States in the Court of
37   Claims for the recovery of his reasonable and entire compensation
38   for such use and manufacture.

39   "For the purposes of this section, the use or manufacture of a
40   registered design or an invention described in and covered by a patent

1   of the United States by a contractor, a subcontractor, or any person,
2   firm, or corporation for the Government and with the authorization
3   or consent of the Government, shall be construed as use or manufac-
4   ture for the United States.

5   "The court shall not award compensation under this section if
6   the claim is based on the use or manufacture by or for the United
7   States of any article owned, leased, used by, or in the possession of
8   the United States, prior to, in the case of an invention, July 1, 1918,
9   and in the case of a registered design, July 1, 1978.

10   "A Government employee shall have the right to bring suit against
11   the Government under this section except where he was in a position
12   to order, influence, or induce use of the registered design or invention
13   by the Government. This section shall not confer a right of action on
14   any registrant or patentee or any assignee of such registrant or pat-
15   entee with respect to any design created by or invention discovered or
16   invented by a person while in the employment or service of the United
17   States, where the design or invention was related to the official func-
18   tions of the employee, in cases in which such functions included
19   research and development, or in the making of which Government
20   time, materials, or facilities were used.".

21   TIME OF TAKING EFFECT
22   Sec. 233. This title shall take effect one year after enactment of this
23   Act.

24   NO RETROACTIVE EFFECT
25   Sec. 234. Protection under this title shall not be available for any
26   design that has been made public as provided in section 209(b) prior
27   to the effective date of this title.

28   SHORT TITLE
29   Sec. 235. This title may be cited as "The Design Protection Act of
30   1976".

Passed the Senate February 19, 1976.
    Attest:

                                        FRANCIS R. VALEO,
                                          Secretary.

Index